Throughout the course of American history the broad frontier exercised a profound influence on the men and women who settled it. Here, amid hardships that were at once discouraging and challenging, a rough democracy grew up that was compounded of individualism, unshaken optimism, and a belief in equality. Boundless faith in themselves and the nation they had created enabled Americans to weather the storms of rapid industrialization, civil war, and severe economic depression, and to emerge with the same type of grim determination that inspired their pioneer forefathers.

PICTORIAL HISTORY
of
AMERICA

By the EDITORS of

YEAR

Foreword by
ALLAN NEVINS

The dramatic story of the United States and Canada from the Age of Discovery to the Atomic Era, told in 2500 pictures, 200,000 words and 55 historical maps in full color

EDITOR

Baldwin H. Ward

MANAGING EDITOR

M. Tugrul Uke

ASSOCIATE EDITORS

John Gudmundsen   Jack B. Palmer

CONTRIBUTING EDITORS

William Adams
Anne Allen
Joan Biles
Florence Brill
Zelda Cini
Katherine Daubenspeck
David Farrelly
Helene H. Fox
Patrick Flaherty
Ann Funk
Bernard Goldman

James L. Graham
William Graydon
David Greenwood
Robert Hare
Austin Heywood
Joseph Howard
Marjorie Howard
Barbara Jenings
Hugh Jenings
Rosemary Jones
D. H. Johnson

Austin Kalish
Barbara Kreibich
Jean Lopin
Walter E. McArthur
Remi Nadeau
Marlen Neumann
Ruth Neumann
Maury Norrell
William Orr
William G. Oxx, III
Eugene Pfrommer

Richard Powell
Frank Rand
Peter Rankin
Thomas F. Smith
Richard Sweeney
Robert Tholsen
Jean Uke
William Van Hemert
Sidney Warren
Susan Wise
Reinhold Wulf

EDITORIAL ASSISTANTS

Betty Jane Peyer
Department Head

Suzan Barker
Josephine Bearcroft
Carl Brogden

Dolly Henkel
Marjorie Lane

Ida Lees
Jill Morse

Barbara Parker
Ethel Parrish
Phyllis Schmutz

RESEARCH STAFF

Helen Pickler
Department Head

Marie Crummett
John Cheney

Mary Donatoni
Peter Durlauf
Betty Hopper

Aleen Kiel
Rene LaBelle
Jacqueline Major

Euena Matthews
Lee Petersen

ART DEPARTMENT

Edith Sully
Art Director

Stanley Dennis
Don Eldridge
Thomas Hext
Duane Higgins
Joan Ingoldsby

Ross Kerlin
Michael Kuranoff
Gerardus Leeflang
Dolores McLoughlin
LaVon Moore

Sylvia Newman
Jane Parsons
Allen Repashy
George Saris
Jean Shaw

Arseny Spilewsky
Erma Tackett
Olej Tatarenko
William Ulman

Published by the Editors of YEAR and NEWS FRONT

 **PICTURE NEWS ANNUALS** **NEWS FRONT**
PICTURE HISTORY BOOKS THE PICTURE NEWS MAGAZINE FOR MANAGEMENT
PICTURE NEWS MAGAZINE

235 East 42nd St., New York 17, N.Y.

ALLAN NEVINS
PROFESSOR OF HISTORY
COLUMBIA UNIVERSITY

Foreword

American history is a multicolored pageant. We often think of Europe and Asia as richer in pictorial incident than the United States, but those who study this illustrated record carefully will question that idea. Our record already covers four centuries. It begins with the red man, the buffalo and the wolf — with the prehistoric surge of the Iroquois from the Mississippi Valley toward the Atlantic, building their long houses as they went; it runs down to the jet airplane, the atomic-energy plant, the tall skyscrapers, and the massive dams of today. Unlike the history of Britain, France, or Italy, it covers a continental domain. It treats of the fusion of human stocks from all over the world. Far more than the record of any other Power, it tells a story of unbroken progress, without disaster or heavy defeat. Pictures can only begin to present this march of the American people; but pictures, reinforced by text, can speak to the imagination as nothing else does.

American history may be viewed from various standpoints. Some (younger readers especially) will like to look at it as a long adventure story, a romance. Full of adventure it is, from Coronado traversing the Great Plains and John Smith penetrating the Chickahominy swamps to the hardy modern scientist conquering infantile paralysis. One respect in which our past most differs from that of the Old World lies in its comparative peacefulness.

We had no major war from 1783 to 1861, and none from 1865 to 1917. Our martial exploits from Lexington to Kwajalein are many and lustrous, but they do not make up the main stream of American adventure. We find that in the perils and achievements of the explorer, hunter, and trapper; the risks of the sailor before the mast, the steamboat pilot on the Mississippi, the cowboy on the Texas range; in the hard-won victories of such inventors as Fulton, Morse, and Edison; in the readiness of reformers like Garrison to face abuse and derision; in the willingness of the penniless Greeley to stake everything on a newspaper venture, and Henry Ford on his tiny automobile factory; in sacrifices Thoreau made for his books. What other land since 1776 has had so much *peaceful* adventure?

The American past may also be viewed as a great success story. Indeed, it is in some respects the brightest success story in the annals of nations. People came to America for certain well-defined objects; more political liberty, wider religious freedom, the betterment of their material position. By and large, they achieved these aims. With the advantage of freedom from feudal restrictions and social caste, with rich natural resources never before tapped, with a pervasive individual enterprise, they achieved a higher standard of living than any other nation. This standard included a better general provision for education, health, and recreation. It included the harnessing of productive energies on a scale never before known. Until the Second World War, most Americans did not realize that their output in steel, in some other metals, in textiles, in breadstuffs, in automotive units, and in other goods came near equalling that of all the rest of the globe.

Involved in both the adventure story and the success story is the repeated transformation of American society. We began with a thin coastal frontier. The wide wilderness frontier followed, population rolling west to the Missouri; then the very different frontier of the high plains, which could not be conquered until new implements (barbed wire, the windmill, the six-shooter, the combine) were provided. For two hundred and fifty years America was primarily an agricultural nation, exporting its food surplus. Then after the Civil War the industrial revolution rapidly conquered the land, with all its bright and dark accompaniments; the great city, the slum, the thronging immigrants, the new social problems, the multimillionaire, the labor union. Still the transformations go on. Coal power has largely given way to oil and electrical power, and the power of the atom looms ahead. The role of government has vastly expanded; the nation has become part of a close knit world society.

The most significant element in our American Story, however, is the growth of a truly American character and culture. Even in the 18th century Crevecoeur pointed out that a new man was rising from our soil, while in Benjamin Franklin we produced a truly American figure — versatile, energetic, ruggedly independent, optimistic, idealistic. The frontier did much to mould a distinct American character. Lincoln, its greatest son, exemplified the qualities we like to believe truly American; patience, homely sagacity, kindness, magnanimity, belief in the future, and faith in human brotherhood, all mixed with certain crudities and imitations.

Into the American character went the expansive humor of Mark Twain; the independence of Walt Whitman saying, "I wear my hat as I please, indoors and outdoors"; the democracy of Jefferson declaring, "I am not one of those who fear the people"; the progressive instinct of the business magnate who advised, "Never sell America short." Along with the growth of the American character came a more and more vigorous culture of our own.

A huge colorful panorama it is, which should be endlessly interesting to all of alert mind, and inspiring to all of hopeful vision.

Allan Nevins

PUBLISHER'S NOTE

When it was decided to undertake the publishing of YEAR'S *Pictorial History of America,* the challenge of recording four and one-half centuries of history in a single volume (even though it would contain more than 400 large pages), was accepted with full knowledge of the problems involved.

A staff of 10 expert researchers and 40 writers spent two years in extensive search and study in libraries and museums throughout America gathering material to make this book as authoritative and complete as possible. The work entailed studying the endless stream of materials that was "begged, borrowed or bought" from countless sources in the United States, Canada and overseas . . . general and specialized picture agencies, historical societies, art galleries, private collections, rare historical books, and business institutions—insurance firms, railroads, banks, chambers of commerce, etc.

For illustrations unobtainable elsewhere, original art was specially prepared for *Pictorial History of America* by artists Gerardus Leeflang of Rotterdam, Holland, and Edith Sully and Arseny Spilewsky of Los Angeles.

Up to the Civil War, line drawings, paintings and steel etchings predominate; from that point on, the book becomes essentially photographic, with selections more strongly influenced by historical significance than photographic effect. This may explain the nostalgic lingering over America's colorful early days.

Those readers who are particularly interested in current history (from 1900 on), will want to refer to *Your Lifetime In Pictures,* YEAR's 2,300-picture companion volume of the turbulent 20th century, from the days of Teddy Roosevelt up through the Eisenhower administration. Also, YEAR'S pictorial news annual series, beginning in 1948, offer intensive pictorial coverage of the present years. In addition, YEAR has published *Flight, A pictorial History of Aviation, The Pictorial History of the Bible and Christianity* and will soon publish YEAR'S *Pictorial History of the World.*

A book as all-encompassing as YEAR's *Pictorial History of America* cannot be the work of editors and writers alone. Grateful acknowledgment of kind and generous cooperation is hereby made to the scores of individuals and institutions whose help was instrumental in producing this volume.

YEAR's special appreciation for invaluable contribution is expressed to Alice Parker, Virginia Daiker, Milton Kaplan, Hirst Milhollen, Carl Stange, Donald Holmes of the Library of Congress; to Josephine Cobb and Thomas Ray of the National Archives; Corcoran Gallery of Art, National Gallery of Art, L. C. Handy Studios (Washington), Romana Javitz of the New York Public Library, Arthur B. Carlson of the New York Historical Society, Frick Art Reference Library, Museum of the City of New York, Whitney Museum of American Art (NYC), Sons of the Revolution (Fraunces Tavern, NYC), The Old Print Shop (NYC), Museum of Modern Art, Metropolitan Museum, Peter A. Juley & Son (NYC), Dr. Louis Sipley of the American Museum of Photography (Philadelphia), Historical Society of Pennsylvania, H. Maxson Holloway of the Chicago Historical Society, Los Angeles Public Library, Santa Monica Public Library, West Los Angeles Public Library, Academy of Motion Picture Arts and Sciences (Hollywood).

Our gratitude is also acknowledged to hundreds of institutions who by their cooperation, added greatly to this project; especially to the Museum of Fine Arts (Boston), Boston Public Library, California Historical Society, Society of California Pioneers, Wells Fargo Bank & Union Trust Co., M. H. de Young Memorial Museum (San Francisco), Bancroft Library of the University of California (Berkeley), E. B. Crocker Art Gallery, California State Library (Sacramento), Peabody Museum of Archaeology and Ethnology of Harvard University (Cambridge), Fogg Art Museum of Harvard University, American Antiquarian Society (Worcester, Mass.), Wadsworth Atheneum (Hartford), Confederate Museum (Richmond, Va.), Mariners Museum (Newport News, Va.), Colonial Williamsburg, Yale University Art Gallery, Yale University Press, Peabody Museum (Salem, Mass.), Essex Institute (Salem, Mass.), New York State Historical Association (Cooperstown), Enoch Pratt Free Library (Baltimore), Maryland Historical Society (Baltimore), Keystone View Company (Meadville, Pa.), L. J. Bullard Co. (Cleveland), George Eastman House (Rochester), Ohio State Archaeological and Historical Society (St. Louis), City Art Museum of St. Louis, Peoria Public Library, Wisconsin Historical Society (Madison), Tulane University (New Orleans), Louisiana Historical Society (New Orleans), Woolaroc Museum of the Frank Phillips Ranch (Bartlesville, Okla.), Ellison Photo Co. (Austin, Texas), Denver Public Library, Nebraska State Historical Society (Lincoln), Historical Society of Montana (Helena), Utah State Historical Society, Washington State Historical Society (Tacoma), Oregon State Highway Department (Salem), Vermont Historical Society (Montpelier), F. St. George Spendlove and Kenneth E. Kidd of The Royal Ontario Museum of Archaeology (Toronto), Public Archives of Canada (Ottawa), National Gallery of Canada (Ottawa), Saskatchewan Legislative Library (Regina), British Museum (London), Historisches Bildarchiv (Bad Berneck, West Germany), National Museum (Mexico City), Picture Post Library (London), National Portrait Gallery (London), Bibliotheque Nationale (Paris), John Morrell & Co. (Ottumwa, Iowa), John Hancock Mutual Life Insurance Company (Boston), Continental Distilling Corporation (Philadelphia), Stackpole Company (Harrisburg), America Fore Insurance Group (NYC), American Factors Ltd. (Honolulu), House of Seagram (Montreal), Title Guarantee and Trust Company (New York City), National Life Insurance Company (Montpelier, Vt.), Glen Falls Insurance Company, Wyeth Laboratories (Philadelphia), ANSCO (Binghamton, N. Y.), Douglas Aircraft Company (Santa Monica), Canadian Pacific Railway, Union Pacific Railroad Co.

To commercial picture agencies for their tireless efforts, our appreciation goes wholeheartedly to Harry Collins of Brown Brothers, Henry Grund of Wide World, Powell Gulick of International News Photos, Jay Culver of Culver Service, Milton Davidson of Underwood & Underwood, and to many other individuals and sources we can here only inadequately acknowledge.

BALDWIN H. WARD, PUBLISHER

Special Titles in the Pictorial History Series published by the Editors of YEAR

WORLD HISTORY

BIBLE and CHRISTIANITY

FLIGHT

YEAR

SCIENCE AND ENGINEERING

THE TURBULENT 20th CENTURY

CONTENTS

AGE OF DISCOVERY

Men of the Renaissance, seeking new route to the wealth of Cathay, find potentially greater riches in their explorations of the New World

The discovery of America in the 15th century was not new to history, but only to the men of Columbus' day. It had been discovered before. The Norsemen made repeated voyages between 986 and 1347, and even established settlements, but these were gone and forgotten by the dawn of the Age of Discovery. Medieval Europe was not prepared to expand into a new world. The Renaissance which brought Europe back to life, also gave birth to America. In the vigorous surge of the new intellectual life, men began to apply their scientific curiosity to nature and the universe. With the compass and the astrolabe it was possible for a navigator to travel the oceans, keeping track of his direction and position. No less interested in the rest of the world than the scientists were the merchants and traders. Their land routes to the East cut off by the Turks, they eagerly sought new ways of access to riches of the Orient. The voyage of Columbus was very different from the voyages of the Norsemen. Officially sponsored by powerful monarchs, he travelled in an age when news was beginning to spread rapidly. Immediately after his return, the word of what he had found, or thought he had found, reached the other great powers. In 1497, John Cabot sailed off from Bristol seeking the shores of Cathay, and returned to report his success. Columbus died believing he had reached Asia. Those who followed him sought fabled cities, gold, silver and even fountains of youth. It was a long time before the explorers realized they had discovered an undeveloped wilderness, a whole new continent. Even then, they regarded it as merely an obstacle to be overcome on the Cathay route. Balboa's crossing of the Isthmus of Panama to the South Sea (the Pacific) in 1513, fostered the theory that the new land was not very wide and probably could be traversed easily by simply following the eastern rivers to their sources, then descending the mountains to the sea on the other side. This idea was followed for years, the explorers fully convinced that each mountain range would be the last.

Spanish Claims

By virtue of discovery, and their supremacy at sea, the Spanish laid first claim to the New World, and they were indefatigable explorers. Large groups of soldiers and adventurers, accompanied by priests equipped with horses and weapons, assaulted the wilderness with a courage that was admirable, if their intentions were not always the best or their handling of the Indians humane.

In 1513 Juan Ponce de Leon, conqueror of Puerto Rico, explored much of Florida. Between 1539 and 1543 Hernando de Soto led 600 men from Florida to the Mississippi in a brave but fruitless march that cost his own life and those of half his men. In 1540 Francisco Vasquez de Coronado, resplendent in plumed helmet and gilded armor, set out from Mexico in search of the fabled Seven Cities of Cibola, travelling hundreds of miles over the arid lands of New Mexico, Arizona and Colorado. Meanwhile a Spanish ship commanded by the Portugese Magellan had sailed around the world, enabling the Spanish to establish a spice route across the Pacific to India. The fruits of Spain's conquests in Mexico and Peru gave reality to the legends of the New World's treasures. Spanish galleons laden with silver and gold sailed back across the Atlantic and were regularly chased down by England's gentlemen pirates. England was not strong enough before the defeat of the Spanish Armada in 1588 to vie with Spain for a place in the New World. But Elizabeth's "sea dogs" chased the galleons with gusto. On one trip Sir Francis Drake's "Golden Hind" was said to have collected five million dollars in treasure, in addition to valuable charts that later aided English exploration. In 1577-1580 Drake sailed around the Horn and up the Pacific coast of the Americas as far as Canada, putting in for repairs at a bay north of what is now San Francisco. Another great Elizabethan, Sir Walter Raleigh, spent his own fortune in several unsuccessful attempts to establish English colonies on the middle Atlantic coast, and his military commander, Captain John Smith, made detailed explorations from Virginia to New England.

The French, also desirous of a share in the new land, but equally eager to steer clear of the Spanish, concentrated their attention on the north. In 1534 Jacques Cartier sailed from France, discovered the St. Lawrence and visited the future sites of Montreal and Quebec. The next French move did not come until 1608 when Samuel de Champlain founded Quebec and began exploring the Great Lakes. He was followed by missionaries, fur traders and more explorers. Without fanfare, often alone, the Frenchmen paddled their canoes along the lakes and rivers, opening routes to the West, and seeking the furs that were to be their treasure.

CHRISTOPHER COLUMBUS

Land of Wealth

As reports of the explorations were circulated in Europe, it gradually dawned that this new land was in itself a great discovery. The writers were astonished by the rich vegetation, the abundance of game. The land of Georgia, said De Soto, was "abundant, picturesque and luxuriant, well watered." Captain John Smith was unceasingly amazed by the variety and quantity of fish to be found in New England waters. And the French explorers, Pierre Radisson and Sieur des Groseilliers—first white men to enter the Mississippi basin, explore Lake Superior, and visit the northwest country of the Sioux—found the land to their liking. Drifting through the lakes in his canoe in 1659, Radisson wrote, "I can say that in my lifetime never have I seen a more incomparable country." The cities of gold, the fountain of youth, were not to be found; but there was wealth in the wilderness, waiting only for men with eager hands and stout hearts to cultivate and develop.

★   ★   ★

THORFINN KARLSEFNI, in 1003, led the most extensive Viking expedition to the New World, almost 500 years before Columbus "discovered" it. Settling in a place he called "Straumfjord," on the northwest shore of Hudson Bay, he and his company remained in North America for three years, until hostilities with the natives forced them to abandon the colony in 1006. Although there remains some disagreement among scholars as to the precise locations of the early Norse settlements, there is no doubt of their having actually existed. Accounts are found in medieval literature.

INDIAN ARTISTRY and craftsmanship varied in quality and diversity from region to region. While the pottery of the Plains and Northeastern tribes was unadorned, that of the Indians of the Southwest excelled in its orna-mentation, style and form. Southwest Indians were known also for the intricate designs of their basketry. Elaborately carved masks and totem poles were developed among the Southwest Eskimos in the Aleutians.

INDIANS OF AMERICA

New World first settled by Asiatics who arrived thousands of years ago

Threading their way sporadically across the narrowest point between Asia and North America — the Bering Straits which divide Siberia from Alaska — the earliest inhabitants of the Western Hemisphere came to the North American continent as long as 15 to 20 thousand years ago. They were the ancestors of the American Indian, whose Mongoloid features, such as straight black hair, black eyes, and high cheek bones, mark him as a descendant of the earliest Asiatic racial stock. (See Plate 3 in atlas.)

Primarily, these first migrants who roamed prehistoric America were hunters. Following the hunt, they spread southward, and gradually established civilizations of varying degrees of complexity throughout North, Central, and South America. By the time of the European explorations, there were an estimated one and one-half million Indians in North America, and from three to four million in Central and South America.

In all regions, the Indians were masters of their environment. They found and made use of the best materials for their weapons, their homes, and for their crafts. Thus canoes made of birch bark skimmed the lakes of the Northeast, "bull boats" made of bull hide crossed the rivers of the treeless plains, and the "dug-out" log canoe carried the Indians of the East and South along their wooded streams and rivers.

A profound devotion to nature characterized the Indian, who developed elaborate myths about the origin of the oceans, of the forests, of rain, and of the sun. He was remarkable for his eloquence as well as for his silence; for his wisdom and for his folly; for his fierceness and cruelty in war and for his complete devotion to his tribe. He relied on his own efforts in all his endeavors. The dog was his only domesticated animal as horses were not known until introduced by the Spanish who came to explore.

The highest levels of Indian culture were attained in South and Central America, where the Mayas of Yucatan, for example, contributed the 0 (zero) to mathematics, thus surpassing even the Egyptians, Romans, and Chinese in astuteness. The Incas of Peru were known for their skill as architects and engineers and the Aztecs of Mexico for their development of an exact calendar and for the detail, beauty, and symmetry of their art.

In comparison with the Indians of South and Central America, the tribes of the North American continent were very backward. They failed to develop a civilization or culture which could compare in complexity and advancement.

PASSING THE PIPE was a custom common to many tribes. Among the Mandan Indians of the Plains, who lived in earthen lodges, it was used in receiving guests and represented friendship.

HAWAII'S NATIVE population, the Polynesians, came from Asia and reached the islands by way of the Malay peninsula and Java. They had soft musical language, built on only twelve letters.

TRIBAL COUNCILS were the governing bodies in most regions. Among the Iroquois, women played an important political role. Descent was in the female line and property and land were owned by the women, who also had a vote in the tribal councils. This was not the case among most other tribes.

TRIBAL ENCAMPMENTS often were placed along the shores of lakes and river banks. Many Indians were semi-nomadic, moving with the seasons and returning again to former camping grounds. They were very adept at using available materials such as clay, hide, grass, bark, in their dwellings.

ALONG THE SHORES of the Pacific, on the Midwest plains and in the Eastern forest regions, the Indians depended largely on hunting and fishing for their livelihood. Seed gathering provided food for some Western tribes, but agriculture was a late development in most cases.

BURIAL CUSTOMS differed among the various tribes. Sometimes the body was wrapped in a skin or blanket and placed upon a scaffolding to protect it from animals. Some tribes practiced cremation. Elaborate rites, sometimes lengthy, were often held upon the death of a tribesman.

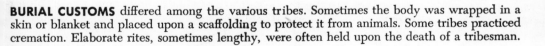

INDIAN WARRIORS, particularly of the Plains region, dressed brilliantly. Their headdresses and blankets were elaborately decorated and indicated the stature of the man by depicting the important deeds he had performed. The Indian of the Plains depended largely on the bison for his clothing, and on bones and horn for his ornaments. The tribes of the forest dressed less elaborately. Mostly, clothing consisted of one wrap.

VIKINGS

Norsemen first to settle America;
Sagas tell of the early explorations

It was probably enterprising Teutons of the Norse sagas, not Columbus, who first "discovered" the New World. Setting out in their swift vessels, the Norse came to America by means of two stepping stones, Iceland and Greenland.

Iceland, a barren, treeless island of lava, fjords and open grass, had little to offer new arrivals. However the Norsemen, many of whom were prompted to leave Norway to seek political freedom, set out to colonize it. These colonies survived and today descendants of this ancient stock still live in Iceland.

The next link in the discovery of North America was provided by Eric the Red. Outlawed from Norway for manslaughter, he came to Iceland, where he was again outlawed for the same crime. Eventually he landed in Greenland, where he established a home in 985. The bright carpet of summer grass on the hills of Greenland lent the island its name, but gave no hint of the rigorous winters. Eric was followed by other Norse settlers who raised cattle and sheep, built stone houses and churches, and continued to trade with their homeland and with Europe, exporting cattle hides, seal skins, walrus ivory and other products of their environment.

One of the chief traders was called Herjulf. He made yearly voyages to Norway. His son, Bjarni, driven off course on his way to Greenland, sighted new lands, but did not explore them. He may have been the first to set eyes on continental North America.

Stories of these new lands seen by Bjarni reached Leif Ericson, the son of Eric the Red. Determined to explore these new lands, he bought a small ship, took 30 hearty men, and sailed from Greenland about the year 1000. It was summer and soon he came upon a land which had a soft climate, gentle breezes and was rich in vegetation, probably near present-day Cape Cod. He built huts, and stayed through the winter. One day a German in the party, Tyrker, excitedly reported finding grapes like those in his native Germany. Accordingly, Leif named this land Vinland (Wineland)

Norse Establish New World Colonies

Most distinguished of Norse explorers was Thorfinn Karlsefni. He set out in 1003 to colonize the New World, taking with him 151 men, seven women, and also cattle and sheep. He set a more northerly course than Leif, possibly settling in the Hudson Bay area or the Gulf of St. Lawrence. During his three years in the area Karlsefni conducted numerous expeditions in search of warmer climates and better conditions. A saga tells that he encountered forests full of beasts, brooks which swarmed with fish, excellent pasture land and grapes like those found by Leif. Hostilities with the natives forced him to give up the colony in 1006 and return to his former life in Greenland.

Although there were a few other expeditions, the Norsemen vanished from North America. Except for the possible record left in the Kensington Stone, there is no record of any other Norsemen reaching the New World until the Swedes came to Delaware in 1638. Nevertheless, there is no doubt of the authenticity of their early explorations, which are recorded in sagas and also in such early histories as the *Hamburg Church History*, by Adam of Bremen, a canon and historian of high authority who died in 1076.

The Norsemen were not the only pre-Columbian explorers of North America. Diderick Pining and Hans Pothorst, two Germans who led a combined Danish-Portuguese expedition, and Johannes Scolvus, famous Polish pilot, are believed to have sailed to Iceland and the West, but the extent of their voyages is not known. There is some evidence of pre-Columbian expeditions by the Portuguese. Andrea Bianco, for example, must have sailed past the coast of South America because his map shows the definite outline of Brazil.

It is certain that Columbus was neither the first white man to "discover" America, nor the first to explore it. However, the 15th century did bring with it more extensive explorations and more determined colonization, marking the effective beginning of present-determined colonization by men of greater vision, marking the effective beginning of present-day America.

BOLD AND INDEPENDENT, the Vikings were daring navigators who knew how to calculate their course by sun and moon, and how to measure time by stars. Their early voyages are recorded in famous Icelandic sagas.

NORSE EXPEDITION into the heart of America is recorded on the Kensington Rune Stone, discovered in Minnesota in 1898. Its authenticity has never been established, and like the Old Stone Mill at Newport, R. I., its origin remains a point of dispute. The inscription has been translated as follows: "We are 8 Goths and 22 Norwegians on exploration-journey from Vinland over the West. We had camp by two skerries (islands) one day's journey from this stone. We were out and fished one day. After we came home we found 10 of our men red with blood and dead. Ave Maria. Save us from evil. We have 10 of our party by the sea to look after our ships 14 days' journey from the island. Year 1362." No other evidence remains.

LEIF ERICSON, prompted by stories of new lands seen by trading vessels, set sail from Greenland about 1000 A.D. He came upon a land which he named Vinland because of its grapes. It was probably near Cape Cod.

LAND was first sighted by a sailor aboard the *Nina*, on Oct. 12, 1492. Columbus landed at San Salvador (now Watling Island) in the Bahamas the same day, after sailing 4,492 miles, the longest continuous voyage then known. The crew, many of them mutinous during the anxious passage, now prostrated themselves at Columbus' feet and joined him in prayer. Awestruck Indians cautiously approached the explorers with peace offerings.

COLUMBUS DISCOVERS AMERICA

Exploration for a westward passage to Orient uncovers new continent

Christopher Columbus, a Genoese, set sail from Palos, Spain, Aug. 3, 1492, to find a western route to Asia. The real voyage into the unknown began September 6 from the Canary Islands. Columbus commanded the *Santa Maria*, some 80 feet long, slower and slightly larger than his other two ships, *Nina* and *Pinta*. The expedition totaled 120 men.

For nearly 15 years Columbus had sought this chance, appealing to four monarchs, the Genoese senate and various nobles. Finally, King Ferdinand and Queen Isabella of Spain equipped him with three caravels.

The 15th century was a period of oceanic discoveries and Columbus, a sailor at 14, heard stories told of land beyond the Canaries and west of Ireland. Imaginary islands to the west appeared on accredited mariners' maps as early as 1375. One of these islands, Antillia, Columbus hoped to en-

counter about 2500 miles out. The weather was calm but tangled weeds of the Sargasso Sea and variation of the magnetic needle terrorized his crews. Symptoms of mutiny were frequent. Only by pleading and cajoling could Columbus prevent them from turning back. He changed course from west to west-southwest and on Oct. 12 landed at San Salvador in the Bahamas, going on to find Cuba and Haiti (Espanola), which he identified as Japan. After the *Santa Maria* was wrecked, he was forced to leave 37 of his men at Haiti.

Columbus, on his return to Spain, was received with high honors and confirmed Admiral of the Ocean Sea and governor of all islands he found in the Indies. A second expedition of 17 ships and 1500 men was immediately organized. It found Puerto Rico, Virgin Islands and Jamaica (1493-

96). The original fort at Haiti had been wiped out by natives but a second attempt at colonization was made.

When gold was discovered, Columbus, a poor administrator, failed to quell the ensuing chaos and resentment flared against him. On his third voyage Columbus discovered Trinidad and the coast of South America. But during his absence a new governor, Bobadilla, replaced him and, in a bid for popularity, arrested Columbus at Haiti and shipped him to Spain in irons. He was speedily restored to favor by the King and Queen and granted a fourth fleet. With failing health, Columbus set out in 1502 to remake his reputation, exploring the inhospitable south shore of the Gulf of Mexico. In 1504 he returned to Spain and died two years later, disillusioned, discouraged and almost forgotten.

COLUMBUS PLEADED twice with Spanish monarchs. Rejected initially, he appealed in vain to Portugal and England, finally caught ear of Queen Isabella who agreed to grant him ships.

HIGH POINT of Columbus' career was his triumphal return to Spain. He displayed before the throne trophies of the New World: 6 ornament-clad Indians, 40 parrots, fauna and flora.

COLUMBUS DIED in Spain, May 20, 1506, a broken man. In 1542 his remains were taken to Hispaniola. Among the last records of his life was a license to ride muleback, issued in 1505.

SPANISH ADVENTURERS

In the 50 years after the discoveries of Columbus, the proud, ruthless, devout conquistadors staked out for Spain an empire in the New World twice the size of Europe.

They came first to conquer and loot. They brought with them horses, pigs, sugar cane, grain, measles and smallpox. They returned with gold, pearls and tobacco. The Indians, terrified by the horses, revered the Spaniards as gods. Hunger and fatigue were the conquerors' worst enemies.

Hernando de Soto and Francisco Coronado explored North America. (See atlas, plate 2). De Soto landed at Tampa Bay in 1539 (left) and for four years wandered over 350,000 square miles of wilderness. He discovered the Mississippi river. Here he died and his men set his body afloat on the river (below). After De Soto and Coronado failed to find more gold, the Spaniards settled down to colonizing their holdings.

JUAN PONCE DE LEON first came to the Indies with Columbus, as did explorers Vicente Yanes Pinzon, who discovered sub-equatorial South America, and Juan de La Cosa, who explored the coast of Guiana and Venezuela. In 1508 Ponce de Leon led an expedition to Puerto Rico, where he became governor. Determined to find a rumored fountain of perpetual youth on the island of "Bimini," he set sail in 1513. On April 8 he landed near the present site of St. Augustine. When he returned in 1521 to conquer the land he named "Florida," he was mortally wounded by an Indian arrow.

BARBARITY OF SPANIARDS killed off the frail, mild mannered natives of the West Indies in less than 100 years. Resistance and revolts were met with savage hunts with dogs, burnings and wholesale slaughter. Captured, they were made serfs or sold as slaves. Many preferred suicide to Spanish masters. One Spaniard arose as the "Apostle of the Indians," Bartolome de Las Casas (left), who sailed with Columbus, took holy orders at Haiti. Revolted by the massacres, he repeatedly appealed to the Crown for temperance and in 1542 succeeded in banning use of natives for forced labor.

CORONADO tramped into New Mexico and Arizona in 1540 looking for the "Seven Golden Cities of Cibola." His hopes were bolstered by Cabeza de Vaca, one of two survivors of a 400-man expedition to Florida, who had made his way in eight years across the continent. To both Coronado and De Soto, Vaca embroidered on the stories he had heard of gold to the north. Two vessels with Coronado's large expedition kept a parallel course along the Pacific coast, hoping to find the long sought for waterway linking the Atlantic and Pacific. The seven golden cities turned out to be the seven pueblo villages of the Zuni Indian confederacy. Coronado discovered the Grand Canyon and sighted ancient cliff dwellings (right). Fed another golden rumor, he searched eastward into Kansas, returning defeated, in 1542. The bloody trail he left behind incited Indians against future explorers.

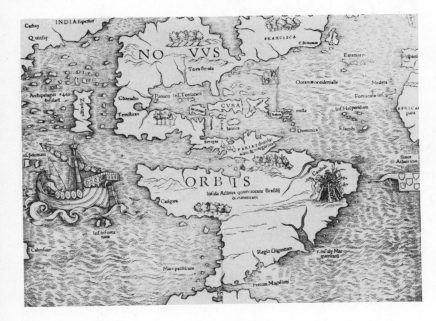

SPANISH EXPLORATIONS in North America after 1543 mainly retraced and filled in gaps between the wanderings of De Soto and Coronado. Santa Fe was founded in 1605 on the site of Indian pueblo, as was Taos (above).

◀ **CONTINENT OF AMERICA** had begun to take shape in this map of 1540. But until Magellan's world circling voyage (1519-22) it was still considered a part of Asia. As early as 1507 it had begun to be called America after Amerigo Vespucci, famous navigator who widely publicized his trips.

FRANCISCO PIZARRO, who was with Balboa at the discovery of the Pacific, conquered Peru with Diego de Almagro. Capturing the Inca king, he held him for $16 million ransom, killed him. After sacking Cuzco in 1533, they fell out. Almagro was executed; Pizarro killed.

HERNANDO CORTES set out to conquer Mexico with some 500 Spaniards, 16 horses and 10 cannon. Landing at Vera Cruz he was met by Aztec emissaries with gifts of gold as a bribe to return. Defeating the Tlascalan Indians, who then joined him, he marched on Tenochititlan, and was received cordially at the Aztec capital Nov. 8, 1519, by the weak, reflective Montezuma (left) who considered him a god. Defeating at Vera Cruz an expedition sent to recall him, he returned to find the Aztecs in revolt. Montezuma was killed by his people. The Spaniards fled the city but with the aid of Indians retook it Aug. 13, 1521.

SAMUEL DE CHAMPLAIN was for more than 30 years a key figure in the building of New France. In 1609, accompanying a party of Huron and Algonquin Indians to Lake Champlain, he became involved in a battle with the Iroquois which helped spark the longstanding enmity between Iroquois and French. In 1629, Champlain was forced to surrender Quebec, which he had founded in 1608, to the English (l.). The city was returned to France in three years.

NEW FRANCE

Daring Frenchmen create foundations of an empire in the New World

French interest in the New World was first aroused when the Breton navigator Jacques Cartier led two expeditions to North America in 1534-34. Cartier discovered the St. Lawrence River, visited Indian settlements and took the great Huron chief Donnaconna home with him to France. (See plates 2 and 3 in atlas.)

Little was done about the discoveries until 1603 when a new expedition, headed by Champlain and Pontgrave, was dispatched at the instigation of the fur merchants of Rouen and St. Malo. This time settlements were established at Port Royal in Acadia and in Quebec. Almost immediately conflicting French and British claims set off a two-century struggle for control of the new territories in America.

In 1627, Cardinal Richelieu organized the Company of New France, also called Company of The Hundred Associates, composed of a group of hand-picked leaders who were given a monopoloy of the fur trade. In return they promised to send out colonists and establish missions.

Two fleets were forced back by the British and, in order to fulfill its obligations, the Company began granting seigneurial tracts to individuals agreeing to take out colonists. One such grant in 1640 gave the island of Montreal to the Sulpician Order of Paris. With the building of a hospital, mission and schools, Montreal soon became a flourishing outpost.

Problems of the colony's religious life became too burdensome for the Recollect friars who had joined Champlain in 1615, and in 1625 the richer, better-organized Jesuit order sent out a group of priests. They plunged into missionary work and exploration, recording their efforts in the famous Jesuit *Relations* series, which stimulated great interest in France.

In 1649 the French fur trade suffered a serious setback when marauding Iroquois, armed by the English and Dutch, attacked and wiped out the Huron Indians who had long been helpful to the French traders.

The Company of New France was dissolved in 1663 when Louis XIV and his minister Colbert took over direct control of the province. Peace was established with the Iroquois and an era of great prosperity began. The fur trade resumed its importance and Indians in fleets of canoes descended the rivers each spring to barter skins for guns, tools, blankets, jewelry and brandy — the latter much against the will of the good fathers. Important in the fur trading picture were the colorful *coureurs de bois,* adventurers who lived among the Indians, emerging periodically to sell furs.

Missions established around the Great Lakes aided exploration and development of the interior in the latter part of the 17th century. With their Indian friends the Jesuits roamed the forests and waterways, carefully recording their discoveries. The Count de Frontenac, named governor in 1672, established a series of forts along the lakes and rivers and sponsored the explorations of La Salle, who in 1682 carried the king's banner to the Mississippi Delta, and opened a vast but short-lived empire.

JOHN CABOT, citizen of Venice, was among the first explorers to visit the New World. After news of Columbus' voyage reached him in England, Cabot sailed from Bristol to coast of North America, which he believed to be the Orient.

JACQUES CARTIER of St. Malo led the first official French expeditions to North America in 1534-35. He explored the Gulf of St. Lawrence, discovered the St. Lawrence River and visited the sites of present-day Montreal and Quebec.

FRENCH DOMAIN was extended to the Gulf of Mexico when Robert Cavelier, Sieur de la Salle, obtained royal patent to build forts, conduct fur trade and explore the interior. In 1679 he astonished Indians by constructing a sailing ship, the "Griffin" on Lake Erie (l.). After one trip the fur-laden ship disappeared. In 1682, La Salle descended the Mississippi to its mouth, claimed the rich river valley for France and named it Louisiana (above). Returning by sea two years later he missed the river, landed on the Texas coast. Soon afterward La Salle was murdered by one of his men.

FIERY COUNT DE FRONTENAC was Canada's outstanding governor. He built chain of forts along the waterways, turned English from Quebec in 1690 with a haughty refusal to surrender.

FRENCH FORT on the Chicago River was typical of outposts established during the 17th century. Explorers, missionaries and fur traders roamed the lakes, rivers and forests of New France, establishing forts and missions that eventually formed a chain from Quebec to the mouth of the Mississippi. These settlements gave the French a firm hold on interior of the continent, left English hemmed along the Eastern seaboard.

PIERRE RADISSON was one of the most famous *coureurs de bois*. With his partner Medard des Groseilliers he explored Lake Superior, the Hudson Bay area, helped found Hudson's Bay Co.

FLORIDA HUGUENOTS

With Protestantism becoming wider spread in France, both supporters and opponents of the new movement began to consider the possibility of establishing colonies for its followers — as dumping grounds or refuges, depending on the point of view. In 1562 Jean Ribaut, backed by Protestant Admiral Gaspard de Coligny, led Huguenots to Florida, already claimed by Spain, founding Charlesfort, later abandoned.

In 1564 a second Huguenot group built Fort Caroline on St. John's River. Next year Ribaut brought out a fleet to reinforce the colony. Meanwhile Philip II of Spain had dispatched a fleet under Pedro Menendez to drive the French from Florida. He built the fort of St. Augustine (c.) as a base for his campaign. When Ribaut's ships were wrecked in a hurricane, the Spaniards marched overland, destroyed Fort Caroline and massacred its occupants (r.) This marked the end of French colonial efforts in Florida.

EARLY MISSIONARIES played a vital role in development of New France. Recollec friars arrived in 1615, the first Jesuits in 1625. For half a century they controlled much of the economic and social life in colony.

OUTSTANDING FIGURE among Jesuits was Father Jacques Marquette, missionary and explorer. After founding two missions on the Great Lakes, Marquette, with Louis Joliet, made the first descent of the Mississippi in 1673. Taken ill on a later voyage, he wintered in a crude hut on the Chicago River (upper). He died following spring while trying to reach his mission.

RECOLLET PRIEST Father Louis Hennepin, discovered Falls of St. Anthony, where Minneapolis stands, was first white man to see and describe Niagara. With typical exaggeration he tripled actual height of falls.

HENNEPIN'S WRITINGS were prolific, colorful and extremely popular, although often quite unreliable. Boasting cheerfully of his great personal courage, he described his journeyings with La Salle, his own explorations of the upper Mississippi. His narrative told of his capture by the Sioux, and also described his subsequent rescue by the voyageur Duluth.

JESUIT PRIEST Jean de Brebeuf was among the first group to reach Canada. He established missions among the Hurons. Later he was tortured and killed during Iroquois attack in 1649.

JEAN NICOLET spent fifteen years among the Indians before he was dispatched by Champlain to seek the reported water route to the west. He was the first European to reach Sault Ste. Marie, travelled up Green Bay, met the Winnebagoes who told of a "great water" at three days journey. But Nicolet did not make trip that would have led him to the Mississippi.

JESUIT MARTYRS were almost commonplace in 17th century Canada. Amid famine, disease and incredible hardship the black-robed fathers toiled in missions and schools. Under constant attack by warlike Iroquois, they remained with their Huron friends, calmly facing death and horrible torture. Composite picture above shows incidents of Jesuit martyrdom in Canada.

PORT ROYAL in Acadia, founded in 1605, was the first successful French colony in America. After a difficult beginning, colonists enjoyed a good year under guidance of De Monts and Baron de Poutrincourt. Delighted Indians were regular guests at nightly banquets which featured game, fish, fowl and fine wines. However, colony was temporarily abandoned in 1607.

WIVES FOR COLONISTS were dispatched in shiploads under Colbert's program for developing New France. A free 100 acres was granted to fathers of 12 children. Some petitioned for double acreages, claiming 24 or more offspring. Present population of three million or more French-Canadians are chiefly descended from 30,000 17th century immigrants.

COLONIZATION OF NEW FRANCE continued into the early 18th century. Quebec in 1730 (top) was a thriving city, the gateway to a series of frontier settlements bearing such famous names as Detroit, St. Louis, Natchez, Biloxi, Mobile and New Orleans. Biloxi was scene in 1720 of John Law's notorious "Mississippi Bubble" real estate promotion scheme.

BUILDING FIRST SETTLEMENT at Port Royal, colonists laid out an attractive quadrangle of wooden buildings around a large court. French and English alternated occupation of Acadia several times during the succeeding years.

ENGLISH EXPLORERS
In the latter half of the 16th century, England sponsored a number of voyages in the hope of discovering the much-desired northwest passage to the Pacific. In 1579, Francis Drake, sailing north in the Pacific, beached the *Golden Hind* for repairs some thirty miles north of San Francisco Bay. He called the land New Albion and took possession of it in the name of Queen Elizabeth (l.). Martin Frobisher, shown above with Drake, made three voyages across the Atlantic in search of the passage, but discovered nothing more than some rocks bearing false gold. In 1583 Sir Humphrey Gilbert (r.) sailed to Newfoundland and informed crews of the fishing fleets that he was claiming the land for England. On his return trip Gilbert's ship was lost in a storm near the Azores. These explorers laid the groundwork for English claims in New World.

COLONIAL ERA

Groups of oppressed Europeans, seeking economic and religious freedom, look westward in the 17th century to find hope in the unspoiled New World

Driven by poverty, persecution and oppression, a tide of emigrants swept westward in the 17th and 18th centuries as Englishmen and Continentals sought increased freedom and opportunity in a new land. This vast folk-wandering to the raw wilderness of the New World created a culture which was to mark the new nation.

The colonial period in American history first established the continent's role as a "melting pot," assimilating many nationalities into a way of life with distinct characteristics of its own. Although the colonists reflected their European background, the reality of establishing a society in a wilderness impressed its individual stamp on the culture of the colonies and the character of the inhabitants.

Religious persecution in England offered the first stimulus to emigration. A Separatist group was the first of these to seek opportunity in the New World, founding a Pilgrim colony at Plymouth on Dec. 25, 1620. The ascension of Charles I to the English throne in 1625 caused Puritan leaders to seek haven elsewhere, leading to establishment of the Massachusetts Bay Colony.

Other religious leaders followed the same pattern. William Penn, dissatisfied with treatment of Quakers in England, founded the colony which bears his name, Pennsylvania. Cecil Calvert offered similar haven to English Catholics in Maryland.

The economic depression, however, which swept England in the early 17th century spurred emigration more than religious or political tyranny. Many English lived in poverty and even skilled laborers could not find work. The promise of economic opportunity was a lure they could not resist. Colonization in Virginia was stimulated by a turn in political fortunes. Many Cavaliers or "king's men" decided to cast their lot with the colonies when Oliver Cromwell came to power in England as a result of civil war. These Royalists became "country squires."

Europeans Emigrate

Although early settlement was conducted mainly by the English, the same factors of poverty, persecution and political oppression in Europe swelled the emigrant tide during the latter part of the 17th century. Thousands of Germans, Dutch, French, Swiss, Scotch-Irish and other Europeans emigrated. These nationalities adopted the English language, laws and customs, modifying them with their own habits and traditions, creating a culture peculiarly American.

Diverse backgrounds were not alone in producing differences in the colonies. Since the colonies depended on trade with England for many of the necessities of life, early colonial development was limited to the seaboard. In New England, a short growing season and shortage of tillable land turned the settlers to trade, industry and fishing as sources of income. The strong influence of the Puritan church was felt in both government and everyday life.

While New England was predominantly commercial and industrial, the Middle Colonies were more cosmopolitan. Here commerce

and agriculture flourished side by side. In the South, rich lands and long growing seasons tended to create an agrarian economy, revolving around plantation life. Virginia, the first colony to survive in the New World, centered its economy around cultivation of tobacco, which found a market in Europe. Further south, the Carolinas evolved a more diverse economy, based on rice, indigo, naval stores.

Colonial development faced more problems than conquering the wilderness. Wars which racked Europe also extended to America. Rivalry between the French and English for development of the continent led to many conflicts. These included King William's War, Queen Anne's War and King George's War. The French and Indian War in America was the counterpart of the Seven Years' War in Europe. Even with the settlement of these conflicts, settlers living on the fringes of the colonies faced constant trouble with the Indians. These wars and Indian skirmishes developed a self-reliance and unity among the colonies, binding them together in time of adversity.

Just as economic life was varied in the colonies, differences also existed in political and social life. The Puritan influence was strong in New England, imposing severe restrictions on society. Although the church was a dominant factor in political life, the urban structure of the economy led to limited self-government through the medium of the town meeting, held to enable citizens to work out mutual problems in a manner satisfactory to all.

Education Becomes Important

In the Middle Colonies, European influence was strongest, producing a culture that reflected Continental tastes and manners. In New England and the Middle Colonies education was of primary importance. Colleges were founded to further religious teachings and provide the leaders needed by the colonies. Harvard, the first college in America, was established in 1636. Distances between plantations in the South deterred central schools so private tutors were the rule. Plantation owners often sent their sons to England to finish their education.

THE PRESS, GUARDIAN OF FREEDOM

Spanish colonization contrasted strongly with English. The Spaniards ruled harshly, exploiting native populations and depredating the land. In the Southwest, the major Spanish colonization was conducted by Jesuit and Franciscan missionaries.

The English came to stay. The Crown, however, did not exercise authority at first and the colonists developed self-reliance which stood them in good stead during the French and Indian War. The French, conversely, were handicapped by close royal supervision.

The lack of control of English colonies also had two far-reaching effects. First, colonists were forced to establish their own governments and second, the lack of centralized control tended to drive America away from Britain. Thus, when friction occurred over controversial legislation, the self-reliant colonies were able to resist the authority of the Crown, paving way for eventual bid for freedom.

★   ★   ★

◀ **RELIGIOUS PERSECUTION** led a small band of Separatists to leave England, first for Holland and eventually for the New World. Forerunners of a wave of emigration to the New World, these Pilgrims faced the problem of creating a home in a strange country, cultivating friendship with the

Indians and conquering the wilderness. Despite privation and disease, which took a heavy toll in the early months of settlement, the Pilgrims remained steadfast in their effort to create a home where they might worship as they believed. Their success encouraged others to follow to America.

FIRST ENGLISH CHILD born in North America was Virginia Dare. Born August 18, 1587, in the first English colony in America, Roanoke, she was the granddaughter of the first governor, John White. She was named Virginia in honor of England's virgin queen, Elizabeth, for whom Sir Walter Raleigh also named land in which colony of Roanoke was founded.

LOST COLONY of Roanoke, founded by Sir Walter Raleigh in 1585, had vanished in 1591 when John White's expedition found only the word "Croatoan," the name of an Indian tribe, carved on a tree where the 200 colonists had been. Because of his persistence in founding the Roanoke colony, Raleigh is known as the true parent of North American colonization.

SOUTHERN COLONIES

Roanoke and Jamestown, the first English Colonies in North America

England's colonization of North America stemmed from divergent reasons, including a desire to weaken expansion-minded Spain. Colonization also offered a chance for merchant-adventurers to gain easy profits, and for many it was an escape from religious and political persecution.

The first English claim to North America was made in 1497 by John Cabot, who explored Newfoundland in an effort to find a waterway to the Pacific. Later, English slave traders reached the West Indies and privateers, looting treasure-laden Spanish galleons, explored the Caribbean as far north as Florida. But not until 1585 was there any attempt to establish an English settlement

in North America. After peace with Spain was reached in 1605, the seas became more secure. In 1606, a charter was obtained from James I for formation of two companies, the London and the Plymouth, to establish North American settlements. The London company settled Jamestown, Va., in 1607 with 120 men, but faced terrible losses.

Tobacco, introduced to England by Sir Walter Raleigh, became the leading crop and slave trade had its start on the large Southern estates. The county, akin to the English rural county, became the basis of agricultural, social, and governmental division in the South.

In nearly all Southern colonies the Church

of England was supported with public funds and freedom of religious worship was not permitted. In Maryland, however, churches of almost all faiths were allowed.

In 1624 King James dissolved the Virginia company and appointed a royal governor and council. In the years that followed, many quarrels ensued between the colonists and the governors, most notably in 1676, when Nathaniel Bacon and his followers, incensed by Governor Berkeley's refusal to protect the frontier against the Indians, drove the governor out of Jamestown and set fire to part of the town. The rebellion, which soon collapsed, was the first armed resistance to British rule in America.

FIVE KERNELS OF CORN were distributed to each household in the early days of the colonies to prevent starvation. From 25 to 90 per cent of the colonists died annually from severe weather, disease, famine, or Indian raids.

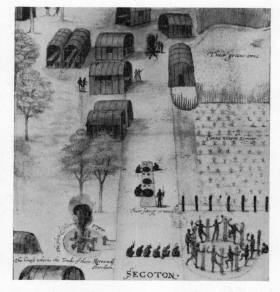

FIRST DRAWING made of early America was this sketch by John White in 1585 of an Indian village near Roanoke, Virginia. The Indians in the South generally proved to be less hostile to the colonists than those living in the North.

FIRST NEGROES in English America were 20 bound servants landed from a Dutch man-of-war in 1619 at Jamestown. However, John Hawkins had brought a large number of slaves to Spanish possessions in the West Indies as early as 1563.

CAPTAIN JOHN SMITH'S LIFE IS SPARED by Indian Chief Powhatan when his daughter, Pocahontas, pleads for Smith's life. Smith, an able leader of the Jamestown colony which was founded in 1607 by the London Company, started friendly trading with the Indians for corn, explored the Chesapeake Bay, Potomac, and Rappahannock Rivers, and organized Jamestown's fight for survival. Pocahontas was taken by colonists as hostage in 1613 until the warring Pequots would agree to a peace. Her marriage to planter John Rolfe in 1614 confirmed the peace made with the Indians.

THE FIRST HOUSE OF REPRESENTATIVES in America convened in Virginia in 1619. The first 11 cities sent two representatives each to the House of Burgesses which acted to restrict British authority.

NATHANIEL BACON, protesting Governor Berkeley's failure to act, led group of colonists against marauding Indians, then turned on Berkeley and oligarchy.

JAMESTOWN SURRENDERED peacefully to Cromwell's fleet sent in 1652 to quell any royalist opposition to the Commonwealth government established after King Charles I was beheaded in England.

CATHOLIC MASS IS HELD AT FOUNDING OF MARYLAND IN 1634, FIRST COLONY TO GRANT RELIGIOUS FREEDOM

LORD CALVERT OF MARYLAND

FOUNDING OF MARYLAND

When, in 1632, King Charles granted George Calvert, first Lord Baltimore, a patent for land to start a colony, it was named Maryland for Charles' wife. Calvert died before charter was approved but his son, Cecilius, reached St. Mary's (later called Baltimore) in 1634. Lord Baltimore, Roman Catholic convert, sought charter to establish refuge for members of his faith. However, charter provided freedom which was re-inforced by the passage of the Tolerance Act of 1649. Thus the colony became a haven for those fleeing religious persecution and soon the majority of colonists were Protestant.

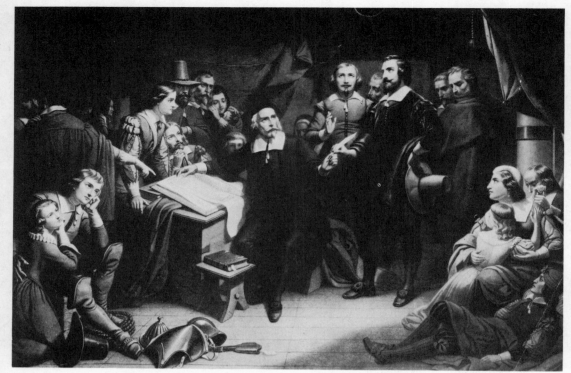

THE PILGRIMS were a group of Separatists who emigrated to Leyden, Holland, in 1609 to escape religious persecution in England. In 1617 they sent two of their leaders, John Carver and Robert Cushman, to London for financial aid to start a colony in America. With two patents granted them for land within Virginia, 73 men and 29 women set sail in one ship, the *Mayflower*. Bad weather and the rugged seacoast forced them to land near Cape Cod in November, 1620, where they founded their colony, New Plymouth, December 25, 1620. Since their patent had no force outside Virginia, they united aboard ship and signed "The Mayflower Compact" as a political document binding them.

PILGRIMS' ARRIVAL

Band of exiles establish the first permanent colony in North America

By the end of the 16th century English explorers had visited New England and brought back reports of its rich stock of fish and furs. But there were no English colonists in New England until 1607, when George Popham attempted a settlement on behalf of the Plymouth Company. However, this colonization attempt failed.

In 1620 the Plymouth Company, reorganized as the "Council for New England" obtained a new charter. The Pilgrims, some 35 of a band of Separatists who had been living in exile in Holland for more than 10 years, sailed with 67 others from London to found a colony in Virginia. Sidetracked by weather, they debarked outside the land grant, so they banded together politically as they had done religiously by signing the "Mayflower Compact" before landing. In spite of severe winters, disease, and scant supplies, the colony survived.

The Massachusetts Bay Colony, a fishing settlement established in 1623 at Cape Ann, was reorganized and resettled in Salem in 1626 and was joined in 1628 by John Endecott and 60 colonists. In 1629 the Massachusetts Bay Company obtained a charter making the colony a trading corporation which was run as a religious commonwealth of Puritans. When the Massachusetts Bay Company moved its seat of government from England to New England, it transformed itself from a British trading company into a self-governing commonwealth.

Religious dissension brought other colonies into being. Roger Williams, banished from Massachusetts, established Providence in 1636; Anne Hutchinson left Masschusetts to settle Portsmouth, R.I., in 1638; and Thomas Hooker was the spiritual force behind the formation of Connecticut the same year. All the colonies but Rhode Island persecuted religious non-conformists and conducted "witch hunts."

Indian raids took their toll of early settlers, but as more and more colonists arrived, the Indians were subdued and driven off their lands. In New England both the Dutch and French protested that the English colonists were encroaching on their lands, but the English so outnumbered them that little was done to prevent it.

The only real good fortune experienced by the Pilgrims was to stumble on deserted fields ready for tillage on their arrival at Plymouth, and to find a friendly teacher in the Indian, Squanto. The remainder of the long, hard pull found the novice adventurers strictly on their own. Nearly half the small band perished that first winter, and many of the quick were dangerously close to the starvation point.

Severe winters, threat of Indian attacks, and a childish inexperience in the wilderness combined to nearly blot the community out of existence. But the Pilgrims' faith held a stubborn, tenacious streak that would not yield to adversity or privation. Like Plymouth Rock, they were there to stay.

MILES STANDISH RETURNS to the Pilgrims after five weeks of exploration up and down the coast in search of habitable land and a plentiful water supply for the new colony of Plymouth.

BUILDING THE COMMON HOUSE at Plymouth was one of the first tasks. The colony, at first a communal system, began to prosper in 1624 when individual enterprise was inaugurated.

THE FIRST THANKSGIVING was celebrated by the Pilgrims after the first harvest in 1621. They invited Massasoit and 90 of his Indian braves to join them in their three-day feast of gratitude.

CHIEF MASSASOIT, head of the Pokanoket tribes on whose land the Pilgrims had settled, journeyed more than 40 miles to meet with the Plymouth colonists. As a result, a treaty of friendship between the Pokanokets and the Pilgrims was signed by Massasoit and John Carver, first governer of Plymouth. Peaceful relations continued for more than 50 years. Squanto, a Pokanoket Indian who had learned to speak English, remained with the Pilgrims and was of great service to them as their guide and interpreter. He taught them how to raise corn and to fish.

GOVERNOR WINTHROP arrived in Salem (r.), capital of Massachusetts Bay Colony, in 1630 with 900 colonists who were fleeing from religious persecution in England. Salem was originally founded four years before by Roger Conant, who led colonists to the area from a small fishing settlement near the mouth of the Kennebec river. In 1628 a patent was obtained for the land from the Plymouth company and John Endecott and 60 settlers joined the colony. A year later nearly 400 more colonists arrived and the King granted the company a trading charter. The colony actually was a trading corporation run as a religious commonwealth. After 1630 the government became representative. The first voting by ballot started in 1634.

CAPTAIN MILES STANDISH MARCHED on Merry Mount in 1628 on orders of the Pilgrims to destroy the settlement. The Pilgrims were outraged by colony head Thomas Morton's uninhibited life and success at Indian trading. Standish arrested Morton, who was then shipped back to England.

PURITAN CUSTOMS were austere and religious, usually having righteous practicality as a basis. Weddings were simple ceremonies and usually included a procession from the church. Their social life was stern and disciplined and seldom did they allow themselves comforts and pleasures in life.

PRISCILLA AND JOHN ALDEN were romantic figures in the Plymouth Colony. Their plain, homespun garments typify the Puritans' laws which opposed frivolity of action or of dress.

ENDECOTT CUTS THE CROSS from the King's ensign at a muster of the Salem militia in 1635. Roused to this action by the fiery preaching of Roger Williams who opposed union of church and state, Endecott's act was decried as rash and indiscreet at a time when the authorities in England were stirred against the colony and there was danger of their revoking the Massachusetts charter.

ROGER WILLIAMS, BANISHED FROM SALEM (left) was sheltered by the Narragansett Indians in the winter of 1636 after he wrote a pamphlet saying that the King of England was an intruder on Indian lands and had no right to grant American lands to colonists. Therefore, he claimed, all existing titles were invalid. He was ordered back to England, but escaped, lived with the Indians, and went south with five followers to establish Providence in 1636. An outspoken and fiery critic, he was famous as an apostle of religious toleration and as an advocate of liberal democratic government. Williams' regard for Indian rights was noteworthy. Friendly relations he established with Narragansetts aided colonies in Pequot War.

ANNE HUTCHINSON WAS TRIED at Boston in 1637 for her preaching, which questioned the legality of the Puritan religion. Ordered to leave the colony, she and her followers started a colony in Rhode Island in 1638, free from religious dictates. She was killed by Indians some five years later.

WITCH HUNTS were held throughout New England except in Rhode Island. The Massachusetts Body of Liberties of 1641 authorized capital punishment for witchcraft. Trials and executions, started in 1648, ran more than 40 years until witchcraft epidemic ended in 1693.

MASSACRE OF THE PEQUOTS was one of the bloodiest Indian battles in early American history. Colonists in Connecticut under Captain James Mason attacked and burned Indians' chief village, slaughtered more than 400 Pequots in 1637. The remaining Pequots either were killed or given as slaves to neighboring tribes. Their lands were divided among colonists.

RETURN OF THE MAYFLOWER to England in April, 1621, left the Pilgrims alone in their new settlement to eke out a living in the wilderness. About half of the settlers died during the first winter. Those who survived were so weak that the Indians could have killed them easily if an epidemic a few years before had not drastically reduced the New England tribes.

QUAKERS PERSECUTED

Religious minorities did not fare well in New England. Flogging (left) was a regular item on the agenda for those who gave "scandal" by their unorthodox views on religion. The first Quakers to visit Boston (1656) were imprisoned, whipped, and expelled from Massachusetts. They incurred Puritan ire because they did not believe in consecrated churches or ordained ministers. In addition, the Quakers refused to take oaths or remove their hats for anyone, matters considered a threat to Puritan rule. They were punished severely throughout the New England colonies (trial, right) with the singular exception of Rhode Island.

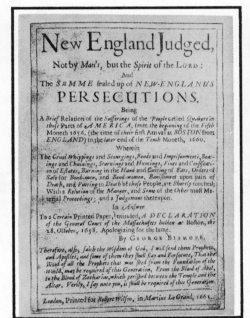

'H' FOR HERETIC frequently was branded on the hand of admitted Quakers. A heavy key was tied in the mouth of Humphrey Norton to silence him at his trial. Norton was whipped, branded, fined and then banished. A Dutchman paid his fine.

DEATH PENALTY faced Quakers who returned to Massachusetts after banishment. Mary Dyer was expelled to Rhode Island. She was taken into custody on a visit to Boston, and hanged in June, 1660. London pamphlet (left) decried harsh treatment of Quakers.

REV. THOMAS HOOKER'S SERMON in Connecticut in 1638 on the principles of establishing a government were framed in the "Fundamental Orders," the first known written constitution that created a government without reference to a king, charter, or patent. A liberal follower of Anne Hutchinson, Hooker created the framework of the United States constitution. No religious test was imposed on voters and a truly representative government for all was initiated.

ENGLISH AND DUTCH QUARRELS were bitter over land claimed by both in Connecticut. Although arbitrators settled on a satisfactory boundary line in 1651, war between the New England colonies and Dutch was imminent over question of land encroachment.

HENRY HUDSON, English navigator and explorer who was commissioned by the Dutch East India Company to find a northwest passage to China, was forced south along the Atlantic coast by calms and mutiny.

Guiding his *Half Moon* into New York Bay in September, 1609, Hudson rounded islands into the river that bears his name. Though shallow waters stopped him at the site of Albany, he had penetrated into the continent.

NEW NETHERLANDS

Dutch found New Amsterdam, settle Hudson Valley and carry on fur trade

Sponsored by Dutch West India Company, Capt. Cornelis Jacobsen May brought 30 families to New Netherland in 1624. Putting ashore in what is now New Jersey, they established the first permanent Dutch settlements in America. Two years later, Willem Verhulst and Peter Minuit founded New Amsterdam on Manhattan Island. Other

Dutch colonists settled in Connecticut, Delaware, Fort Orange (Albany), and the patroon estate of Rensselaerswyck. Three vessels named the *Sheep, Horse,* and *Cow* brought livestock from Holland to give the farmers in the New World a start.

Formed originally for trading purposes, and to destroy Spain's power in the New World, the company exercised tight control over the settlers' lives, dictating crop plantings and external trade. Its major difficulties were finding additional colonists and securing good officials. Although New Amsterdam enjoyed a thriving fur trade and had an abundance of fish, game, timber and lime, the colony suffered from incompetent leadership and the unruliness of its people.

The colony struggled through a succession of dictatorial though colorful governors from ineffectual Verhulst and Director Minuit to Van Twiller and Peter Stuyvesant. The settlers chafed under the rule of the landed aristocracy, but their fight to obtain representation councils was unsuccessful.

Infiltration of New Englanders into Dutch settlements and the advice of his mediators persuaded Stuyvesant to deliver New Amsterdam to the British without bloodshed in

1664. The Dutch re-occupied New York briefly in 1673-74, but the English had come to stay. However, Dutch influence continued in New York. It was reflected in commerce and trading, establishment of the Dutch Reformed Church, and in property holdings of such families as the Roosevelts and Van Burens, as well as in architecture.

FAMOUS BARGAIN, the purchase of Manhattan Island from the Indians for $24 worth of trinkets, kept peace with local tribes and secured lands for farmers from besieged forts.

DUTCH SURRENDER to Duke of York in 1664 followed lands, trade disputes. English based claims on Cabot's discoveries. Stuyvesant capitulated; New Amsterdam became New York.

BARBAROUS ATTACKS under Director Kieft brought Indian revenge on the settlements near New Amsterdam. Peace was restored in 1645 by treaties and land purchases for settlements. Early colonists tried to maintain neutrality in Indian feuds and encourage peaceful trade, but were endangered when they took sides. Cruelest of Dutch directors was Kieft. He levied heavy tributes and sought to wipe out Indians on upper Manhattan to avenge the murder of a Dutch wheelwright. After the treaties, the Dutch kept peace with Five Nations and promoted fur trade with Iroquois.

◀ SOUTH RIVER, as the Dutch called the Delaware, was first claimed by a group of Dutchmen led by De Vries, who later headed Governor Willem Kieft's Council of Twelve. De Vries' followers built Fort Nassau and Swannendael, a colony which was razed in 1632.

EX-GOVERNOR Peter ▶ Minuit of New Netherland led first expedition of Swedish settlers, who built Fort Christina on Delaware for their young queen, and colonized river's west bank. New Sweden Company also had settlement problem; it united with the Dutch.

SWEDES IN DELAWARE

Swedish and Finnish colonists were led by Peter Minuit after his dismissal by the Dutch. They built trading posts and forts on the Delaware at the site of Wilmington, proclaiming New Sweden in 1638 over the protest of the Dutch.

Another Dutchman, Peter Ridder, extended the settlements in the 1640's. Prosperity seemed on the way with a good fur trade and fine grain and tobacco crops, but as immigration waned, the colonists faced the unruly Indians and hostile New Netherland neighbors. In 1648 the Dutch built a blockhouse on the site of Philadelphia, opposite the Swedish settlement. Johan Printz, strongest of the Swedish directors, razed the Dutch fort, only to have Stuyvesant retaliate a few years later by constructing a new garrison blocking the Delaware. The Swedes captured the fort and changed its name to Trinity, but Stuyvesant reaped the final glory by securing both Forts Trinity and Christina in 1655.

Swedish officers were deported, settlers forced to swear allegiance to Holland, and Fort Trinity was re-named New Amstel. Though completely under Dutch rule, Swedes continued to live in the area, merging with the Dutch, English and Finns. Remnants of their culture — log cabins, wood carving, folk tales, and the strongly entrenched Swedish Lutheran Church — persisted on Atlantic frontier.

DEERFIELD MASSACRE of settlers in western Mass. took place during "King Philip's War." Organization of the United Colonies of New England in 1643 was partly due to Indian threat. In 1675 King Philip, son of Massasoit, united the Indian tribes of Massachusetts and declared war. Philip was slain in 1676. The Five Nations of the Iroquois Confederacy (Mohawks, Oneidas, Onondagas, Senecas and Cayugas) made early peace with the Dutch and English in New York and greatly aided the settlers in the wars against the French who found allies among the Algonquin Indians.

COLONIES THRIVE

Great overseas migration spurs America's rapid pre-Revolution expansion

Colonial America was the promised land to the beleaguered peoples of Europe and the British Isles. Under the triple lash of religious persecution, political oppression and pauperism thousands sought haven.

Most of the immigrants were hard-working farmers. They sought no gold like the Spaniards, nor fur like the French, but a chance for freedom of thought and action.

Waves of Germans, Scotch-Irish, French Huguenots and Swedes joined the influx from England. Native customs prevailed in some areas, but the mingling of peoples was general. Common use of the English tongue fashioned a strong bond between colonies.

The 13 original colonies were of two kinds: *charter* and *proprietary*. Under charters granted to settlers by the English Crown, colonists elected their own governors and assemblies. Proprietary colonies were established by great landed proprietors such as William Penn and Lord Baltimore. Here they appointed governors, but the freemen elected their own assemblies.

In most cases the charters and proprietorships were later revoked by the Crown and the colonies became Royal Colonies. Governors were then appointed by the Crown. However, the Provincial Assemblies continued to be elected by the colonies. They retained a strong voice in local government and control over appropriated money.

Thus, from the first, the principles of self-government guided the political life of the colonies, although tax and property laws allowed only a few adult men to vote.

While the colonists responded similarly to their new freedoms and to the abundance of the virgin land, the long coastal strip from Maine to Georgia became divided into four fairly distinct regions during the 18th century: the New England Colonies, Middle Colonies, Southern Colonies, and the Back Country. Political problems and cultural developments varied between sections.

THE LONG RIFLE was a family's best defense against the Indians in the wild Back Country. West of the burgeoning seacoast ports of New England and the Middle Colonies and the rich coastal plantations of the Southern Colonies lay the frontier. Here a man could buy land for a few shillings an acre or homestead it for nothing. Settlements were widely scattered.

Here and there a stockade like that at Fort Dummer (left) offered some defense. But all too often Indian raids wiped out rude cabins and resulted in men and women being led into captivity. In 1754 Mrs. James Johnson (center) was carried away into what is now Vermont. More fortunate was John Kilburn (right) who fought off an all-day attack in 1775.

WITCHCRAFT trial of George Jacobs resulted in his execution in 1693 at Salem, Mass.

At the time of the Revolution the 700,000 people in New England were mostly of English descent. Puritanism remained strong, except in Rhode Island, where the more liberal views of Roger Williams persisted. Previous to 1700 the union of church and state in Mass. ruled both political and religious life. Fanaticism of Puritans reached climax in 1692-93 when 20 were executed as witches.

Dissenters from the harsh demands of Puritanism settled the regions of New Hampshire and Connecticut. The settlements of Connecticut were united under a royal charter granted by Charles II in 1662. New Hampshire in 1679 became royal province.

John Clarke obtained a charter for Rhode Island from Charles II granting complete independence and providing for self-government and religious tolerance. The territory of Maine was granted to Sir Ferdinando Gorges and John Mason in 1623 by the Council for New England.

During the Colonial period, New England was largely a maritime region. Fishing, shipbuilding and trading built the great merchant fortunes of Salem and Boston.

ALARMED by the growing spirit of independence in New England, the British Crown revoked the Massachusetts charter in 1684. Sir Edmund Andros was made royal governor of several colonies in 1686, ruling as a despot. Upon rise of William and Mary, Andros was imprisoned. Mass. became a royal colony.

FIRST TRADING POST at Oswego, New York, was established in 1722. Canny Dutch and English traders lost no time in developing trade with the Back Country. And the stern Puritanism of Salem was diluted as large numbers of Germans and Swedes flooded into Middle Colonies. New York was made a royal province in 1685; New Jersey in 1702. Philadelphia and New York rose swiftly to challenge Boston for trade.

CAPTAIN KIDD, most famous of pirates, was no pirate at all! He sailed under a royal warrant from the King of England. One of his backers was Lord Bellomont, Governor of New York, who later for political reasons caused Kidd's arrest, trial and execution in England for piracy. Shown above (l.) is the arrival of Kidd in New York for the purpose of recruiting seamen. Above (r.) is Kidd's handsome residence in New York. Privateering and piracy were common during the days of colonial commerce. In contrast to the Puritanism of New England, New York seemed closer to London, and reflected the latest fashions of European capitals. There was laughter and gaiety, balls and folk dancing, silks and powdered wigs. "Free thinking" and passionate political discussion flourished. Where men would one day gamble on Wall Street, it was natural then to gamble on a bold sea rover and his luck in capturing a treasure ship of the Great Mogul in the Indian Ocean or a rich Spaniard in the far reaches of the Caribbean.

TWO BEAVER SKINS was the annual rent paid by William Penn to the English Crown for his vast grant of land in America. Penn first landed in his colony (above) in the fall of 1682. In that same year he laid out Philadelphia, the "city of brotherly love," which rapidly grew and prospered. By 1755 it was the largest city in the American colonies, and for years was the capital of Pennsylvania.

UNDER THE GREAT ELM at Kensington near Philadelphia, Penn made a treaty of peace with the Indians in 1683. Wrote Voltaire: "This was the only treaty between these people and the Christian that was not ratified by an oath and that was never broken." Unmolested by Indians until the defeat of Braddock (1755), industrious Quakers and Germans dotted countryside with well-ordered farms.

William Penn
Founds Pennslyvania as haven for Quakers

Greatest proprietor of the American Colonies was William Penn. He was granted the huge area between New Jersey and Carolina in 1681 to satisfy money which was owed to him by the Crown of England.

Penn, son of a famous British admiral, became a preacher in the Quaker faith. He founded Pennsylvania as a refuge for Quakers and was sole owner and governor of the vast fertile territory.

In addition to Quakers, Penn granted religious freedom to all and encouraged the immigration of large numbers of Germans. They settled Germantown and gave rise to the term *Pennsylvania Dutch.*

By permitting election of freemen to his assemblies, by friendship with the Indians and by careful planning and organization he enabled his colony to flourish. However, the colony did not bring in the personal profits Penn had expected, and it eventually involved him in debt, prison and financial ruin. Delaware was granted to Penn as part of his holdings. However, at the time of the Revolution it became a separate colony.

The Southern Colonies

While the colonial New Englander was busy tilling his frugal acres and building wealth through maritime pursuits, a far different society was developing in the Southern Colonies. Wealthy Cavaliers, fleeing the Civil War in England, began vast plantations in the rich tidewater area and grew tobacco, rice and indigo. A single holding in Virginia or the Carolinas might cover sixty thousand acres and contain the complete facilities of a town. Owners traded directly with European markets in their private vessels, thus eliminating the need for a merchant class. Because of this, the urban growth of the South lagged far behind the New England and Middle Colonies.

Unlike New England's open town meetings and representative assemblies, civil power in the Southern Colonies rested almost exclusively with the landed aristocracy. Yet back of them lay the lesser planters and small farmers who clung tenaciously to their British rights. Dissention and even open rebellion were common among the smaller landowners, and many were forced into neighboring areas or the Back Country.

In 1632 a grant embodying most of Maryland was made to George Calvert, first Lord Baltimore, who desired to establish a refuge for persecuted Catholics.

A group of religious dissenters from Virginia made the first permanent settlement in North Carolina at Albemarle about 1650. And in 1670 William Sayle with 200 followers established Charlestown in South Carolina. Charles II granted the territory between 29° and 36° 30′ N latitudes to the Pacific Ocean to eight "Lords Proprietors" in 1663. Eventually this huge grant of territory was divided into two royal colonies.

FIRST NAVY in America was formed in Pennsylvania and included this small gunboat. Action helped discourage pirates along coast and rivers. Boundary disputes harried Pennsylvania from the first. Southern boundary was finally set at latitude 39° 43′ N after survey by Mason and Dixon in 1763-67. Western boundaries were settled by the Continental Congress.

INDEPENDENCE HALL in Philadelphia was built in 1732. In early days it was known as the State House. Here the second Continental Congress met on May 10, 1775. Here, on June 15, Washington was appointed commander-in-chief of army. On July 4, 1776, Congress adopted Declaration of Independence to the pealing of the old Liberty Bell in this famous hall.

THROUGHOUT THE COLONIAL PERIOD, as settlers pushed farther into the Back Country, the Indians were an ever-present threat. This rugged region stretched from the Green and White Mountains of New Hampshire through the Mohawk Valley and along the eastern slopes of the Alle-ghenies into the Piedmont country of the Carolinas. One of the most successful Indian traders was Sir William Johnson, a British soldier, who built a large hall (above) in western New York. As superintendent of northern Indians, he concluded Treaty of Fort Stanwix with Iroquois in 1768.

OGLETHORPE

Debtors prisons in England were opened to provide most of the 120 colonists who followed James Oglethorpe (above c.) to Georgia. It was his idea to found a haven for the poor debtor classes in England and for persecuted Protestants. An English soldier and Member of Parliament, Oglethorpe obtained a charter for the most southerly portion of the Carolina grant in 1732. In 1733 he landed in Georgia (above l.), purchasing a tract of land from the Creek Indians and settling Savannah as the seat of his enterprises. Many German Protestants soon followed and the colony prospered. When war broke out between England and Spain in 1739, Oglethorpe, under royal orders, attempted unsuccessfully to conquer Spanish Florida with a force of Creeks and Carolinians (above r.). A Spanish fleet attacked forts at Frederica in 1742 but was beaten off. Later a Spanish landing force was severely defeated in Battle of Bloody Marsh. Shortly afterwards, discontent broke out in the colony, primarily as a result of restriction on land tenure. Consequently, Georgia was placed under provincial government in 1752.

TAKEN BY ARMS from France in 1745, key Canadian defense fort of Louisbourg was returned by Treaty of Aix-la-Chapelle, 1748. Mass. Gov. William Shirley is shown directing preparations for expedition which, under William Pepperrell's command, besieged fort 49 days before it fell.

GALLEY SLAVES were taken from Iroquois captured by the French prior to King William's War (1689-97). British successfully wooed the Five Nations (Cayuga, Mohawk, Oneida, Onondaga, Seneca) despite French promises at conferences like this in 1684 between Gov. La Barre and chiefs.

INDIAN CRUELTY to prisoners (here a captive is lashed to horse before torture) was well known to colonists. Queen Anne's War (1702-13) was mostly massacres like that at Deerfield, Mass., where more than 100 were slain. Many women were taken prisoner; some wed Indians, few escaped.

CONTEST FOR EMPIRE
French and Indian War decisive

During the 17th and 18th centuries wars blazed frequently in the New World. Although bitter fights themselves, they were extensions of conflicts which racked Europe.

The French colonies were ruled from Paris, which led to the same intrigues and corruption in America which infested the French court. French governors were instruments for transmitting the orders of the autocratic king. The English, however, allowed their colonists limited self-government, generating a self-sufficiency which helped win the French and Indian War. Often, however, English colonial assemblies quarreled with royal governors harder than they fought the French or Indians. Many colonists were slain while assemblies debated political strategy instead of raising militia for defense.

Wars fought over control of the rich bounty of America and the treaties which ended them were King William's War, Treaty of Ryswick in 1697; Queen Anne's War, Treaty of Utrecht in 1713, and King George's War, Treaty of Aix-la-Chapelle in 1748. (See atlas, plates 6, 7, 8.) These struggles were inconclusive, often returning captured areas to their original owners.

The French and Indian War in America was the counterpart of the Seven Years' War in Europe. French attention was centered on the Continent, while the English concentrated on building its fleet as well as on land battles. Thus control of the seas was a big factor in England's New World victory when the Treaty of Paris was signed in 1763, ending the Seven Years' and French-Indian Wars.

CHAIN OF FORTS from Quebec down the Great Lakes, Ohio, Missouri and Mississippi rivers to New Orleans for fur trade and to block English expansion westward, was France's plan prior to French and Indian War. Shown is founding of St. Louis (1764) on site chosen by Pierre Laclede.

EXPELLED FROM HOMES in 1755, 6,000 Acadians were resettled in British colonies to the south. Expulsion resulted from devout Catholic Acadians' refusal, at behest of French priests, to give allegiance to British king. Many later returned to land renamed Nova Scotia.

REDCOATS WERE SLAUGHTERED when British Gen. Braddock's men fought in massed ranks in their first battle with French and Indians, who fired from forest ambush. French power was then at peak in 1755. Less than ten years later, the English ruled New World.

FUTILE ATTEMPT by Louis Joseph de Montcalm-Gozon Marquis de Saint Veran to set fire to English ships besieging Quebec in 1759 is shown in Samuel Scott painting. British sea supremacy, blocking French efforts to supply Montcalm, counted heavily in English victory.

DEATH CLAIMED BOTH Montcalm and his brilliant opponent, Gen. James Wolfe, 32, at crucial battle of Quebec, Sept. 13, 1759. A clever ruse enabled Wolfe to get 5,000 British regulars from ships in St. Lawrence to Plains of Abraham, and defeat 4,500 Frenchmen there. Full of hope when sent to Canada, Montcalm was deterred by Gov. Vaudreuil's corruption.

OVERWHELMED BY FRENCH four-to-one superiority, 2,200-man garrison at Ft. William Henry surrendered to Montcalm in August, 1757. Unable to control his Indian allies, Montcalm personally intervened to try and save captured British, many of whom were butchered by savages. Ironically, a British relief army under Gen. Webb was but 14 miles from Ft. William Henry when the slaughter occurred.

SEVERAL DEFEATS were inflicted on George Washington in his early military career with the British. In 1754, Gov. Dinwiddie of Virginia sent Washington into the Ohio Valley to order the French out. The French refused and Washington started home, only to get into a battle at Ft. Necessity which resulted in his surrender on July 4. Washington also was with Braddock at the Monongahela defeat.

MONTREAL FELL to the British after a three-pronged drive planned by commander Gen. Jeffrey Amherst. Aiding British was Canadians' lack of faith in Gov. Vaudreuil, after his currency was found to be worthless. Without Canadian forces, city surrendered on Sept. 8, 1760. In revenge for French-incited Indian slaughter of English settlers, Amherst made French depart, disgraced, without weapons.

ROGERS' RANGERS played an important role in opening new western territories. An intrepid explorer and soldier, Robert Rogers is pictured here leading his men back from an expedition against the St. Francis Indians in Canada. They reached the Passumpsic river in Vermont to find still-warm campfires of a rescue party which, fearing Indian attack, had just fled to the south. Many of the Rangers starved there. Rogers' great unrealized desire was to find a northwestern route to the Pacific.

PONTIAC IN WAR COUNCIL with Indians from other tribes. Pontiac tried to lived peaceably with the whites, but their aggression, open hatred of Indians, and other factors, caused him to rebel. He rallied the tribes into a confederation to drive the English back across the mountains. The Indians struck on May 7, 1763, when Pontiac led an army of his men against Detroit. Pontiac's successes were many and outstanding. His rebellion lasted for two years before a peace was finally effected.

DANIEL BOONE, hunter, trapper, pioneer is shown leading first party of settlers through the Cumberland Gap into Ky. in 1767. As the agent of Col. Richard Henderson of the Transylvania (land) Co. he made another trip to Ky. in 1775 and established a fort at what became Boonesborough. In 1778 he was captured and adopted by the Shawnees, but escaped. He lost his land in Kentucky country because of faulty titles, but later received a grant in Missouri, where he hunted and trapped.

WESTWARD MIGRATION

Frontier expands over and beyond Alleghenies

The 1763 Treaty of Paris gave England incalculably rich territories in the New World. East and West Florida were ceded by Spain. France ceded Cape Breton Island and the vast lands of Canada. Under the same treaty, France ceded Louisiana and all French claims west of the Mississippi to Spain. (See atlas, plates 6, 7).

The Ministry and the Crown in London, with little first hand knowledge of conditions in America, recognized the seriousness of the Indian problem. In an effort to establish a region exclusively for the Indians, the Royal Proclamation of 1763 was issued.

The Proclamation organized the British acquisitions into four new governments: Grenada (West Indies), East and West Florida and Quebec. It reserved territory across the Alleghenies for the Indians, to the extreme displeasure of the colonists.

Pontiac's Rebellion was under way long before the Proclamation was issued, and it was not settled for over two years. (See atlas, plate 8.) The colonists, territorially restricted by orders from London, were infuriated and made constant, sharp protests. They were not placated by the Proclamation's provisions for the future acquisition of portions of the reserved land.

Proclamation defied

As the Indian rebellion subsided, the westward movement of the colonists intensified in defiance of the Proclamation. George Groghan, a Pennsylvania trader and soldier, the man who actually effected the final peace treaty with Pontiac, was one of the many who promoted westward expansion. He secured early monopolies on trade with the Indians, and provided garrisons with supplies. The rewards were rich until fur trade in the overtrapped area south of the Great Lakes shrank to a profitless level.

The land speculators, their appetites whetted by traders' tales of fertile and richly timbered lands, expanded operations. Individuals and groups acquired thousands of acres of land. Some, who had suffered losses during Pontiac's war, banded together and petitioned the Crown for huge land grants. One of these companies sought to secure 1,200,000 acres along the Mississippi.

A dozen new provinces and colonies were proposed, including New Wales, Vandalia, Transylvania and Charlotina. It was a period of ruthless acquisition.

These turbulent years drew to a close as the Quebec Act of 1774 annexed all land north of the Ohio to the Province of Quebec. At one stroke the Western claims of many colonies were wiped out.

AN ANCHOR in the chain of 21 California missions founded by the Franciscans between 1769 and 1834 was Mission Dolores. It was set up by Frs. Palou and Cambron where Dolores Creek enters San Francisco Bay on the western shore.

HORSE RACING, fiestas and other simple pleasures were enjoyed by Californians of the Mission and Mexican Eras. Cattle, with their hides and tallow the most valued parts, plus some agriculture, were mainstays of the area's economy.

OTHER MISSIONS were founded, starting in late 1500s, in New Mexico and Texas, before California chain was begun. Typical construction, with Indian-made tile roof and a bell tower is displayed at Santa Clara, founded in 1777.

BEAUTIFUL EXAMPLE of California Mission architecture is Mission San Luis Rey, founded in 1798. Many missions were partially or wholly destroyed by 1812 earthquake. Some were rebuilt by missionaries before secularization.

SPANISH SOUTHWEST

Driven by zeal to expand their king's domain and carry Christianity to the savages, Spaniards explored the Southwest thoroughly between 1500 and 1700. New Mexico had a church and colony as early as 1598. (See Atlas, plates 2, 6.)

Not all exploration was done on the coast. Juan Bautista de Anza found an overland route to link New Mexico and California missions, but a massacre by Yuma Indians in 1780 made this trail unsafe for travelers for many years.

By 1821, Mexico had broken from Spain and Spanish holdings in California and the Southwest were under Mexican control. The revolution, however, had no marked effect in far-off California.

Catholic missionaries slowly moved from the southern tip of lower California northward. Missions were well-established on the lower California peninsula long before settlements were established in the main portion of the area.

PRESIDIO, or fort, was established at Santa Barbara and three other missions. Franciscans converted 90,000 Indians to Christianity before secularization in 1830s. Dependent on padres, Indians lapsed swiftly when clerics were gone.

ONE OF BIGGEST missions was San Gabriel Archangel, founded Sept. 8, 1771, by Fr. Junipero Serra on expedition with Portola to Monterey. Fr. Serra founded nine missions before his death in 1784 at Carmel, where he is buried.

FATHER JUNIPERO SERRA

UNEQUAL TOWERS identify Mission San Carlos, founded in 1770 at Monterey. The harbor for many years was a refuge from pirates for the Manila Galleons as they sailed to Spain from the Philippines with their cargoes of rich treasure.

JUAN CABRILLO and Bartolome Ferrelo explored California coast in 1542-43. Despite early discoveries, Spain did no colonizing until Mission San Diego was founded in 1769.

FOOD WAS SO SHORT on early Spanish exploring and mission founding trips that it was sent north by ship from La Paz, Mex. California Indians were basket weavers and hunters before the missionaries taught them the arts, agriculture and other occupations.

NOT ALWAYS PEACEFUL, Indians sometimes rose against Spanish. Smarting under cruel discipline, they revolted in 1680 in New Mexico, slew 21 friars, were reconquered by 1692.

DON GASPAR DE PORTOLA missed recognizing Monterey on his 1769 expedition, instead went on to discover San Francisco Bay. Scurvy hit his troops severely on the long trek.

HANGING FROM THE "GALLOWS-CROOKS" (pothooks), kettle and pot share the warmth of kitchen fireplace with New England family and the traveler savoring his host's tobacco. Usually offered in hospitality, the long "churchwarden" pipe of fine, glazed clay was imported from England.

A Yankee invention was the swinging iron back-bar in the hearth, replacing the dangerous lug-poles of green wood used by first settlers to suspend pots. Butter churns were scarce at first; later, churning became household duty (above)—not required by law, as was flax spinning in several colonies.

COLONIAL CONTRASTS

Life in the colonies mirrors varying social and religious backgrounds

The Puritan traveler, leaving the compact communities of New England, must have wondered at the unequal divisions of land in New York. The proprietary manors of East Jersey must have been equally puzzling, while the plantations and smaller farms of the South must have seemed like a different world.

But it was from different worlds of social background and religious beliefs that the early settlements sprang into being, each bearing the stamp of its founders on every phase of community living.

Thus, the almost equal distribution of land in New England was in marked contrast to the "gentlemen's seats" dominating large portions of New York and the huge estates of the tidewater country in the South.

Religion dominated much of the life in the colonies, coloring social and cultural as well as spiritual life. Here again, sectional differences were marked. The New England Congregationalists, with their allocation of meeting-house seats by rank and their intolerance of other religions, contrasted vividly with the experiment of religious tolerance in Maryland.

ONE O'CLOCK AND ALL'S CALM

Friends, or Quakers, were followers of George Fox, establishing their experiment of a City of Brotherly Love in Philadelphia. They were persecuted for their missionary zeal in New England while extending their influence by emigration to West Jersey. Another religious influence in Pennsylvania was the Moravian sect, which had been persecuted in its homeland, Germany.

Catholics found haven from intolerance in Maryland, while in Virginia and the Carolinas the Anglican church was predominant.

Social life varied from the austerity of Puritan New England to the comparative luxury of the Southern plantations. Distances hampered the spread of education in the South, where private tutoring prevailed. Many planters sent their sons to England for university training. In New England, public education was beginning under the Free School Act of 1694. American colleges offered training grounds for Northern scholars. This was especially true in the ministry. By 1693, 107 of 123 ministers in Massachusetts and Connecticut were graduates of Harvard.

INVITING FRONTIER. The territory back of the colonies, reaching from the drainage area of the St. Lawrence to the highlands of Carolina, was a lure to colonists. Early menace was the Pequot, driven east by invading Mohawks, planning Pequot War. End of war in 1637 brought founding of new settlements, many with secret hiding places (left) for safety of women and children during attacks. Marauding Indians often possessed firearms (center), in spite of laws forbidding their sale to Indians. Frequently, captives from Indian raids (above) were sold as servants in Canada.

BANNING THE USE OF TOBACCO was tried in 1638 by William Kieft, Governor of New Amsterdam, thrusting his cane through haze of smoke clouding his doorway in protest of edict. A brazier (center foreground) is kept within reach for relighting the long-stemmed porcelain pipes the Dutch settlers brought from Holland. In New England, use of tobacco was forbidden near meetinghouses from sunset Saturday to sunset Sunday. Use of tobacco was widespread. Even women of the lower classes smoked. It is told that one, dropping her pipe during a seizure, burned to death.

SPARE THE WHISPERING ROD and communication was virtually impossible between young folk, confined to the heavily-chaperoned hearthside of a Puritan home. Words for her ears alone could be transmitted through the hollow instrument. Nor were there secluded spots on the Sabbath (c.) under the order in town-meeting that "one householder or more walk every Sabbath day in sermon time with the constable to every Publick House in ye town to suppress ill order, and if they think convenient, to private houses also" (r.). Usual penance for offenders: Confession before congregation.

DOGMA AND DOGGEREL went hand in hand in Calvinistic A B C Book (r.), as New England's early "free" education was held to strict Puritan limits. New Massachusetts charter of 1691, abolishing church control over state, widened scope of instruction, gave rise to present concept of school district. "Moving schools" were held in different sections of town at different times to reach more pupils and hold taxes down. The usual setting was a log schoolhouse.

COLONIAL SPORTS ranged from mild game of bowls (above) to such brutal amusements as cock fighting, bear baiting, and gouging. Horse racing was feature of colonial fairs, especially in the South where there was a jockey club. Sport of hunting led to improved firearms.

GRACIOUS LIVING IN THE SOUTH

In contrast to closely-knit Northern communities, the South was an area of vast estates and plantations. Unlike many Northern cities of uniform architecture, the South showed a wide variety of styles. The Colonial Governor's mansion at Williamsburg, Va. (above) a fine example of Georgian architecture, was completed in 1720. It was the official residence of the king's visitors to the colony. Seven royal governors and Patrick Henry and Thomas Jefferson, the first two governors of the Commonwealth, lived there. It was surrounded by ten acres of formal gardens including a maze, canal, bowling green and fish pond. Vying with it for grandeur were many private mansions. Some Southern planters maintained way of life by going into debt to English merchants, one reason for later support of independence. The middle-class planter got start by leasing tracts from South's landed gentry.

CONTEMPLATING JOB'S TROUBLES on Sunday was distinct from the task of "setting a Job's Trouble" (a hexagonal pattern) into the design of a patchwork quilt during the week. Generous neighbors (c.) contributed time and precious material to quilt-making. The quilting frame of four wooden bars, supported on the backs of chairs, was the center of much colonial sociability. As the finished portion was rolled under, work and gossip continued. Two wooden bars supported sedan-chair of fashionable women (r.). First sedan-chair in America was taken from Spanish galleon.

MARRIAGE CONTRACT in Virginia was signed in presence of the county clerk after the banns of matrimony had been read three times in public. This often followed custom of "bundling," putting courting couples to bed fully clothed.

FAREWELL TOAST to their hostess is offered by guests at moment of departure. Tavern prices were low from Maryland to Georgia as a result of the custom of planters entertaining travelers. Poor planters relinquished own beds to visitors.

FASHION'S VICTIM is not only milady receiving the lacing, but also the husband tugging at the corset strings. She with her "French head", he with his "grave full-bottom" wig were victims of Europe's fashions, brought to colonies.

FIRST COLLEGES FOUNDED

John Harvard, Puritan clergyman, died in 1638, leaving half of his estate and his library to help endow the new seminary at Cambridge for which the general court of Massachusetts Bay Colony had provided 400 pounds. The school, which became Harvard, was founded in 1636, the first college in North America. A more liberal curriculum drove its former heads to join Connecticut church leaders in establishing a new school at Killingsworth, 1701. It was moved to New Haven, 1716, and named Yale College, 1718, in honor of Elihu Yale (r.), a former governor of East India Co., who gave financial support.

WILLIAM AND MARY (top, l.) named for ruling monarchs, was established in 1693, the first college in the Southern Colonies. Later, the need for a trained ministry brought the establishment of Princeton (top, r.) in 1746 by the Presbyterians, and Dartmouth College (bottom), a training school for Indian preachers. The first class at King's College in New York City (r.), founded by the Anglicans in 1754, had a wide curriculum. King's College later became Columbia University. Queen's College (Rutgers University) was Dutch Reformed; College of Rhode Island was Baptist.

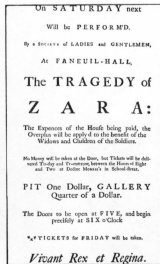

COLONIAL DRAMA

Plays, like fashions, were nearly all imported from England. Performed by amateur companies at first, perhaps the earliest was given before Governor Spotswood at Williamsburg in 1716. Lewis Hallam brought the first professional company to America in 1752. Mrs. Hallam, appearing as "Marianne" (l.) in *The Dramatist*, was the first leading lady. In 1754, Hallam's company broke down the Quaker opposition to theater in Philadelphia and, in 1766, the first permanent theater in America was built there. Later, the first American tragedy was performed in it. Playbill (c.) advertises a play by *Ladies and Gentlemen* at Faneuil Hall, Boston (r.).

RELIGION DOMINATES COLONIAL LIFE

Religious zeal was evident among all groups of colonists. Anglican benediction (above) is bestowed on Virginia colonists whose faith followed them from England. Dissenting groups were scattered throughout the colonies, mainly in the North. By 1750 they had made huge gains, especially among the common people. Baptists, Anglicans and Quakers opposed forced contributions to New England Congregational churches, while many Virginians and Carolinians in turn opposed the practices of established Church of England.

CODE OF LAWS for administration of Puritan justice in Massachusetts was drawn up by John Cotton in 1636. Though code was not adopted, it offset belief that harsh and arbitrary justice of the Puritan magistrates was divinely inspired.

WITCHCRAFT HYSTERIA reached its height in 1692, spurred by the works of Cotton Mather. Support of inoculation during a small pox epidemic made Mather a target for persecution, but saved more lives than "witch hunts" cost.

PUBLIC FRENZY accompanied each of the 20 victims of the witchcraft trials of 1692 to the gallows. About 150 others were imprisoned. Evidence was "spectral" rather than legal—hysterical accusations growing out of the mass hysteria resulting from the writings of Cotton Mather. However, after the excesses of the trials, there developed a strong wave of revulsion against witchhunting in the colonies.

PUNISHMENT FOR GOSSIPS was the ducking stool, an ingenious device for punishing lesser law infractions in Puritan New England, where human weaknesses were disapproved. The parson presided at such public punishment spectacles because of his dominant position. Asked if he were the "parson who serves here," Parson Phillips of Andover replied: "I, sir, am the parson who rules here."

SEEDS OF DEMOCRACY were sown by dynamic preachers like Jonathan Edwards, who gave impetus to religious revival which swept colonies in 1740's, crumbling sectional barriers. He introduced the "violent" saving of sinners.

"APOSTLE TO THE INDIANS," John Eliot (r.), established communities of "praying Indians" who often huddled in his home for protection from the vengeance of their tribes. Also receiving Eliot's protection during a long winter was the Jesuit, Father Druillettes (l.). Eliot, broad and just in thinking, made an exhaustive study of the Indian language, then translated the Bible into their tongue. He also translated the metrical version of the Psalms, known as the Bay Psalm Book, which he had written with Richard Mather and Thomas Welde. He endured great hardships in carrying out his work. His converts were invaluable allies to the colonists in King Philip's War, but suffered at hands of the English as well as from vengeance of their own race.

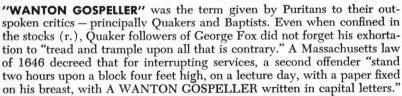

"WANTON GOSPELLER" was the term given by Puritans to their outspoken critics — principally Quakers and Baptists. Even when confined in the stocks (r.), Quaker followers of George Fox did not forget his exhortation to "tread and trample upon all that is contrary." A Massachusetts law of 1646 decreed that for interrupting services, a second offender "stand two hours upon a block four feet high, on a lecture day, with a paper fixed on his breast, with A WANTON GOSPELLER written in capital letters."

"INNER LIGHT" was held superior by Quakers to external trappings, both in dress and meetinghouses. Seeking the "new and living way" urged by George Fox, Quakers showed racial tolerance, and opposed war and severe forms of punishment. They used the workhouse and hard labor to punish offenses, thus laying the groundwork for prison system in America.

TOLERATION ACT of 1649 gave religious freedom to all Trinitarian Christians who settled in Catholic Maryland. It was repealed later after a local civil war in which the Protestants were victorious.

STORM-TOSSED MORAVIANS, the German brotherhood almost extinguished in the Thirty Years' War, came to Georgia in 1735. Later, they moved to Pennsylvania. John and Charles Wesley, crossing the ocean with them, took inspiration from their confidence amid storms.

POLITICS

Colonists experience new feeling of unity

LIBERTY BELL was ordered from London in 1751 for Philadelphia's State House (Independence Hall). Twenty-five years later its chimes proclaimed Declaration of Independence adoption.

VILLAGE INN with its colorful sign was an important center of colonial life. With development of roads, stagecoach lines and posts, inns were well supplied with latest news and gossip.

Eighteenth century America has been described as a perfect example of the change which occurs when an old civilization is challenged by a new environment. Though most colonists were still loyal to the Crown, they had developed customs and institutions that were slowly separating them from England. Government was a disorganized mixture of imperial and local elements. Each colony had a legislature and though voting was restricted to property owners, the assemblies were active and vocal. The "gentlemen's party" and "country party," representing conservative and progressive politics, stood together when their inherited "rights as Englishmen" were in any way infringed.

JOIN, or DIE.

BEN FRANKLIN'S WARNING TO THE COLONIES

VERMONT SETTLERS used the famous "beech seal" (left) to defend their homes against holders of doubtful land grants. After warning intruders with the "high chair treatment" (right), irate settlers often resorted to use of beech whips. Disputes arose when Crown gave conflicting Vermont grants to New Hampshire and New York. Ethan Allen's Green Mountain Boys were formed to defend settlers.

TRIAL OF PETER ZENGER

A milestone in establishment of freedom of the press was the trial of a New York printer, John Peter Zenger, for seditious libel. Zenger, publisher of the *Weekly Journal*, printed a series of articles by deposed Chief Justice Lewis Morris. The articles attacked New York's governor, William Cosby, raising the question of corruption in government. Morris had denied Cosby's right to establish a special court without the consent of the Assembly. Cosby promptly dismissed Lewis who then wrote the articles for Zenger's *Journal*. Copies of the paper were seized and burned (l.) and Zenger was placed on trial in 1735 (below). The jury was instructed to decide only whether or not Zenger was guilty of publishing the offending articles. The decision as to their libelous character was reserved for the judges of the trial. However, Andrew Hamilton appeared as Zenger's defense council and argued the accusations in the article were known to be true, therefore, they could not constitute libel. Ignoring instructions of the judges, jury acquitted Zenger in the first real test of a "free press" in the American colonies.

ALMS HOUSE AND HOSPITAL in Philadelphia were indicative of civic development and concern for public welfare that had grown up in major centers by mid-18th century. Pennsylvania hospital (l.) opened in 1750; in 1765 Philadelphia College founded a medical school. Of five largest centers in Boston, Newport, New York, Charleston and Philadelphia, the latter had the most phenomenal growth. By the Revolution it was the second city in population in British Empire. Visitors from Europe were often surprised by bustling American cities and by rarity of poverty and unemployment.

IMPROVED TRANSPORTATION facilities were of utmost importance in helping to weld the 13 colonies into a single unit. Roads and bridges like the toll bridge (l.) were still primitive, but stage coach lines (r.) maintained regular schedules. Colonists moved freely throughout the provinces. Expansion of the post office stimulated exchange of information. As newspapers were exchanged from one province to another, Americans became aware of a growing unity, realizing the similarity of their problems, especially in relations with England. By 1758 the post office which had carried newspapers free, fixed special rate as quantities sharply increased.

NEW YORK'S GROWTH in less than 100 years from a tiny Dutch fort to a busy seaport is shown in early engravings. The Hartgers View (right) depicts fort of New Amsterdam about 1626-28 and is earliest known view of New York. The Burgis View (below) covers the period 1716-45. It was issued in 1719 but additional landmarks were added by later engravers. In colonial period, New York's commercial development was slower than that of rival centers because access to interior was blocked by Iroquois. However, it profited by fur trade and commerce with West Indies. The Dutch made a lasting impression and a century after English had officially taken over city, a visitor described its inhabitants as "more than half Dutch."

t' Fort nieuw Amsterdam op de Manhatans

A South Prospect of y Flourishing City of New York in y Province of New York in America

47

FUR TRAPPERS were the first to explore new regions. Trading with the Indians began as early as 1524. In 1670 the Hudson's Bay Company was chartered and during the height of the fur trade 40,000 skins were sent annually to England. But by 1699 supplies declined and trappers moved westward, opening the Mississippi Valley. So bitter was rivalry for control of the fur trade that French and English allied with Indians against one another.

SHIPBUILDING was one of the earliest industries. Lumber was plentiful and the colonists soon became excellent shipwrights. On the eve of Revolution, one-third of British ships were American built, and Americans owned 2,000. Before acquiring American colonies, England depended on Baltic forests for masts, pitch, tar.

EARLY INDUSTRY

America's wealth lay in her natural resources

Colonial America was primarily agricultural. New England and the Middle Colonies traded mainly with the Continent and West Indies. The South, however, shipped five-sixths of its exports, which exceeded that of other colonies combined, to England.

The population, almost all English, was 700,000 in 1700. By 1776 it had swelled to 2,750,000 and become cosmopolitan, with the immigration of large numbers of Scotch, Irish, Germans and Huguenots.

England, intent upon strengthening British mercantilism, passed various restrictive laws affecting colonial trade and industry. The second of these (1651) was a Navigation Act requiring all goods entering England or the colonies to be carried only on British ships. Other laws, such as the Iron, Wool, and Hat Acts, curtailed competitive industries in the colonies. Certain items, as tobacco and rice, could be shipped only to English ports. Under Walpole these laws were loosely enforced. More progress in manufacturing and production was made than officially recorded. These Acts handicapped industrial development, but not as severely as did the lack of skilled labor and capital. When George III came to the throne and tried to enforce these laws and new ones, the colonists joined to resist them.

FISHING and commerce were the chief sources of wealth in New England. The colonists brought fishing tackle with them. By 1765 the industry, which engaged 300 ships to carry fish to foreign ports, yielded $2 million annually.

AGRICULTURAL CONDITIONS as well as the leading crops, tobacco, Indian corn, rice and indigo, were new to Englishmen. Indians taught them to plant quickly by burning underbrush, girding trees later; how to dry and store food.

LUMBER was one of the earliest marketable commodities sold to England and West Indies. There was also great demand for it in the colonies. A lumber business sprang up with each new community; many sawmills were built.

CAPTIVE NEGROES WERE MARCHED TO PORTS

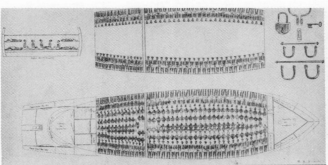

SLAVE SHIP, SHOWING ARRANGEMENT AND PADLOCKS

SLAVES WERE BOUGHT IN AFRICA WITH RUM

SLAVES AND TOBACCO

Tobacco was the greatest single export of the colonies. It was profitable and easy to grow. As early as 1618, Jamestown colonists exported 20,000 pounds, tripling this in three years. They were so intent on tobacco, they traded their weapons to the Indians for food, a policy which resulted in a massacre. Before the 19th century more than 100 million pounds were exported yearly. Tidewater Virginia produced half.

In the South tobacco brought about the plantation system of production. Huge feudal-like estates evolved. Sufficient labor was a problem. A European servant could work out the cost of his passage over in three to seven years, then set out for himself. His treatment and duties were regulated by law. In 1671 there were 6,000 indentured servants in Virginia, only 2,000 Negroes. By 1700 a sharp drop in tobacco prices wiped out most small planters, making only large slave-worked plantations profitable. Negroes were found to be the cheapest labor and the only ones who could stand the harsh work of the rice and tobacco fields. By 1775 there were 400,000 Negroes in the colonies. Of these, more than 350,000 were in the South.

EASIEST WAY WAS TO ROLL TOBACCO TO THE WAREHOUSE

ENGLISH TRADE CARD

BE MERRY AND WISE
SURBY'S
Best Virginia

BIG PLANTATIONS HAD THEIR OWN WHARVES AND SHIPS

PHILADELPHIA forged ahead of Boston in the middle 18th century to become the largest city in the colonies, with a population of 28,000 in 1770. Benjamin Franklin promoted its paved, well-lighted streets. The fertile, temperate Middle Colonies were known as the "bread colonies" for their production of wheat and baked goods. Their many flour mills were the most effective of all colonial industries. Oliver Evans perfected a mechanical means of processing grain from milling to barrelling without manual intervention. The Pennsylvania Germans in 1730 began the manufacture of rifles. They also designed the sturdy freight carrier, the Conestoga wagon, which in time became the famous Prairie Schooner.

BEN FRANKLIN, ENTERPRISER

The "wisest American," as Franklin is often called, was born in Boston (1706-90), the son of a soapmaker. At 17 he ran away to Philadelphia to become a printer. He acquired the *Pennsylvania Gazette* and soon afterward published *Poor Richard's Almanack*, a handbook of sayings which have become American proverbs, such as "Honesty is the best policy." He aided many civic reforms and founded or promoted the circulating library, fire company, American Philosophical Society and University of Pennsylvania. His autobiography is considered one of the finest in any language. As postmaster general (1753-74), he reorganized the postal system, making it efficient and profitable.

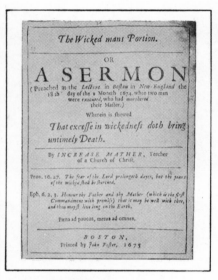

FRANKLIN WAS A PRACTICAL SCIENTIST who believed in experience and experiment. Flying a kite during a thunderstorm proved the identity of lightning and electricity. It was one of many experiments which won him world fame. As America's first scientist, he invented such diverse articles as bifocal spectacles, lightning rod, and the Franklin stove.

FIRST PRESS in the colonies was set up in 1630s. Early efforts were newssheets and pamphlets. First book printed in Boston (above) was by Puritan clergyman Increase Mather.

BOSTON NEWS-LETTER was the first successful American newspaper (1704-76) and first to be distributed by mail. Publisher John Campbell was postmaster.

FIRST SUCCESSFUL IRON WORKS opened near Lynn, Mass., in 1643 (above). By 1775 every colony except Georgia had blast furnaces and forges, supplying one-seventh of world's iron.

CANDLE MAKING was one of many small shop industries that took over work formerly done in the home. Colonial craftsmen turned out furniture, silverware, felt hats and wool cloth equal to those made in England.

COLONIAL PAPER MONEY was unsound and promissory notes were often substituted. With ban on English coin shipments, foreign money was general.

BLACKBEARD MET DEATH (above) at the hands of Lt. Maynard. A daring and ruthless pirate, Captain Edward Teach (Blackbeard) preyed on shipping and coastal towns from Virginia to the West Indies (1716-18). His winter quarters were at North Carolina, whose governor shared his booty. Despite such protection, Virginia's governor sent two sloops to destroy him. The story of his death became a popular colonial ballad. Pirates, like Blackbeard, traditionally disposed of mutineers by forcing them to walk a plank blindfolded into the ocean as jeering crew looked on.

THE PIRATES

In the 16th century there was no stigma attached to piracy. Exportation of gold and silver from Spain's American colonies and development of the slave trade made it highly profitable. European states condoned attacks on the commerce of rival powers.

Many buccaneers began as privateers, carrying a commission during wartime to attack enemy vessels. In the French-Indian War, 11,000 Americans were so engaged. During the 17th and 18th centuries English pirates of the Spanish Main often divided their spoils with the crown and received pardon. Buccanneers such as Henry Morgan became national heroes. He was knighted and made governor of Jamaica. However, Captain William Kidd and others were hanged, under the Act of 1699 which made piracy a capital offense. Piracy reached its height about 1720, declined soon afterward.

PIRATES raided coastal areas and extorted tribute from townspeople (above). Later, as peaceful visitors, they were welcomed in several colonies, as they bought goods with scarce gold.

SMUGGLING was prevalent along coasts during the colonial period. It was carried on by the picturesque buccaneer (above) or respectable merchants angry at Trade and Navigation Acts.

CUNNING AMBUSH preceded looting of many a merchantman. Losses were so high in early 1700s that shipping fell off. In 1735 first colonial insurance office opened. Underwriting cargoes helped in offsetting the losses.

SPANISH TREASURE SHIPS from the New World, after defeat of the Spanish Armada in 1588, fell prey to English, Dutch and French pirates, who often sailed in fleets, once took booty at Vera Cruz worth $30 million.

THE REVOLUTION

Craving for liberty, at first by a few, grows into revolt against British rule and the founding of a nation based on the principles of freedom

Surprising lack of agreement exists concerning the causes, and even the nature of the American Revolution. Its history has been written and re-written. Fresh interpretations constantly appear. One school holds that it was occasioned primarily by economic causes, that American merchants and capitalists wanted freedom to trade and manufacture unrestrained by Britain's mercantilistic regulations. Others maintain the Revolution was chiefly a political and constitutional movement, a struggle between Parliament and the Colonial assemblies. The philosophical approach it in terms of Thomas Paine — as the fruition of eighteenth century liberalism. Still another school holds that there was no ruinous material damage to America in Britain's restrictions, but that differences in ideals were paramount, differences produced by the bold, new American environment.

Each generation interprets the Revolution according to the prevailing climate of opinion, and there can be no complete objectivity. Suffice it to say that no narrowly economic, political or social view is entirely adequate, and perhaps none is totally wrong. More likely, analysis of the movement must take account of all prevailing interpretations and attempt, if possible, to synthesize them.

There were in truth two wars: a War of Independence of England, and a Revolution; a struggle for home rule and a struggle to decide who was to rule at home. The desires of the artisan or small farmer in regard to relations with England often were opposed diametrically to those of the tidewater planter, and his to the New York merchant. Beginning in early colonial times a rift appeared between the landed aristocrat and the upcountry farmer, the lawyer and the ruling clique. Representation in the colonies was for the most part restricted to the rich and propertied. Rebellions such as those of the North Carolina Regulators and the Green Mountain Boys attested to the bitterness held by the underprivileged toward the privileged, of the average man toward the "twice two thousand for whom the world was made."

Many Americans apathetic

The American Revolution did not, however, become a social movement to the extent that either the Russian or French Revolutions did later. Before hostilities began the initiative was seized by radicals such as Thomas Paine and Samuel Adams, but control passed gradually into moderate hands, and the demanded reforms did not all follow immediately upon Independence. Paine and Adams and the other radical leaders at the beginning of the Revolution played only minor roles after the war.

That the Revolution was not a popular cause is indicated by the few who actively participated. Washington's army sank to as few as 3,000 effectives. Loyalists were many, and were to be found among all classes. They included persons sentimentally tied to England, small farmers who opposed independence mainly because landed aristocrats favored it, and conservatives who feared the revolt would swing leftward and engulf them as it went. Among many of those who did fight there was an appalling lack of determination. Only too eager to join in "bushwacking" expeditions of short duration under popular leaders like Francis Marion, they had little taste for sustained campaigns, and simply wandered off home when it came time to get the hay in, or when the fighting was taking place in an alien part of the country.

Yet independence was achieved. How? Certainly the timely aid of France, who was anxious to strike back at England after her defeat in 1763, contributed substantially. The help in terms of troops and ships, and the inspiration and leadership of men like Lafayette, Rochambeau and Admiral DeGrasse, turned the tide in favor of the insurrectionists. To a marked extent Britain lost by default. Involved in other theaters of war, she also suffered from lack of determined leadership. The counterpart in England to Loyalists in America were men who felt the colonists' cause was just. And although the American army was small, the dedicated body of men who carried on were patriot soldiers, imbued with an idealistic cause, as opposed to the professional and foreign mercenaries that England employed.

"Gentleman Jack" Burgoyne regarded the war so lightly that he took his service of plate, his champagne and 30 wagons of personal baggage on all his campaigns. Baron Riedesel, commander of the Brunswick mercenaries, took his wife wherever he went, battle or no, and held picnics along the route of march.

A New American Type

What manner of men were these upstart Americans who dared oppose the greatest power in the world? How were they different from their European cousins? The French-American, Michel de Crevecoeur, in *Letters of an American Farmer* (written during the Revolution) described his adopted countrymen in a discerning manner.

"We are a people of cultivators," he wrote, "scattered over an immense territory . . ., united by the silken bands of mild government, all respecting the laws without dreading their power, because they are equitable. We are all animated with the spirit of industry, which is unfettered and unrestrained, because each person works for himself. If he travels through our rural districts, he views not the hostile castle, and the haughty mansion, contrasted with the clay-built hut and miserable cabin . . . We have no princes, for whom we toil, starve and bleed; we are the most perfect society now existing in the world. Here man is free as he ought to be . . . Here individuals of all nations are melted into one new race of men, whose labors and posterity will one day cause great world changes."

Freed from religious, political and economic restraints of the Old World, and blessed with a bountiful land, possessing unquestioned faith in himself and his future, the American, though his culture had its roots in the great traditions of Europe, was indeed a new man.

GEORGE WASHINGTON

★

◀ **SPIRIT OF THE REVOLUTION** is symbolized by this soldier at Valley Forge, where Washington brought his army to spend the winter of 1777-1778. A weak Congress with ill-defined powers failed to provide sufficiently for the patriotic force. Men were hungry and suffering from the cold. Few had sufficient clothing. In place of shoes they wrapped their feet with rags. Complaints were strident and desertions many. But a loyal group stuck by their commander and the following summer Washington was able to marshall an army for attack on the British at Monmouth, N.J.

GEORGE WILLIAM FREDRICK OF HANOVER (1738-1820) ascended the throne of Great Britain in 1760 determined to restore autocratic power to the Crown. Assisted by Lord Bute, his former tutor, George III set out to destroy party government and master Parliament, colonies by patronage.

PATRICK HENRY, A "WESTERN UPSTART," gained political stature by leading a group of young liberals in Virginia's House of Burgesses. Attacking King and the Stamp Act with equal vigor, Henry presented his seven Virginia Resolves, protesting Britain's right to tax without representation.

APPROACHING STORM

Irksome taxation policies of British stir deep resentment in the colonies

After the Peace of Paris (1763) economic grievances did more to promote revolt in the colonies than did ideals of personal liberty or hopes of freedom from England.

Peace brought new colonial problems for England. The cost of war and expense of administering and defending newly-acquired territory increased royal costs in North America five-fold. Thus, English officials thought it only just to obtain more revenue from the colonies to offset the costs.

Under the ministry of George Grenville, appointed by the king in April, 1763, to succeed Lord Bute as Chancellor of the Exchequer, taxes and shipping curtailments descended on the colonies with monotonous regularity, stirring up resentment.

Grenville's Sugar Act (also known as the Revenue Act of 1764) was presented to Parliament together with the advice that further revenue might be extracted from the colonies by means of a stamp tax.

The Sugar Act reduced the duty on molasses, heavily taxed since 1733, but added duties to sugar, wines, coffee, silks, linens, and by giving the admiralty court jurisdiction over revenue cases, put a virtual end to profitable, organized colonial smuggling.

The colonies already had acknowledged Parliament's right to regulate imperial trade by taxing colonial commodities. But the Sugar Act was denounced by Samuel Adams as "taxation without representation." The Stamp Act (Mar. 22, 1765), which was levied through revenue stamps on news-papers and legal documents, pointed up this Parliamentary technique by requiring colonies to contribute part of the expense of maintaining British army in North America.

By the summer of 1765, colonial resentment blazed into violence. Non-importation agreements were drawn up by merchants in Boston, New York, and Philadelphia. The

AMERICA'S FIRST PROPAGANDIST, Samuel Adams, has been called "the true father of the American Revolution." A fiery rebel, he helped organize Correspondence Committees.

boycott brought business to a standstill. Respectable men organized "Sons of Liberty" groups and Patrick Henry castigated the Act with "sublime torrents of eloquence" before the Virginia Assembly. Subsequent publication of Henry's "Resolves" inspired a circular letter from the Massachusetts House inviting delegates to a Congress in New York, the first intercolonial meeting sparked by colonial initiative.

In England, Grenville had been succeeded by the Marquis of Rockingham and a small band of Whigs who brought about repeal of the Stamp Act (March, 1766), but made no effort to stave off passage of a Declaratory Act restating absolute sovereignty of Crown and Parliament over the colonies.

In the jubilation of Stamp Act repeal, colonials overlooked the Declaratory Act until the Rockingham ministry was supplanted by that of William Pitt (the Great Commoner, who had become Earl of Chatham). The course of action pursued by Charles Townshend, Chatham's Chancellor of the Exchequer, who took command when Pitt fell ill, set the fuse which was to ignite the fires of revolution.

Aspiring to reduce British land taxes by increasing revenue from American colonies, Townshend reinvoked the Quartering Act of 1765, pushed through a series of levies (Townshend Acts), and established for the colonies the blood-brother relationship between Parliamentary sovereignty and the arbitrary levying of taxes.

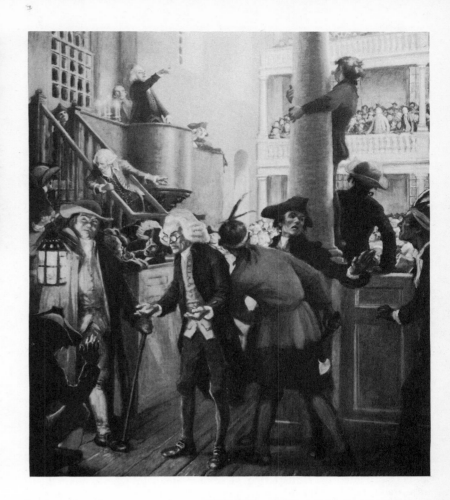

BENJAMIN FRANKLIN, representing Pennsylvania before the English Parliament, was called before the House of Commons in 1766 to explain American opposition to the Stamp Act. Franklin stressed the heavy expenses borne by the colonies during the French and Indian War and their continued expenditures for protection from the Indians. He warned that attempts to enforce the Act with troops might lead to rebellion. Parliament, heeding his warning, repealed the Act. News of repeal brought rejoicing.

PROTEST MEETINGS were held in Boston and Philadelphia after British tried to bolster near-bankrupt East India Co., which had huge surplus of tea. Parliament passed Tea Act in 1773 allowing Company to sell tea in American colonies without paying duty. Import tax on tea was retained, however. Act enabled Company to undercut colonial merchants, who had bought tea at higher prices. Opposition centered on threat of monopoly.

WITH PARALYZING REGULARITY, George Grenville, British Chancellor of the Exchequer, continued to tax colonial commodities. Rice, sugar, molasses, fur, and woolen taxes were protested bitterly. The Stamp Act, a final indignity, was ushered in Nov. 1, 1765, with symbols of mourning in newspapers (above, c.), organized evasion and near riots.

COLONIAL UPRISINGS FOLLOWED protests against the Quartering Act which forced colonists to house and feed British troops. General Thomas Gage (above), British military chief, tried to stem violence resulting from measure.

WILLIAM PITT (above l.) championed the repeal of the Stamp Act, believing Parliament had no right to levy such taxes on colonists. Lord North (left, center) succeeded Townshend as Chancellor of the Exchequer. He believed Parliament should operate under the Declaratory Act and prove its sovereignty by taxes. His port bill in March, 1774, closed Boston Bay

after the Tea Party. Among the supporters of American beliefs in England were Charles James Fox (right, center) and Richard Price (extreme right). For his pamphlet on " . . . War with America" Price won an LL.D. from Yale Corp. in 1781 and Congress offered him citizenship. Fox, member of Parliament, opposed Boston Port bill; sought to eliminate trade barriers.

First Hostilities

Economic and political restrictions provoke colonists to defy England

Burdened by Parliament's restrictions, the colonial economy faltered. British soldiers roaming the streets of Boston and New York only intensified the smouldering resentment. Riots accompanied suspension of the New York Assembly for refusing to comply with the Quartering Act. John Hancock, putting into Boston on the *Liberty* with a cargo of smuggled Madeira wine, had mob help in resisting customs officials trying to collect duties. Governor Bernard, as a result, procured two fresh regiments for the protection of commissioners. In North Carolina, British Governor Tryon put down an uprising of disgruntled "Regulators" and hanged the six leaders.

The impassioned propaganda of Samuel Adams magnified every outbreak; transformed the Tryon episode into the "Battle of Alamance," and a street-brawl between civilians and British Redcoats into the "Bloody Boston Massacre" although only five were killed.

With Britain's efforts to create a civil list in Massachusetts, Sam Adams emerged as a leader, developing the most formidable revolutionary machine in the American colonies with his organization of the Boston Committee of Correspondence (1772). The movement spread like prairie fire as the one Committee became a network.

More violence erupted with Lord North's attempts to save the nearly-bankrupt East India Company by delivering tea directly to the colonies, by-passing colonial merchants. Boston rebels countered with the Tea Party. North's retaliation was swift and deadly. He closed the Boston Port until restitution should be made.

Adams' Committee on Correspondence reacted promptly. By the time the Port Act reached Boston (May 11, 1774), Paul Revere had headed for New York and Philadelphia with a Circular Letter, and the Solemn League and Covenant (advocating immediate suspension of trade between the colonies and Britain) had been drawn up.

New York formed a Committee of Fifty-One and proposed that a Continental Congress be set up to consider Adams' Covenant. One by one the rest of the colonies fell into line and on Sept. 5, 1774, delegates from every colony except Georgia gathered in Philadelphia. The Suffolk Resolves and an organized boycott resulted.

Meanwhile in England appeasement measures were before Parliament. Lord North's Conciliatory Propositions reached New York the day after news of the battles of Lexington and Concord.

BOSTON "MASSACRE" (Mar. 5, 1770) between townsmen and British soldiers exploded over quartering of troops. Small brawl was magnified into "massacre" by Sam Adams who engaged Paul Revere to engrave cartoon (above), later forced Gov. Hutchinson to move troops out of Boston.

THE SCHOONER GASPEE, stalking New England smugglers, ran aground and was burned by colonists protesting customs regulations. British set up a Court of Inquiry, convicted no one, were accused of attacking liberty.

FRANKLIN'S EFFORTS to improve British-Colonial relations were unavailing and led, in Jan., 1774, to the King's Privy Council examining and accusing him of attacking the Crown. Disheartened, he returned home.

DUMPING TEA into Boston Harbor to protest the Tea Tax brought to a head the long-smouldering conflict over home-rule. Colonial rebellion was further unified by British retaliatory laws, later called "Intolerable Acts": closing Boston port to trade until the tea was paid for, changing the form of Massachusetts government, deporting culprits to England for trial.

FROM THE UPROAR attendant to Lord North's "Intolerable Acts" and Boston's severe punishment for the "Tea Party," the colonies banded together and sent 56 delegates to form First Continental Congress in Philadelphia, Sept. 5, 1774. Patrick Henry (l.) fiery Virginia delegate keynoted the attitude with "I am not a Virginian, I am an American." Another Virginia delegate was aristocratic Richard Henry Lee (r.) who had earlier aided Stamp Act resistance and led one of the Committees of Correspondence. George Washington also represented Virginia while other delegates to the Congress included such extremists as Samuel and John Adams of Mass., conservative John Jay of New York and Rutledges of South Carolina.

BOYCOTT VIOLATORS were severely punished by the colonists themselves. For attempting to pocket tea washed ashore after the Boston Tea Party, one culprit found coattail and pockets nailed to whipping post.

ENGLISH CARTOONS lampooned both British and American retaliatory measures. Entitled *Bostonians Paying the Exciseman*, this caricatures a customs officer, John Malcolm, who was tarred and feathered in Boston (Dec. 1773) for threats after the Tea incident.

WHILE CONGRESS MET in Philadelphia, a society of patriotic ladies gathered in Edenton, North Carolina in Oct. 1774 and established America's first woman's club. Purpose was twofold: "engage not to conform to that pernicious custom of drinking tea" and "not promote ye weare of any manufacture of England." British satirists derided the meeting, but Congress later passed non-consumption and non-importation measures enforced by vigilance committees.

PAUL REVERE

On the night of April 18, 1775, when the British marched, Paul Revere leaped on his horse, headed for Concord and immortality. Accompanied by William Dawes, Revere rode to Lexington where he warned John Hancock and Samuel Adams to flee the oncoming British. There he was joined by a third rider, Dr. Samuel Prescott. Enroute to Concord, Revere was captured by the British, taken to Lexington and released. Dawes eluded the British but Prescott was the only one to reach Concord. Aroused patriots already were staked out to protect supplies and powder caches. Colonists had formed volunteer militia of Minute Men after the Suffolk Resolves were passed by the first Continental Congress. Many Minute Men were boys 14 to 16 (top right) and most were farmers (above).

SHORTLY AFTER DAWN on Apr. 19, 1775, Lt. Col. Francis Smith and Major John Pitcairn, of royal infantry, led 700 British soldiers into Lexington, Mass. On a secret mission ordered by Gen. Gage, Redcoats were to capture Hancock and John Adams, rebel leaders, and proceed to Concord to destroy patriots' powder supplies. Warned by Revere, Adams and Hancock escaped. British soldiers were met by Capt. John Parker and 70 colonial Minute Men in crude battle formation (l.). No one knows who fired the first shot, but eight Americans were killed, 10 wounded, and the British marched on to Concord. Here too, the colonists were massed for battle, having already moved most supplies to safety. At Old North Bridge (above) retreating redcoats were subjected to grueling fire from rebels concealed in houses, behind trees and walls, and saved from total rout by the timely arrival of 1200 men led by Lord Percy. British casualties that day numbered 273; Americans, 93. The collapse of British authority had begun and the Second Continental Congress convened in Philadelphia 20 days later.

BUNKER HILL

The battle for Breed's Hill (June 17, 1775), mistakenly credited to Bunker Hill, cost the British more than one-third of the 2,400 men who marched under Gen. William Howe's command to meet withering fire from colonial sharpshooters who were entrenched there under Gen. Israel Putnam and Col. William Prescott (l.). Interested spectators watched the battle from rooftops in nearby Boston, Dorchester and Charlestown (right). Howe's men aided by fresh troops led by Gen. Henry Clinton, brought colonial defeat which the heavy death toll turned to a moral victory. (See Atlas, plate 10.) Battle started when British General Gage sought to occupy Charlestown peninsula by surprise. The colonists, warned by spies, were prepared.

TICONDEROGA, British garrison guarding approaches to Lake Champlain, was captured jointly by Ethan Allen, commanding a small group of Green Mountain Boys, and Benedict Arnold, commanding 400 volunteers, on May 10, 1775. Allen is reputed to have demanded surrender from Capt. William De la Place, fort commandant, "in the name of the Great Jehovah and the Continental Congress." (r.) Lt. Jocelyn Feltham, aide of De le Place, recorded Allen's demand as "immediate possession of the fort and all effects of George III." Not a shot was fired. Crown Point, sister fort of Ticonderoga, fell to Allen the next day. With Arnold commissioned by Connecticut and Allen by Massachusetts, disposition of forts and munitions fell on the Second Continental Congress, meeting in Philadelphia. Decision to hold Ticonderoga intact until dispute with Britain could be settled was rescinded when invading Canada seemed feasible. Cannons were then moved to Albany (above) and in September, 1775, Congress authorized Richard Montgomery and Arnold to attack. Montgomery took Montreal and with Arnold attacked Quebec. He was killed; Arnold retreated.

COLONIAL MILITARY preparations included accelerated manufacture of frontiersmen's rifles adapted from Swiss original. Long, small-bore weapons, custom-made in blacksmith shops like above, were used with legendary accuracy by riflemen who were at first considered elite corps of American army. Ordered by Congress to join Washington at Cambridge after start of hostilities they sniped at British sentries, shot gold epaulets from officers and officers from horses. Frontiersmen used Indian tactics, shooting from behind trees, to the dismay of traditionally-trained British.

THOMAS PAINE

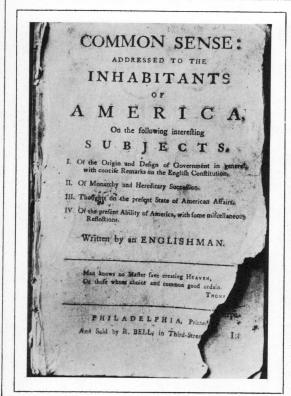

No more popular and persuasive indictment of British rule in America was ever penned than Thomas Paine's fiery *Common Sense* (l.).

Paine (r.), a Philadelphia printer and recent arrival from England, published his pamphlet in January, 1776. Within a few months nearly everyone in the colonies had read it. Its language was simple and vigorous, its philosophy a popularized version of the rationalism that dominated 18th century thought.

Abandoning all sentiment and tradition, Paine attacked the Empire, the Ministry and the theory of monarchy itself. "Government," he wrote, "like dress, is the badge of lost innocence." George III was "the Royal Brute of Great Britain"—an abominable monarch.

Paine urged Americans to cut loose all their ties with England. What benefits would accrue to an independent America! What wealth, once Britain's noxious restrictions were swept away!

Like a true revolutionist, Paine denounced in advance those who would not share his views. To some, he was a dangerous radical, to many, an apostle of light. But none could deny his powerful influence on the course and the outcome of the Revolution.

GEORGE WASHINGTON, Virginia aristocrat and retired colonel, was elected commander-in-chief of Continental Army while serving as a member of Virginia delegation to Second Continental Congress. He was chosen for the post over Gen. Artemus Ward, John Hancock, who refused the post, Charles Lee and Horatio Gates, who was named adjutant-general. Washington, a veteran officer of French-Indian War, attended Continental Congress sessions in military uniform to indicate his willingness to serve. He was endorsed for commander by John Adams; formally nominated June 15, 1775, and unanimously elected. He refused any payment other than his expenses. On July 3 he took charge of troops beseiging Boston. ▶

In CONGRESS, July 4, 1776.

The unanimous Declaration of the thirteen united States of America.

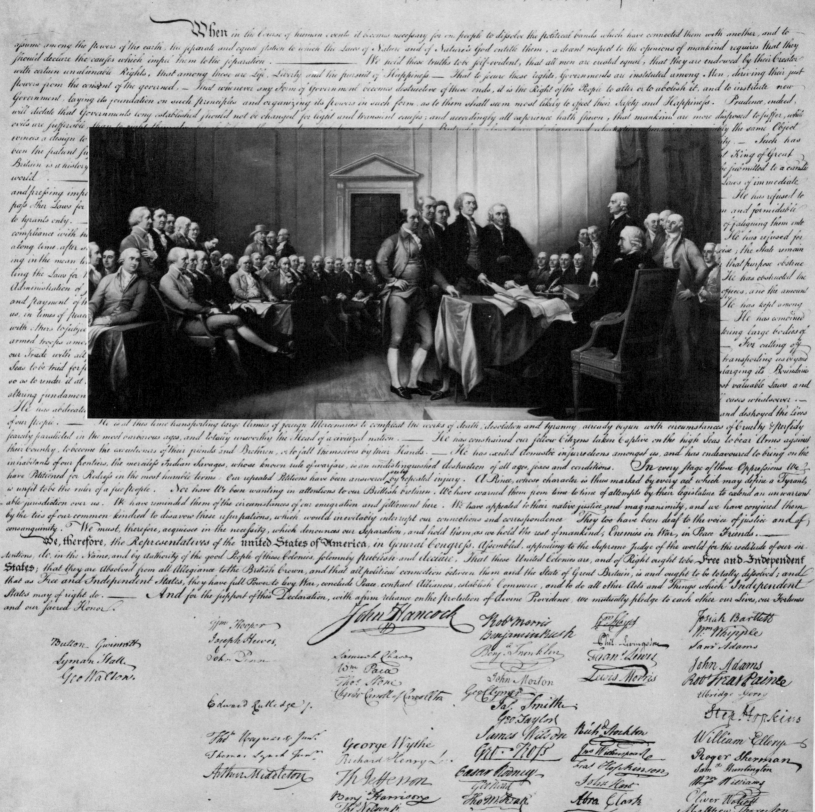

UNANIMOUS DECLARATION OF THE THIRTEEN UNITED STATES OF AMERICA WAS APPROVED BY DELEGATES FROM 12 COLONIES, JULY 4, NEW YORK ORIGINALLY ABSTAINING.

Declaration of Independence Signed

As early as the spring of 1776 sentiment for a complete rupture with England became manifest in the Colonies. The North Carolina Convention instructed its delegates to vote for a declaration of independence. Richard Henry Lee of Virginia put forth a resolution (June 7) that the United Colonies "are, and of right ought to be free and independent States." It was decided to postpone a decision on the resolution until a committee composed of Jefferson, Franklin, John Adams, Robert Livingston and Roger Sherman drew up a formal declaration. A draft of this was presented to Congress on June 28 and on July 2 the declaration was passed. Minor amendments were made, the changed document being approved without dissent and the first signatures were affixed July 4.

INDEPENDENCE

While Congress debates Jefferson's document, Howe takes Staten Island

"We hold these truths to be self-evident, that all men are created equal . . ." wrote Thomas Jefferson, chairman of the committee appointed by the Second Continental Congress to draft the document which would define Richard Henry Lee's resolution for independence. In his original presentation of July 2, Jefferson bore out this premise with a ringing denunciation of slave trade and an indictment of the "abuses and usurpations" of King George III. The slave trade clauses were ordered struck by Southern and New England delegates and much of the virulence against the king was modified before the document was accepted by delegates July 4. The Colonies through Congress, actually declared themselves independent of the Crown in the July 2 pronouncement. The July 4 vote approved plans for independent government.

In the interim (July 3), Sir William Howe, British major-general, landed 9,000 men on Staten Island and prepared to drive American troops out of Long Island and New York City, stronghold of Loyalists (Tories). A week later, New York patriots celebrated news of the Declaration of Independence by razing a statue of King George and ordering it melted down for bullets.

Throughout the colonies, formal pronouncement of independence brought with it the first major cleavage among colonists themselves: the clear-cut division between Loyalists, many of whom had been willing to defend American "rights" but were unwilling to subscribe to absolute severance from the crown, and the patriots who sought to set up a new nation, with "full Power to levy War, conclude Peace, contract Alliances, establish Commerce . . ." On August 2, 1776, the die was cast, the parchment Declaration had been signed.

NEWS OF SIGNING spread from Philadelphia's tolling Liberty Bell to New York where Washington paraded the army and had Declaration read at head of each brigade. In Boston (above) jubilant crowds gathered at Old State House, heard volleys from Fort Hill, and burned royal insignia.

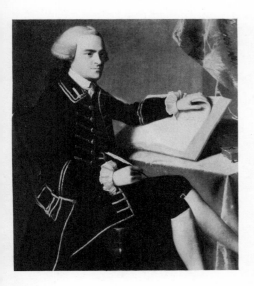

JOHN HANCOCK, President of the Continental Congress, rich young merchant from Massachusetts, was first to sign the Declaration. He later resigned presidency, became his state's first governor.

RESPONSIBILITY for drafting Declaration fell on Thomas Jefferson (r., with paper). John Adams and Franklin made minor revisions. The "self-evident" truths spoken of in the document were based on John Locke's works and formed basis of 18th century political philosophy. Jefferson, unlike Locke, put human rights above property.

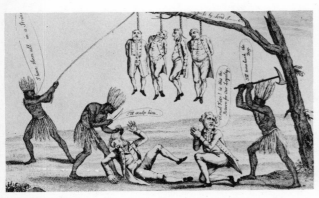

WHEN THE BREAK with Britain became official, colonial patriots set about forcing oaths of allegiance to the United States. Deemed traitors, Loyalists suffered persecution at the hands of patriot committees, even to being thrown into underground mines of Newgate prison. British cartoonists propagandized brutality (above), while generals like Sir William

Howe sought unsuccessfully to recruit volunteers from Loyalist ranks (c.). Benjamin Franklin's natural son, William, Royal Governor of New Jersey, was an ardent loyalist, devoted to furthering the King's cause. Imprisoned by patriots, he was exchanged in 1778 and fled to England where he was feted by royalists (above) and devoted himself to defying his father's work.

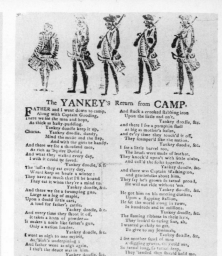

AMERICAN MARKSMEN who learned accuracy at competitive "rifle frolics" (l.) were willing to do a little "bushwacking" but had little taste for sustained warfare. Thus inducements in form of land and money had to be offered volunteers. Massachusetts and Virginia both chose conscription in 1777 as the way out. Washington in a message to the Continental Congress in 1778 suggested that other colonies adopt the draft. The help which came from France postponed any action on the matter. The German engraving (center) of 1775, is probably the earliest picture ever published of the first American soldiers. The song (right) now called "Yankee Doodle," tells of the humors and hardships facing the early recruits.

REVOLUTIONARY ARMY

American woodsmen and farmers prepare to fight Britain's professionals

"Here once the embattled farmers stood and fired the shot heard round the world," wrote Ralph Waldo Emerson, telling the story of the Revolution's first engagement. Through all the long years of struggle that followed that opening battle at Concord, farmers were always in the front ranks of those who fought for liberty and independence. Shoulder to shoulder with them were frontiersmen and sailors, clerks and craftsmen, common men of the Colonies, united in a common cause. They were,Washington admitted, "a mixed multitude"; but as straw gives strength to bricks, the very coarseness of their common clay made them superior to Great Britain's porcelain-slick professional soldiers in backwoods fighting.

Certainly there was nothing professional in the appearance of the average Revolutionary fighting man. A few veterans of the French and Indian War donnèd their old uniforms, but most simply kept on wearing their working clothes, especially in the early years of the fighting. Buckskin-clad backwoodsmen fought alongside farm boys in homespun, and an officer might have only a military jacket or a cocked hat to show his rank. Rank itself meant little in the first days of the fighting. When Washington arrived at Boston to take command of the Army he found an almost total lack of military organization and willingness to obey orders.

Under Washington, the men were trained to function as an army rather than a mob and some semblance of uniform dress was gradually established, but American soldiers continued to show considerable liberty in deportment throughout the entire period of the war years.

When Washington was given command, he was told he would have 20,000 men. His command turned out to number only 17,000, and of these perhaps 14,000 could be called effective. The Revolutionary Army at times fell as low as 3,000 as enlistments expired; and against it were pitted 35,000 trained and well-equipped British regulars and mercenaries.

Yet, despite the disparity in numbers and equipment, the Revolutionists had the one thing their opponents lacked, and it was the deciding factor. They were fighting, not for pay, but for freedom.

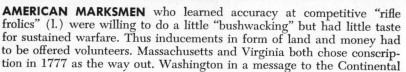

PAPER MONEY, unbacked by gold, originated phrase, "Not worth a Continental."

WOMENFOLK of the Revolutionary soldiers have received far less recognition by historians than they deserve. It was they who continued operating the farms in the face of great difficulties. Thanks to their industry with their needles, soldiers were supplied with such items as shirts and knitted garments. These needs were constantly in short supply at the embryo quartermaster corps warehouses of the colonial army.

HESSIAN TROOPS were hired by George III when he found it difficult to get Englishmen to join the army he was assembling to send to America. When the news spread in the colonies that the King was using German mercenaries, many who had not been in favor of rebellion gave their allegiance to the Patriots.

GENERAL MONTGOMERY was one of the first to die in the abortive attack on Quebec, Dec. 31, 1775. The Canadian campaign was abandoned after this disaster. Benedict Arnold, later turning traitor, shared command with Montgomery.

CELEBRATING the Declaration of Independence on Bowling Green, New York, July 10, 1776, "Sons of Freedom" dragged down lead statue of George III, erected six years before. The legislature ordered it melted into bullets.

THE LIBERTY POLE was erected in Boston to take the place of the Liberty Tree, which was burned for fuel during the siege of the city. Boston's Liberty Tree, an institution which was widely copied by other communities, was used as a place to display colonial flags and effigies.

"THE SPIRIT OF '76," PERSONIFIES THE VIGOR OF THE NEW-BORN REPUBLIC.

GENERAL HOWE committed a tactical blunder when he evacuated Boston on March 7, 1776. He was not aware that the morale of the Revolutionists was at a low ebb and that an attack might have relieved the siege of the city. With Howe's 11,000 Redcoats went 1,100 Boston Tories, and behind them were left military stores of great value to General Washington's army.

SGT. WILLIAM JASPER found immortality at Fort Moultrie on Sullivan's Island near the entrance to Charleston, S.C. On June 28, 1776, the British fleet attacked. The flagstaff was shot down, the flag falling outside the fort and in full line of fire from the ships. Jasper, leaping the parapet, recovered the flag and set it upon a new staff amid heavy and continuous firing.

BRITISH TAKE NEW YORK

Washington believed Howe would return from Halifax and attempt to capture New York, a move which would divide the American confederation in two. Therefore, in the spring of 1776, he fortified Harlem Heights at the north end of Manhattan Island, and Brooklyn Heights, Long Island, whose position commanded New York. As expected, Howe returned. He camped on Staten Island and on August 22 ferried 15,000 men across to Gravesend (center). On August 26 he attacked. The Revolutionists lost 2,000 men in casualties and prisoners; General Putnam's two chief field commanders, Sullivan and Stirling, were captured; and six field guns and 26 heavy guns were taken. Why Howe did not press his advantage is a question, for at the end of the siege the battered remnants of Putnam's forces were backed against the East River. Washington ordered a retreat and under cover of darkness and fog his men were able to cross to Harlem Heights (left). A participant in the day's disastrous action was General Woodhull (right) brigadier of the local militia. While organizing the concealment of supplies, he was taken prisoner and later died of wounds he sustained during the encounter.

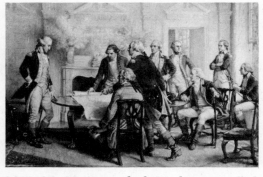

COUNCIL OF WAR which Washington called after his Long Island retreat unanimously supported his decision to withdraw. New York City thereafter became British headquarters and remained in their hands until 1783.

LORD HOWE released Gen. Sullivan, sent him to arrange a meeting which could stop fighting. Rutledge, Franklin and Adams attended, but made recognition of independence a pre-condition to discussion. Howe regretfully withdrew.

BURNING OF NEW YORK occurred as British began to pitch tents there. It was extinguished by soldiers and sailors, but only after about 500 houses were consumed. Origin of fire was probably accidental, but British blamed Americans.

MRS. MURRAY, living in a country house close to what is now Murray Hill, is supposed to have invited General Howe to luncheon. It is related that he accepted, stopping the advance of his army across Manhattan until lunch was over.

NATHAN HALE volunteered to penetrate British lines on Manhattan disguised as a Dutch schoolmaster. Captured, hanged without trial, he lives forever in his farewell words: "I regret that I have but one life to lose for my country."

HARLEM HEIGHTS was where Washington made his stand at the north end of Manhattan Island. Howe's Highlanders (above) fought fiercely, but were checked by colonials and were forced to withdraw with Washington in pursuit.

GEN. HOWE, to outflank Washington in North Manhattan, landed at Pell's Point. Washington moved north to White Plains, and Howe attacked. As Americans retreated, Howe struck garrison at Ft. Washington (above), overwhelming it.

BRITISH FLEET meantime, was forcing a passage up the Hudson between Forts Washington and Lee. It broke the massive chain stretched across to hinder the ships, and then provided the landing craft to ferry the soldiers across.

FORT LEE was the next British objective. Cornwallis landed on the Jersey shore near it, climbed the Palisades (above) but his attempt at surprise was spoiled when a deserter disclosed the move to Gen. Greene, who beat a retreat.

WASHINGTON'S ARMY retreated across New Jersey and dwindled as it went. There were deserters and fainthearts, but there were also men whose enlistment was over. The remainder, added to the men brought by Sullivan and Gates, amounted to about 4,000. Gen. Howe dispatched only a token force of Hessians in pursuit, and these camped at Trenton, on the east bank of the Delaware, since Washington had all the boats. By Christmas, the American army, now 8,000 strong, received word that the Hessians were off their guard because it was a holiday and they were homesick. So Washington seized the opportunity, crossed the Delaware in a snowstorm and defeated the Hessians, capturing 900 of them. It was a heartening victory.

VICTORY AT TRENTON was more than merely the triumph of a mobile force with high morale against dispirited mercenaries in a foreign land; it was an answer, at a moment when an answer was needed, to those who had begun to think of the American cause as completely lost. The British suddenly awoke to the fact that the rebellion was far from being stopped.

CORNWALLIS was sent by Howe to re-occupy Trenton, but Washington was able to out-maneuver him and took up positions on the Princeton road, between Cornwallis and his base. The American commander proved his bravery during victorious fighting that followed. He rode to within 30 yards of enemy to rally wavering troops. This victory changed course of the war.

THIS WAS THE FLAG which served during the transition period between the Union Jack of Britain, and the Stars and Stripes ordained by Congress in 1777, well into the third year of the war. It was called the Jack and Stripes, and it had a significant military meaning in that it was the first visual symbol of the real Union Army Washington was striving to build.

MRS. BETSY ROSS is popularly believed to have been the person who made the very first Stars and Stripes flag. She was an upholsterer who lived in Philadelphia, and the story is that Gen. Washington and George Ross came to her and showed her the new design. She is supposed to have made the suggestion that the stars be altered to have five points rather than six.

PHILADELPHIA OCCUPIED

Late in August of 1777, General Lord William Howe (l.) and 15,000 troops landed at Elkton on the northern tip of Chesapeake Bay. Howe felt that the capture of Philadelphia would deliver crushing blow to the American cause. He encountered and engaged Washington and 11,000 Americans at Brandywine Creek (r.). Germans under General von Knyphausen attacked American center at Chad's Ford while a brilliant flanking movement of Cornwallis defeated the Americans and caused them to retreat toward Philadelphia. (See atlas, plate 10.)

LIBERTY BELL was removed to a place of safety and other measures were taken to prepare Philadelphia for a lengthy siege. General Washington had withdrawn his army to positions north of the city. He knew that the longer he could delay Howe in the South, the better were the chances of defeating Burgoyne's 7,000-man force, half of whom were German mercenaries, now marching from Montreal south along the Hudson. St. Leger and 1800 more Loyalists and Indian allies proceeded up the St. Lawrence to Lake Ontario and turned east to reach the source of the Mohawk, planning to follow it into Albany, where they would join Burgoyne. There both armies would unite with Howe, who was supposed to be advancing north to meet them.

PHILADELPHIA was no problem to the British commander Lord Howe. After routing Anthony Wayne's force at Paoli, he occupied the city on Sept. 26, without experiencing any resistance (left). Congress fled first to Lancaster and then to York. The Loyalists opened their doors to the English, entertained them lavishly (right) and many merchants willingly took British gold in exchange for provisions. The occupiers should have been on the march north to join the forces of Burgoyne and St. Leger in accordance with the orginal plan of campaign. However, not a word of Burgoyne's whereabouts had reached Howe's headquarters.

GEN. NICHOLAS HERKIMER DIED OF WOUNDS RECEIVED AT ORISKANY WHERE TROOPS WERE AMBUSHED

BURGOYNE'S SURRENDER

Colonel St. Leger with a British force of 1800 men, mostly Indians and Loyalists, marched from Oswego against Fort Stanwix on the Mohawk river. On August 3, 1777 he arrived and beseiged the place. But presently he learned that General Herkimer with a force of 800 colonists was moving against him in order to relieve the fort. St. Leger ambushed the Americans as they threaded their way through a wooded swampy area near Oriskany. The Americans fought fiercely and were supported by a timely sortie from Fort Stanwix. The British were defeated and fled. Meanwhile Burgoyne, in want of supplies, had heard of stores at Bennington, Vt., but a short distance from his line of march.

Colonel Baum with 700 troops was sent to seize them. Word of British plans leaked out and 2,600 Americans under command of Gen. John Stark (below, left) intercepted Baum near Bennington. During the night more Americans encircled Baum and thus cut off his retreat. Presently 650 reinforcements sent by Burgoyne arrived just in time to be cut to pieces as was the first column. In these engagements the British lost 4 guns and nearly 1,000 men. Consequently the British were forced back to Fort Edward. Early in September Burgoyne crossed the Hudson and lost two battles against Col. Dearborn and Gen. Morgan. Finally, on Oct. 13, 1777, after failing to make contact with Sir Henry Clinton and Lord Howe, Burgoyne found himself outnumbered and surrounded and was forced to surrender.

GENERAL JOHN STARK

FORT STANWIX

SURRENDER AT SARATOGA

FORT VENGEANCE at Pittsfield, Vt., was east of Fort Edward. Once when a Tory and Indian raid found the townsmen away scouting, firing posts were filled by women until men returned.

MURDER by a group of Burgoyne's Indians, of Jane McCrea, the fiancee of one of Burgoyne's lieutenants, did much to crystalize loyalties and thus recruit militia for the American side.

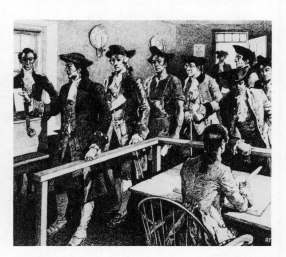

VERMONT in 1777, was the first of the States to adopt universal manhood suffrage. In all other States at that time the right to vote was made dependent upon income or property ownership.

SEPARATED from the force he had brought to relieve beleaguered Fort Henry, Va., Major McCulloch was pursued by renegade Simon Girty's band of Indians. When the savages hemmed him in, he urged his mount over a 150-foot cliff into Wheeling Creek. Both horse and rider escaped.

HORRIBLE MISTAKE occurred in Battle of Germantown (Oct. 4, 1777) when Washington's troops, striking Howe's main force, fired on each other in a dense fog. Climax of the fight took place when the Americans tried vainly to dislodge the British, who were holed up in Judge Chew's house.

WASHINGTON'S GENERALS

Foreign aid to American cause came in the form of superb officers such as Baron Friedrich von Steuben (left), and 20-year-old Marquis de Lafayette (right). Steuben, trained on the staff of Frederick the Great, arrived in time to drill recruits at Valley Forge (center), where Washington took up winter quarters after defeat at Germantown. The Prussian, who was appointed Inspector-General by Washington, introduced strict discipline and sanitation among the rag-tail troops. He became an American citizen in 1786, once nominated Washington for king of the United States. Lafayette, drawn to America out of sympathy for Patriots' cause, was created a major-general and served throughout the war without pay. Other foreign officers who volunteered services were Thaddeus Kosciuszko, Count Pulaski, Baron de Kalb, and the Chevalier du Portail.

WEALTHY LANDOWNER Philip Schuyler (l.) was a veteran soldier at the time of the Revolution. He organized the army for the invasion of Canada, and was put in charge of the Northern Division in 1776. He was succeeded by General Horatio Gates (r.), who defeated Burgoyne. Gates became president of the Board of War in 1778, tried to supplant Washington as chief of the armies by intrigue.

INNKEEPER Israel Putnam (r.) entered the Revolution early and participated in the battles of Bunker Hill, Ticonderoga, and Long Island. He aroused the hatred of the British by hanging Edmund Palmer, an English spy. Putnam once effected a daring escape from Gov. Tryon's troops by riding down the stone steps at Horseneck and racing away. A stroke of paralysis put him out of the fighting in 1779.

EXPERT ON RETREAT Gen. Nathaniel Greene directed the stubborn withdrawal from Germantown after defeat by British.

BOOKSELLER Gen. Knox spent his youth studying military texts, and was a warm friend of Washington throughout war.

BENJAMIN LINCOLN was captured and exchanged, later commanded in South. Lincoln became Sec. of War in 1781.

"MAD ANTHONY" Wayne gained his nickname for his daring tactics, as displayed during storming of Stony Point.

VALLEY FORGE

Barefoot and hungry, Washington's ragged troops spent the winter of 1777-78 at Valley Forge, Pa., while British Gen. Sir William Howe was "revelling on the fat of the land" at Philadelphia. Though the small American army was just 20 miles away, Howe sat it out and made no attempt to attack that winter. While Washington pondered the failure of Congress to provide for his army, the soldiers were put to work building cabins of straw and logs. The camp, strategically situated between the Schuylkill River and steep cliffs, was well fortified by Washington's forces as the winter rolled along.

But lack of food and clothing and the bitter cold caused many desertions. By February, 1778, 4000 men were unfit for duty. Washington gave assurance that he would "share in the hardship and partake of every inconvenience." Disgruntled soldiers, forswearing open rebellion, kept up a cry of "No meat. No meat." When scouts reported that a British foraging party was in the vicinity, Washington could not stir his troops, so lacking were they in food and uniforms. Early in 1778, clothing was in such short supply that Gen. Anthony Wayne wrote to a friend, "They have not a single shirt to an entire regiment." The following winter was even more gruelling.

LAFAYETTE (with muffler), wintering at the Forge, was shocked to learn that Washington was accused in Congress and elsewhere of weakness and ineptitude. To his friend's protests, Washington replied, "Things are not now as they formerly were; but we must not, in so great a conflict, expect nothing but sunshine." Praying for his men, Washington asked that the hearts of his countrymen be touched, and that aid be tendered the wretched soldiers. When a committee of Congress visited camp (right) he pointed out the conditions paralyzing his army. Lafayette made a stirring appeal to the committeemen to ignore the spurious charges being brought against Gen. Washington by Horatio Gates and Gen. Thomas Conway.

WASHINGTON'S HEADQUARTERS at Valley Forge was a stone house, belonging to Isaac Potts, a Quaker preacher. The general spent long hours writing letters to Congress, pleading for badly-needed supplies. Valiantly he sought to cheer the starving troops. Yet he never abandoned his courage, and only rarely, his reserve. Just before striking camp, he was directed by Congress to administer an oath of allegiance to his officers. They were asked to acknowledge the independence of the United States, to renounce allegiance to George III. When Gen. Lee protested that, although he was ready to deny allegiance to the king, he still had scruples about the Prince of Wales, even the staid Washington joined in the ensuing laughter.

FRANKLIN IN PARIS

Franklin and Arthur Lee were sent by Congress shortly after Independence to obtain open or secret assistance from the French, who had been waiting for a chance to strike England since their defeat in 1763. For years taught by Voltaire, Rousseau and Condorcet to admire what they considered Utopian American society, the French welcomed Franklin warmly. While negotiating with Vergennes, minister to Louis XVI, the American was toasted in the salons of Paris, where gentlemen and ladies, unaware of what republicanism would one day bring them, vied for the American philosopher's favor.

AMERICAN MILITARY VICTORY at Saratoga was matched by diplomatic victories: the treaty of amity and commerce and the treaty of alliance with France. Soon after Franklin (center), Silas Deane and Lee (right) signed treaties for U.S., France took the sea against England.

JOHN PAUL JONES

In 1777, Jones was sent to France, where he sought a fleet to harass the English. He was given an old hulk, the *Duras*, which he re-christened *Bonhomme Richard*, plus the *Alliance*, the *Pallas*, the *Cerf* and the *Vengeance*. Off England in September, 1779, he ran into the British Baltic fleet, convoyed by men-of-war *Serapis* and *Countess of Scarsborough*. When the merchantmen scattered, Jones stood for the *Serapis* and ordered his captains to form the line of battle. Two of the *Richard's* guns exploded, killing many of her crew. Jones made the ship fast to the *Serapis* (above, l.) and firing continued at close range. Presently the *Alliance* arrived (r.), firing so wildly she damaged the *Richard* more than the enemy. Jones' men aloft finally turned the tide with skillful use of muskets and grenades. When the *Pallas* captured the *Countess*, battle was over. Jones left sinking *Richard*, sailed off in *Serapis*.

FRENZIED BUILDING of ships occurred along Lake Champlain in 1776. While British transferred fleet from St. Lawrence to the lake, Benedict Arnold's men built 15 vessels of logs from nearby forest. Most of these ships were lost at the Battles of Valcour Bay and Split Rock.

FIRST STARS AND STRIPES to fly on the ocean were hoisted by Capt. John Paul Jones aboard the new 18-gun *Ranger* which he was given June 14, 1777. Angered that 13 inferior officers were promoted over his head, he took an assignment in Europe convoying French and American merchantmen. When treaty was made with France, French were at first eager to pretend neutrality, reluctant to openly recognize U.S., and Franklin was eager that nothing be done to compromise work of the American Commissioners in Paris. But Jones, after sending a boat back and forth to induce French to return gun for gun, was able to induce French flagship (left) to exchange salutes. Though the proud French admiral fired two guns less than Jones, this was the first recognition of the United States flag.

WESTERN FRONT during Revolution was held down by George Rogers Clark (r.) and his "Long Knives." Since the outset of war British had aroused Indians to raid the border. Paying a liberal reward for scalps, they offered as much for female hair as male. After defeating redcoats at Cahokia in 1778 Clark remained there as wondrous Indians gathered to view him, the red-haired, 25-year-old white chief who fought so ferociously. Seeking to put the border at peace, he orated in eloquent Indian manner. When he finished red men went into council. Returning, their spokesman offered peace pipe to the earth, the heavens, the Great Spirit and to the "great white warrior." Soon other bands began to arrive, and to each Clark repeated his speech. Certain Meadow Indians decided to

explode his reputation by taking his scalp. They crept into his camp before dawn, seeking to capture him without arousing his men. He quickly discovered their plan, arrested offending braves, called them "old women" and stripped them. After this supreme insult the warriors begged to die, but Clark spared them and made them chiefs. Eminently successful as a peacemaker, he made treaties with Indians from as far off as Spanish domains beyond the Mississippi River.

GREAT PLAN of Clark was to drive British from Northwest. Gov. Patrick Henry of Va. granted him £1200 and in June, 1778 he and 150 men descended the Ohio. Reaching Kaskaskia his men surrounded the fort. The sentries had deserted their posts to watch a dance given by the commandant. While ball was in progress, Clark appeared at door, told company to carry on, adding they were dancing in Virginia rather than British territory.

VINCENNES was Clark's next objective. Obliged to expend part of his meager force to garrison Kaskaskia, he relied on surprise to take the post. He spoke to Father Gibault, French priest, who agreed to try to bring his communicants to the American cause. His influence was successful. Inhabitants of Sackville, fort of Vincennes, arose in the night and cast off British authority. Clark entered peacefully (above), took the fort for Virginia.

STONY POINT, American fort in N. Y., was seized by Gen. Clinton June 1, 1779. On July 15 Gen. Anthony Wayne led 1200 men in a night-time bayonet attack and recaptured it. He dismantled and soon evacuated it. Used in the engagement were elite American Light Infantry, veterans of General von Steuben's discipline, all between 5′ 7″ and 5′ 9″ tall. Wayne (above, waving hat) was grazed by musket ball but remained in the battle.

OVERSHADOWED by his Mohawk ally Joseph Brant (l.) was Col. Guy Johnson. Brant, leader of Loyalists at Oriskany, joined Johnson and John Butler in terrorizing Cherry Valley in 1778.

HERO of Freeman's Farm in 1777 was Gen. Daniel Morgan. Having once been in Braddock's army, he still carried marks of a British whip on his back. For victory at Cowpens Congress voted him gold medal.

MASSACRE occurred in November, 1775, as John Butler and St. Leger led Loyalists and Indians on a raid through Wyoming Valley, Penn. Men were burned at the stake and roasted over live coals while their horrified families looked on. Queen Esther, a half-breed squaw, chopped off many of their heads.

◀ **MARY LUDWIG HAYS** gained nickname "Molly Pitcher" when she carried water to thirsty soldiers in Battle of Monmouth (1778). When her husband, a member of Pennsylvania artillery, suffered a sunstroke, she replaced him at the cannon. Gen. Washington made her a sergeant and granted her a pension for life.

THAYENDANEGA, or Joseph Brant (l.), was protege of British Superintendent of Indian Affairs, who educated him. Brant joined Episcopal Church, translated part of Bible into his native tongue. As a British ally he led his warriors at Minisink, N.Y., where they fell upon local militia, captured it after a day's siege and massacred all who did not escape. A Major Wood was spared when he made a movement interpreted as a Masonic sign by Brant, who was himself a Freemason. The movement was an accident, but Wood later joined order out of gratitude.

Far to Southwest a British force marched on Spanish-held St. Louis, but vigorous defense (r.) waged by town's inhabitants discouraged attackers, who retired. During same year (1780) Spanish took St. Joseph, Mobile and Pensacola, weakening the British strategically.

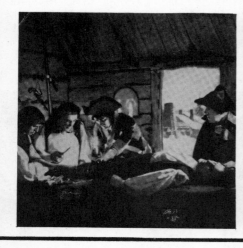

BIRTH OF U.S. MEDICAL CORPS

Having bargained to fight only the British, Continental troops soon discovered they also had to do battle with disease. Much of the weakness of Washington's army was explained by the fact that more soldiers were dying of flux and pneumonia than from wounds. Mounting complaints to Congress that medical facilities were almost entirely lacking resulted in the dismissal of recently appointed Dr. John Morgan, Director General and Chief Physician of Hospitals. His successor was Dr. William Shippen (c.) nominee of Washington, who also took steps to have his men inoculated against smallpox. Shippen and his subordinate, Dr. John Cochran, set about improving and reorganizing military hospitals, "those wretched charnel houses," where disease was more often contracted than cured. At Valley Forge (l.) ampu-

tation of limbs, "frozen until they grew black," was common. Though seemingly as unconcerned as if having their hair cut, 18th century amputees, as pictured in Heister's *General System of Surgery* (above) suffered horribly. Lacking anesthetics, surgeons often resorted to giving patients brandy or knocking them unconscious.

Under the direction of Chief Physician Shippen an enlarged staff of medical officers and male nurses manned hospitals which were often unused jails, barns or even ships. Progress, however, was slow, and Washington complained that, in this reform as in others, Congress "thinks it is but to say Presto, begone, and everything is done." Yet valuable knowledge of surgical practice and disease was gained by doctors such as Morgan, Shippen and Cochran, which they applied and taught in the medical schools that sprang up throughout the Northeastern states after the Revolution was over.

"SWAMP FOX" GEN. FRANCIS MARION AND MEN CROSSING PEDEE RIVER

MARION INVITING CAPTURED BRITISH OFFICER TO DINNER

WAR IN THE SOUTH

In the fall of 1778 Gen. Henry Clinton, successor to Lord Howe, shifted operations to the South, hoping to establish bases there. In December he sent a force that landed near Savannah, crushed the militia and captured the town. A second British force under Gen. Prevost pushed north from Florida. Augusta fell to the British in January, 1779, but for a year little was accomplished by either side.

In December, 1779, Clinton left New York with a force of 8,000, bent on capturing Charleston. Arriving off the Carolina coast on Feb. 1, he took the city by April 11, after a bloody siege. Loss of the 5,400-man garrison and four ships made this the heaviest American defeat of the war. Satisfied that South Carolina was securely in Brit-

ish hands, Clinton left Cornwallis in control, returned to New York.

British optimism about the South was unjustified, however. In Georgia and South Carolina guerrilla bands led by Francis Marion, Thomas Sumter and Henry Lee harassed posts with hit-and-run attacks. Marion was especially effective, striking often at night and retreating swiftly into the swampy fastnesses, earning him the sobriquet of "Swamp Fox." When Gen. Morgan won a smashing victory at Cowpens, Cornwallis pursued him into North Carolina. At Guilford Courthouse, Greene joined forces with him and hit Cornwallis. Though the British won on the field it was a pyrrhic victory, and they retreated, too weak to push on. Greene marched into South Carolina, and while he met defeats, the tide began to turn. By fall, 1781, British control was limited to Charleston. (See atlas, plate 10)

SIEGE OF CHARLESTON, S.C., FEB.-APRIL, 1780

BRITISH RETREAT

BATTLE OF EUTAW SPRINGS, S.C., SEPT. 8, 1781

Cornwallis Retreating!

PHILADELPHIA, April 7, 1781.

Extract of a Letter from Major-General *Greene*, dated CAMP, at *Buffalo Creek, March* 25, 1781.

"ON the 16th Instant I wrote your Excellency, giving an Account of an Action which happened at Guilford Court-House the Day before. I was then persuaded that notwithstanding we were obliged to give up the Ground, we had reaped the Advantage of the Action. Circumstances since confirm me in Opinion that the Enemy were too much gauled to improve their Success. We lay at the Iron-Works three Days, preparing ourselves for another Action, and expecting the Enemy to advance: But of a sudden they took their Departure, leaving behind them evident Marks of Laborle. All our wounded at Guilford, which had fallen into their Hands, and 70 of their own, too bad to move, were left at New-Garden. Most of their Officers suffered—Lord Cornwallis had his Horse shot under him—Col. Steward, of the Guards was killed, General O'Hara and Cols. Tarleton and Webster, wounded. Only three Field-Officers escaped, if Reports, which seem to be authentic, can be relied on.

Our Army are in good Spirits, notwithstanding our Sufferings, and are advancing towards the Enemy; they are retreating to Cross-Creek.

In South-Carolina, Generals Sumpter and Marian have gained several little Advantages. In one the Enemy lost 60 Men, who had under their Care a large Quantity of Stores, which were taken, but by an unfortunate Mistake were afterwards re-taken.

Published by Order,

CHARLES THOMSON, Secretary.

"GIVE 'EM WATTS" cried Pastor James ▶ Caldwell at Battle of Springfield, 1780, as he handed psalm books by Isaac Watts to defenders for use as wadding in their guns. Caldwell and wife were later killed, their house burned.

SCORCHED EARTH policy was practiced by wife of Gen. Schuyler, who burned her wheat fields at approach of British. Another notable woman in the war was Elizabeth Zane, who risked her life to bring powder to Ft. Henry. Because of her heroism defenders won the day.

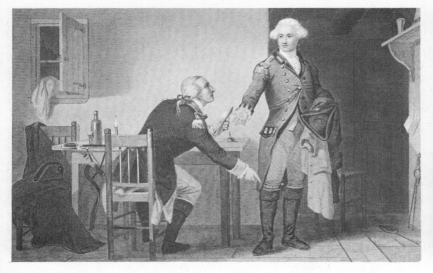

GENERAL ARNOLD TURNS TRAITOR

Benedict Arnold, veteran of Ticonderoga and Quebec, began to feel a change of heart in 1777 when Congress ignored him for promotion and elevated five of his inferiors. Placed in command at Philadelphia during the next year, he married Margaret Shippen, daughter of a Loyalist, lived extravagantly, and went deeply into debt. Court-martialed for misusing his powers, Arnold re-opened the negotiations he had once hesitantly begun with the British. On learning he was about to be put in charge at West Point he wrote Major Andre, Gen. Clinton's adjutant, that he was prepared to deliver the post to the British. Shortly after taking command (Sept. 21, 1780) he contacted Andre, giving him plans of the fort which showed its weaknesses. Hiding the plans in his boot (l.) Andre left, donning civilian clothes, something Clinton had strictly ordered him not to do. Three days later he was captured by three New York militiamen (r.) and the smuggled plans were discovered. Andre did not betray Arnold.

WHEN ARNOLD learned of Andre's capture he sent an excuse to Washington, who was at that moment on the way to visit him, and rushed upstairs to tell his wife. When she collapsed (l.) he rushed from the house, hurried to the nearby Hudson, leaped into his barge, told his men to row downstream. By waving his white handkerchief he was allowed to pass the sentinel at West Point. Reaching the British vessel *Vulture* he waved his handkerchief again and was taken aboard (c.). While he sailed to join Clinton in N. Y. Andre was tried, convicted as a spy, and, over vehement British protests, hanged on Oct. 3 (r.). Arnold was made brigadier-general in the British Army. On his deathbed he asked forgiveness for his treason.

FINANCIER of the Revolution was Robert Morris (r.), who became Superintendent of Finance in 1781. He strengthened credit and secured a loan from the French Government, enabling him to create the Bank of North America, and issued notes based on his personal credit. Merchant Haym Salomon (above) is advancing funds to Morris for war.

PEACE TREATY Military and economic necessity persuaded Britain to sign preliminary peace treaty with U.S. in Nov., 1782, and a final treaty Sept. 3, 1783. Provisions: Britain recognize U.S. independence; U.S. boundaries extend to the Mississippi; all debts between two nations be validated; British forces be evacuated. (See atlas, plate 6.) Shown in unfinished Benj. West painting are commissioners Jay, Adams, Ben Franklin, Laurens and Wm. Temple Franklin.

CORNWALLIS SURRENDERS

Climax of the war was the Battle of Yorktown. Cornwallis, in May, 1781, gathered 7,500 troops, marched into Virginia. Choosing Yorktown as a base he sought to maintain contact with Clinton in N.Y. On Aug. 30 a French force under Adm. DeGrasse set up a blockade outside Yorktown and landed troops, who joined Lafayette's. In a week the British fleet under Adm. Graves arrived and gave battle to De Grasse, who drove it off, then took ships up the Chesapeake to transport troops of Washington and Rochambeau to Williamsburg. From there a combined Franco-American force of 15,000 marched on Yorktown. (See atlas, plate 10.) Cornwallis soon abandoned the outer line of his defenses. The Allies dragged up siege guns and bombarded the camp. Early on the morning of Oct. 17, under the roar of a hundred heavy guns, a British officer waved a white flag. On the 19th, Cornwallis signed the capitulation. Washington delegated Gen. Lincoln (c., on white horse) to receive actual submission of the garrison from Gen. O'Hara, Cornwallis' representative.

COMTE DE ROCHAMBEAU (1.) came to U.S. in 1781 in response to Lafayette's appeal, leading 5,500 troops. In May, 1781, Washington secured his consent for a joint attack against Cornwallis in cooperation with DeGrasse, who offered his entire West Indian fleet and 3,000 men. Rochambeau, who lent $20,000 of his own funds to finance the campaign, is shown (pointing, r.) as he gives last minute orders for the assault on Yorktown. To his left are Washington and the boyish Lafayette. Allied casualties in the engagement were 263 against 552 for British. Five days after Cornwallis' surrender Clinton arrived off Chesapeake Bay with reinforcements, but returned when he learned of defeat. DeGrasse went back to West Indies, Rochambeau north to R. I.

AFTER YORKTOWN Clinton's successor, Carleton, abandoned plans for continuing war, concentrated all British forces on N.Y. seaboard. Except for a few skirmishes in the South, the war was over. Yet British did not evacuate N.Y. until Nov., 1783. City had been in their hands since Sept., 1776. Citizenry cheered Washington's entry and march down Bowery St.

WASHINGTON'S FAREWELL to his officers occurred at Fraunces' Tavern (below) on Dec. 4, 1783. Though a great popular hero, Washington eschewed power, brusquely repelled suggestions that he found a monarchy. After a tour to Annapolis, where Congress was in session, he resigned his commission to that body, and then returned to Mt. Vernon.

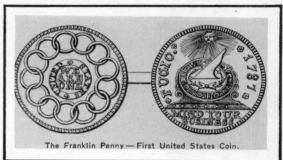

The Franklin Penny — First United States Coin.

FINANCIAL TROUBLES plagued Congress and the states. Debtors in Mass. petitioned the legislature to print paper money but were turned down. Led by Daniel Shays, farmers took up arms and forced the courts to close. In January, 1787, Shays' band attacked the arsenal at Springfield but militia, paid largely by subscription of Boston merchants, dispersed the rebellion.

The Second Continental Congress had issued notes (above) that were merely promises to pay. Congressional currency soon depreciated in value and the phrase "not worth a continental" came into being. Until 1785 no national coinage was established. Instead, foreign coins of silver and gold were circulated, and the copper penny was minted locally by some states.

THE CRITICAL ERA

A weak Confederation causes discontent and disorder in 13 states

Political and social unrest marked the period between the Peace Treaty of 1783 and the adoption of the Constitution in 1788. Economic readjustments necessitated by independence were painful.

Commercial ties were renewed with a reluctant Britain and 75 per cent of all trade took place with British merchants. Yet American ships sailed into other European ports and the Orient. Barbary pirates captured Yankee seamen and went unpunished.

Financial conditions of the Confederation were desperate as many states refused to meet their obligations. Within the states, high prices and a shortage of sound money created debtors who clamored after relief laws. Seven states began to print paper money and thus contributed to the unstable currency. Rivalry between states took on serious proportions as local tariff walls were erected, and disputes over territory added to the difficulties and confusion.

As the 13 states were joined together only in a "league of friendship," they were independent commonwealths. States violated the Peace Treaty in their treatment of the Loyalists and British creditors. On her part, Britain also failed to carry out all terms of the treaty. Diplomatic dealings were difficult; American representatives labored under the handicap of negotiating agreements that the states could set aside at will. It was a critical period in American history.

PICTURES CAN LIE! Thomas Jefferson and Benjamin Franklin were shown by an imaginative artist signing the Treaty of the Hague in 1785. In fact, the Treaty of Amity and Commerce between the U. S. and Prussia was unusual in that it was signed by four persons at four different places on four separate dates. Franklin signed at Passy July 9, Jefferson at Paris July 28.

LAST FAREWELL between two firm friends took place in 1781, when Marquis de Lafayette visited General George Washington at Mt. Vernon. In 1777 the French nobleman had volunteered his services to the American Revolution and Congress made him a major general. He obtained soldiers and financial aid in France for American cause. In 1824-25 he revisited U.S.

Confederation

In general, the Articles of Confederation have been criticized as weak. Actually, at the time they were written and debated (1776-77), the Second Continental Congress proposed as much authority as it dared in the face of avid localism. Maryland was the last state to ratify the Articles and they went into effect on March 1, 1781.

While the Articles were the best form of confederacy the world had seen up to that point, they did not establish strong government. The key to the theory behind the Confederation was Article II: "Each State retains its sovereignty, freedom and independence, and every power, jurisdiction and right, which is not ... expressly delegated to the United States in Congress assembled." It was a league, not a union.

Powers delegated to Congress included those to declare war, conduct foreign relations, requisition revenue, build a navy, borrow and coin money. The most important powers could be exercised only with the concurrence of all of the states. Lesser powers had to obtain the approval of nine states. Success depended completely upon the good will of the states. Congress had no direct authority over them or the people.

No judiciary or executive was created. Congress was the sole organ of government. It was a unicameral body to which each state was entitled to send from 2 to 7 delegates. Voting was on an equal basis and each state had one vote. Congress did establish administrative committees, forerunners of War, Treasury, State, Navy departments.

Two prime powers were lacking in Congress: it could not regulate commerce, nor could it levy taxes. Recognition of the need for improvement came in the form of proposed amendments to give Congress the right to set tariffs. However, the Articles could be amended only by unanimous vote of all the states and this was never done. The practical impossibility of amending the Articles was a fatal defect. The "perpetual union" came to its end in 1789.

A STATESMAN'S WELCOME was accorded Benjamin Franklin on his return from Europe in 1785. As a commissioner, Franklin was sent abroad in 1776. There he remained for nine years, gaining note for his charm and learning. His diplomatic skill was shown when he secured loans and concluded an alliance with France in 1778. With John Adams and John Jay, the "old philosopher" negotiated the Treaty of Paris in 1783. Back in the U.S., he became president of Pennsylvania executive council.

SELF-CENTERED New York, with George Clinton as governor (1777-1795), waged trade wars with its neighbors. Clinton opposed closer union and earned the title "Father of New York State."

TRIPLE-THREAT statesman, diplomat and jurist, John Jay signed the peace treaty with Britain. He was Secretary of Foreign Affairs (1784-90) and first Chief Justice of the U.S. (1789-95).

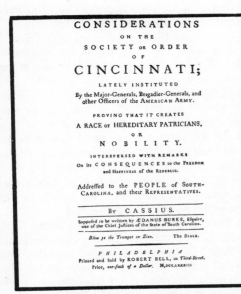

MILITARY INFLUENCE in politics was feared by Aedanus Burke and others who developed suspicions that the Society of the Cincinnati had as its objective the creation of an aristocracy.

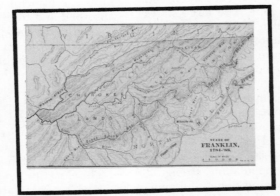

NEW STATE was created by frontiersmen in the northeast corner of present-day Tennessee. The short-lived State of Franklin came into existence when North Carolina ceded its western region to Congress in June, 1784. Yearning for self-government, the settlers drew up a constitution and elected officers. In Dec, 1784, North Carolina repealed the cession act and reinstituted her authority over the area. For two years there were rival sets of officials until John Sevier, State of Franklin's elected governor, was forced to flee.

STATE CLAIMS of territory included all land to the Mississippi river, except Florida. The problem of rival claims was settled by cession and passage of the Northwest Ordinance of 1787.

CONSTITUTIONAL CONVENTION

Federal government supplants Confederation and stability is attained;
work of the Philadelphia framers is approved in every state convention

A controversy between Maryland and Virginia over navigation on the Potomac River produced the first step toward the constitutional convention. Meeting at Mount Vernon in 1785, delegates from those states reached such an amicable agreement that they proposed commissioners from all states should meet at Annapolis, Md., in 1786.

However, men from only five states appeared at Annapolis so the delegates adopted a resolution calling another convention together in May 1787, at Philadelphia. The purpose of the meeting was to recommend changes in the Articles of Confederation. To this idea Congress gave its approval and authorized states to send delegates. Except for Rhode Island, every state took action to comply; deputies were appointed either by state governors or the legislatures.

On May 25 the convention met for its first official session at Independence Hall, and George Washington was elected to preside. Rules of procedure were adopted a few days later. It was decided that voting would be by states and deliberations would be secret.

As James Madison observed years later, a constitution would have been impossible if the convention debates had been made public at that time. Madison himself took elaborate notes even though an official secretary was chosen. His papers, published in 1840, are the most valuable convention records.

The first serious debate took place on the question of what the delegates were supposed to do. Exceeding their instructions, members determined to frame a new form of government rather than to suggest amendment of the Articles of Confederation. In creating this new government, the delegates approached their common task as practical men who had learned their politics at first hand and as men who were familiar with history and the universal political principles which it taught.

Plans and Compromises

Virginia's delegates presented a scheme for a general overhaul of the governmental structure. Introduced by Gov. Edmund Randolph, their plan had been drawn up largely by James Madison. It called for a bicameral legislature, a single executive and a judiciary. Powers established for the national government were broad in scope. The large states would have had a distinct advantage if this plan had been adopted. Led by William Paterson of New Jersey, a counter proposal was put forth which provided for a unicameral legislature (each state having one vote), a plural executive and one Supreme Court. Powers of Congress were somewhat enlarged.

Other minor plans were presented to the convention, but it was the Virginia plan that was accepted in principle. Plans advanced by Alexander Hamilton and Charles Pinckney received no support.

For five crucial weeks the delegates debated various issues, but one main question divided the small and the large states: should the states be represented equally or on population strength? Two Connecticut delegates, William S. Johnson and Roger Sherman, finally suggested a solution. The "Connecticut Compromise" called for equal representation in the upper house and representation in proportion to population in the lower house. Later, a provision was adopted that no state should ever be deprived of equal representation in the Senate without its consent. Other compromises followed. Slaves would be counted as three-fifths in apportioning representatives and for direct taxes; the slave trade would not be stopped but would be allowed to continue for 20 years; treaties required a two-thirds majority for enactment into legislation.

In general terms the major debates revolved around three issues.

First, it was agreed that the new government should be republican in form, but what did this word mean? To James Madison there were three aspects of republicanism: representation, sovereignty resting on the people, decisions based on majority rule. The essence of Alexander Hamilton's position was that representation had to include a Senate which contained the permanent will of the society. To Luther Martin, Roger Sherman and William Paterson, republicanism meant state sovereignty which required a legislature based on state representatives. After the "Connecticut Compromise," a new view emerged in which there was representation both of the states (in the Senate) and of the people (in the House).

The problems of representation geared into that of federalism, the second concern of the convention. Where does political power come from, the people or the states? This issue was compromised so that states were looked at in two ways: as districts composed of people in corporate units and as areas made up of individuals. Federal government thus stemmed from states; national power flowed from the people.

Suffrage — key to representative government — brought forth views which indicated that the framers were anxious to curb the dangers of popular rule. Said Madison on June 6, "interference with the security of private rights and the steady dispensation of justice were evils which had more perhaps than anything else, produced this convention." Worried about factions and the leveling spirit, the only politic solution was to leave voting qualifications up to each state. And Article I, Section 10, prohibited certain state legislation which would encroach on central government prerogatives.

ONLY 39 of 55 delegates signed the original Constitution which is now preserved in helium at the Library of Congress in Washington, D.C.

Sources and Principles

While the Constitution was a new document, its roots are traceable to European sources and earlier American experiences. Words and phrases were repeated from the Articles of Confederation and from several state constitutions, especially that of Massachusetts. From John Locke, James Harrington and Baron Montesquieu came political ideas and principles of government which the framers had obviously absorbed and translated into the new document.

Looking at the debates as a whole, the Constitution was offered as a solution to the problem of government as stated by Madison: "to secure the public good and private rights . . . and at the same time to preserve the spirit and form of popular government." The framers accomplished this by creating constitutional devices to check and control the various interests. Three particular devices were employed: a *federal* structure; *representative* government in which persons of the wiser breed got into power; *balanced* government, with two houses (to check one another), an executive to check the legislature, and an independent judiciary to cap the structure.

The Constitution was transmitted to Congress with the recommendation that it be ratified by conventions chosen by the people in the states. It was to go into effect when nine states consented.

Delaware ratified first, on Dec. 7, 1787, and the ninth state, New Hampshire, did so on June 21, 1788. However, two of the most important states (Virginia and New York) had not ratified, and the new Union could not be successful without them. In both states the struggle was bitter, but by narrow margins the Federalists in each state convention obtained a majority. As a condition for ratification, anti-Federalists insisted upon a Bill of Rights, in order to guard against the possibility of government tyranny. The first 10 amendments to the constitution comprise the Bill of Rights.

"AN ASSEMBLY OF DEMI-GODS," wrote Jefferson from Paris when he read the list of delegates to the Constitutional Convention at Philadelphia in 1787. George Washington (on rostrum) is shown addressing the members who elected him their presiding officer. The average age was 42; Franklin at 81 (left, with cane) was the eldest. Small farmers and working men were not represented. Most delegates were educated, professional men who had wide experience in public affairs. All had business or financial interests to guard, yet the document they wrote protected civil and political liberties as well as property rights. The meetings were secret, but James Madison (standing, center) kept detailed notes, published years later.

FEDERAL PARADES were held in large cities to celebrate ratification of the Constitution. New York's rally included ovation to Hamilton, foremost proponent of Federalism in the state.

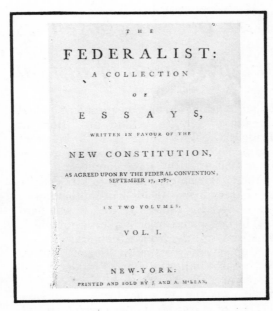

ESSAYS on the meaning of the Constitution were written by Hamilton, Madison and Jay to secure ratification in New York. These *Federalist Papers* are best American government treatise.

ADVOCATE of strong government, Hamilton of New York opposed even the Randolph plan as "pork still, with a little change of the sauce." Nevertheless, he worked hard for ratification.

SOUTHERN STATESMEN ably represented their section at the convention. James Madison (l.) earned the title "Father of the Constitution" by his role in the debates and his stout support of ratification. Governor Edmund J. Randolph (l.c.) presented the Virginia plan, the endorsement of which precluded any revision of the Articles of Confederation. George Mason (r.c.) held strong democratic views and opposed ratification because he believed the new government would lead to aristocracy or monarchy. Gen. Charles C. Pinckney (r.) opposed the election of representatives by popular vote.

A DEVOTED FATHER and family man, Washington spent many of his spare moments with his wife and family at Mount Vernon. Edward Savage has portrayed this family scene (l.) where Washington is reviewing a plan for the location of the capitol city with his wife and her two children. Born into wealth, Washington lived the gracious life of a country squire and plantation owner and did not especially enjoy the responsibilities of the presidency, which kept him away from home. The famous Gilbert Stuart portrait (r.) is a study of poise and stately bearing of nation's first president.

THE LEGEND of Washington and the cherry tree is an illustration of the honesty and truthfulness he was accorded, even as a small child. This later served to make him a great man, able to assume the responsibilities for his actions.

WASHINGTON

War hero is chosen as the first head of nation

When Washington became president he had already a full life behind him. Born at Bridges Creek, Virginia in 1732, he spent the first years of his childhood in a four-room house on the Rappahannock.

Young Washington moved to Mt. Vernon in 1743, to live with his half-brother Lawrence after his father's death. It was here that he began his career as a surveyor, which took him into the frontier country.

After several years in the Virginia Militia, he became aide to Gen. Braddock and shared in his defeat. He then served as commander of the Virginia forces, resigning in 1759, to live at Mt. Vernon, which he had inherited. He later married, and took up the quiet and peaceful life of a planter. No one believed more strongly than Washington that armed conflict was inevitable when Britain's restrictions became unbearable. He was chosen head of the colonies' forces in 1775. His subsequent career stands as a model and a challenge to all who followed.

AS A YOUTH Washington wanted to go to sea. He had a midshipman's warrant and his baggage was on a man-of-war when his widowed mother refused consent. Torn between love of home and sea, Washington obeyed his mother.

A SCIENTIFIC FARMER, Washington practiced crop rotation and experimented with various types of seeds and fertilizers. He was the personal overseer of Mount Vernon, which produced almost everything needed for household.

THE MARRIAGE of Washington and Martha Custis was a union of two prominent Colonial families, and a social event of the time. Of note is the dark hair of Washington, who was seldom pictured without the fashionable powdered wig.

THE HAPPIEST YEARS between the war with France and the Revolution were spent by Washington in the role of a gentleman farmer. He enjoyed traditional fox hunt with his neighbors.

ELECTED PRESIDENT unanimously, Washington received the news with mingled gratitude and reluctance because it meant giving up his quiet life as a gentleman farmer at Mount Vernon.

A SHORT TWO DAYS after being elected, Washington left peaceful Mount Vernon, Virginia, to take oath of office as president in the national capital, at that time in New York.

THE INSTALLATION of first U.S. president into office was a momentous event for the people of New York. In public ceremony on the balcony of Federal Hall, Washington took the oath of President (upper left) in the presence of those men who had aided him in the formation of the new government. His inauguration was greeted with wild acclaim by the public (right) as even his political opponents admired him greatly. The reception which followed, and other social functions of the new president, were lavish affairs (lower left) which met with criticism from the opposition.

FIRST PRESIDENCY

George Washington sets a standard of integrity for all future Presidents

The new nation began putting itself on a running basis. Hamilton was chosen Secretary of the Treasury, and Jefferson Secretary of State. Hamilton, the Federalist, believed in a strong central government; Jefferson favored a looser union.

The former submitted his fiscal policy, including the Funding Bill, authorizing the Treasury to accept old securities at par in payment for new bonds. Other legislation included the Assumption Bill, assuming the debts of the states; The Bank of the United States; and an excise tax. He argued tariff protection, but the first tariff in 1789 was primarily a revenue measure.

The First Judiciary Act of 1789 established the Supreme Court pre-eminent over the other courts. This act also assured the Supreme Court's right to hear appeals from state courts, establishing judicial review.

THE FIRST CABINET was a gathering of imposing statesmen. The fiery Jefferson and aristocratic Hamilton, at opposite political poles, kept Washington busy arbitrating their disputes.

Washington acquiesced to a second term as President. Political parties had taken form from the issues of states' rights and a central government. France, at war with England, desired the help of the new nation, but Washington refused such aid in his Proclamation of Neutrality.

In the Treaty of San Lorenzo, Spain agreed to the American claim of the 31st parallel as a southern boundary, settling one of the primary problems of the West, opening the Mississippi River.

Washington refused a third term. In his *Farewell Address* he cautioned against sectionalism, urged that neutrality be maintained by avoiding any permanent alliances with foreign nations.

PEARL AND CHERRY Streets in New York was the location of the first Presidential Mansion, while plans were being drawn for the site of the capital. Philadelphia was favored by most as the site for center of newly formed government.

PHILADELPHIA was rapidly becoming the financial center of the new nation, especially with the establishment of the United States Bank. It was set up early in 1791 to provide added banking facilities and a sound currency system.

THE LACK OF a Federal capital made it necessary to provide other locations for government functions. Congress Hall in New York was utilized for Congressional meeting until 1800, when Capitol was opened at Washington, D. C.

THE WESTERN FRONTIER was opened in the summer of 1794 by the Treaty of Greenville in Ohio. Gen. "Mad Anthony" Wayne is shown at the treaty signing, in which Indians ceded the southeast section of the Northwest Territory. The removal of the Indian problem in the area enabled the new government to expand, utilizing the western land. The "crowded" cities and towns of the eastern seaboard witnessed a mass exodus as citizens sought the trans-mountain lands. (See atlas, plate 14).

CITIZEN GENET, minister of the French Republic, called upon United States to fulfill terms of alliance with France. Washington and Hamilton demanded his recall, asserting that treaty with executed Louis XVI was no longer valid.

OUTRAGED farmers in western Pennsylvania started revolt to protest excise on whiskey they produced. Excise officers at times were tarred and then feathered (right). Militia put down uprising in a test of ability of the federal government to enforce the law.

BILL OF RIGHTS

Many Americans objected to the Constitution because they felt their individual rights were not guaranteed sufficiently. James Madison submitted 12 amendments to Congress Sept. 9, 1789, and 10 of these were ratified by Dec. 15, 1791, to make up the Bill of Rights. Its provisions: (1) freedom of religion, speech, press and assembly; (2) establishment of a militia; (3) no forceful quartering of soldiers in private homes; (4) freedom from unreasonable searches and seizure; (5) due process of law; (6) trial by jury; (7) right of common law; (8) prevention of excessive fines, bail, punishment; (9) listing of certain rights in Constitution would not deny other rights retained by the people; (10) powers not delegated to the United States by the Constitution be reserved to states or to the people.

AN UNPOPULAR treaty was made by Chief Justice of the Supreme Court John Jay (l.), who was sent to persuade Great Britain to fulfill the treaty of 1783 and to stop her impressment of American seamen. Jay made many concessions, and the question of impressment and seizure of U.S. ships was not settled. The treaty was so ill-received that Jay was burned in effigy at New York (r.) The Senate, after a series of bitter debates, finally ratified the treaty in the June, 1795, session.

VERMONT JOINED the union in 1791, the first state to be added to the original 13. Statehood came after New York's claims to the area had been put aside. The creation of the new states beyond the Appalachian mountains was soon to follow.

JOHN ADAMS

Struggle for leadership weakens the cabinet as French crisis looms

John Adams was second only to Washington in the official capacities in which he had served his country. When he became the second president, he retained Washington's cabinet, most of whose members looked to Federalist leader Alexander Hamilton for advice. The ensuing struggle for leadership weakened Adams' administration.

England and France, at war with one another, were both seizing U.S. ships. At the moment France, angry at the Jay Treaty, was the worst offender and American efforts to negotiate ended in the "XYZ Affair." Until then the U.S. had been progressively pro-French, electing Thomas Jefferson, leader of the pro-French Republicans, as vice-president. But Americans reacted with patriotic fervor. Hasty preparations were made for war with France. The Navy Department was created May 3, 1798, and Lt. Gen. George Washington was recalled as commander-in-chief of the Army. In June commercial intercourse was suspended. By July treaties with France were abrogated. An undeclared naval war broke out.

Meanwhile, the Federalist government enacted the Alien, Naturalization and Sedition Acts, aimed at immigrants, pro-French, and non-conformists. Under these laws the president could deport "such aliens as he shall judge dangerous to the peace and safety"; residency for citizenship was raised from 5 to 14 years; and it was made a crime to write or publish "any false, scandalous and malicious" statements about the president or congress. The few convictions under the Sedition Act caused widespread alarm. Kentucky and Virginia adopted resolutions denouncing these laws, claiming they violated the constitution and state's rights.

Adams Puts Welfare of Nation Above Party

Early in 1799 Adams learned that the French would receive a new mission cordially. Without consulting his hostile cabinet nor the pro-war Federalist leaders in Congress, he appointed a minister to France. The resulting Treaty of 1800 assured peace when it was imperative for U.S. development and paved the way for purchase of Louisiana. But Adams, by putting nation above party, doomed his own career and destroyed the Federalists' power. In the 1800 contest Adams and the Federalists were soundly defeated. Jefferson won the majority vote but tied in the electoral vote 73-73 with his running mate Aaron Burr. Under the original system electors voted for two candidates without designating presidential preference. The election was thrown into the House, still controlled by the Federalists. Jefferson, on the 36th balloting, was chosen president. This weakness in the electoral system was changed by the new congress with the 12th Amendment.

Adams, in his last hours, appointed Federalist John Marshall as Chief Justice of the United States and bitterly left Washington next day before the inauguration ceremonies began.

JOHN ADAMS, learned, aristocratic, vain, was also, as Vice-President Thomas Jefferson said, as "impartial as the God who made him." During his presidency, Abigail Adams (l.) lived often at their Massachusetts farm to economize. Late in his term, when the capital was changed from Philadelphia to Washington, the Adams' family become the first occupants of the White House.

CARTOON OF 1799 shows U.S. reaction to "XYZ Affair." Mission sent to France to negotiate with revolutionary government was met by three officials (termed XYZ by Adams). They demanded bribe and loan to avert war. Americans cried "Millions for defense, but not one cent for tribute."

UNDECLARED NAVAL WAR with France (1798-1800) was waged mainly in West Indies against French privateers attacking U.S. merchantmen. Britain gave U.S. guns and ammunition and exchanged naval code signals. The frigates *Constitution* (l.), *United States* and *Constellation* were hastily completed. In a spectacular 77-minute action (r.) the latter made *L'Insurgente* strike her tricolor flag in abject surrender.

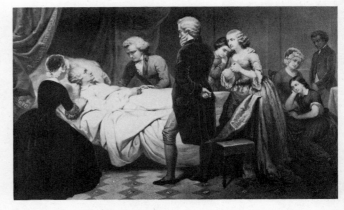

WASHINGTON'S DEATH Dec. 14, 1799, at Mt. Vernon was brought on by an attack of quinsy, badly treated by doctors who bled him. Among his last words were: "I die hard, but I am not afraid to go." The United States went into mourning. France's Napoleon and even the British honored his memory.

U. S. MOVES WEST

Expanding America proves democracy is more than theory, but crisis looms over slavery issue

"I have no fear," wrote Jefferson, "but that the result of our experiment will be, that men may be trusted to govern themselves without a master." This, indeed, was what the young Republic had set out to prove, and with Jefferson's election to the Presidency in 1800, it would be put to its purest test. For while the "Revolution of 1800," as Jefferson called it, was still not a truly democratic election of popular balloting, it brought the triumph of democratic principles over the stern rule of the Federalists. Jefferson himself proved to be a strong and decisive president, but by this very process he showed that government can be democratic without being weak.

Almost alone among the earth's inhabitants, Americans answered to no man — and were proud of it. In 1812 they went out of their way to assert themselves by declaring a second war on Great Britain. In 1823 their President boldly served notice on European rulers that they could henceforth keep out of the Western Hemisphere. In 1836, American settlers in the Mexican province of Texas revolted and set up their own republic. When the dispute with Britain over the Oregon boundary waxed hot in 1844, Americans elected a President on the campaign cry, "54-40 or Fight!" Finally, in 1846, they proceeded to take the rest of the Far West from Mexico by outright conquest. But if Americans were too cocksure, this was a trait of a youthful people with a taste of liberty.

JEFFERSON OF MONTICELLO

Americans Conquer Wilderness

Americans also had enough resolve and imagination to tame a continent within a few decades. The entire Mississippi Valley was teeming with trade and population by the Civil War. Even the formidable Western plains were no barrier. As early as 1804 Lewis and Clark had explored overland to the Pacific Coast. By the 1840s, following trails blazed by trappers and traders, pioneer families were crossing the plains to the green valleys of California and Oregon.

After 1848, when gold was discovered in California, they poured West by the hundreds of thousands. To a world accustomed to seeing history made by kings, they were proving that it could also be made by the common people. These people carried with them their belief in freedom.

Popular Government Thrives

Americans were demanding, and getting, a more direct voice in government. By the time Jackson was elected President in 1828, the electoral college was a formality and the popular will a reality. Equally dynamic was the new American economy. With such inventions as the cotton gin, the power loom and the steamboat, Industrial Revolution reached America in earnest. Railroads, canals and riverways were employed in a thriving trade which gave new life to such eastern centers as New York and Baltimore, and fostered such western cities as Cincinnati, Chicago and St. Louis. Even American art flowered in these early decades. This was the Golden Age of U.S. painting — of Trumbull, Stuart, Copley and Sully. In the field of letters, the era bore the monumental stamp of Emerson, Hawthorne, Bryant, Longfellow, Poe and Cooper.

But even while the nation was proving the possibilities of freedom, it was approaching its sternest crisis. For contained within the American system of equal rights was a deadly flaw — Southern slavery. It might have persisted far longer before the inevitable clash, because much of the North was too preoccupied with a flourishing commerce to raise an ideological battle. But the American frontier forced a showdown. Neither side could afford to give way on the issue of whether slavery should be freely extended into the new West. Finally, the election of 1860 confirmed what the South had long feared — a political alliance between the North and West. The time was ripe for the vital and significant test of Jefferson's promise that men could be trusted to govern themselves.

★　　★　　★

◄ **JEFFERSON'S** purchase of Louisiana Territory from France in 1803 gave U.S. control of New Orleans, removing last obstacle to vast Mississippi River trade. Four years later Robert Fulton perfected the steamboat, which first appeared in New Orleans in 1812. From then until the Civil War, the Mississippi Valley thrived on a flourishing river trade. New Orleans became the nation's third largest city, these floating palaces the symbols of American commerce, industry and resourcefulness.

THOMAS JEFFERSON (left) was a paradox of his time. Born a Virginia aristocrat, he championed the people. Although he had expensive personal tastes, he stressed frugality in government. A great politician, he died in poverty. An author, musician, inventor, scientist, lawyer and architect, he was also a natural statesman. The classic influence of Europe, where he traveled, was shown in his house at Monticello, which he designed himself. The home, which he built near Charlottesville, was a haven during his two presidential administrations

THE JEFFERSONIANS

Republican-Democratic administration ends 12 years of Federalist rule

Inauguration of Thomas Jefferson as President in 1801 brought new political philosophies and methods to American government. Federalist power was ended and the Republican-Democrats assumed office.

Emphasizing simplicity and economy, the new administration aimed to abolish Federalist pomp and aristocracy. In his inaugural speech, Jefferson stressed need for "wise and frugal" government, payment of debt.

Equal opportunity and protection of individual freedom highlighted his speech. He urged support of state's rights, spread of education, majority rule and peace with all nations — entangling alliances with none.

Although the third president, Jefferson was the first to take office in Washington. Moved in 1800 from Philadelphia to a site on the Potomac called District of Columbia, the half-finished capitol was dismal and isolated when Jefferson took office.

Following inauguration Jefferson chose a distinguished cabinet, including James Madison as Secretary of State and Albert Gallatin as Secretary of the Treasury.

Governmental changes and quarrels with the Judiciary followed. Internal Revenue Act, Naturalization and Judiciary Acts were repealed. When Alien and Sedition Act died, persons convicted under it were pardoned.

Chief Justice John Marshall made history with the first annulment of an act of Congress in the Marbury vs. Madison case. Ruling on the appointment of a justice of the peace, Court held that a section of the judiciary act was in conflict with the Constitution and thus was invalid. This established the right of the Supreme Court to review and rule on the constitutionaliy of acts of Congress.

Republican conflict with the Federalist judiciary resulted in the impeachment and dismissal of Judge John Pickering. An attempt to remove Justice Samuel Chase backfired, however, so campaign was dropped.

JAMES MADISON was Jefferson's protegee and the gentleman of distinction of his day. An experienced statesman, he served two terms as Secretary of State. Dolly Madison, his wife, was White House hostess for the widowed Jefferson.

CONFIRMED FEDERALIST John Marshall was appointed Chief Justice by outgoing President John Adams. Serving on Supreme Court bench 34 years, Marshall established the court's right of judicial review of all acts of Congress.

FINANCIAL WIZARD Albert Gallatin, treasury chief, put government finances on sound basis, reduced national debt and introduced first budget. Swiss-born Gallatin's motto was "turn the other cheek to avoid war — it's less expensive."

BURNING OF THE PHILADELPHIA marked a high point of the war. Captured after grounding on a reef, the warship was refloated by Tripolitans for use against the Americans. Lt. Stephen Decatur, Jr., and 70 volunteers slipped into Tripoli harbor in February, 1804, blew the ship sky-high and escaped under intense enemy fire. Bainbridge and the crew of the *Philadelphia* remained in the Pasha's prison for 19 months, but the feat gave Preble's ill-supplied squadron a shot of confidence and increased U.S. prestige. Lord Nelson called the feat the "most daring act of the age."

TRIPOLITAN WAR

United States Navy enters Mediterranean to defeat Barbary pirates

The Tripolitan War, a series of naval encounters in the Mediterranean, had a bearing beyond its own results. It prevented the Navy from being budgeted out of existence, and served as a training ground for the War of 1812. In addition, it spurred Congress to establish the United States Military Academy at West Point in New York in 1802.

Buying protection for merchant ships from North African states was common practice, and by 1800, the U.S. had paid more than $2 million in tribute to Algiers, Morocco, Tunis and Tripoli.

Jefferson's firm stand against added bribes to the Pasha of Tripoli brought a declaration of war from that portly individual in May, 1801.

The president, with a fleet he could count on his fingers, dispatched a squadron to the area. But the listless course of action pursued by Commodore Richard Dale and Capt. Richard Morris resulted in little more than an ineffectual blockade.

Capt. Edward Preble was placed in command in mid-1803 and the action picked up tempo. Preble's disciplinary views, tempered by a tenacious loyalty to his men, achieved positive results. Officers like Sommers, Wadsworth, Israel, and the two Decaturs led several successful bombardments against the walled fortress and generally made life uneasy for the Pasha.

Major U.S. setbacks were capture of the *Philadelphia,* and loss of all hands when the *Intrepid* blew up prematurely on a sabotage mission into Tripoli Harbor.

An interesting sidelight was an attempt by William Eaton, U.S. naval agent, to restore the Pasha's brother to the throne. Eaton's rag-tag army captured Derne after a 600-mile desert march. But the adventurer had to call off an attack on the capital and restore Derne when Col. Lear concluded a peace treaty with the Pasha in 1805. However, the Barbary pirates in other states continued to receive tribute until 1815, when Algiers was forced to respect the U.S. flag.

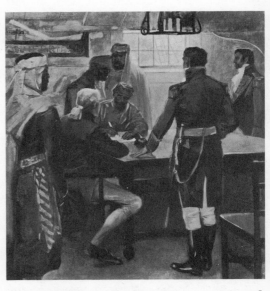

WOUNDED SEAMAN Daniel Frazier saved Decatur's life by stopping a cutlass blow with his head. In another clash, Lt. Trippe of *Vixen* received 11 wounds before he and 10 tars overpowered the crew of a large Tripolitan gunboat.

UNREALISTIC PEACE TREATY was negotiated in 1805 by Col. Tobias Lear. The pact involved paying the Bey $60,000 even though Tripoli was threatened by a U.S. naval squadron and approaching land army led by William Eaton.

END OF NAPOLEON'S dream of an American empire came when he sold vast Louisiana Territory to United States for $15,000,000. Above, American negotiators Robert Livingston and James Monroe sign the Purchase treaty in Paris, April 30, 1803. At left, soldiers salute the lowering of the French flag and raising of the American flag in the Cabildo at New Orleans where the transfer was actually accomplished, Dec. 20, 1803. This purchase doubled the area of the United States, giving it control of the Mississippi and its watershed, and made possible American expansion to the Pacific.

PURCHASE OF LOUISIANA

Aquisition of the vast French territory was a great stroke of diplomacy

The unsettled lands east of the Mississippi river began to fill rapidly with settlers under the new land act of 1800. The act allowed them to buy tracts as small as 320 acres at $2.00 an acre for an initial deposit of 10 cents per acre. Payments spread in installments over four years. By the spring of 1803, Kentucky had 250,000 people, Tennessee had 100,000, and Ohio was admitted as the 17th state with a population of 55,000.

The only cheap and practical outlet for their commerce was down the Mississippi river to New Orleans. But the river and all the land west of it, and the land on both sides of the Mississippi at its mouth belonged to Spain. Since 1795 Spain had permitted Americans to use the river freely and to transship their cargoes at New Orleans without paying duty. Three-eighths of U.S. commerce passed through this port in 1802.

That fall the Spanish intendant at New Orleans closed that city to foreign commerce and abrogated the American right of deposit there. At once Americans assumed that he had acted on orders from Madrid dictated from France, as it was rumored that Spain had ceded Louisiana to France. She had, on Oct. 1, 1800, but it was still a secret. Americans feared that France might be too strong a neighbor.

Rivermen began to say that navigation of the Mississippi could never be secure unless New Orleans and West Florida belonged to the United States. Western wrath at the closure of New Orleans began to kindle. Some talked of sacking New Orleans.

The Federalists, who had previously opposed most Western desires, now began demanding that the West's interests be protected.

President Jefferson, reluctant to provoke war with France, decided to see what diplomacy might achieve. He sent James Monroe, his favorite trouble-shooter, to Paris. Monroe, well-liked by the Westerners, was to act as a special envoy and help Robert Livingston, the American minister there, who had already been trying to persuade France to sell part of Louisiana. They were authorized to pay up to $10,000,000 for New Orleans and as much land east of the Mississippi as they could obtain.

In the meantime, the troops Napoleon had intended to send to Louisiana were decimated by yellow fever and bitter war in

UPPER LOUISIANA'S TRANSFER to the United States did not occur until March 9, 1804, when official ceremonies took place in St. Louis. The area was transferred by the Spanish Lt.-Gov. to Major Amos Stoddard, commissioned as the French representative. The following day Maj. Stoddard delivered it up to the United States.

Santo Domingo. Reinforcements were delayed in Europe. Thus, two days before Monroe arrived in Paris, Napoleon, who needed money to launch new military campaigns in Europe, suddenly decided to sell not only New Orleans but all of Louisiana as well. Monroe and Livingston had no authority to buy land *west* of the river, nor at such a price, but it was a case of all or nothing. They agreed to buy, for $15,000,000 in cash and claims.

Jefferson, who was a strict constitutionalist, feared that this exceeded his powers and was tempted to ask for a constitutional amendment to sanction such a purchase. However, he was persuaded that Napoleon might withdraw his offer before such a move could be completed. He finally presented the treaty as it was to the Senate, which ratified it on October 20, 1803, by a vote of 24 to 7. (See atlas, plate 7.)

Jefferson's first term in office ended in a glow of success, financial, diplomatic, domestic. Some embittered New England Federalists held out in strenuous opposition against the Louisiana Purchase and talked of secession. They even planned a union with Canada to escape the political power which they saw shifting to the South and West. However, their voices were so weak against the general chorus of approval that, when Jefferson ran again for the presidency, he won the electoral vote of every New England state except Connecticut. Delaware was the only other state against him. It seemed to President Jefferson, as he took office a second time, that "not a cloud appeared on the horizon."

FIRST AMERICANS TO CROSS the continent to the Pacific, Meriwether Lewis and William Clark, might never have succeeded without the help of the Shoshone Indians, whom they met (above) near the source of the Missouri. The Shoshone chief Cameahwait was found to be the long-lost brother of their guide Sacajawea, the Bird Woman. Only 16 when she joined the expedition, she was invaluable through knowledge of trails, weather, edible plants. She gave birth to a boy Feb. 11, 1805, while expedition was in winter quarters. The child was carried to Pacific and back.

ANOTHER DARING EXPLORER, Lt. Zebulon Pike, discovered the great peak now named for him while on a mission for the U.S. in western Louisiana Territory and Southwest in 1806-07.

BURNING OUT LOGS after the Indian fashion, Lewis and Clark with their 23 soldiers, three interpreters, and a Negro slave built boats at Celilo Falls on the Columbia River to take them to the Pacific. They had spent their first winter with the Mandan Indians in what is now North Dakota, and resumed journey in April, 1805. They crossed the Great Divide in September and in October reached this spot.

AMERICAN CLAIMS TO THE OREGON COUNTRY made 40 years later were considerably strengthened by the fact that the Lewis and Clark Expedition wintered on the south bank of the Columbia River, near its mouth, from Nov. 15, 1805 to March, 1806. Their reports of their journey did much to encourage the later flow of settlers to the Northwest. They waited in vain all winter for a trading vessel to come to the mouth of the Columbia.

AN ENCOUNTER WITH UNFRIENDLY INDIANS in the Dakotah country, pictured above, was typical of many such meetings experienced by Lewis and Clark. A firm show of force and a pow-wow paved the way for peaceful passage. On their return trip they explored the area between the Clearwater and Yellowstone rivers, otherwise following much the same route they had taken westward. They reached St. Louis again in September 1806.

ALEXANDER HAMILTON, co-author of *The Federalist* and first Secretary of the Treasury under Washington, was responsible for revolutionary fiscal and economic measures which marked the first 18th century break with the theories of Adam Smith. Idea of a U.S. National Bank originated with him.

AMERICAN EXASPERATION over British impressment of their deserters from American merchant ships reached a peak when the American warship *Chesapeake* was searched, June 22, 1807. Four deserters were taken off. Jefferson immediately ordered British warships out of American waters.

NEUTRAL RIGHTS

Embargo on export of U. S. goods fails to bring warring nations to terms

Jefferson's second term as President (1805-09) was filled with troubles. France was at war with England; and the United States, being an important neutral shipper, suffered in the naval rivalry between these two giants. Their restrictions on neutral trade grew so severe that by December, 1807, an American ship could hardly go to Europe without being seized as a prize.

Despite this, American owners made handsome profits. In 1805 some 70,000 tons and some 4,200 seamen were added to the American merchant marine. Sailors' wages rose from $8 to $24 per month. By 1807, a year when many American ships were seized, American foreign trade was bigger

($246,000,000) than it was again until 1835. Had confiscation of ships and cargoes been the only United States grievance against England and France, the country probably would never have gone to war.

What irritated Americans particularly was the way British frigates hovered off American ports, searching all ships for evidence of something irregular. The issue of impressment was the most important. President Jefferson became convinced that a policy of "peaceful economic coercion" would force England and France to repeal their restrictions on neutral trade. So, over Federalist opposition, he pushed a sweeping Embargo Act through Congress in De-

cember 1807, which practically forbade the export of any U.S. goods by sea or land.

Although the Act was not strictly enforced, loss of trade was damaging to the country and loud protests were aroused. A huge smuggling trade across the Canadian frontier grew up. England was harder hit by the Embargo than France.

The defunct Federalist party revived, especially in New England. Threats of secession were heard there. Three days before Jefferson ended his second term, Congress repealed the Embargo and replaced it with the Non-Intercourse Act of 1809 which left Americans free to trade with every nation except England and France.

BITTER ABOUT POLITICAL ACCUSATIONS, Aaron Burr (c.) challenged Alexander Hamilton to a duel, during which, on July 11, 1804, Hamilton was killed. Public reaction was intense, and Burr had to flee. He decided in 1805-06 to revive his political fortunes by a Western venture. With General Wilkinson, Governor of Louisiana Territory, he assembled a small force of armed men and sailed down the Mississippi on flatboats. Whether Burr intended to set up an independent state in the Mississippi Valley or in Spanish territory is still a mystery. He was arrested in 1807, tried for treason before Chief Justice Marshall in a U.S. Circuit Court, and acquitted. He lived in Europe in self-imposed exile before returning to New York.

MADISON

U.S. becomes involved in European conflict

When James Madison was elected president in 1808 there was a depression at home. The raging Napoleonic wars abroad at the same time were an ever-increasing threat to America's peace.

Madison continued Jefferson's policy of peace, hoping to avert war with France or England, which he felt would be useless and unwise. His attempts at conciliation, however, were ill-managed and a series of diplomatic blunders led the country into war. He was hampered by wide dissension in Congress and in the ranks of his own Democrat-Republican party.

England's obnoxious Orders in Council and France's Berlin and Milan decrees restricting American trade continued in effect. In March, 1810, Napoleon issued another decree at Rambouillet ordering the confiscation of American ships detained in ports under French control.

Napoleon's Duplicity Leads Nation Toward War

Since Jefferson's embargo had proved ill-advised, Congress passed the Macon Bill No. 2 as a substitute measure. This bill provided for open trade until March 3, 1811, three months after adjournment of Congress. If by this time one of the belligerent countries should rescind its orders or decrees, the U.S. would again proclaim non-intercourse with the other. Napoleon, anxious to align America on his side against England, responded in an ambiguously-worded decree purporting to revoke his previous decrees. Actually they continued in effect. England refused to recognize Napoleon's decree which was contingent upon her revoking her Orders in Council, or America's "causing her rights to be respected." But Madison fell into Napoleon's trap and resumed non-intercourse with England as France had hoped.

Sentiment in the South and West was strong for war. Indian attacks such as the Tippecanoe Massacre, as westward-moving pioneers encroached on Indian lands, were blamed on British incitement. A victorious sea encounter of the U.S. *President* over the British *Little Belt* increased the popular enthusiasm for war throughout the nation.

Pressed by the "War Hawks" in Congress who clamored for the annexation of Canada, Madison finally capitulated. On June 18, 1812, war with England was declared for the protection of America's rights on the seas. Ironically, Parliament had suspended the Orders in Council two days before, but the news of this act, obviating the need for war, had of course not reached America. Thus the nation entered a war it was not prepared for, a war which was unnecessary and could have been averted at several junctures before declaration.

DOLLY MADISON, charming and gay, was noted for her hospitality. Born Dolly Payne in 1768, she was the Quaker widow Todd when she married Madison.. She served as White House hostess for widower Jefferson, later ruled as Washington society's queen dowager.

FOURTH PRESIDENT of the U.S. was James Madison of Virginia. Born in 1751, he lived to be 85. His great claim to fame lies in his being "Father of the Constitution." Small, quiet, James Madison was an able legislator, but lacked executive ability as President of the United States.

EVASION of Jefferson's Embargo Act was attempted by many American shippers. The *Hercules* of Salem is shown here in the French-held Bay of Naples in 1809. United States ships which were at sea when the embargo began remained in foreign waters and continued their trade with belligerents. Napoleon's Bayonne Decree ordered the seizure of all American vessels which entered ports of France and Italy and the Hanseatic cities. In two years the French confiscated more than $10 million in U.S. goods and shipping, despite vigorous American protests.

TIPPECANOE MASSACRE occurred on cold dawn of Nov. 7, 1811, when William Henry Harrison burned Indian village in retaliation for attack on his troops camped nearby. Above, he and Indian leader Tecumseh meet at Vincennes.

WAR HAWKS Annexation of Canada was desired by an enthusiastic group of young Republicans in the House after elections of 1810. With hot-headed, 34-year-old Henry Clay (l.) as speaker, the group included Peter B. Porter (c.) and 29-year-old John C. Calhoun (r.). They embraced the optimistic belief that Canada could be taken easily from England. They roused the Westerners with claims that England was inciting Indian attacks on frontier settlements, using the Tippecanoe incident to advantage. As prosperity had returned to shipping, Easterners were not interested in war. To them the "War Hawks" orated fervently on "freedom of the seas," kept alive resentment against earlier British impressment of American seamen. Opponents claimed that this influential group made war a condition of President Madison's renomination in 1812 election.

THE FAMED "CONSTITUTION" under command of Captain Isaac Hull destroyed the British frigate, *Guerriere*. This victory on Aug. 19, 1812, was hailed with particular enthusiasm as the *Guerriere* had caused the impressment of many American seamen. On Dec. 29, 1812, with William Bainbridge in command, she defeated the British *Java*. Left, an English commander boards an American ship and takes a sailor for duty in the British Navy. Impressment of American sailors, claiming them as British citizens, became one of the chief reasons for the War of 1812.

WAR OF 1812

U.S. invades Canada as Britain blockades coast

GALLANT LITTLE "WASP," 18-gun American sloop of war, captures British *Frolic* off Virginia coast with odds even, Oct. 18, 1812. On the way home with his prize, Captain Jacob Jones lost both of the little ships with small glory to the much larger 74-gun British *Poictiers*.

The United States was totally unprepared for the War of 1812 despite the fact that it had been long threatening. The tiny fleet was pitifully inadequate against the most powerful British navy. On the other hand, England was reaching the climax in the long fight against Napoleon and her navy could spare but a small effort for the war with the United States.

Early sea battles of the war were brilliant American victories. In the first six months there was but one American loss while six British warships surrendered. American privateers were raising havoc with British commerce, capturing more than 300 vessels. In December, 1812, the British journal *Pilot*, called its readers to "serious reflection . . . down to this moment not a single American frigate has struck her flag

. . . Nothing chases, nothing intercepts, nothing engages them but yields them triumph."

In the spring of 1813, the British navy began to gain ascendancy. On May 31, 1814, shortly after Napoleon's abdication, the whole American coast was placed under blockade. Scarcely a ship was able to leave home ports. New England was plunged into depression. The exports from New York dropped from $12 million in 1811 to $200,-000 in 1814. The government resorted to borrowing by public subscription, since no national bank existed, but little help came from anti-war financiers in the Northeast.

Though the naval war was in reality Britain's victory, the triumphant early sea duels left the impression in the popular mind that it had been a glorious triumph for America. (See atlas, plate 11.)

PRIDE OF THE BRITISH NAVY, the *Macedonian*, was captured (l.) by the frigate *United States* under command of Captain Stephen Decatur (c.) on October 25, 1812. Americans were jubilant over their glorious battle victories early in the war. The U.S. *Essex* defeated the *Alert* in August, 1812. The U.S. *Hornet* sank the *Peacock* in February, 1813. As the war progressed, more of the victories went to the British ships. In June, 1813,

the American *Chesapeake*, after losing her commander, was forced to surrender to the *Shannon* under Captain Philip Broke. It was a terrible 15-minute battle with much bloodshed on both sides. Captain James Lawrence is seen (r.) as he died aboard *Chesapeake*. Richard Rush wrote of this crushing American defeat: "I remember the public gloom . . . 'Don't give up the ship,' the dying words of Capt. Lawrence — were on every tongue."

SERVING HOT SHOT, a woman aids in the defense of Fort Niagara at the mouth of the Niagara River. The British bombarded and captured the fort on December 30, 1813, in retaliation for the burning of Queenston. The war became more and more barbarous as British marauding parties burned farms and villages. Buffalo, then a small town, was raided and destroyed.

TECUMSEH MET DEATH in Battle of the Thames, Sept. 12, 1813. The Indian leader had been commissioned a brigadier-general in the British army and had fought in the campaigns of 1812 and 1813. This battle was Gen. Proctor's last stand in his retreat from Detroit, pursued by Gen. William Henry Harrison. It completed recapture of Northwest for Americans.

While the valiant little American **navy was** making history on the sea, the army was failing shamefully in its early campaigns in the Northwest. A three-pronged drive into Canada was planned by the War Department. Gen. Henry Dearborn was to advance upon Montreal by way of Lake Champlain. Gen. Stephen Van Rensselaer was to strike the Niagara River front, and Gen. William Hull was to launch an attack from Detroit against Upper Canada. The expedition commanded by Gen. Hull ended in his falling back to Detroit where on Aug. 16, 1812, he surrendered his troops to Gen. Sir Isaac Brock's much smaller army. After Gen. Van Rensselaer was unable to get his raw militia to cross into Canada at the Battle of Queenston Heights, he retired in disgust. Gen. Alexander Smyth assumed the command, but his leadership was equally ineffective. Gen. Dearborn, in command

of the main army at Plattsburg, marched his forces to the Canadian frontier where on Nov. 19, 1812, they sat down and refused to cross the border. Detroit and Ft. Dearborn (Chicago) had fallen to the British, and the Canadian border had been pushed down to the Wabash and Ohio rivers.

After the Battle of Lake Erie in the fall of 1813 (see pg. 94), the British were forced to retreat and the Northwest was recaptured. After the fall of Napoleon in April, 1814, England was able to send large veteran reinforcements to Canada. Meanwhile incompetent generals had been cleared from the American army. Fighting on home ground with such generals as George Izzard, Jacob Brown, Peter S. Porter, Winfield Scott and Andrew Jackson in command, the American forces, then better trained and disciplined, were able to hold their own against the British.

FERRYING ACROSS THE NIAGARA from Lewiston, 1,000 American troops under command of Major General Stephen Van Rensselaer attacked British at Queenston and met defeat on Oct. 13, 1812. Some 5,000 troops of New York militia comprising the rest of Van Rensselaer's forces refused to leave the boundary line of their state, calmly watched the disastrous defeat from across the river. Canadian commander, General Sir Isaac Brock, was killed in this encounter, known as the Battle of Queenston Heights.

DEARBORN MASSACRE occurred on Aug. 15, 1812. On orders from Gen. Hull, Fort Dearborn was evacuated and surplus stores were divided among the Indians. Escorting inhabitants to safety of Fort Wayne, garrison was attacked by savages. All whites were killed or captured and 12 children were butchered mercilessly. Next day fort (above) was sacked and burned.

FORT GEORGE, on the Canadian side of the Niagara, was captured by some 4,000 American forces on May 27, 1813. The second fleet under Captain Isaac Chauncey enfiladed the beach while Winfield Scott's troops advanced along the shore. About one-third of the garrison of British regulars were killed or wounded. American loss totaled 160 killed and wounded.

BATTLE OF THE LAKES

"We have met the enemy and they are ours; two ships, two brigs, one schooner and one sloop," was Commodore Oliver H. Perry's message to General William Henry Harrison, leader of the land forces. The American fleet of nine vessels with 57 guns had met and defeated the British squadron of six ships and 63 guns on Lake Erie. Perry is pictured above as he directed the engagement. His tactics were brilliant and the result was a decisive American victory on Sept. 10, 1813. With the support of the British fleet gone, General Proctor decided to abandon Detroit and retreated with the American Army in hot pursuit. A year later, British General Prevost with 10,000 veterans of the Duke of Wellington's Spanish campaigns invaded the Northwest from Montreal. Prevost's flotilla of lake boats were met on Lake Champlain by an American fleet. Though the American ships could only throw a broadside of 759 lbs. against the British 1128 lbs., Commodore Thomas MacDonough (l.) brought the Americans through to victory. U.S. forces consisted of some 1,500 regulars and a few militia. But Prevost, having lost the waterway, withdrew his 10,000 troops. (See atlas, plate 11.)

"OLD IRONSIDES" was the apt nickname given to the 44-gun U.S. frigate *Constitution*. It was heavily planked and timbered and threw tremendous broadsides. After a long, magnificent record, the frigate was rebuilt and preserved.

◀ **INDIAN WARS** inflamed the frontier during the War of 1812. Gen. Andrew Jackson, after the massacre of Ft. Mimms, humbled the Creeks of the Alabama country, forcing them to sign a treaty relinquishing two-thirds of their lands. Meanwhile, in 1814, Gen. Henry Dodge (l.) defeated the Miami tribe of the state of Ohio.

"CITY OF MAGNIFICENT SPACES" was the term applied to Washington, D.C., by European visitors in early 1800's. Laid out with a view to later growth, public buildings were widely separated. The site, chosen by Washington in 1790, was far from promising. Malaria infested and dusty, it did not grow to magnificence until Civil War. Congressmen, forced to leave families at home, fought for rooms in boarding houses.

MADISON'S LAST TERM

The election of 1812 was a strong indication of the division of sentiment in the country over the war. Federalists and anti-war Republicans voted for DeWitt Clinton. The votes from the 13 original states were evenly divided. The issue was decided by the West and Madison was reelected 128 to 89.

The administration was seriously hampered in the war effort by the lack of cooperation in the New England states. Some states refused to send militia to the aid of the regulars. Their increasing dissatisfaction led to the Hartford Convention. It was called by the Massachusetts legislature for the purpose of considering a revision of the Constitution. Some of the more radical members such as Timothy Pickering even talked of secession. However, activities of the Convention ceased after news of Jackson's victory at New Orleans.

War was officially ended by the Treaty of Ghent Dec. 25, 1814. Though the treaty did not touch upon the question of the rights of neutral commerce or impressment of American seamen, it was received with great joy.

Despite its cost to the U.S., the War of 1812 had taught the nation valuable lessons. The lack of government revenue as a result of the British blockade stifling American commerce, New England's refusal to cooperate in loans, and total cost of the war had left the government bankrupt. The Tariff of 1816 was passed by Congress for revenue as well as for the protection of manufacturers. Madison, "surmounting the prejudices of a lifetime" signed a bill on April 10, 1816, providing for a Second U.S. Bank.

To avoid having to depend again on an unreliable militia, Congress voted to maintain a 10,000-man regular army. And New England, having learned the danger of depending too much on commerce, began to turn to manufacturing.

"THE STAR SPANGLED BANNER" was written by Francis Scott Key as he watched the defense of Fort McHenry during the night of Sept. 14, 1814. Having boarded a British ship to arrange for the release of a prisoner of war, he was detained for security reasons until the morning, when the attack was over.

THE BATTLE OF NEW ORLEANS was fought without the knowledge that the peace had been signed two weeks before. On Jan. 8, 1815, General Andrew Jackson (r. mounted) with some 5,000 men, fought off Sir Edward Pakenham's 7,500 troops in a great American victory. British loss was 2,036, American loss, 71. Gen. Pakenham (l.c.) was killed in action.

WASHINGTON WAS BURNED by the British on an August night in 1814. President Madison fled to the woods, Dolly Madison saving the famous Stuart painting of George Washington. The White House, Capitol and other public buildings were set afire but destruction was checked by storm.

ON CHRISTMAS EVE, 1814, the peace treaty ending the War of 1812 was signed at Ghent, Belgium. American commissioners were John Q. Adams, James A. Bayard, Henry Clay, Jonathan Russell and Albert Gallatin. Provision was made for the restoration of territories taken by either country.

VIRGINIAN JAMES MONROE'S election as fifth President of the United States continued the rule of the Republicans and marked the end of the Federalists. Monroe carried all the states except Massachusetts and Connecticut, receiving 183 electoral votes. His Federalist rival Rufus King received only 34 votes. Despite British cartoons such as that above, attacking "American Justice" for Gen. Andrew Jackson's execution of two British subjects, diplomatic relations between America and England were good. By the 1817 Rush-Bagot Agreement both nations agreed to limit their naval forces on the Great Lakes. A treaty of 1818 fixed the northern boundary of the Louisiana Purchase and joint occupancy of Oregon for ten years.

MONROE ADMINISTRATION

Foreign relations peaceful but Missouri Compromise prolongs slavery issue

The greatest political battle of Monroe's first term in office concerned the admission of Missouri to the Union.

Since 1802 Congress had been preserving the political balance between Northern free states and Southern slave states by admitting alternately new slave and free states. By 1819, when Missouri applied for statehood, there were 22 states in the Union, 11 free and 11 slave. The House passed an amendment to the Missouri Statehood Bill that no more slaves should be imported into Missouri and that children born of slaves there, after it became a state, should be freed at the age of 25. However, the Senate rejected this amendment and a storm of controversy arose.

Before anything was settled, Maine applied for separation from Massachusetts and statehood. After much debate and the passage of different bills in House and Senate, the Missouri Compromise was finally reached March 3, 1820. Maine was admitted as a free state, Missouri as a slave state, and slavery was excluded from the rest of the Louisiana Purchase north of the line 36°30′.

Perhaps the most satisfactory diplomatic negotiation during Monroe's administration, apart from the boundary treaties with Great Britain, was American purchase of the Floridas from Spain, included in the Adams-Onis Treaty of 1819. This also defined the western and southern boundaries of the Louisiana Purchase from the mouth of the Sabine River on the Gulf of Mexico to the Pacific Ocean. Spain thereby surrendered her claims to the Pacific Northwest. At the same time, the U.S. renounced its claims to Texas. (See atlas, plates 13 and 20.)

GENERAL ANDREW JACKSON (left) was sent into Spanish-owned East Florida late in 1817 to subdue the Seminole Indians whom Spain could not control. He captured Spanish cities right and left. At St. Marks he found two rebellious Seminole chiefs, Francis and Himollemico, prisoners on an American warship and had them brought ashore (center) to be hanged. He also executed by court-martial two British subjects, Alexander Arbuthnot and Robert Ambrister, caught stirring up the Indians. William McIntosh (right) was a halfbreed Creek Indian chief who served with Jackson after notable service in the War of 1812. The captured posts were returned to Spain. In 1819 Spain ceded Florida to the U.S. for $5 million.

MONROE DOCTRINE

It was Secretary of State John Quincy Adams who persuaded President Monroe to state America's views on intervention in the Americas openly to foreign powers. The President's message was delivered to Congress on December 2, 1823.

"The American continents," stated Monroe, "by the free and independent condition which they have assumed and maintain, are henceforth not to be considered as subjects for future colonization by any European powers ... The political system of the allied powers is essentially different ... from that of America ... We owe it, therefore, to candor and to the amicable relations existing between the United States and those powers to declare that we should consider any attempt ... to extend their system to any portion of this hemisphere as dangerous to our peace and safety. With the existing colonies or dependencies of any European power we have not interfered and shall not interfere. But with the Governments who have declared their independence ... we could not view any interposition for the purpose of oppressing them ... by any European power in any other light than as the manifestation of an unfriendly disposition toward the United States."

Europe paid little attention then to this bold hands-off announcement but Monroe's name lives today because of it.

CABINET DISCUSSIONS like the above gave birth to the Monroe-Adams Doctrine in the fall and winter of 1823. It was an anxious time. Five of Spain's major colonies in South and Central America had revolted and freed themselves. Austria, France, and Russia were reported ready to help Spain recover them. England wanted the U.S. to join in a declaration that they did not want the Spanish colonies but would not let any other power try to conquer them. Pres. Monroe's Cabinet decided to act alone.

SLAVE-COFFLES were a familiar sight in Washington, D.C. and the Southern states. The great debate in 1819 over admission of Missouri to the Union as a slave state stirred deep passions and foreshadowed the sad events of the 1860's.

ELECTION DAY AT THE STATE HOUSE, painted by John Krimmel about 1818, with its groups of arguing men, the roistering crowd of drunkards (left), and serious voters (right) is typical of elections in Monroe's time. The eight years of his administration have been called the "Era of Good Feeling." But below the placid surface, political factions were forming, sectional interests again threatened to break into the current of national unity which had begun to set in after the War of 1812.

THE RUSSIAN-AMERICAN Company extended its trade in 1816 from Sitka, Alaska (above) to Spanish California. In 1821 the Czar claimed the northwest coast of America as far south as the 51st parallel. England and U.S. protested.

WESTWARD-BOUND WAGON TRAINS became a familiar sight as thousands of native Americans, and German and British immigrants moved where land was cheap and fertile. While the population of older states remained almost static, the new states were doubling and tripling their inhabitants. By 1820 one fourth of the people in the U.S. — 2,600,000 out of 9,600,000 — lived west of Alleghenies. However, friction was growing between the industrial North, the planters' South, the farmers' West.

STRATEGIC NEW ORLEANS was jostled into awareness of its full potential after the War of 1812 just as it was getting used to life under a third flag. Founded by the French in 1718, the city passed to Spanish rule, then reverted briefly to France before the Louisiana Purchase. Surge of civilization west, plus opening of abundant new cotton lands, and invention of the steamboat made the bustling port a focal shipping point for the entire Mississippi and Ohio valleys and interior river systems.

MARQUIS DE LAFAYETTE was given a tremendous ovation after landing at Castle Garden, New York, in 1824 for a year's tour of the United States. The gallant volunteer, who had assisted Gen. Washington in handing Cornwallis a decisive defeat at Yorktown in 1781, proved an extremely popular ambassador of goodwill for France. Lafayette visited his old friend, John Quincy Adams, in the White House. He was voted $200,000 and a township of land out of gratitude on part of Americans.

THE WHITE HOUSE was far from a pleasure palace for Adams. Stung by Jackson's charges and rejected by a popular majority, the austere New Englander flung himself into a rigid work schedule, broken only by swimming in the Potomac, long walks and writing in his diary. Adams (r.), son of the second president, had studied for government service from boyhood. Educated in France and at Harvard, he was Minister to the Netherlands, Prussia, Russia, and Great Britain as well as secretary of state before becoming the president.

John Quincy ADAMS
Losing popular vote he still wins Presidency

John Quincy Adams served his country for nearly 60 years. It is ironic that his term as President represented such an inconsequential phase of his long career.

In 1824 there were four candidates to succeed Monroe: Adams, Secretary of State; William Crawford, Secretary of the Treasury; Henry Clay, Speaker of the House; and Andrew Jackson, the old campaigner.

Jackson led easily in the popular voting, but failed to gain the required majority in the Electoral College. The election was referred to the House, and there the influential Clay, no longer a contender, became a president-maker.

The House leader often had opposed Adams, but there was little doubt he preferred the learned, steady New Englander to Jackson. The House vote tallied: Adams, 13; Jackson, 7, and Crawford, 4.

Adams named Clay as Secretary of State, probably the most unfortunate decision of his career. Jackson's enraged supporters charged a political deal, and John Randolph of Virginia provoked a bloodless duel with Clay by calling it the "coalition of the Puritan and the black-leg". The President was deeply hurt by the charge and Jackson's star continued to rise.

Adams, who had hoped to improve the intellectual and moral outlook of his countrymen, as well as their material lot, found his program hamstrung by the corruption cry, and by an adverse Congress. His term also was unmarked by conflict, threat of war, or any major decisions. The man who played a giant's role in establishing American foreign policy in the formative years found no demand for his special talents.

Swept out of office in 1828 by a wave of Jacksonian sentiment, Adams re-entered public life in 1831 as a representative from Massachusetts. There for nearly two decades "Old Man Eloquent" remained the recognized legislative leader of the anti-slavery forces, which grew in strength.

The scrappy 80-year-old statesman, who never compromised on his principles and never avoided a good fight, collapsed on the floor of the House in 1848, and died a few days later. The nation mourned the passing of one of its most selfless benefactors.

John Quincy Adams — who played a vital diplomatic role in pushing the nation's boundaries beyond the Mississippi, in securing Florida from Spain, and who deserved much credit for the Monroe Doctrine — seldom won the warm plaudits of his contemporaries. But in death, as in life, he earned their grudging respect.

CHINA FUR TRADE inspired some of the most spectacular early ventures in the far west. Captain James Cook on his last voyage inadvertently discovered that sea otter skins, obtained from the Indians for a few pennies worth of beads, sold in China for 100 dollars each. British and Americans vied for the trade. In 1792 Captain Robert Gray, sent out by Boston merchants, made his historic discovery of the Columbia river (above). In 1811 John Jacob Astor (left) launched his Astoria project in hopes of gaining a monopoly of the northwest trade. He planned to send regular shipments of barter goods by sea from New York (right).

EXPLORERS
Americans move west seeking land and furs

FUR TRAPPERS played an important role in exploration of the American continent. Pushing constantly into more remote areas, often living among the Indians, they mapped rivers and mountains passes, paving way for later settlers.

HOSTILE INDIANS shown above attacking a typical heavily laden keel boat on the Missouri river, endangered the fur traders. However, profits from furs were enormous and traders usually managed to come to terms with Indians.

Official explorations of the West were spurred by Jefferson's enthusiasm for the area. He was eager to solidify the American position and prevent European powers from moving in, and he realized the economic importance of developing fur trade.

American claims were aided by Captain Gray's discovery of the Columbia river and by the momentous journey of Lewis and Clark. Jefferson wanted to trace the Red river to its source, but two parties were turned back by the Spanish.

While Zebulon Pike explored the country between the Arkansas and Red rivers, fur traders were plying the upper Missouri. Important expeditions were headed in 1807 by Manuel Lisa and Pierre Chouteau, who later formed a fur company to exploit the trade in the Northwest and Southwest. Indian attacks caused the company to fail, but it added much to knowledge of the West.

Pike considered the West an arid wasteland, an idea supported by Major Stephen Long who explored from the Mississippi to the Rockies in 1820, terming the region the "Great American Desert."

ROCKY MOUNTAIN PASS leading to beaver-rich Green River Valley was discovered by scouts of William Ashley's Rocky Mountain Fur Company. This opened thousands of square miles to trappers, brought a plentiful decade.

In 1808 John Jacob Astor conceived a spectacular scheme to set up posts from the Great Lakes to the Pacific, with headquarters on the Columbia. He sent a group by sea from New York to establish the post of Astoria while a second party crossed by land, suffering severe hardships. But the War of 1812 ended the operation.

In the central region the Rocky Mountain Fur Company, formed in 1822, was active for a decade and made many important explorations. By 1828 Astor's American Fur Company enlarged its operations by penetrating the central Rockies, adopting the already established "rendezvous" system whereby trappers met to dispose of peltry.

CAPTAIN JAMES COOK was first European to visit Hawaiian Islands. He arrived in 1778, named them Sandwich Islands. On return visit in 1779, he was received by King Kalaniopuu, greeted as god by natives who later killed him.

FORT ARMSTRONG (now Rock Island, Ill.) was typical of outposts which early explorers and fur traders used as their bases. Innumerable forts dotted western waterways, serving more as trading posts than as military installations.

SOLITARY TRAPPER was a picturesque figure. Equipped only with guns, traps and simplest camping equipment, trappers roamed every corner of the Rockies, emerging only to sell furs and obtain new barter goods at spring "rendezvous."

FAIRVIEW INN at Baltimore, Md. (l.) was a favorite stopping place for travelers on the Frederick Road, one of the major westward routes. The road typified those in the North, where improvements in transportation far exceeded those in sparsely settled South. Canals also provided important link between the East and new states in Great Lakes region. In the West, frontiersmen struggled to subdue the wild country and keep peace with Indians (r.). Settlers became self-reliant, resourceful, courageous. The West developed a stark democracy with political, social equality.

WESTWARD MOVEMENT
Problems of Industrial Revolution beset America

ELI WHITNEY, noted for his cotton gin (1793), later became a small arms manufacturer. His armory at Whitneyville, near New Haven, turned out muskets for the U.S. Army during the War of 1812. Whitney employed a system of interchangeable parts and factory division of labor, becoming the originator of mass-production.

The new nation which emerged from the Revolution was a nation only in a constitutional sense. In most respects, it was still a mere geographical expression, a country inhabited by peoples of widely divergent interests sprinkled in a vast area.

The first census in 1790 revealed the nation had four million inhabitants, nine-tenths of whom lived on farms. Only eight cities had a population of more than 8,000.

Virgin woodland exceeded cultivated areas to such an extent that some European visitors viewed the nation as one vast forest. For many years rivers were used in place of roads, which were either non-existent or so poor as to be of scant use.

By 1830 great strides had been made. Canal and road building proceeded apace, especially in the North. New England turned increasingly from agriculture to manufacturing, capturing the shipping trade between the United States and England. Production of coal and iron began and textile factories sprang up in the valleys of eastern rivers. Along with industrial growth, however, sectionalism widened. The agricultural South was fast developing a distinct society based on plantation life and slavery. In the West, mecca of the restless and discontented, a rough, new democracy was growing up, increasingly resentful of Eastern control. The East, in turn, viewed with dismay the radicalism of the West.

The Industrial Revolution brought a new class, the propertyless worker who made his grievances known through "benevolent societies," forerunners of trade unions.

The new nation was expanding by leaps and bounds, suffering growing pains. The growth of the West served as a check on the East and, although sectionalism was a problem, no one area dominated the nation.

KING COTTON ruled much of the South. The 1820 crop of 160 million pounds doubled in 10 years. Growers left worn-out land to move to Louisiana, Alabama, Mississippi. Farms were semi-feudal, producing owners' own necessities.

STRIKES of shoemakers in 1799 and sailors (above) in 1803 were among first attempts of workers to get fair wages and hours. Many strikers were tried, convicted of conspiracy.

SLAVE TRADE was an important item in colonial commerce. Growth of southern plantations increased the need for slaves to work on them. Trade flourished as Congress was forbidden by the Constitution to interfere with it until 1808. Much of slave trade was conducted with the West Indies.

JOHN FITCH'S STEAMBOAT.

Fitch made the trial of the steamboat with a screw propeller on the Collect Pond, where the Tombs now stands, in New York City, in the summer of 1795. In 1787 he had successfully run the *Perseverance* at the rate of seven miles an hour on the Delaware, several years before Robert Fulton tried out his boat on the Seine River. Fitch's boat was a long-boat or yawl, about eighteen feet long and five feet beam, with square stern and round bows with seats, and was steered by an oar at the bow and went about six miles an hour. Fitch took with him as passengers Robert Fulton and Robert R. Livingston, and was aided in running the boat by a boy, John Hutchings, all of whom are represented in the above picture. The State of New York granted Fitch a patent for his invention, but he later abandoned the boat with part of its machinery, leaving it to decay on the shore of the pond, and to be carried away in pieces by children for fuel.

FULTON'S FORERUNNER was John Fitch of East Windsor, Conn., who built first model of steamboat in 1785. His pioneer screw propeller craft (above) made successful run on Collect Pond in New York City in 1795. Fitch was able to obtain patents from New York, Delaware, New Jersey, Pennsylvania and Virginia, but he could not raise sufficient cash for further development.

"FULTON'S FOLLY" struggled upstream 150 miles on Hudson river from New York City to Albany, August 17, 1807. The *Clermont*, first successful steamboat, made the trip in 32 hours. Speaking of the vessel, Fulton later said, "It will give quick and cheap conveyance . . . on the Mississippi, Missouri and other great rivers, which are now laying open their treasures."

INDUSTRIAL REVOLUTION

Inventions and new factory system begin to transform the face of America

The Industrial Revolution which swept England in the late 18th century was retarded in America for several reasons. Chief among these were that U.S. capital was invested in agriculture and foreign trade and capitalists were afraid home factories could not compete with English industries. Poor means of transportation over broadly scattered settlements meant restricted local markets. During the first decades of the 19th century these obstacles were overcome with rapid growth of population, phenomenal westward expansion, and a new willingness of merchants, who suffered from the blockade during the War of 1812, to invest in manufacturing, rather than only shipbuilding and commerce.

New inventions provided the impetus for capital investment in industry and the raw new West, rapidly being linked to the East by roads and canals, provided a growing market.

Important was the rise of the textile industry. Samuel Slater, using recently perfected Ark-

IN 1790, seventeen years before Fulton launched the *Clermont*, Fitch advertised steamboat trips in Philadelphia paper.

wright machinery, first spun cotton by power in 1790. By 1800 seven Arkwright mills were operating. The founding of mills at Lowell, Mass., in 1822 marked the extension of new developments in textile manufacture, and by 1830 belt transmission of power began to be widely employed in textile manufacturing.

While the Northeast turned increasingly to the factory system the South, profiting from Eli Whitney's revolutionary cotton gin, became more a feudal aristocracy, based on slavery and large landholdings.

The immediate effects of the Industrial Revolution were obvious, but far more important than the mere accumulation of inventions were the fundamental economic and social changes that grew out of industrialization. The imminent passing of Jefferson's beloved agrarian republic would be attended by new problems, but the transformed nation would attain heights undreamed of by the philosopher of Monticello.

PIONEER STEAMBOATS were *General Pike* (left), *Walk-In-The-Water* (center) and *Savannah* (right). On August 20, 1818, the *Walk-In-The-Water* started its run from Buffalo to Detroit, becoming the first Great Lakes commercial vessel running on a schedule. In November of 1821 she was wrecked in a gale. Named after Indian chief who was her boiler maker, the "elegant steamboat" had a length of 145 feet, and accommodated 100 passengers. On May 24, 1819, the *Savannah*, a steam-sailing vessel built by Francis Fickett sailed from Savannah, Georgia, reaching Liverpool 25 days later, after having used her steam engines for a small part of the voyage. Captain of approaching British cruiser *Kent* thought her afire.

ELI WHITNEY'S cotton gin, invented in 1793, made possible use of short staple upland cotton, difficult to separate from seed. Result was vast extension of plantation system into piedmonts. Whitney also pioneered in use of interchangeable parts in manufacturing, thus fathering mass production.

RAPID GROWTH of turnpikes and toll roads during early 1800's led to the establishment of roadside inns and stagecoach systems. The Philadelphia Turnpike Co. was established in 1792 for construction of 62 mile toll road. Many bridges were built, eliminating slow ferries on important trade routes.

NEW ENGLAND SILVERSMITHS were kept busy by the thrifty who often converted silver coins into readily identifiable silverware. Craft declined with rise of banks and paper currency.

GEORGE WASHINGTON'S VISIT to first cotton mill in Beverly, Massachusetts in 1789 forecast the swift growth of the New England textile industry, outgrowth of Southern cotton boom.

POSTMASTER BENJAMIN FRANKLIN established New England postal system under Continental Congress, led way to 1794 revision of postal laws making possible U.S. Postal System.

HOME CONSTRUCTION was encouraged by Asher Benjamin's book, *The Country Builder's Assistant*. It told returning Revolutionary soldiers all a man needed to know to build a house.

WIDE CONNECTICUT RIVER was bridged in 1784 by Enoch Hale. Disregarding jeers of his neighbors, he spanned the turbulent rapids at Bellows Falls with covered bridge 365 feet long.

FIRST U.S. PATENT issued over signatures of Washington and Jefferson went to Samuel Hopkins of Burlington, Vt., July 31, 1790, covering process of leaching wood ashes to produce soap.

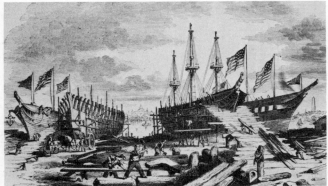

◄ **COASTWISE SHIPPING** and Atlantic fishing grounds made Boston, Mass. important ship building center. Expanding whaling industry grew in Boston and Salem shipyards.

STEAM SHAVING SHOP ►
was lampooned in early newspaper political cartoon. This was one man's view of limits to which mechanical absurdities eventually might reach.

ERIE CANAL
The dream of De Witt Clinton, governor of New York, came true in 1825 with opening of Erie Canal. Clinton was given honor of officially opening new artery. It stretched from Buffalo to Albany, thus connecting Lake Erie with the Hudson river and opening a link between Mid-West and port of New York. Canal quickly became chief route for emigrants passing from New England to Great Lakes country and contributed directly to agricultural boom in West.

WHALE OIL for the lamps of America established whaling as a main industry of New England coastal towns. Adventurous whaling captains like twenty-one year old **Nathaniel Palmer** explored Antarctic regions and led to U.S. Navy Antarctic Expedition of **1838**. Rich profits were returned to financiers of whaling ships, but oppression of seamen, **poor** food and pay led to riots and mutinies. Discovery of petroleum was **death-blow to industry.**

AMPHIBIAN MONSTROSITY, forerunner of World War II's LVT was Oliver Evans' steam driven vehicle, capable of travelling on land and in water. Evans prophesied in 1804 that people would go three hundred miles a day by steam.

AMERICAN OF 1827 satisfied his urge for a speedy vehicle by straddling and shoving this ungainly two-wheeled velocipede. Lack of roads in this era made social outings a challenge only the hardiest adventurer would accept.

AMERICA'S FIRST balloon ascension was made by Frenchman Jean Blanchard, Jan. 9, 1793. The voyage from Philadelphia to New Jersey lasted 45 minutes. Blanchard carried "passport" from Pres. Washington asking people to aid him.

FIRST RAILROADS
Early railroaders depended largely on horses but other methods of locomotion were also employed. Cars which descended slopes by gravity were hauled up by stationary engines, horses or both. Even sail-cars were used. As early as 1806, Thomas Leiper of Ridley township, Pennsylvania, devised a horse-drawn railway (left) to transport stone a distance of one mile from his quarries at Crum Creek. Cars had wheels of cast iron with flanges. The first real American railroad was the Granite Railway Company of Massachusetts, chartered in 1826. It was a three-mile track, designed to carry granite for the Bunker Hill monument from Quincy to Charlestown, Mass. The line was operated by gravity, two horses and a stationary engine. The first passenger coach (right) also was built for the Quincy line. In 1827 a second railroad was built to carry coal along a nine-mile track from Carbon County, Pa. Early rail lines supplemented existing waterways.

THEATER

Although American prose and poetry began to show promise during the early years of the republic, the infant theater racked up few laurels. Chief among the obstacles to good drama were lingering puritanical disapproval of such "frippery" and slavish imitation of European models. These imitations, moreover, did not come off well, and were often rank caricatures. Professional theaters were established in New York, Philadelphia and Baltimore. The first profes-

sionally acted American play was Royall Tyler's *The Contrast*, 1787 (r.), purporting to show the superiority of the Yankee over Europeans. It was produced by Hallam's London company, one of many English companies of gifted actors (like Edmund Kean, c.) that came to America. New York's leading theater, the Park, built in 1798, is shown (l.) during a performance of Moncrieff's *Monsieur Tonson*, with Charles Mathews and Miss Johnston. Admission was $1.00 for box seats, 50 cents for gallery seats.

SOCIAL LIFE

The sheer struggle for existence absorbed the energy of most citizens of the new nation, but in many of the larger cities genteel society began to develop. The cultured and wealthy presided over salons on the French model (l.) while the middle class restricted themselves to giving simple teas. Musicales (c.) were frequently held in the homes of rich, urban merchants and Southern aristocrats. Appreciation of classical music was considered a badge of dis-

tinction among the upper classes. The "gentleman," however, fared badly in the young, equalitarian republic. Pretensions to art or learning were sneered at by the rank and file, who preferred the rough-hewn man of action, the frontier type. A familiar sight on the city streets was the "oyster girl" (r.) whose wares were popular confections. Liquor was consumed in staggering quantities by all classes. Salaries of country preachers were sometimes paid in rum, and many citizens drank whisky at breakfast.

FASHIONS

In early America the well-to-do looked to France for fashions in dress. When the French Revolution, ruinous of traditions of all sorts, decreed an end to powdered wigs and satin knee-britches for men and elaborate brocaded dresses for women, style-conscious Americans followed suit. American ladies donned the daring low-cut, high waisted gowns of the Directoire and Napoleonic periods, and gentlemen began to accept high hats of silk or beaver and long trou-

sers, previously considered the mark of a country bumpkin. Martha Washington (l.), as first lady, set the style for the older, more conservative generation, and simple, homespun fashions of an earlier period (c.) prevailed in the country. A duke's mixture of fashions is revealed in the 1804 painting, at right, of a Philadelphia family on the way to church. The gentleman's costume is 18th century except for the hat. The ladies, though their skirts are short, wear the modest bonnet of the farm girl.

COUNTRY FAIRS, a tradition inherited from England, were a popular feature of rural life. Farmers exhibited prize stock, vied for awards, exchanged information on agriculture and animal husbandry. Horse races, plowing contests and competition among women for best preserves and handicraft were added attractions. During the Revolution 95 per cent of Americans lived on farms, number decreased but slowly in next 50 years.

FARM LIFE   In contrast to the rich, well-watered farm shown at the top of the page, many holdings, especially in New England and the mountain regions of the South, were rocky and unproductive. A farmer could eke out only enough to support his own family on a subsistence level. But well-knit rural life had its compensations. Neighbors were friendly, and when one fell sick, others rallied to keep his farm going (c.). Land titles were often tenuous, and some were tricked into buying plots belonging to others (l.). Many farmers, as the one at right, tired of laboring on barren acres, set out with family and belongings for promised land in Ohio Valley or northern Great Lakes area.

SPORTS   Organized sports were slow to develop in America on a large scale, but many participated in such activities as skating, gymnastics, bowling on the green. There were few games a lady could play, however, and still remain a lady. Though horsemanship was common to all America, it reached its highest development in the South. Decorum dictated that ladies ride side-saddle, and many pioneer women crossed the entire continent in that fashion. Fencing, taught by French and Italian masters, was part of the training of every correct young man, though single combat in earnest was forbidden by law. On the frontier, rugged pastimes as bear-baiting, cock-fighting, wrestling were popular.

NATION'S FIRST CAPITOL WAS DESIGNED BY THORNTON AND HALLET

BUSTLING BOSTON HARBOR CROWDED WITH WHALERS, CHINA CLIPPERS

Growth of cities marks period; influences architectural trends

Growth of the nation spurred rivalry between New York and Philadelphia for recognition as the leading city. New York won out, primarily because of its harbor which attracted world shipping, and the Erie Canal, which made it the terminus for farm products from the West and North.

Between 1790 and 1830 New York grew from a population of 33,131 to 202,589. During the same period, Philadelphia expanded from 42,520 to 161,410; Boston, 18,038 to 61,392 and Charleston, 16,359 to 30,289.

In the West, New Orleans, the Mississippi river outlet for western produce, was the only metropolis, numbering 46,310 people in 1830. Pittsburgh was growing in importance but Chicago and St. Louis were still small frontier settlements.

The trend towards urban growth brought marked changes in American architecture. Buildings reflected a growing sense of nationalism, although continuing to rely on Roman symbolism or Greek and Gothic imitations. The resulting combination was to

be seen in churches, banks, mansions and state capitals and some industrial units.

In the South, plantation homes and urban construction reflected the gracious living of the area. Thomas Jefferson was influenced by revived classicism of the 18th century.

Shifting of the nation's capital and its redesigning also influenced architecture. Benjamin Latrobe, seeking a distinct American style, used Indian corn columns in modifying the Capitol in 1803. Slowly architecture was throwing off European influence.

ARTIST JOHN AUDUBON CAPTURED TRANQUILITY OF NATCHEZ, MISS. IN 1822

ENTIRE TOWN TURNED OUT TO LUG BUCKETS AND AID FIREMEN OF 1776

SLEIGHBELLS JINGLED IN MONTREAL WITH WINTER'S FIRST SNOWFALL

NEW YORK HARBOR WAS CENTER OF THE CITY'S BRISK TRADE ACTIVITY IN 1828

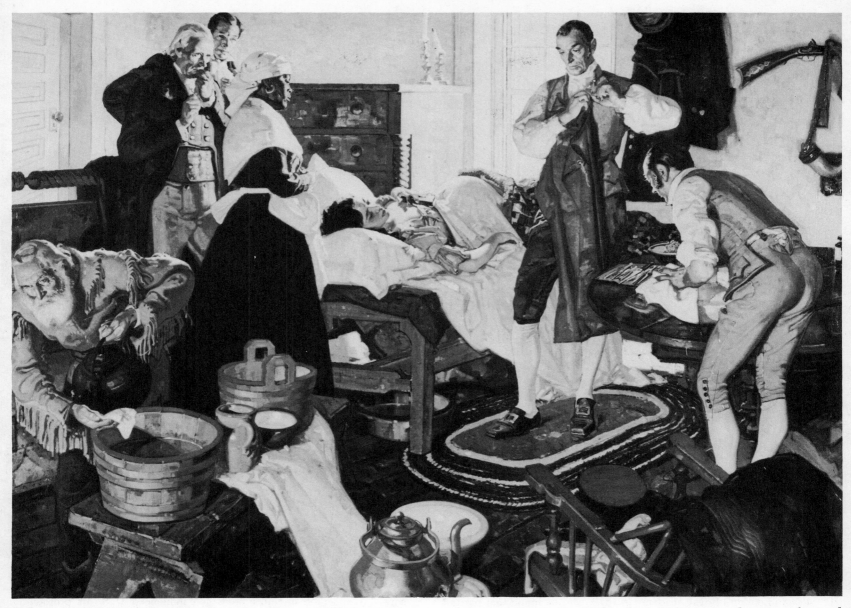

WORLD'S FIRST OVARIOTOMY was performed successfully by pioneer surgeon, Dr. Ephraim McDowell, on Jane Todd Crawford in Danville, Ky. in 1809. Local physicians thought she was pregnant, but McDowell diagnosed an ovarian tumor. Within the next few years, despite professional disapproval, he performed the operation on 12 other women, seven times successfully. McDowell is regarded as the father of abdominal surgery.

MEDICINE
A Primitive Science

Although medicine resembled a pseudo-science during the first decades after the Revolution, increasing progress was made by a small body of dedicated men. When Dr. John Jeffries gave his first lecture on surgery, the public, violently opposed to dissection, mobbed him. Despite this opposition research continued, and knowledge of the subject was advanced point by point.

Philadelphia's new dispensary was overtaxed in 1793 when an epidemic of yellow fever, the worst in U.S. history, ravaged the town. Out of it grew improved sanitary conditions and water supply systems.

Between 1810 and 1840, 27 new medical schools were founded. Pharmacopoeias and medical textbooks were published, and in 1812 Dr. Benjamin Rush published his *Diseases of the Mind,* which anticipated modern psychoanalysis. Hospitals and insane asylums grew up throughout the East. Medicine was coming of age.

FIRST RELIABLE INFORMATION on digestion was reported by Dr. William Beaumont in his classic study of the digestive processes of the stomach through the permanent gastric fistula of Alexis St. Martin at Ft. Mackinac, Michigan in 1825. Beaumont's extensive studies also expanded knowledge of the secretion of the gastric juices, effects of humor, anger, and other emotions on digestive process.

SAMUEL MORSE, inventor of the telegraph, is less-known for his paintings, such as this study of Niagara Falls. Morse exhibited his painting, *The Dying Hercules*, in London's Royal Academy in 1813. But he found that portrait work, which he disliked, was the only way he could make a living in art, so he turned his interest to electricity and organization of the National Academy, a democratic organization which influenced U. S. art profoundly.

SEMINARY ART flourished in young ladies' schools. Classes in use of watercolors and oils were part of training as gentlewomen. Velvet, silk, glass, canvas, were among materials used.

THOMAS BIRCH painted important naval battles of War of 1812. *Philadelphia from Petty Island* here shows view of his home. He changed to marine subjects after beginning as portraitist.

ART'S GOLDEN AGE

Romanticism keynotes American painting

Artistic development in America during the Revolution and post-war period presented a paradox. While the nation broke away from former political traditions, artists continued to rely on European influence.

Towering above his contemporaries was Benjamin West, who was a paradox himself. Born in Pennsylvania of Quaker parents, he found fame and made his home far from the land of his birth. West became court painter to King George III and remained in England during the Revolution. However, he remained a loyal American and retained the confidence of his countrymen.

West's London studio was a focal point for many of America's young artists studying abroad. Coming under his influence were John Copley, Samuel Morse, John Trumbull, Gilbert Stuart, Washington Allston, Thomas Sully, Charles Peale and John Vanderlyn, of America's first art "school."

European influence on American art evolved from the belief of young artists in the need for studying abroad in a "friendly climate." Rome and London were prime attractions for these expatriates, many of whom never returned to the U.S.

Careers in America were based mostly on portrait painting. In this field Stuart was the leading figure. Although many of America's European-trained artists scorned such work as the "lowest art form," economic necessity forced them into it.

One of these was Peale, a member of a family of artists. Peale's three sons, his brother, a nephew and two nieces all gained recognition as American artists.

Itinerant artists also stimulated art interest in the new nation. These untrained painters, using "primitive" techniques, brought art to new areas. Work of both professional and primitive painters is reproduced in this book (see picture credit list).

The new stirring of interest stimulated by these painters led to the establishment of academies in major cities, where artists studied relatively free from European influence, slowly evolving a truly American art.

BENJAMIN WEST became most famous American painter of his era, still ranks as one of best in nation's history. He influenced entire generation, including Copley, who painted his portrait (r). West's own work showed influence of classic background, as illustrated by his *Christ Rejected* (1). His canvases were heroic in concept and large in scope. Later he came to prefer more realistic picturizations. He is buried in St. Paul's Cathedral.

MINIATURE PAINTER Robert Fulton captured his own likeness in this portrait painted on ivory. Many artists concentrated fruitfully on this sort of specialized work, but Fulton soon gave up the brush for engineering and became one of the first men to construct a successful steam boat.

SEA CAPTAINS CAROUSING was painted by John Greenwood of Boston. Rollicking scene is tavern in Dutch Guiana port where artist migrated. From there he moved to Holland, then England, where he gained notice with exhibitions of mezzotint engravings. He was often confused with another John Greenwood, noted dental pioneer who made the ill-fitting teeth for George Washington.

THOMAS SULLY, shown in a self-portrait with his wife, studied with both Stuart and West. He was noted especially for his portraits of women and also for his skillful brushwork.

ROBERT FEKE, one of first American artists, made his first rude paintings while prisoner in Spain. From proceeds of them he returned to U.S., specialized in portraits such as this of Ben Franklin. His works, dating from 1746, reflected aristocratic leanings of American colonial life.

HOMESPUN SCENES such as the *Yankee Peddler* hawking his goods were captured by artist-illustrator John W. Ehninger. Primarily a genre painter, Ehninger also had a rich background of European training. His first popular success was the result of a plate illustrating Irving's *Peter Stuyvesant*. He also drew book designs, and was known as one of the best draftsmen in America.

CHARLES W. PEALE in his museum, first in the country. Peale painted eight portraits of Washington, was America's first taxidermist, and participated in Revolutionary War.

LITERATURE AND RELIGION

"Who reads an American book?" scornfully asked an English critic of 1820. A reply came quickly when such authors as William Cullen Bryant and Washington Irving burst forth to world-wide popularity with *Thanatopsis* and *Tales of a Traveler*.

At the time of Irving's birth, only one American had gained fame as a writer — Benjamin Franklin. Before the author of *The Sketch Book* died, the United States had entered its golden age of literature.

Many of the outstanding works of this era were of a religious nature, for America was burgeoning forth as heartily in theology as it was in other fields. The North led the South in the development of artists of all varieties, as well as newspapers, but such was not the case in matters relative to religion. The liberating doctrine of transcendentalism rose in the North hand-in-hand with the rise of Francis Asbury and the Methodism in the South.

But, while congregations in New England continued their attendance of all-day church meetings, worshippers in Maryland and the states farther south were visited by circuit preachers. So faithful were these men that they were the basis for the saying concerning inclement weather, "There is nothing out today but crows and Methodist preachers." The spirit of expansion and pioneering that came to characterize the men from Tennessee and the Carolinas took more quickly to individual consideration than to tradition. Significant for the intellectual history of New England was the founding (1819) of the Unitarian Church by Wm. Ellery Channing. Unitarianism, a liberal doctrine, stressed the unity of God.

LITERARY GIANTS such as those assembled by the artist in a fictitious gathering (l.) towered over the American scene during late 18th and early 19th centuries. Shown together are Wm. G. Simms, Oliver Wendell Holmes, Fitz-Green Halleck, as well as Nathaniel Hawthorne, H. W. Longfellow, Nathaniel Parker Willis, William H. Prescott, Washington Irving, James Kirke Paulding, Ralph Waldo Emerson, William Cullen Bryant, John Kennedy, J. Fenimore Cooper and George Bancroft. First to begin this new dawn of vital American writing was Washington Irving, whose story of "Rip Van Winkle" captured the hearts of Americans for generations. Here Rip (r.) hesitantly enters his home, still finding it difficult to comprehend that he has had a nap of not one night, but twenty years.

ST. JOHN'S CHAPEL dominated New York's old Hudson Square. It was designed by John McComb, Jr., who also drew up the plans for the small fort at the Battery. The delicate spire of St. John's stood as a religious reminder from its completion in 1807 until 1918, when it was torn down for construction of West Side subway.

ADONIRAM JUDSON went to Burma in 1813 to lead the first American Protestant mission outside the Western Hemisphere. Cast into prison during the Anglo-Burmese War of 1824, Judson is shown here being visited by his heroic wife, Ann Hasseltine, who secured his release. He worked on in Burma until his death in 1850.

FEATHER TREATMENT was meted out to dozers during lengthy New England church services. At this time Puritan influence was waning, but preachers still delivered their half-day sermons.

INCREASING VARIETY of established religious sects in America was illustrated by the Shakers of Lebanon, who earned their nickname by practice of holding hands and whirling in circles that literally made the building shake. In the years following 1776, a crusade was launched in all the colonies to separate the church and state, and to establish complete religious liberty. The struggle lasted until all the churches lost their special privileges. The Congregational church in Massachusetts retained its power to tax until 1833. The Evangelical church groups enjoyed rapid growth in the formative years of the United States, following a period of recession during years of the American Revolution.

FRANCIS ASBURY in 1787 became first bishop of Methodist Church in America. He organized circuit preachers and helped his church become largest Protestant denomination in the country.

EDUCATION

New England led in the development of adequate school systems in the United States, but by 1805 colleges were numerous throughout the East, and stretched westward as far as Ohio and Indiana. New institutions often convened in barns, churches, or homes, but older schools had firmly-established traditions of procedure. Dartmouth classes met at the call of a conch shell sounded by a sturdy freshman (l.), and fraternities began at Union College in Schenectady. Also beginning were several new State universities, an idea uniquely American. Lower-level and country schools were slow to improve, however. As many as six grades often were lumped into one room, to be taught by a youth who had only slightly more knowledge than his charges. Confusion and disinterest (c.) were sometimes the result. High schools for girls were unknown, and no college in the world admitted women until Emma Willard began her Seminary in Vermont (r.). This pioneer in education, who also composed the song *Rocked in the Cradle of the Deep*, later established the now-famous Emma Willard School in Troy, N.Y. in 1821.

STRAYED,

On WEDNESDAY, 14th inst.

A Red Cow,

She is marked with white on her flank, on her back, and between her horns, which are small and denote her to be about nine years old; she is also remarkable for having lost nearly half her tail. Any person who will return her to the Subscriber, at No. 180, Pearl-Street, or the upper end of Broad-Way, near Sandy Hill, shall receive Five Dollars Reward.

ANDREW OGDEN.

PRINTED BY G. & R. WAITE, No. 64 & 38, MAIDEN-LANE.

CLASSIFIED ADS made their appearance on the scene as newspapers and magazines multiplied. By 1790, there was a newspaper in every state, and cities such as Boston had as many as five.

APPLES, TREES AND LEGEND grew out of the dream of John Chapman, who became the "Johnny Appleseed" of the pioneers. He was born in New England and lived in Pittsburgh. He took apple seeds from the cider presses and planted them in the wilderness of the Ohio Valley. He lies buried (l.) in Indiana, but his orchards still flower and stories of the kindly white-haired man (r.) live on.

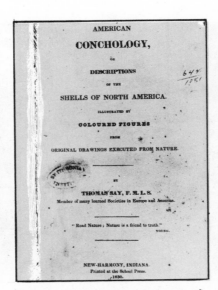

CIRCULATING LIBRARIES were the natural result of the awakening American interest in knowledge and the printed word. The first circulating library in Vermont was established in the township of Brookfield in 1791, and has vied with other libraries nearly as old in continuous operation.

UTOPIAN Robert Owen founded a model community in New Harmony, Ind. Among the colony's accomplishments was this pioneer work employing the color print process.

NOAH WEBSTER'S "Dictionary of the English Language" was published in 1824, and still is considered to be authoritative. Author was one of the founders of Amherst College, as well as a noted teacher and lecturer on history and law.

ANDREW JACKSON (1767-1845), seventh President of the United States, was a typical son of the frontier. Born in North Carolina, he early migrated to Tennessee, studied law, held prominent local offices, and served in both houses of Congress. His national fame resulted from his military leadership in Indian expeditions and in the defense of New Orleans. Of meager education, he was a born leader who could act decisively, express his ideas clearly and forcibly. His romance with Rachel Donelson Jackson (r.) endured throughout his life. Rachel was a woman of boundless generosity, but she was attacked by gossips because, through error, the Jacksons were married before her first husband obtained a divorce. A second ceremony was performed when divorce was granted. She died just before inauguration.

JACKSONIAN DEMOCRACY

Era of common man arrives with new concepts of popular government

Jackson's entry into the White House in 1829 marked a break with the political past. With property qualifications for voting removed and with direct choice of Presidential electors for the first time, the landslide victory made "Old Hickory" truly the people's choice as Chief Executive.

The "spoils system" resulted from the president's belief that men who supported the party should be rewarded. At the same time he put into practice the democratic idea that no intelligent man should be barred from office holding because of his humble background.

Jackson re-asserted the independence of the Executive from Congress and the Judiciary and asserted his leadership vigorously. He vetoed the Maysville Bill, providing for a state road at Federal expense, despite its popularity, because he considered such a project was unconstitutional.

His Indian policy was characteristic of the frontiersman. He concluded 94 treaties with the Indians, but when the redmen failed to move quickly enough, he aided the settlers in forcibly pushing them westward.

Though reputedly a "states' righter," Jackson opposed nullification sentiment in South Carolina. In his political battles he was guided by a "kitchen cabinet" of unofficial political friends who were more influential than his official family.

Antagonistic to the vested interests of his day, President Jackson remained popular with the masses who had elected him throughout his term of office.

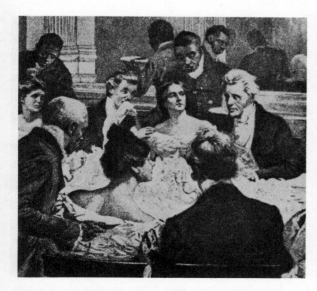

PEGGY O'NEILL EATON, wife of the Secretary of War, had been the daughter of a Washington tavern keeper. She was snubbed by cabinet wives, even at White House functions. Jackson's anger was aroused and situation led to a wholesale cabinet resignation.

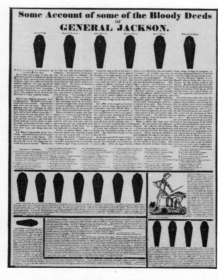

COFFIN HANDBILL, a propaganda document used by Whigs in election of 1828, proported to show that Jackson was bloodthirsty. He was charged with illegally executing militiamen.

RESIGNATION of Jackson's cabinet in 1831, satirized above, climaxed the Peggy Eaton affair. With appointment of new cabinet officers and Calhoun's later resignation as Vice-President, Van Buren emerged as the heir-apparent of President Jackson.

WEBSTER'S REPLY TO HAYNE inspired this famous painting by George P. A. Healy. The great debate on the U. S. Senate floor between Daniel Webster of Massachusetts and Robert Y. Hayne of South Carolina was a brilliant display of oratory. It was touched off by a resolution, supported by the industrial East and opposed by the agrarian West and South, to limit for a period the sale of public lands. The debate quickly branched off into an examination of Constitutional fundamentals. Hayne defended the principle of state sovereignty while Webster insisted that the Union was a creation of all the people of all the states and therefore national supremacy must prevail. The conflict was eventually settled on the field of battle.

A TYPICAL LOCAL MUSTER of the militia in 1832. Military drill was still primarily a social occasion, with participants often dressed in gaudy outfits and little if any equipment available. From the earliest days of the nation a standing army had been considered dangerous to the safety of the Union.

TRIAL OF RED JACKET as depicted by the famous painter of Indians, John Mix Stanley. The scene shows the Seneca making his defense against a charge of witchcraft brought by Chief Cornplanter. In the circle is shown one white man, supposedly Samuel Kirkland, a missionary to the Indians.

ROBERT Y. HAYNE, blond, mercurial, was at 38 one of the ablest men in the Senate. In his great debate with Daniel Webster, he gracefully and skillfully urged the West to unite with the South against the growing power of the Northeast.

THE INDIANS were pushed steadily westward beyond the Mississippi. The Sauk and Fox tribes were evicted from their homes near present-day Rock Island, Illinois, but Black Hawk (left), one of the chiefs, defied the treaty. He led his people back across the river to their homeland, now rapidly filling up with white settlers. The militia was called out and inflicted a severe defeat on the Indians at Bad Axe (right). Abraham Lincoln and Jefferson Davis were fellow officers in the Black Hawk War.

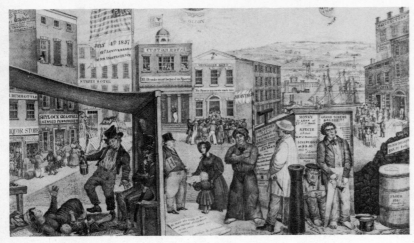

PANIC OF 1837 hit nation in the closing weeks of Jackson's last term. Resulting from reckless speculation partly prompted by destruction of Bank of United States, the financial debacle grew in proportion during March, when mobs of unemployed in New York held demonstrations and sacked city's warehouses. Banks suspended specie payments; sale of public lands fell off; inflation ensued and scores of businesses were ruined by the panic.

SECOND BANK OF THE UNITED STATES was regarded by cartoonist as a nightmare to Jackson. Above, he battles the dragons of Nicholas Biddle's institution while the public, presumably tired of the fight, attempts to drag him away. In 1832 Jackson vetoed a bill to recharter Bank. Through a compliant Secretary of the Treasury he then effected the gradual withdrawal of government deposits, thus insuring the death of the Bank.

OSCEOLA, a Seminole chief, waged a long, bloody war to prevent removal of his people from Florida. The war lasted from 1835 to 1842 but Seminoles pursued it half-heartedly after Osceola's death in 1838 following capture. Challenging validity of one treaty, Osceola drew his knife and plunged it into council table, saying: "The only treaty I will execute is with this."

SPANISH DOMINATION in the Western Hemisphere crumbled during the 1800's as such leaders as Simon Bolivar led So. American colonies in successful revolts. By 1830, Spanish holdings in the hemisphere had been reduced to Cuba (Havana bay, above) and Puerto Rico.

ANDREW JACKSON

Elected for second term

King Andrew, as he was dubbed by the opposition, was re-elected in 1832 by an overwhelming majority. He continued to prove a deadly foe in political combat, triumphing on the two great issues of his administrations—the Bank and the tariff.

Although the rates of the tariff law of 1832 were somewhat lower than those of the "tariff of abominations" four years earlier, it put the principle of protectionism on a permanent basis. The legislature of South Carolina, bitter at the rising influence of northern industrialism which this indicated, promptly enacted an ordinance of nullification. The President countered with a threat of military force to uphold federal law in Calhoun's state. A compromise tariff the following year averted a showdown.

In the conduct of a foreign policy Jackson's new type of "shirtsleeve diplomacy" was eminently successful. He induced Great Britain to reopen the West Indian trade, closed since the Revolution, thereby increasing commerce from $100,000 to $2 million annually. He extracted from France a satisfactory claim settlement for spoliations to American shipping during the Napoleonic wars, which had been a touchy issue.

Texas, which had revolted from Mexico and set up an independent republic, was eager for admission to the Union. Jackson was sympathetic. But formidable Whig opposition in the Senate and Mexican protests forced him to act cautiously and he reluctantly had to leave the decision on annexation to a successor.

Andrew Jackson retired from office as he had entered—in a blaze of glory and popular approbation—to spend the remainder of his life at his beloved Hermitage.

FIRST THIRD PARTY in U.S. history was Anti-Masonic party, which grew out of resentment towards secret societies and mysterious disappearance of William Morgan, who wrote supposed expose of Freemasonry. Unproven charge arose that Morgan was killed by Masons and such literature as above was circulated. Party opposed Jackson, a Mason, but later died out.

HENRY CLAY, using Bank issue to embarrass Jackson, introduced a resolution in the Senate that "in relation to the public revenue" the President had violated the Constitution. Above, cartoonist depicts Clay's attempt to prevent Old Hickory from protesting against the resolution.

"TRAIL OF TEARS" climaxed removal of the Cherokee nation from northeastern Georgia to the Indian Territory. The Cherokees, most civilized of the southern tribes, had kept their federal treaties faithfully. They built neat homes, roads, published books, and adopted a constitution in 1827.

But, with discovery of gold in the area in 1829, Georgia found it expedient to scrap the U.S. treaties and claim the Indians as its subjects. Jackson ignored Chief Justice Marshall's ruling in favor of the Indians, and the uprooted Cherokees were forced to make their long trek westward.

LITTLE VAN

An inherited depression nearly swamps Jackson's "Little Magician"

Paradoxical Martin Van Buren prompted Davy Crockett, the unpoetic Texan, to write:

> "Good Lord, what is Van? For simple though he looks,
> 'Tis a task to unravel his looks and his crooks,
> With his depths and his shallows, his good and his evil,
> All in all, he's a riddle must puzzle the devil."

Jackson's successor, the first President content to be known as a politician, stepped lightly on the sands of time. None of his speeches or writings made a dent on posterity. Yet this soft-spoken New Yorker whose lifetime spanned from Washington to Lincoln, exercised a potent influence on the national political scene from 1828 to 1848. He was a Democrat on all questions but that of slavery.

Born at Kinderhook, New York, in 1782, the farmer's son was reading law in the village office at 14, and entered politics at an early age. He became successively state senator, attorney general, U.S. senator, and governor of New York.

Van Buren delivered the important New York vote for Jackson in 1828 and was named Secretary of State. He became the President's advisor and friend, and at the 1832 Democratic convention, "Old Hickory" forced his nomination for the vice-presidency.

As Jackson's hand-picked candidate in 1836, Van Buren defeated Hugh White, Daniel Webster, and Gen. Harrison, piling up 762,000 votes against a total of 735,000 for his opponents.

Swept into office on a wave of Jacksonian sentiment, the "Little Magician" was almost inundated by the Panic of 1837. But he withstood pressure to re-establish a national bank, and in 1840 had the satisfaction of seeing his plan for an independent sub-treasury pass through Congress.

Depression and the growing Abolitionist movement marked Van Buren's term, but there were no major conflicts. Defeated in 1840, Van Buren ran again in 1848 as a Free Soil candidate, splitting the Democrats, and eliminating a political enemy, Lewis Cass.

CHEAP LAND was advertised in New York (r.) and throughout the country. State-assisted internal improvement programs stimulated a transportation boom. This resulted in heavy land speculation, which was a major factor contributing to the Panic of 1837, which reached its peak during Van Buren's first year in office. With financial chaos, elaborate development schemes collapsed. The sale of public lands fell off from 20 million acres in 1836 to 3,500,000 acres in 1838. Effects of panic persisted in South and West until 1843.

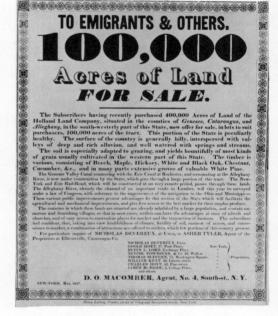

TO EMIGRANTS & OTHERS.

100,000 Acres of Land FOR SALE.

The Subscribers having recently purchased 400,000 Acres of Land of the Holland Land Company, situated in the counties of *Genesee, Cataraugus,* and *Alleghany,* in the south-westerly part of this State, now offer for sale, in lots to suit purchasers, 100,000 acres of the tract. This portion of the State is peculiarly healthy. The surface of the country is generally hilly, interspersed with valleys of deep and rich alluvion, and well watered with springs and streams.

D. O. MACOMBER, Agent, No. 4, South-st., N.Y.

WILLIAM LLOYD GARRISON, editor of *Liberator,* was dragged through Boston streets with a rope around his neck by an anti-Abolitionist mob in 1835. He never relented in his 35-year war on slavery.

MARTIN VAN BUREN drew his greatest support from radical wing of N. Y. Democrats, called "locofocos" after name of matches they used to light up party caucus when conservatives turned out the lights.

WHIGS PUT UP this banner (l.) at Philadelphia in 1840 in an attempt to corral some votes for "Tip and Ty." Enthusiasm for the "Hero of Tippecanoe," General William Henry Harrison (c.), grew rampant as the election neared. The aged general was pictured as a rustic of simple tastes. His backers wore coonskin caps, and carried cider barrels and miniature log cabins as a regular feature of the torchlight parades and huge mass meetings.

HARRISONIAN

KEEP THE BALL ROLLING.

WILLIAM HENRY HARRISON THE FARMER OF NORTH BEND

RALLY!

A General Meeting

Will be held at the Old COURT ROOM, [Riey's building]

On Saturday Evening,

The 18th instant, at early candle light. A punctual attendance is requested.

MESSRS. DAVIS, BOTKIN, KEATING

And others, will address the Meeting.

R. P. TODD, *Chairman*

"LIBERTY, EQUALITY, FRATERNITY" was title of this 1848 Punch cartoon by John Leech. England, which had freed West Indian slaves in 1833, often jibed at the U.S. ideals of liberty.

WHIGS WIN

"Tippecanoe" is elected over Martin Van Buren

In 1840, Van Buren was pitted against his old Whig rival, Gen. Harrison, and lost by an electoral count of 234 to 60. The severe depressions of 1837 and 1839 were blamed on Van Buren. In addition, the colorless New Yorker was no match for the "Hero of Tippecanoe" in popular appeal.

The election campaign became extremely lively as the Whigs made intensive efforts to defeat the "Kinderhook Fox." Van Buren summed up his loss briefly as: "Lied down, drunk down, and sung down."

The 68-year-old general, a wealthy Ohio landowner, was portrayed as the "log cabin-hard cider" candidate whose door was always open to an old comrade-in-arms. Van Buren was shown as a corseted dandy reclining in a Washington palace.

Torchlight parades rang with the cry, "With Tip and Tyler, we'll burst Van's biler," and "Van, Van is a used-up man." Western hens were supposed to cackle, "Tip, tip, tip. Tip, tip, tip, Tyler."

Harrison's brief stay in the White House was not pleasant. He spent most of it dodging office-seekers eager for election spoils.

NAT TURNER, a trusted Negro preacher, led a slave uprising in Virginia in 1831 in which 55 whites died. Panic was widespread, but the incident proved isolated. Turner and his men were executed and their heads set up in warning.

FIRST ABOLITIONIST MARTYR was Elijah P. Lovejoy, minister and editor of the Alton, Ill., *Observer*. In reply to his anti-slavery articles, drunken anti-abolitionists burned his office, shot him and carried his corpse through the streets.

HENRY CLAY, perennial presidential candidate, straddled a slavery plank to avoid splitting the Whig Party. But in 1839, the Kentuckian aroused the Abolitionist ire by opposing any "emancipation scheme, gradual or immediate."

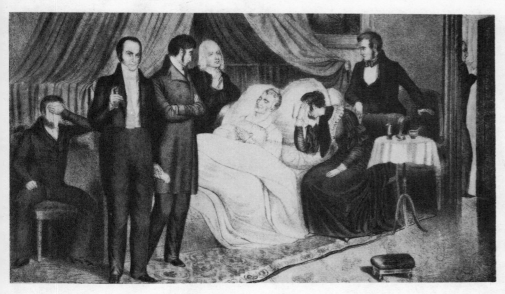

TRAGIC DEATH of President William Henry Harrison occurred only a month after his inauguration. Probable cause was pneumonia. His most notable act was to appoint as Secretary of State veteran statesman Daniel Webster (above, second from left). John Tyler (r.) became first Vice-Pres. to assume presidency due to death of incumbent president.

CLAY VS. TYLER

President clashes with the Whigs; Henry Clay reads him out of party

John Tyler, a former Democrat, had been nominated by the Whigs for Vice-President solely to gain Southern votes for the party. His only bond of union with the Whigs was a common hatred for Jackson.

Henry Clay hoped to charter a new Bank of the United States and abolish the Independent Treasury, to raise the tariff and to distribute to states the proceeds from the sale of public lands within their borders.

A bill for abolition of the Independent Treasury was passed and reluctantly signed by the President, but Tyler vetoed two successive bills for creation of the Bank. As a result of this, five cabinet officers resigned, at Clay's request, leaving only Daniel Webster of the original Harrison appointments. Tyler calmly filled the vacancies with men of his own stamp.

The President signed a bill raising the tariff, but refused to consider Clay's public land policy. Having thus ruined the plans of the Whigs, Tyler was read out of the party. Clay resigned his Senate seat, charging the President with being the captive of his "corporal's guard" of Virginia friends. Irate Whigs considered his impeachment.

Webster remained in the Cabinet only to complete important negotiations with Great Britain. Among the sources of irritation with the British government were the Oregon question (the territory had been jointly occupied since 1818) and the boundary between Maine and New Brunswick. In the latter area a minor clash (the Aroostock War) had already occurred. Through the able diplomacy of Lord Ashburton and Webster the Maine boundary was settled by compromise, but the Oregon problem remained unsolved, largely because of

American expansionists, who demanded that the northern boundary extend far into British Columbia.

Since the 1820's American settlers had been moving into East Texas and by 1836 had declared their independence of Mexico (see page 118). Tyler pressed for annexation and John C. Calhoun, the new Secretary of State, resumed negotiations. Since Texas would come into the Union as a slave state, Abolitionists and many Whigs were opposed to its admittance. Clay said annexation would be tantamount to a declaration of war on Mexico, but changed his mind as the elections of 1844 drew near. Although he was chosen as his party's presidential candidate, his vacillation on the Texas question lost him votes on all sides. The Democratic nominee, annexationist James K. Polk, won by a slim margin.

ARDENT states' righter and champion of slavery was John C. Calhoun, former Vice. Pres. As Sec. of State in 1845 he helped bring about annexing of pro-slave Texas.

FOREMOST ORATOR of his day was Daniel Webster. Great opponent of Henry Clay, he served as Senator, Secretary of State, negotiated the Maine boundary treaty.

HENRY CLAY, the "Great Compromiser," was presidential candidate in 1824 and 1832, served in House and Senate, ran for presidency in 1844 on Whig ticket.

JAMES G. BIRNEY was twice an unsuccessful candidate for the presidency on Liberty party ticket —in 1840 and again in 1844. His party was moderately anti-slavery.

FALL OF THE ALAMO followed by the massacre at Goliad gave Texans a rallying point and a battlecry in their fight for freedom from Mexico. When the Mexican army under Santa Anna invaded San Antonio, the Texan garrison took refuge in a former mission, the Alamo, which had been converted to a fort. In the ensuing siege all 183 men in the Alamo were killed. At Goliad, Texans taken prisoner were massacred at Santa Anna's orders.

REPUBLIC OF TEXAS

After winning freedom from Mexico, "Lone Star State" joins the Union

Governed first by the Spaniards and then by the Mexicans, Texas became independent when Sam Houston defeated Santa Anna The victory on April 21, 1836, at San Jacinto helped assure that the political connection between Texas and Mexico was "forever ended." President Jackson recognized the independence of Texas, but Congress refused to admit it to the Union.

Mexico never recognized the liberty of Texas and the Mexican Congress regarded the treaties signed at Velasco with Santa Anna as "scraps of paper." After Mirabeau Lamar was elected president of Texas, he attempted to secure an understanding with Mexico, but soon resorted to force.

Lamar's final act was the sending of an armed expedition to Santa Fe. That, in the opinion of the Mexican government, was an invasion of Mexican territory. Feeling rose to fever heat when Mexican troops retaliated and crashed across the Texas border in 1842 under Vasquez and captured San Antonio. The invasion was short-lived and the invaders soon withdrew across the Rio Grande. The last of the Texan attacks on Mexico was the Snively expedition of 1842. On this occasion Colonel Snively, by authority of the Texas government and with the aid of about 180 men, captured a richly-laden Mexican wagon train enroute from St. Louis to Santa Fe. He and his men were promptly taken prisoner by U.S. troops who claimed the Texans were on U.S. soil. Later this decision was rescinded and the Texas government was remunerated.

Gradually the U.S. government veered towards incorporating Texas into the Union. It was growing in population and wealth, and England had eyes on it as a possible protectorate of the British Empire. On Dec. 29, 1845, Congress voted to accept Texas as the 28th state of the Union and the Lone Star flag of Texas was replaced by the flag of the United States.

JAMES BOWIE (wielding his famous two-edged bowie knife) and Texas patriots defended the main door of the Alamo after the outer wall had been scaled by the enemy.

WILLIAM TRAVIS commanded the doomed troops at the Alamo. Earlier, he led a band of Texans in opposing the Mexican forces at Battle of Anahuac.

GEN. SANTA ANNA led Mexican army against Texas. His early successes were reversed at San Jacinto in 1836.

STEPHEN AUSTIN helped form Texas republic, but lost bid for Texas presidency, 1836.

LONE STAR REPUBLIC was founded by delegates at Washington on the Brazos while Santa Anna's army was besieging the Alamo. Since Texan families were fleeing the advancing Mexican armies and bands of men were hurrying from all over to join the army of defense, the Washington convention found little attention given its work. A log hut was the meeting place. Under the leadership of Richard Ellis, a committee drafted a declaration of independence which was adopted on March 2, 1836.

SAM HOUSTON was chosen commander-in-chief of Texan army which defeated Santa Anna. He served as president of Texas, 1836-38, and again from 1841-44. On admission of Texas into Union in 1845 he became senator, later governor.

TEXAN SOLDIERS were few and poorly equipped. Shown above is detachment braving the cold during winter of 1835-36. Hearing news of the spectacular defense of the Alamo and eager for the liberal land offers of the Republic, hundreds of American adventurers came to Texas and joined army. President Jackson made no attempt to stop this non-neutral activity.

MASSACRE took place at Goliad shortly after the fall of the Alamo. Houston ordered Col. J. W. Fannin to blow up fort (above) and retire. Before Fannin could comply, Gen. Urrea arrived and engaged Texans at Coleto Creek (March 19). Fannin's men were surrounded and capitulated. Terms of surrender stipulated freedom. Instead Santa Anna had them slaughtered.

"REMEMBER THE ALAMO," shouted the 700 Texan troops under Houston on April 21, 1836, as they attacked Santa Anna's force of 1,500 at San Jacinto (above) while the Mexicans were taking their siesta. In a few hours most of the Mexican soldiers were killed or captured. Houston's own losses were two killed and 23 wounded. Since Mexico made no serious effort to reconquer Texas (except for a minor foray in 1842) the battle of San Jacinto was decisive. Texans regarded massacre of Goliad as avenged.

CAPTURE OF SANTA ANNA occurred a few hours after the Battle of San Jacinto. The wounded general was brought to Houston, and the two agreed on an armistice. When news of the victory reached *ad interim* President Burnet of Texas and his cabinet, they came to Santa Anna and concluded the Treaty of Velasco (May 14), providing for withdrawal of all Mexican troops beyond the Rio Grande and for Santa Anna's pledge that he would take up arms against Texas again. Houston sent him to Washington.

OREGON COUNTRY was the goal of the first pioneer families to venture into the Far West. In 1836 Marcus Whitman established a Protestant mission (above, lower r.) near the site of Walla Walla, Wash. By the 1840's the influx of Americans brought to a climax the rival territorial claims of Britain and the United States. Representing British interests at time was the chief factor of Hudson's Bay Co. in the territory, Dr. John McLoughlin, "the Father of Oregon." He is shown (above, upper r.) greeting Mrs. Narcissa Whitman and Mrs. Eliza Spalding, first white women to cross the plains to Oregon. In 1843 American settlers met at Champoeg (upper l.), near Salem, decided by a margin of two votes that Oregon should go to U.S.

MANIFEST DESTINY

Hordes of pioneering Americans start westward to settle frontier lands

America's frontier of settlement was stalled at the great bend of the Missouri River until the 1840s. Yet even the forbidding Great Plains could not stem the restless spirit of young America.

The growing trade with the Mexican city of Santa Fe and the explorations of traders and "mountain men," were fast proving that the Far West was inhabitable. Rumors of the green fertile valleys of Oregon and California reached frontier farms. Beginning in 1841 a small but irresistible flow of humanity moved by ox team over what came to be known as the Oregon Trail. Main jumping off point was Independence, Mo., long the eastern terminus of the Santa Fe Trail. The wagons followed the Platte river, moved through Wyoming's South Pass, and at Fort

Hall, Idaho, branched off the Trail going either to California or Oregon.

However, these new territories were not American. California and the Southwest belonged to Mexico. The vast Oregon territory, comprising the present states of Oregon, Washington, Idaho and most of British Columbia, was jointly held by the U.S. and Britain. Mexican authorities in California looked upon the American influx with suspicion. In Oregon, clashes occurred between Hudson's Bay Company men and American trappers. For the first time, the great westward movement became an international issue which had to be solved.

To this dilemma, cocksure America had a ready answer. Occupation of the continent from coast to coast was the republic's

"manifest destiny." Nothing could halt it, and the sooner American acquisition was achieved, the better. Negotiations were opened with Britain, and a joint provisional government was set up by vote of the Oregon settlers in 1843. Meanwhile, President Tyler was claiming all territory up to Russian Alaska, while the British proposed a boundary at the Columbia river. As for California, U.S. intentions were partly revealed in 1842 when Commodore Thomas A. Catesby Jones heard a rumor that the U.S. was at war with Mexico, promptly seized the California capital of Monterey, then realized his mistake and bowed out two days later. For a few years at least, the slavery issue gave way to "manifest destiny" as the chief topic in the nation.

EARLY CALIFORNIA life, depicted by this Charles Nahl painting, was both carefree and strenuous. After the secularization of the missions in the 1830s, the ranchos were the dominant factor. Rodeos, dances and other social events sparked an otherwise monotonous, pastoral existence. The coming of the Yankees changed all this.

JAMES K. POLK was elected President in 1844 on an expansionist platform, including annexation of Texas and acquisition of all Oregon territory to the Alaska boundary.

NORTHERN OUTPOST of Mexican California was Sonoma, where General Mariano G. Vallejo maintained a garrison of troops against possible encroachment by the Russian forces at Fort Ross. However, by 1841 the Russians had abandoned California and withdrawn to Alaska. Also at Sonoma was California's northernmost mission.

PATH OF EMPIRE in the early Far West was the Missouri River. Through the 1830s steamboats were used in fur trade. Eventually paddlewheelers reached as far as Fort Benton, Mont.

MOST FAMOUS mode of travel was the "prairie schooner," which could mean anything from the boat-shaped Conestoga wagon to a buckboard with a canvas top. Usually drawn by several oxen, wagon trains required entire summer to get from Missouri river to Pacific slope. With these "ships of the plains," pioneer families braved cloudbursts, torrential rivers, savage Indian attacks, buffalo stampedes, barren deserts. American men and women met their sternest physical test in this great trek.

FORT LARAMIE, Wyoming was one of the great mileposts on the California-Oregon Trail. Built in 1834, it served as trading center, military post, and refitting point for wagon trains. Indians came hundreds of miles to trade here.

TIRELESS MISSIONARY among the Northwest Indians was Pierre-Jean De Smet, Jesuit priest. Here he is shown receiving Indian welcome.

ANNUAL RENDEZVOUS of Indians, trappers and traders was held at prearranged places each year along the Green River in Wyoming and Utah. Begun by American traders in 1825, this picturesque institution spanned the great years of the beaver trade. The rendezvous was not strictly business; it included feats of horsemanship, shooting contests, gambling and considerable carousing. After several days the participants returned to the wilds. The season's catch of furs was marketed at St. Louis.

MAINSTAY of the Plains Indians was the American bison, or buffalo, which provided not only food, but also clothing and shelter with its thick hide. In contrast to Indian methods, white hunters usually fired from a stationary, concealed position near the herd. The animals, often too confused to run, were picked off one by one. Once ranging as far east as Ohio, the buffalo was virtually wiped out east of the Mississippi river by 1810. In the Far West, the animals were hunted commercially for their hides. In the 1840s more than 100,000 buffalo robes were sold annually. The slaughter increased until 1883, when great herds which once numbered 50 million were practically exterminated. This was the death blow to Indian resistance. Shorn of his subsistence, he depended on government for existence.

"CIVILIZING INFLUENCE" of the white man on his Indian neighbors often did more harm than good. At left, warriors are gambling for possession of the deer. But it was the sale of liquor to Indians which had the most tragic results. White missionaries unanimously reported that the worst problem encountered with the Indians was whisky, furnished by unscrupulous traders. Yet the Indian way of life was tenacious. For 70 years the red man fought white invasion of his last stronghold, the Far West. He had the advantages of familiarity with the ground, ability to endure hardships, and such special tricks as communication by smoke signals (r.) One U.S. general, a veteran Indian fighter, paid his opponents the highest military compliment by calling them "The greatest light cavalry in the world."

BRIGHAM YOUNG (r.) and Mormon followers set out westward in spring of 1847, seeking peaceful land for settlement. In the "Pioneer Band" were 143 men, three women and two children traveling in 72 wagons. Their own invention, the odometer, was used to measure distance traveled. Midway on the trek they met Sam Brannan, Mormon leader who earlier took group around Cape Horn to San Francisco. Brannan tried to persuade them Zion was to be found in California, but Young wanted isolation for colony and pressed on toward desert. Brannan, his plan rejected, returned to California. Young fell ill as his wagon reached Big Mountain. Rising from his bed he beheld the Salt Lake Valley and decided to settle his people there.

MORMONS MOVE WESTWARD

Religious persecution forces them to abandon homes and seek new lands

While "Manifest Destiny" was being pushed to fulfillment in the Mexican War, settlement of the West was suddenly aided by an unrehearsed and unexpected factor. Persecuted for religious differences and polygamy, the Church of Latter-Day Saints had moved from one community to another. When the Saints, known as Mormons, were expelled from Nauvoo, Ill., they determined to migrate beyond the reach of religious persecution (see page 148).

Leading the church was the stern and fearless Brigham Young, who started from Kanesville, Iowa (now Council Bluffs) with an advance party in the spring of 1847. Braving rigors which were unknown in the settled Midwest, the covered wagon train pushed along the Platte River into the Rockies. In July, 1847, the weary band descended from the Wasatch Mountains into Great Salt Lake Basin. (See atlas, plate 14.)

At this place Brigham Young founded the new capital of his church, Salt Lake City. The main body of Mormons, which had gathered at Council Bluffs, soon followed, and the great inland colony was firmly established.

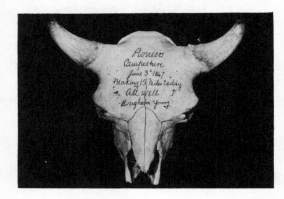

BUFFALO SKULL shown here was used by Brigham Young as trail marker in the Great Migration. For years route was called Mormon Trail.

Streams were dammed for irrigation, and the desert was literally made to "blossom as the rose." The second harvest was threatened by a plague of grasshoppers, but the timely arrival of numbers of hungry seagulls helped to save the colony.

In 1849 the Mormons organized a provisional government, claiming all of Utah and Nevada and parts of seven other states. Expanding and proselytizing in the area, they founded 100 towns in 10 years. Their claims beyond Utah were not recognized; neither was their bid for statehood in 1849. Instead, Utah became a territory in 1850 with Young named as the first governor.

Complaints from non-Mormons about federal law violations brought a punitive expedition under Col. Albert Johnston. The affair was settled, but not before a serious clash occurred between Mormons and California-bound emigrants at Mountain Meadows, where the passing train was massacred.

"THIS IS THE PLACE" was exclamation of Brigham Young as he first viewed Salt Lake Valley. On this spot the Mormon leader founded Salt Lake City on July 24, 1847. Despite hardships, the settlement thrived by the industry of its people and its fortunate location near California Trail. During Gold Rush, Salt Lake was stopping place on the way to California.

TITHING STORE at Salt Lake symbolized the cooperative economic and religious life of the Mormons. Settlers would bring their farm produce to the store as tithing payments. The goods were, in turn, sold to colonists and passing travelers. Proceeds were then turned over to church treasury. Cooperative life did not hurt individualism of Mormons, who prospered.

GEN. ZACHARY TAYLOR led Americans to victory at Fort Brown, Palo Alto, Resaca de la Palms, Metamoros, Monterry, and Buena Vista. His resulting popularity alarmed President Polk. He became Whig nominee for President in 1848.

MEXICAN WAR

American forces march on to the Halls of Montezuma

While the annexation of Texas in 1845 was the immediate cause of the Mexican War, other factors contributed to the tension leading to armed conflict. These included the failure of the Mexican Government to honor claims put forth by Americans; restiveness in California to be free of Mexican rule; and disputed areas of New Mexico claimed by both sides.

President Polk ordered a detachment under Gen. Zachary Taylor to the southwestern border of Texas to guard against a possible attack by Mexico. When Polk's offer to purchase California and New Mexico was not taken up, he ordered Taylor to cross the Nueces into disputed territory. War was declared over the violent protests of Whigs who had opposed such a move.

Under the leadership of Generals Taylor and Winfield Scott, the American forces reached Mexico City and were victorious on Sept. 14, 1847. By the Treaty of Guadalupe-Hidalgo, Mexico ceded two-fifths of her territory to the U.S. in return for $15 million and the assumption of American claims by the United States Government.

"VOLUNTEERS FOR TEXAS," as the militia in the Mexican War were called, came mainly from the South and West. This 1846 cartoon shows typical Eastern derision of the "warlike" West.

BATTLE OF PALO ALTO (near Brownsville, Texas) was one of the earliest actions in war with Mexico. Amid claims of aggression by both sides, forces under Mexican General Mariano Arista crossed the Rio Grande River. On May 3, 1846, guns of Matamoros put an advanced American position at Fort Brown under fire. Moving in quick defense, General Zachary Taylor went on to defeat the Mexican forces at Palo Alto four days before receiving news of a formal war declaration by the U.S.

CAPTURE OF MONTERREY, capital of Nuevo Leon, was completed Sept. 25, 1846, after six days of fighting. American forces in two groups under Zachary Taylor and William J. Worth sustained 120 killed, 349 wounded in the engagement. Respect for the courageous defense staged by his opposition prompted Taylor to relent on his original demand for unconditional surrender. On Sept. 26, therefore, he allowed Mexican army to march unmolested from the city with their arms, wives and followers.

BATTLE OF BUENA VISTA was one of the worst in the Mexican war. Outnumbered three to one, Taylor suffered 746 casualties. But the Mexican army under Gen. Santa Anna suffered losses in excess of 5,000. At first depressed by news of impending defeat, the American public greeted the hard-won victory with enthusiastic acclaim. Congress conveyed the thanks of the nation to Gen. Taylor and the Whig party nominated him as their candidate for President. He was elected over Cass and Van Buren.

NAVY LANDING AT VERA CRUZ put 12,000 troops ashore in support of General Scott's expedition there. Beginning in mid-afternoon, and led by General Worth in the first boat, a steady stream of men were rowed ashore. Much to their surprise, they landed without a shot being fired in opposition.

BOMBARDMENT OF VERA CRUZ followed naval landing and continued almost unremittingly for four days. Considerable damage was inflicted upon the city, but there was little loss of life on either side. Surrender on March 29 gave Americans a harbor and complete control of Gulf of Mexico.

CERRO GORDO PASS was the next obstacle on Scott's march to Mexico City. Clever American strategy brought surrender in two days. Americans captured over 8,000 of the enemy and routed Santa Anna's forces. Scott's route through Mexico was same one followed by Cortes in 16th century.

MOLINO DEL REY was attacked Sept. 8 after an armistice of one month had failed to bring agreement. During interlude, U.S. troops enjoyed rest in lush orchards and orange groves of Valley of Mexico. Furious battle, described as "blood bath," was under direct command of Gen. W. J. Worth.

ASSAULT AT CONTRERAS "was a great victory," Scott reported. "One road to the capital opened; 700 of the enemy killed; 813 prisoners; 4 generals; 22 pieces of brass ordnance — half of large calibre; thousands of small arms; 700 pack mules, many horses, etc. — all in our hands" (Aug. 19-20).

STORMING OF CHAPULTEPEC, a savage assault lasting two days, ended with victory for the Americans and access to the capital on Sept. 14, 1847. The heroism of its "boy defenders" from nearby military school has made Chapultepec a symbol of glory to the people of Mexico. It still stands.

WINFIELD SCOTT became a national hero for his bold leadership in the southern phase of the Mexican War.

FRANKLIN PIERCE was a brigadier general of volunteers in the Mexican War. Future president fought valiantly at Battle of Churubusco although he was injured by fall from horse early in the course of the action.

ULYSSES S. GRANT was a 25-year-old lieutenant when he fought in the Mexican War. At Chapultepec he cleverly mounted a howitzer in the belfry of a church, surprising the Mexican defenders, who fled before his fire.

COL. ROBERT E. LEE served with the Engineers in the Mexican War. He was commended by Gen. Scott for his part in fall of Vera Cruz.

FORT KEARNEY was built on the Platte in 1848 to protect emigrants against Indians along Oregon-California Trail. Army life at these frontier posts was characterized by hardship and monotony. Covered wagons were main transportation on this route until Overland Stage Line was founded in 1858 by John Butterfield, Wm. Fargo.

EMIGRATION TO CALIFORNIA was encouraged by reports of John C. Fremont, who began exploring Far West in 1842. Seeking a shorter route to Oregon, he set out from Ft. Laramie, entering California in 1843.

SUTTER'S FORT, built by Capt. John A. Sutter on a grant given him by Mexican governor, was the emigrant's first sight of civilization upon entering California. From here the newcomers moved on and settled the rich farm lands of Napa, Sonoma, Sacramento Valley and coastal slope.

"ARMY OF THE WEST," under command of Col. Stephen W. Kearny, was sent westward by President Polk at outbreak of Mexican War. On Aug. 18, 1846, Kearny raised the Stars and Stripes at Santa Fe.

REPUBLIC OF CALIFORNIA

Yankee boldness wins fabulous new territory

While acquisition of California was not an issue in the election of 1844, it was a major part of President Polk's plan of expansion. Capt. John C. Fremont, "The Pathfinder of the West," was on his second expedition to California when war broke out with Mexico. Hostilities in California were opened by a party of American settlers at Fremont's instigation. A month after the Mexican War began, but before word of it reached California, they raided the military outpost of Sonoma. Mistakenly, they captured the commandant Mariano G. Vallejo, who was sympathetic to their cause. The settlers raised an improvised flag with a bear pictured on it, and proclaimed the "California Republic."

The "Bear Flag Revolution" lasted only until the American seizure of Monterey on July 7, 1846. Meanwhile, Fremont was consolidating the American hold on northern California, and soon after, Commodore Robert F. Stockton captured the main California ports. The conquest would have been over except for the unruly spirit of Los Angeles. Chafing under strict military occupation, its citizens rebelled and drove the Americans out in September, 1846.

For three months the southern Californians outwitted and outfought the Americans. But the revolt was doomed. Fremont was marching south, and Col. Kearny had brought his force across the southwest to capture the new territories. Kearny and Stockton took Los Angeles in January, 1847, and the Californians surrendered three days later to Fremont. The entire region from Texas to the Coast was ceded by Mexico in the treaty of Guadalupe Hidalgo, Feb. 2, 1848 — nine days after gold was discovered at Sutter's mill. (See atlas, plate 17.)

REACHING CALIFORNIA, Kearny's force subdued the California lancers at the battle of San Pascual (above). Earlier, Commodore John D. Sloat had sailed into Monterey Bay. On July 7, 1846, he raised the American flag over Monterey (below), took it in the name of United States.

FREMONT POSES with Kit Carson, who guided his expeditions. After San Pascual, Carson broke through enemy lines and got help at San Diego for Kearny, who then marched northward.

GEN. KEARNY, reinforced by troops of Commodore Stockton, ended resistance by capturing Los Angeles in January, 1847. The retreating Mexicans soon surrendered.

DRIVING FORCE in the conquest was Commodore Robert F. Stockton, who relieved Sloat in July 1846 and proceeded to seize the California ports. Main fighting occurred later when Angelenos revolted.

LEADING Californian at time of invasion was Gen. Mariano Vallejo, seized in Bear Flag Revolt.

MEXICAN RESISTANCE ended when Gen. Winfield Scott marched into Mexico City on Sept. 14, 1847. Accompanying the army was a U.S. diplomatic representative, Nicholas P. Trist. Although President Polk had already relieved him of his duties and ordered him home, Trist went ahead and negotiated a peace treaty with Mexico at the town of Guadalupe Hidalgo on Feb. 2, 1848. Its terms included U.S. annexation of all territory west of Texas and south of Oregon in return for $15 million and cancellation of U.S. claims against Mexico. Unauthorized treaty was ratified by U.S. Senate.

ORIGINAL PICTORIAL
ROUGH AND READY MELODIES
No. 3.

UNCLE SAM.—You look very pretty, Mr. Cass, but you can't come in; I've had so many of your sort already that I hardly know my own farm.

OLD ZACK TAYLOR IS THE MAN!

TUNE—"*Yankee Doodle.*"

Old Zack Taylor is the man,
  His countrymen select him,
To fill the chair of Washington;
  And surely they'll elect him.

Chorus—Old Zack Taylor! keep him up!
  Honest, Rough and Ready!
We've a voucher in his life
  He's good as he is steady.

When Uncle Sam last let his farm,
  Right sorry soon he'd done it,
He saw them knock his fences down,
  And *poke*-weeds overrun it.
Chorus—Old Zack Taylor! keep him up, &c.

But once again in careful hands,
  The right sort will be growing;
As Uncle Sam found out one day,
  A Taylor apt at *sow*-ing.
Chorus—Old Zack Taylor, &c.

The politicians now must learn
  'Tis not for them to reap all;
Though *they* may mark out party lines,
  We've none for the whole people.

Chorus—Old Zack Taylor is the man, &c.

Polk thought when first the war began
  How grand *he'd* be in story!
He little dream'd how Zack would rise,
  And carry off the glory.
Chorus—Old Zack Taylor, &c.

In politics' mysterious ways
  Good often comes from evil;
So Polk's ascendancy has brought
  His party to the ———— !
Chorus—Old Zack Taylor, &c.

In Zack we know we've chosen well—
  The noble, the undaunted——
One who's "no private ends to serve,"
  Is one we long have wanted.
Chorus—Old Zack Taylor, &c.

Good cheer to every patriot's heart—
  The field is to the trusty—
"When thieves fall out, then honest men"—
  The proverb's old and musty.
Chorus—Old Zack Taylor, &c.

So gassy Cass, why you must pass—
  You shifting, sly pretender—
We've tried the tricksters long enough—
  We'll try our flag's defender.
Chorus—Old Zack Taylor, &c.

NEW-YORK: Published by Horton & Co. Engravers and Publishers, 60 Nassau Street.

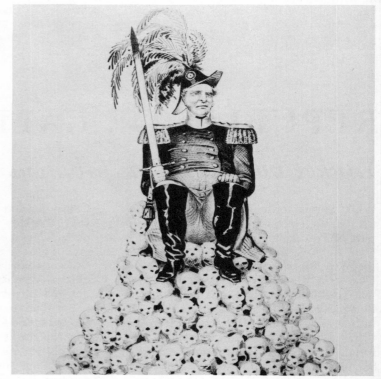

NEWLY-ACQUIRED TERRITORY brought the nation face to face with the old slavery issue in the election of 1848. Two years before, Congressman David Wilmot had proposed a measure outlawing slavery in any new territory acquired from Mexico. The "Wilmot Proviso" had failed to pass, but it persisted as an issue. So sharply was the nation divided that both parties tried to avoid the slavery question in 1848. Though dominated by the South, the Democratic Party sidestepped the slavery issue in its platform and nominated Lewis Cass of Michigan. The Whigs offered no platform and nominated the war hero, Zachary Taylor, a Southern slaveholder. Anti-slavery men of both parties formed the "Free Soil Party," nominating ex-President Martin Van Buren. Pro-Taylor cartoon (l.) shows Uncle Sam in unfamiliar garb driving Democrats from White House. Anti-Taylor cartoon (upper r.) attacks his military qualification. Cartoon (lower right) derides Democrats, who lost Presidency but retained Senate control.

GOLD RUSH began with breathless period in which first prospectors hurried to tell others of new discoveries (above). Crime was then rare. But as news spread throughout the world, peace departed. Millrace where gold was first found by James Marshall on Jan. 24, 1848 (above) symbolized the human torrent that soon swept into California. Competition for wealth brought on an era of violence. Theft and murder became commonplace.

"GOLD RUSH!"

Discovery of gold at Sutter's Mill brings horde of '49ers to California

Gold was found in California years before the 1848 discovery. Early explorers heard stories of it, and mines near Los Angeles were worked in 1842. But it was not until after the American occupation, when James Marshall found gold in the race of Captain Sutter's mill at Coloma, that men's imaginations were inflamed.

Outside of California, the news spread slowly. Easterners, skeptical of western tales, jeered at early reports. Then came an official letter to the War Department from California's Governor Mason. Gold was there; enough, he wrote, "to pay the cost of the Mexican War a hundred times over." At last people believed. Toward California began the greatest flow of humanity since the Crusades. The territory was soon full of adventurers from everywhere.

Before the rush started, San Francisco was a village of 812. In the first year of the rush, 40,000 landed there to produce chaos that can only be imagined. The flow continued; California's 1847 population of 15,000 mushroomed to 379,994 in 1860.

Around the mining towns, which boasted such boisterous names as You Bet and Git-up-and-git, a skilled miner put about $50 into his poke on an average day. If lucky, he did better: one panful of dirt yielded $1,500 in gold, and two miners, working a 100-foot trench, shoveled up $17,000 in a week. But a majority were neither lucky nor skilled. The total gold found in the five peak years of the rush equalled day-laborers' wages for the hordes seeking it.

When found, gold did not always remain with its finder. Gamblers and thieves had ways of relieving a miner's burden. If he evaded such perils, the Forty-niner often found himself giving up his gold for food and materials. Most gold rush fortunes were made, not by miners, but by enterprising merchants. Eggs reached $36 a dozen, potatoes brought $1.50 per pound, and all tools and equipment were similarly priced. Since few would perform menial tasks, laundry was shipped to Hawaii and even China.

The mining area rapidly broadened. Supply towns such as Stockton and Sacramento blossomed into cities. Steamboats plied the rivers between the diggings and the coast and wagon trails criss-crossed the wilderness. Although the rush slackened within the next few years, gold had become the cornerstone of early California.

GOING BY LAND, Forty-niners took more than six months to reach gold fields in covered wagons. Fifty thousand started across plains in spring, 1849. Many died during the long trek.

CLIPPER SHIPS sailed from East Coast around Cape Horn to California, carrying passengers. Record-holder *Flying Cloud* made trip in 89 days. Betting on duration of voyage was lively.

WIVES and families, journeying west to rejoin Forty-niners, often were startled by rags. But clothes were no index of wealth. Miners prided themselves on rough attire and often continued wearing it after they had found their fortunes.

WAGONS of Forty-niners had hard going in the Sierras and sometimes were lowered from cliffs by ropes. Prior to American occupation, trails across these mountains were traversed only by Indians and a few adventurous white explorers.

WESTWARD from towns and cities went young men seeking California wealth. Many Easterners formed mining companies, traveling together to gold fields or relying on the success of a delegate whose trip they financed for share of profits.

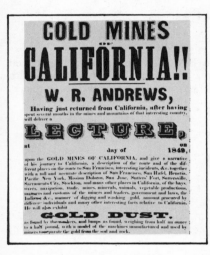

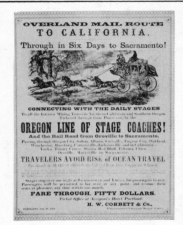

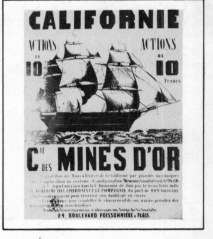

SALESMANSHIP of California boosters and transportation line operators is seen in these early posters. At left, a lecturer who had returned from the mines offered to tell of his experiences. Few such speakers had genuine knowledge. Some even wrote books explaining California conditions without having ventured from their eastern offices. Overland mail stage lines reached California in 1858 (trip from St. Louis to West Coast took 24 days). Second poster describes run from Portland, Oregon, to Sacramento, Calif. "Good news for miners," heralded by the poster above, carefully avoided any mention of prices. Items from eastern points were often extremely expensive. French advertisement shows how gold caught worldwide attention. French gold seekers formed cooperative mining companies, including more women than early American groups. Thousands joined rush.

FORTY-NINERS heading for the gold fields were joined by crews of ships that unloaded them at San Francisco. Many of the abandoned vessels never went to sea again. The shoreline was filled in and ships, surrounded by earth, were used as warehouses, stores and hotels. Miners soon learned that glowing tales of gold for the taking were greatly exaggerated. Many returned home bitter.

MINING FOR GOLD was a novelty to most men who came to California, and many methods were tried. Sutter had provided his men with only knives and pans. Picks and shovels were soon added. In panning gold-laden gravel, water was put in a pan, shaken until the heavy gold particles settled to the bottom, then water was poured out and the sand and gravel scraped off. What was left might be gold. The cradle or rocker (above) employed the same principle. More efficient was the sluice, a long inclined trough with riffle boards at the bottom. Gravel was shoveled in and stream of water was directed at it. The current carried off sand and gravel, leaving gold in the cross strips. Ingenious but worthless contraptions for extracting gold, sold in the East, were abandoned when green miners learned facts of the trade. Mining was hard work, often calling for long hours of back-breaking labor in ice-cold streams.

TWO SEA ROUTES to the gold fields were available. The shortest was by way of the Isthmus, but the Pacific part of this trip was always overcrowded, as in upper picture. A voyage around the Horn (above), was more likely to be comfortable, but meant three or four months at sea.

WAGON TRAINS traveling west met incredible hardships. Indian attacks, although common, were usually to steal horses rather than to massacre. Greater dangers were disease, thirst and starvation. Five thousand emigrants died of cholera in one year. Desert stretches were dotted with dead cattle. Starvation is illustrated by story of Donner Party (1846). Eighty-one were marooned by snow; 36 died, some of the survivors resorted to cannibalism.

SUNDAY in the mining towns was a rip-snorting day, liberally sprinkled with games, races, and dancing. Females were lacking, so the rugged Forty-niners were forced to brush beards with heavy-footed partners, as shown here.

CHINESE immigrants posed a complex political problem in California as mine and rail owners formed them into cheap labor pools. The state, after its formation in 1850, instituted a special tax on the profits of all the foreign miners.

GAMBLING was the biggest industry in cities. Professional gamblers set up parlors that were show-places. Bets, always in gold, were rarely less than $5, and thousands were often wagered. The largest recorded bet, in faro, was $20,000.

BANDIT Joaquin Murrietta was famous in tales of gold rush days. He began to rob out of revenge. After being wronged by miners, Murrietta (l.) swore to kill them. He did so, then went on to rob stages, camps. A reward of $5,000 in gold was put up for his capture, but he eluded pursuers for several years. Many robberies blamed on him, like the stage holdup at left, may have been performed by other bandits of those lawless days. Murrietta's ex-wife, La Molinera, told a posse where to find him. He was shot to death near San Jose in July, 1853. His head, pickled in alcohol, was exhibited.

FORMAL DEDICATION of a California mine in 1859 shows the changes made in 10 years. The brawling, free-for-all days of the Forty-niners were ended. Gold mining was now a businesslike operation depending more on scientific methods than on luck. It was still a big industry, (1860 gold production was $45 million as compared with an all-time peak of $81 million in 1852) but as it inevitably tapered off other industries came to the forefront. San Francisco had grown from a village into a major port boasting foundries, flour mills and shipyards. Settlement spread from coastal strip to interior valleys. With rapid growth, demand grew for railroad to the East.

VIGILANTES

The former village of San Francisco had grown into a busy port, and new problems cropped up as its polyglot population entered into an era of civic life not based on a gold economy. Chief among these problems was crime and punishment. The Gold Rush brought in many criminals, along with unethical lawyers and unscrupulous politicians. Between 1849 and 1856 more than 1,000 murders took place, but only one legal conviction was secured. For a time San Francisco's law-abiding citizens were too busy to clean up the courts, and in the meantime the underworld had become solidly entrenched. Finally, decent people took matters into their own hands. Forming a Vigilance Committee, better known as the Vigilantes, these citizens armed and drilled volunteers as policemen and began enforcing the law. Several murderers, confidently awaiting mock trials and exoneration, were given fair hearings and, after being found guilty, were publicly hanged as in the 1856 scene above. More than 800 criminals hastily left the city. The next election gave San Francisco a local government which enforced order.

TRANSITION from simple pastoral economy of padres to advanced agriculture is typified in this picture of American plowing on old mission lands. Wheat and barley were early crops. When superior vines were imported, grape growing flourished. Mexican land grants were disposed of to settlers, but it was hard to prove titles. Many settlers simply "squatted" on land.

STOCKTON began as a small settlement, known first as Tuleberg and later as New Albany. Strategically situated on the San Joaquin river, it became a supply center for the mines during the Gold Rush. During the "Fabulous Fifties" it was known as a center of lawlessness and haven for criminals. It is seen above in 1856 as rebuilt after a series of devastating fires.

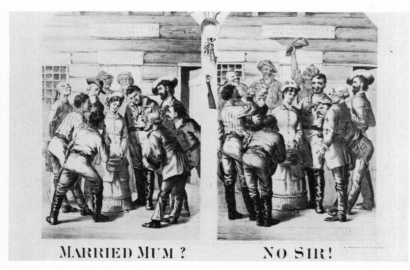

ABSENCE OF WOMEN in early California had a marked effect on the character of society. Enterprising men advertised in Eastern papers for wives, but the first female arrivals generally found their way to the gambling halls instead of the hearth. Virtue later gained ascendancy as spouses were sent for and maiden ladies came to "visit relatives" in Calif.

FORT DEFIANCE was established in 1851 in what is now northern Arizona but was then New Mexico Territory. Its purpose was to stop Navajo Indian raids on California-bound emigrants. Vast new territories, added to the Union through the Mexican War, were now causing controversies in far-off Washington as to whether they should become slave or free states.

MILLARD FILLMORE, who came into office on Zachary Taylor's death, won enemies by signing the Fugitive Slave Act. "Doughface" was coined as a name for any Northerner favoring slavery.

THE UNDERGROUND RAILWAY was a network of hiding places through which slaves were spirited into Canada by Northern abolitionists. The loss in labor force for the South was negligible, but Southerners complained that operation of the "railway" was a violation of the Compromise of 1850. Abolitionists displayed fugitive Negroes to Yankee crowds to further movement to wipe out slavery.

TAYLOR AND FILLMORE

Territory added by Mexican War causes tension between North and South

Zachary Taylor, called "Old Rough and Ready" because of his military exploits, had little interest in politics. When nominated by the Whigs, he had not even voted for some years. Furthermore, he was a Southerner and owned slaves, and the question of slavery was developing toward a point where a President needed both impartiality and political skill. But Taylor accepted the nomination and, after an unexciting campaign, he became the 12th President.

Technically, he was the 13th chief executive. Inauguration Day, March 4, 1849, was a Sunday, so Taylor's inauguration was delayed until Monday. But James Polk closed his term as President when Congress adjourned early Sunday. Polk's vice-president, George Dallas, had already resigned. Thus, the president of the senate, David Rice Atchison, became President until Taylor took office on Monday.

The technicality mattered little. Taylor, like a good general, had already taken action. Shortly after election he sent a Congressman west to advise New Mexico

PRESIDENT for a day, David Rice Atchison served shortest term in U. S. history (see text).

and California to form constitutions and seek admission to the Union. California asked entry as a free state. This would have ended the deadlock then existing between North and South, giving preponderance of power to the anti-slavery faction. After nine months of debate, a temporary truce was reached through Clay's compromise, but Taylor did not live to see it. After a short illness, he died on July 9, 1850, and Vice-President Millard Fillmore became the chief executive, taking the oath of office July 10.

Fillmore, who might never have become President except for this accident, became unpopular with Northern Whigs by signing the Fugitive Slave Act, by which federal officers could compel any citizen to aid in capture and return of runaway slaves.

Also achieved was first step towards a Panama Canal, the Clayton-Bulwer treaty. By its terms, United States and Great Britain agreed not to seek exclusive control over a Central American canal and guaranteed neutrality of any canal built by private capital.

LOCAL ELECTIONS were colorful events. Bingham painting shows election results being read from court house steps in Missouri town. Wagering was high, feelings were strong, and celebration of winners was lively. In 1850's slavery issue was dominant. Addition of each new state tended to upset delicate North-South balance, especially in Missouri and the border states.

HENRY CLAY, "The Great Pacificator," early in 1850 made a great speech advocating peaceful compromise. Admit California as a free state, he suggested; let future states, New Mexico and Utah, decide slavery themselves; and enforce a drastic new Fugitive Slave Act. Southerners were displeased with this, but Clay's suggestions were adopted in Compromise of 1850.

FRANKLIN PIERCE

An unwilling candidate attempts to perpetuate slavery in America

Franklin Pierce was the second "dark horse" nominee to become president. His nomination was politically expedient but not well calculated by the Democratic leaders.

After floundering through 35 inconclusive ballots, the Democratic convention chiefs of 1852 trotted out Pierce. They offered him to the disorganized delegations as the only "safe" man for the South's pro-slavery platform, although he was a New Englander. On the 49th ballot Pierce was chosen, 282 votes to 2.

Pierce, proclaiming a broad party platform of territorial expansion, support of the Missouri Compromise and slavery, defeated the Whig candidate, Winfield Scott. Actually, slavery was on its way out elsewhere. The British West Indies, Nicaragua, Mexico and many others had abolished it. Spain was considering freeing slaves in Cuba. But to maintain its position in the face of strong free-land sentiment growing throughout the United States, the Pierce administration embarked on a series of pro-slavery moves.

Expansionist policies, designed to incorporate more slave territories, embraced Alaska, Hawaii, the lands surrounding the Gulf of Mexico and key South American areas. During this period, adventurer William Walker exploited a civil war in Nicaragua and managed to set himself up as dictator. He opened Nicaragua to slavery until a coalition of neighboring republics forced the U.S. Navy to remove him. These maneuvers followed Lopez' attempts to eliminate anti-slave tendencies in Cuba, failure of which resulted in such policies as the shameful "Ostend Manifesto" of 1854.

Meanwhile, Senator Stephen Douglas, contemplating a rail route to the Northwest, introduced the controversial Kansas-Nebraska Bill, which voided the Missouri Compromise. Pierce signed the bill, violating a campaign promise. He did not anticipate that these territories might go to the Free State Party of anti-slaver Charles Robinson. No longer bound by the Missouri Compromise, the new territories became a battleground for pro- and anti-slave factions.

Pierce's action split his administration as effectively as his election had broken the Whig party. Bitter dissatisfaction with the Pierce policies caused a group of Whigs, anti-slavery Democrats, and Free-Soilers to meet at Ripon, Wisconsin, on Feb. 28, 1854. They chose the name, "Republicans", adopting it officially at Jackson, Michigan. Thus, was the present-day Republican Party born.

ROUGHHOUSE TACTICS used by framers of the infamous "Ostend Manifesto" were parodied in anti-administration cartoon showing James Buchanan, then U.S. Minister to England, being attacked by ruffians using power principles of the Manifesto. This controversial doctrine, inspired by pro-slavery elements, demanded that Spain cede Cuba to the U.S. as a slave possession or "lose it by force." Buchanan co-authored the ultimatum.

LAME COW belonging to Mormon emigrant train wandered into Indian camp in Nebraska in 1854. A brave butchered it. Mormons reported loss to Fort Laramie commander, who sent troops to recover cow. When the soldiers shot the chief, Indians massacred them. Next year Gen. Harney led 1,500 men into area, in turn massacred offending Indians. So began 40 years of war on Plains.

POWER POLITICS blossomed when the Tammany Society, formed for the care of revolutionary patriots and their kin, finally became an important influence in political matters. The organization was opposed to anti-immigrant policies of the Know-Nothings and the Native American Party. It succeeded in abolishing property ownership as a qualification to vote and led the fight for the five-year limitation for acquisition of citizenship. Tammany Hall aided the naturalization of foreigners. The oppositionist press pictured Tammany members as literally black-jacking foreigners into supporting Hall policies. The poster at right hoped to induce "emigrants" and the public in general to settle in the Territory of Minnesota, just before it became a state. Promises of colorful enterprisers such as John Nininger and the exploiters who signed the poster lured thousands of immigrants into distant frontier lands of the United States, where they established their homes.

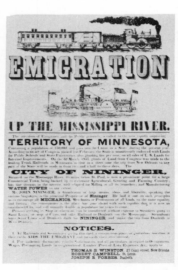

HANDSOME Franklin Pierce had few friends as President, but many friends outside of politics, including Nathaniel Hawthorne. Pierce, like his father, was a New Hampshire Democratic leader. He shunned public life to join Scott in Mexican War, became a general. Constant political turmoil made Pierce's tenure in White House an unhappy one.

LOPEZ AND CUBA

Gen. Narciso Lopez tried three times between 1849 and 1851 to overthrow the Spanish government in Cuba, with U.S. recruits. Failing in his first two attempts, he landed at Morillo in 1851 for a third try. Fifty Southern volunteers were captured and executed and Lopez was hanged at Havana. Cartoon (right) hints his Cardenas expedition of 1850 was financed by pro-slave interests in America.

ANNEXATION

of California pointed up the need for a canal in Panama. The U.S. concluded a treaty with New Granada (now Colombia) guaranteeing neutrality of Isthmus and New Granada's sovereignty in exchange for certain canal rights. American capital backed a railroad across the Isthmus which reached the summit in 1854 and was completed in 1856. It aided travel to California.

FILIBUSTERER WALKER

Retreat of Costa Ricans from San Juan del Norte (l.) showed the continuing political upheaval, paving the way for many opportunists in the Latin Americas. Typical of these was William Walker, who in 1853 marched against Mexico, invading lower California. When his conquest failed, he retreated to the U. S. and was tried and acquitted of violating neutrality laws. Aided by U.S. sympathizers, Walker led an expedition against Nicaragua, became its president in 1856. He did away with Nicaragua's anti-slavery laws, thereby hoping to gain support of the pro-slave states in the U.S. When the U.S. failed to recognize his government, his troops (right) revolted. Walker sought refuge in U.S. custody but jumped bail. He was executed after leading a revolt in Honduras.

KANSAS-NEBRASKA ACT

In 1854, Congress voided Missouri Compromise by passing the controversial Kansas-Nebraska Act. The compromise amendment, enacted in 1820, had provided that all territories north of 36° 30′ except Missouri should remain free of slavery. The new act, sponsored by Sen. Stephen Douglas, applied Lewis Cass' principle of "popular sovereignty" to the territories of Kansas and Nebraska. It allowed the admission of new territories with or without slavery — according to the decision of the settlers. By signing the bill into law, President Pierce opened the door to actual warfare in the areas. Pro-slavery advocates from Southern states streaming into Kansas were tabbed "Border Ruffians" (l.) by opposition. They fought a series of guerrilla skirmishes with anti-slavery factions, including the followers of Charles Robinson. A physician and journalist, Robinson supported squatter sovereignty and had worked against establishment of slavery in California. In 1854 he became the leader of the Kansas Free State Party and was elected governor of the territory the following year. The "bogus" legislature indicted him on charges of treason and conspiracy and he was imprisoned for a period of four months. After a sensational trial (c.) Robinson was acquitted by a Federal grand jury and he returned to serve out his term as governor. The trial put an end to the so-called "Bogus Laws" (r.) and paved the way for admission of Kansas into the Union as a free state. But violence continued for years.

LIEUT. S. BENT, USN, PASSING JAPANESE BOATS IN BAY OF YEDO, 1853

U.S. NAVY PERSONNEL EXERCISE BEFORE IMPERIAL COMMISSIONERS, 1854

Commodore Perry Opens Japan

Isolationist in policy for 200 years, Japan found herself approached on all sides in the 19th century by nations eager to trade.

The Gold Rush brought American steamships into the Pacific, and the consequent need for coaling stations spurred the first effective American mission to Japan, entrusted to Commodore Perry, brother of the hero of Lake Erie.

American attempts to establish commercial relations with Japan dated back to 1791, but it was not until Perry anchored his armed squadron in Yedo Bay in July, 1853 that important results were obtained. Perry's display of force impressed the Shogunate, who broke precedent by receiving his credentials and referring him to the Mikado. Perry left shortly after, in order

to allow the Japanese time to consider his trade proposals. He returned in 1854 with ten ships and negotiated the treaty of Kanagawa, the first between Japan and an Occidental power. The United States was allowed to establish a consulate and American ships were given the right to visit certain specified ports. Perry's work brought Japan permanently into family of nations.

JAPANESE COMMISSIONERS BEING ENTERTAINED AT DINNER ON USS POWHATAN

PERRY, JAPANESE VERSION

PERRY, AS PHOTOGRAPHED

COMMISSIONERS representing Japan visited U.S. in 1860, were received by President Buchanan on May 17. Their trip to the United States was made aboard *U.S.S. Powhatan* and included a warm welcome in San Francisco and a journey via Panama to Washington. This was the first of many expeditions by which Japan proved her eagerness for commerce.

CHINESE FACTORIES were established by several nations, including the United States, Great Britain and France. American trade with the Chinese flourished many years before Commodore Perry's first contact with Japan. Trade was conducted under severe restrictions imposed on foreigners until 1844 when Caleb Cushing negotiated a treaty opening China's ports.

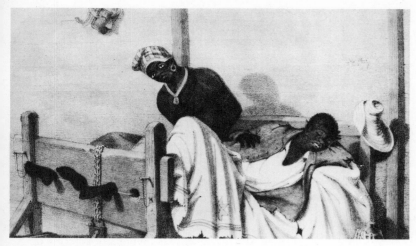

FEAR OF TORTURE often kept slaves in check. They worked just hard enough to avoid flogging, or worse punishments, such as the stocks or torture mask (background, on wall). Kept in ignorance, slaves were not as efficient as free Northern labor, knew nothing of work-saving machinery. About nine-tenths of all cotton grown in South in 1850 was picked by slaves.

BRUTAL ASSAULT on Sen. Charles Sumner of Mass. was waged by Preston Brooks, nephew of Sen. Butler of S. C., whom Sumner had attacked in a speech. Brooks caught Sumner in Senate Chamber, caned him mercilessly. Sumner never fully recovered. Although Brooks became a hero in the South for trouncing, he later complained: "I shall go down in history as a bully."

BOOTH AFFAIR occurred in Wisc. as a Mr. Booth kidnapped a recaptured runaway slave, was himself caught and imprisoned by Federal officers. The poster protests this villainy of "slave-catchers."

RUNAWAY SLAVES were sought by public advertisements. This 1853 notice identifies owner of runaway as a Marlboro, Md. lady; the slave as a substantial fellow. Reward of $200 depended on his being secured in jail for the owner.

COTTON was picked by Negroes of all ages and packed into bales by a huge press. Less than 5% of the eight million whites in the South owned the three and one-half million slaves who picked it. Cotton was ruinous to the soil and produced vast wastelands.

FIRST REPUBLICAN candidate for Presidency was John C. Fremont, soldier and explorer. In 1856 at Philadelphia, Republican convention nominated him for President on platform that Congress was sovereign over territories and should forbid slavery in them. "Free soil, free speech, and Fremont" was battle cry. Southerners threatened secession if Fremont was elected.

FORTY YEARS of government service in many branches qualified James Buchanan for the Presidency. A lawyer, he entered politics as a Federalist and later became a Democrat. In the campaign of 1856, with Tammany backing, he defeated General Fremont in the campaign for the presidency. Engraving shows a Buchanan poster hung outside Tammany Hall, New York.

BORDER DISPUTE between the U.S. and Mexico resulted in the Gadsden Purchase, ratified in 1854, in which U.S. acquired control of 45,000 square miles of land in what is now southern Arizona and New Mexico (see atlas, plate 12). Treaty of purchase was negotiated by James Gadsden, U.S. minister to Mexico. Area was regarded as desirable route for railroad to Pacific.

BUCHANAN

A house dividing: slavery issue produces an irrepressible conflict

Few presidents inherited a more formidable burden than James Buchanan. Few were less capable of managing their legacies. The questions of slavery and state's rights had become dominant, pervading almost every aspect of American life. Whether or not to allow the South's "peculiar institution" in the newly acquired territories continued to aggravate the conflict.

A stronger chief executive might at least have impartially dedicated himself to easing out the wedges of separation, but Buchanan was neither a strong nor a consistent man. Failing to grasp the essence of the great divisive issues, he sought to preserve the Union merely by enforcing the Fugitive Slave Law and preventing abolitionist agitation. After every passing crisis of his administration he considered the slavery issue settled.

Milestones along the road to war appeared one by one in the years following his inauguration. Hinton Helper's *Impending Crisis*, like Stowe's *Uncle Tom's Cabin*, was a strong indictment of slavery and broadened the gulf between North and South. The Supreme Court's decision in the Dred Scott case, ruling that negroes were not citizens and protecting slaveholders in their property even outside the South was another wedge. It meant that Congress had no right to prohibit slavery in the territories and that the Missouri Compromise had been unconstitutional from its enactment.

Equally serious was the continuing strife in Kansas. Pro-slavers in the territory, by a fraudulent vote, pushed through the Lecompton Constitution in 1857, hoping to enter the Union as a slave state. Buchanan approved of the move and pressed for Kansas' admission. When Congress rejected Kansas' bid, the North in general and the Republican party in particular were the gainers, but only in a short term sense for no permanent good could accrue to any faction from hollow victories in what was amounting to a fraticidal conflict.

A fresh element of reason was injected into the widening conflict with the emergence of Lincoln, whose seven debates with Stephen Douglas are among the greatest in the English language. In Freeport, a small Illinois town, Lincoln placed his opponent in a corner by asking him if the people of a territory could lawfully exclude slavery from their midst. If Douglas rejected the Dred Scott decision he would have to separate himself from the Democratic party by defying the Court. But the clever "Little Giant" found a way out by stating that while Congress could invalidate any law passed by a territorial legislature, it could not compel it to pass a given measure. Douglas' subsequent victory at the polls was a blessing for the nation, freeing Lincoln for the fearsome task ahead.

JOHN BROWN'S BODY fell to the hangsman in 1859 but his soul in truth "went marching on." The fanatical abolitionist had seized the federal arsenal at Harper's Ferry, Virginia, and prepared to hand out arms to slaves. But too few responded and Brown was captured by Col. Robert E. Lee after stubborn resistance. The South accused Republicans of inciting the slave insurrection. The North, seeing only the principle for which he stood, enshrined the bearded Brown as a martyr in the anti-slavery fights.

LINCOLN-DOUGLAS DEBATES Whole country listened when Abe Lincoln challenged the right of Stephen Douglas to his Illinois Senate seat in 1858. In a series of debates the contenders eloquently defended opposing doctrines. Douglas accused Lincoln of promoting sectional conflicts, sneered at "Black Republicans" who demanded racial equality, and expounded his own doctrine of popular sovereignty. Lincoln, who was no abolitionist, fought for confinement of slavery to the states in which it already existed, where he believed it would die out. Douglas was re-elected but the debate catapulted Lincoln from comparative obscurity to national prominence. It also intensified the rift in the Democratic Party and made the "rail-splitter" new leader of the growing Republican Party.

CARICATURES of President Buchanan were helped by upstanding forelock, habit of carrying head cocked to one side like a listening parrot. "Old Buck" was first bachelor president. In his inaugural address, he called slavery "a difference of opinion, a matter of little practical importance," and "bleeding Kansas," was to him "an agitation that shall pass away."

CRUELTIES that Northerners heard were inflicted on Negroes were often absent when they visited slave sales. But the sight of man, wife and child on auction block was enough to stir their anger all over again. Buchanan's government turned its back on illegal slave trade conducted in South.

TENSION IN CONGRESS was so great by 1859 that members carried concealed weapons. Floor had become wild debating area for question: "Is slavery right or wrong?" Disruptive force of sectionalism proved stronger than party loyalty. Democratic discord was aid to Republican solidarity.

ENGLAND'S PRINCE OF WALES paid U.S. a visit in 1860, was taken on tour of Washington's Mount Vernon estate by Buchanan. To mark the visit, the royal visitor planted a young horse chestnut tree on mound not far from the first President's tomb, returned to cutter *Harriet Lane* for dinner.

BLEEDING KANSAS was small-scale rehearsal for coming Civil War. After pro-slavery Lecompton constitution was forced through in 1857, conflict broke out anew between opposing factions resulting in scenes like Marais des Cygnes Massacre (above). Both sides were guilty of wanton savagery.

40,000 BUSINESSMEN milled about Wall Street on eve of Panic of 1857. Collapse was caused by speculation in railroads and real estate. There were more "paper cities" in Kansas than actual cities in Mid-West and Northern states combined; too much was tied up in paper, not enough in cultivation. Panic was over in 30 days; South escaped almost untouched.

FUGITIVE SLAVE Dred Scott was taken by master to North. On return to Missouri, Scott sued for freedom on ground of having resided on free soil. Supreme Court found: Negroes were not citizens; Congress couldn't deprive citizen of property without due process; Missouri Compromise was void.

THE "STOURBRIDGE LION," first locomotive in America, thundered along at 10 miles per hour "amid deafening cheers" at trial run on Aug. 8, 1829. The *Lion* was brought from England by the Delaware & Hudson Canal Company for its 16-mile Carbondale and Honesdale Railroad. Locomotive weighed seven tons and proved too heavy for the track of wood rails topped with an iron strap rail. The trestle was fully 35 feet high.

STEAM AND STEEL

Railroads, clippers and steamboats open new vistas of trade and settlement

Spectacular improvements in transportation provided the spark that set off the unprecedented development of the 19th century. Cumbersome wagons and jolting stagecoaches, laboring over impossible roads, had kept travel beyond the eastern seaboard a project reserved for the most adventurous citizens, who to a great extent, had to rely on Indian trails for roads.

Suddenly, in rapid succession, railroads, steam locomotives, new canals, clipper ships, steamboats appeared on the scene. The young country expanded across mountains, plains, prairies and deserts in an unparalleled spasm of growth.

By 1835 there were only a thousand miles of railroads in the country, mostly short lines connecting existing waterways along the eastern seaboard. By 1860 more than 30,000 miles of railroads were in use. The railroads, combined with steam navigation on the lakes, rivers and canals, opened the lands across the mountains to settlers, and provided them with a sure means of bringing their produce to the eastern markets.

Meanwhile, speedy China clippers and Atlantic packet lines provided an outlet for America's surplus production and an opportunity to obtain needed imports from European and Asiatic countries.

SMOKE-BELCHING LOCOMOTIVES were regarded with some dismay by citizens as trains hurtled by at unbelievable 15-mile-per-hour clip. Early stage coach type passenger cars soon were replaced by rectangular design.

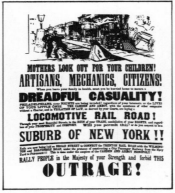

ALARMIST POSTER published in New Jersey in 1830 was characteristic of futile attempts to discourage railroad builders.

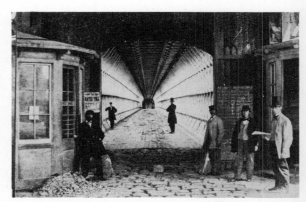

SUSPENSION BRIDGE over Niagara Falls was great achievement of the 1850's, eliminating need to ferry trains across river above Falls. Bridge was designed by engineer John Roebling of Brooklyn Bridge fame.

THE "GREAT EASTERN," was the biggest vessel ever built when she sailed from England to New York in June, 1860. With space for 4,000 passengers plus 400 crew she was 680 feet long, displaced 18,900 gross tons. Her paddlewheels were driven by a 1000-horsepower engine and her six masts carried 6,500 yards of canvas. She was also the biggest white elephant in maritime history. Withdrawn from passenger service after a series of catastrophes she was eventually used to lay the trans-Atlantic cable, the only vessel capable of holding enough cable to reach across the Atlantic.

THE "BELLE CREOLE" shown at New Orleans, was typical of the brave little steamboats that paddled up and down the Mississippi before the railroads took over. Steamboating already was established in the East, both for river and coastal service, when Nicholas Roosevelt built the first Mississippi River steamboat, the *New Orleans*, in 1811. Within 10 years 60 steamboats worked the river. Their role grew in importance for passenger and freight transport for half a century until the spreading rail network made their commercial use impractical. But many remained as excursion boats.

STEAMBOAT RACING was a popular sport on the Mississippi. Favorite boats and skilled pilots attracted heavy bets up and down the river. The winner of one classic covered 1,218 miles upstream from New Orleans in three days, 18 hours, 30 minutes. The quaint riverboats often were fitted out in a luxurious manner, leading one traveler of the period to describe them as "fairy structures, of oriental gorgeousness and splendor." To be a pilot often was the greatest ambition of youngsters growing up in the Mississippi Valley, a dream achieved and immortalized in fiction by Mark Twain.

STEAM AND SAIL were combined on ocean-going vessels like the *California*, designed to handle the West Coast portion of a government subsidized mail service. Mail from New York went to Panama by sea, across the Isthmus by land and water, and up the Pacific coast via the *California* and her sister ships. During the gold rush they also transported tons of mining machinery and hundreds of '49ers who gathered in clamoring throngs at Panama, offering up to a thousand dollars for a berth. Returning, they found themselves carrying gold itself, $280 million worth in seven years.

CLIPPER SHIP "RAINBOW" launched in 1843, was first of a series of fast sailing vessels that won international fame in maritime commerce. The sleek clippers were designed for the China trade where time was vital in getting precious cargoes of tea, spices and fruits to market in good condition. The *Rainbow*, for a time the fastest ship in the world, made her first round trip from New York to Canton in six months, 14 days, including loading time. Previously the run required four to six months each way. Clippers crossed Atlantic in 13 days, sailed from New York to California in 89 days.

AMERICAN WHALING recovered from the setback of the Revolution and returned to commercial importance by the mid-19th century. The whaling fleet in the 1840's included more than 700 vessels, most of them working the sperm whale fisheries in the Pacific. In the 1850's the whalers turned their attention to the hunt for right whales in North Pacific and Arctic waters which soon became the industry's center. Whaling vessels worked under sail, did not use steam until 1866. Declining as rapidly as it had grown, the whaling fleet dropped to 38 ships by the turn of the century.

AGRICULTURE

The 19th century witnessed the sharp rise and fall of the cotton kingdom in the South and the westward spread of farmlands. With improvement of the cotton gin and growth of the textile industry, production of cotton soared from just over 300 million pounds a year in 1830 to more than two billion pounds in 1860. Cotton culture spread westward into Alabama and Mississippi and across to Arkansas and Texas, depleting the fertility of the once rich "black belt" by the 1860's. Vast plantations with hundreds of slaves, as shown (above left) served King Cotton, and steamboats dotted the rivers, carrying the crop to the Gulf ports for shipment. The tide of immigration pushed the farm frontier to the edge of the forest lands and new arrivals were obliged to move out onto the prairies. They were aided by the increasing spread of the railways, and by new inventions like the reaper that facilitated large grain operations. But in some areas old methods remained. Oxen and mules were widely used, and in New England in 1860 there were still as many oxen as horses.

CHICAGO

The most phenomenal growth of all the American cities that sprang up in the 19th century was experienced by Chicago. The village of 1830, (top left) was no more than the few wooden buildings of Fort Dearborn, out in the middle of Indian country. After the Black Hawk War of 1832, settlers began to arrive and by 1837 there were 4,000 inhabitants. Development of canals, railroads and steam navigation on the lakes brought more newcomers. The population jumped to 30,000 by 1850, to 80,000 by 1855, to 110,000 by 1860. Chicago had become the commercial center of the Midwest. Less than five years after the first shipment of grain from her docks (top right) 20 million bushels were being handled annually, and Chicago was the largest primary wheat depot in the world. Eleven trunk lines with 74 trains a day made it the railroading center of America by the mid '50's. Lake shipping cluttered her waterways (bottom left). Everything was done on a big scale. Entire blocks of buildings (bottom right) were raised four feet when the land under them began to sink. This combination of departing frontier and erupting industry brought incongruities. Wooden cabins stood beside handsome public buildings, and cows wandered on the streets. Sanitation was primitive and the water supply often polluted. Civic affairs were in constant turmoil, but the young giant kept right on growing.

BUFFALO was transformed from a village to a metropolis by the development of Great Lakes shipping after the opening of the Erie Canal. Improvement of machine-powered grain elevators made the city an important grain storage and milling center. Buffalo's population climbed from 2,500 in 1825 to 81,000 in 1860.

PHILADELPHIA was outstanding in civic development, noted for its educational and charitable institutions. From 1850, aided by improved transportation from the anthracite coal fields, it led the country in total value of manufactured products. After consolidation with county lands it became the second U.S. city in size.

BALTIMORE shown above in the 1850's, outstripped New Orleans in size by 1860. Long an important tobacco port and shipbuilding center, Baltimore benefited greatly from railroads. With access to wheat areas of Virginia and Maryland it developed a large milling business, producing and exporting 500,000 barrels of flour a year.

DUBUQUE had been closed to white settlers for many years prior to the Black Hawk War. Reopened in 1833, it underwent a spectacular development in the 50's as one of the points of entry for immigration to fertile Iowa farm lands. Spurred on by drought in Ohio Valley, farmers poured through the city at the rate of 600 a day.

DETROIT, like Buffalo, received a rush of settlers when the Erie Canal opened. Within weeks 4,000 newcomers arrived and the land boom was on. Established as a fort by Sieur de la Mothe Cadillac in 1701, Detroit was not incorporated as a town until a century later, when its population was still under 2,000. Arrival of the railroad in 1838 complemented the Canal to turn it into a flourishing city of 45,000 by 1860. But its great industrial development came only after the Civil War.

NEW YORK was firmly established as the commercial center of the U.S. by the mid-19th century. The Erie Canal and the new steam railroads connected its busy harbor with the productive interior, and Atlantic steamship service, inaugurated in 1838, provided swift access to European markets. By the 50's New York had 272 churches, 8 great markets, 115 fire companies, 29 omnibus lines, five theaters and 25 hotels. Broadway is shown above as it appeared in 1835, in a view made from Canal Street.

NEW ORLEANS, the "Queen of the Mississippi," outranked even New York in the value of her exports during the 1830's and early 1840's. Until railroads and Northern canals were well-established, New Orleans shipped out the bulk of the production of the entire Missouri and Ohio valleys, receiving the cargoes of 4,000 flatboats and 450 steamboats each year. But as transportation facilities in the North improved, New Orleans soon found herself losing ground to Northern rail and shipping centers.

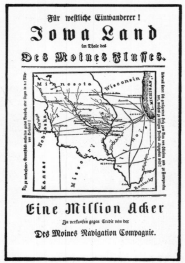

IMMIGRATION soared after Irish potato famine of 1845-46 and German revolution of 1848. In two decades four million immigrants arrived. Many headed west (l.), lured by posters in Europe. A few dissatisfied immigrants returned to Europe (r.).

NATION FORGES AHEAD

Trouble in Europe spurs immigration and American industrial growth

In 1830 there were less than half a million foreign-born persons in the United States. By 1860 more than five million immigrants had arrived. Total population of the country leaped from 13 million in 1830 to 31 million by 1860. Newcomers included 1,800,000 Irish and 1,500,000 Germans, with the remainder of the arrivals English, French, Swiss, Dutch and Scandinavians.

Not all were members of the lower classes. Many skilled and well-educated migrants came to join friends or relatives already established in the United States. About half the new arrivals became farmers or merchants immediately on arrival, rather than joining the ranks of common laborers.

Many moved west, taking up farms just beyond the line of settlement. The remainder, lacking special skills or without funds, made up a vast labor pool for rapidly developing industries of the East. Establishment of the factory system with its demand for concentrated groups of workers created an industrial urban population and cities grew by leaps and bounds.

With the cotton gin and power loom in general use, production of cotton in the South, and cotton cloth in Northern mills became all-important. Despite the growth of cotton culture and opening of new farmlands, industrial production outstripped agriculture. In 1859, the value of domestic manufactures amounted to almost $2 billion, while the entire production of Southern agriculture, including cotton, tobacco, sugar and rice was worth $204 million.

Increasing population and improved transportation in the North had a serious effect on Southern economy. The cotton planters, resisting attempts to industrialize, were interested only in expanding raw cotton production, and cotton prices dropped accordingly. Southern goods went directly to Europe by sea, but the returning ships unloaded their cargoes in Northeastern ports which had better access to the most highly populated areas. Foodstuffs produced in the Northwest were shipped east by rail, bypassing the New Orleans route.

Meanwhile the population moved steadily westward. By the middle of the century the frontier extended from eastern Minnesota south through eastern Arkansas to Texas. Then it hop-scotched a thousand miles to

the Pacific Coast. Federal land grants to railroads amounted to 130 million acres, sometimes extending as much as 40 miles on either side of the tracks. Publicizing and disposing of these lands, the railroads attracted many settlers and speculators.

The decade 1850-1860 was a golden age of development for the United States. The value of its farms increased 103 per cent; of total manufacture, 87 per cent; of manufactures for export, 171 per cent and of railroad mileage, 220 per cent. Within the 10 year period the nation's total wealth more than doubled, increasing 120 per cent.

SETTLEMENT OF OREGON was inspired by missionaries whose efforts to obtain funds publicized the area and encouraged a group of 150 farmers to blaze the famous Oregon Trail in 1842. Mural in state capitol shows scene at Salem in 1859 when Oregon was admitted as state.

WESTWARD BOUND, pioneer families made last-minute purchases at final assembly points before the wagon trains set out across the plains. In 1820, of a total population of 9,638,00, only 2,217,000 lived west of the Alleghenies. By 1860 there were 15,407,000 settlers in the West.

FIRST OIL WELL was brought in on August 27, 1859, at Titusville, Pennsylvania, by Colonel Edward L. Drake, right foreground. After drilling to a depth of 69 feet, Drake struck his "gusher," which flowed at the rate of eight to ten barrels a day. The value of oil for illuminating uses already was known, but quantities floating to the surface had been of negligible commercial value. Drake's strike started the first "oil rush," and within three years the oil industry, firmly established, was threatening the whaling industry.

FIRST TRAVELING SALESMAN carried fruits of civilization to the ever-advancing frontier. His rickety wagon, laden with pots, pans, tools, books, and the new printed cottons from the mills of New England provided sorely-needed comforts for the pioneers and paved the way for future commerce.

ICE CUTTING became a major winter enterprise in New England. At Spy Pond in West Cambridge, Mass., as many as 6,000 tons a day were cut and stored during a good season. Sawdust-packed ice was shipped to Africa.

GIANT TRIP HAMMER at Nashua Iron Company in New Hampshire typified development of industrial machinery in 19th century. Trip hammers weighing up to seven and one-half tons were used widely for metal work.

ARCTIC OIL WORKS at San Francisco was an outgrowth of the great whaling industry in North Pacific and Arctic regions. It handled whale oil used for illumination before petroleum, gas lighting came into widespread use.

HOOPSKIRT FACTORY of the 1850's employed 1,000 girls and turned out 90,000 hoopskirts a month, using 150,000 yards of muslin and 100,000 feet of whalebone. This type of work paid four dollars a week to "smart girls."

OLIVER WENDELL HOLMES, physician-poet is shown reading his work on childbed fever to the Boston Society for Medical Improvement in 1843. Born at Cambridge in 1809, the 34-year-old Harvard graduate practiced medicine in Boston and was made professor of anatomy and physiology at his alma mater four years later. Best known for his popular writings, his brilliant medical work remains today a model of careful scientific reasoning.

SCIENCE AND INVENTIONS

New discoveries set the stage for era of medical and industrial progress

The United States was entering an era of scientific progress, heralded by the telegraph of Morse and the sewing machine of Howe. Medical science also was taking giant strides. In 1840, Baltimore College opened the first dental school in America.

The most humane discovery of mankind was anesthesia. First used by Dr. Crawford Long of Georgia, sulfuric ether fumes were employed at the Massachusetts General Hospital soon after Dr. Morton's famous demonstration in 1846.

Dr. William Beaumont, observing the stomach interior of a severely wounded fur-trapper, was able to explain the action of gastric juices and the laws of digestion to the medical world in 1827.

Epoch-making inventions destined to create giant industries followed one another in rapid succession. Joseph Saxton built the first electric dynamo in 1833. Samuel F .B. Morse laid the first underwater telegraph cable in New York harbor in 1842 connecting the Battery with Governor's Island.

A retired paper manufacturer, Cyrus W. Field, made two unsuccessful attempts to lay initial Atlantic cable from Ireland to Newfoundland. The third try suceeded, linking the two continents on Aug. 5, 1858. Queen Victoria and President Buchanan exchanged historic greetings over the cable shortly before it went dead. The link was not reestablished until 1866.

In 1836, David Bruce of New York patented the first type casting machine, opening the way for the great daily newspapers. The most nostalgic invention of this productive age was by Henry Shreve, who constructed the first double deck, shallow draft Mississippi River steamboat in 1842. This famous craft soon achieved immortality in American folklore.

Of undeniable importance to the development of the West was Samuel Colt's invention of the revolver in 1835. He developed manufacture of interchangeable parts, the basis of modern production lines.

DR. JOHN W. DRAPER took first photographic portrait in 1839 by using focusing mirrors to direct sunlight on subject's face. This cut exposure time from hours to seconds. Draper also took the first photograph of the moon in 1840.

PHYSICIST JOSEPH HENRY pioneered the idea of an electromagnet in 1831, indispensable to development of commercial telegraphy. First director of the Smithsonian Institute, Henry also laid foundation for U.S. Weather Bureau.

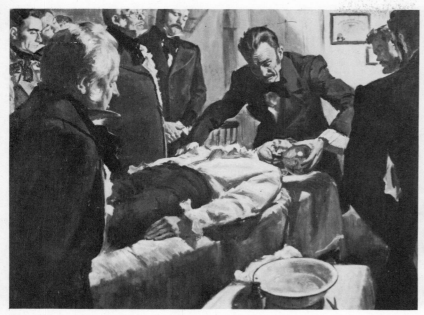

TRIUMPH OVER PAIN was result of Dr. William Morton's experiments with sulfuric ether fumes. First use of anesthesia in general surgery occurred in 1846. Dentist Horace Wells tried nitrous oxide gas for extractions but ceased experiments when a patient died from overdose of gas. Dr. Morton turned from gas to ether fumes, brought to his attention by Dr. Charles Jackson, who noted that medical students inhaled the fumes at "ether-jag" parties. Doctors Morton and J. C. Warren demonstrated action of anesthesia at an operation (r.) in Mass. General Hospital, Oct. 16, 1846.

SAMUEL F. B. MORSE transformed a scientific toy into a practical telegraph. Born at Charleston, Mass., in 1791, Yale graduate Morse first conceived the telegraph after observing a crude magnetic spark instrument in England. In 1836 he perfected workable telegraph sounders (right) that reproduced letters by means of electrical shorthand later to become famous as "Morse Code." Congress appropriated money to build experimental telegraph line from Baltimore, Md., to Washington, D.C. On May 24, 1844, first instantaneous transfer of human thought between two isolated communities occurred when words "What hath God wrought?" were flashed over the wires.

WEIRD IDEA of Carlincourt Lowe was a balloon-supported ship for trans-Atlantic service. Never built, the airship was inspired by 1,150 mile free balloon flight in 1859 of Professor Wise from Missouri to New York.

MILLION DOLLAR IDEA was originated by Elias Howe Jr., who patented his famous sewing machine in 1846. Howe's invention held cloth by a curved resettable baster plate. The unit made a lock stitch by combination of curved, grooved eye-pointed needle and a speedy shuttle action.

CYRUS HALL McCORMICK patented his horse-drawn reaper in 1834 and sold it to farmers on the installment plan. This revolutionary machine was marketed in Chicago, grain capital of the world. Growth of the Midwest grain belt was due largely to use of the mechanical reaper.

VULCANIZING PROCESS was discovered accidentally by Charles Goodyear in 1839. The hardware merchant found adding sulphur compound to natural rubber turned sticky mess into usable substance. Goodyear developed various processes to pave way for growth of industry.

LETTERS
Romanticism awakens Literary Golden Age

"THE FOREST MOANED AND SHUDDERED" at the anguished cry of Hiawatha, seeing his lovely Minnehaha (Laughing Water) dead of hunger. Written in 1855 the *Song of Hiawatha* — with *Evangeline* (1847)—established Henry Wadsworth Longfellow's reputation as America's most popular narrative poet. The *Courtship of Miles Standish* in 1858 and the *Golden Legend* (1872) secured it. This "poet of the mellow twilight of the past," as Whitman termed him, concerned himself chiefly with romanticism. The lilt of his verse, his buoyant optimism captured hearts of unlettered people.

Period from 1830 to 1860 frequently is called the Golden Age of American literature. Growing urbanization in the East and increased leisure time created a public hunger for esthetic nourishment, and American authors offered a wide variety of solid reading matter to fill that need.

The ballads of a Harvard professor of letters, Henry Wadsworth Longfellow, struck the right chord, attaining a startling popularity at home and abroad. Versatile Edgar Allen Poe was exerting a potent influence on U.S. poets and French symbolists, and in addition aiding the development of the detective story. In the South, Sidney Lanier was enchanting a generation with his lyrical verse on nature themes.

Sharp contrast to the dark prose of Nathaniel Hawthorne was provided by a dean of Harvard medical school, Oliver Wendell Holmes, with his *Wonderful One-Hoss Shay* and *Autocrat* series. Washington Irving, in the twilight of his career, Francis Parkman, James Russell Lowell, George Bancroft, and John Greenleaf Whittier contributed their significant talents to the gradual literary awakening.

Foremost in the ranks were the Transcendentalists who shared Jefferson's belief in the ultimate perfection of man. They had learned, however, that men who were not free spiritually could not be liberated by free institutions. Centered at Boston and led by Emerson and Thoreau, the Transcendentalists exercised a dominant influence on American literature from 1820 to 1860 and affected theology as well.

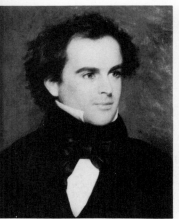

SALEM AND COOPERSTOWN, widely separated in character, nurtured distinct expressions of the romantic spirit in early novelists. Nathaniel Hawthorne (l.) perceived the beauty and tragedy of life, remained preoccupied with sin, as exemplified in his masterful *Scarlet Letter*. James Fennimore Cooper's *Leatherstocking Tales* and sea stories provided vicarious adventure for readers throughout the world.

POET AND JOURNALIST William Cullen Bryant was publishing poetry at 13 and wrote the lofty *Thanatopsis* (1817) at 18. During a busy life, Bryant also practiced law, helped found the *New York Review* and edited the *N. Y. Evening Post*.

HERMAN MELVILLE'S *Moby Dick* utilized Captain Ahab's conflict with the great white whale to symbolize man's eternal struggle with the forces of evil. Melville renounced his earlier primitive style (*Typee*, 1845, and *Omoo*, 1847) when he fashioned his masterpiece in 1851. Turning to mystic misanthropy, Melville culminated his literary effort with *Billy Budd*, 1891.

"IN SILENT SUSPENSE," William Hickling Prescott's memory held details which he wrote with a noctograph guiding his finger. Virtually blinded by a biscuit thrown carelessly in the commons hall at Harvard, Prescott wrote boldly and vividly. His works included *History of Ferdinand and Isabella, Conquest of Mexico, Conquest of Peru,* and *The Reign of Philip II.*

QUAKER POET John Greenleaf Whittier was filled with moral fervor and love for his fellow man. Whittier used his pen to war on slavery, but won a far wider audience with his emotional ballads, *Barbara Frietchie, The Barefoot Boy, Maud Muller,* and *Snow-bound*. His unmatched descriptions of nature, childhood, and rural life endeared him to the American public.

EMOTIONAL POWDER KEG was ignited with publication of Harriet Beecher Stowe's *Uncle Tom's Cabin* in 1852. Criticized as an exaggeration, this vivid account of slave life touched off storm of indignation in the North and bitter resentment in the South. The novel sold 300,000 copies within a year, and an adaptation played in six London theaters simultaneously, gaining international reputation for Stowe. Scenes depicted added fuel to raging slavery issue.

PROLIFIC Edgar Allen Poe fashioned America's first mystery stories, with his *Murders In The Rue Morgue*, serving as model for A. Conan Doyle. Poe's brooding genius *(The Raven, Tell Tale Heart)* earned a unique niche in letters.

JULIA WARD HOWE penned *Battle Hymn of the Republic* after visiting the Union Army on the banks of the Potomac after retreat of Bull Run. Its measured cadence and grand sweep exercised a profound reaction throughout North.

NINE CENTS A DAY was Henry David Thoreau's budget during two years he led hermit's existence at Walden Pond. A firm believer in individualism, Thoreau wrote *Civil Disobedience*, a work that swayed India's Mahatma Gandhi.

HIGH PRIEST of democracy was Ralph Waldo Emerson, foremost of the Transcendentalists. Emerson, whose essays remain as models of lucidity and strong conviction, called for American culture free from any European bondage.

HORACE GREELEY

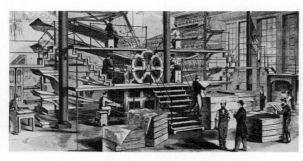

PRESSROOM OF GREELEY'S NEW YORK TRIBUNE

JAMES GORDON BENNETT AND STAFF

PRESS Early American newspapers were largely dominated by political parties. But the appearance of penny dailies in the 1830's brought human interest and wider, more objective coverage to more people. The *New York Sun,* appearing in 1833, was a pioneer in this field.

Another "penny" paper, the *New York Morning Herald,* was founded in 1835 by James Gordon Bennett, who promised in his first edition on May 6 to "support no party . . . to care nothing for any election." His aim was circulation through "lively, saucy, spicy" reporting, while pioneering coverage of society and financial news.

A "moral war" against the *Herald* in 1840, along with desire of the Whigs for a penny paper, led to founding of the *New York Tribune*

by Horace Greeley in 1841. Attempts by *Herald* and *Sun* to stem its immediate success brought first great circulation war. Fearlessly advocating unpopular causes, Greeley opposed Mexican War, supported women's suffrage. Strong against slavery, his influence was great. Bennett, on the other hand, opposed anti-slavery movement.

On Sept. 18, 1851, a newspaper appeared, aiming, as Charles A. Dana later wrote, at a "middle course between the mental eccentricity of the *Tribune* and the moral eccentricity of the *Herald*." The *New York Daily Times* was begun by Henry J. Raymond, in 1851.

Of wide popular appeal was *Frank Leslie's Illustrated Newspaper,* appearing in 1857, about the time (the old) *Gleason's Pictorial* died. *Harper's Monthly* was founded 1850 by James Harper.

EDUCATION and RELIGION

Schools and churches revitalize the nation

Religious and social institutions of the first half of the 19th century reflected the nation's struggle to attain maturity. The rugged individualism inherent in the new frontier life caused men to exchange "hell and damnation" doctrine of Calvin for a modified evangelical Protestantism.

The new look in religion swept America like a prairie fire. To a firmly-based belief in an Almighty Being, it added the philosophy that man should make a real effort to improve his lot on earth. It taught also that in creating a moral law to govern men's actions, God had given man a conscience to comprehend that law.

Enthusiasm for the new philosophy took three directions. The hope of a millennium was viewed as almost a certainty by those who practiced Mormonism and Millerism (known today as Seventh-day Adventists). With others, rejection of the 'mother church' of Rome became so complete that anti-Catholicism approached the proportions of a crusade in the 1830's. A third group, the intellectuals, searching for a simple religion based on reason, turned to Ralph Waldo Emerson's Transcendentalism.

During the same period Unitarianism was also organized as a church. It was founded by William Ellery Channing in 1825. Five U.S. presidents were Unitarians.

Evangelical Protestantism influenced the Abolitionist movement, the fight for women's suffrage, improvement of prisons and asylums, and effected labor reforms.

The temperance movement also received momentum from the new philosophy, and universal education found support within its framework. America had decided that man was master of his own destiny.

ST. PATRICK'S SPIRES symbolized new hope to European immigrants searching for a better way of life in America. The New York landmark, initiated by Archbishop Hughes in 1858, was held up by the Civil War stress, completed in 1878.

FIRST BAPTIST CHURCH at Broad and Arch streets was an imposing Philadelphia landmark. Baptists by 1850's were one of most dynamic of Protestant denominations. Especially effective on frontier, they organized schools, newspapers, home missionary work. Slavery issue caused separation of Southern Baptists.

CAMP MEETINGS provided means of carrying the gospel to isolated frontier settlements. The rousing meetings served as an outlet for religious fervor, gave wayward believers an opportunity to purge themselves publicly. They also filled a real social need for many lonely settlers.

HENRY WARD BEECHER, famed pastor of Plymouth Church of Brooklyn, placed emphasis on individual liberty tempered by self-control. He departed from the concept of a stern God raining down "fire and brimstone"; pictured a merciful Saviour comforting the lost sheep.

CHURCH OF JESUS CHRIST OF LATTER-DAY SAINTS was founded by Joseph Smith (right) at Palmyra, New York, in 1830. Smith reported a direct revelation from heaven with divine authorization for establishment of his church. Vigorous missionary zeal spurred rapid growth of Mormon sect, and resulted in construction of such imposing temples as one (below, l.) at Nauvoo, Ill. They were persecuted because of their religious beliefs and their practice of polygamy. The Mormons, after the assassination of Joseph Smith in 1846, migrated to Utah under Brigham Young's direction.

RIGHT TO STRIKE did not become legal until 1848 although labor groups had existed in Eastern cities since 1770. At Lynn, Mass., in 1860, 800 women and 4,000 men marched through a heavy snowstorm during the shoemakers' strike to dramatize their appeal for improved working conditions.

ONE ROOM SCHOOLS received their initial financial support from lotteries and tavern taxes. Less than eight of 10 Americans went beyond primary grades, but free education in the one room school was an important development.

COMPELLING ORATORY OF HORACE MANN jerked Massachusetts out of a lethargic attitude toward education and brought about formation of State Board of Education in 1837. Mann's plan, based on the Prussian school system, replaced inept local control across the land. The crusading educator stumped for colleges to train teachers, and also pleaded for public land grants and direct taxes to aid schools, noting that education was one means of reducing poverty and crime in urban centers.

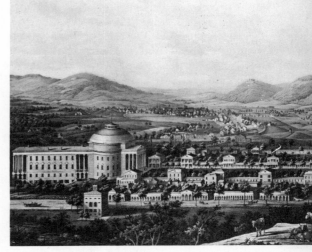

UNIVERSITY OF CHICAGO, which had been founded initially in 1857 by Stephen A. Douglas, was abandoned in 1886. Rechartered in 1890, school exercised vital force on higher education under direction of Dr. William Harper.

NATION'S FIRST COED was admitted to Oberlin College, Ohio, in 1833. Sacramento Academy, Calif., opened a Female Institute in 1854. Situated in a "healthful, retired" neighborhood, its courses varied from embroidery to science.

THOMAS JEFFERSON'S role in American education often is neglected. He introduced the initial proposal for a free school system to the Virginia legislature in the 1780's, founded University of Virginia at Charlottesville, in 1819.

SUFFRAGETTES

Man was fighting a losing battle. American womanhood was on the march. Quickly consolidating hard-won gains, the Suffragettes launched fresh sorties in new directions. Education, a primary target, was among the first to succumb to the determined attack. Mary Lyon (left), a proponent of higher education for women, founded the Mount Holyoke Female Seminary at South Hadley, Mass., in 1837. Women also concentrated on politics in an effort to revamp laws that prevented them from voting or holding office, gave them no legal control of children or property. Margaret Fuller (right), influential literary critic of the *New York Tribune*, used her pen and took to the lecture platform to sustain the cause. Counter-attacks were launched against the Suffragettes, as in the cartoon (center). But achieving equal rights with men was not a humorous subject to the crusaders and their band of followers. Males soon learned that it was not a joking matter.

DANCING THE POLKA was popular with American couples at mid-century. Northern country folk enjoyed the clog while fiddles played "The Arkansaw Traveler." Boston society favored the quadrille. At left is seen the "unobtrusively designed" interior and furniture in elegant apartment of a wealthy merchant's mansion.

GROWING LEISURE

New interest in sports, theater, music, and arts brought forth by prosperity

Rapid growth and expansion of American cities and the great increase in wealth brought about two important changes in the habits of urban Americans. First, they discovered that they had a growing amount of leisure time in which to play. Second, they were able to afford more expensive pleasures than they ever had before. Ironically, however, as a people, they knew little about playing and utilizing their leisure time to its best advantages. Even the word *vacation* was not in their vocabulary. They knew drinking (the chief American vice), gambling, and card-playing from their earlier rustic, pioneer period, and the only sport that might be termed a national pastime was horse-racing. Dancing was popular all over the country, for it provided desirable occasions for the sexes to mix. In the West, a dance was an occasion for a riotous revel that lasted all the way through the night or for an entire week.

Yet, psychologically and practically, the Americans were ready by mid-century to take the preliminary steps to develop a national leisure-time play life. The results opened up many new fields of entertainment in sports, theater, circuses and side-shows, art, and music.

In the field of sports, Americans had not yet completely submitted to the discipline of team play. They therefore had emphasized games of individual skill, such as hunting, fishing, wrestling, boating, and horse-racing. However, the formation of baseball clubs in the 1850's, the overgrowth of cities, and the transcontinental railroad system gave rise to the development of sports and the out-of-doors movement.

The theater, rapidly becoming an American institu-

"THE POLKA" appeard in the *Ladies National Magazine*, 1844.

tion, was one of the first media of entertainment to respond quickly to the new demands of the people. In the growing cities, the theater was the chief source of entertainment, particularly for the aristocratic social circles. In New York, which wrested theatrical supremacy away from Philadelphia, Boston, Baltimore, and Charleston, audiences were able to see some of the finest artists America had developed. The names of Edwin Forrest, Charlotte Cushman, E. L. Davenport, and Joseph Jefferson were star attractions of their day, and their contributions to the stage enriched their profession. Foreign artists also delighted native audiences, while wandering players entertained small groups in Shakespearean plays. Even the opera houses of San Francisco featured wildly gesturing Hamlets.

The "common people" were amused by other types of entertainment. Shrewd showmen like P. T. Barnum learned to appeal to public tastes. They staged circuses and side-shows, attracting people to see industrious fleas, educated dogs, jugglers, ventriloquists, living statuary, fat boys, giants, dwarfs, rope dancers American Indians, and Negro minstrels (most of whom were white men painted in the familiar blackface style).

Painters received little encouragement, for most Americans had little time to cultivate the arts. While the people's chief pleasure was to see themselves in portraits, they were also fond of seeing nature in woodland scenes and landscapes.

In the musical arts, opera companies were just beginning to appear on the American stage, while many vocalists, like Jenny Lind, became public favorites.

JOHN WANAMAKER and Company in Philadelphia gained reputation as America's "finest clothing house," featuring latest fashions. Illinois store (r.) advertised suits for $7 to $12 in 1855. Store also offered shotguns, groceries, with "produce taken same as cash."

WAR DECLARED
AGAINST OLD GOODS AND HIGH PRICES.
WM. H. KELLY.
DRY GOODS
READY-MADE CLOTHING.

ELEGANT JEWELRY AND SILVERWARE were offered to Boston's wealthy citizens at Stanwood's store. Although the day of huge fortunes had not arrived yet, the standard of living was improving. Modest fortune was $10,000, while $20,000 represented great wealth.

NEW YORK'S WINTER GARDEN, fashionable social meeting place and a deluxe beer garden (right), was patronized by capacity crowds of German immigrants on Sundays. Well-dressed city folk promenaded and danced to the music of a conservative orchestra on the second tier, as other interested spectators lined the balcony sections on either side. On the ground floor, waiters serving beer and other refreshments were busy satisfying demands of customers.

Beer drinking was one of the gayer aspects of entertainment and social life which helped to break down the older, austere Puritan tradition of weekdays spent in hard work and Sabbaths devoted to contemplation and quiet relaxation.

Another famous upper-class drinking place in New York was the Gem Saloon, an adjunct of the Broadway Theater on the west side of Broadway. The Gem boasted the city's largest mirror, and at its long bar, celebrities could rub elbows with Tammany bigwigs, leading New Yorkers, and substantial German immigrants.

Other respectable establishments of this type sprang up in numerous cities, such as Cincinnati, St. Louis, Louisville, Chicago, and Milwaukee, where the German population was large. By 1860 New York had the third largest German population of all the cities of the world, including those in Germany itself. This was another indication that the United States was fast becoming a "nation of nations."

EXCLUSIVE SUMMER RESORT at Saratoga, N. Y., was popular with the wealthy, who liked its elegance and formality, as well as medicinal springs. Later, Southerners began to pass up Northern resorts in favor of such Southern vacation resorts as Old Point Comfort, Fauquier White Sulphur Springs.

MOST FASHIONABLE of the sea-bathing resorts was Newport, R. I., where society gathered in summer months to relax in its cool breezes. Elaborate homes, cottages and hotels dotted the shoreline. Along the beach mixed bathing in cumbersome bathing suits of the day became a popular pastime.

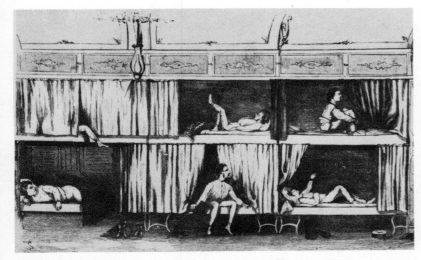

FIRST SLEEPING CARS were built by George Pullman in 1858, containing tiers of bunks on one side of the car only. He remodelled two old coaches into ten sleeping sections and two washrooms. They were furnished in cherry, upholstered in plush, lighted by oil lamps, heated with big stoves.

WONDERS OF NATURE, such as Natural Bridge, Va. (above), were visited by many Americans as part of the movement to develop their free-time out-of-doors activities. The writings of Thoreau, Emerson and others encouraged people to re-discover beauties of nature and preserve them.

STEAM CALLIOPES were installed in luxury steamboats or hauled in horse-drawn carts. Patented by Joshua Stoddard in 1855 and considered his masterpiece, the calliope survives today only as a circus curiosity.

CORN HUSKING was one of the popular "bees" enjoyed by the early American rural family. When labor was scarce or illness or accident struck, the folk of nearby farms displayed their characteristic spirit of cooperation by gathering together to perform the necessary tasks of the harvest. Finishing all the work in one day, they were treated to the best food the farm could afford, enjoyed dancing and genial fellowship in the evening.

NEW YORK SHAKERS literally shook the building as they enjoyed a good rousing barn dance. Pledged to a life of strict celibacy regarding marriage and reproduction, Shakers were intent on building a perfect community.

SPELLING MATCHES gave the winner prestige because he could "spell down" the other country folk. Nearest to a game organized into teams, even though the victory sought was an individual championship, the hard-fought spelling bees also enabled rural folk to increase their vocabularies.

SCAVENGER PIGS roamed city streets, fed on refuse, but were "too deficient in organization" to keep the streets clean. Roving pigs became so numerous in Cincinnati and New York they were often rounded up by police (above) and either sold at auction or driven to the pound.

◀ **MAY DAY** traditionally was moving day in New York. Custom originated from a city ordinance requiring anyone planning to move to do so by May 1, so that the city directory could be completed on schedule. Some society ladies were ashamed to occupy same house more than year. House servants were kept on run.

SPORTS

Organized pastimes encourage relaxation

Early American settlers, intent on conquering a wilderness, had little time for organized sports. Relaxation was rough and ready, emphasizing individual skill.

By the mid-19th century, however, Americans, especially in cities, turned more to organized sport. English influence was visible in the development of cricket clubs, especially in Philadelphia. The first cricket club was organized in 1842 and matches with Canadian teams were started in 1853.

Baseball appeared on the scene later with the first formal club organized in 1845. But the sport spread rapidly, gaining wider popularity than cricket. Amateur clubs sprang up during the 1850's.

In the years before the Civil War, horse racing fell into disrepute as gambling elements gained control. At the same time, rural America became interested in trotting races as improved roads stimulated the popularity of speed. Friendly matches between owners of trotters widened into organized racing. By 1840 most cities had courses laid out for trotting races.

Boxing, although frowned on in many areas, had a certain popularity on the rough frontier. One of the most popular boxers of the era was John Morrisey, who won the heavyweight championship in 1853 and remained unbeaten until he retired five years later to enter New York politics.

German influence on sport was reflected in the growing importance of gymnasiums. Prussians, fleeing persecution in the 1840's, brought gymnastic sports with them. Although individualistic Americans cared little for military-type drills, the gymnasium stimulated fencing and wrestling.

Yachting also gained popularity, encouraged by the victory of the *America* in an international yachting race in 1851.

Despite the growing interest in organized sport, Americans did not abandon their individual pursuits. Hunting and fishing were major pastimes and pleasure of a buffalo hunt lured Eastern sportsmen to the plains.

BASEBALL, THE NATIONAL SPORT, was invented by Abner Doubleday at Cooperstown, N. Y., in 1839. Familiar with English rounders, town and barn ball, one-old-cat, four-old-cat played on a square field, Doubleday outlined a more systematic game on a diamond-shaped field, with a team limit of 11 men. Each team batted until three men had been put out. The team that scored 21 runs first was declared the victor. Hitting the base runner to get him out ("soaking") was soon discontinued.

FIRST BASEBALL TEAM was the New York Knickerbockers, organized in 1845 by Alexander J. Cartwright. Their code of rules outlined the modern game, calling for nine men on a side, flat bases, a diamond with bases 90 feet apart. Wearing blue trousers, white shirts, straw hats, they played the first match game ever held between two ball clubs, June 19, 1846, losing to the New York Nine.

"OUT-OF-DOORS" MOVEMENT made sleighing and skating two of the most popular winter sports. The Boston Neck (l.) was turned into a perfect race course during sleighing time, and was the scene of many exciting competitions involving the fastest horses, the most beautiful sleighs. This popular diversion also permitted young ladies to join the men in sleighing frolics. Outdoor skating had been a popular sport since colonial days. In pursuit of "manly outdoor exercises," huge crowds flocked to lakes, rinks, any frozen stream or pond, or to New York's Central Park (right).

WRESTLING was a favorite amusement in Midwestern communities, where rough-and-tumble activity attracted an audience that needed no tickets. There were few, if any, rules. The object was to get the opponent down — by any means.

PRIZE-FIGHTING was considered by the press as an uncivilized British importation. It was not unusual for death or disfiguration to result from brutal fighting with bare knuckles and lax laws. Laws prohibiting boxing in America were numerous. In 1849, to escape the law, a bout was held in the backwoods of Maryland in which, for $10,000, Tom Hyer beat Yankee Sullivan. By 1860 boxing grew popular as a spectator sport, moved uptown, providing the public with the excitement it craved.

COCK FIGHTING appealed to many spectators, provided them with an opportunity to gamble and to witness gory spectacles. An especially popular pastime in the South and West, it was practiced under cover in New England towns.

TROTTING MATCHES as well as horse racing had long been accepted as a national sport. Particularly popular in Boston, light harness racing was a highlight of almost every state and county fair in the country. Utilitarian, in that it improved the speed and stamina of horses, trotting also avoided the heavy commercialism that characterized race track betting. Hiram Woodruff, the era's most beloved sports figure, was the country's master reinsman. His career (1833-65) mirrors the story of trotting.

CELEBRATED FIGHTING PIG, "Pape," defeated a heavier dog in 37 minutes on March 18, 1849. Like cock-fighting, this grisly spectator "sport" was accompanied by furious betting, and attracted its followers from all walks of society.

ROPER'S GYM was one of many established after Charles Follen and Charles Beck, following German methods, first taught gymnastics in U.S. in 1825. After the German emigration of 1848, Turnvereins became centers of physical education in German communities, like Milwaukee, Cincinnati.

HUNTERS' PARADISE was America in the mid-19th century, as many enjoyed shooting matches for ducks, turkeys, and buffalo. During this period game abounded in most of the country. Combining profit with pleasure, hunting gave Americans an outlet from business strife, city life.

HARVARD FOOTBALL GAME between freshmen and sophomores (in top hats) was a rugged affair frequently ending in a bloody free-for-all fight. It served as an expression of inter-class rivalry in most colleges. The game was played by a freshman ball carrier in the center backed up by all his teammates resisting an attack by the sophomores. The latter tried to recover the ball and push, throw, or kick it over the opponent's goal. The riots that usually followed led Harvard and Yale to abolish the game in 1860. First organized team in the U.S. was Oneida Football Club, formed in 1867 by Gerrit S. Miller, who recognized that football would be improved by a team of players cooperating to advance the ball and defend the goal line.

PAUL BUNYAN, legendary lumberjack, shaped the earth into a ball so Columbus could discover America. With Babe, his great blue ox, he plowed the ditch for the Mississippi River. On another occasion, he reversed a train so its whistle could catch up with the engine. Tall tales of Bunyan's prowess caught on rapidly in U.S., were matched only by Texas cowboys.

YACHT AMERICA surprised the world August 22, 1851, by trouncing the 14 swiftest vessels of England's Royal Yacht Squadron, the most distinguished sailing club in existence. For its victory on the difficult 60-mile course around Isle of Wight, the yacht was awarded "The America's Cup." Famed trophy remained in U.S. despite efforts of British yachtsmen.

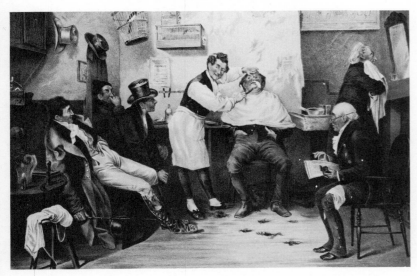

INTEREST IN SPORTS of every sort grew to such heights that people of all classes eagerly awaited the latest news of athletic contests. The barber shop rated as a favorite meeting place where the games and players of the day were discussed, argued, and gossiped about by partisan fans.

"AMERICAN FOREST SCENE," a Currier lithograph, depicts maple sugar time, one of the most picturesque features of rural life in the spring. To those who participated in sugar-making in the maple woods, it was as much an occasion of recreation and social get-together as it was work.

AMERICA'S FIRST GREAT native actor was Edwin Forrest, who entertained theater-goers throughout country for more than three generations. As a personality, he aroused violent enthusiasm or bitter hostility because of his imperious vanity. Nevertheless, he impressed critics and audiences with his sincerity and the strong individuality of his interpretation. Forrest's acting was flavored with a rough, crude spontaneity and by a flair for oratory.

CHARLOTTE CUSHMAN was recognized as America's greatest actress. Her impressive appearance and brilliant vitality established her as a personality fitted for roles embodying majesty, great passion, and tragedy. She was outstanding as Lady Macbeth, Nancy Sykes, Meg Merrilies, and even in men's roles as Romeo, Cardinal Wolsey. As the leading stock actress for several companies, "Our Charlotte" charmed New York, Boston, London.

"PET AND PRIDE" of California was the title given to Lotta Crabtree, who scored her first major success in the role of Topsy. Several sentimental melodramas about the waif who regenerated drunken miners were written for her.

AMERICAN STAGE
Theater becomes respectable entertainment

The American stage was gaining in popularity by the middle of the 19th century. The nation, entering an era of expansion, found the theater keeping pace. More than ever before, it was satisfying the public's desire for stimulating entertainment. Urban playgoers and their country cousins cheered the heroes and hissed the villains as stock companies toured the land.

Although many visitors from abroad played to U.S. audiences, the American stage asserted its independence by performing more American plays and by developing native actors. Edwin Forrest, Charlotte Cushman, E. L. Davenport, Mrs. Mowatt, Joseph Jefferson, Lotta Crabtree, "Yankee" Hill, and William Warren Jr. were among the nation's first matinee idols.

Several theaters were built at New York, each establishing a stock company, and specializing in a given type of entertainment. The Bowery Theater, most imposing in the country, seating 3,500, opened Oct. 23, 1826. Boston also busied itself organizing theatrical companies as Puritan opposition began to be replaced by polite sophistication.

"FUNNIEST MAN who ever lived" was title bestowed on Billy Burton. His farcical, broad-humor roles won him a solid following through the country. With his wife (above), he appears as Falstaff.

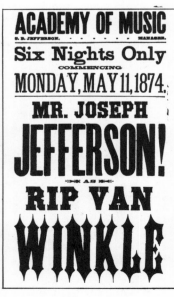

JOSEPH JEFFERSON III, "a poet among actors," attained popularity in the role of *Rip Van Winkle* which he played throughout the United States and in England.

BLOODY RIOT at Astor Place Opera House occurred in 1849 when British tragedian William MacReady appeared there. Anti-English mobs, resenting the superior attitude of European actors, rioted in the streets and set fire to the theater. Jealous Edwin Forrest incited the mobs. Twenty-three rioters were killed in the bloody fracas.

CASTLE GARDEN (above), originally a fort and later transformed into a theater, was the scene of Jenny Lind's triumphant New York debut. Barnum's American Museum (below) became nation's greatest entertainment palace.

P. T. BARNUM, MASTER SHOWMAN

"The American people love to be humbugged," was the watchword of Phineas Taylor Barnum. The fabulous success of the great showman proved his point. Born at Bethel, Conn., in 1810, Barnum went to work at thirteen. Jobs as clerk, storekeeper, lottery agent, newspaper editor, and boarding house keeper sharpened his insight into human nature.

TOM THUMB AND WIFE

Barnum broke into show business by buying a 161-year-old Negress — supposedly George Washington's nurse — for $1,000. A post-mortem after her death revealed 80 years had been tacked on her birth certificate, but Barnum already had pocketed the $1,500-a-week receipts.

Broke again in 1841, he purchased Scudder's Museum at New York, renamed it Barnum's Museum and paid off his debts within a year. Barnum hit pay dirt the following year when he found Charles Stratton at Bridgeport, Conn. Stratton, a midget less than two feet tall and weighing only sixteen pounds, was signed promptly by the promoter, who retitled him "General Tom Thumb." He was shown throughout U.S. and Europe.

Unique Barnum attractions included the world's tiniest midget, the famed Commodore Nutt, Japanese mermaids, a living white whale, automaton writer, and an Albino Negress. In addition to the exhibits, the museum held a "Moral Lecture Room" where uplifting dramas and farces were presented. Within a short time, the museum was a "must" for New Yorkers and rural visitors. His philosophy of "flattering the public so judiciously as not to have them suspect your intention" was paying off.

While he was presenting Gen. Tom Thumb to awed European audiences, he "discovered" Jenny Lind (r.), one of Europe's outstanding concert figures. He signed her for a tour of America at the unheard-of salary of $1,000 a night. It was a gamble that appealed to the adventurous Barnum.

"The Swedish Nightingale" made her spectacular debut at Castle Garden on September 11, 1850. The overflow crowds, lured by Barnum's publicity, battled for tickets and launched the singer on her extraordinary tour. Miss Lind gave 95 concerts and Barnum saw to it that towns along the route had ample advance notice. The nine-month tour grossed more than $700,000 for the pair. They are shown together in a sleigh (above).

MISS JENNY LIND

ADVENTURESS Lola Montez was the most notorious woman to appear on U.S. stage. Born in Ireland, she became famous at an early age as a beauty and dancer. Expelled by scandal from London, she toured Europe, captivated the Czar, became mistress of Ludwig of Bavaria. On U.S. trip in 1851, she toured Calif. mining camps, danced in ballet written for her.

COL. WOOD'S MUSEUM at Chicago originally consisted of a display of natural history specimens, a hall of paintings, and panorama of London. In 1864, Col. Wood re-built and enlarged the museum, turning it into a theater. He organized a stock company that became active in Chicago theatrical circles until building was destroyed by the great fire of 1871.

ART

Painters reflect life in the pre-Civil War era

Because Americans had little leisure in which to cultivate the arts, artists received scant encouragement. Nevertheless, there were significant developments in the painting of portraits, nature scenes, landscapes, and all types of genre subjects.

With professional photography still in its infancy, the desire of the people to see themselves in portraits stimulated a number of artists to develop this craft. New York became the home of a number of excellent portrait painters — Chester Harding, Robert Weir, Charles Elliott, William Page, G. Baker, and Daniel Huntington — who had the gift of catching a likeness in addition to creating a canvas that looked handsome on the wall. A few portrait painters grew wealthy.

Fondness for nature found expression in a group of painters known as the Hudson River School. They were chiefly self-taught, conscientious workmen who approached their subjects with a reverent spirit. Thomas Cole was the first American to paint landscapes professionally. Some of his contemporaries included Thomas Doughty, Asher Durand, Henry Inman, Thomas Hill, and Frederick Church, who painted fresh and vigorous scenes, dusky woodlands, mists, mountain peaks. Striving to learn a more faithful photographic representation of nature, many painters went to Germany to study. For twenty years or more, their improved technique showed the effects of this European training.

Extremely popular were such artists as John Mix Stanley, Charles Wimar, Carl Bodemer, and George Catlin — all of whom sought to capture the spirit of the American West before it passed into history.

"PAT LYON AT THE FORGE," by John Neagle, was one of the first American portraits free from the florid conventions of the time. Influenced strongly by Gilbert Stuart, leading portrait painter of the period, Neagle showed a firm understanding of character and used a sturdy and naturalistic method.

WILLIAM SIDNEY MOUNT was the first American to make a specialty of genre paintings, and pioneered in the discovery of the common people as subjects for paintings. Possessing a keen eye for humorous traits of rustic life and a shrewd observation of human nature, Mount utilized these abilities to create a limited number of striking paintings, such as *Ringing the Pig,* 1842 (l.), *Bargaining for a Horse,* and *The Truant Gamblers.*

STUDY OF INDIANS was the absorbing interest of German-born artist Charles F. Wimar, whose *Buffalo Hunt* (below) illustrates the prowess of the Plains' Indian in hunting the animal that was food, shelter, fuel and clothing for him. Though Wimar spent fifteen years in America learning his craft, his work revealed the influence of Lessing's Dusseldorf (Germany) school, which many American painters attended.

"JOLLY FLATBOATMEN" was one of many river scenes painted by George Caleb Bingham in the 1840-50 era. After studying at the Pennsylvania Academy of Fine Arts and in Europe, he moved to Missouri. Known as the "Mark Twain of the Mississippi Valley," he captured the spirit of the vigorous young nation with more accuracy and charm than any genre painter of the period. Bingham's fame also rests on colorful, humorous scenes of small town politics, such as *The Stump Speaker*. For another example of his fine works see *Verdict of the People*, on page 131.

EMANUEL LEUTZE, born in Germany, devoted himself to works of early American themes, such as the famous *Westward the Course of Empire Takes Its Way*, now in Capitol at Washington.

"INDIAN SURVEYING" by De Witt Clinton Bontelle (1855) symbolically portrays the dispossessed Indian. A warrior views his former hunting grounds, dotted with houses and farms.

"AN OSAGE SCALP DANCE," by John Mix Stanley (1845) shows a chief during the triumphant dance stopping one of his warriors from striking woman (since only men were scalped).

"POWER OF MUSIC" by genre painter William Mount showed his Dutch influence. He was one of the first American artists to study Negro face and character.

FLOWERY COTTON print (1847) depicts Gen. Zachary Taylor at the Battle of Palo Alto. Such prints were popular as draperies during the era.

RUSSIAN claims north of 51st parallel along American Pacific Coast were portrayed in Chinese print.

DAGUERREOTYPE, invented by Louis Daguerre of France in 1839, was first permanent photograph, gained rapid popularity.

STEPHEN FOSTER
Foremost among American song writers, Stephen Collins Foster (1826-1864), received his musical inspiration from the songs of the southern slaves. Born at Lawrenceburg, Pa., of Scotch-Irish parents, he showed an early proficiency with the piano, the flageolet, and the flute. Educated mostly by tutors, he attended Jefferson College for only a few weeks. He worked for a short time in his brother's business at Cincinnati, but, convinced that music was his life, returned to composing, which brought him eventual fame and a measure of financial success. His *Massa's In De* *Cold, Cold Ground, Old Black Joe, Nelly Was A Lady, Oh Susannah, Nellie Bly* and *My Old Kentucky Home* (painting at left) were widely known and sung. Christy's Minstrels, with whom he made an agreement in 1851, and other groups, popularized his songs throughout the nation. Foster is shown at right with his friend George Cooper, lyricist of *Sweet Genevieve*. Taken only two weeks before the composer's death, the photo apparently refutes some of the lurid accounts of his last years, which depicted him as a drunken slum dweller. Foster died in poverty, but left more than 150 songs which live for their melody, simplicity, and feeling.

CRYSTAL PALACE, a structure of glass and iron, housed the first world's fair to be held in the United States (1853). Titled "The Exhibition of the Industry of All Nations," the New York fair epitomized the industrial era which was revolutionizing the country. The *Palace*, heralded as an outstanding architectural achievement, was short-lived. It was totally destroyed by fire in October, 1858.

FOUNDERS and members of the New York Philharmonic Society assumed this sober pose after sponsoring the group's initial concert in 1842.

WASHINGTON MONUMENT, world's tallest masonry structure (555½ feet), was planned as early as 1833, though the cornerstone was not laid until 1848. The monument, not completed until 1884, reached height shown above in 1853.

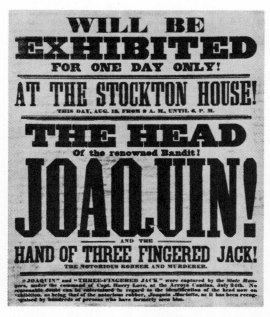

CALIFORNIA'S ROBIN HOOD, Joaquin Murrietta, and his aide, "Three-fingered Jack," were leaders of a band of desperadoes. After their capture Murrietta's head and one of Jack's hands were pickled in alcohol, auctioned off for $36.

FOUR ACES is the winning hand in this poker game on a Mississippi riverboat, where games of chance attracted both professionals and amateurs. Traveling by steamboat was popular with southern planters, on their way to New Orleans.

FASHIONS

New York society belles were typical fashion plates. Women wore pounds of clothing, favored velvets, silks, satins of many colors (decorated with fluttering ribbons, silk tassels), and rich cloaks with gaudy hoods and lining. Enormous bonnets, sleeves full above the elbows, tiers of skirts were popular out-of-doors (l.). View of bedroom (r.) shows a conservatively-decorated nightgown. The stiff petticoat, standing on the floor, was a popular fashion highlight of this era.

BLOOMER COSTUME was introduced by Elizabeth Smith Miller at Seneca Falls, New York (1851), as a new dress style "to give a more correct idea of the human form." It symbolized the suffrage movement which sought to give women a position of equality with men. The attempts of femininist editor Amelia Bloomer to popularize the style attached the name "bloomer" to the costume ridiculed by males.

LATEST FASHIONS OF 1857 featured large full skirts and slender waists. For indoor wear the two ladies (l.) have lace-trimmed brown silk, violet terry velvet. The ball dress is of white tulle with blue silk, the opera cloak of white cashmere, trimmed with pink plush over double-skirted pink silk dress. Amount of detail varied.

WINTER FASHIONS of 1849-50 found gentlemen sporting high silk hats and mutton chops. Increased popularity of silk hat dealt a hard blow at beaver trapper faced with a dwindling market. Beards, which were experiencing a periodic decline in the public esteem, did not regain favor in urban areas until Civil War years.

DISASTERS

Fire constituted an ever-present threat to American cities, constructed largely of wooden buildings. Volunteer firemen were considered a lesser peril by some citizens. Some volunteers were so eager to answer the alarm that they dressed on the run or at the scene of the blaze. The spirited competition to get there first frequently led to fist fights and near riots while the fire raged unchecked. Cincinnati was the first American city to establish a salaried fire department (1853). In the summer of that same year, an $800,000 fire at Oswego, New York (above), destroyed much of the city's business area. It burned 45 acres, 113 buildings, and left almost 2,000 persons homeless overnight.

STEAMBOATS of all types were equipped with comforts and conveniences to attract excursionists, especially on the Mississippi. The increased traffic resulted in many accidents, explosions. On Sept. 8, 1860, the *Lady Elgin*, returning from Milwaukee to Chicago with excursionists, was rammed by a lumber schooner on Lake Michigan. It sank with a loss of 297 lives.

NETWORK OF RAILROADS comprising more than 9,000 miles of track by 1850 created a revolution in the nation's life. Railroads helped fulfill the American's dream of progress and desire to conquer distance. Railroad disasters, however, took their toll. On Aug. 29, 1853, an accident on Camden and Amboy Railroad near Burlington, N. J., killed 21, injured 75.

A HOUSE DIVIDED

Union is split as South forms Confederacy; Lincoln steers nation through Civil War, but his leadership is lost for the critical Reconstruction years

Contrary to popular belief, the Civil War was not fought over abolition of slavery. And despite the fast growing strength of Northern abolitionists, neither Lincoln nor his party had intended to wipe out the South's "peculiar institution." But most Northerners had come to feel that while they might overlook Southern slavery in order to preserve the Union, they had no moral right to permit its extension into the new West. The unavoidable task was, in Lincoln's words, to "arrest the further spread of it, and place it where the public mind shall rest in the belief that it is in the course of ultimate extinction."

To this the Southerners, who had been accustomed to dominating federal policy, could never submit. So long as Democrats or compromising Whigs held the government, a showdown was postponed. But in 1860 Lincoln and the Republican Party, strongly committed to halting the extension of slavery, captured more electoral votes than the other three tickets combined. The South saw itself permanently outnumbered and the day of compromise past. It could only uphold "Southern rights" by withdrawing from the Union and establishing its own government — the Confederate States of America.

At this point a broader belief took over — whether, as Lincoln put it, "in a free government, the minority have the right to break up the government whenever they choose." The new President, a Westerner whose faith in popular rule was as strong as Jefferson's, saw this more clearly than his advisers. While others urged the South be allowed to go its way, Lincoln stood for preserving the Union. "If we fail," he said, "it will go far to prove the incapability of the people to govern themselves."

In this situation, armed clash was inevitable. Lincoln announced in his Inaugural Address that he intended to hold the "property and places belonging to the government, and to collect the duties and imposts." When he tried to supply Fort Sumter in Charleston Harbor, Southern batteries opened fire and war began.

Short War Expected

Few Americans on either side expected the fighting to be long or costly. With the Union defeat at the first Battle of Bull Run, however, the opposing sides prepared for real war. In this the South had an advantage in the brilliant generalship of Robert E. Lee, and the aroused spirit of a people who believed they were defending their rights. But the North had more telling strength: the sound judgment and firm leadership of Lincoln; a flourishing industry for the support of modern war; a preponderance of population; and a navy with which to blockade Southern ports.

Most of the action occurred on the major front in the 100 miles between the two enemy capitals — Washington and Richmond. For the first two years events were shaped by Lee's masterful strategy. While Lincoln looked in vain for a general who could win battles in the East, Union troops on another front were pounding through the enemy's back door — the Mississippi West. Largely under the leadership of Gen. Ulysses S. Grant, federal forces cleared the Mississippi

LINCOLN OF ILLINOIS

River and struck across the lower Appalachians into the deep South.

In the summer of 1863 Lee invaded Pennsylvania, attacked strongly-entrenched Union forces at Gettysburg, and suffered a defeat which has been called the turning point of the war. But it was actually the blockade of Southern ports and the invasion of the Western army which brought the Confederacy to its knees. By 1864 Lee had an opponent along the Potomac — Gen. Grant — who matched him in daring and persistence, if not in strategy. Finally, with a Union Army marching northward from Georgia along his very line of supply, the harrassed Lee was obliged to surrender to Grant at Appomattox in April, 1865.

Southern Support Firm

For four years the people of the South had supported their cause with gallantry and fortitude. Even the slaves remained faithfully at their duties throughout the war, releasing more whites for service. In the North support for the war was generally firm, though in some instances lacking. An example was the 1863 draft riot in New York City. In the five slaveholding border states remaining loyal to the Union, feeling was bitterly divided.

As the figure of Washington at times virtually held the Revolution together, so the figure of Lincoln piloted the nation through the storm of civil war. Recognizing that for both foreign and domestic support the North needed a "cause," he announced the freeing of the slaves in his famous Emancipation Proclamation of January 1, 1863. Had Lincoln lived, Reconstruction might have been different. But his assassination was followed by bitterness.

The new President, Andrew Johnson of Tennessee, was well-meaning but unequal to the situation. Congress, led by Sen. Thaddeus Stevens, an implacable foe of the South, became the dominant branch of government. It pursued a program of Southern "reconstruction" designed to humiliate secessionists and make mere tributary provinces of the Southern states. When President Johnson opposed this, his opponents in Congress contrived to bring impeachment charges against him, but failed by one vote to get the necessary two-thirds majority for conviction.

Reconstruction was imposed on the South by the armed power of military occupation, and carried out largely by Northern opportunists known as "carpetbaggers." By 1870, ten Southern states had been re-admitted to the Union with the native white population shorn of power, and with corruption rampant. The election of Gen. Grant to the presidency had, by his indifference, given the despoilers free rein. Not until President Hayes withdrew federal troops in 1877 did Reconstruction come to an official close. Its scars — a one-party South and slow progress for Negro rights — have persisted ever since. Slavery had been abolished, the Union saved, and popular government vindicated; but new problems, of great magnitude, had arisen to replace the old.

★ ★ ★

◀ **NUMBER DEAD** on both sides in this "bloodiest American war" was about 600,000 — at least half of them by disease. This photograph of a wounded Union soldier guarded by a comrade in a deserted camp shows the fatigue and pain of men hurt in battle. Heavy casualties were partially caused by

frequent use of newer, more accurate weapons while tactics remained the same — free movement and open maneuvers. The South, scene of most of the fighting, naturally suffered most. With more than four million men engaged, however, impact of the war was brought home to all Americans.

FOR PRESIDENT
ABRAHAM LINCOLN
OF ILLINOIS

FOR VICE PRESIDENT
HANNIBAL HAMLIN
OF MAINE

CAMPAIGN PICTURES of the 1860 election include the fine photographic study of Lincoln above. It was made by Brady in New York at the time of the Cooper Union address less than three months before the nominating convention. Lincoln once remarked that this portrait and that speech made him president. The traditional lithographed campaign poster at right shows Lincoln and his running mate, Hannibal Hamlin of Maine, the Vice Presidential candidate of the Republican party. The scathing political caricature below it, entitled "Miscegenation," attacks Lincoln's reputed devotion to the cause of abolition. It is typical of the rough and ready political tactics of the period, which witnessed many abusive attacks on Lincoln.

LINCOLN ELECTED

Secession in the South follows 1860 election

The seeds of civil war ripened in the early spring of 1860 when the nation's two great parties called their nominating conventions for the presidency. The strife-ridden Democrats convened in April at Charleston, S. C. They were met by a demand flung by William L. Yancey of Alabama for complete guarantees of the continuance of slavery, or independence for the South.

Senator G. E. Pugh of Ohio answered for the North. "Gentlemen of the South, you mistake us — we will not do it." The Alabama delegation walked out and the convention adjourned without making a nomination. The Southerners called their own convention at Baltimore and nominated John C. Breckinridge of Kentucky. The regular Democrats nominated Stephen A. Douglas, who believed the issues of slavery could be resolved by compromise.

The new Republican Party met at Chicago in June. The leading contender for the nomination was Sen. Seward of New York. Abraham Lincoln of Illinois appeared as a compromise candidate. His pro-Union sentiments were well known, and he had gained some notice the previous February in an address at Cooper Union in New York. The convention nominated him on the third ballot because he was the man with fewest

"WIDE-AWAKERS" was name of Republican campaigners who paraded in Hartford, Conn., and in other Eastern cities in a uniform of cambric capes and caps.

EXTREME PESSIMISM expressed by James Gordon Bennett's New York *Herald* is lampooned in this *Vanity Fair* cartoon which shows Bennett shutting up shop while cattle graze in streets of New York after election of Lincoln. Horace Greeley fiddles over desolation at right. Bennett and Greeley, influential editors, were very partisan.

SOUTHERN NOMINEE John C. Breckinridge of Kentucky was the candidate of insurgent Southerners on pro-slavery ticket and carried the South. Chosen as his running mate was Joseph Lane of Oregon.

VICE PRESIDENT of the Confederacy elected at the Montgomery convention of 1861 was Alexander Stephens of Georgia. Stephens was an old friend of Lincoln and accepted the appointment sadly out of a sense of duty to his home state for he privately felt the Confederacy was doomed from the start to fall before the economic might of the industrial North. As late as Nov. 14, 1860, he expressed himself as opposed to secession.

JEFFERSON DAVIS

The President of the Confederacy and his wife posed for this daguerreotype before he was elected to the office which he held throughout the Civil War. Davis was a former U.S. senator, Sec. of War, planter and slave owner. He was a moderate in politics and exercised his almost dictatorial war powers with the utmost restraint. Davis was a West Pointer and a fellow officer of Lincoln in the Black Hawk War. During the Mexican War he served as a colonel of Volunteers and won distinction at the battle of Buena Vista. His military background led him to pry incessantly into military matters. Many of his generals resented the constant military advice which Davis persisted in giving.

enemies. The remnants of the American and Whig parties convened at Baltimore, formed the Constitutional Union Party, and chose John Bell as their Presidential candidate.

Although Lincoln received no electoral votes in the South (which Breckinridge carried), he won 1,866,352 popular votes; Douglas received 1,375,157; Breckinridge, 849,781; and Bell, 589,581. Lincoln had clearly benefited from the sharp division among his opponents.

Learning of Lincoln's election, the South Carolina legislature called for a state convention, which met at Columbia on Dec. 20. The delegates voted unanimously for the secession of their state from the Union, declaring that the step was necessary because of the North's continuing attack on slavery and because of the accession to power of a President and party that were purely sectional, "whose opinions . . . are hostile to slavery." Secession extended as seven other states joined S. C. in a convention in Montgomery, Ala., in February, 1861. They formed a provisional Confederate government and framed a constitution stressing states' rights. Jefferson Davis, former U.S. Sec. of War, was chosen President, Alexander Stephens, Vice President. A distinguished Cabinet of Southern leaders was named.

A compromise proposal, introduced into the U.S. Senate by John Crittenden of Ky., to allow slavery south of 36°-30′, was rejected. Southern troops began to seize Federal arsenals in the South. The war had begun.

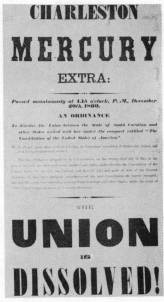

SECESSION is proclaimed in flaming headlines by this extra issued by the Charleston *Mercury* after South Carolina withdrew from the Union.

CONFEDERACY inaugurated its president, Jefferson Davis, as the hands on the Statehouse clock at Montgomery, Ala. pointed to 1 p.m. on Feb. 18, 1861. Simultaneously Abraham Lincoln traveled to Washington for inauguration.

CONFEDERATE CAPITOL throughout the Civil War was the Statehouse at Richmond, Va. The Confederate Congress sat in its Hall of Delegates. There also sat President Davis, shown with his cabinet (center) in conference with Gen. Lee. The government of the Confederate States was transferred from Montgomery, Ala., to Richmond on July 20, 1861. At the same time Davis moved his wife and family to the new executive mansion in Richmond (right). Davis and his family fled from the house before the victorious Federal troops when Richmond fell in 1865. The mansion, known as the Confederate White House, was turned into a museum which now houses the South's largest collection of Confederate memorabilia.

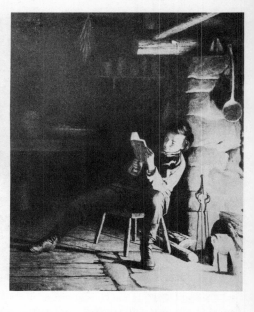

LINCOLN'S LIFE

Abraham Lincoln was born on Feb. 12, 1809, in his pioneer father's log cabin in Hardin County, Kentucky. He went three years to a grammar school. Beyond that he was largely self-taught. Despite his lack of formal schooling, Lincoln was well educated by reading at night by his cabin fire. Hard work was the rule of the frontier and Abe found employment as a young man splitting fence rails. The nickname "rail splitter" followed him when he went into politics.

YOUNG LINCOLN worked at one job and another, never settling on one thing, until he began the study of law. He worked in a country store where he read books between customers' visits. In 1828 and again in 1831 he made the long river voyage on a flatboat to New Orleans. There he saw the infamous slave market which, it is recorded, aroused his indignation at its barter of human lives. Lincoln finally settled upon the law, which he read as a clerk until he was admitted to the bar. Then he buckled down to the life of a successful, circuit-riding country lawyer, a career he loved.

LINCOLN, THE LAWYER, was gregarious, popular and increasingly successful. His wide acquaintanceship on the judicial circuit he followed won him a seat in the Illinois State Legislature. He became a man of importance in Springfield, where he established his law practice. In 1846 he was elected to Congress by the Whigs and had his first photographic portrait made (left). From this point on Lincoln was continuously in politics and a power in the state of Illinois, although he did not seek reelection. During this middle period of his life he was perfecting the speaking techniques which brought him to national fame in his 1858 debates with Stephen A. Douglas. It is in this period that the full-length photo at left portrays him. It was his earliest full-length portrait and shows his figure clearly.

LINCOLN'S HOUSE at Springfield, Ill., is the only one he ever owned. At first a simple one-and-a-half story dwelling, it was enlarged by Mrs. Lincoln, who felt that it lacked prestige.

LINCOLN'S FAMILY PORTRAIT includes Mrs. Lincoln, Willis, Robert, Thomas (Tad) and the President. A fourth son, Edward, died in infancy. At left, Lincoln poses with Tad for Mathew Brady, famed photographer. He married Mary Todd Lincoln (r.) in 1842.

Inauguration

Lincoln becomes President and offers the South peace

War was in the air that bleak Feb. 23rd of 1861 when Abraham Lincoln rode into Washington to receive the Presidency of a divided nation. He had come secretly and by night through Baltimore where his advisors feared a plot upon his life. Only 17 days earlier the Confederacy had been formed in Montgomery, Ala., and Washington was full of federal troops summoned to keep order during the inauguration.

In Lincoln's pocket was a list of cabinet choices which was to reveal his broad grasp of the powers of the Presidency and his faculty for laying aside personal feelings in distinguishing true ability. The new Republican Party was little more than a coalition of conflicting elements united only in a desire to save the Union. To consolidate these elements into a working government was Lincoln's first great task. He had defeated for the Republican nomination the great William H. Seward of New York and Sen. Salmon P. Chase of Ohio as well as veteran politicians Edward Bates, Simon Cameron of Pennsylvania and William L. Dayton.

Coalition Formed

Lincoln saw in these leaders of various wings of the party a coalition which would strengthen the nation for the struggle ahead, and named his bitterest political foes to his cabinet. He chose Seward as the Secretary of State and the great abolitionist Chase as Treasury Secretary. He appointed Cameron Secretary of War; Edward Bates, a St. Louis conservative, as Attorney General; Gideon Welles of New England as Secretary of the Navy; Montgomery Blair of Maryland, Postmaster General, and Caleb B. Smith of Indiana, Secretary of the Interior.

Seward and Chase were both powerful men and political rivals. Lincoln had to appoint Cameron to fulfill a convention commitment. Welles was a political enemy of Seward. Blair was aligned politically against both Seward and Chase. Lincoln relied upon judgment and dominance to weld such personalities into an effective administration.

Lincoln's cabinet was still incomplete when he rode up Pennsylvania Avenue with President Buchanan to take his oath at the Capitol. The new President made there in his inaugural address a final effort to conciliate the South. His speech, gentle in tone, contained three main points: Lincoln pledged himself not to interfere directly with slavery in the states where it then existed; he promised to enforce the Fugitive Slave Law; and he declared he would maintain the Union. "In your hands," he told the South, "is the momentous issue of civil war. The government will not assail you." But he warned: "No state, upon its own mere motion, can lawfully get out of the Union."

LINCOLN'S INAUGURATION was recorded for history in this photograph by Brady. In his inaugural address the new President pledged himself to enforce the law and support the Union. He had arrived from Springfield ten days earlier after passing through Baltimore, perhaps in disguise, as Thomas Nast drawing above shows, because of the violently Southern sympathies of many in Baltimore. Brady photographed him on day of arrival looking tired and worn (right) after journey from Illinois.

CABINET which Lincoln selected represented a coalition of opposing factions in the Republican Party. Throughout the war it served to hold the support of diverse elements. In this portrait are, seated left to right, Edward Bates, Attorney General; William H. Seward, Secretary of State; Salmon P. Chase, Secretary of the Treasury; Mr. Lincoln; Caleb Smith, Secretary of the Interior; Simon B. Cameron, Secretary of War. Standing, left to right, are Gideon Wells, Secretary of the Navy; Montgomery Blair, Postmaster General, and Lt. Gen. Winfield Scott, the Chief of Staff. Cameron, a Pennsylvania political boss, resigned after a series of procurement scandals, but the rest remained throughout most of the war. Only Lincoln's tact kept peace within this assemblage of brilliant but hostile minds.

UNFINISHED CAPITOL dome looms starkly over the scene of Lincoln's first inauguration. Raising of the dome and construction of wings at either end of the building was not completed until 1863. Lincoln kept the work going during Civil War to boost public confidence in Union.

PRIVATE SECRETARIES to Lincoln are shown with the President. At left is John G. Nicolay. At right is assistant secretary John Hay, 22. The pair later collaborated on official biography and document collection of Lincoln. Hay became Sec. of State in 1898.

SEC. OF STATE William H. Seward, a brilliant and temperamental New Yorker, tried at first to dominate Lincoln and his cabinet. He later came to respect and admire Pres. Lincoln and served him ably.

"STAR OF THE WEST" steamed into Charleston Harbor on the night of Jan. 9, 1861 to deliver supplies to Major Anderson's garrison on Fort Sumter. A South Carolina harbor battery discovered the vessel and opened fire on it. The unarmed steamer beat a hasty retreat. Lincoln's attempts at provisioning the fort were as ineffectual as Davis's demands for federal withdrawal. Shortly after 4:30 a.m., April 12, heavy Southern guns opened on Fort Sumter (r.) in Charleston Harbor. The fortress fell to Confederate Gen. P. G. T. Beauregard's troops on April 13. The Civil War had begun.

HOSTILITIES BEGIN

War provoked by the Union's effort to reinforce beleaguered Fort Sumter

Abraham Lincoln, in his eloquent and moving address, on March 4, 1861, declared: "We are not enemies, but friends. We must not be enemies. Though passion may have strained, it must not break our bonds of affection." But the fall of Fort Sumter severed all ties.

The "Black Republican's" call to loyal state "war governors" for 75,000 volunteers was met with enthusiastic support. Border states, meanwhile, took sides. Virginia, Arkansas, North Carolina and Tennessee joined President Jefferson Davis's new Provisional Confederate Government. Delaware, Maryland, Kentucky and Missouri remained loyal to the North. Western counties of Virginia confirmed their allegiance to the Union by breaking away from Virginia to form the state of West Virginia in 1863.

The United States, or the Federal Union, consisted of 23 states with a population of 22,700,000. The Confederacy comprised 11 states with a white population which totaled only 5,500,000.

As the two governments, Federal and Confederate, took stock of their respective resources, it must have seemed to the former, remarked historian Ralph Volney Harlow, "that the war was won before it began, so great was its superiority in all material assets." The Confederacy controlled 57,000,000 acres under cultivation to 105,000,000 for the North. The Union's nearly 22,000 miles of railroad, forming an integrated network, more than offsetting the South's meager 9,000 miles.

EDMUND RUFFIN, the Southern partisan, fired the first shell on Sumter.

In terms of industrial manpower, the North had 1,300,000 factory workers and the Confederacy 110,000. The Southern cause was further assisted by 3,500,000 Negro slave laborers who contributed substantially to the war potential by performing such economic tasks as farming, road building, railroad construction and building substantial military fortifications at New Orleans, Charleston, Richmond and Vicksburg.

The marked discrepancy in physical and material numbers was in part made up by the obvious geographical advantages which the Confederacy enjoyed. By fighting on the defensive, the Southern forces were able to maintain shorter lines of communication. Moreover, Southern terrain was strategically served by numerous rivers which facilitated Confederate movements, thereby rendering the Federal commanders' tasks in the field more difficult.

The naval disposition of the opposing factions, on the Atlantic, from Maine to the West Indies, favored the North. The Union had an advantage of 90 ships, mounting 783 guns, manned by some 9,000 seamen and well trained officers. The South had neither sufficient ships nor seamen, and her ports were closed after Lincoln pronounced a blockade of the Confederate coasts, from South Carolina to Florida on April 19, 1861. (See atlas, plate 21, for maps of all subsequently mentioned military and naval campaigns of Civil War.)

"GOING TO THE FRONT!" intermingled with boisterous cheering from thousands of throats, as New York's 7th Regiment marched past the Astor House. On April 15, Lincoln issued a proclamation calling upon the governors of the loyal states for 75,000 militia to serve for three months.

FIRST BLOOD OF WAR was shed in Baltimore when a citizen-soldier melee broke out. As Boston's 6th Massachusetts Volunteers marched through Maryland's capital, hissing, stone-throwing and shooting forced the exasperated troops to resort to fixed bayonets, leaving 100 dead in their wake.

UNION VOLUNTEER of 1861 like one in old tintype (l.) joined army for three-month enlistment, was termed a "summer soldier." When enlistments were up many of the Civil War's eager summer participants refused to re-enlist. Skylarking "Boys in Gray" at Richmond (c.) made light of war.

Over-confident soldiers on both sides approached the first Battle of Bull Run, the first severe lesson of the war, in the same jocular spirit. A private in Company F, 4th Michigan Infantry (r.) attests to the youthfulness of many volunteers who did not realize long, hard, grim fighting they faced.

HECTOR OF THE SOUTH, a Northern version of a Southern officer, "a'going to war in a rockin' chair wif mint julip and especial refinements by his side," indicated the North's contempt for the South's "gentleman army." Both antagonists said war would be over in six months. It was a common boast in the South that one Southerner could lick at least four Yankees. Many Southern officers had seen service with the U.S. army against England in 1812 and in Mexico in 1846-47. And many Union officers, like Gen. Wm. S. Harney, although born in the South, threw in their lot with the North after a period of indecision.

"AN ATTACK ON WASHINGTON" is anticipated, said a Northern poster (left), as "rumors floated about daily of Confederate plans to seize the capital." On April 22, Winfield Scott, 75, General-in-Chief of the Union armies, thought the capital "partially besieged, threatened, and in danger of being attacked on all sides in a day or two or three."

In 1860 the Regular Army consisted of 16,367 officers and men. There were, in addition, a number of graduates of West Point or of the Citadel and the Virginia Military Institute. In the South, Jefferson Davis's March 16, 1861 proclamation, calling for 100,000 volunteers for one year's service, was met with wild enthusiasm as thousands rallied behind the rebel cause. Lincoln's April 15 call for 75,000 troops proved inadequate, and on May 3 he urged an additional 500,000 for three years' service. A series of calls, varying in number, followed thereafter. Altogether the Union was required to **raise 2,763,670 militiamen, and furnished 2,772,-408,** which included some re-enlistments.

TWENTY-FOUR HOUR WONDERS burst upon the main street of every city when the war broke out. In the first flush of martial enthusiasm, over-zealous merchants and their clerks "left their ledgers to don handsome uniforms . . ."

BATTLE OF BULL RUN

The war's first major engagement, a "fumbling, sloppy bit of execution by dead green troops," took place halfway between Centreville and Manassas, Va., on July 21, 1861. Major Gen. Irvin McDowell's 30,000 Yankee soldiers, eager to seize the capital at Richmond, succeeded for a time in driving back Gen. Pierre Beauregard's 23,000 Confederate troops. McDowell hastily telegraphed the "victory" to Washington. Tide was turned suddenly in favor of the South by the arrival of Gen. Joseph E. Johnston's 9,000 men from Shenandoah Valley. The Union retreat melted quickly into a near-rout as officers and men ran for their lives.

BARBARA FRIETCHIE'S DEFIANCE of the South was hurled upon the figure of Stonewall Jackson during his entrance into Frederick, Maryland. An angered trooper raised his rifle but was stopped by Jackson, who admired the woman's courage. This legend inspired Whittier's famous poem.

"STONEWALL" JACKSON was regarded by Lincoln as "a seedy, sleepy-looking old fellow . . . who bestrode a regular Rosinante of a horse." Tenacious Maj. Gen. Thomas J. Jackson helped Beauregard and Bernard Bee terrorize the Union troops at Bull Run. Wounded, Gen. Bee rode down the Confederate line. "Look!" he cried. "There stands Jackson like a stone wall!"

FOOLISH CONGRESSMAN Alfred Ely of New York rode out of Washington to see the "grand fight" at Bull Run and promptly landed in a Richmond "pogey."

EDWIN M. STANTON'S jaw dropped upon hearing that his old political foe, Lincoln, had appointed him Secretary of War. Lincoln's choice proved a wise one.

GUERRILLA WARFARE broke out in Missouri between the forces aligned with Governor Claiborne Fox Jackson, an ardent secessionist, and friends of the Union cause. Called upon to join the North, Jackson cried out bitterly that he would send "no men to furnish or carry on such an unholy crusade." Numerous citizens opposing the secessionists' views were hanged and their homesteads set to the torch. Franz Sigel (r.) came to America as a Prussian refugee. In 1861 he raised the Union Third Missouri Infantry and became major general of volunteers after Pea Ridge battle.

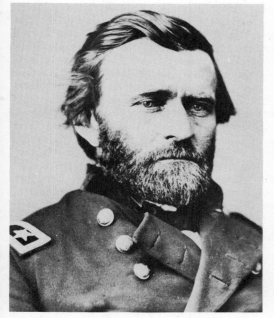

ULYSSES SIMPSON GRANT was described as a man "who knows how to do things." A fellow Union officer said: "He habitually wears an expression as if he had determined to drive his head through a brick wall, and was about to do it."

At Springfield, Ill., in 1861, a shabby-appearing new colonel with a short stogey jutting between clenched teeth rode into the camp of the 21st Regiment on an old white horse named "Mathusalem." A sentry saluted him airily — "Howdy, Colonel!" The adjutant was drunk and the troops disorderly. This was Grant's first command. He soon whipped the unruly troops into a disciplined army. On Feb. 6, 1862, Grant captured Fort Henry and 10 days later took Fort Donelson (r.) to open the way for Union advance in Tenn.

The great battle at Shiloh, on April 6th and 7th, was the opening salvo in the western campaign. Grant won his first major success here, pushing Gen. Albert S. Johnston's 40,000 troops back to Corinth, Mississippi.

AMERICA'S FIRST FIELD HOSPITAL for battle casualties was established at Shiloh, April 7, 1862. "Up to this time," said Grant, "surgeons with the army had no difficulty in finding room in the houses near our line for all sick and wounded, but now hospitals were overcrowded." Surgeons worked under hardship, "cutting off legs and arms with a most businesslike air."

WAR IN THE WEST constituted one-half of the Union's task in subduing the defensive-minded Lee. The eastern campaign was to be the other half. The object of the war in the West was to secure the Mississippi Valley, then strike at the heart of the Confederacy from the west. After Shiloh, Beauregard, Bragg, A. S. Johnston retreated from Corinth, Miss. (above).

OUTPOST AT ISLAND NO. 10 was built by Maj. Gen. Henry Halleck's three western armies to prevent an attack on the lower Mississippi. Following the loss of Forts Henry and Donelson, the Confederates made their stand at this stronghold, situated just opposite the northern boundary of Tennessee. The island fell on April 7, 1862, to Commodore Foote's boats.

BATTLE OF THE RAMS took place when a large Federal fleet of warships with armor plate and revolving gun turrets steamed downstream on June 6, 1862, to seize Memphis. Half the city's population lined the bluffs to cheer on their defenders. Commodore Davis took possession of Memphis, after a fight of 20 minutes, destroying seven of eight Confederate gunboats.

THE CAPTURE OF NEW ORLEANS by Flag-officer David G. Farragut, U.S.N., was planned in the spring of 1862. The utmost haste was necessary, since the Confederates were completing construction of four ironclads, all of the *Merrimac* type. Failing to silence the forts protecting the Mississippi, Farragut decided to run by them. Seventeen vessels, comprising five frigates, three sloops and nine gunboats, aided by David G. Porter's mortars, burst across the bars into the river. For six days Porter's 20 heavy schooners, armed with 13-inch mortars, bombarded the two Confederate forts. Fort Jackson became "a perfect wreck" on April 16.

Farragut, in the flagship *Hartford*, led his fleet across the tortuous, tricky waters off Forts Jackson and St. Phillip in a determined sortie past the rebel batteries. On April 24, Farragut smashed the bulk of the South's river fleet, including the powerful ram *Manassas*. The Federal squadron lay before New Orleans, and "the great seaport, the largest, the wealthiest, the strongest city of the Southland," surrendered on April 29 to Gen. Benjamin Butler's militia. Butler took over the command of New Orleans on May 1 and retained control until replaced by General Banks on December 17, 1862.

RAILROAD CONSTRUCTION was an important logistical phase of Union campaigns. The Elk River bridge was built by U.S. Army Engineers during the advance into Tennessee in 1862. While Northern rail-building proceeded apace, the South suffered gravely from a shortage of rails and rolling stock. Although cut off from Northern foundries and European factories, deprived of skilled labor, and faced with congested troop movements, the Confederate government was so restrained by laissez-faire ideas that it failed to assume control of transportation before February, 1865.

MONITOR AND VIRGINIA

The sunken U.S. steam frigate *Merrimac* was raised by the Confederacy and $172,500 appropriated to convert her into the ironclad *Virginia*. Oddly enough, few ever referred to the ram by her newly-christened name. Built by Lieut. J. M. Brooke, the *Virginia* made a bold attempt on March 8 to break up the blockade by demolishing the Union frigates *Cumberland* and *Congress* off Hampton Roads, Virginia. The North, shocked by the losses, thought the Navy doomed. The following morning, the *Virginia* was intercepted by the strange, deck-washed *Monitor*, invented by the Swedish engineer, John Ericsson (r.). Sailors at left pose on her deck, barely above the water line. As the *Monitor*, armed with two large cannon in a revolving turret, hove into view, the rebels chortled and immediately dubbed her the "Yankee cheese-box on a raft." The Southern attempt to break the blockade was thwarted.

YORKTOWN

The month-long siege of Yorktown in the spring of 1862 took place at the orders of Maj. Gen. McClellan. After Bull Run, Lincoln put the Army of the Potomac under his command. The objective was Richmond, but instead of advancing directly on the city, McClellan took his army down the Chesapeake. Washington newspapers had full acounts of the Lincoln-McClellan debates. Gen. Joseph Johnston followed them with interest. It seemed incredible to him that "any commander could be such an ass as thus publicly to announce that he was going to surprise his enemy, with date and place." Laboriously, McClellan arrayed his huge 20,000-pound 13-inch mortars against Yorktown. By nightfall of May 3 all batteries were ready. The big guns, however, never fired a shot for, by dawn, the rebels withdrew. McClellan squandered $7 million worth of stores (r.), and Richmond remained in Confederate control under Gen. Robert E. Lee, given command when Johnston was wounded.

PENINSULAR CAMPAIGN

NORTHERNERS were fully aroused to the seriousness of the war after Union's tragic defeat at First Bull Run. Gen. George B. McClellan replaced Winfield Scott as commander of Army of the Potomac, a portion of which is seen at left.

McClellan reorganized, drilled and equipped his army for an advance on Richmond. "More regiments poured in; under the blazing trees of autumn, 190,000 men, the mightiest army the world had seen, now complete with cavalry, artillery and engineers, wheeled to the orders of the young Napoleon." Ordered by Lincoln to set his army in motion, he proceeded, between March and July, 1862, from Yorktown to Williamsburg, to Fair Oaks, and thence within sight of Gen. Joseph Johnston's scouts outside Richmond. There he waited in vain for reinforcements from Gen. Irvin McDowell's forces.

The Peninsular campaign, culminating in the Seven Days' Battle (June 26 to July 1) failed, in spite of Federal victories, because Johnston and Robert E. Lee thwarted, in the end, McClellan's attempt to take Richmond.

JOHNSTON'S DUMMY GUNS overlooking the Heights of Centreville literally hypnotized the Army of the Potomac into a dead standstill. General McClellan's laughable winter-long wait forced indignant Northerners to ask: "If logs had immobilized him for winter, what would real guns do?"

SWAMP AND FLOOD and nature seemed to work against the Peninsular advance. "Heavy guns became bogged and the horses were unable to drag them." Fortunately for McClellan, the Grapevine Bridge, built by the 5th New Hampshire Infantry, enabled Federal troops to turn tide at Fair Oaks.

FAIR OAKS
Gen. McClellan, splitting his forces on both sides of the Chickahominy River, moved one arm beyond Fair Oaks to within five miles of Richmond in May, 1862. Union soldiers (l. completing an unfinished redoubt) were isolated by the flooding river when Gen. Johnston attacked. Only the timely arrival of an army corps which managed to cross the river saved the Union from a disastrous defeat. Casualties were heavy on both sides. On June 26 the Seven Days' Battle broke out, including action around Savage Station, Va. (r.), as Gen. Lee, who succeeded Johnston, sought to drive McClellan off the peninsula. McClellan inflicted heavy losses while withdrawing across the river.

JACKSON'S BRILLIANT PERFORMANCE at Bull Run earned for him the command of the vast Shenandoah Valley. "The grand strategy of the Valley campaign was Lee's and, to some extent, Joe Johnston's; but the tactics were Jackson's — and the resolute spirit that gave them meaning." In three months, April-July, 1862, Stonewall Jackson's 18,000 rebels immobilized a good part of the Union army, chased the Federal artillery over Virginian ravines (above), defeated Milroy, Banks, Shields and Fremont, and "proved the value of the Valley as a threat to Washington and the North."

PROFESSOR LOWE'S BALLOONS

In the gondola of his observation balloon *Intrepid* (left) Prof. L. S. C. Lowe ascended carrying telegraph and wire during the Battle of Fair Oaks to telegraph war reconnaissance information from aloft for the first time. "It was one of the greatest strains upon my nerves that I have experienced," he related, "to observe for many hours an almost drawn battle, while Union forces were waiting to complete the (Grapevine) bridge to connect their separated army." *Intrepid* (r.) was inflated with hydrogen, using special apparatus for speedy inflation. Rebel sharpshooters prevented closer observation.

LAST TO RETIRE from the position of honor on the firing line at Gaine's Mill was John Tidball (far l.), shown with staff. Cannon such as this 10-pounder Parrott covered the Federal withdrawal across the Chickahominy. Tidball was promoted rapidly, being brevetted a major general at the battle of Petersburg.

GEORGE A. CUSTER, later famous for his heroic "Last Stand" against Sitting Bull, swapped yarns with former West Point classmate Lt. J. B. Washington (r.), who fought for the South. Washington was captured by Northern pickets at the battle of Fair Oaks. He was held prisoner-of-war.

ENGINEERS AND INFANTRY of Brig. Gen. Herman Haupt's United States Military Railroad Construction Corps performed services of immense value by building hundreds of rail bridges similar to that on the Orange and Alexandria Railroad (above). Haupt's most famous was the Potomac Creek Bridge, 82 feet high, 414 feet long, using 204,000 feet of timber.

It was built in 40 hours in May, 1864. Abraham Lincoln once fondly remarked that it was "the most remarkable structure that human eyes ever rested upon . . . over which loaded trains are running every hour, and . . . there is nothing in it but beanpoles and cornstalks." Negroes said: "The Yankees can build bridges quicker than the Rebs can burn them down."

RAILROAD BRIDGE at Harper's Ferry, where the Shenandoah joins the Potomac, was pounded into rubble by McClellan's retreating troops. Confederate soldiers managed to save valuable rifle-making machinery, which was quickly removed to Richmond. McClellan was relieved of his command, but his hapless successor, Gen. John Pope, suffered a disastrous defeat at the hands of Jackson's 25,000 soldiers in the second Battle of Bull Run. Lee's army took 7,000 prisoners and 30 guns, while Pope's Army of Virginia "went flying back to Washington in confusion and completely routed."

BLOODIEST DAY OF THE WAR accounted for 2,700 Rebels and 2,108 Federals at Antietam, Sept. 17, 1862. After Pope's "Second Manassas," McClellan was recalled, as he put it himself, "to save the nation for a second time." The two opposing armies met at Antietam, and Gen. Lee's wearied troops were compelled to retreat. McClellan, who "always saw double when looking rebelward," was loath to follow.

LINCOLN AND STAFF OFFICERS of Gen. McClellan met at the headquarters of the Army of the Potomac on Oct. 3, 1862. Lincoln was disturbed by McClellan's constant demands for more time, more troops, and more supplies. Bitterly, Lincoln felt that his army seemed to dwindle "like a shovelful of fleas tossed from one place to another." The President's patience hit the boiling point when McClellan asked for more cavalry horses. Lincoln exploded: "Will you pardon me for asking what the horses of your army have done since the battle of Antietam that fatigues anything?" On Oct. 6, Gen.-in-Chief Halleck ordered McClellan to "cross the Potomac and give battle to the enemy," but "Little Mac" continued his old habit of delay.

DRAMATIC MEETING between the President and McClellan (l.) in early October, 1862, was to be their last. One month later, General Ambrose Burnside (r.) assumed control of the Potomac Army of 113,000 men, in six army corps. To the group of hero-worshipping officers who surrounded McClellan his removal was a devastating blow. Many irreconcilables were in favor of marching on Capitol and seizing Government in a coup d'etat.

PRUSSIAN, BRITISH, FRENCH and other European military strategists assiduously studied strategy employed in the war. Count Zeppelin, of the Prussian Army (second from right), who later received world acclaim for development of dirigibles, was inspired by the use of Civil War balloons. To his right is Swedish Lt. Rosenkranz. The fighting was, in many respects, "a modern war, one that anticipated the 'total' wars of the 20th century."

"SOUTHERN COMMANDERS"

CONFEDERATE COMMANDERS of the "War for Southern Independence" surround their beloved leader, General Robert Edward Lee (standing fourth from the right). Others (left to right) in the group are: Captain Raphael Semmes, Confederate States Navy; Brigadier Gen. Bell Hood; President Jefferson Davis (seated); Brigadier Gen. James Ewell Brown ("Jeb") Stuart; Lieut. Gen. Thomas Jonathan ("Stonewall") Jackson; Gen. Lee; Gen. Nathan Bedford Forrest; Gen. Joseph Eggleston Johnston and Gen. Pierre Gustave Tautant Beauregard. The Civil War produced in Lee "one of the supreme military geniuses in history." Lee was only less of a hero than Lincoln, and Union Army had no figure so glamorous as Jackson.

DARING REBEL RAID into Pennsylvania occurred as McClellan made his way toward his destination, the Potomac River, shortly after Antietam. On Oct. 10, 1862, the audacious Gen. J. E. B. Stuart began his spectacular ride around McClellan's slow moving army. "Jeb" Stuart's 1,200 cavalry rode with impunity to the west of "Little Mac's" Army of the Potomac (left), crossed north of it through Chambersburg, seized quantities of clothing, boots, small arms and 500 horses (right), before cutting back through Cashtown, thence down Emmitsburg road and across river to rejoin Lee.

BATTLE OF FREDERICKSBURG

Dec. 13, 1862, was the day that Gen. Burnside's 113,000 soldiers could never forget. Noting that Gen. Lee's rebels were widely scattered, Burnside unwisely moved his "Grand Divisions" at Falmouth, Va., to a position opposite Fredericksburg on the Rappahannock. Lee's 75,000 troops and 306 guns waited entrenched behind the heights; with "Stonewall" Jackson commanding the rebel left, Gen. Longstreet the right. Burnside hurled his troops across the river (above), in a series of desperate, vain charges. The battle was a colossal blunder. More than 10,884 Federals were casualties, at a cost of 4,656 rebels. Brady's photo of Union artillery under fire (l.) was first combat photo. During truce, Union photographers (r.) shot views of Lee's troops.

SUPPLY STEAMERS AT NASHVILLE on Dec. 18, 1862, rushed stores and artillery reinforcements to the Federal army base 13 days before the Battle of Murfreesboro opened near Stone River, at which point Confederate Gen. Braxton Bragg was threatening Nashville. While Lee in Virginia was preparing for invasion in the North, Union and Southern forces stepped up preparations for renewed war in the West. On the snow-covered wharf (above) are piled barrels of whiskey, or "Cincinnati rot-gut," barrels of sugar, hogsheads of molasses to be mixed with battlefield-brewed coffee.

CONFEDERATE ARMY operating in Kentucky withdrew into Tennessee, after a clash at Perryville. Bragg then pitted 38,000 men against Gen. W. S. Rosencrans' 47,000 Federals at Murfreesboro, Dec. 31, 1862-Jan. 2, 1863. The Union lost 9,222, Bragg 9,239, before retiring to Chattanooga.

"ADVANCE AND GIVE THE COUNTERSIGN" was a challenge respected in both camps. Nevertheless, relations between the Confederate and the invading Federal armies were "somehow, good-natured: the very names combatants had for each other, Johnny Reb, Billy Yank, testified to this!"

SOUTHERN HOSPITALITY (l.) struck a sour note whenever a Federal column arrived at a planter's house. "Away from home, in the enemy's country, and without any inbred sense of discipline or firm officers, many of the soldiers were (in contrast to the scene, r.) indeed, 'awfully de-

praved', running the gamut from drunkenness and profanity" to "theft, pillaging, and murder." Wrote Private Charles Wills, 8th Illinois Infantry: "Most of the mischief is done by the advance of the army, though, God knows, infantry is bad enough. The d--d thieves even steal from Negroes."

Emancipation Proclamation

Prior to Fort Sumter's collapse, Lincoln had declared: "If I could save the Union without freeing any slave, I would do it; and if I could save it by freeing all the slaves, I would do it." Political pressure and military reverses changed all that. Lincoln, in 1862, declared that the best interests of the nation would be served by abolishing all slavery, because it would unite the North, gain world sympathy, and put to an end the South's last hope of obtaining foreign aid.

Any proclamation calling for the abolishment of slavery while General Robert E. Lee's armies continued to win victory after victory in the Eastern campaign would appear absurd. President Lincoln, therefore, chose to wait for a Union victory. The moment came when Gen. G. B. McClellan thwarted a Confederate invasion of western Maryland during the battle of Antietam.

Although Antietam was not a great victory, if a victory at all, Lincoln seized upon the event to issue his Emancipation Proclamation on Sept. 22. In this public declaration, he asserted that, unless the Confederate States returned to their allegiance by Jan. 1, 1863, the slaves in all districts rebelling against the Union "henceforward shall be free." Southern leaders regarded Lincoln's decree as madness, but on the date set, Lincoln carried out his promise. What is often forgotten is that Lincoln intended that all slaveholders be fully compensated for their lost Negroes. The vindictiveness of the North after the war prevented the eventual carrying out of this policy.

Actually, the emancipation thus proclaimed was little more than a war measure and a promise for the future. It did not abolish all slavery. It proposed only to emancipate slaves in places then offering resistance to Union authority.

Moreover, it was unconstitutional until Congress in January, 1865, on the urgent advice of Lincoln, sent to the states the 13th Amendment, liberating some 3,500,000 Negroes living in servitude.

LINCOLN READ first draft of Emancipation Proclamation to his Cabinet, July 22, 1862, but was persuaded to withhold it by Sec. of State Seward (with hand in coat) so that it could be issued when victory was near. On Sept. 22, just after Antietam, Lincoln issued preliminary document, which stated that slaves in rebellious states would be "then, thence-forward, and forever free" as of Jan. 1, 1863.

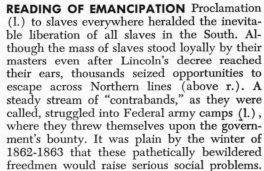

READING OF EMANCIPATION Proclamation (l.) to slaves everywhere heralded the inevitable liberation of all slaves in the South. Although the mass of slaves stood loyally by their masters even after Lincoln's decree reached their ears, thousands seized opportunities to escape across Northern lines (above r.). A steady stream of "contrabands," as they were called, struggled into Federal army camps (l.), where they threw themselves upon the government's bounty. It was plain by the winter of 1862-1863 that these pathetically bewildered freedmen would raise serious social problems.

"CONTRABAND OF WAR" was Gen. B. F. Butler's term for the Negro who had made his way within the Federal lines and who, while no longer a slave or a piece of property, was not yet accepted as a person. "Contrabands" served the Union as army teamsters and helped build fortifications.

"COME AND JOIN US BROTHERS!" and similar Union sentiments induced 150,000 free Negroes to join Federal army. In 1862, 54th and 55th Mass. Regiments were formed, and after Jan. 1, 1863, Negro refugees were to "be received into the military and naval service of the U.S. Corps."

WAR VETERANS AT PLAY during the Army of the Potomac's stay at Brandy Station in the winter of 1863-64 serves as a vivid illustration of camp life. Troops of the 14th Pennsylvania Regiment played cards, loafed, strolled about or gossiped, while two of them engaged in a boxing match.

Of the 3,559 organizations in all branches of the service in the Union armies, the individual states furnished 3,473. By late 1863 American volunteers on both sides were drilled and well disciplined, giving to Grant and Lee some of the finest soldiers to ever fight in an American uniform.

STONEWALL JACKSON
Lee's success at Chancellorsville, May, 1863, had been a costly one. In darkness of evening Jackson (r.) was returning to his line from a tour of the front when he and his staff were mistaken by the 33d North Carolina for Federal cavalry. His troops assumed an "attack was forward," rose for a volley — and slew Jackson. On May 10, the great general died. Lee was shocked by the loss. Said Major Brinton, a Federal surgeon: " . . . the feeling of the Northern Army was one of pity, I might also say of regret, that so great a soldier was passing away." Wrote the British military historian, Henderson: "The fame of 'Stonewall' Jackson is no longer the exclusive property of Virginia and the South; it has become the birthright of every man privileged to call himself an American." Gen. Lee's triumph (l.) at Chancellorsville was the South's last great victory. The three days of fighting, May 2 to 4, 1863, took a total of 3,240 lives.

BATTLE OF GETTYSBURG, July 1-3, 1863, was the war's most bitterly contested campaign and the greatest single battle ever fought in North America. Lee, with 75,000 veterans under his command, was confident that a decisive victory on Union soil would cause the disheartened North to sue for peace. Meade's 88,000 Federals pursued him. The field of battle was selected inadvertently when a Confederate unit, foraging for boots, struck a Union cavalry picket west of Gettysburg, Penn. Neither Lee nor Meade wanted to do battle on this terrain, but the fighting was precipitated on July 1, north of the town. During that night Meade's troops, driven south through village streets, dug in on a line along Cemetery Ridge.

RHODE ISLAND ARTILLERY supporting the right center of the Federal line, fired across the stone wall upon oncoming gray rebels. "Gettysburg was won and lost, on the second day, and the outcome . . . was determined by geography, or by enterprise of the Union commander in taking advantage of geography."

HAND TO HAND COMBAT, stabbing, stone throwing and rifle fire continued throughout July 2 at Little Round Top, the Devil's Den, the Wheat Field, Peach Orchard, Culp's Hill, Spangler's Spring, as Lee's Confederates tried unsuccessfully to dislodge the Northerners.

FROM PRIVATE TO GENERAL was the achievement of Brig. Gen. James Madison Robertson (first on left below). A private in battery F of the Second United States Artillery in 1838, he became first-lieutenant in 1852, and was named brigadier-general for distinguished battle service in 1864.

"WITH HIS LONG BROWN RIFLE," John L. Burns, 70, Constable of Gettysburg, was honored by Bret Harte's popular poem, as the only civilian who joined the Federals at the Battle of Gettysburg.

MEADE AND SEDGWICK (in round hat at right) before the Federal 6th Army Corps advance that resulted in Major Gen. John Sedgwick's death by a Confederate sharpshooter's rifle at Spotsylvania.

Battle of Gettysburg

Gen. Robert E. Lee inflicted a disastrous defeat on Burnside at Fredericksburg in December, 1862, and at Chancellorsville, May, 1863. Lee's 60,000 troops out-fought a force of 130,000 men under Burnside's hapless successor, "Fighting Joe" Hooker.

Lee decided once more to lead his capable army of 75,000 veterans in an invasion of the North. Washington was stifled with "prickly heat and strange rumors; a spy in the streets of Chambersburg had counted Lee's marching host up to 90,000 . . ." Pennsylvania roads ahead of Lee's advance were choked with fleeing humanity and beast of burden alike, as farmers drove cattle relentlessly before them. Negroes fled to the woods in peril of their lives.

Northern cities seethed amid incredulous disbelief and mingled terror as the rebels pushed northward from Fredericksburg through Winchester, Harpers Ferry, Sharpsburg and Hagerstown in the Shenandoah Valley. "If the head of Lee's army," Lincoln inquired of Hooker, "is at Martinsburg and the tail of it on the plank road between Fredericksburg and Chancellorsville, the animal must be very slim somewhere. Could you not break him?" "Impossible," cried Hooker. "I cannot divine his intentions as long as he fills the country with a cloud of cavalry . . ." "I am outnumbered, I need a reinforcement of 25,000 men."

News of Lee's advance spread fast while Hooker penned another bad-tempered note to Washington: "I must have more men. This is my resignation else."

Lincoln promptly appointed Gen. George G. Meade head of the Union Army. Meade's 88,000 blue-clad Federals followed Lee north. For three bloody days, July 1 to 3, 1863, the armies of the Blue and the Gray thundered before Gettysburg. The high-tide of Pickett's charge left its scars on Cemetery Hill. Lee's savage thrust through Maryland and Pennsylvania was stopped by Meade, and his army retreated to Virginia.

PICKETT'S CHARGE Lee's voice rang out in "calm exaltation" as he explained his plan for July 3. "The Federals' best troops were fought out, their right had been effectively turned by Ewell, their left smashed by Hood." Lee planned to bury Meade under a cascade of artillery fire, then thrust Pickett's 15,000 Virginians like a thunderbolt straight through the Union's weak mid-section. Longstreet urged Lee to reconsider his plan and proposed instead that he outflank the Federals, but Lee refused to budge. Longstreet ordered the charge.

LONGSTREET'S ARTILLERY ceased fire at 3 P.M., as Pickett's three brigades, advancing in three lines, swept down the slope on the Confederate side. Furiously charging gray cavalry and Union guns and rifles crashed together at 3:15 P.M. Federal troops mowed Pickett's front ranks as if with fiery scythes. By 3:30 P.M. Pickett's brigades were crushed at the Bloody Angle, ending hopes of victory.

WAR DEAD AROUND DEVIL'S DEN near Gettysburg, illustrates the devastating accuracy of sharpshooters in gray who picked off many Union officers, among them Gen. Stephen Weed and Colonel Vincent Strong. A minie ball, weighing an ounce or more, produced large ugly wounds, and could kill a man nearly a mile distant. In the field the regimental hospital was serviced by two small tents for officers and medical supplies, another for the kitchen and a larger one for the sick. The surgeon (l.) is about to amputate a soldier's leg. By 1864 the U.S. Surgeon General's 892 hospitals were assisted by volunteer nurses including Dorothea Dix, Clara Barton, Kate Cumming. Poet Walt Whitman served also as a Civil War nurse.

"THE WORLD WILL LITTLE NOTE nor long remember what we say here," Lincoln told his listeners at Gettysburg — but his words came to be among the best known in the English language. At the time, they made little impression. Not all of the 15,000 listeners could hear the President, and many who heard had been so dulled by two hours of ringing oratory that they were unmoved. The newspapers were also unimpressed; some were downright critical. It remained for succeeding generations to put President's statement into the context of history, and recognize its true greatness.

GETTYSBURG ADDRESS

Four score and seven years ago our fathers brought forth on this continent, a new nation, conceived in Liberty, and dedicated to the proposition that all men are created equal.

Now we are engaged in a great civil war, testing whether that nation, or any nation so conceived and so dedicated, can long endure. We are met on a great battle field of that war. We have come to dedicate a portion of that field, as a final resting place for those who here gave their lives that that nation might live. It is altogether fitting and proper that we should do this.

But, in a larger sense, we cannot dedicate — we cannot consecrate — we cannot hallow — this ground. The brave men, living and dead, who struggled here, have consecrated it, far above our poor power to add or detract. The world will little note, nor long remember what we say here, but it can never forget what they did here. It is for us the living, rather, to be dedicated here to the unfinished work which they who fought here have thus far so nobly advanced. It is rather for us to be here dedicated to the great task remaining before us — that from these honored dead we take increased devotion to that cause for which they gave the last full measure of devotion — that we here highly resolve that these dead shall not have died in vain — that this nation, under God, shall have a new birth of freedom — and that government of the people, by the people, for the people, shall not perish from the earth.

Lincoln at Gettysburg

The President was invited to speak at Gettysburg as an afterthought. A Pennsylvania commission in charge of dedicating the battlefield cemetery had asked Edward Everett to deliver the dedicatory address on Nov. 19, 1863. Everett was the outstanding orator of the time. He had served in turn as president of Harvard, governor of Massachusetts, United States senator and Secretary of War.

As a courtesy, the President was invited to attend. He surprised the commission by accepting and was then asked to make a "few appropriate remarks." The record indicates Lincoln took the invitation to be extended in good faith.

There are in existence five separate drafts of the Gettysburg Address in his handwriting. He carried two of them with him. Lincoln arrived by train Nov. 18 and was lodged in the spacious home of Mr. Wills in Center Square. At 10 o'clock the following morning he joined a procession which included Cabinet officers, judges of the Supreme Court and members of Congress. At noon thousands listened as Everett made a two-hour oration, followed by a hymn.

Then Lincoln arose. He spoke for less than five minutes. The 10 sentences he read to the crowd at Gettysburg were to become the most famous speech in American history.

LINCOLN WORKED ON HIS SPEECH in his special train to Gettysburg. Next morning, he mounted a horse and rode in an elaborate procession to the cemetery. Picture shows an infantry regiment in the parade marching out to dedicatory exercises. "... We here highly resolve," Lincoln said, "that these dead shall not have died in vain — that this nation, under God, shall have a new birth of freedom — and that government of the people, by the people, for the people, shall not perish from the earth."

DESPITE CARES OF WAR and his work-stacked White House desk (above), Lincoln took time to proclaim first national Thanksgiving holiday in November, 1863. He acted at urging of Mrs. Sarah J. Hale, editor of *Godey's Lady's Book*.

"THERE ARE PERFECT shoals of womenkind now in the army," wrote Theodore Lyman in February, 1864. The picture shows a gentlewoman, probably the wife of an officer, at headquarters of the 1st Brigade, Horse Artillery. The Union army also had many camp followers of lower station.

At right is a company of Union soldiers in the trenches before Petersburg. In the Civil War as in all wars soldiers spent much of their time sitting and waiting while officers deliberated. Within 30 miles of their trenches lay Gen. Lee's Confederate army. It was ragged, hungry, but still full of fight.

THE SOLDIER'S LIFE

Conditions improved in the North but Confederate troops went hungry

The great armies of North and South were formed amid the wildest confusion in 1861. The United States had only a few regiments of regulars when war broke out, and most of these were stationed on the far-off frontiers. Lincoln's first call brought 75,000 men to the colors and a half-million followed in the ensuing months. For these raw troops there were few arms and little equipment.

Government was victimized, in its rush to equip the new armies, by unprincipled manufacturers and contractors. Soldiers drew uniforms of wool shoddy which fell apart within a few days, and shoes with paper soles. The scandal which followed resulted in the resignation of Secretary of War Simon Cameron. He was succeeded by stern but efficient Edwin M. Stanton. Under Stanton the army bought good equipment and found good officers. As the organization improved, the lot of the common soldier was bettered. War Department records show that a daily ration for a soldier included: hard tack, 16 ounces; beef (salt or

fresh), 20 ounces; pork or bacon, 12 ounces. For every 100 men there was issued 15 pounds of beans, 10 pounds of rice, eight pounds of coffee, 15 pounds of sugar, and seasonings for their food.

As the men grew accustomed to soldiering they devised ways to supply themselves with the creature comforts. The "A" or wedge tent was standard with the Northern

UNION SOLDIERS in the mess line draw part of their daily ration of 22 ounces of soft bread and 20 ounces of beef. The bread is stacked at left.

army by 1863. It held four to six men comfortably when the sides were built up with logs, an outside chimney added and the gaps chinked with mud.

The lot of the Union soldiery improved as the war progressed, but the Southerners suffered in greater measure. The Northern blockade strangled imports into the South, and the Confederate army grew increasingly ragged with time. Uniforms were of homespun supplied by the wives, mothers and sisters of the troops. Food was scarce and consisted by the end of the war mostly of sweet potatoes, corn pone, acorn coffee.

A Confederate private wrote in the fourth winter of war that "our men have built them good log cabins, and we are near a forest, where there is plenty of fuel for fires. The cabins are covered with slabs, but have no plank floors. We had no nails to fasten the roofs, and so the slabs are held in place by logs laid on top. Of course the cabins are nothing like the neat ones when we had both plank and nails."

INDUSTRIOUS Union trooper takes advantage of a lull to do his washing in an improvised laundry tub in winter quarters. A cheerful group (center) gathers before a tent to pose for a picture while the members engage in the pastimes of soldiers. One is cleaning his rifle, another writing a letter

and a third paring his toenails with a knife. At right, the dignified non-commissioned officers of Company D, 93rd New York Infantry, sit down to dinner in the field on folding chairs at a folding table in their well-equipped mess. The photograph was made in 1863 by Timothy O'Sullivan.

HARDSHIPS of war were always present with the troops of the Union and Confederate armies. But soldiers have always waited in bivouac more often than they have fought. Civil War armies were no exception, and during the periods of inaction the men were kept busy improving their more permanent camps like the one at left. More than a million soldiers in the Union army were under 21 and the Confederate army contained even a larger percentage of boys. These youthful soldiers rallied quickly from the bloody toil of war and in camp found entertainment in games, boxing and wrestling. Soldiers at Gen. O. B. Wilcox's headquarters (above) found diversion watching a cockfight.

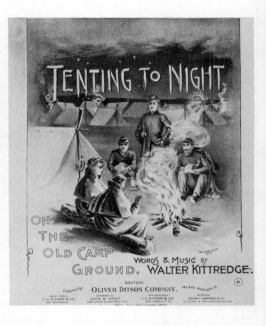

MUSIC PLAYED an important role in maintaining the morale of the troops during war which lacked formal entertainment for the army. Commanders recognized the value of marching music and many bands served with the armies of both sides. Such a group of field musicians was Taltry's fifers and drummers above. Fife and drum corps were the mainstay of most regiments. Gen. Horace Porter reported that he once encountered one of Sheridan's bands under heavy fire playing *Nelly Bly* as cheerfully as if they were at a picnic. A different type of music, the sentimental ballad based upon the hard military life, was popular both at home and at the front. Such a song was "Tenting Tonight," written after the war but inspired by camp life.

◄ **FURLOUGH** at home was destination of these convalescent soldiers. They are men of McClellan's army on their way home by sidewheel steamer on the James River. Most had been stricken by typhoid.

RELIGION became more important to the new armies as hardships and death became commonplace. At right are chaplains of 9th Army Corps at Petersburg. Both armies experienced a revivalist movement. ►

SUTLER'S SHACK was the Civil War post exchange. Most units had a merchant who accompanied the troops, selling tobacco, whisky and various necessities and frequently discounting soldiers' paychecks at ruinous rates.

MAIL FROM HOME was recognized as vital to the soldier's morale. Each regiment in the field had a postmaster to collect and distribute troopers' letters. Men designated as postmasters were freed from all other duty.

MATHEW BRADY

The world's first great photographer was a Cork Irishman with an Irish temper. He photographed Lincoln and the other great Civil War figures, and his documentary pictures of war are still unsurpassed. By a special commission from the War Dept. he followed the armies into the field to record the scenes of camp and combat. The wagon in which he carried his clumsy wet plate outfit is shown at left. The picture (right) of Brady himself was made after his return from Bull Run, where he had been lost and had wandered unarmed on the battlefield until a company of N. Y. Zouaves gave him the sword which he wears under his coat. Photographer Alexander Gardner also made notable war pictures in the North. Southern photographers included George S. Cook, J. D. Edwards, and A. D. Lytle.

WAR CORRESPONDENTS

Newspaper and magazine reporters who covered the Civil War were the first to establish the correspondent's place with the army. They argued with censors, railed against security regulations and battled for combat zone and headquarters privileges. Here a correspondent for the New York *Herald* pauses at a press camp site during a lull in the fighting. He traveled in the horse-drawn wagon at right. Photo-engraving was unknown during the Civil War and newspapers depended upon sketch artists whose work they reproduced in woodcut form. At lower left A. R. Waud, a staff artist for *Harper's Weekly*, sketches the field at Gettysburg in 1863. The contemporary sketch (below center) shows Northern correspondents under fire on the battlefield interviewing Union soldiers returning with a Confederate prisoner. Newspapers were as eagerly sought after by soldiers then as now, and the newsboy (lower right) with his horse-drawn cart is peddling the latest news from the home front to Union cavalry troopers in camp during November of 1863.

SECRET SERVICE

Allan Pinkerton, the most famous detective of his day, was the first intelligence officer of the Union army. McClellan appointed him to organize the intelligence service which functioned with the Army of the Potomac until McClellan was removed in November, 1862. Here, at his headquarters near Cumberland Landing, Pinkerton sits smoking in the middle background with his scouts and guides about him. At left he appears (in derby) as Lincoln's bodyguard during the President's visit to the camps at Antietam. Despite his fame as a secret agent, he is blamed by some for overestimating the size of Lee's army of northern Virginia. McClellan acted overcautiously as a result. Had he known that he greatly outnumbered the enemy, the war in the East might have ended in 1862.

MILITARY INTELLIGENCE fell into neglect after Pinkerton departed, until Gen. Hooker assumed command of the Army of the Potomac and put Col. George H. Sharpe of New York in charge of the new Military Information Bureau. Sharpe, (extreme left) served until the end of the war and gathered a notably resourceful staff. Seated next to him is his chief aide, John C. Babcock. When Sharpe overhauled the intelligence service he replaced Pinkerton's civilians and Pamunkey Indian scouts with soldiers from the ranks. The North was filled with Southern sympathizers and the advancing armies overran much territory occupied by Southern families. As a result the North was honeycombed with rebel spies and counter-intelligence was a major activity of the Federal secret service. There was also the usual quota of "double agents" who sold information to both North and South. Many spies of both sides were captured and executed.

SPIES Brave and shrewd women served as spies for both North and South. Among the cleverest were those appearing here. Bell Boyd (left) and Mrs. Greenhow, with her daughter, were Confederate agents. Mrs. Greenhow was a member of a prominent Washington family and remained in the capital when other Southerners left. She relayed to the South the intelligence reports which led to the Union defeat at Bull Run. In August, 1861, she was arrested by Pinkerton and eventually lodged, with her eight-year-old daughter, in the old Capitol Prison. In May, 1862, she was released and sent to Richmond, where she received the personal commendation of President Davis. At the right is Pauline Cushman, an actress who served as a Northern spy. Her expulsion from Nashville as a Southern sympathizer was faked by General Mitchel, and she was welcomed by the Confederates. Until her arrest, she accumulated and transmitted to the Union forces maps and drawings of primary importance.

MILITARY TELEGRAPH was of the utmost importance to the Union forces. The army had no telegraph service at beginning of the war, and the Signal Corps was restricted to visual signaling. Secretary Stanton incorporated civilian operators into the War Department, put them in charge of Col. Anson Stager and Major Thomas T. Eckert. Their military telegraphers strung 15,000 miles of special wire, often under fire, as the drawing at left shows. The field telegraph station (above) was one of those by means of which Gen. Grant kept in touch, from his headquarters at City Point, with four armies numbering 250,000 men and directed operations over 750,000 square miles. Telegraph corps suffered more than 300 casualties.

SUPPLY TRAINS consisting of mule-drawn wagons supplied the marching armies of both North and South. Northern armies adopted a policy of bringing up their own supplies instead of foraging off the country. This made necessary an elaborate transportation corps and thousands of mule trains like this one. Wagon trains fought mud, sleet, snow and the enemy in turn, to keep contending armies supplied with food, vital ammunition.

RIVER BOATS supplied Federal armies as they advanced through the South. Above the heads of the Negro dock workers in the picture above may be seen masts of some of the scores of small craft which brought supplies up to the wharfing areas. At right is a general view of the maga-zine wharf at City Point, Union headquarters in 1864. The big sidewheel steamer and the barges and lighters around it were employed to bring military supplies up the James River to be unloaded and shipped by wagon train. Rail, water transport gave the armies an elaborate support system.

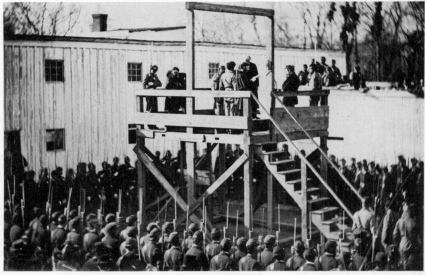

CIVIL WAR PRISONERS

By war's end there were about 200,000 Confederate prisoners in Federal prison camps, and about the same number of Union prisoners in Confederate hands. Each side made propaganda of the treatment of prisoners by the other. In fact, neither side was blameless for prison camp cruelties. The cocky Confederate prisoners, photographed by a Federal war photographer shortly after Gettysburg, were probably taken to the U.S. military prison at Rock Island, Illinois. There, more than 300 Confederate prisoners died in a single month from lack of food and clothing. Andersonville prison in the South was the favorite target of Northern atrocity propaganda. Capt. Henry Wirz, the commander of Andersonville, was tried on atrocity charges and hanged in the grim execution above. Bad prison conditions were due more to breakdown of supplies than to intentional brutality of captors.

PRISON CONDITIONS were poor both in North and South. The highest death rate was at Andersonville, Ga. (r.) where for a time over 100 men died each day and were buried in a communal grave. Starvation and neglect of prisoners was charged against the Confederates, but Southern armies and civilian population were also suffering privation.

Northern prison camps reduced rations in retaliation for treatment accorded Northern captives in the South. Northern prison system did not suffer the supply breakdowns which were caused in the Southern prisons by invading Union armies. The South had prisons also at Richmond, Va., Point Lookout, Md., and Belle Isle. Beside Rock Island, the prisoners of the Union were held at Ft. Lafayette, N. Y., Ft. McHenry, Md., and Fort Delaware, in the Delaware River. War prisoners, prisoners of state and political captives were held in these fortress-prisons.

LIBBY PRISON was a notorious Confederate jail for officers. A remodeled warehouse in Richmond, Va., it was crowded and the inmates complained about the inadequacy of the food. During the entire war, some 125,000 Union officers were held in the prison under conditions depicted above.

After the Southern defeat and the capture of Richmond, the tables were turned, and Libby was filled with Confederate soldiers. In the photograph at right, the prison is guarded by Union soldiers; among the prisoners is the former commander, Maj. Thomas P. Turner, later acquitted of atrocity.

UNION PRISONERS at Salisbury, N. C., play a game of baseball. During the early years of the war, a prisoner exchange was maintained by the opposing forces. In 1862, a Northern river steamer, the *New York*, con-veyed the paroled prisoners between Aiken's Landing and City Point on James River. Federal prisoners were brought to Annapolis and, because they were under oath not to fight the South, went west to fight Indians.

CIVILIAN RELIEF

The Sanitary Commission was formed by the Federal government in 1861 to care for the sick and wounded, and the dependent families of soldiers. It was supported by private contributions, particularly by "Sanitary Fairs" — fund-raising benefits held in the large Northern cities. Numerous other relief organizations were formed in the North and South. The largest, next to the Sanitary Commission, was the United States Christian Commission sponsored by the Young Men's Christian Association. During four years of service, it distributed to soldiers nearly $3,000,000 worth of goods, and over four million library books, Bibles and magazines. It gained the volunteer services, for six-week periods, of nearly 5,000 men whom it commissioned as "delegates."

Some $2,500,000 was received and spent. In the picture at left, men and women of the Commission are pictured in an army camp at White House, on the Pamunkey River, distributing foods and delicacies to wounded soldiers. In the photo above, food is distributed at a Commission office. The merchant, John Wanamaker, right, raised many millions for relief.

PENSION records were kept in the field by Union army surgeons. At left is the clerical office of the 1st Division 9th Corps in 1864. Here mortality statistics were compiled at the portable field desks for later use when claims were filed.

SOUTHERN relief was conducted largely by the Women's Relief Society headed by Mrs. Felicia Grundy Porter (right). When war broke out she established hospitals in Nashville for wounded soldiers and her agency later spread throughout the Confederate states.

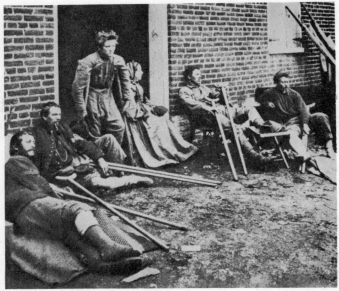

SICK AND WOUNDED

The basis of the modern military medical system was established during the Civil War. Medical care was generally inadequate and at best primitive when the war started. Wounded men, such as those shown (above, l.) resting after the battle of Chancellorsville in 1863, received only the barest treatment, and amputations were common for comparatively minor wounds. As the war progressed the demands for medical aid grew and the medical services were improved. The newly-formed ambulance corps (r.) is shown in a drill directed by a surgeon (beside ambulance). The Union army finally worked out a system for providing forward aid stations in the field at the rear of each regiment. Seriously wounded soldiers were moved from the aid stations to divisional field hospitals in the rear. Ambulances were used to transport the wounded and supply train wagons also were pressed into service. Hospital trains (below, r.) were utilized also to move wounded soldiers to hospitals. From May 1, 1861, to June 30, 1865, the number of patients treated by military hospitals in the North totaled 408,000 with more than 36,500 deaths. Carver hospital (below, l.), near Washington, D.C., was one of 230 Northern hospitals.

YOUNGEST Northern soldier to receive battle wounds was William Black. More than 800,000 youths of 17 or under served in Union ranks and among these 200,000 were under 16; 100,000 were 15. Confederate army also had many boys.

CLARA BARTON, founder of the American Red Cross, was an employee of the U.S. Patent Office when the war broke out. As she began collecting and distributing supplies for the men injured on the battlefield, her organization grew rapidly.

DR. MARY WALKER was the only woman doctor in the Union ranks during the Civil War. She wore men's clothing by a special dispensation and won special decorations for distinguished service to the Federal army's medical corps.

RECURITING

On July 2, 1861, the President called for 300,000 volunteers for the Union army. He got only 88,000. By March 3, 1863, Congress was forced to enact a conscription law. In another year the people had become so war-weary that desertions were commonplace. Executions of deserters, like the one above, also became commonplace, but deserting continued, often by men who re-enlisted to claim another bounty. Bounties were freely offered in an effort to attract volunteers, as the picture at right indicates. More than 200,000 Confederates deserted during the war, and at start of the second winter campaigns more than 100,000 were absent without leave from the Northern armies. Federal agents abroad procured the recruiting of thousands of alien immigrants for the United States army on payment of transportation and bounty.

DRAFT RIOTS

The Federal draft act had an escape clause under which a draftee could avoid service by payment of $300 or by providing a substitute. This obviously unfair provision worked a hardship on the poor, who rose in New York City on July 13, 1863, when the first draft was drawn. In the wild rioting which followed, the mobs hanged Negroes and killed about 1,000 persons and burned 100 buildings, including the office of the provost marshal. The sketch at the left shows the lynching of a Negro, while at right the maddened mob fights police. After four days, Federal troops were called and restored order. Under strong military guard the draft proceeded without further incident.

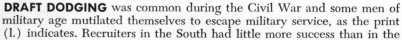

DRAFT DODGING was common during the Civil War and some men of military age mutilated themselves to escape military service, as the print (l.) indicates. Recruiters in the South had little more success than in the North and desertions were higher as many men left the armies to return to their fields and produce a crop for their hungry families. Print (r.) shows some of the fancied "persuasions" used to induce recruiting in the South.

Home Front

War caused a tremendous drain on the manpower of both North and South. The armies required thousands of the strongest young men while the factories at home were called upon to increase their output to support the armies. The result was that women went into business and industry for the first time. The Treasury Department hired women clerks and a leading cartoonist of the time feared that women would sometime become soldiers and even receive officers' commissions (at right). Business boomed throughout the North under the impact of war and profiteers grew rich. War financing was also a concern of the folks at home and $400 million in small denomination bonds were purchased by Northern public. Since there was little industry in the South, women had to make own clothes and raise food to help keep their hungry families alive.

READY-MADE clothing manufacturers expanded their business with contracts for uniforms. By 1863 almost 100,000 operators were employed by 100 firms in New York City. Dividends on woolen mills stocks rose 40 per cent, but wages lagged 40 per cent behind prices, creating labor strife.

FOOD became so scarce in the Confederacy that the government had to seize civilian stocks of flour to feed the army. The food shortage caused a bread riot in Richmond in 1863. Here deeply humiliated Southern women in area occupied by Union Army apply at a Federal commissary for food.

NEW TAX LAW of 1862 made the home front feel the impact of war as taxpayers like these lined up in the assessor's office. The Federal government raised $667 million during the war by direct taxation while it borrowed some $2½ billion. The nation's first income tax was levied in 1861.

HEAVY CONSTRUCTION during the war called for increased iron and steel manufacture. North produced 13 million tons of coal in 1860 and 21 million by 1864. Pig iron production went from 821,000 tons in 1860 to 1,014,000 tons by 1865.

DRAMA was not all at the war front. Above is a sketch by a contemporary artist of Ellsworth's brave company of Zouaves successfully fighting a blaze which threatened to destroy Willard's famous hotel in Washington, D.C., during war.

INDIAN TREATIES were violated while the government concentrated on the war. In 1862 the Sioux rose in Minnesota and killed some 400 whites when government annuities were held up. Thirty-eight Indians were hanged together.

PONY EXPRESS AND TELEGRAPH

Communication with the Far West was vital to the Federal government and to the people of the Western states. The great freighting firm of Russell, Majors and Waddell attempted to capitalize on the need for rapid communication by founding the Pony Express in April, 1860. The 60 riders of the Pony Express carried the mail, at $1 a letter, from the end of the railroad at St. Joseph, Mo., to San Francisco in 10 days. They rode 40 to 125 mile relays and changed horses every 25 miles. The venture was short lived. The Western Union telegraph was driven forward from both east and west under the spur of war. When the wires were joined on Oct. 24, 1861, the Pony Express passed out of existence. The riders of this romantic service carried the post a total of 650,000 miles during 16 months and only lost one mail. Pictured are an original Pony Express poster and express riders attempting to outrun Indians and passing the telegraph workers (left).

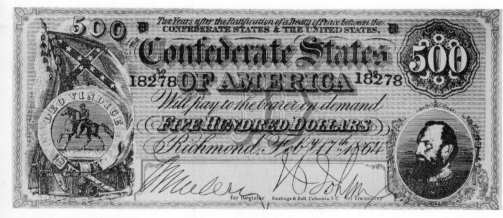

INFLATION

The Confederacy had little hard money and most of that went abroad to buy military supplies. The states were requested to raise quotas of money by taxation. Finally paper currency like this was circulated in the amount of about one billion dollars, although even the treasury did not know exactly how much.

GREENBACKS, unbacked by specie, were issued by the government. Total issue of $450 million was authorized. Here are bull market speculators at doors of New York Stock Exchange. Union defeats meant profits to them.

OIL was discovered in Pennsylvania in 1859 by Col. J. E. Drake, who sold it as a patent medicine. The use of petroleum for illumination was soon discovered, and by 1865 industry boomed.

COMSTOCK LODE

Out in the Washoe Range of Nevada, gold had been mined for several years. A troublesome "blue stuff" made gold mining difficult. In 1859 the "blue stuff" was found to be almost pure silver. The great rush that followed developed mines which helped to fill the Federal war coffers. The discovery is pictured here.

CONFEDERATE RAIDERS

Aside from the regular Confederate armies there were marauding bands in the West who terrorized Union frontier states with their lightning raids. The notorious renegade Quantrill and his brilliant cavalry officer, Brig. Gen. John H. Morgan (top r.), were known to the Union as the most daring guerilla leaders. On July 4, 1863, Morgan's 8,000 raiders left Knoxville, Tenn., swept through the Kentucky mountains, thence across the central and eastern part of the state. Nearly two million dollars in property was destroyed. On July 8, Morgan led 2,500 cavalrymen across the Ohio River into southern Indiana and Ohio. He was captured by Federal pickets in late July and imprisoned.

The wily general and several companions escaped on Nov. 26, leaving a "polite note" to explain the details of their work. In September, 1864, Quantrill was killed during a brief foray at Greenville, Tenn. Nast's portrayal (above) gave the artist's conception of Morgan's activities and proved an effective bit of anti-Confederate propaganda.

Col. John S. Mosby, 43rd Battalion, Virginia Cavalry (l.), operated in northern Virginia and Maryland, set afire Federal ammunition depots, and tore up rolling stock, telegraph lines and railroads. Maj. Gen. Nathan B. Forrest (bottom r.), leader of a band of swift and silent night-raiding irregulars, hated Yankees and Negroes alike. Forrest later became the First Grand Wizard of the Ku Klux Klan. During the war 29 horses were shot under him, and "that devil Forrest," as he was vehemently referred to, is supposed to have uttered, "I have with my own hand killed a man for every horse I lost in the war, and I was a horse ahead at its close." The panic resulting from the costly and, at times, barbaric raids of Morgan, Mosby and Forrest kept Federal troops busily engaged.

MISSISSIPPI BLOCKADE at Vicksburg was by-passed by Admiral David Porter's fleet on April 16, 1863. Porter's action cut Vicksburg off from all rebel relief from the north, south and west. Grant then humbled Vicksburg from the east after a six weeks siege.

GEN. GEORGE H. THOMAS (l.), standing on the left of Rosencrans' Union line (r.), repulsed Confederate assaults at Chickamauga on Sept. 19, 1863. Thomas stood firm, frustrated Bragg's attempts to turn his flank, and became known to the world as the "Rock of Chickamauga." Later, his troops captured Lookout Mountain and Missionary Ridge, where he put the Confederates to rout from the positions that they had held so confidently for previous two months.

GENERAL U. S. GRANT (r.) was often tobacco-stained and sometimes drunk. But, as Lincoln said, "he fights!" His military ability was further demonstrated by the victory of Sherman and Thomas at Chattanooga, Tenn., Nov. 24-26, 1863. In early 1864, Congress revived the rank of lieutenant general (the first time since George Washington held it). Lincoln promoted Grant to that rank and made him Commander-in-Chief. Grant, with his staff (l.) soon decided on a bold, twofold drive: a thrust against Lee in Virginia, with Richmond as his goal, and a thrust against Atlanta to be led by Sherman.

IN THE WILDERNESS

General Ulysses S. Grant decides to "fight it out"; victory in the west

July 4, Independence Day, was celebrated with rejoicing in the North as Meade's victory over Lee at Gettysburg was announced. While victory bells rang in Baltimore, Washington, Philadelphia and New York, telegraph wires flashed an incredible piece of news: an aide had ridden into Holly Springs, Miss., plastered with mud and incoherent with excitement. He said Grant was in Vicksburg, that Gen. J. E. Johnston's Confederate Army of the West was cut off, and that "our general and troops are safe."

The Vicksburg campaign lasted from November, 1862, to July, 1863. Supported by Admiral Porter's fleet, Grant managed, after great effort, to place an army of 70,000 men and 200 guns in such a position as to besiege the strongly-fortified city. Gen. Johnston's 25,000 troops, meanwhile, were prevented by Major Gen. William Tecumseh

Sherman from joining Gen. J. C. Pemberton's army. For 47 days Pemberton's 25,000 rebels held out, capitulating on July 4, 1863. The fall of Vicksburg, together with the strongest Confederate Army in the West, gave Grant's 98,000 Federals complete control of the Mississippi and severed Arkansas, Louisiana, and Texas from the remainder of the Confederacy.

UGLY PROTESTS were hurled by retired Gen. McClellan and Northern press at Grant's "hammer tactics." Lincoln, however, stuck by Grant.

It was now possible for Grant to shift troops eastward to join in the campaigns there. In March, 1864, Grant was transferred east and appointed Commander-in-Chief of all the Union armies. He put his most trusted lieutenant, General Sherman, in command of the three veteran armies of the West. Sherman promptly selected McPherson as head of the Army of the Tennessee, which had captured Vicksburg. The Army of the Cumberland, which had fought at Murfreesboro and Chickamauga, remained under Thomas. Command of the Army of the Ohio, which had fought with Burnside at Knoxville, was given to Gen. John Schofield. Thus threatened, the Confederacy's days were numbered.

GRANT'S COUNCIL OF WAR at Bethesda (l.), just before the battle of Cold Harbor, ended in a tremendous decision on June 2, 1864. After losing 17,000 men in the Wilderness, May 5 and 6, and more at Spotsylvania, May 10 and 12, Grant gravely announced: "I propose to fight it out on this line if its takes all summer." It took all summer, all winter ,and 43,000 more lives. Northern patriots and the Northern press howled with anger. "Unconditional Surrender Grant" now became "Butcher Grant." Union troops (r.) protected Federal rail communications during campaign.

SIEGE OF PETERSBURG

Grant's failure at Cold Harbor, June 3, 1864, destroyed his last chance to turn Lee's right flank north of Richmond. Petersburg, situated just 21 miles south of Richmond on the southern bank of the Appomattox, stood between Grant and Lee. On June 16, the Army of the Potomac under Meade crossed the James River. Mortars like 13-inch, 17,000 pound "Dictator" (above), hurled 200-pound exploding shells two miles against Beauregard's Petersburg garrison. Between June 18-30 Grant's frontal assaults together with the crater engagement cost 14,000 men. General Grant settled for a long blockade, ending in April, 1865.

BLOODSHED AT THE CRATER within Elliott's salient thwarted the attempts of Burnside and Meade to storm Petersburg. The Federals blew a big crater in rebel works on July 30, but Confederate Gen. W. Mahone's 18,000 gallant rebels (above) repulsed 50,000 Federals ranged along a 10-mile front and smothered 4,000 Yankees in debris of Petersburg crater.

OLD WESTOVER MANSION, located in Charles County, Va., was built by William Byrd, II, and designed by Taliaferro around 1730. Westover Mansion was occupied by Federal troops during eastern campaigns and, as painting depicts, one wing was destroyed by Union artillery. Many southern estates were wrecked during advance of Grant, Sherman and Sheridan.

SIDELIGHT in the fighting of 1864 took place on May 15, when the cadet corps — the entire student body — of Virginia Military Institute participated in Battle of New Market, Va. (right). Ten cadets were killed, 47 injured. In retaliation, Gen. David Hunter attacked the Institute. All of the cadets escaped as Hunter approached, but his forces looted and burned the school buildings, including the barracks (left). Many Confederate officers were graduates of VMI. Others took their training at Citadel in Charlestown, and before the war, West Point drew heavily from Southern families.

WASHINGTON, D. C. THREATENED

Only once were McClellan's elaborate fortifications protecting Washington seriously threatened. That threat took place when Gen. Jubal Early's 10,000 cavalrymen confronted the capital in July, 1864. Union troops were rushed northward and Early withdrew. Northern insistence that Washington be strongly defended was a strategical error. The numerical superiority of the Army of the Potomac as compared with Lee's Army of Northern Virginia had been considerably reduced by McClellan in 1861 when Federal troops (l.) were assigned to "guard the Potomac." In 1864, Grant revised McClellan's policy, left only a few heavy artillery regiments (r.) to defend Washington. Grant then outnumbered Lee in the field.

TO WHITE HOUSE went six soldiers whose records assisted them to the Presidency. They were Brig. Gen. Benjamin Harrison (l.), Brig. Gen. A. Johnson, Gen. U. S. Grant, Maj. Gen. Rutherford B. Hayes, Maj. General James A. Garfield, and Major William McKinley.

LT. ARTHUR MacAR-THUR (r.) was one of the Civil War's youngest Medal of Honor winners. Promoted to colonel shortly after the war, MacArthur, father of Gen. Douglas MacArthur of World War II fame, served along western frontier, and during Spanish-American War.

THE RODMAN GUN in Battery Rodgers, near Alexandria, Va., was the largest standard battery weapon of its kind at the opening of the Civil War. The 15-inch mammoth rifle, rising from atop a bluff 28 feet above the Potomac River, was erected to guard the south side of Washington from an attack by the Confederate Navy. The huge 117,000 pound gun was designed by Capt. T. J. Rodman.

SHERIDAN'S RIDE

Major General Philip Henry Sheridan's famous ride from Winchester and final charge at Cedar Creek (below r.), 20 miles distant, on Oct. 19, 1864, overwhelmed Gen. Jubal Early's Confederates. Southern troops paused, found themselves attacked by the Northern Army of the Shenandoah that they had just defeated. Then, "finding the Federals not only in superior force but with completely changed morale, they broke before the excellent charge of their united enemy." Infantry, cavalry, and artillery all pressed on to Union victory. Gen. Sheridan (below l.) was the leader who relieved the Union cavalry from waste of energy and forged it into an arm of the service as effective and terrible to the Confederate cause as the Southern cavalry had been to the Northern efforts at the outset of the war.

SHERMAN'S MARCH TO THE SEA climaxed the greatest military drive of the war. Sherman's decision to break his own line of communications and live off the land proved fatal to Lee. The Army of the West marched into Savannah, and then turned north, through the heart of South Carolina.

Federal cavalry officer Judson Kilpatrick was ordered to "forage liberally on the country" — and he did. His men burned, destroyed and looted everything in sight. More than $100 million in property was devastated during long march. On Feb. 17, Sherman seized Columbia, enroute north.

GEN. SHERMAN was the Union's chief exponent of the tactical belief "that long marches count as much as fighting." When the Atlanta City Council asked Sherman to spare the fallen city, he replied: "You might as well appeal against the thunderstorm." Atlanta was burned.

General William Tecumseh
SHERMAN
takes city of Atlanta,
then marches to the sea

While Thomas held the rebels out of Tennessee, Grant began his Wilderness campaign and advanced toward Richmond May 7, 1864. Simultaneously, Sherman, with 100,-000 men, cut loose from his base of supplies at Chattanooga and began his giant 100-mile pincers movement against Georgia.

Johnston, who had replaced Bragg after Chattanooga, faced Sherman with 60,000 troops. He succeeded in slowing down Sherman by a series of defensive actions at Resaca, May 13-16; New Hope Church, May 25-28; and Kenesaw Mountain on June 27. On July 17 Sherman crossed the Chattahoochee River, only eight miles from Atlanta. As a result of this Johnston was removed from his command. His successor, Gen. J. B. Hood, offering battle, was defeated July 22.

While Atlanta burned, Sherman organized a select army of 62,000 in two wings, under Howard and Slocum. Sherman then turned his back to the west and his face toward the sea and prepared to "make Georgia howl!" Federal troops systematically destroyed rebel property on a 60-mile front. Emerging at Savannah, Sherman made that city a Christmas present to Lincoln. Then turning northward, he seized Columbia and compelled the surrender of Charleston.

HOOD'S RETREAT forced the demolition of the Georgia Central Railroad and Rolling Mill. As Hood withdrew from burning Atlanta for Tennessee, six engines, about 100 abandoned box cars loaded with ammunition, were blown up.

JOHN BELL HOOD, brigadier general, was "a magnificent human animal, six feet, two inches tall," who had lost the use of an arm at Gettysburg, a leg at Chickamauga, and who during his heroic defense of the manufacturing center of Atlanta, "had to be strapped to his horse."

CHARLESTON FALLS

The South Carolina city, as seen from the Circular Church, itself reduced to bare blackened walls, was devastated by fire from naval bombardment. The abandonment of Charleston had not been the result of any Northern military assault, but of Sherman's advance through the heart of South Carolina. The Confederate stronghold capitulated to the Federal Navy on Feb. 17, simultaneously with the entrance of Sherman into Columbia. The entire Northern army, Gen. Sherman wrote, "is burning with an insatiable desire to wreak vengeance upon South Carolina. I almost tremble at her fate but feel that she deserves all that seems in store for her."

"THE WALLS CAME TUMBLING DOWN" — illustrates the fate of the stone blocks of Fort Sumter after the Confederate-manned fortress had been breached by the pounding of Rear Admiral John A. B. Dahlgren's heavy, rifled guns. Numerous earth-filled gabions (or baskets) were thrown up around the walls as naval guns dislodged the earthworks. On July 9, 1863, Dahlgren demanded the surrender of the fort. Major Stephen Elliott replied: "Come and take it." Fourteen months and eight days later, after a relentless cannonading by units of Atlantic Fleet, the fort was evacuated.

FARRAGUT AT MOBILE BAY

By the close of 1863 Union ships controlled all the important ports except Wilmington and Mobile. Blockade-runners found it more difficult to carry their trade from ports in the West Indies. Federal blockading fleets destroyed 1,150 vessels, with their cargoes, valued at $30 million. Mobile became the Confederacy's main shipping point after New Orleans' capture. Farragut's fleet, with the *Hartford* leading, gathered in July of 1864 for an assault. His famous order to "DAMN THE TORPEDOES! FULL SPEED AHEAD!" sealed doom of Admiral F. Buchanan in ironclad *Tennessee*. Mobile surrendered Aug. 23.

FARRAGUT AND GRANGER met inside captured Fort Gaines on Dauphin Island after the battle of Mobile Bay to discuss plans for a combined land-sea assault on **Fort Morgan**. Farragut's aggressiveness at New Orleans, and again at Mobile, had accomplished what was deemed impossible. Mobile finally surrendered to Gen. G. Granger.

FORT MORGAN, at Mobile Bay, bore the brunt of 3,000 missiles from Federal artillery and naval guns. General Page was finally induced to raise the white flag of surrender on Aug. 23.

SUBMARINE *H. L. Hunley* was accepted by critics as either an "underwater menace," a "fish," or a "floating coffin." Opinions were revised after the Confederate *Hunley* sent the *Housatanic* to the bottom of North Channel in Charleston harbor.

KEARSARGE'S OFFICERS (above) pose beside one of the warships' two 11-inch pivot-guns which sent Confederate Admiral Semmes' raider *Alabama* to bottom off Cherbourg, France, on July 17, 1864.

CHARGING GUNBOAT *SASSACUS* thwarted the ram *Albemarle's* single-handed attempt to run through the Northern blockading flotilla off North Carolina in May, 1864. Six months later, *Albemarle* was blown up during the darkness of night by Lt. W. B. Cushing.

BRIGHT FACED LITTLE "POWDER MONKEY" leans picturesquely against the pivot-gun of the warship *New Hampshire* off Charleston to pose for the cameraman who has preserved this typical scene of sailors' idle hour. No educational qualification was required, and some of the seamen could scarcely speak English.

SAILORS ABOARD THE *MENDOTA* congregate on the after-deck for checkers, banjo-playing, and other diversions. Men from inland towns and farms as well as experienced seamen from coast joined Union Navy. Higher navy pay and a slice of the prize money made it increasingly diffi- cult for many foreign ships of commerce to procure merchant-seamen. Englishmen, Norwegians and Swedes, Danes, Russians, Frenchmen, Germans, Portugese and Spaniards were found on United States warships. Nautical terms and orders, sea-language were the same the world over.

"LONG ABRAHAM a little longer" was the title of this satirical sketch of Lincoln in *Harper's Weekly* after his re-election in Nov., 1864.

DEMOCRATIC SUPPORTERS of Gen. George B. McClellan parade streets of New York in campaign of 1864. McClellan joined forces with Lincoln's political foes after "Little Mac" was dismissed by the President. Democrats included peace advocates but McClellan was in favor of continuing struggle.

LINCOLN RE-ELECTED
Harassed President expected to be defeated

Lincoln's prospects for re-election in 1864 seemed so remote that he once publicly promised to "cooperate with the president-elect."

A group of violent abolitionists split from the Republican party. They nominated Gen. John C. Fremont for president. The Regular Democrats convened in Chicago to bring together the "Copperhead" elements in the North. This group nominated Gen. George B. McClellan.

Lincoln had been renominated in Baltimore in June by the Republicans on a Union platform designed to draw the support of the "War Democrats." Radical abolitionists led by Henry Winter Davis of Maryland and Ben Wade of Ohio called a convention in September to seek Lincoln's retirement.

Politics were in a turmoil; people were tired of the war, which was going badly. Lincoln's defeat was generally forecast.

Then news came from Georgia which electrified the nation. Gen. Sherman had routed Hood's army from Atlanta in one of the most disastrous Confederate defeats, and Farragut had won the battle of Mobile Bay. The President issued a proclamation on Sept. 3 setting a day of thanksgiving for the great Northern victories. The opposition collapsed at home and Fremont withdrew his candidacy.

Lincoln received an electoral vote of 212 against 21. The popular vote was Lincoln, 2,330,552 and McClellan, 1,835,894.

On March 4, 1865, Lincoln took the oath of office. It was an hour of personal triumph for the President, but there was no triumph in his voice as he spoke the moving words of his Second Inaugural Address: "With malice toward none, with charity for all, with firmness in the right, as God gives us to see the right, let us strive on to finish the work we are in ..."

SOLDIERS voted heavily for Lincoln, encouraged by their commanders, who were openly in favor of the President. Here, men of Army of the Potomac line up to cast their ballots while a politician speaks persuasively to voter on sidelines.

COPPERHEAD Clement Vallandigham, of Dayton, Ohio, was arrested for sedition by Union soldiers. Lincoln ordered him expelled into the Confederacy. He termed war "wicked, cruel," returned North, campaigned against Lincoln.

"WRETCHED CONDITIONS" of the Southern Commissioners" is the title of this Northern cartoon which depicts the Confederate agents abroad as mendicants. The Southern mission was then engaged in an effort to borrow foreign capital and did, in fact, receive $15 million from the French.

BRITISH WORKERS in the textile industries of Lancashire were thrown on charity when a Southern embargo on export of cotton closed down the mills. More than three million Britons made their living in the cotton mills and the South hoped by embargo to force British to intervene in the war.

FOREIGN AFFAIRS

"King Cotton" fails to obtain recognition from European powers for the Southern cause

"Cotton is King" was the watchword of the Confederate diplomats. Southern diplomacy was based upon the assumption that England and France would intervene before they would see their cotton supplies cut off. It was on this premise that Confederate Secretary of State Robert Toombs sent off a commission on March 16, 1861, to seek recognition from England, France, Spain, Belgium and Russia. The mission gained one important concession. England and France granted the Confederacy the legal status of a belligerent.

U.S. Secretary of State William Seward then embarked on a campaign of threats, cajolery and bluff to prevent the recognition of the Confederacy. Lord John Russell, the British foreign secretary, would have liked nothing better than to see the United States divided and weakened. He was supported in this view by Emperor Napoleon III of France, who was busy putting Maximilian of Austria on the throne of Mexico in defiance of the Monroe Doctrine.

By alternate threats and professions of friendship, Seward waged such a war of nerves on Napoleon and Lord Palmerston, the British prime minister, that neither was willing to provoke the United States. America and England came very close to war when an American ship seized Confederate Commissioners James M. Mason and John Slidell from the British merchantman *Trent* at sea. Then Seward backed gracefully down in the face of an aroused Britain. Mason and Slidell were released and the United States apologized. In his apology Seward noted impishly his pleasure that Britain was so opposed to search and seizure on the seas — the very type of British acts which a half a century earlier had provoked the War of 1812.

Seward's tactics also persuaded the British to seize two powerful ironclads being built for the Confederacy at Liverpool where the Southern raider *Alabama* had earlier been launched.

Jefferson Davis even offered in the end to abolish slavery in return for recognition. By then it was too late. The South had played its cards on the basis that Cotton was King — and Seward had held the Ace.

FRIENDLY RUSSIA sent a fleet on a goodwill mission to the United States. Only Russia, stinging from her defeat in the Crimea, favored the North in the Civil War. Here in the harbor of Alexandria, Va., the crew of the Russian frigate *Osliaba* pose for their picture.

FRENCH EMPEROR Napoleon III intervened in Mexico while U.S. was busy with war. French occupied Mexico City June 7, 1863, and Napoleon put Austrian Archduke Maximilian on Mexican throne. After Civil War ended, Sec. of State sent French an ultimatum, demanding withdrawal. Gen. Sheridan and 50,000 troops were sent to the border. French withdrew in spring of 1867. Mexican partisans, led by Benito Juarez, executed Maximilian (above), June 19, 1867.

RICHMOND FALLS

Confederate armies, trapped between Sherman in the south and Grant in the north and reduced to slow starvation, were no longer able to withstand the pressure. In the spring of 1865, General Lee was appointed Commander-in-Chief of all Confederate forces. He promptly restored Joseph E. Johnston to command. At Bentonville, March 19-20, Sherman and Johnston met in their last battle. Pushing the rebel army before him, Sherman moved into Goldsboro, N. C., on March 21, where he joined Gen. Schofield.

The dashing cavalry officer, Sheridan, destroyed the agricultural resources of the Shenandoah Valley so completely that "a crow flying over it would have to carry its own rations." On April 1, Sheridan won the battle of Five Forks and thus forced the evacuation of Petersburg the following day. The Richmond government issued decrees against conspiracy. Transportation broke down and the blockade tightened. Hunger, disease, desertion and death spread throughout the South. Riots and demonstrations against the Confederacy and the food speculators broke out in Southern cities. On April 3, Richmond (l.) surrendered. Lincoln visited the burning capital of the Confederacy the next day.

LEE SURRENDERS AT APPOMATTOX

In April 1865, Grant, with all his armies, pursued and encircled Lee's army of 30,000 near Lynchburg. Sheridan seized the rail juncture at Burkesville, thus preventing Lee from moving south toward Danville and joining forces with Johnston. On April 7, after five years of continuous combat, the Army of Northern Virginia was forced to yield. Lee asked for terms.

He met Grant in the McLean house at Appomattox Courthouse (r.) on April 9. As Gen. Grant penned the terms his eyes fell upon Lee's magnificent sword, a presentation from the the State of Virginia. Grant immediately added a clause exempting the side-arms of the officers. Then Grant asked for any further suggestions; whereupon Lee explained that the mounted Confederates owned their horses. Grant added that all soldiers could retain private mounts. Lee concluded: "It will be very gratifying and do much toward conciliating our people."

JUBILANT SOLDIERS AND CITIZENS gathered in front of historic Appomattox Courthouse and waited for Lee's departure. When negotiations were over, Grant issued orders to his troops to discontinue firing victory salutes. "The war is over," he said, "the rebels are our countrymen again . . ."

◀ **GENERAL RUFUS INGALLS,** chief quartermaster of the Army of the Potomac (left), is shown astride his veteran war horse "Charger." Other famous cavalry mounts that bore proud names were Lee's "Traveller"; Grant's "Cincinnati"; Kearny's "Bayard" and A. S. Johnston's "Fire-Eater." Great numbers of horses and ability to feed them helped North win war.

GEN. ROBERT E. LEE

The prospect of secession had caused Lee endless anguish from the beginning. When civil war became a certainty, Lincoln offered him command of the Federal forces in the field. Political and economic arguments for Southern independence made little impression on Lee. The issue rested solely upon a conviction that his first allegiance was due his state, Virginia. Lee declined Lincoln's proposal.

After Fort Sumter, Virginia authorities offered Lee command of the forces of the State of Virginia. His colonial mansion at Arlington, Va. (l.), was thereafter seized by the Union. In May, 1862, Gen. Joseph E. Johnston was severely wounded and Lee was given command of the Army of Northern Virginia. His contributions to the art of war earned for him the reputation of being "one of the truly great modern soldiers and probably the most eminent American strategist."

FINAL ACT of the great Civil War drama occurred in April, 1865, at Point Lookout Prison, Maryland (l.). Confederate prisoners took the oath of allegiance to the flag of the United States under which they stood, their hands touching Bibles, one held by each group of four. Union war loss statistics cite 67,000 killed in action, 43,000 dead of wounds, and 248,000 from disease and other causes. Southern losses totaled 368,000 in all categories. War expenditures for the Union totaled $4 billion compared with Confederate expenditures of more than $2 billion. A wounded colored soldier (r.) stands erect as "Fader Abraham," liberator of his race, visited the 18th Corps of the Union Army at City Point, Virginia, as war ended.

FLIGHT OF JEFFERSON DAVIS across the Carolinas ended on May 10, at Irwindale, Ga. The President of the Confederacy was captured by Federal cavalry and an ambulance was ordered to convey him to Fortress Monroe, Virginia, for confinement as a prisoner of state.

TWO HUNDRED THOUSAND MEN IN BLUE swung down ➤ Washington's famous Pennsylvania Avenue in Grand Review on May 23, 1865. Citizens and officials in silk hats lined the avenue again on June 8 (r.) for the march of Sixth Corps of Potomac Army.

ASSASSIN John Wilkes Booth slipped into the President's box in Ford's Theater when Lincoln's guard, a besotted Washington policeman, reeled away to get a drink. Booth shot Lincoln in the head, then stabbed Major Rathbone, who attempted to seize him. The surgeon-general and other

physicians were summoned immediately. An examination of the President's wound showed there was no hope for recovery. Ford's Theater was immediately closed. Theater was draped in mourning and guarded by soldiers (l.) when this picture was taken a few days after the assassination.

LINCOLN'S GROWTH in stature through the years is depicted in this sketch. When Lincoln became President he was a well known public figure, but of less consequence than many of his day. The war elevated him to top rank and he continued to be revered when contemporaries were forgotten.

DEATH BLOW

Nation mourns for slain president

Five days had passed since Appomattox and Washington was in a holiday mood. On this Good Friday (April 14, 1865) the President and Mrs. Lincoln went to Ford's Theatre in company with Major Rathbone and his fiancee to see *Our American Cousin*. Shortly after 10 o'clock an actor named John Wilkes Booth entered the President's box. The guard had wandered off for a drink of whisky. Booth stepped inside and fired a Derringer pistol into the back of Lincoln's head, then leaped to the stage, breaking his leg in the fall. With a melodramatic flourish of a dagger he staggered out the stage door and into the night. Lincoln was carried to the Peterson house across the street. There he died at seven o'clock the next morning without regaining consciousness.

His death plunged the nation into an agony of grief such as it had never known. The great President, who was reviled and maligned in life, became in death a hero even to his enemies.

History has since taken the full measure of Abraham Lincoln. The Kentucky back-country rustic without formal schooling raised himself by his own intelligence and determination to the rank of prairie statesman and learned lawyer and famous orator. In his gnarled oak character were mingled humor and reverence, shrewdness and frankness, humility and courage, and above all, complete confidence in himself. Chance placed in his hands the presidency on the eve of civil war, and probably no man in America was better fitted to the task. The history of the Civil War is symbolized by Lincoln's iron devotion to the Union and by his firmness in the right as God gave him to see it.

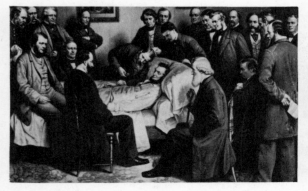

LINCOLN DIED in a house across the street from Ford's Theatre ten hours after he was shot, while his cabinet and his family stood by. The nation was grief stricken. The President was given a public funeral such as America had never witnessed. Towns were draped in black along the route of his

funeral cortege and thousands turned out. The center photo shows the ornate funeral catafalque outside Independence Hall in Philadelphia where soldiers hold back the crowd. Notables were assembled outside Lincoln's home in Springfield, Ill. (right), for the funeral and burial services.

THE CONSPIRACY

Lincoln's assassination was part of a plot led by John Wilkes Booth, an actor and a member of a notable stage family. Booth was apparently less a Southern sympathizer than an opportunist in search of a spectacular stroke to gain attention. Financed by Southern agents in Canada, he had hatched a scheme to kidnap the President. This plan was finally rejected in favor of assassination. Booth was detailed to kill Lincoln while another conspirator, Lewis Powell, or Payne, a Confederate deserter, made an attempt to kill Secretary of State Seward. The attempt nearly succeeded and Seward's throat was cut, although not fatally, as he lay in his bed recovering from injuries received in a carriage smashup. Powell posed defiantly for his photograph (above) shortly after his capture. A third member of the gang, George A. Adzerodt, a middle-aged Confederate spy, was supposed to kill Vice-President Johnson, but lost his nerve. After the shooting Booth fled on horseback southward, accompanied by his personal aide, David Herold. The government issued offers of a reward (above) for the capture before they were trapped in a barn near Port Royal, Va. Herold surrendered. Booth was killed. He is shown at right being tempted by Satan.

DEATH ON THE SCAFFOLD awaited the conspirators. After a trial by a special military court, David E. Herold, George A. Adzerodt, Lewis Payne and Mrs. Mary E. Surratt, keeper of a Washington boardinghouse where the conspirators met, were sentenced to be hanged. The sentence was carried out, as this picture shows, in the Washington prison yard on July 7, 1865. Michael O'Lauchlin, Edward Spangler, Samuel Arnold and Dr. Samuel A. Mudd were convicted of conspiracy and sentenced to imprisonment. O'Lauchlin died in a military prison. Others were later pardoned.

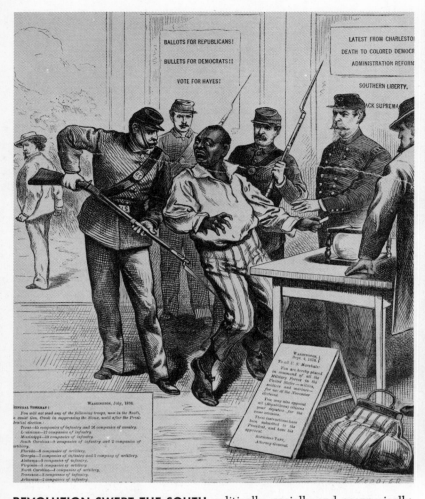

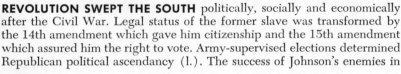

REVOLUTION SWEPT THE SOUTH politically, socially and economically after the Civil War. Legal status of the former slave was transformed by the 14th amendment which gave him citizenship and the 15th amendment which assured him the right to vote. Army-supervised elections determined Republican political ascendancy (l.). The success of Johnson's enemies in socially degrading the Southern whites is shown in the composition of the South Carolina legislature of 1868 (u.r.). Of 146 members, 90 were Negroes, few of whom could read and write. The absence of slave labor, which had been indispensable to productive system, caused economic prostration. Soldiers returned to bread lines supervised by the Union army (r.).

RECONSTRUCTION ERA
Carpetbaggers and Radical Republicans create antagonistic South

Andrew Johnson, who once told a Washington street crowd he would hang Jefferson Davis and all the "diabolical" secessionists if he ever got a chance, adopted a different course when he actually became President. He proclaimed a general pardon for the Confederate rank and file, while Davis and the other leaders were held in confinement.

The initial phase of Southern Reconstruction was carried out by the Freedmen's Bureau, which assigned abandoned land to former slaves, protecting them against forced labor. Johnson carried out Lincoln's plan for restoring civil government in the South. By July, 1865, provisional governors had been named for all of the Confederate states. Constitutional conventions declared the ordinances of secession were invalid and abolished slavery in the states forever. Elections were held throughout the South and governors and legislatures were chosen.

As Johnson's lenient plan for leaving Southern reorganization to the white electorate became clear, a break with radical members of his party seemed inevitable. When the 39th Congress met Dec. 4, 1865, revengeful extremists led by Thaddeus Stevens in the House and Charles Sumner in the Senate seized control and denied recognition to members elected from rebel states. They created a Joint Committee on Reconstruction, which sponsored the 14th amendment, giving citizenship to Negroes. The Reconstruction Act followed on March 2, 1867, dividing the South into five military districts. The act ordered constitutional conventions with delegates to be elected by Negroes and loyal whites. Constitutions provided for Negro suffrage and election of legislatures pledged to ratify 14th amendment.

ANDREW JOHNSON, uncouth ex-governor of Tenn., was a devout Unionist and had been nominated Vice-President in 1864 to illustrate inclusion of the South in the Republican party.

VINDICTIVE Thaddeus Stevens, Congressman from Pa., wanted Confederate leaders severely punished, Southern plantations confiscated and Southern political reorganization postponed.

OUTRAGED by the treachery of Secretary of War Edwin Stanton, in approving Reconstruction Act, Johnson suspended him from office. Tenure of Office Act, which had been passed by Radicals to keep Johnson from removing civil officers, made the President guilty of a misdemeanor for his act. On Feb. 24, 1868, the House adopted a resolution calling for impeachment of Johnson for high crimes and misdemeanors in office, inaugurating the first Presidential impeachment proceedings in history.

The trial, beginning March 13, soon degenerated into the farcial question of whether Johnson should be deposed because of opposition to Congress—not whether he was guilty of any crime. Conviction failed by one vote. Elements which triumphed in making new Southern constitutions ordered by Reconstruction Act were mainly politically ignorant freedmen led by Northern "carpetbaggers" and native whites contemptuously called "scalawags."

Following ratification of new constitutions in 1868, Congress restored Arkansas, the Carolinas, Georgia, Florida, Louisiana and Alabama to representation. In a bid for political power, Congress saw to it that several million ex-soldiers received pensions (r.) on eminently generous terms.

"SEWARD'S ICEBOX" was name given to Alaska after purchase of the territory by U.S. Sec. of State William Seward was asasiled for buying a "dreary waste of glaciers and icebergs." But Alaska more than repaid purchase price before turn of the century. Cartoon (l.) depicts Seward leaving for Alaska's "genial climate" after retirement. Alaska purchase agreement was signed hours after Russian czar offered to sell. Seward is shown (right) with pen in hand at signing. U.S. paid Russia $7.2 million but only $1.4 million actually was applied to the purchase. Remaining $5.8 million was paid for the expenses of Russia's "friendly naval demonstration" for the North in New York harbor during the Civil War.

HAMILTON FISH worked actively for election of Grant in 1868 and was rewarded with appointment as Secretary of State. Only cabinet member to serve through both of Grant's terms, Fish brought integrity and competent leadership to the office of U.S. foreign relations.

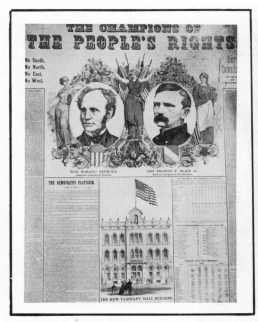

ELECTION OF 1868 saw triumphant and popular Gen. Ulysses S. Grant winning on a Republican platform which enthusiastically approved Congressional Reconstruction, condemned Johnson and the Democrats, and advocated payment of the national debt in gold. Grant was swept into the arms of the Radicals after a violent quarrel with Johnson. Above, Union veterans carry torches for Democratic nominee Horatio Seymour, in a New York parade (r.). Seymour, governor of New York, campaigned for lower taxes, less Reconstruction and more greenback money. Grant's running mate was Schuyler Colfax, an Indiana Radical. Grant captured 26 of 34 states. Left, campaign poster for Seymour and running mate, Gen. Francis Blair.

GOLDEN SPIKE ceremony at Promontory, Utah, May 10, 1869, marked the completion of the first transcontinental rail route. Construction was undertaken from the East by Union Pacific from Omaha and from the West by Central Pacific, headed by Leland Stanford. First through train from California to New York arrived July 29, 1869, after six-and-one-half day run.

RAIL CONSTRUCTION from the West, by coolie labor, was heavily subsidized by the government. Union Pacific's machinations with the corrupt Credit Mobilier yielded huge profits for stockholders and government officials. The eight years following the Civil War witnessed construction of 35,000 miles of track. Rail stock overspeculation helped cause 1873 panic.

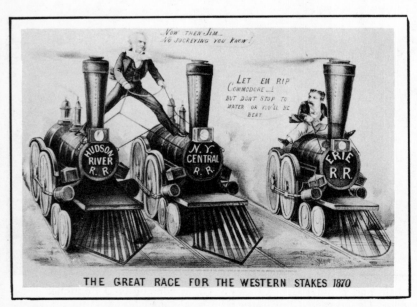

GREAT RACE for the western stakes came in 1870, as competing Eastern lines ventured west. Shipowner Commodore Cornelius Vanderbilt transferred his capital to railroads, obtaining controlling interests in large number of eastern lines and extending his system to Chicago. He is shown in cartoon racing Jim Fisk who, with Jay Gould, controlled Erie railroad.

BOOM YEARS

Railroads link the industrial East with expanding Western frontiers

At the end of the Civil War the United States had hardly advanced beyond the Missouri, its railway system was modest, and ony $1.5 billion was invested in manufacturing. By 1877, settlement had expanded to the Pacific, American railroads were the finest in the world and manufacturing investments had doubled.

The North's wartime boom continued unabated. Capital was abundant and with credit inflated, banks flourished as never before. Big business expanded at a phenomenal rate. There were more cotton spindles, iron furnaces, steel mills, more coal and copper mines, more lumber mills and more manufacturing than during any equivalent period in the nation's history.

Ten years after its start in England, the modern steel process reached America. By 1875, there were more than a dozen important steel works flourishing, especially in Pennsylvania, with the major portion of the output going to railroads.

Other industries grew as rapidly — meat packing, oil, shoe manufacturing, clothing, watches, sewing machines, farm implements. As more consumer goods were made in factories managed by corporate boards, industrial growth led to a fever of speculation and the rise of financial institutions.

More and more people were lured to the great West as railroads advanced. Settlers acquired homes through provisions of the Homestead Act and other land-grants. In 1871-72, 6,000 homesteads were granted. By 1876, settlers had acquired 26,000 more. Tillable lands went to small holders, eastern clerks and artisans and European immigrants, who settled in national groups in certain areas.

The plains states concentrated on farming and ranching. Mineral resources, however, were the lure to settlers in the mountain states and Far West. Survey parties explored the canyons of western rivers, seeking silver, gold and other metals. The mountain states became a hive of mining camps and boom towns.

Closer contact with the East was maintained by way of the new railroads. The ever-growing number of settlers in the West developed a cultural pattern based on the East but influenced by the West's rugged individualism. Social order was brought to the West with schools and churches slowly taming an area which had been known for its restless, warring Indians, famed Indian scouts and the cowboy — an individual roughened to face rugged Western life.

The boom years also were inventive years. Out of the period came the refrigerator, oil tank and Pullman cars, Westinghouse's automatic air brake and other railroad developments. Oil pipelines also helped speed the transportation of petroleum. Great strides were made in communications and farm equipment. Even the severe depression of 1873, though it ended the boom, did not halt America's steady growth and expansion.

VANDERBILT

PULLMAN

STANFORD

INDUSTRIAL TYCOONS built their fortunes from meager beginnings. At 16, Cornelius Vanderbilt bought his first boat to ferry passengers and goods from Staten Island to New York City. George Pullman began as a building contractor. In 1859 he made a sleeping car, since developed into the "Pullman," and organized the Pullman Palace Car Co. Leland Stanford went West in 1852, established a mercantile business, and formed Central Pacific with Collis P. Huntington, Charles Crocker and Mark Hopkins.

ATLANTIC CABLE, constructed by efforts of Cyrus Field and cooperating English and American capitalists, and reaching to London, was completed in 1858. The first cable was soon destroyed by use of too strong current but another was laid in 1866 and many more thereafter. Third cable was laid by *Great Eastern,* largest steamship of its time. U.S. businessmen and newspapers profited from cable by gaining quicker knowledge of world affairs.

NEW YORK DOCKS reveal the shipping and trading activity of the boom. Sidewheels, steam and sailing vessels carried goods to coastal and European ports. "Jubilee Jim" Fisk, Jr. made his first New York appearance as negotiator for the purchase of trading ships. Commerce with Europe brought interchange of ideas and inventions. The postal card was introduced from the Continent; Edison, Bell sought telegraph, telephone communication.

JOHN D. ROCKEFELLER, richest man in the world in his day, entered the produce commission business at 19 and two years later was engaged in the oil business in Cleveland. From the firm of Rockefeller and Andrews in 1865, he expanded and formed the Standard Oil Company of Ohio in 1870. Keen competition was driving the small refineries out of business. They were absorbed by Rockefeller, who had the capital required to bring the industry under virtually single ownership. Most phenomenal development in oil field activity was in the Pennsylvania area. From Col. E. L. Drake's first well in 1859 near Titusville had sprung a 400-square-mile district dotted with derricks and producing more than two million barrels a year. Overnight oil towns such as Funkville (above) and Pithole City sprang up. Rockefeller controlled 90 per cent of refineries by 1882, a near monopoly.

MODERN STEEL PROCESS, begun by Bessemer in England, revolutionized the industry after the Civil War. Captain Eber S. Ward of Detroit became first U.S. steel king, later surrendering his patent to Alexander M. Holley, who held Bessemer rights. Demand was created for cheap steel, and by 1875 Carnegie, Phipps, Frick and Schwab were turning out steel products. Carnegie's company was largest interest in formation of U.S. Steel in 1901.

FIRST ELEVATED TRAIN created a stir in New York, where overcrowding in central areas looked to new transit developments for relief. The "El" went through in spite of claims by property owners and surface transportation lines that the noise would ruin business and the elevated tracks would detract from the natural beauty of the city's arteries. First such rapid transit system, the Gilbert Elevated Railroad, passed over Sixth Ave. in 1878.

CUSTER'S LAST STAND

Massacre of Gen. George Custer and his men by Sioux Indians was a tragic incident in the long fight to pacify the redman. Push of settlement deprived Indians of lands and food supply of elk and buffalo. Cheating and maltreatment also led to increasing restiveness of Sioux tribes. Indians under Sitting Bull and Crazy Horse ignored orders to return to reservation. They fought ferociously when troops pursued them. During campaign Custer and 264 men were lured into ambush at Little Big Horn River, June 26, 1876. All were slain. Sitting Bull escaped to Canada. Crazy Horse, regarded as greatest cavalry leader of his day, was captured.

BUFFALO BILL CODY

CALAMITY JANE

THE SQUAW MAN

WILD BILL HICKOK

SCOUTS

In addition to the Indian fighters, most of whom were Civil War veterans, the West developed other colorful characters. One of the famous Indian scouts was Buffalo Bill Cody, who helped organize some of the hunts which virtually removed the buffalo from the face of the Western prairies. Cody spent his early life among Indians on the Western frontier, but at the beginning of the Civil War offered his services as a Union Scout. He later served with troops which protected laborers during the construction of the Union Pacific Railroad and took the contract to supply the entire force with fresh buffalo meat. Later he collected a band of Indians, cowboys, rough riders, among them Calamity Jane, unbroken bronchos and a small herd of buffalo and toured the nation with his "Wild West Show." Wild Bill Hickok was a tall, lithe frontiersman, who, though mild-mannered, had slain many antagonists. He was dismissed from Custer's command following a saloon brawl with lawless soldiers. A scout during the Civil War, he served under Custer as a companion of Buffalo Bill and California Joe. Yellowstone Kelly, a scout for General Miles, was sent on long missions into Indian country, once to Sitting Bull's camp north of the border. The latter, a Sioux chief, was the consulting head of 5,000 warriors in 1876. "Liver-Eating" Johnson, a cavalry scout, denied the story that he had once eaten a small piece of an Indian's liver.

YELLOWSTONE KELLY

CHIEF SITTING BULL

LIVER-EATING JOHNSON

CALIFORNIA JOE

INDIAN WARS

Gen. Nelson A. Miles (l.), a Civil War officer, campaigned against hostile Indian tribes in the West, subduing the Sioux in Montana and driving Sitting Bull across the border into Canada, "the land of the Great Mother." In 1877 the Nez Perce Indians went on the warpath in protest against being moved from the Wallowa Valley in northeastern Oregon. Only 500 warriors held off more than 5,000 soldiers while Miles made a 2,000-mile devious march through the mountains to reach Canada. At Bear Paw Mountain, within 50 miles of the Canadian border, Chief Joseph and his Nez Perce braves were surrounded by Miles and forced to surrender. Many years of fighting and more than $20 million were required to subdue the restive Indians. Both the army and the Bureau of Indian Affairs agents played an important part. Military officers accused Indian agents of sentimentality, weakness. Bureau officials said the army was guilty of organized murder.

ABSENCE OF LAW ENFORCEMENT was one of the factors contributing to the rise of desperadoes who rustled cattle, attacked and robbed trains and cross-country stages, and terrorized helpless settlers. Jesse (c.) and Frank James (l.) were the leaders of a notorious gang whose criminal career is a part of the history of the West. Young Bob Ford (r.), one of James' henchmen, led a group of gunmen to call on Jesse at his St. Joseph, Mo. hideout on April 3, 1882. They planned to kill him and share the $10,000 reward. Jesse James, who was unarmed in order not to arouse the suspicions of a passerby, rose to straighten a picture and was a perfect target for Ford's bullet.

TIBURCIO VASQUEZ turned to crime after trouble during a fight with Americans at his dance-hall. He led an outlaw band, terrorizing Calif. with kidnapping, robbery and stagecoach holdups until captured.

YOUNGER BROTHERS, Bob, Jim and Cole, headed another notorious gang of outlaws. Their attempted robbery of the bank at Northfield, Minn., in 1876, resulted in their imprisonment in the penitentiary at Stillwater, Minn., where this photograph with their sister, Henrietta, was made in 1889.

LAW WEST OF THE PECOS was Judge Roy Bean, who held court with "one law book and a six-shooter" and tended bar between sessions. Bean was justice of the peace in a lawless Texas area and heard all types of cases. He rendered "unorthodox but witty" decisions and his judgment in such cases as the murder of a Chinese ranch cook by a cowboy often depended on the amount of money the defendant had with him or could raise to pay his fines.

SECRET AGENCIES were South's answer to rigid military control. Ku Klux Klan terrorized Negroes and disciplined carpetbaggers. Klan was formally dissolved after irresponsible men joined, committing outrages on innocent persons.

MEXICAN AMERICANS were integral part of San Antonio life and customs. When painting of Market Plaza was made in 1879, Mexican population was larger than that of whites. "Cowtowns" sprang up along tracks of the Santa Fe railroad and developed into large communities. Dodge City, Abilene, Kansas City and Wichita are a few cities which grew on the railroad. Other cities thrived on trade with miners en route to gold fields.

PLANK STREET was the pride of Grass Valley, California. Plentiful lumber from nearby Sierras made Mill Street one of few mudless ones in rough and dirty mother-lode towns. Wood-block paving was also used, proved more durable than planks and still exists.

FIRST PHOTOGRAPH of Helena, Montana, was taken in 1865. Gold had been discovered in Last Chance Gulch on July 14, 1864, by four prospectors. One year later Helena had become center of mining activity, with discovery of quartz lodes leading to rich long-term mining and steady development; a contrast to most boom towns.

LOS ANGELES became the center of a thriving wine industry after importation of superior vines from Europe. First carload of oranges was sent east in 1877, beginning a new era of prosperity. Los Angeles doubled in population every decade.

"THAR'S GOLD! in them thar hills" brought fortune hunters swarming to Cherry Creek, Cripple Creek and Pike's Peak, between 1858 and 1890. Mining of gold, carbonates, and silver created Denver, Central City, Leadville, and a host of other mountain towns. Main commercial streets of Denver were Blake (above) and Larimer, both robust mining stems that ran to Cherry Creek. Visitors included Oscar Wilde, Buffalo Bill, Duke of York.

COW CAPITAL of America was Dodge City, on the sunny plains of southwestern Kansas. A riotous Western town, Dodge City boasted dusty streets, cowboys, buffalo hunters, bullwhackers and muleskinners. It was the shipping center to Kansas City and Chicago packing plants for herds of cattle driven up from Texas. Fast-riding cowhands, whipping the stampeding Texas longhorns into line in the town's wide streets, were a common sight.

BOLD RACE of Plains Indians (such as these Omahas) looked with growing apprehension on encroachments of whites, whom they believed were bent on exterminating them. Red Cloud, an Ogalala Sioux chief, organized formidable resistance. On Dec. 21, 1866, a party left Fort Phil Kearny to gather wood. When Indians attacked them, Capt. Fetterman and 80 men rode out to rescue, and were in turn massacred by Red Cloud's warriors.

RIVER MERCHANTS were the principal contact with the East for some rapidly growing cities not touched by rail routes. The Mississippi was the nation's north-south artery, while the Missouri riverboats carried goods into the West. On Pacific Coast, Washington's and Oregon's rivers floated logs and traders. Greatest activity was on the Father of Waters, with the South procuring Northern manufactured goods in exchange for cotton and crops.

MAIL AND EXPRESS were enterprise of Henry Wells (l.) and William Fargo (r.). In 1843, Wells competed with the government by running mail between New York City and Buffalo at less than government rates. He teamed with Fargo in 1852 to form Wells, Fargo and Company. It handled express, mail, and pay shipments between New York and San Francisco. Wells was a stammerer and established many schools for those similarly afflicted. W. G. Fargo became president of the American Express Co. when it merged with Wells-Fargo. A brilliant public administrator, he served Buffalo as Mayor from 1862-1866. Line-up of coaches in Ashland, Oregon (above), meant communication and exchange with rest of world. Ashland was fringe-town of Wells-Fargo and would not have existed except for it. The railroad and the stage coaches were the life lines of the country.

WANTON DESTRUCTION of redwoods deprived California and Oregon of countless trees, valuable to soil conservation. John Muir, spent large part of his life fighting for the conservation of American forests. His efforts helped initiate vast conservation program and aided passage of the Yosemite National Park Bill.

RAILROAD SURVEY PARTIES in the Western states met with difficulties in rugged ranges like northeastern Utah's high Uintahs. Smithsonian Institution and Interior Department also conducted surveys under the most adverse conditions.

BARBARY COAST of San Francisco was a center of gay life. Gambling and lawlessness were commonplace. San Francisco became West Coast's chief port, experienced a boom during Nevada's silver rush. Isolation was broken with the completion of transcontinental railroad in 1869.

GRANT ERA

Moral debacle follows war years

The history of the Grant era was a story of blatant public plunder on the national, state and municipal levels. It was the result of the aftermath of war in considerable part, and the frenzied industrial expansion which followed the conflict.

Frauds, chicanery and graft riddled the Internal Revenue Bureau, the Indian Land Office, the Customs Office — practically every department of the government. The infamous Credit Mobilier railroad scandal involved leaders of Congress. "Grantism" became a well-known synonym for corruption.

Administration policies of Grant soon raised sharp opposition. Debtors protested the deflation that resulted from retiring paper money. Advocates of Civil Service reform castigated the President for refusing to deal forthrightly with the issue. The high tariff policy became a subject of heated debate.

Another outstanding example of corruption was the attempt by Jay Gould and James Fisk to corner the gold market. They schemed to force the price of gold upward and reap their profits by forcing short sellers to buy from the stocks they had purchased secretly. The result was "Black Friday," Sept. 24, 1869. Panic and ruin followed for many innocent dealers.

"Salary grab" bills passed by Congress gave the lawmakers a windfall. Cabinet officers were involved in questionable deals with men who stood to benefit from such transactions. Such corruption was not Grant's making. Personally honest, Grant, however, encouraged the forces of corruption by default. He stood by his friends regardless of the crimes they committed, thereby ignoring the interests of the taxpayers and tarnishing the honor of his office.

Discontent in the party culminated in a split which led to the formation of the Liberal Republican party in 1872. The liberal branch of the party chose Horace Greeley as its Presidential candidate. The Democrats, weak and disorganized, hoped to capitalize on the Republican split by also endorsing Greeley. But the choice of the New York editor proved to be a fiasco. A subject of ridicule, he died shortly after the election.

The blunder in picking Greeley, plus Grant's great personal popularity as a Civil War hero, his support from the veterans and national prosperity combined to re-elect him with a substantial margin.

The major positive aspect of the Grant administrations lay in the field of foreign affairs. Secretary of State Hamilton Fish was a notable exception in a Cabinet of mediocrities. Skillful diplomatic negotiations brought about the Treaty of Washington, settling the Civil War dispute between Great Britain and United States. Both countries agreed to submit to an international arbitral tribunal, America's claims against Great Britain for damage (estimated at 100,000 tons with cargoes) done to Northern merchant marine by British-built Confederate raiders, including the *Alabama*. The tribunal awarded U.S. $15.5 million, far short of earlier demands of $2,125 million.

ULYSSES S. GRANT, Civil War hero, was unanimously nominated for the Presidency by the Republicans on the first ballot. A brilliant military leader, he was completely unqualified to lead the nation in a critical period. Grant was an innocent in politics and without either a political or economic philosophy. Having failed at farming and in business, he had an exaggerated regard for the materially successful. He served for two terms (1868-77) despite united efforts of Democrats and rebellious Republicans to defeat him for re-election. Above, Grant is shown with his family.

TWEED RING, headed by William Marcy Tweed, ex-chair-maker and volunteer fireman, robbed New York City of millions annually, increased its debt tenfold in a decade. The brilliant cartoonist, Thomas Nast, fought Tweed mercilessly in *Harper's Weekly*. An attempt to bribe the magazine finally turned the public against the politician. Nast cartoon (above) shows Tweed in ruins of Tammany Hall, which came tumbling down as a result of exposures, prosecutions of machine leaders. Tweed, convicted of stealing $6 million, escaped to Spain, was extradited, died in jail in 1878.

CORRUPTION in the nation fed on a largely inexperienced investing public and the absence of restrictive regulations. Economic adventurers watered stock or sold it in bogus enterprises, turned security exchanges into gambling casinos. In 1869 the notorious James Fisk (l.) and Jay Gould (r.) cornered the gold market after having persuaded the naive President not to interfere. On "Black Friday" gold rose from 132 to 160 and disaster was averted only when Grant finally had $4 million in gold put on the market. The President's act toppled gold prices to 135, ruining many speculators.

REPUBLICAN PARTY split in 1872 as the liberal wing, discontented with Grant's administration, nominated Horace Greeley, New York *Tribune* editor, for President. Democrats, hoping cooperation would defeat "Grantism," also nominated Greeley, who had attacked their party for years.

Greeley, eccentric in dress and manner, was ridiculed in cartoons (l.) as were the Democrats for supporting him. Whitelaw Reid, Greeley's second in command, also was ridiculed (r.) for criticism of Reconstruction policies under Grant. Reid became *Tribune* editor when Greeley died shortly after.

WHISKY RING, partly composed of high governmental officials, defrauded Treasury of enormous sums in revenue. Even Grant's private secretary, General Babcock, was involved, and the President himself received gifts from the ring.

RECONSTRUCTION in the South, President Grant believed, should be left in the hands of those who had controlled the region after 1865. This meant Radical Republican domination. Each of the Southern state legislatures contained a substantial number of freedmen, and in South Carolina they were in a majority. Above, cartoon of the era attacks Grant and Radical Republicanism. At right is shown scene in the Louisiana legislature as a white member forces a Negro from the speaker's chair in 1875.

PETER COOPER, wealthy inventor and industrialist, was Presidential candidate of Greenback party in 1876. Composed of labor leaders, farmers, and small business men, it advocated an inflationary policy of currency expansion. Cooper received less than one per cent of votes.

INFLATIONARY SENTIMENT had succeeded in blocking legislation against paper currency. But in 1875 a law was passed authorizing Sec. of the Treasury to resume paying gold dollars in exchange for paper dollars in January, 1879. Above, cartoon attacks "hard money" policy.

SAMUEL J. TILDEN ran against Republican R. B. Hayes for the Presidency in 1876. Manipulation of the South's electoral votes by Northern politicians caused a disputed election. Not until the eve of inauguration was outcome in Hayes' favor determined by an electoral commission.

INDUSTRIAL GROWTH

United States becomes world's greatest manufacturing nation, but labor unrest and revolt in the West lead to sectionalism in political parties

The United States came of age as an industrial nation in the last quarter of the 19th century. Stimulated by the post-Civil War boom, expanding settlement, new inventions and natural resources the nation's economy was transformed. For the first time, value of manufactured goods exceeded agriculture, marking the transition from an agrarian to an industrial economy.

Increased foreign trade created part of the new demand. The nation gained a favorable trade balance for the first time, exporting more than it imported. The greatest stimulus, however, came from railroads which spanned the continent, opening new markets for manufacturers. Railroads demanded steel for construction and industry responded. Development of refrigerator cars lent impetus to the meat-packing industry. Invention of the telephone and the many new uses for electricity which came from the laboratories of Thomas Edison also spurred industrial production in the nation. The demand for farm machinery to cultivate new lands in the West was another stimulus to production.

Rise of the Industrial Baron

Expansion brought the rise of a new figure on the American scene — the industrial baron. Seeking wealth and power, ruthless, selfish but efficient businessmen came to the fore, convinced that "all natural resources should be transferred to private control as soon as possible."

Giants of industry were such men as Hill, Vanderbilt and Morgan in railroading; Armour in meat-packing and Rockefeller in oil. The *laissez-faire* policy was their byword as the government failed to check their growing power.

Industrial growth brought new problems. A new tide of immigrants supplied the cheap labor that factories needed. New arrivals settled mostly in cities, where employment was available. Often they became pawns of corrupt city political machines. Low wages forced them to live in slum areas, creating additional problems for city governments.

While the power of the barons grew, unchecked by the federal government, their policies did not pass completely unchallenged. Labor, seeking its rights and just compensation, began to organize, resorting to strikes to gain its ends. Industrialists countered with lockouts and black lists to keep unions from gaining strength. Violence followed, especially in bitter strikes involving the railroads and the steel industry.

Labor organizations made little progress during the period, although the American Federation of Labor, founded and guided by Samuel Gompers, slowly gained strength.

Labor unrest was paralleled by a restive stirring among farmers. Tremendous expansion of cultivated land pushed the United States to the top in agricultural production, but farmers were almost smothered economically by the surpluses created as a result. Unable to control rail rates or storage facilities on which they depended, farmers turned first to such cooperative efforts as the Grange, then organized politically. Although shrugged off at first as "agrarian radicals," the Populist party showed its power in the election of 1890 and became a force to be reckoned with. Efforts were made to align labor and agriculture politically, but the divergence of their interests doomed such a move to failure, leading to the creation of many "splinter parties."

Politically, it was an era of reform, hesitantly advancing. Following the scandals of the Grant administration, succeeding Presidents heeded the desire of the people for a change. Hayes, Garfield, Arthur and Cleveland pushed through civil service reform to control spoils system abuses. Post Office corruption was cleaned up, and other political scandals were dealt with. The hold of the Republican party on the Presidency, starting with the Civil War, was broken in 1884 when many Republicans deserted their own party to support Grover Cleveland, a Democrat. Republicans were united four years later, however, and returned to power.

Tariff debates were a bitter political issue. Farmers and labor sought low tariffs to keep prices down, except when they feared being undersold by foreigners. Industry favored high tariff to eliminate foreign competition. Business won out in the McKinley tariffs. Manufacturers also learned that domestic competition could be ruinous and turned to the formation of trusts, pools and holding companies. The first hint of government regulation came with the Interstate Commerce Act in 1887 and the Sherman Anti-Trust Act of 1890. Although these laws were full of loopholes and were weak, they "marked the twilight of *laissez-faire*."

EDISON CHANGED EVERYONE'S WAY OF LIVING

Social Reform

Late 19th century also saw the nation develop a social conscience. Prison reform, women's rights and social work were eagerly pressed. Rivalry developed in the newspaper field as sensationalism, aimed at increasing circulation, created an era of "yellow journalism."

The 1890's marked the emergence of the United States in the world's councils. Unrest in Cuba, at the nation's doorstep, led to the Spanish-American war. In four months, the United States drove another Old World power out of the Western Hemisphere and for the first time gained overseas commitments in the Philippines. The nation also played an important role in establishing the Open Door policy in China and in settling the Boxer Rebellion.

On the eve of the 20th century, United States stood as a young giant, flexing its industrial muscles and taking a place in world affairs. The nation faced the future with zest and anticipation for the momentous events that were about to unfold in the new century.

★ ★ ★

◀ **GIANT** in the era of industrial barons was Andrew Carnegie, the poor immigrant boy who became one of the dominant figures of the age. Carnegie was born in Scotland, emigrated to U.S. when he was 13. He began manufacturing steel and pig iron in 1865. With the aid of a remarkable group of assistants, Will Jones, Henry Frick and Charles Schwab, he became the world's greatest steel manufacturer. In a period of tremendous corporate growth, Carnegie was one of the most powerful leaders. Selling to J. P. Morgan, he devoted his time promoting education, health, peace.

LABOR

Immigration supplies workers for industry

In the turmoil of recovery from Civil War, America had begun to exploit the resources which were to make her the world's richest nation. By 1880, manufactured products accounted for 65 per cent of the nation's output, zoomed in value from $4.23 million in 1870 to $5.37 million in 1880.

Railroads linked the Atlantic to the Pacific and crisscrossed 163,000 miles of countryside by 1890. The widening demand for coal brought discovery of new coal fields — 500,000 square miles of bituminous coal, essential to the vital new steel industry. Mechanical aids followed: the compressed air drill, combination cutter-breaker-loader, sorting screens, and machine tools and dies.

Labor needs kept apace. From Europe and China, 457,000 immigrants flooded into the U.S. in 1880, start of a mass influx which was to continue for more than a decade.

Rapid growth brought its own problems. Industry spawned a breed of strong and ruthless leaders. To gain bargaining strength wage-earners banded together in unions such as the Knights of Labor. Led during the '70s and '80s by Terence V. Powderly, the Knights attempted to amalgamate all labor unions. Farmers, representing 44 per cent of the nation's populace, formed their own group, Patrons of Husbandry, for mutual protection and, as members of The Grange, sought to spread agricultural education, and build their own grain elevators and farm machinery. Strikes and rate-wars plagued the railroads.

Political parties were formed to represent these various elements in the national economy. Labor unrest led to the formation of the Greenback, Laborite and Anti-Monopolist parties to oppose the interests of big business. The many conflicting interests ill prepared the U.S. for the panic of 1884.

CROWDED DEPOTS were common in European ports as emigration to the U.S. accelerated steadily during the latter half of the 19th century. About 457,000, mostly from northern and western Europe, were admitted to the U.S. in 1880; 789,000 in 1882, turning the racial balance for the first time to more Scandinavian and German than English. After 1890, most came from eastern, southern Europe.

CHINESE IMMIGRATION, swelling American cities with quantities of cheap, unskilled labor, reached a peak in 1882 with 39,600 entries; precipitated United States' first immigrant curb — Chinese Exclusion Act.

"THE LAST YANKEE," title of this cartoon of the '80s, was a sardonic way of looking at America's new polyglot population as immigration continued to soar.

LONG WORKING DAYS gave industrial labor its first major reason to organize into unions. National drive for eight-hour-day, no cut in pay, began after Civil War, gained impetus as competition for jobs increased. In 1886, strike occurred in East St. Louis. Deputy sheriffs, with court backing, fired into crowd, killing six, only one of whom happened to be a striker.

EARLY RAILROAD STRIKES were among bloodiest in U.S. history. In West Va., July 16, 1877, workers protested sudden wage cuts with riotous strike, dragged engineers and firemen from trains, destroyed railway property and were subdued by state militia and U.S. Regulars. Other outbreaks followed in Penn., Maryland, elsewhere. All were bloody and won little.

CENTERS OF AGITATION for farmers, hard-hit by the panic of 1873, were meetings of the Grange, started as the "Patrons of Husbandry," in 1867, by a Bureau of Agriculture clerk, Oliver H. Kelley. Farmer members sought state regulation of railroads, worked to free themselves from "tyranny of monopoly." Movement declined in 1876 and was replaced by Farmers' Alliance and Agricultural Wheel in South, Northwest Alliance in North.

HARVEST TIME in the U.S. in 1880 meant gathering 552 million bushels of wheat, 436 million bushels of corn. In the decade 1870-1880, the number of farms more than doubled, with farm property and implements valued at $12.5 billion, one-fourth of the country's national wealth. Demand created new farm machinery, 12,000 patents, 200 companies to manufacture inventions like Withington's self-binder, Marsh's automatic harvester.

FARM PROBLEMS MOUNTED with rising cost of land, scarce money, high interest rates, while news of wealth to be made in the cities filtered back. Result was widespread migration, despite warnings from country press and pulpit of the city's evil. In 1870 only 20.9 per cent of U.S. population lived in areas of 8,000 or more; by 1900 figure had risen to 33.1 per cent. Scarcity of itinerant farm worker encouraged farm families to keep sons at home.

LOUISIANA SUGAR HARVESTS almost rivaled post-Civil War rice crops but 12,000-acre plantations like Millandon, near New Orleans, had dwindled in value. Once worth $1.25 million, land and sugar mill sold for $300,000. Similar plantations were divided, nearly doubling number of farms. Tenant farmers tried to eke out living on small exhausted holdings.

CALIFORNIA WINEMAKING started with Father Junipero Serra's first vineyard in 1769, spread northward with his missions, proved agricultural potential of the state. News of the mild weather, plentiful labor, coupled with railroads' rate-war in 1884, brought many immigrants. Farm values rose from $262 million in 1880 to $697 million in 1890; mining dropped.

MONTGOMERY, WARD & CO. innovated mail-order merchandising in 1872 specifically "to meet the wants of the Patrons of Husbandry." The firm won rapid support in rural areas through illustrated catalogs which farmers called "wishing books." 1875 catalog featured Granger Hat, $1.25.

F. W. WOOLWORTH'S FIRST successful store opened June 21, 1879, in Lancaster, Pa., grossed $127.65 the first day. Woolworth revolutionized retail sales method by selling for spot cash, fixed prices (5 & 10 cents), displaying goods freely on counters. By 1899, Woolworth owned 54 stores.

NEW ORLEANS PROSPERITY had ended with the Civil War. The decline of steamboat traffic, only partially offset by railroad building, added economic strain, intensified with disastrous Mississippi River flood of 1882. Levees were increased, port was improved, but the golden age was over.

PRICES WERE FIXED and garments were marked by Alexander T. Stewart, Irish immigrant, who initiated a system in 1870s to end common retail practice of haggling. Clothes were mass-produced in store's sewing room, "sweatshop" forerunner. Girls worked 7:30 a.m. to 10 p.m. for $5 a week.

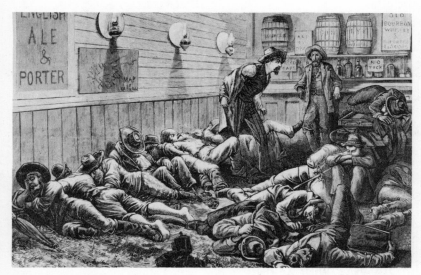

BOOMTOWN BEDROOMS were any place a miner could sleep. In Leadville, Colo., discovery of silver-bearing carbonates of lead in 1877 turned Oro City from abandoned gold-mining camp to one of world's biggest silver centers. Population jumped to 40,000 in 1880; beds rented at "25c a night."

DINING CARS APPEARED on cross-country luxury trains with George M. Pullman's "Delmonico" in 1868. First inventor-builder of sleeping cars, Pullman soon added chair and vestibule cars. He founded Pullman, Ill., for employes in 1880. It was site of one of U.S.'s most famous strikes in 1894.

HAYES

"His Honesty" fights graft and corruption

The disputed election of 1876 carried Rutherford Birchard Hayes to the presidency. His intelligence and strong moral fiber combined with tolerance and generosity in proportions eminently suited to meet the disturbed conditions of reconstruction.

Hayes' chief problems were: 1) reconstruction and ending military occupation of the South, 2) re-establishment of the national currency, 3) reforming civil service.

In a conciliatory gesture toward the South he flouted the arguments and machinations of the Stalwarts and ended military occupation. Republican carpetbag governments fell, and the South went solidly Democratic.

Currency problems sprang largely from the greenbacks issued during the Civil War. Hayes fought efforts to cheapen the currency. However, over his veto in 1878, Congress passed the Bland-Allison Act, which required the Sec. of Treasury to purchase large amounr of silver for coining purposes at prices favorable to silver interests.

True reconstruction of the South did not take place until after Federal troops left. Profound economic and social change gave rise to a New South as the old aristocracy disintegrated. In agriculture the plantation gave way to small holdings and sharecropping. Northern industry gradually took cognizance of Southern resources and cheap labor. Increased investment began an industrial revolution in the area after 1880. The Carolinas began to threaten New England as the chief textile-producing area. By 1896 the South supplied 18 percent of the nation's iron output. Tobacco, paper, furniture, and cotton seed-processing factories sprang up. Industrialization profoundly altered the Southern economy as well as culture.

PRESIDENT and Mrs. Hayes had this portrait picture taken on their silver wedding anniversary in the White House in 1877. Hayes was very devoted to his wife, Lucy Webb, one of the most active women in public life during her time. The high moral qualities of Hayes were a beacon in an era rank with corruption and misgovernment. He brought to his cabinet men of similar caliber. Their efforts contributed greatly to turning the tide against political immorality, which plagued the Grant administration. In cleaning up the New York port customs collection agency, Hayes fired Chester A. Arthur and Alonzo B. Cornell. In the confirmation of new appointees, he fought stiff opposition from Arthur's friend, Sen. Roscoe Conkling. Hayes finally won the fight by exposing the graft in the agency, Conkling's prestige suffering.

NEGROES PUSHED AHEAD CULTURALLY during Hayes' regime. One of the great men of the South and most outstanding among Negroes was Booker T. Washington (r.). Born a slave, he founded the Normal and Industrial Institute at Tuskegee, Alabama, in 1881. He urged those of his race to solve their problems by making themselves indispensible through education and hard work. Negroes went increasingly into skilled professions although they met with great prejudice.

CONKLING, THE CURLED CONGRESSIONAL CÆSAR.

Though the Custom House founder in politics whirl. He still keeps his neat back and Hyperion curl.

ARDENT OPPONENT OF REFORM was Sen. Roscoe Conkling (l.). Politically powerful and arrogant, Conkling hindered Hayes' efforts to improve civil service. Hayes received warm support from his Sec. of the Interior, Carl Schurz, former senator from Missouri. Opponents caricatured Schurz, German immigrant, as theoretical tinkerer.

"CINDERELLA" of the Republican party and her haughty sisters" was the title of this cartoon. Hayes asserted, "He serves his party best who serves his country best." This principle brought him athwart the "Stalwarts" faction of the Republican party, led by Conkling. In 1880 Grant (c.) and Conkling (r.) snubbed "Cinderella" Hayes (l.) at convention, chose instead James Garfield.

VANCOUVER ISLAND was the discovery of George Vancouver, English navigator and veteran of Capt. James Cook's second voyage around the world. He was commissioned in 1791 to take territory at Nootka Sound assigned to England; also, to survey N. Pacific coast. Later, settlement of Canadian-American dispute over Oregon boundaries confirmed British sovereignty of the region. Vancouver Island was made a Crown Colony. In 1866 it became part of British Columbia. Vancouver's explorations also took him to the Hawaiian Islands, which he accepted for Britain in 1794.

CANADA UNIFIES

Britain's largest colony enters era of discovery, turmoil and growth

While colonists in America were still waging war for independence from British rule, French and English Canadians co-existed uneasily under the after-effects of the Quebec Act of 1774. No longer governed by authority of royal proclamation and in official possession of France's western claim — Quebec — the country sought to live under French civil law and English criminal law.

Revolutionary refugees from America poured into Nova Scotia, 20 shiploads at a time, as early as 1783. Even colorful Joe Brant, Indian Chief Thayendanega, led a sizable migration of Mohawks to Canadian soil. To all these Loyalists, the King made liberal grants of land, cash compensation amounting to nearly 4 million pounds, and granted tools and farm implements.

British-Americans brought problems which found partial solution in the Constitutional Act of 1791 modifying the French-type government. Passed by British Parliament, it divided Canada at the Ottawa River into two provinces: Upper and Lower, with a Governor General over all Canada, a Lt.-Governor for the Upper province, preponderately English. Lower Canada, chiefly French, retained its old system of laws. Upper Canada modeled its new rule after the British.

Col. John Graves Simcoe, first Lt.-Governor of Upper Canada called his first legislature Sept. 17, 1792, in Niagara (later Newark), moved capital to Toronto, which was heavily populated by displaced "Americans."

In Lower Canada, where there were already language barriers, politics, like culture and religion, were dominantly French. Before resentment could flare into uprising, Britain and America were involved in the fruitless War of 1812. When boundaries were settled and peace restored, Canada returned to solving internal problems.

The extensive explorations of seafaring men like George Vancouver, John Meares and Captain James Cook had given Britain a firm hold on what is now British Columbia. Courageous Alexander Mackenzie had cut an overland route from the arctic to the Pacific in 1793. The fur-trading monopoly of Hudson's Bay Company had been threatened by Northwest Company, an upstart, with which "the Bay" finally merged.

Steamboats plied inland waterways as the building of the St. Lawrence canals began in 1821. Canada's first railway lumbered out of Toronto in 1836.

In 1837, the long-seething revolt exploded and Lord Durham was dispatched to investigate. His *Report on Canada*, 1839, set the pattern for the 1840 Act of Union which united Upper and Lower Canada under one government, one legislature, free votes for all and English its language of record.

In the continuing imbalance of English and French speaking peoples, Sir John MacDonald was able to create a "Liberal Conservative" party in 1854. Result was British Upper Canada had won Roman Catholic schools by French vote, Lower Canada a militia by English vote.

The American Civil War spurred the union of British North America. In a stalemate of government in 1864, rival leaders John A. MacDonald and George Brown agreed to seek a confederation of provinces which would allow local separation of the Canadas under one dominion government.

Irish Fenian invasion from U.S. strengthened their resolve; the British North America Act (1867) made confederation a fact.

LOYALISTS fled the American Revolution into Canada by the shipload. In 1783, 10,000 flooded into Shelburne, making it the largest "town" in the country. King gave Loyalists liberal land grants and cash amounting to 4 million pounds.

FRENCH FUR TRADERS fought for survival against British-Canadian monopoly of trade routes. Battling Hudson's Bay control, independents enlisted French-Canadian aid, formed rival Northwest Co., with Montreal as trade base.

NOOTKA SOUND, natural harbor on west coast of Vancouver, was visited in 1788 by John Meares, British Naval officer turned explorer and fur trader. On its shores he built a trading post for Hudson's Bay Co.'s great rival, the Northwest Co., and a ship, *North West America,* first to be launched in British Columbia. A year later, Spain seized the Nootka Sound and Meares' property, nearly caused armed conflict with Great Britain.

ALEXANDER MACKENZIE set out in the interests of Northwest Co.'s fur trade in July, 1789, made his way over land and down stream from Saskatchewan to the Pacific, arriving July 22, 1793, first white man to cross the continent north of Mexico. His *Voyages,* published in England in 1801, gave detailed description of terrain and was translated into French for Napoleon, who had considered a "back-door" conquest of Canada.

PROVINCE OF QUEBEC, mostly French, was known as Lower Canada after Constitutional Act of 1791. Quebec's resentment against British-type rule fired into Revolt of 1837, precipitating Lord Durham's 1839 *Report,* led to 1840 Act of Union, joining upper and lower Canada.

MONTREAL, among first French settlements in North America, received large influx of Loyalists after American Revolution. By 1836, city was connected by rail with Portland, Boston and Toronto, and by 1856 with Chicago. It became the capital of United Canada from 1844-1849.

FORT GARRY was early trading post named for Nicholas Garry, head of Hudson's Bay Co., who arranged merger with rival Northwest Co. there in 1821. Once center of authority for Manitoba and Red River traffic with what became North Dakota, fort was razed, city of Winnipeg arose.

BATTLE OF LUNDY'S LANE on July 25, 1814, was, for Canadians and Americans alike, a decisive contest in the indecisive War of 1812. Five hours of bloody warfare between 3,000 British troops and 2,600 U.S. effectives ended with 1,689 casualties, 42 prisoners and withdrawal of American military from Canadian side of Niagara frontier. Canadians had successfully repelled three U.S. invasions, turned early U.S. naval victories into later defeats. With Treaty of Ghent, Dec. 24, 1814, *status quo ante* was restored. Disregard for causes of controversy showed war's futility.

TWO GOVERNORS GENERAL of turbulent periods in Canadian history were Sir George Murray (l.) and James Bruce, 8th Earl of Elgin. Murray served from 1813-1815, a period of disturbances marked by the War of 1812. Lord Elgin served from 1846-1854, basing his government on the plan outlined by the famous report of his father-in-law, Lord Durham. Elgin was largely responsible for promoting harmony between French and English Canada, granted French Canadians the right to use their language officially, non-officially. He negotiated 1854 Canada-U.S. treaty reciprocity.

FREQUENT REBELLIONS dotted the calendar during the early part of the 19th century. Colonel Wetherell's Bivouac (above) at St. Hilaire de Rouville, P. Q., came during the Lower Canada Rebellion of Nov. 23 and 24, 1837. This action, precipitated by Louis Papineau (right), popular, explosive leader of the French Canadians, rose out of differences between the French and English, and the conviction of the French that they were unjustly treated. Papineau was conceded to be right in his beliefs, but his methods did not receive the backing of the Roman Catholic clergy. Therefore the revolt was not widespread. Upper Canada, too, saw a small rebellion in 1837, under the leadership of fiery William Lyon Mackenzie (left). A trend toward Americanization of the region, land reserves of the Crown and the clergy, and unfair land grants all contributed to the uprising. Mackenzie tried to rally his followers, overthrow the government and establish a republic. The revolt failed, and Mackenzie fled to the U.S.

FIRST LOCOMOTIVE AND TRAIN IN CANADA RAN SMOKILY BETWEEN LePRAIRIE AND ST. JOHN'S, QUEBEC. THE ROAD BEGAN OPERATING JULY 21, 1836.

FENIAN RAIDS harassed Canada after U.S. Civil War. Fenians were Irish-Americans who sought freedom for Ireland and hoped to impress their cause on England by such raids. Fenians first invaded Canada in 1866. Near Freleysburg, Major P. O'Hara and 15 Fenians routed the British Voluntary Cavalry (l.). Fenian raiders also captured Fort Erie, but later were defeated. Remnants of forces surrendered to U. S. warship. Raids of 1870 (r.) also failed.

FIRE swept through St. John, New Brunswick, June 20, 1877, destroying most of the older part of the city. The fire broke out early in the afternoon and was soon beyond control. It burned throughout the night. Residents rebuilt damaged portions of the city with brick and stone.

DOMINION OF CANADA came into being July 1, 1867, through efforts of the "fathers of Confederation," shown here. John MacDonald (standing, c.) was the first prime minister of the Dominion. Seated at his left is Georges Cartier, French-Canadian leader. The union came from necessity. Upper and Lower Canada were united in the legislature, but divided by racial lines, English and French, creating a deadlock. Formation of the Dominion eliminated such dualism. Only four provinces were in the original Dominion: Nova Scotia, New Brunswick, Quebec and Ontario. Others followed.

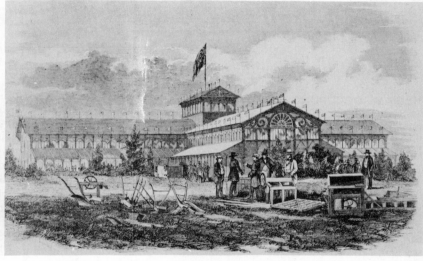

ROYAL VISIT TO CANADA in 1860 witnessed the country outdoing itself in showing hospitality to the heir to the British throne. The Prince, who became King Edward VII four decades later on the death of Queen Victoria, graciously participated in social events and in political and business conferences wherever he went. He laid the cornerstone of the new Parliament building at Ottawa. At left, above, the Royal Squadron arrives at Quebec to be greeted by salutes and rockets. At right is shown the Agricultural Exhibition of Upper Canada at Hamilton. This and other expositions were opened, or attended by, His Royal Highness. Relations between Canada and the mother country were vastly improved by the Royal visit.

HIGH COMMISSIONERS of the United States, negotiators of the 1871 Treaty of Washington are shown above. The treaty gave Canada many advantages in fishing, trading, and the use of border waterways. Left to right: Ebenezer Hoar, George Williams, Judge Samuel Nelson, Gen. Robert C. Schenck, Sec. of State Hamilton Fish, and J. C. Bancroft Davis.

FIRST ONTARIO PARLIAMENT followed closely the establishment of the Dominion in 1867. With the newly-organized government, the people were assured of more equitable representation than they had previously known. Trade was improving at home and abroad, agriculture expanding, and all Canadians were looking forward to continually expanding prosperity.

BOXING WITHOUT GLOVES was the custom when John C. Heenan, the Benecia Boy, fought John Morrissey at Long Point, Canada, on Oct. 20, 1858. Heenan lost the decision when he hit a spike and broke his hand. Morrissey later refused to grant him a return bout, and Heenan went to Europe to win heavyweight laurels. Men (foreground) are ring keepers.

WINTER SPORTS early claimed the interest of Canadians. Athletic events also had social aspects. Here a meeting of the Sleigh Club at St. John, New Brunswick, in 1837, shows smart rigs of the era with horses harnessed in tandem. Canada's widespread fur-trade made possible luxurious use of pelts for sleigh decorations. Men, women wore furs for practical reasons.

THE GAME OF CURLING came to Canada with the Scots and quickly became one of the most popular winter pastimes. Here, Prince Arthur, on Royal visit to Provinces, officiates at opening of the Caledonia Curling Rink at Montreal.

SOCIAL LIFE was not neglected by Canadians during the early part of the nineteenth century. The Grand Masonic Ball of Montreal was typical of social events in cities and towns. In smaller communities, folk dancing prevailed.

A QUEBEC MERCHANT became honorary chief of the Huron Tribe in a ceremony that took place about 1850. For more than two centuries French Canadians had been cementing relations with Indians with resulting goodwill.

LIFE IN CANADA

Undeterred by political upheavals, hardships, French, British pioneers create unified nation

While the history of Canada was being molded by statesmen and explorers in the century between the American Revolution and Canada's Confederation, the people of British North America were pursuing the vigorous destinies of pioneers anywhere.

Mammoth land holdings, granted by the Crown or purchased with profits from strategic manipulation of stock in the great fur-trading monopoly of Hudson's Bay Company, metamorphosed from backwoods settlements to thriving cities. Colonel Talbot's Lake Erie grant grew from 5,000 acres to 650,000. John Galt converted subscribed money into 2.5 million acres in the western peninsula, persuading the government to accept the building of roads, schools, churches and bridges as part of his 20,000 pounds per year payment. Lord Selkirk bought 116,000 square acres in the Red River basin and started a colony with a group of approximately 800 Highlanders from Prince Edward Island.

To these colonies, and other areas of Canada, came waves of immigrants, uprooted by wars elsewhere. From America, Loyalists fled the Revolutionary War. From the continent of Europe after the collapse of Napoleon, 98,000 refugees poured to the safety of the gigantic American colony. By 1834, 403,000 British settlers had arrived. During the period from 1850 through 1854, an unprecedented 1,639,000 people were building lives in the new land.

Hardships were part of the bargain. In the Talbot settlement salt, when available, was $12 per bushel. Everywhere there was work at hand: land had to be cleared, building had to be done.

In Lower Canada, French culture, language and religion survived almost intact.

In literature, Quebec became the center of an intellectual movement led by Abbe Raymond Casgrain, Antoine Gerin-Lajoie, Hubert Larue and Joseph-Charles Tache. Patriotic poetry made an appearance in the works of Octave Cremazie, first French Canadian poet, who wrote nostalgically of the French

In Upper Canada, histories of Canada's political and exploratory travail abounded, but in the preoccupation of building cities, factories and railways, Canadian artistry lagged. Talent was needed elsewhere.

Canadians found relaxation in sports; ice-skating, sleigh rides, curling, in "round dancing" and, in the big cities where court tradition lingered, in sumptuous balls.

Steamboats plied the waterways; railroads cut through the wilderness tying together the provinces which had already been linked by the Act of 1840 and were to be unified still more by the Quebec Conference of 1867.

Uprisings and rebellions sputtered across the country, the War of 1812 came and went. Canadian boundaries were set and reset as fur traders cut deeper into U.S. claims, and Canadian fishing vessels sailed into U.S. competition.

Distinguished visitors, French unrest, or the influence of the Church on political affairs were faithfully reported in the Toronto *Globe* in 1844, as George Brown, journalist and statesman, wielded the advantages of being editor and managing director. The *Globe* was to grow from weekly to tri-weekly and then to daily newspaper, with political and social influence unequaled in Canada.

Thus, in the great swirling movement of pioneers and politics in a new country, the people of Canada created a nation.

FORT VANCOUVER, on the Columbia River opposite present site of Portland, Oregon, was western base of Hudson's Bay Company before 1846. U.S.-Canada Oregon Treaty, which set boundary at 49th parallel, forced Co. to move.

MONTREAL STEAMBOAT LANDING flourished in the middle of the 19th century. Montreal Island and Mount Royal were discovered in 1535 by Cartier. In 1611, Champlain laid out a settlement there, although the city was not founded until 1642. Montreal early became the fur center of the region. The location of the city on the St. Lawrence made it a fast growing commercial center.

NEW UNIVERSITY COLLEGE at Toronto was one of the numerous educational institutions in eastern Canada. James McGill founded the McGill University in Montreal. Laval University of Quebec received Royal charter in 1852.

LONDON, ONTARIO, sprawled on the edge of the Thames River, was the site originally selected by Col. John G. Simcoe, first lieutenant-governor of Upper Canada, as the capital of Upper Canada in 1792. Unfortunately, his plans did not mature and settlement was delayed until 1826. In 1838, British troops were garrisoned in London and by 1858 the town had developed extensive factories.

TORONTO, capital city of Ontario, was first named York. This view shows King Street. The burning of public buildings, first in York, by U.S. troops, in War of 1812, later gave British their excuse for burning Washington, D.C.

ICE FOR THE PEOPLE came from lakes and ponds in the 19th century. Blocks of ice were cut, skidded onto the surrounding solid ice, and then hauled away to ice houses sufficiently insulated so that ice remained frozen all year.

CLEARING LAND for the town of Stanley, New Brunswick, followed the decision of surveyors, who selected the site on the Nashwaak River as the most suitable location. Proof of the fallibility of planners was the fact that Stanley, established in 1834, never grew beyond a small community. The town, named for Lord Stanley, Secretary of State, exemplified government-sponsored expansion.

PROGRESS OF MEDICINE was accelerated through efforts to standardize known medications, mostly imported from Europe until after 1852, when American Pharmaceutical Association was formed by William Proctor (above). Physicians brewed their own formulas, often prescribed on theory that double doses were twice as effective. A.P.A. sought to restrict dispensing of medicine to qualified pharmacists, revised *U.S. Pharmacopoeia*.

WAR SPURS INVENTIONS

American way of life changed as inventors provide new ideas for industry

Every facet of American life was touched or changed by the fever of progress which gripped U.S. after the Civil War. Industry flourished on invention and discovery, and at no time in history was the need for new methods and processes greater.

For the trains, already speeding across the continent, Eli Janney patented a coupler. Andrew Hallidie's cable car appeared on San Francisco streets, and in New York the first electrically powered streetcar began its shuttle service, in 1874, the invention of Stephen Dudley Field.

Industries no longer needed to doubt a bookkeeper's accuracy. Edmund Barbour invented an adding machine which printed totals and sub-totals in 1872. William S. Burroughs topped him, in 1888, with the first successful recording adding machine, and Dorr Felt produced the first accurate comptometer in 1884.

Alexander Graham Bell's telephone performed its communications revolution in 1877, four short years before Thomas Edison introduced a system of central power production in New York City.

George B. Selden took out the first auto-mobile patent in 1879, but Henry House had built a steam-operated car in 1866.

Immigration provided labor, but it also brought congestion to cities and increased danger of disease. Medical research evolved

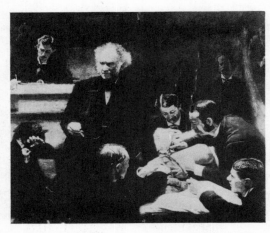

SAMUEL DAVID GROSS was among first in U.S. to teach pathological anatomy and surgery, founded American Medical Assn. in 1847. Photo shows surgical technique at Gross Clinic, 1875.

its own discoveries and inventions.

Surgical techniques leaped ahead, aided by one of the first U.S. medical journals, *Annals of Surgery*, started in 1885, partly through the help of the American Public Health Association, formed in 1872.

In New York's Bellevue Hospital, the first school of nursing was established the following year and 15 such schools had grown up by 1880. Medical schools developed concurrently, with 112 established between 1873 and 1890.

Women made their first entry into the realm of medicine in 1849 with Elizabeth Blackwell, first woman in the U.S. to receive a medical degree. Eight years later, with her sister Emily and a friend, Marie Zackrzewska, she founded the New York Infirmary and College for Women.

Chemical findings of M. Carey Lea brought impetus to the art of photography and Josiah Willard Gibbs in this period became "founder of chemical energetics."

And looking even higher, as the 19th century sped toward its close, scientists had photographed the moon. Asaph Hall had succeeded in discovering Mars' satellites.

BELL'S CRY FOR HELP after being burned by battery acid in a laboratory accident proved that articulate speech could be carried through distance by electrical impulse. Alexander Graham Bell and his assistant, Tom Watson, had invented the telephone. First practical demonstration of the mag-

neto-electric model was held in Boston, March 10, 1876. Bell Telephone Co., for commercial development and application of the invention, was founded in 1877. Born in Scotland, Bell and his father, Alexander Melville, were pioneers in "visible speech" for the deaf. Bell became citizen in 1882.

MACHINE EXHIBITIONS vied with fairs for popularity. The curious clustered around Richard Hoe's web press of 1871. First installed at N. Y. *Tribune*, it printed both sides of a continuous roll of paper simultaneously, made 18,000 impressions per hour. Co-designer was Stephen Tucker. Hoe also invented form folder.

ALLEN'S TYPEWRITER of 1876 lost out to one by Christopher Sholes, first patented in 1868 with Carlos Glidden and Samuel Soule. Sholes sold his improved model to E. Remington & Sons in 1873.

ASA GRAY, era's leading botanist, helped found Nat'l Academy of Science, American Academy of Arts and Sciences. He was Darwin's confidant, chief defender of Darwinian theories.

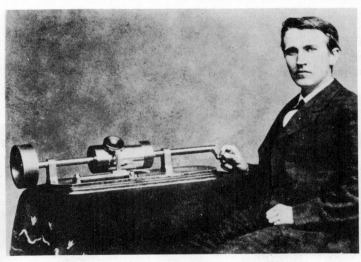

FIRST ELECTRIC LIGHT   **INVENTOR EDISON WITH HIS 1876 PHONOGRAPH**   **NEW MODEL, 1877—TINFOIL TALKING-MACHINE**

EDISON

The man who was to emerge as one of world's most practical scientists patented his first invention, an electrographic vote recorder, in 1869, while working for Western Union Telegraph Co. in Boston. Moving to New York, he joined an electrical engineering firm which sold out in 1870, netting him $40,000. With this Edison formed his own company, nucleus of an investment destined to light the world. Except for discovery of the "Edison Effect," demonstrating that incandescent lamps could be used as valves to admit negative

but not positive electricity, Edison made no notable contribution to pure science. His practical experiments, however, embraced a wide range, from the earliest phonograph to the incandescent lamp whose crude beginnings in 1879 set the stage for his almost concurrent system of distributing electricity for light and power — generators, motors, light sockets. Crowning achievement was New York's Pearl Street installation (1881-82), first electric light power plant in the world. Much of his success was due to his skillful hiring of assistants to further research.

POEMS OF THE PEOPLE came from the pen of Walt Whitman. A new voice among poets, he wrote of workers, wives and the West. A nurse during the Civil War, he relived his experiences in verse, sometimes harsh, always sensitive. *Leaves of Grass* (1855) was his major work, still stands as living monument.

FIRST GREAT WRITER OF THE WEST was Mark Twain (Samuel L. Clemens), who took his pen-name from cry of riverboat captains. His life (1835-1910) spanned industrialization of America. His gift of imagination and ever-young outlook created whole new worlds of wide-eyed fun. His two boys, *Tom Sawyer* and *Huckleberry Finn* (1884), became part of American folklore, as did flamboyant personality of creator.

PRESS AND LITERATURE

Post-war writing tends to reflect local color; "giants" of the press arise

Literature in post-Civil War America increasingly reflected local color. Sarah Orne Jewett delineated New England character with exquisite care. Edward Eggleston, a Methodist preacher, enriched letters with his portrayals of small town life in Indiana. Walt Whitman sang lustily of such a neglected place as Brooklyn. Foremost of the school was Mark Twain, who charmed his generation with tales of the Mississippi Valley. The breezy optimism of his earlier books gave way, however, to biting social criticism, so apparent in certain chapters of *Huckleberry Finn*, and *The Gilded Age*.

Large newspapers and magazines became part of the national scene, with giants like Greeley, Reid and Dana dominating the journalistic world. They were matched on the educational side by Matthew Vassar, who founded the first important college for women in the country, and Henry Barnard, whose efforts were primarily responsible for the tax-supported public school system in America. Land-grant colleges mushroomed into being all over the United States.

In education and in literature, the South began to fulfill its earlier promise, with Sidney Lanier, Joel Chandler Harris, Thomas Nelson Page and George Washington Cable.

Tales of adventure—such as those of Bret Harte — and the early novels of Herman Melville were almost equalled in popularity by the works of historian Francis Parkman, who chronicled the great Anglo-French struggle for mastery of North America.

Three women, Emily Dickinson, Amy Lowell and Louise May Alcott, emerged to prove that the nation was ready to admire the product of talent without regards for sex.

WEST AND EAST met happily in the work of William Dean Howells. Born in Ohio, he went East in 1866 to become editor of *Atlantic Monthly,* succeeding Fields. He wrote many novels, one *Rise of Silas Lapham*.

LINOTYPE machine, invented by Otto Mergenthaler in 1886, revolutionized publishing business. Entire line of type could be set quickly, allowing more, cheaper printing. Every town soon had its own paper.

FURTHER SPREADING of news was hastened by invention of rotary press by Richard M. Hoe in 1847. Modern newspapers still employ variation of same type of machine.

AVID COMPETITION between major big-city newspapers resulted in more general insight into events. Charles A. Dana built *Sun* into position alongside other N. Y. newspapers such as *Tribune* and *Post*.

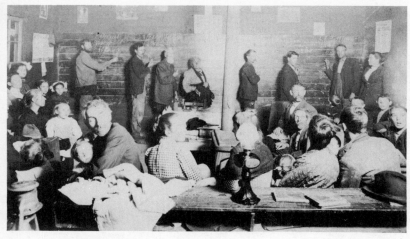

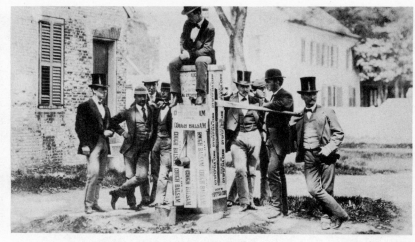

EAGERNESS FOR "BOOK-LARNIN'" hit all generations, resulting in classes attended by whole families. Settlers in new areas set up "common schools" to give rudiments of education, producing famous Americans.

YALE CLASS OF 1870 (above) was to be famed as first group privileged to study for doctors' degrees in an American university. Yale began offering Ph.D. work in 1871, with other colleges not far behind in advancement.

POET, EDITOR, CRITIC, professor was James Russell Lowell, who was first editor of *Atlantic Monthly*, followed Longfellow at Harvard, wrote tart *Bigelow Papers*.

BE GOOD, GET RICH philosophy of Horatio Alger became credo of all American boyhood. Such books as *Luck and Pluck* inspired deeds of virtue in hope of future success.

LOOK OUT, NOT IN, was creed of such poets-preachers-philosophers as Edward Everett Hale, whose *Man Without a Country* did much to awaken a newly united nation.

SOUTHERN REVIVAL of education, literature was led by Sidney Lanier, whose *Poems* were published in 1877. He distrusted new realism, saw it as idealism threat.

FOREMOST HISTORIAN, whose works attained popularity of novels, was Francis Parkman. *The Oregon Trail* gives what is probably best picture of early West.

DEEP INSIGHT, light touch of Dr. Oliver Wendell Holmes enabled him to sugarcoat basic philosophy with satire, as in *The Autocrat of the Breakfast Table,* his best work.

NEGRO FOLKLORE entered literary scene with Joel Chandler Harris' *Uncle Remus.* Stories of Br'er Rabbit and his friends of the Briar Patch made the Georgian famous.

EDUCATIONAL REFORM fight was led by Henry Barnard. End result was widening of opportunities and basic public-school system, and equal rights for women.

FOREMOST FEMININE WRITER of age was Louisa May Alcott, whose *Little Women* recalled romanticism to American letters, started trend toward sentiment.

POSTHUMOUS FAME came to recluse Emily Dickinson, who never meant her work for publication. Peculiar quality of "near rhyme" in verse brought protests.

INNOVATOR from a famed family was poet Amy Lowell, whose poems spanned gap between new, old forms. Most famous collection is *Sword Blades and Poppy Seeds.*

REVERSE TWIST was success of Bret Harte, Easterner who dug literary gold out of California. Most-read tales concern mining camps, as *Luck of Roaring Camp.*

235

WINSLOW HOMER, one of America's most powerful painters, was among first masters to express American scene in ruggedly realistic, unconventional terms. Through careful observation of nature and with sober workmanship, he depicted the gaiety of rural life (above, *Snap the Whip*) in paintings of husking bees, croquet games and schoolrooms. Profoundly moved by a certain wildness in man and nature, he painted longshoremen, pioneers, farmhands in fields, humble Negroes, soldiers around campfires, and, as his finest work, sombre dramatic epics of ocean and marine life.

GREATEST LANDSCAPE PAINTER of his day was George Inness, whose vitality and variety gave him an undisputed eminence. Although Inness had visited Europe many times, he surrendered to no foreign masters, but discreetly selected their excellence in expressing his own inimitable methods. *Lackawanna Valley* shows Inness' skill in portraying panoramic richness.

EASTMAN JOHNSON, prolific genre painter of everyday life "with a story," received $1,000 for each member of the well-to-do Hatch family (including the newborn baby) appearing in this group portrait in 1871. Among the vanguard who fought for realism in art, Johnson achieved a quiet, often humorous mood, and supported it by fine lighting and coloring.

PAINTING

A native American art develops

The new crop of millionaires that grew up after the Civil War turned to art collecting as a means of enhancing their respectability. Though their taste was questionable, their checkbooks were ready. Merchant and railroad magnates began large collections, making their selections from English and French art dealers, or with the advice of American art-scouts.

Many native artists reaped some of the bounties of this financial harvest, and began to establish new techniques. Edward L. Henry painted the customs of early American days, and Eastman Johnson, the prolific genre "story-teller" and one of the great artists of the period, was a strong advocate of realism. Self-taught genius John La Farge had the rare quality of color, noticeable first in his flower pieces, then in decorative work for private and public buildings.

Meanwhile, a native American art was developing more strongly through the work of Winslow Homer, Thomas Eakins and George Fuller. Homer, shunning conventionality and relying upon a careful observation of nature, captured the roughness and wildness in man and nature, especially in marine life, his favorite subject in later years. Eakins demonstrated a rugged masculine power in *Operation* and *Christ on the Cross,* but was neglected by the public. The strongest exponent of poetic, emotional painting, Fuller interpreted quiet scenes, idealized visions of shadowy outlines (*The Romany Girl, Psyche*). In the field of landscapes, Albert Bierstadt, Frederic Church and Thomas Moran captured distant scenes of grandeur and bigness with depth in scope.

Important changes took place in the middle seventies. Many eager students had gone to Paris and Munich schools, returning with new ideas on every subject, and with new skills.

In 1876, religious mural painting had its renaissance with the work of La Farge, who was engaged to do the entire mural decoration of the new Boston Trinity Church. In 1878, the Society of American Artists was founded, and opened a school offering free instruction. One of the leaders of the movement was George Inness who, while still comparatively unknown, was destined to become America's greatest landscape painter. Favorite artists' subjects included animals, street scenes, Indians, portraits and flower arrangements.

FANNY DAVENPORT was one of the most gifted stars presented by autocratic Augustin Daly, New York's most powerful producer. Playing a wide range of parts (above, Nancy Sykes in *Oliver Twist*), she had deserved popularity.

THEATER Georgie Barrymore, sister of John Drew II, who was considered one of the most distinctive actors on the American stage, joined Daly's company in 1875. After a season with him, she played leading roles with Edwin Booth, Lawrence Barrett, John McCullough and Helen Modjeska. Shortly after 1876, she married a handsome ex-law student, Maurice Barrymore, with whom she had appeared. When Georgie died in 1893, she was survived by her husband and three children (above), Ethel, Lionel and John, all of whom later distinguished themselves on stage, screen.

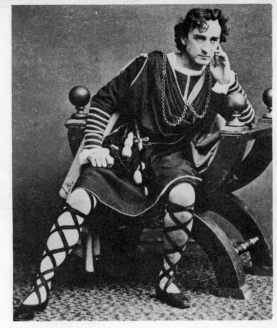

EDWIN BOOTH was the foremost American actor of his day. Endowed with a melodious voice, unusual grace, eloquence, artistic temperament, he was superb in tragic Shakespearean roles of Hamlet (above), Iago, Shylock, and King Lear.

MISSISSIPPI MINSTREL, usually a white performer in blackface, had his greatest vogue after the Civil War when the returning soldiers carried popular Negro songs all over the country.

NEW YORK'S MADISON SQUARE GARDEN, SCENE OF STUPENDOUS SHOWS.

SOUNDPROOF LOGE at the Metropolitan Opera House, opened in 1883, was a satiric suggestion designed to isolate loquacious boxholders who had little appreciation of music, came only to be seen, and indulge in scandalous gossip.

VOLUME OF NOISE was often more appreciated by music lovers than quality of music, and extravagantly staged concerts were popular. Recitals by a single artist, even though he was renowned, were not generally well received. At a music festival in staid Boston in 1872 in honor of Johann Strauss, who was touring America, Irishman Patrick S. Gilmore presented a chorus of 20,000 voices, an orchestra of 2,000, an Anvil Chorus of 100 Boston firemen pounding on real anvils (above, in rehearsal), and the firing of artillery for an audience of 40,000 persons. Strauss wrote music for momentous occasion.

INCREASED INTEREST in music was reflected in the home where children enjoyed singing around the piano. After the Civil War, conservatories sprang up, while native composers, grand opera, musical societies were encouraged.

FASHIONS

Bustles gained in popularity after the Civil War. Best-dressed ladies copied the Empress Eugenie, who set the style trend for America. First made of crinoline, Yankee ingenuity soon designed bustles made of whale bone and metal which, once sat upon, would rise again. So far as women were concerned, legs did not exist. It was indecent to expose so much as an ankle in alighting from a carriage. The stage finally ended such false modesty, but not without protests from ladies with tape measures. Beaches along the Long Island and Jersey shores became popular. Men and women were required by propriety to swim fully clothed. Men never approved of the bustle, but it was the ladies themselves who finally instituted dress reform along more natural lines. Physicians declared the corset was doing as much to destroy the female race as alcoholism was doing to destroy men. The "wasp waist" was much admired, and some women prided themselves on measuring 18 inches around the middle.

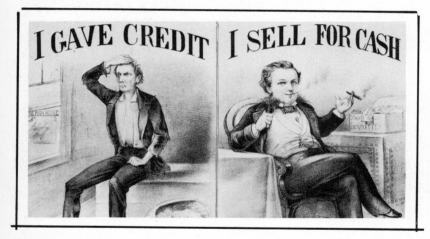

MONEY TALKED in the growing cities as rapid expansion made credit hazardous. Even major transactions were conducted on a cash basis. Credit was necessary in rural areas where farmers had to await harvest to pay.

MINIATURE ADULT fashions aped those of parents with little thought given to growth needs or comfort. High button shoes worn over long cotton stockings were musts for young set. Even swimming togs copied adults.

FAUST'S RESTAURANT in St. Louis was one of the most famous in the West. Restaurant featured the first roof beer garden in the United States. Faust also installed first electric lights in St. Louis. Such beer gardens, offering free lunch with huge schooners of beer, were popular throughout nation.

BILLIARDS was a popular and respectable diversion for the whole family in the homes of the wealthy, where ornate game rooms were maintained. Major business was frequently transacted at the billiard table. Pool halls early fell into disrepute as gathering places for loafers and the underworld.

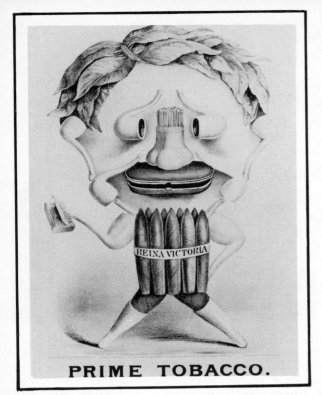

PRIME TOBACCO.

ADVERTISING became more important as a merchandising medium after the Civil War. Tobacco ads emphasized the pleasure-giving qualities of pipes and cigars. Cigarette smokers were laughed at as "dandies."

TEN-CENT STEAKS were featured on San Francisco menus of the 1870's. Most items were a dime; butter was free with 15-cent orders. Rooms were $1 a week.

CYCLING was a popular form of recreation with the high-wheeled variety preferred. The feminine version was dictated by modesty and required no little amount of talent, poise to ride.

WEEK-END HOLIDAYS became increasingly popular as employers began to shorten working hours. As transportation improved, Saturday and Sunday excursion boats (above) were filled to capacity. The wealthy were able to extend their holidays to include a sojourn at spas such as Saratoga, where the gentry gambled and "drank the waters" thought to be beneficial.

VICTORIAN DECOR was grand and ornate. This drawing room of the Tiffany House in New York was relatively restrained. Gew-gaws, Chinese bric-a-brac, beaded curtains and plaster statuary cluttered the high-ceilinged living rooms. One decorator of era remarked that so long as there was space to walk around, one could hardly put too much into a room.

FIRE FIGHTERS of the 19th century manned horse-drawn wagons, carrying their own water with them. When water could be found at the scene pumping was done by hand but often proved ineffectual. Firemen were joined by volunteers, roused by the alarm, who often rushed, pajama-clad, to aid comrades. Crowded tenement conditions added to the fire hazards.

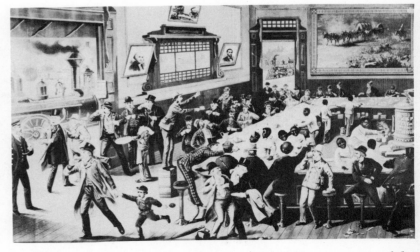

RAILROAD TRAVEL was made more desirable with the appearance of the first dining car in 1863. Before that, passengers were given ten minutes to take refreshment at railroad lunch counters while the train waited. People of modest means still did much of their traveling by road coach and spent the night in small towns, sleeping at boarding houses instead of hotels.

DEMANDING "EMANCIPATION OF WOMEN" through the right to vote, militant suffragists asserted that women were as fit to cast their ballots as were ex-slaves. In the face of newspaper ridicule, and often spattered with rotton eggs and epithets, the National Woman Suffrage Association under president Elizabeth Cady Stanton (r., with son and daughter), made noticeable headway. Organizers were sent to all major political party nominating conventions. A few states reluctantly conceded women the right to vote in school elections. Wyoming Territory (l.) established complete political equality in 1869. A host of professional reformers joined Susan B. Anthony (c.) and Mrs. Stanton in advancing freedom for women.

RELIGION AND REFORM

Era is marked by social advance, religious revival and labor strife

Postwar industrial growth and consolidation led to the inevitable organization of labor. As corporations grew in size, individual employee bargaining power lessened.

In an attempt to cope with low wages, long hours, or bad working conditions, the Order of the Knights of Labor was organized in 1869. Building upon spadework done by the earlier National Labor Union, the Knights sought to unite all laborers, skilled or unskilled, of whatever crafts, in "one big union." It favored an eight hour day, abolition of child labor, and the use of arbitration as a substitute for strikes.

Union membership advanced sharply after Terence V. Powderly became its head in 1878. Labor unions, however, were not yet strong enough to withstand both public unwillingness to accept them and the power of big business. The closing of troublesome plants and circulation of industry "blacklists," making it difficult for agitators to get jobs, broke the back of union demands.

When the Civil War ended, humanitarian performers turned once again to bettering the lot of unfortunates. While actions were piecemeal and little effort was made to find the underlying causes of insanity, poverty, and crime, improvement of existing conditions was immediate. Boards of charities were set up to deal with relief in many states. State schools for the deaf and blind were established. Recognition of juvenile delinquency as a separate problem began with Massachusetts opening an industrial school for delinquent girls. Humane treatment for animals was even demanded.

"Demon Rum" and the liquor interests were met head on by the Evangelical churches and by Women's Christian Temperance Union, headed by Frances Willard.

Religious leaders were concerned principally with attempting to digest the Darwinian doctrine of evolution. In attempts to resolve conflicts that arose between an infallible Church or infallible Book and the evolutionary theory, many American churchmen placed emphasis upon proper conduct, holding it more important than belief. Intellectuals began to disturb the air with a social interpretation of Darwinism.

INFLUENTIAL preaching by the gifted Episcopal Minister of Boston's famous Trinity Church, Phillips Brooks, did much to stimulate and maintain Protestant appeal to incoming immigrants.

BUILDING of the main Mormon temple in Salt Lake City started after Mormons were thoroughly established in 1870's. The famous Tabernacle had been finished earlier. Friction with federal government increased after Mormon acceptance of plural marriage resulted in federal laws aimed solely at Utah.

EVANGELIST Dwight L. Moody's leadership in America's post-war religious revival was evidenced by the tens of thousands, both in America and Great Britain, who attended his very colorful meetings.

IMMIGRANT LABOR that worked for "coolie wages" far outweighed the effectiveness of striking employees during the 1870's. Chinese laborers in California, originally used to build the Central Pacific Railroad, turned to other jobs, accepting wages on which a white man would starve. A Massa-chusetts shoe factory owner fired his striking employees, replacing them with low-paid Chinese. Cartoons above demonstrate the popular prejudice against foreign workers. In 1882 Congress passed the Chinese Exclusion Act, but an unending supply of low-cost labor still poured in from Europe.

HENRY GEORGE'S *Progress and Poverty*, first published in 1871, gained increasing recognition in Europe and America. George believed a single tax on land would meet costs of government, unburden capital and labor of taxes on output, eliminate monopolies and depressions.

BLOODIEST STRIKE the United States had ever seen followed sudden Eastern railroad wage cuts of 10 per cent in July, 1877. More than 50 strikers and soldiers were killed in riots and 126 locomotives were destroyed. Two weeks passed before state and federal troops completely broke up the strike.

PRISON REFORM was led by Dorothea Dix, who personally investigated hundreds of jails and prisons. Her shocking revelations of how brutally the insane were treated resulted in the founding of many state hospitals for the insane.

PUBLIC FLOGGINGS still continued in some states such as Delaware despite earlier movements toward more humane forms of punishment. Within prisons and insane asylums, chaining, whipping were means to enforce discipline.

EDWARD BELLAMY startled country with his novel *Looking Backward, 2000-1887*. It described experiences of man who fell asleep, awakened a century later in an ideal society. Book inspired chain of socialistic "Nationalist Clubs."

SPORTS
British got an early look at the new American sport of baseball. The champion Boston Red Stocking and former-champion Philadelphia Athletics sailed to England in 1874 and played a series of exhibitions. The tour came only five years after the first professional baseball team, the Cincinnati Red Stockings, had been organized, and two years before formation of the National League was completed in 1876.

◀ **GAS-LIT ERA** fathered one of greatest boxers in sports annals, fabulous John L. Sullivan. America's first great sports hero, the Boston Strong Boy was unbeatable for 10 years. A cloud of disapproval hung over boxing and every state in the Union had outlawed it until Sullivan came on the scene. He was first athlete to be followed in the streets by admirers.

TURKEY SHOOTS became the rage for gentlemen sportsmen. Hunting and fishing were popular, thoroughbred racing came into its own and horse and carriage driving was still the favorite outdoor sport for sedentary citizens.

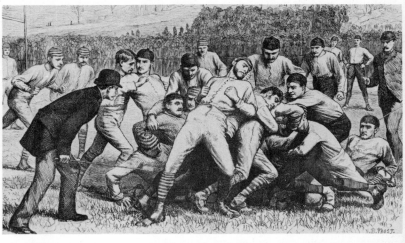

FOOTBALL was a push and pull affair based on power and brawn. The forward pass and open game were yet to come. Mass tackling, as shown above in Yale and Princeton game of 1879, was rule rather than exception.

WOMEN APPEARED on archery ranges by 1879 to enjoy their part in perhaps the greatest upsurge of sports in American history. Labor saving devices meant more time for sports. Both men and women began to recognize recreational and social advantages of athletic participation.

GENTLE GAME of croquet was first game played by both men and women in America. It was a social amusement rather than a skill, became so popular the National Croquet Association was formed in 1882. The fair sex not only began playing games, but visited such events as dog races.

ORIGINAL SIAMESE TWINS were Chang and Eng (shown with children), born in Siam in 1811. Sold by their parents, they were exhibited in U.S. by P.T. Barnum. From their profits, they settled down in North Carolina as farmers, adopted name "Bunker," married twin sisters and fathered 22 children. They died at 63; Chang outlived Eng two hours.

AMERICANS BECAME AIR-MINDED with building of Prof. T. S. C. Lowe's balloons. Dr. John F. Boynton and Miss Mary Jenkins of New York (above) went aloft to sign their marriage contract. Papers called it "Sacred compact of Holy Matrimony solemnized above the clouds."

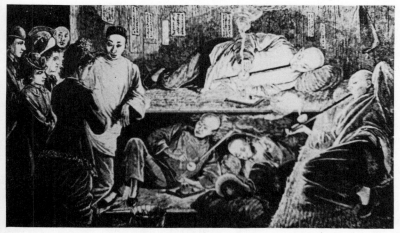

CRIME Lawlessness bred in the opium dens (above) and honky-tonks of San Francisco's Barbary Coast and in the rich mining regions of California and Nevada, producing such colorful bandits as "Sheet-iron Jack," "Rattlesnake Dick," and Dick Fellows. The most successful and feared was dapper "Black Bart" (l.), who held up 28 stagecoaches in eight years without firing a shot. Between jobs he posed as a mining engineer, lived comfortably in San Francisco. He was finally caught in 1883 by Wells-Fargo detectives, sentenced to six years in prison.

CHICAGO FIRE The great fire started night of Oct. 8, 1871, when, says legend, Mrs. O'Leary's cow kicked over a kerosene lantern. Prolonged drouth and high winds turned the rambling wood-built city into a tinder box. With the waterworks burned, the fire swept unchecked for three days over 2,124 acres, destroying nearly $200 million worth of property and killing several hundred people. Of the 300,000 inhabitants, 100,000 were left homeless. When Chicago was rebuilt, it was made a city of steel and stone.

WRECK OF THE S.S. SCHILLER May 7, 1875, was a major marine disaster. The Hamburg mail steamer out of New York was stranded at night in dense fog off Scilly Islands, on the coast of Cornwall, England. According to contemporary accounts, of the 385 aboard, only 15 passengers, three officers and 25 of crew were saved. Captain died at his post.

THEATER FIRES took a heavy toll of life due to few exits, poor construction and inadequate fire protective measures. In Trenton, N. J., in 1872, 600 persons were killed. Four years later 283 died in Brooklyn. The American Theatre in the Bowery burned in 1856 (above); was rebuilt.

FARMER GARFIELD
Cutting a Swath to the White House.

JAMES A. GARFIELD, born in 1831, had worked on farms as a youth and supporters stressed this (l.) and his Civil War record in campaign of 1880. Garfield represented the "Half-Breeds" of the Republican party, a faction which desired to reform the "Stalwart" system of political patronage. This led to his assassination (r.) by Charles J. Guiteau, a "Stalwart" who had failed to get a political appointment. Guiteau shot Garfield in July, 1881, but the President did not die until September. Guiteau claimed his motive was to give control of government to "Stalwart" Vice-Pres. Chester Arthur.

CHESTER A. ARTHUR (r.) shown at Yellowstone Park in 1883, was born in 1830. As Collector of Port of N. Y. (1871-78), he was accused of graft, but served as honest, upright President.

GARFIELD AND ARTHUR

By a tragic coincidence, James Garfield, the second President to be assassinated, was a close friend of the first martyred chief executive, Abraham Lincoln.

During his short term as President, Garfield began reforms in accordance with the principles of the "Half-breeds," his faction of the Republican Party. Among these was action against "Star Route frauds," Post Office Department graft whereby contractors were paid for non-existent mail routes.

Garfield's death was a blow to James G. Blaine, leader of the "Half-breeds," whom Garfield had made Secretary of State. He had already begun ambitious international plans, including one to promote friendship between North and South America by a Pan-American Congress.

Blaine left the Cabinet when Chester A. Arthur became President; and since Arthur was a "Stalwart" it was expected that the administration would now be graft-ridden. To the surprise of many, however, Arthur handled his position with dignity and honesty, carrying on Garfield's reform program.

Blaine was the Republican candidate for President in 1884, but opponents made much of past mistakes and many of the reform element in his party voted for Democrat Grover Cleveland. Democrats cried out in derision: "Blaine! Blaine! James G. Blaine, the continental liar from the state of Maine." Republicans, in turn, learning Cleveland had fathered an illegitimate child, chanted: "Ma! Ma! Where's my pa? Gone to the White House. Ha! Ha! Ha!"

CHINESE PROBLEM came to a head during Garfield-Arthur administrations. Allowed entry without control during California's Gold Rush, Orientals worked for low wages and antagonized white job-seekers. After many riots had occurred like that at left, in Denver, China agreed to a treaty allowing the U.S. to regulate Chinese influx. In 1882 President Arthur signed a bill halting Chinese immigration for 10 years and prohibiting Chinese from becoming citizens.

FAMOUS PAINTING of ancient Greek courtesan Phryne before the Tribunal suggested this 1884 cartoon. Whitelaw Reid of the New York *Tribune* unveils James G. Blaine before the Republican convention and reveals marks of past political sins. Among these are the "Mulligan Letters," so-called because one James Mulligan possessed them, which showed that Blaine had once helped an Arkansas railroad in obtaining land grants. Nominated, Blaine lost the election.

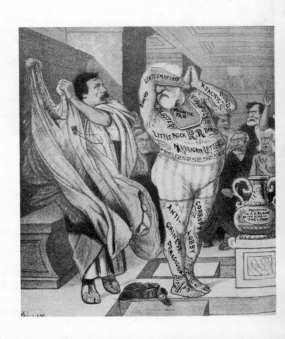

CLEVELAND

Democrats win after interval of 24 years

Courageous was a word to describe Grover Cleveland. Frugal was another. As sheriff of Erie County, N.Y., he refused to incur expense of a hangman when murderers were hanged, and sprang the trap himself. He became "Vetoing Mayor" of Buffalo, then crusading governor of New York. Like Theodore Roosevelt after him, he stressed morals in politics, but his opponents never let him forget his own misdemeanors. Accused of fathering an illegitimate child, his admission of guilt plagued him.

As the first Democratic president since Buchanan, Cleveland set out to demonstrate that his party could still conduct good government. He took for his motto the prosaic phrase "Public officials are trustees of the people," which a reporter translated into: "A public office is a public trust." The new President was beset by hordes of office-seekers, whose demands for spoils he reluctantly met; but he offset this compromise by extending the civil service employee list.

Turning to the pension controversy, he censured Congress for passing countless private aid bills in behalf of their war veteran constituents, many of whom were not deserving. After close study of governmental finance, he decided to work for tariff reform. The simple fact was this: the government was collecting more money than it could spend. Eschewing wasteful projects, Cleveland channeled surplus funds into the creation of an enlarged Navy, but his tariff proposals died in a sharply divided Congress.

Most vexing were the problems of restive labor and nascent agrarian revolt, but because Cleveland's first administration was corrective rather than constructive, their solution was deferred.

Opposing a well-financed Republican campaign in 1888, the Democrats went down in defeat. The presidency went to Benjamin Harrison who, lacking a popular majority, captured the electoral vote.

SOCIAL WASHINGTON regarded Cleveland's bachelorhood with suspicion during his first year in office. Despite an unassailable reputation as a public figure, his personal life had been colored by scandal. Criticism dwindled when in June, 1886, the 49-year-old President married 22-year-old Frances Folsom, daughter of his former law partner, in a dignified White House ceremony. John Philip Sousa provided the music. Mrs. Cleveland ruled Washington society as a brilliant hostess and gathered additional fame as the nation's most beautiful First Lady. She later bore Cleveland five children.

GERONIMO Cleveland's government was beset by problems arising from banditry in the West. Most formidable of the troublemakers were outlaw Apaches (l.) in Arizona. After the Civil War, Southwestern Indians were ordered onto reservations, but many bands, longing for their former life, broke out and carried on plunder and pillage. Greatest of their leaders was Victorio. After his death in 1880,

Geronimo came to the fore. In 1882, Gen. George Crook, veteran Indian fighter, took the field against him. The Apache chief was persuaded to return to the reservation, but three years later he escaped with his band and resumed his attacks. Again he surrendered, but his men fled into Mexico. He is shown (crouching) after his capture. Woman with hand to face had end of her nose cut off by tribesmen as punishment for adultery.

ANTI-LABOR and anti-Catholic sentiments are expressed in cartoon asking: "Does the Catholic Church sanction mob violence?" Workers are members of Knights of Labor, founded in 1869. Union embraced skilled and unskilled workers alike (many of them Irish Catholics), rose to a membership of 700,000 laborers. Series of violent strikes in the mid-1880's led to popular condemnation of union.

LONDON-BORN Samuel Gompers gained experience in Cigarmakers' Union, was one of a group of delegates who, in 1881, founded what became American Federation of Labor. Gompers foreswore Utopian goals, worked for practical, short-term benefits for labor. He kept A. F. of L. restricted to skilled workers. From 1885 until his death in 1924 he was its president.

MAY DAY STRIKES of 1886 involved 340,000 men throughout U.S. seeking eight-hour working day. In Chicago's Haymarket Square, foreign-born anarchists (above) addressed workers, exhorting them to overthrow the state. Police rushed in, killed and wounded several. Next day anarchists stirred up protest meetings. Police appeared again, and someone threw bombs, killing seven. Eight were jailed.

POLICE ATTACKED when Chicago street railway strike of 1877 erupted into violence. Ironically, the Knights of Labor received blame for much of labor strife though favoring arbitration.

WM. VANDERBILT, when asked why he did not give more consideration to the public in operating his railroads, allegedly said, "The public be damned." Cartoon pictures him riding over all classes of society. In 1887 Congress created Interstate Commerce Commission to correct abuses.

HOMESTEADERS like this family in Nebraska often lived in dugouts or huts made of sod cut from treeless prairies. First sod houses leaked badly in rains, turned to mud. A community "soddy" building day became festive occasion for plains settlers, when all those in area would help with the job.

TECHNOLOGICAL REVOLUTION in agriculture rapidly altered farming methods. Such inventions as Hussey and McCormick reapers in the 1830's, Marsh harvester in 1858, chilled steel plow in 1869, and John Appleby's twin binder in 1878, increased the speed of harvesting. Scientific methods of farming further increased grain production. Such methods, plus opening of new land for settlement, created surpluses which plagued farmers.

POPULIST ORATORS like "Pitchfork" Ben Tillman, "Sockless" Jerry Simpson, Mrs. Mary Lease preached an agrarian radicalism which offended Eastern conservatives and infuriated Western Republicans. Above, a Populist being beaten.

VIOLENCE in the mining fields during the 1890's resulted from strikes in protest of poor pay and working conditions. The Western Federation of Miners, established in 1893, waged bitter strikes for the next decade. Armed miners fought armed strikebreakers imported by owners. State and Federal troops assisted in crushing strikes. Above, troop train leaving mining area.

POPULISTS
Agrarian crusade for a people's government

As the country's industrial development forged ahead in the post-Civil War decades, the economic plight of the farmer grew steadily worse. Drouth, over-expanded credit, low prices, and victimization by the railroads contributed to mounting discontent. Their grievances ignored by both major parties, the farm groups of the South and West organized into the National Farmer's Alliance and Industrial Union in 1889.

Winning some notable victories in the elections of 1890 convinced the farmers of the wisdom of forming a national party. The Populists held their first convention in Omaha in 1892. Advocated were such reforms as a graduated income tax, direct election of Senators, public ownership of railroads, the initiative and referendum and postal savings banks. Most insistent was the demand for inflation; that is, abandonment of the gold standard for a policy of free and unlimited coinage of silver at the ratio of 16 to one. General James B. Weaver, candidate for President in 1892, polled more than a million popular and 22 electoral votes. Two years later six senators and seven representatives were elected to Congress, convincing Eastern politicians of their strength.

In 1896 the golden-tongued orator, William Jennings Bryan, captured the Democratic convention at Chicago with his impassioned plea for a silver plank in the platform. With his nomination as Presidential candidate, the radical, inflationary wing of the party captured control. Bryan was to be the party's dominant figure for years.

Endorsed also by the Populists, Bryan was defeated but only by half a million votes. Prosperity returned, new issues engaged the voters and the Populists gradually disappeared from the American scene. Many of their demands, revolutionary then, later were to become commonplace and accepted as conservative measures.

WORKING MEN resorted to extra-legal means to defend their jobs when every other means failed or when attacked by armed thugs. In 1892 strikers (top) at the Carnegie Homestead Steel Plant killed some strikebreakers imported from the Pinkerton Agency to take their jobs. Mining town above was typical of many. Miners' lot was untenable in face of implacable owners.

"CZAR" REED, Speaker of the House under Harrison, won his title when he ruled against the minority practice of refusing to answer the roll call when a quorum was needed. He ordered the clerk to count a quorum from the members he saw in attendance, whether they chose to vote or not. A set of House rules bearing his name was permanently adopted.

◀ **FAMILY PORTRAIT** of Benjamin Harrison was taken at White House. Harrison, a compromise candidate, was selected after James G. Blaine, once defeated, refused to run. Harrison was an able speaker, but his cold personal manner won him few friends. A dignified figurehead, he was completely overshadowed by Blaine and party wheelhorses.

MONOPOLY, pictured above as demanding tribute from all ranks of society, became embarrassing to the Republicans. More as political expediency than desire for business regulation, 51st Congress passed Sherman Anti-Trust Act, forbidding any combination to carry on interstate commerce in restraint of trade. It made attempts to gain monopoly illegal.

HARRISON

Republicans control 51st Congress

When Benjamin Harrison took office it was the first time in many years that one party controlled all three branches of government.

The Republican Congress hoped to erect high tariff walls, but before they could move in this direction, a sop to the Western and agrarian elements was necessary in order to gain needed support. As a result, the Sherman Silver Purchase Act — replacing the Bland-Allison law — was passed in 1890, designed to appease debtor farmers and Western silver mining interests. The price of silver had been dropping. The new act required the government to purchase nearly twice as much silver as before and to issue Treasury notes based on these purchases. The step was ineffectual, however, and the Treasury surplus threatened to disappear. The public began to lose faith in the government's power to redeem greenbacks and Treasury notes. As a result of the consequent rush on the Treasury, gold flowed out and paper flowed in. Toward the close of Harrison's term, economic crisis seemed inevitable, and, in an effort to stave it off until the next president assumed office, the administration took bold and drastic steps.

Republican Hegemony Short Lived

The Treasury asked New York banks to exchange $6 million in gold for its paper. This step kept the gold reserve in precarious balance for the time being, saving the Republicans — or so they hoped — from the odium of catching the blame for whatever panic might ensue.

Secretary of State Blaine re-issued invitations to a Pan-American conference. He presided over the meeting of 1889-90, which produced the Pan-American Union. A controversy between Germany, Britain and the United States concerning the Samoan Islands threatened to erupt into war, with each power striving for preferential rights. The matter was settled, for the time being, when the three nations agreed to rule the islands under a tri-partite protectorate.

The Democrats captured Congress at the mid-term elections, upsetting the Republicans' legislative program. Blaine was considered for the presidential nomination, but by the time he spoke up on the matter, the convention was pledged to Harrison. In the elections he went down in rousing defeat to Grover Cleveland.

GROWING CITIES, crowded with immigrants from southern and eastern Europe, presented social and political problems. Corrupt politicians used immigrant votes to stay in power. Manufacturers relied on cheap immigrant labor, forcing new arrivals to live in slums. Trusts, however, came under attack for such exploitation and were accused of tearing at America's vitals.

INVASION of last frontier started at the bark of the U.S. Marshal's gun on April 22, 1889. In what is now Oklahoma, land-hungry settlers raced to claim home-sites in what had been Indian Territory. The government re-tained part of the area for Indians and threw the rest open for settlement. The remainder, known as the "Cherokee Strip," was similarly settled in 1893 after the Indians were provided with 160 acres of land per family.

PLAINS INDIANS, terrified of extermination, found a prophet among Nevada Indians who initiated the ceremony of the Ghost Dance. When it spread to Dakota reservations, frightened whites called in troops (l.) under Gen. Miles, who needlessly attacked camp at Wounded Knee (1891), slaughtered 200, mostly women and children. Chiefs pose (r.) with Buffalo Bill at the Pine Ridge Reservation.

SITTING BULL (in white) poses with chiefs and agents after return from exile in Canada fol-lowing Custer massacre. During Ghost Dance craze, Indian police killed him in cold blood.

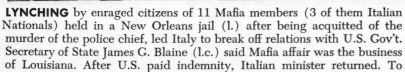

LYNCHING by enraged citizens of 11 Mafia members (3 of them Italian Nationals) held in a New Orleans jail (l.) after being acquitted of the murder of the police chief, led Italy to break off relations with U.S. Gov't. Secretary of State James G. Blaine (l.c.) said Mafia affair was the business of Louisiana. After U.S. paid indemnity, Italian minister returned. To obtain money for expansion U.S. firms sold bonds in England. Americans with little understanding of financial matters complained about this "eco-nomic vassalage." Cartoons (r.c.) decrying the British were widely pub-lished. In contrast to Mafia affair, when U. S. sailors were later attacked in Valparaiso (r.), Blaine demanded and received apology from **Chile.**

COMMONWEALTH OF CHRIST, otherwise known as Coxey's Army, began its march on Washington at Massillon, Ohio, Easter Sunday, 1894. Comprising about 500 of the four million unemployed after Panic of '93, horde was led by "General" Jacob Coxey and Carl Browne. Organized to force Congress to legislate relief work programs, the "army" was dispersed when Coxey was arrested for walking on the White House lawn.

Cleveland's 2nd Term

Major depression grips nation as economic problems become more acute

Speculation, extravagance, uncertain currency and the prospect of changes in the tariff combined to make Grover Cleveland's second term in White House a stormy one.

While his supporters collected election bets, Cleveland contemplated the lack of gold in the Treasury. He called a special session of Congress and successfully pushed repeal of the Silver Purchase Act. He discarded bi-metallism in favor of a gold standard, and persuaded Congress to authorize the sale of government bonds to the public in exchange for gold.

He was much criticized for his money policies, especially when he made a deal with J. P. Morgan and the Rothschilds of Paris to permit them to buy a $62 million issue of bonds below their market value.

The purchasers agreed to procure gold from abroad. The Treasury was saved. The Administration further secured reductions in tariffs, although the new tariffs were not as low as Cleveland desired.

The loss in revenue was to be made up by levying a two per cent tax on incomes over $4,000. Republican opponents charged the bill was "socialism, communism and devillism." The next year, the Supreme Court declared the tax unconstitutional.

The so-called "panic" of 1893 was a major, world-wide depression, but Cleveland, viewing the problem in 19th century terms, did not believe it the duty of the government to bring back prosperity. Widespread labor troubles developed as a consequence of the depression. Cleveland sent the Army

to restore order in the Pullman strike, acting under the Sherman Anti-Trust Act. He charged labor with acting in restraint of trade by striking.

When Great Britain tried to force Venezuela to accept her terms in the boundary dispute, Cleveland stood firmly behind the Monroe Doctrine. Congress established a commission which set the boundary, and both parties signed an agreement settling the dispute amicably.

In 1896, the Democrats repudiated Cleveland, embraced Populism, and put forth William Jennings Bryan for President. Republican candidate William McKinley, ably supported by Mark Hanna, won an easy presidential election victory over Bryan despite his extensive campaign.

PANIC AND UNREST marked the spring of 1893. 1892 had been a year of reckless borrowing and speculation. Severe panic resulted when credit was curtailed. Defunct banks totaled 158; 74 railroads went into receivership; more than 15,000 commercial failures were recorded; unemployment and strikes were prevalent. Among these, the Pullman strike of 1894 was foremost. Strikers protested lay-offs and demanded restoration of wage cuts. Labor leader Eugene Debs was jailed for "conspiring to obstruct the mails." Cleveland sent Army to quell riots. Workers dispersed and strike failed.

TAMMANY BOSS Richard Croker marched in parade at Cleveland's inauguration although he was one of the president's sternest enemies. He advocated the old spoils system and wanted control of the New York political patronage.

SILVER-TONGUED ORATOR, William Jennings Bryan, won nomination at Democratic convention in 1896 with impassioned speech in favor of free silver, later labeled his "Cross of Gold" speech. Arthur Sewell was his running mate. The issue of free silver was one Republicans hoped to bypass, but Bryan carried it to the people. The campaign was fierce. Terms like "gold bug" and "popocrat" were tossed back and forth. Republicans dogged his footsteps calling for some sound money policies.

SUFFRAGE was repealed in Hawaii by Queen Liliuokalani in 1893. Revolution followed and Queen was deposed by American interest. Hawaii was annexed as territory in 1898, when it was deemed advisable to have mid-Pacific base.

"THE LAW AND DUTY" appeared in *Harper's Weekly* in 1895. As police commissioner of New York City, Theodore Roosevelt met opposition in enforcing existing laws, as he had in Washington, D.C., in his tenure as Civil Service boss.

STRONG MAN of the Republican Party, Marcus Hanna, was a businessman who felt government existed to help business. By shrewd maneuvering he was able to secure McKinley's nomination in 1896 on first ballot at convention.

FRONT PORCH campaign conducted by McKinley won him the presidency. Behind the scenes was Mark Hanna, collecting enormous campaign funds and spending them on hundreds of speakers to follow the campaign of Bryan and preach the gold standard. On eve of election, 150,000 businessmen, clad in black, marched in support of sound money in New York.

TRAVELING CANDIDATE William Jennings Bryan covered 18,000 miles and gave 600 speeches in support of his free silver platform. First to take his case to the people, he began a new era in political campaigning. While McKinley won the election, 271 to 176 electoral votes, Bryan was not downcast and wrote an account of campaign entitled, *The First Battle.*

SPARK that ignited the conflict was the explosion of the *Maine* in Havana Harbor on Feb. 15, 1898. The craft, a second class battleship, was ordered to Cuba on the pretext of preserving order. The disaster killed 266 members of the crew, wounded 66 others. Many in the U.S. jumped to the conclusion that the Spanish were responsible. "Remember the *Maine*" became the nation's battle cry. Parties of Spanish and American divers examined the sunken hull. The Americans claimed explosion came from outside, Spaniards said from inside. Responsibility has never been fixed.

SPANISH-AMERICAN WAR

U. S. acquires an overseas empire, enters the arena of world politics

Spain by 1898 retained only Cuba and Puerto Rico as remnants of her once-great American empire. Cuba had long been the target of filibustering Americans, and the Cuban nationalists had repeatedly tried to gain the support of the United States in their struggle for independence.

The Cuban revolt which broke out in 1895 was aided by Spain's inhuman colonial policies, which served to unite the Cubans in bitterness against her. Slavery persisted on the island and the peon was no better than a serf. The pure-blood Spaniards exercised an iron-fisted rule and were proverbially corrupt.

Maximo Gomez, the insurrection leader, was hailed in America as a Cuban George Washington. American newspaper correspondents flocked to the island to report the progress of the revolt for sensation-hungry readers, but Cleveland refused to be stampeded into war. When McKinley assumed office he, too, attempted to forestall U.S. intervention. In response to stern notes sent at his direction, the Spanish government agreed to relax its harsh practices in Cuba and offered the Cubans autonomy; but the rebel leaders would be satisfied with nothing less than independence.

The situation grew tense when a letter, written by the Spanish Minister to the U. S., was stolen from the Havana post office by a rebel spy and printed in the newspapers. In it, the Spaniard had referred to McKinley as "a spineless politician." American indignance rose to fever pitch. Theodore Roosevelt had referred to the President (for his hesitancy to ask for war) as having "no more backbone than a chocolate eclair." Americans permitted such talk from their own politicians, but for a foreign official to say the same was inexcusable.

Following upon this came the explosion of the *Maine*. The yellow press in the United States cried out for war. Sec. of State William Day demanded an immediate armistice in Cuba, but the Spanish government hesitated, fearing a revolt at home if it obeyed. But on April 9, 1898, in response to a joint peace plea sent to the United States and Spain by the European powers, Spain accepted in their essentials all the U.S. demands. McKinley, however, felt by this time that only by yielding to the popular clamor for war could he hold his party together. On April 11 he asked for a declaration of war and Congress eagerly complied. It meant that the United States had abandoned her policy of isolation and, for good or bad, had embarked on a new career as a world power.

EVIL HAND behind Cuban war (in the eyes of U.S. extremists) was Alphonso XIII of Spain, a boy of 12. His mother, Maria Christina, served as regent during his minority, attempted vainly to preserve peace amid clamor for war.

WILLIAM McKINLEY took office amid the Cuban revolt. His efforts to prevent war with Spain were hampered by public hysteria, excesses of the press and by his Asst. Sec. of Navy, Theodore Roosevelt, who longed for a good scrap.

"BUTCHER" (Gen. Valeriano) Weyler, Spanish commander in Cuba, won nickname for stringent measures he took against Cuban rebels. He ordered all those living in the troublesome areas to be concentrated in specified areas where they could be watched, also set up internment camps. Many Cuban prisoners died of tropical diseases or starved in the wretched camps.

CUBAN INSURRECTIONISTS under Maximo Gomez avoided pitched battles, concentrated on guerrilla warfare, set fire to Spanish plantations. Many Cuban rebels escaped to the U. S. to become naturalized, then returned to Cuba. Thus if mistreated by Spaniards they could appeal to the U.S. government for help as citizens. They hoped in this way to involve the United States on Cuban side.

ADMIRAL CERVERA led Spanish squadron to Caribbean. At his approach, Americans in Atlantic seaboard cities grew alarmed, demanded protection. Cervera evaded U.S. blockade and reached Cuba, but was defeated off Santiago.

EXECUTION of rebels was unenlightened Spanish method of dealing with insurrection. All Cubans found outside designated areas were regarded as rebels and tried as such. The insurrectionists were equally brutal and killed, besides Spaniards, whomever they suspected of loyalism. Cuban insurrection had been going on intermittently since 1868. Danger of United States intervention was near in 1873 when Spanish seized an American ship bringing arms to the insurgents, but war was averted.

CAPT. ALFRED MAHAN of U.S. Navy gained world renown for books on the influence of sea power. His call for large Navy was eagerly answered by Congress in 1890s. A great proponent of building an empire, he influenced Roosevelt.

UTTER CONFUSION characterized transport of troops to Cuba. Tampa (above) was poor choice for port of embarkation, lacked proper facilities. Same ships were mistakenly allotted different regiments. Rough Riders went minus horses.

WM. RANDOLPH HEARST, in the midst of circulation war with Joseph Pulitzer, filled his papers with atrocity stories about Spaniards, urged war. He once stated it cost him $3 million to bring about United States intervention in Cuba.

ROUGH RIDERS were a cavalry regiment raised by Roosevelt (beneath flag). Riders were "a motley array of ex-cowboys, college athletes, and adventurers." Command went to Col. Wood, but T. R. was effective head. Group trained at San Antonio, where informality prevailed. T.R. joked and drank with his men. When word of Dewey's victory came, he feared war would end before Rough Riders saw action, wrote letters to prevent this.

◀ **U. S. ARMY** at the outbreak of Spanish War was small and poorly organized. There was no general staff. Commanding was Gen. Nelson Miles, the Indian fighter. Not until after it passed war resolutions did Congress appropriate additional funds for the army. New law permitted acceptance into army of three volunteer cavalry regiments. Most famous was that of T. Roosevelt shown (l. to r. front row) with Gen. Wheeler, Col. Wood.

LANDING TROOPS in Cuba was a hectic, mismanaged operation. Each regiment hoped to get ashore before the others. Horses brought along for officers were thrown overboard to swim to land. Rough Riders were chided by infantrymen for being horseless. Two men drowned in the surf. Troops marched to a point called Las Guasimas. There Rough Riders and Gen. Young's cavalry separated, hit Spaniards individually, won a small victory.

BATTLE PLAN was frequently changed. Finally it was agreed troops would attack Santiago, in whose harbor Cervera's squadron was bottled up. Cavalry reached ridge above town known as San Juan Hill, July 1. Americans foolishly revealed their exact position and came in for heavy bombardment when they raised an observation balloon. Climax of battle was reckless charge by Rough Riders. Painting above is by Frederick Remington.

HEFTY Gen. William Shafter organized Cuban campaign. The 325-pound general suffered from gout and was so fat he had to be hoisted into saddle. When fighting became heavy before Santiago, he considered retreat, then begged Navy for help. He was severely criticized for not going to front, but he pleaded illness. So unafraid of him were his inferiors that they countermanded some of his orders.

SPANISH GOVERNMENT ordered Cervera to escape Santiago harbor. On July 3, he steamed out. U.S. commanders Sampson and Schley combined forces and sank or beached all Spanish ships. Spanish casualties were 400; Americans: one killed, one wounded. U.S. troops then moved into Santiago, received surrender (above) July 16.

ROOSEVELT, while Asst. Sec. of Navy, showed great independence. While Sec. of Navy Long was out to lunch, T. R. ordered entire navy put on war footing and cabled Commodore George Dewey, then in Hong Kong, to take fleet to Philippines. When war came, Dewey easily took Manila (above).

"WILLIAM, YOU'RE TOO LATE" is title of cartoon picturing Germany's Kaiser discovering the Philippines in U.S. hands. After Dewey's victory, British and German ships appeared in Manila Bay. German squadron could have destroyed Dewey, but American fears were exaggerated.

DEWEY had left Mirs Bay, China, Apr. 27, 1898, after re-fitting his six-ship squadron. Disregarding rumors of mines, he steamed into Manila Bay, Apr. 30. In seven hours, on May 1, Dewey's fire destroyed Admiral Montojo's Spanish fleet and killed 381 Spaniards. The U. S. fleet had only 8 wounded.

RETURN OF CONQUEROR DEWEY to U.S. was cheered by crowds lining New York Harbor. Flagship *Olympia* is seen at right. Dewey and his men paraded through the city, were accorded a tremendous ovation. Left, Dewey appears on speaker's stand with McKinley. There was no useful purpose to be served in Dewey's sinking of the decrepit Spanish fleet. Since war was being fought for Cuba, ships in Philippines could have been ignored. Peace of Paris, Dec. 18, 1898, gave U.S. the Philippines, Puerto Rico and Guam. Spain was ordered to relinquish Cuba. Spanish objected strongly to the loss of the Philippines, pointing out that they had not been an issue in the dispute that led to war. Necessary two-thirds vote in the Senate on the treaty was delayed by "anti-imperialists" led by Wm. Jennings Bryan, House Speaker Reed, and Andrew Carnegie (among others). Bryan, who could not imagine a democracy possessing an empire, finally compromised, suggested treaty be signed, then the Philippines set free.

WASHINGTON VOLUNTEER INFANTRY FIRING LINE IN ACTION

CALIFORNIA VOLUNTEERS CAPTURING FILIPINO STRONGHOLD

PHILIPPINE INSURRECTION

Dewey's victory at Manila Bay by no means secured the Philippines for the United States. Spanish troops still held Manila, and Dewey had no forces to oppose them.

Since the Spanish were occupied by a native revolt, Dewey asked Washington to send an expeditionary force to aid the insurgents. In July, 1899, an army of 11,000 under Gen. Wesley Merritt arrived. By this time, however, the Spanish and Americans

were beginning to fear the rebels more than one another. Consequently the Spanish agreed to surrender Manila if the insurgents were kept out. The Americans were amenable, and received the city on August 14.

When the rebels discovered that, far from gaining their freedom, they had merely exchanged Spanish rule for American, they took arms against the U.S. forces, whom they earlier regarded as liberators.

The fighting lasted more than two years. Aguinaldo and other leaders, heading 75,-000 Mohammedan Moros and Igorrotes and Catholic Filipinos, fought a savage guerrilla warfare. The Americans experienced their most desperate fighting since the Civil War.

The legacy of hatred created by U.S. actions disintegrated, however, with enlightened rule that prepared the islands for eventual independence.

FILIPINO WOUNDED AWAITING MEDICAL CARE

AMERICAN SOLDIERS FIRING FROM BEHIND A CAPTURED FILIPINO BREASTWORK

GEN. ARTHUR MACARTHUR (second from l.) father of Douglas MacArthur, is shown with staff. MacArthur fought insurgents in Luzon for two years. He succeeded Gen. Otis as military governor of islands in 1900. Filipino rebels inflicted severe punishment on American troops.

EMILIO AGUINALDO, in exile in 1898, was returned to the Philippines by Admiral Dewey. Head rebel leader, he welcomed the U.S. at first, then led fight. He was capured in 1900.

WM. HOWARD TAFT (c., greeting natives) headed commission to Philippines in 1900, lingered to become Islands' first civil governor. Respected by the natives, whom he called "little brown brothers," Taft brought enlightened rule.

GOLD SEEKERS, taking the Alaskan panhandle route to the Klondike, suffered great hardships. Above, miners drag sleds up "Jacob's Ladder" across ice, at Sheep's Camp, near Skagway. Snowslide nearby buried 68. Entombed, they were dug out by 1,500 men. Seven, buried 3 hours, were alive.

DYEA FLATS became a thriving tent city during rush. Settlement was stopping place on route to Klondike. Prior to gold discovery, Dyea had only one inhabitant, a trader. Beside tents are stacked piles of cumbersome miners' equipment. Horses, dogs and even goats were used to haul sleds.

LAW REQUIRED each miner to register his claim. Many waited three days in line. Swedish miner was sold a supposedly worthless claim by confidence men for $600. Undaunted by jibes, Swede dug furiously, tapped $1,250,000 mine.

WHALES, "the Eskimos' commissary," were ignored as sources of wealth by miners. Specimen above is being cut into blubber. Tongue and jaws are visible. Eskimos, when taught to play chess, amazed miners with their skill at game.

ACTRESSES (here wearing corsets under their slacks) flocked to mining towns. At Dawson, dancehall girl threw kerosene lamp at rival, causing disastrous fire. As a result, all disreputable women were moved to Louse Town.

KLONDIKE

Gold Rush takes place in "America's icebox"

In 1896, the American people, muddling through a severe depression, were electrified by news of a fabulous gold discovery in the Klondike. Where or what the Klondike was became the prime question. The Alaska Commercial Company, founded the year after Alaska was purchased from Russia, provided the answer, in illustrated guide books. The Klondike proved to be a river valley in the Yukon district of Alaska, approachable by two main routes, both served by steamship lines from Seattle and San Francisco. A gold-seeker could sail either to the mouth of the Yukon River or to the Alaska panhandle and journey by land and water to gold fields. (See atlas, plate 26).

The Klondike gold rush, with its hordes of "stampeders," produced scenes reminiscent of the days of '49 in California. It also proved Alaska's worth. Although the bulk of gold was extracted in Canada, the value of ore taken from Alaska exceeded by 50 times the purchase price of the territory.

Here in the frozen North, "where strong men rust from the gold and lust," the intrepid gold seeker, if he were not hardy, fell by the wayside. Many froze; a few starved. Gunfights and general lawlessness accounted for several deaths in Alaska Territory; but on the Canadian side, crime was held at a minimum by the omnipresent Royal Mounted Police. Miners were at first exasperated at the Mounties, who examined every man entering Canada. They grew to respect them, however, for it was the Mounties who rescued and protected miners.

The gold rush had ceased to attract the multitudes by 1900, but it served to reveal the vast mineral resources of the Northwest. It enriched American literature and folklore as well, with tales of Ruthless Ruth (the maid uncouth), of Yukon Jake, the Killer (who would rake the dive with his .45 'til the atmosphere grew chiller), of Dangerous Dan McGrew (and the lady that's known as Lou). On the debit side, the rush produced a boundary dispute with Canada that was only settled after deep bitterness was engendered.

SKAGWAY boasted 67 saloons. When gambler Soapy Smith's thugs relieved miner Two-Fisted Mike of hard-earned dust, he shot up Clancy's saloon. Schoolteacher Frank Reed challenged Soapy to gun duel. They shot each other dead.

CHILKOOT PASS, near Dyea, was gateway to the gold fields. First stampeders struggled up slope unaided. Later a rope tram line was installed. Average miner packed 50 pounds over pass. A husky Indian once carried 350 pounds.

BOXER REBELLION broke out in China in 1900. Boxers originated as an athletic society, were given nickname by Europeans. Movement was directed against foreigners. Above, U.S. Marines guard American legation as Boxers attack. Eventually all foreigners took refuge in British consulate.

CHINESE TROOPS hold maneuvers while officers observe from hill in background. Imperial Chinese Army was being reorganized on Western lines in 1890s, though few troops had modern uniforms or weapons. Imperial troops of Empress Dowager cooperated with Boxers against foreigners.

GREAT WALL of China is visited by troops of U.S. Sixth Cavalry under Gen. Chaffee. The United States organized a contingent of 15,000 men to fight Boxers, but only 5,000 arrived in time to participate in the capture of Peking. The other powers supplying troops for the expedition were Japan, Britain, France and Russia.

OPEN DOOR POLICY
United States acquires a stake in the Orient

Acquisition of the Philippines made the U.S. a Pacific power, whether it wanted the role or not. In 1899, when it looked as if China would be dismembered by European powers and Japan into spheres of influence (which would exclude U.S. trade and endanger its strategic position) Secretary of State John Hay drafted his Open Door note to Britain, Russia and Germany, asking them to adopt a policy of equal trade for all in China. Only Britain responded favorably to Hay's note.

In 1900 a violently anti-foreign movement, led by a group known as the Boxers and supported by the Empress Dowager, broke out in China. Foreigners were in-sulted, attacked and even killed. In Peking, they locked themselves in the British consulate. As a result, a joint U.S.-European and Japanese expeditionary force landed at Taku and fought its way to Peking, where it relieved the besieged consulate.

Hay again put forth his proposal and this time the powers accepted the Open Door. China was required to pay an indemnity of $333 million. The U.S. later reduced the amount due to her and devoted payments to education of Chinese students in America. The sum of events added up to permanent U.S. interest in the status of China and to a feeling in China that the United States was its "moral ally."

JOHN HAY, U.S. Sec. of State, advocated Open Door policy, subscribed to in theory by the powers after Boxer Rebellion. Actually, idea originated with British, fearful of Russian motives in China, and having a large stake there.

VICTORIOUS TROOPS of U.S. and Europe pose between stone elephants along China's Avenue of Statues. After coming to the rescue of their besieged countrymen, soldiers of the associated forces mercilessly looted Peking, engendering violent antagonism.

RUSSIA AND U.S. were pictured as "young giants" reaching out over Pacific and East Asia. After Boxer Rebellion, Russia kept troops in Manchuria, despite promises to withdraw and U. S. protests.

OLD GUARD

McKinley triumph in 1896 marks downfall of Populist movement

Triumph of McKinley and the Republicans in 1896 heralded the downfall of Populism and all it stood for and marked the resurgence of the industrial elements of the Northeast. Although the domestic policies of the administration were overshadowed by war and by the appearance of the nation on the international scene, they were not unimportant, nor were they treated as such.

Feeling they had been given a mandate to make business the first concern of the government, the Republican House and Senate put through the highly protective Dingley tariff and passed the Gold Standard Act, to the great satisfaction of the financiers and hard money advocates. Big business was given a clean bill of health. The ineffectual Sherman Anti-Trust Act held no terrors for entrepreneurs who believed the government had conceded the legality of monopoly.

Fortunate for the Republicans was the close coincidence between their triumph at the polls and the return of prosperity. One reason for the healthy recovery was a vast increase in the world's money supply, brought about partly by the discovery of gold in the Klondike and elsewhere.

Republicans firmly entrenched

There were many in both parties, however, who were not pleased with the status quo, and the elections of 1900 brought the issues into sharp focus. A growing number had lost their taste for "imperialistic adventures" and stoutly opposed annexation of the Philippines. Democrats asserted that it was inconsistent for a democratic nation to suppress the aspirations of another people to gain their independence. The Republicans countered with the argument that the Filipinos were incapable of governing themselves, and that, in default of U.S. occupation of the islands, they would fall prey to some other power.

It was a foregone conclusion that the Republicans would renominate McKinley. The best the Democrats could do was to resurrect Bryan and the free silver issue, both regarded by some as time-worn, and to plump for tariff reduction. The Republicans, taking "The Full Dinner Pail" as their slogan to please workers, and chanting "Let Well Enough Alone" to reassure business, won the election by a vast majority. Notable in the contest were a large number of minor parties that put forth candidates: the Populists, Socialists and a Prohibition party.

Six months after his inauguration McKinley was assassinated. It was plain that Roosevelt, as his successor, would not carry out the McKinley domestic policies to the letter; but there was no doubt that he would plunge with vigor into the job of administering the newly-gained empire.

ELIHU ROOT, Sec. of War (1899-1904), effected vast improvements in War Dept. and in organization of the Army. He founded Army War College, helped direct U.S. policy in Cuba and Philippines, later served as Secretary of State.

"BOSS" PLATT was a N. Y. senator (1897-1909) and powerful force in politics of his state. Largely responsible for election of Roosevelt as Governor of N. Y. in '98, he later became concerned with T. R.'s popularity and opposed him.

INCONGRUITY of Rough Rider Roosevelt as vice presidential candidate is asserted in 1900 cartoon. The war hero was reluctant at first to accept nomination, thought office a blind alley. No vice pres. had ever been elected president.

HEAVY SMOKER McKinley was said to be suffering heart trouble from the habit. Unsympathetic Democratic cartoon pictures him with cigar labeled with party scandals. Looking over shoulder is power-behind-throne Mark Hanna.

ANARCHIST Leon Czolgosz shot McKinley Sept. 6, 1901 after the President made speech in Buffalo. Assassin, pretending to be an admirer, approached with a gun concealed in handkerchief, fired twice. McKinley died Sept. 14. Roosevelt, vacationing in the Adirondacks, was met by a guide who brought the news. Next day he was sworn in as President.

HORSELESS CARRIAGE

Paves way for new era

From the days of its founding, the conquest of distance was one of America's most pressing problems. The vast size of the country and the tendency of its inhabitants to wander off to its furthermost corners made adequate and cheap transportation a vital factor in American living. Inventors concentrated their best efforts on development of new methods of getting people and goods from one place to another, and financiers were ready to pour capital into new schemes that seemed likely to satisfy the demands of the public for such transportation.

By far the most world-shaking development of the late 19th century was the appearance on the American scene of the "horseless carriage." In their first decade, steam, electric and gasoline cars developed side by side, with steam leading in popularity. In 1895 there were five "horseless carriages" in the United States. Five years later there were 8,000, and the automobile was no longer a laughing matter.

U.S. railroads found their startling expansions somewhat curtailed in the 1890's. The panic of 1893-96 threw 13 major lines into receivership. But by 1900 there were 258,784 miles of track, with 37,663 locomotives, 24,713 passenger cars and 1,365,531 freight cars in operation. During the decade, almost all equipment was fitted with the new automatic couplers and automatic air brakes for greater safety.

Supplementing the railways locally were the new streetcars, elevated lines and subways. The first electric streetcar lines were built by Frank Sprague in Richmond and Boston in 1888. During the 90s the idea was adopted by cities all over the country and the horsecar was virtually abandoned. Boston's Tremont Subway, opened in 1897, was the first underground line in the U.S. New York was first with an elevated railway, helping solve early day traffic problems.

HENRY FORD AND HIS FIRST CAR, the "Quadricycle," which he operated successfully in Detroit on June 4, 1896, are shown here. Car had a two cylinder gasoline engine developing four horsepower, went forward but not backward. In the 1890's Ford was just one of many experimenters in the "horseless carriage" field. Though destined to wield the greatest influence of any single individual in the automobile world, Ford actually was late starting. He failed twice in efforts to launch manufacturing companies before his Ford Motor Company got under way in 1903 with a total capital of $28,000.

THOMAS EDISON is shown with Mrs. Edison in an early electric automobile for which Edison supplied the batteries. The smooth, quiet electrics enjoyed a great vogue around the turn of the century, traveling at 15 miles an hour, with a range of up to 40 miles on a battery charge.

STANLEY TWINS, F. E. and F. O., built the most successful American steam car in 1897. Next year a Stanley broke world speed record and brothers opened a factory. By 1900 steam cars were foremost in popularity. The Stanleys remained in business until after World War I.

CHARLES E. DURYEA is shown with one of his gasoline cars in Peoria in 1898. Duryea and his brother Frank designed and built the first successful gasoline-engine automobile in America in 1893. Their Duryea Motor Wagon Company was the first to produce gas cars commercially, and its business boomed when a Duryea car won first U.S. auto race in Chicago.

BARNEY OLDFIELD graduated from bike racing to auto racing when Henry Ford began experimenting with racing cars. He is shown with Ford and the famous gas-engine racer "999," in which Oldfield set a world's auto speed record of mile in 55-4/5 seconds. Ford built several racing cars before Ford Motor Company was formed and often raced them himself.

"EMPIRE BUILDER" JAMES J. HILL (right, wearing light suit) made an immeasurable contribution to development of the Northwest. When the panic of 1873 threw many U.S. rail lines into bankruptcy Hill, who had started out as a shipping clerk, seized the opportunity to gain control of the scattered St. Paul and Pacific Railroad. By the 1890's Hill was the president and guiding genius of the Great Northern and Northern Pacific roads and recognized as one of the outstanding railroaders in the country.

BROOKLYN BRIDGE, dedicated in 1883, was crowning work of the ▶ great engineer John A. Roebling (inset) though he did not live to see it completed. Roebling, who developed and perfected modern techniques of building safe suspension bridges, had spent two years completing plans for record-breaking 1595½-foot span when he died in 1869. His son carried on.

SAN FRANCISCO'S CABLE CARS were first introduced in 1873, the invention of Andrew S. Hallidie. They were widely adopted by other cities, notably Chicago. By '90s cable cars carried thousands of passengers daily.

NEW YORK'S TRANSPORTATION in late 19th century included streetcars, elevated railways and even fleet of electric taxis. Picture shows workmen laying cable for Broadway Surface Railroad's line at Union Square.

STEAMSHIP *NEW YORK* in 1888 still augmented steam with sails. The late 19th century was a dim period for America's merchant marine. American shipping seemed unable to recover from the setback of the Civil War. By the turn of the century only 14 American steamers were engaged in foreign commerce. Ninety per cent overseas trade was handled by foreigners.

LUSITANIA, pride of Britain's Cunard line, was greeted at dockside by a shiny fleet of hansom cabs. The 40,000 ton vessel carried 2,800 passengers. She regained for Britain the "blue ribbon" for transatlantic speed. Sinking of the unarmed *Lusitania* by the Germans in 1915, with loss of 1,154 lives, including 114 Americans, severely damaged U.S. relations with Germany.

SCOTSMAN ANDREW CARNEGIE used Horatio Alger route to fame. A young telegrapher, he became train dispatcher, superintendent, and directed railroad activities during Civil War. After War, Carnegie founded bridge company, worked into steel industry by buying rolling mills and furnaces. Not a technician, he was forerunner of modern administrator, and was noted for his gift of picking proper people for associates. In 1911 he established Carnegie Corporation with gift of $125 million. Early mill (above) shows crude techniques and muscle power used in first forges.

MATHEMATICAL PHYSICIST Josiah Willard Gibbs of Yale published classic papers on vector analysis, thermodynamics and electromagnetic theory of light during the period 1858-1870.

SCIENCE AND INDUSTRY
New developments transform living in U.S.

America was changing overnight. The industrialization of the country brought about by the rich years of scientific development, industrial growth and rapid expansion of the country to the Pacific was beginning to shower its benefits upon the land. Electric lights were illuminating the larger cities. The telephone, typewriter, phonograph, trolley car, and the motion picture camera were at hand, ready to stimulate industrial growth by their use.

In 1892 a new toy appeared in America. It was the first horseless carriage. These early automobiles created a great amount of excitement, but few persons thought them practical. They were left for the next century to develop. The catalyst for the forthcoming great industrial expansion was the discovery in 1890 of the rich Mesabi iron range, north of Duluth, Minn., by the Merritt brothers. Rockefeller money was used to open this immense natural resource, and nearby water transportation on the Great Lakes provided cheap passage of the ore to Pennsylvania and Indiana steel mills.

Lumbering became a major industry during the late 19th century, especially in the Rockies and Pacific Northwest. Big sawmills moved into the forest areas, stripping all trees and leaving a wasteland. Such land was soon eroded and almost useless.

By the turn of the century, conservationists decried this wasteful, destructive practice. They sought federal legislation to protect the nation's timber resources.

Great scientific advances followed this industrial expansion. The ground work for Einstein's theory was established in 1881 by physicists A. A. Michelson and E. W Morley when they developed the *interferometer* and proved that the velocity of light was constant, regardless of the velocities of the transmitter or of the receiver. Henry Rowland, professor at Rensselaer Institute conducted investigations on magnetic induction and permeability, and made the first precision diffraction gratings for spectrum analysis. In 1900 he received grand prize at Paris Exposition for his synchronous multiplex system.

THOMAS ALVA EDISON made first practical motion picture camera in August, 1889. Encouraged by George Eastman, Edison erected studio in West Orange, N. J. First film was a prize fight sketch starring "Gentleman Jim" Corbett, celebrated boxer. Edison (l.) is shown in Menlo Park shop with improved 1895 model projector.

RAILROAD MAN George Westinghouse invented air-brake in 1872, developed automatic air-operated signalling system in 1878. He also built dynamos for Niagara Falls' power plant and, in 1866, built first commercial A-C lighting plant. (l., Westinghouse; r., Lord Kelvin.)

WONDER of centennial exposition of 1876 was gigantic steam engine. Designed by George Corliss, revolutionary engine ran all machines in the exhibition, and was later purchased by the Pullman Co. to power its Chicago plant.

"HELLO GIRLS" of 1888 handle 3500 lines in new Cortlandt exchange in New York City. Forty women operators were used after it was found that male operators were too prone to argue with subscribers. Use of telephone allowed high concentration of people in offices and accelerated business activity. Dial phone system was patented in 1889, and the finger-wheel in 1898. From 1876 to 1900 the telephone had grown from Bell's primitive device to unified system of 1,355,900 subscribers.

SERBIAN AMERICAN Nikola Tesla was famous in the 1880s for his contributions to science of electricity. He invented the induction motor, and formulated the system of high power transmission by use of step-up transformer, high tension line, and distribution transformer. His "Tesla coil," famous to high school student as laboratory device, was used for short range radio transmission in 1900.

SLAUGHTERERS AND PACKERS joined forces in 1880 to produce famous Chicago meat trust. Led by Philip Armour, stockyard procedure was systematized, and purchase and selling prices were fixed. In 1874 Gustavus Swift invented refrigerator car, which allowed frozen meat to be shipped to east coast from midwest areas. Upton Sinclair's novel *The Jungle* (1906) exposed stockyards, brought him job on Roosevelt's investigating board to effect reform in slaughter-houses.

DRYGOODS CLERK Marshall Field had the magic touch for retail business. His store, organized 1865-81, had developed into $40 million business by 1895. Philanthropist Field donated much of his wealth to charities, and founded Field Museum of Natural History in Chicago.

CLOTHING SALESMAN John Wanamaker started his Philadelphia store in 1876, buying freight depot of Pennsylvania Railroad for his low overhead salesroom. Appointed Postmaster-General by President Harrison, Wanamaker also served as secretary and president of YMCA.

GERMAN-BORN A. A. Michelson established the absolute meter in 1892 when he compared French meter with wavelength of cadmium light. He was recipient of 1907 Nobel Physics Prize for his work on *interferometer* and study of effects of earth's velocity on speed of light.

DOCTOR WILLIAM OSLER, teacher and surgeon, stops enroute to clinic to talk with patient on the grounds of Philadelphia General Hospital. Osler revolutionized the teaching and study of medicine by revising courses to include bedside and clinical studies as well as textbook work. A Professor of Medicine at McGill University of Canada, Dr. Osler taught at University of Pennsylvania (1884-1889) and then at Johns Hopkins Medical School (1889-1904). He conducted original research on diseases of spleen and of blood stream. He also wrote brilliant papers on heart disease and malaria.

MEDICINE

Foundations of modern medicine established in "Gay Nineties" era

Turn of the century was the formative period in the development of modern bacteriology and medical practice. New techniques, new teaching methods and acceleration of research were combining to improve medical standards. The government was paying increasing attention to the health of its citizens. U.S. Army Medical Director George Sternberg, a leader in the field of bacteriology, pioneered this advance when he appointed a committee headed by surgeon Walter Reed to attack the problem of yellow fever, the scourge of the tropical and semi-tropical areas.

In other branches of medicine, equally important progress was made. The Chicago Dental Infirmary was established in 1883, and in 1885 William Halsted developed a successful local anaesthesia. Wealthy merchant Johns Hopkins bequeathed more than $3 million to open a modern hospital and medical institute. In 1889 the Johns Hopkins Hospital opened, setting a precedent by admitting women students to practice medicine. In 1896, the Carville (La.) Leprosarium was begun by the Sisters of Charity, and the first course in medical physchology was offered to students in 1900.

GAMBLE WITH DEATH was taken by volunteers in effort to conquer dreaded yellow fever. Dr. Walter Reed (center) was leader of group. Dr. Jesse Lazear is shown inoculating Dr. James Carroll with virus of infected mosquito. Event occurred at Columbia Post Hospital of U.S. Army in Cuba.

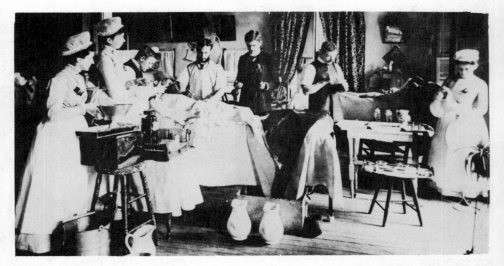

BELLEVUE HOSPITAL operations were performed in wards with other patients observing. The nurses shown in this 1892 photograph were some of earliest professionals in practice. Women's Hospital of Philadelphia graduated nurses in 1872, and nursing at Bellevue Hospital, based on the Florence Nightingale system, was established during late 1873. The first colored nurse, Mary Mahoney, was graduated from New England Hospital in 1879.

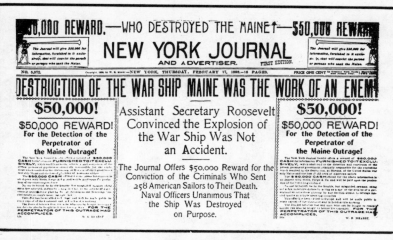

YELLOW JOURNALISM had a field day with Spanish-American war news. Propaganda in Hearst's New York *Journal* and Pulitzer's *World* excited war fervor. Scare headlines blamed the war on Spain. Circulations skyrocketed but profits of papers dwindled because of the high cost of war coverage. Competition faded when Pulitzer abandoned circulation drive.

EDWIN GODKIN, crusading editor of New York *Evening Post,* championed social reform. He attacked Tammany so fearlessly he was sued for libel but won case.

SENSATIONALISM and innovations of modern journalism developed under Hungarian-born Joseph Pulitzer's N. Y. *World* ownership. He created Pulitzer Prize.

BOOKS AND PRESS

New economic and literary trends appear at the close of 19th century

American intellectual maturity was reflected in the significant advance of the press, literature and social sciences at the end of the 19th century. Realism became the vogue in literature, statistical analysis and psychological experiment invaded the social sciences and great newspapers and editors rose to power in the outburst of "yellow journalism" which rocked the nation.

Favorite authors of the 1890's were Stephen Crane and Henry James. A perfectionist for style, James was known as a "novelist's novelist." He displayed his unusual powers in such works as *Daisy Miller, The Ambassadors, The Bostonians* and *Washington Square.*

Tempestuous Stephen Crane flashed his down-to-earth novels and short stories at a startled public. A true disciple of realism, he tried to live the experiences of his stories. Although his descriptive epic of the Civil War, *The Red Badge of Courage,* brought him fame, he had not personally taken part in the war. His short story, *The Open Boat,* was called "the finest short story in the English language" by H. G. Wells.

The leading historical writer of the day was Henry Adams, whose nine volumes of U.S. history, covering the administrations of Jefferson and Madison, won him renown. Later he published *The Education of Henry Adams,* denouncing politics and his failure to find a scientific philosophy.

Meanwhile, the predominating spirit of realism made itself known in philosophy and social science. Experimental philosophers like William James and Josiah Royce deserted the contemplative armchair for the objective laboratory. With James' *Principles of Psychology* and his creation of the demonstrational laboratory, psychology became an empirical science. Royce's philosophy in *The World and the Individual* combined mathematics and metaphysics. He anticipated later developments in physics. Scientific investigation brought about new concepts of economics and sociology as expounded in William Graham Sumner's *Folkways* and Lester Frank Ward's *Dynamic Sociology.* Statistical research came into its own with Thorstein Veblen's economic theories.

In the field of journalism, spectacular changes and innovations occurred from 1885 to 1900. The U.S. became a nation of newspaper readers. New York with its giant dailies became a mecca for newspapermen. Luminaries of the New York press included Joseph Pulitzer, publisher of the *World,* and William Randolph Hearst, of the *Journal.* Competition in sensationalism brought on the Hearst-Pulitzer "war of the Sunday papers."

Conservative Edwin L. Godkin, editor of the *Post* and the *Nation,* and Adolph Ochs, owner of the *Times,* disdained to follow the lead of yellow journals. By 1900, sensationalism was on the way out.

SUPER-REALIST Stephen Crane shocked readers of 1890's with *Maggie: A Girl of the Streets.* Short-lived Crane gained fame with his *Red Badge of Courage.*

WILLIAM JAMES, philosopher and psychologist, influenced world thought. His distinguished works include *Principles of Psychology.* He founded Pragmatist school.

NOTED HISTORIAN Henry Adams gained instant renown with his volumes on U.S. history and with his vital autobiography, *The Education of Henry Adams.*

ICONOCLAST Thorstein Veblen lambasted showy middle class with his theory of "conspicuous consumption." Veblen left his mark in many fields of thought.

MODERN FICTION advanced with the work of Henry James, a leading exponent of psychological novels. He wrote of society life.

CALIFORNIAN Josiah Royce set new standards for systematic philosophy. An idealist, he wrote on influences of loyalty and religion.

HORDES OF IMMIGRANTS were crammed into tenement districts of large cities, like Hester Street in New York's lower East Side (left), where families huddled together in indescribable poverty. At the same time, workingmen were coming to an awareness of their power to organize. These New York City laborers (above) are striking for an eight-hour day. Tenement life seemed to breed alcoholism; often the corner saloon relieved the wage earner both of the miseries of his condition and of money his family needed for bread. The Women's Christian Temperance Union, organized by Frances Willard (right), became increasingly active in fighting the "demon rum" which it believed was responsible for ills.

SOCIAL REFORM

New industrial society creates urban problems requiring fresh ideas

Rapid industrialization, the flood of new immigrants from southern and eastern parts of Europe, and the consequent growth of teeming urban life in the late 19th century, put forth problems of immediate urgency. Great social reformers, labor leaders, educators and churchmen emerged, to work for their eventual solution.

It was a period of labor violence but under the guidance of Samuel Gompers the American Federation of Labor, a grouping of craft unions with such limited objectives as shorter working hours and higher pay, raised labor's prestige. Radical and anarchist elements began to lose ground.

At the same time, the misery of the poor came to wide public notice. Jacob Riis, a Danish immigrant who struggled up from a New York slum to become a reporter for the *Sun*, published *How the Other Half Lives* in 1890. His work on behalf of slum clearance and public parks alerted the public, and resulted in the formation of necessary welfare agencies.

In 1889, Jane Addams founded the famous Hull House in Chicago. The settlement movement spread to other cities. The first National Congress of Parents and Teachers was called in 1897, to take legislative steps toward abolishing child labor and improving living conditions for children of families living in the tenements.

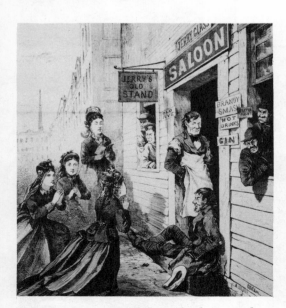

LADIES OF THE WCTU brought their attack on alcohol directly to the saloon itself. Their tactics of singing psalms and kneeling in prayer for the drinkers were to prove more effective than previous attempts to bring about prohibition in the U.S. by determined political action.

SPIRITUAL LEADER who understood the new social problems was the popular Cardinal Gibbons of Baltimore. He interceded with the Pope to remove a ban against the Knights of Labor, explaining that this "secret" union had no pledge prejudicial to the confessional of the Church.

MARY BAKER EDDY, who organized the First Church of Christ, Scientist in Boston, was the first woman of the modern era to found a new religious sect. In poor health for years, she made a dramatic recovery after reading the accounts of healing by Jesus in New Testament.

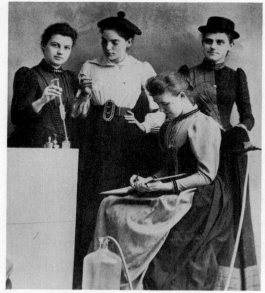

COLLEGES FOR WOMEN were growing in number. Wellesley was first to install laboratories for scientific experiments (above). Admission of women to universities gained impetus with the addition of Barnard at Columbia in 1889 and of Radcliffe College at Harvard in 1894.

NEGRO EDUCATORS AND SCIENTISTS lent valuable talents to human progress. Dr. George Washington Carver, born of slave parents, worked his way through high school and Iowa State College, then went to Booker T. Washington's Tuskegee Institute in Alabama. There he devoted his life to agricultural research, taught Southern farmers to diversify crops. He found many new industrial uses for peanuts and sweet potatoes. Harvard graduate William E. B. DuBois joined faculty of Atlanta U., taught sociology, and wrote world famous books on Negro history and the problems of his race.

PUBLIC EDUCATION took a forward leap, with enrollments reaching 15,000,000 at the turn of the century. One-room, ungraded schools like that of Miss Blanche Lamont in Montana (above) were still common in many rural areas.

COLLEGE ATHLETIC COMPETITIONS had as forerunners such courses in physical education as this one at Amherst. At the same time, great strides were made in the curricula of established schools. Dean of Harvard Law School Christopher C. Langdell introduced the "case method" of teaching law. Under the presidency of Seth Low at Columbia, Nicholas Murray Butler and John W. Burgess created a graduate school of political science, the first in the country organized for such work.

INNOVATIONS in American education were made by the newly-organized University of Chicago's first president, Wm. Rainey Harper. He divided the university year into quarters, the courses into majors and minors, and introduced extension courses and the summer sessions.

ANDREW DICKSON WHITE'S idea of a nonsectarian university, and the system of free elective studies he introduced, were considered radical. He and a fellow N. Y. State senator, Ezra Cornell, founded the land grant college which later became Cornell University in 1865.

VITAL FORCE on the educational scene was Charles W. Eliot, president of Harvard for 40 years. Under his administration, the standards for professional degrees were raised, all courses of study were revised, and the various schools were integrated into a fully modern university.

DR. JAMES NAISMITH was the inventor of only sport purely American in origin — basketball. The game was officially born January, 1892, when Dr. Naismith printed the first set of regulations under the heading, *A New Game*. He devised the game to serve as indoor recreation for the football players at the Y.M.C.A. Training College at Springfield, Mass., where he was a physical education teacher. He nailed two peach baskets to the railing of the gym balcony, directed players to shoot at them with a soccer ball and basketball was born. Women were quick to take up the new game (left). Sports were becoming more popular than ever. Boxing soon came of age, and the first glove bout for the heavyweight title was held in 1892.

BASEBALL outgrew its swaddling clothes in the late 1800's. By 1872 it was hailed as the national game of the country, and big leagues became big business. Connie Mack (c., middle row) managed his first team, Pittsburgh. The White Stockings, under Cap Anson, were the outstanding team of the era. Such names as Buck Ewing, Cy Young, Albert G. Spalding, Mike "King" Kelly, Ned Hanlon and "Wee Willie" Keeler were heroes to U.S. baseball fans.

SPORTS GAIN NEW FANS

Sports in the United States staged a tremendous surge of popularity during the last quarter of the 19th century.

This period marked the emergence of practically all types of sports as well as the advent of something new in America, the "sports hero." It also marked the beginning of large-scale attendance at sporting events.

Following formation of the National Baseball League, the Intercollegiate Football Association and the Intercollegiate Track and Field Associations, more sports organized and the list continued to grow: Rowing Association of American Colleges (1871); American Hockey Association (1887); and U.S. Golf Association (1894).

Basketball was invented and baseball increasing in popularity. International rifle-shooting got under way in 1874 and American athletes, in the first modern Olympic Games at Athens in 1896, captured so many track and field events that they were accused of being professionals.

Golf enjoyed rapid growth as did tennis, although both games were looked upon as being a rich-man's sport. They were played almost exclusively by Easterners.

The first cinder track was built by the New York Athletic Club in 1868 and the first intercollegiate track meet was held at Saratoga in 1874.

John L. Sullivan, who boasted he could "lick any man in the world," took on all comers, anytime, anywhere, to reign as champion for 10 years (1882-1892). "Gentleman Jim" Corbett and Bob Fitzsimmons gave boxing two of its greatest champions before the 20th century dawned.

SHOVE-AND-PULL mass power plays in football led to a brutal game producing slugging and injuries. Weight and momentum characterized such formations as the flying wedge (above) in which the ball carrier was hidden from view and protected by a human battering ram. Fatal injuries sometimes resulted when two teams met head on from such a flying start. The captain of team was in charge, picking team and running it. Coach was merely an advisor and, in some colleges, could be fired by the captain.

DOMINATING FOOTBALL circles until the late 1880's were the Big Three of Yale, Harvard and Princeton. Annual Thanksgiving Day game between Yale and Princeton (above) was country's outstanding football attraction. Perhaps the game wasn't as violent as the artist indicates, but it was rough enough that colleges soon got together in an attempt to stop swearing and slugging. Unless a serious injury was incurred, the 11 men who started a game finished it. Unconsciousness was the only excuse for leaving the field.

HEYDAY OF THE BICYCLE followed its introduction on the stage by the Hanlon Brothers. A small army of cycling enthusiasts formed bicycle clubs in the 1870's and the craze continued for two decades. It played a big role in liberating women from bonds of Victorian behavior. Men, as usual, made more vigorous use of the machines and cycle racing (above) soon became the rage. Climax of the fad was advent of six-day bicycle races in 1891.

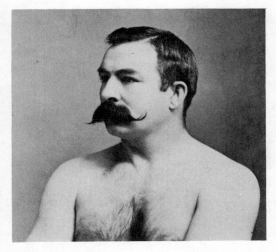

MIGHTY John L. Sullivan was amazingly fast for a big man and packed one of the most vicious punches in ring history. He won the title from Paddy Ryan in a nine-round bare-knuckle fight.

"GENTLEMAN JIM" CORBETT (right) was anything but a gentleman in the ring. A student of the game, he defeated Sullivan by craftiness and fast footwork at New Orleans in 1892. His five-year reign as champion came to an abrupt halt when lanky Bob Fitzsimmons (left) administered the famous "solar plexus" blow to him in 1897. James J. Jeffries took Fitzsimmons' belt away two years later.

FIRST PERMANENT GOLF CLUB IN U.S., SIX-HOLE COURSE AT YONKERS, NEW YORK

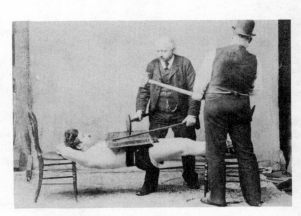

IVAN SKOBEL, THE SIBERIAN STRONG MAN

SPORTING FEVER gripped the country as a sport for every taste appeared on America's athletic menu. New interest in art of fencing evolved from influx of European masters. Rules were set for volley ball in 1895. A fast man named Charles Murphy became famous as "Mile-a-Minute" Murphy, cycling a mile in less than 60 seconds. Dives from Brooklyn Bridge became mode for dare-devils. "Strong men" titles for strength were commonplace.

BULKY TENNIS ATTIRE HINDERED WOMEN

DAY AT THE BEACH

FENCING INSTRUCTION AT THE U.S. NAVAL ACADEMY

JULIA MARLOWE became identified with Shakespearean plays (above, as Juliet, 1897) and appeared in many successes. Co-starring with E. H. Sothern, a great actor of his day, she later married him, and together they toured U.S. in Shakespearean repertory.

RICHARD MANSFIELD, an eccentric, dominating personality, a great tragedian, created many picturesque, romantic character portraits. His Richard III (above, 1889) was in the best theater tradition.

PENSIVE JULIET was Maude Adams. She became national figure because of her charming delineation of James M. Barrie's *Peter Pan*. Under Charles Frohman's management, she did other Barrie plays, starred with John Drew.

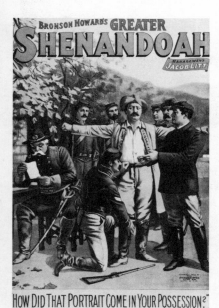

HOW DID THAT PORTRAIT COME IN YOUR POSSESSION?

BRONSON HOWARD'S *Shenandoah,* flamboyant Civil War melodrama, produced in 1889, gave Charles Frohman his first fame.

THEATER
Stage features new talent in late 19th century

The end of the 19th century was rich in development of actors and playwrights. Richard Mansfield, Robert Mantell, E. H. Sothern, Julia Marlowe, Maude Adams, William Gillette, John Drew, and Mrs. Leslie Carter were distinguished names in American theater history.

Playwrights contributed qualities of realism to their theatrical portrayals of familiar American scenes. One of the first successful examples was James A. Herne's *Shore Acres* (1893), a drama of rustic New England life. Augustus Thomas, author of *Alabama* and *Arizona,* was considered the most representative American playwright of his time. Prolific Clyde Fitch wrote 33 original historical (*Barbara Frietchie*) and social dramas. William Gillette also starred in his best known work *Secret Service,* and later as the detective in his *Sherlock Holmes.* With *The Girl I Left Behind Me,* David Belasco launched a long and unique career.

The personality who dominated the period, however, was theater manager-producer Charles Frohman, a kind, loyal, hardworking man for whom it was considered a privilege to work. Called the "maker of stars," Frohman elevated a tremendous number of players to stardom each year. "C.F." also believed that "an actor is made by the audience." Thus, satisfying the public was his prime criterion in selecting playwrights, plays, stars, production methods. In New York and London, his theaters were worth more than $5 million. His salaries paid to more than 10,000 employees averaged $35 million yearly. Frohman met a tragic death on the *Lusitania* in 1915.

BOX OFFICE APPEAL was shrewdly achieved by exploiting "shapely" figures as well as dramatic performances. (Left to right) Florence Baker in *Revels* was striking in coat of mail. Lydia Thompson, London dancer and pantomimic, who in 1868 had shocked audiences in a burlesque show, is decked out as *Robinson Crusoe.* Annie Sutherland, daring in an 1886 costume, blows smoke rings. Grace Vaughn was an 1890 burlesque queen.

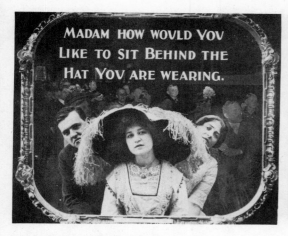

FIRST MOVIES

As labor-saving machines created more leisure time, moving pictures, among other attractions, arose to fill the void. The first movies were slot-machine peepshows in penny arcades, where customers peered through the eyepiece at the top of an Edison Kinetoscope. Edison, who at first saw no future in pictures projected on a screen, built the first movie studio, the Kinetoscope Theater ("Black Maria," painted black both inside and out) in West Orange, New Jersey, for $636.67. It rested on a revolving base, enabling it to follow the sun, thereby keeping the actor always brightly lighted. Comedian Fred Ott was the first subject to be filmed in the "Black Maria" in 1893, and *Fred Ott's Sneeze* has become a historic film.

In 1894, Woodville Latham perfected a machine that could project pictures on a screen so that large audiences could see them. Almost from the start, movies became a medium of mass entertainment, presented in a new, dynamic language. Lecturer Lyman Howe was one of the pioneer exhibitors who presented "High Class Moving Pictures" that were educational as well as entertaining to millions.

Early movie slides (above) stressed decorum and courtesy in the movie theater. The first movie kiss was this now historic scene from *The Kiss* (below, left), starring May Irwin and John C. Rice in 1896. Filmed from their play, *The Widow Jones,* this prolonged buss scandalized audiences, evoked denunciation from the clergy, yet broke all attendance records. *Cripple Creek Barroom* (below, right), an 1898 Edison film, helped audiences realize the screen could tell a connected story vividly.

MOVIE EPIC OF 1896, *THE KISS*, SHOCKED VICTORIAN PUBLIC

CRIPPLE CREEK BARROOM, 1898, WAS A ROUSING HORSE OPERA

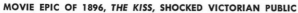

JOHN PHILIP SOUSA, THE MARCH KING

THEODORE THOMAS, FAMOUS CONDUCTOR

EDWARD MacDOWELL, AMERICAN COMPOSER

MUSIC

Although Americans still regarded concerts as entertainment in minstrel show class, large orchestras were established all over the country, playing the world's great symphonies to clamorous, though ill-mannered crowds. Audiences still preferred their musical entertainment on grandiose lines: tremendous choruses and orchestras, circus-style showmanship. Theodore Thomas, famous conductor of the New York Philharmonic and Chicago Orchestras, did the most to improve the taste of a "people led out of the musical wilderness." In 1897-98 Walter Damrosch began symphony concerts for children in New York, musical clearing house of the country. American composers, like playwrights, sought themes which were indigenous to the soil. Edward MacDowell, professor of music at Columbia University, composed *Indian Suites.* John Philip Sousa wrote many popular, stirring marches. Later he became leader of the United States Marine Band. Concerts by chamber music and choral societies, and by foreign virtuosi (who returned home from extended concert tours with well-filled purses) continued in vogue with metropolitan society audiences.

"GLASS BLOWERS OF MURANO," is by Charles Frederick Ulrich, whose photographic realism, and strong textures, won the Academy of Design's Clark Prize in 1884.

VIVID COLORS of the rocks and skillful attention to detail give sensational effect to Thomas Moran's *Grand Canyon of Arizona*, one of many paintings of the places he visited. Through such works the nation discovered the natural wonders of the United States.

ART

OUTSTANDING painter was Thomas Eakins, whose genius won him little acclaim. Rarely has American art been so emphatically a man's art as in *Between Rounds* (above), and *Salutat*.

"MADAME X" was an elegant interpretation of a beautiful Parisienne, painted by John Singer Sargent.

"SHOOTING THE RAPIDS" was Winslow Homer's last canvas, left uncompleted (missing oar, facial details) by his death. In his later years, Homer's main interest was marine life, which he depicted with energy, rugged truth, seeking out the ocean's many moods.

JOHN LA FARGE'S gift to art was his rare ability as a colorist. A fine craftsman in painting (above, *The Muse of Painting*), murals, decorating, he also made use of pictorial stained glass.

AMERICAN SCULPTURE was epitomized in the work of Augustus Saint-Gaudens, whose classic *Abraham Lincoln* is in Chicago.

JAMES A. M. WHISTLER was, like La Farge, an experimentalist, eclectic, many years ahead of his time. His painting of his mother, refused at the Royal Academy, found no buyers in U.S., but was bought by France and transferred to Louvre.

LONELY VIGIL over a prisoner, told with photographic realism, was the dramatic story of Henry Farny's *The Captive*, one of his many paintings depicting Indian and Western Life. Born in Alsace, Farny came to live in Cincinnati. Later he worked for Harper Brothers, illustrating their publications, including sketches of the Cincinnati Opera Festival (1883) and the Chicago Auditorium (1889), where Theodore Thomas first conducted.

PAINTINGS which reconstructed the manners of early America were the notable contributions of Edward Lamson Henry. Though he studied in Paris, his work showed little foreign influence. Above, *Country School*.

AUTHENTIC interpretations of the West by Frederick Remington strongly appealed to a generation that realized the frontier was closing forever. Mule packs, deserts, cowboys were his subjects. Here, *Mexican Major*.

LIFE IN BACKWOODS camps was the theme of a painting by Oscar Kunath, inspired by the famous Bret Harte short story, *The Luck of Roaring Camp*. Above, the men file in to inspect their new foundling mascot.

"BOWERY AT NIGHT," a watercolor by W. Louis Sonntag, Jr., was representative of trend towards use of realistic, even tawdry, subjects. Painters who succumbed to the trend were termed "ash can school" and condemned.

"WETS" AND "DRYS" were fighting it out with new Anti-Saloon League entrenched against the $269 million liquor manufacturing industry, which included "malt tonics" (top) as a healthful sideline. On the domestic front, new appliances like washing machines became available.

◄ **STATUE OF LIBERTY,** a gift from France, was unveiled at the entrance to New York harbor on Oct. 28, 1886. The French people raised $450,000 to pay for the statue and Americans contributed $350,000 for the pedestal. The statue was designed by Frederic A. Bartholdi.

THE GAY NINETIES

FASHIONS In the 1890's styles were becoming "a shade more sensible." Street-sweeping garments like those worn by the ladies riding in Lord & Taylor's new elevator (center), were shortened for daytime wear to a more practical shoe-top length (right). Womanliness was the keynote. Waist-pinching corsets yielded slightly to frantic reform efforts of health addicts. Hats grew larger and more heavily laden with assorted fruits and flowers. Parasols were almost mandatory. Height of fashion was worn by First Lady Mrs. William McKinley, shown at left.

CORNELIUS VANDERBILT RESIDENCE was one of the famous homes that became New York landmarks. Led by Henry Hobson Richardson and Richard Morris Hunt, both of whom studied in Europe, American architecture began to flourish. Prominent social figures hired the best architects to design their mansions. Fifth Avenue soon sprouted a series of magnificent homes combining assorted European styles, complete with balconies.

BIKES AND BUGGIES were the everyday transportation of the nineties. High-wheelers were nonchalantly manipulated down busy city streets, and on Sundays the cycle clubs took over the countryside. When the "safety" bike with lower wheels of equal size was developed, manufacture of a million bikes a year scarcely met demand. Shopkeepers complained of business because "hardly anyone walks any more," but most hailed bike as boon.

"FLAT-IRON" BUILDING at the intersection of Broadway and Fifth Ave., became a New York landmark. It was notable more for its peculiar shape than for its architectural qualities. Its design had the unexpected effect of increasing wind turbulence at the corner to such an extent that during storms windows were shattered and pedestrians blown from the sidewalk. The first "skyscrapers" were built in Chicago, but New York forged ahead.

ATLANTIC CITY BEACH at height of season was a solid mass of bathers, sporting latest beach fashions. For ladies, black stockings, full, knee-length skirts, blouses with wide middy collars were favored. Gents wore dark or horizontally-striped suits, short-sleeved and with pants reaching just above the knee. Americans of the nineties were very health conscious, and the period saw a great increase in all sports and outdoor activities.

KINGSTON POINT PARK, located up the Hudson River from New York City, was a favorite rendezvous for city dwellers on a Sunday afternoon. New York residents took an excursion steamer up the river to stroll through the pleasant park, enjoying the view, band concerts and picnic lunches. For the young there was the attraction of the new Ferris wheel. Such leisurely diversions were typical of the calm, more peaceful life of the "Gay '90s."

FANCY DRESS balls were the main social function of the well-to-do in the 1880's. The middle class was enjoying new forms of entertainment like tennis, bicycling, picnics and week-end excursions. Local opera houses sprang up; Chautauqua assemblies, intellectual study groups were formed.

FEUDING FAMILIES of Cap and Devil Anse Hatfield of Welch, West Virginia, are shown as they were in 1899. Hatfields feuded with the McCoys and the two families virtually destroyed each other. Though no one can remember the cause of the argument, even efforts of the law failed to end it.

COURT OF HONOR at the Columbian Exposition in Chicago was erected to commemorate 400th anniversary of the discovery of America. Opened in 1893 at a cost of $25 million, it played host to more than 27 million visitors. The buildings were destroyed by the great fire in May of 1894.

MOB VIOLENCE resulted when body of three-year-old Myrtle Vance was found. The brutal killing touched off a series of race riots in the vicinity which culminated in the lynching of her Negro assailant in Paris, Texas, on Feb. 1, 1893. A crowd of thousands watched the public execution.

FAITH HEALERS were popular in the 1880's. In Denver, Colorado, hundreds of afflicted are fed as they await the ministrations of the healer who is passing through the city. Such scenes were common in era.

PRISON LIFE in the '90's was gruelling. Prisoners were chained together in work gangs during the day and chained to beds at night. Group above was employed on a turpentine farm in the swamps of Florida.

◀ **SUBMARINE** inventor John P. Holland tested his ninth model in 1898. The Irish-born American was first to launch successfully such a ship. His principles were basis for the early models of U.S. submarine.

DEPOSED QUEEN Liliuokalani ▶ of Hawaii declared the suffrage of white residents void and touched off a revolution in which she was ousted and the Islands made a republic. The U.S. annexed Hawaii in 1898.

GREAT FLOOD at Johnstown, Pa., on May 31, 1889, caused tremendous damage to homes and steel mills in the area when the downpour of rain caused the dam 10 miles above the city to break. A courier rode a wild race with the water to warn the town, but in spite of his efforts more than 2,200 residents were drowned or crushed under tons of debris. Most of the townspeople were employees of the Carnegie Steel Mill or the several mines in the area. A nationwide movement was organized to relieve distress of survivors and help clean up vast amount of wreckage which remained.

TORNADO in St. Louis in 1896 left a path of destruction in its wake. The new American Red Cross, organized in 1881, played a great role in relieving the suffering caused by the disaster. It aided in other calamities such as the ruinous Galveston flood of 1900 and the great Seattle fire of 1889.

TALK OF THE TOWN in 1888 was the great blizzard in New York which filled the streets with drifted snow, kept residents snowbound and the city virtually paralyzed for several days. Any snowstorm thereafter was compared to the great blizzard, but always fell short in severity by comparison.

DESTROYED BY FIRE in the 1880's was the luxurious playground of the rich, the Mt. Vernon Club at Cape May, New Jersey. Other great fires of the era included the Boston fire of 1872, which destroyed the richest section of the city. Horse-drawn fire fighters lacked the speed and facilities to control the flaming holocausts.

NEW DESIGN for capitol was drawn by architect Thomas Fuller for the building at Albany, N. Y. Construction lasted from 1868 until 1897 and cost nearly $5.5 million. In 1911 the white granite structure was gutted by fire. Rebuilding restored the original.

TWENTIETH CENTURY

Violence and progress keynote first two decades as United States adopts

a Big Stick policy, enters First World War and emerges a world power

While millions of Americans basked in unprecedented prosperity, an assassin's bullet cut down one president, raised up another and keynoted the course of history. The 20th century had begun.

The man in the street saw nothing prophetic about the bullet. He had no way of knowing that another assassin in another land would shortly embroil the whole world in a "war to end wars" which the United States would enter to "make the world safe for democracy." Impervious to the speed of bullets or the rate at which the world around him hurtled into the future, he trudged on to his 10- to 12-hour work day, carrying the full dinner pail President McKinley had promised him. All seemed fairly right with the world.

Now President McKinley was dead. In his place, the irrepressible Theodore Roosevelt took over the White House, full of bombast and high spirits, ready to "walk softly and carry a big stick."

In the seven years to follow, Teddy did not always walk softly, but there was no mistaking his use of the Big Stick. Before its hefty swing, U. S. isolationism crumbled. America embraced, instead, a budding imperialism and the world sat up and took notice.

To a handful of sprawling possessions acquired under McKinley, Roosevelt added the Panama Canal Zone, personally turning the first shovelful of earth on the debut of U. S. construction outside her own boundaries. Roosevelt, "the warmonger," approached the belligerents in the Russo-Japanese War with an olive branch; mediated peace acceptable to the two countries and brought back to America the Nobel Peace Prize for his efforts.

Wheels, Wings and Wireless

At home, the U. S. was growing up to wheels, wings and wireless. Across the land, farms had fallen back to let railroads through. Wilbur and Orville Wright conquered the air in their power-driven plane in December, 1903. In 1910, Teddy Roosevelt became the first ex-president to fly, and in 1911 daredevil Calbreath Rodgers spanned the continent in solo flight. In the midwest, Henry Ford's "Model T" took form and the "horseless carriage" which had frightened horses now began to replace them. By 1920, every 13th American was to own an automobile.

Factories, mines and industries, nurtured by the financial wizardry of men such as Morgan, Rockefeller and Carnegie, multiplied like amoeba. Big companies gobbled up little ones and then absorbed each other. Railroads covering one-quarter of the U. S. merged into the $400 million Northern Securities company, formed by James J. Hill and J. P. Morgan. What happened to railroads happened also to steel, petroleum and other industries.

Teddy's Big Stick dealt a resounding blow to the threat of national monopoly. Invoking the Sherman Anti-Trust Act, Roosevelt belabored 44 major combines, Northern Securities among them, in a seven-year fever of "trust-busting" which made him a hero. A sad commentary on history is the fact that the glory rightfully belonged to his successor, the more placid and kindly William Howard Taft,

who pushed through 90 anti-trust prosecutions in only four years as president. But rambunctious Teddy was more colorful.

The genial Taft, Roosevelt's personal selection as president, won the 1908 election by a million votes. More conservative than his predecessor, Taft put away the Big Stick and turned his ample back on the work of Congress' rising young Progressives. By 1910, led by Wisconsin Senator Robert M. LaFollette, these insurgents, whom Roosevelt accused of "exceeding the speed limit," had provided several states with direct primaries, initiative, referendum recall, and beat the drum for the 17th Amendment, adopted in 1912.

In the sweep of these and other progressive reforms, the fiber of the Grand Old Party weakened. New Jersey elected a Democratic governor named Woodrow Wilson in 1910; Ohio defeated a Republican gubernatorial candidate named Warren G. Harding.

As the 20th century progressed, violence erupted along the labor front where "Big" Bill Haywood led the radical "Wobblies" through a series of uprisings. Socialism flourished and Eugene Debs, vociferous defender of railroad workers, became a perennial candidate for President. The first man in U. S. history to be nominated for that high office while serving a prison sentence, Debs polled 919,799 votes in 1920. In 1919, the U. S. Communist Party was formed.

But in 1912 the country was concerned with the antagonism between old friends Roosevelt and Taft, both candidates for Presidency. "I feel like a bull moose," Teddy proclaimed, giving a new name to the Progressive half of the GOP. Taft remained conservative, and when the votes were in, he had polled more than Roosevelt. But the damage was done. Woodrow H. Wilson, Democrat, became the 27th President, solidly backed by a Democratic House and Senate. Where T. R. had taken "righteousness" as his watchword, the new chief executive took "scruple."

DOUGHBOYS IN FRANCE

New Freedom and World War

Instituting a "New Freedom" reform program which reduced tariffs, tightened anti-trust laws and pushed through Congress a Federal Reserve Act, Wilson dusted off the Big Stick Taft had laid aside. Across the Atlantic, an Austrian archduke was assassinated and the whole world went to war, the U.S. among the last, for the preservation of an ideal. When the holocaust was over, America emerged the richest and most powerful nation in the world. Democracy seemed safe and President Wilson sought to keep it that way with his ill-fated League of Nations. Failure of his plan and his Fourteen Points broke his health and cost him his life. The Treaty of Versailles was signed, but America had wearied of world affairs. The nation turned its attention to domestic things, amended the Constitution to give women the right to vote and legislated against anyone's right to drink alcoholic beverages. With Prohibition came another age, another way of life. The fabulous twenties, era of public and private lawlessness, of political conformity and intellectual iconoclasm, was ushered in with a rain of gangsters' bullets.

★ ★ ★

◀ **POWERED FLIGHT,** long a dream of mankind, became a reality early in the 20th century. The first flight of the Wright brothers at Kitty Hawk, N. C., on Dec. 17, 1903, marked the dawn of the air age, an era which was to remold the concepts of the world. The airplane soon was under consideration as a weapon of war. In 1907 the Wrights built the first airplane for the United States Army (left). By the end of the first two decades of the 20th century, the airplane had already become a deadly instrument of war. It was soon to become an important factor in the domestic economy.

TEDDY WIELDS

Backs peace and a "square deal";

First American president to intervene to settle a strike rather than break it, Theodore Roosevelt worked vigorously for a "square deal" for capital and labor alike. To achieve this he practiced the South African adage "walk softly and carry a big stick." He believed in the use of arbitration, both national and international. To popularize it he occasionally resorted to the "big stick," as in the cases of the coal strike and Venezuelan dispute with Germany and Britain.

To Roosevelt the great issue of the day was to bring under Federal regulation the giant monopolies which were strangling the national economy. As opening gun in his battle with the trusts he dusted off the long-shelved Sherman Anti-Trust Act to bring successful suit for the dissolution of Northern Securities, a railroad holding company which threatened to place under single control the entire Western railroad system. Throughout his administration Roosevelt pushed prosecutions under the anti-trust act. His second line of attack was through the Interstate Commerce Commission. He demanded and got two bills enormously increasing the Commission's power and scope. The Elkins Act of 1903 outlawed the widespread practice of railroad rebating, a device used by the "Christian Men of Property" to crush competition. The Hepburn Act, passed three years later, extended the jurisdiction of the Commission to pipe-lines, express companies, sleeping car companies, and private freight lines. By commission and Congressional investigation Roosevelt both exposed the evils of the trusts and rallied public opinion against them.

HUNTER and rancher, historian and naturalist, "Rough-Rider" and reformer, Theodore Roosevelt was catapulted into the White House by the bullet that killed McKinley. Son of a loving and public-spirited father, he was born and raised in mid-town New York. Through willful tenacity he conquered an early asthmatic handicap and developed a constitution he later claimed was "strong as a bull-moose." After graduating from Harvard he shocked his friends by turning career politician. Aggressively sincere in challenging corruption wherever he found it, Roosevelt's crusade against monopoly as governor of New York led Boss Platt to arrange his exile as Vice-President. But McKinley's death brought hunter his biggest game.

"BIG STICK" clubbed coal, rail, oil, sugar, meat trusts, but its purpose was regulation and not ruin.

JUSTICE DEPARTMENT jammed federal courts with anti-trust suits. New laws provided for priority.

LASTING CONTRIBUTION to national welfare resulted from Roosevelt's energetic support of forestry chief Gifford Pinchot's conservation program. Dakota ranch life and Western hunting trips had alerted Roosevelt to the reckless exploitation of resources and to the Western water problem. On

his initiative Congress adopted conservation and reclamation programs and set aside national park areas for public use. Other welfare measures passed at Roosevelt's insistence included meat inspection laws regulating sanitary conditions in packing houses and a federal pure food and drug act.

THE BIG STICK

urges strong Navy, Panama Canal

As Colonel of the "Rough-Riders" Theodore Roosevelt fought the war with Spain. As president he faced the problems of peace. From Cuba to the Philippines the United States had acquired islands to defend and sea lanes to keep open.

Roosevelt, one-time Assistant Secretary of the Navy, saw that strategic necessity now dictated a strong navy He called for the laying down of a minimum of four new ships a year, but Congress cut the number to two. He nevertheless used the available fleet to serve notice on the world that the United States could and would defend its vital interests. When Germany threatened Venezuela in 1902, Roosevelt drew the Kaiser's attention to the American fleet, and the Kaiser changed his plans. Somewhat later Roosevelt sent a section of the fleet on a world cruise, believed impossible by many.

The Spanish war had pointed up the strategic as well as commercial need for a canal linking the Atlantic and the Pacific. Roosevelt promptly set to work on long dormant plans to construct such a canal at Panama. His arbitrary treatment of Columbian claims fired Latin hostility, but he regarded his action taken at Panama as his greatest feat. Roosevelt also concerned himself with the problems of world peace. He advocated arbitration of international as well as national disputes and his personal intervention helped to end the Russo-Japanese conflict of 1905. Again in Morocco, Roosevelt's quick action in calling a conference of powers, which met at Algeciras, Spain, temporarily averted a Franco-German crisis.

PANIC SWEPT WALL STREET in 1907. Roosevelt blamed "malefactors of great wealth." The financiers claimed Roosevelt's attacks on business had undermined confidence and caused currency collapse. Banks closed, Wall Street trading ceased. Morgan reorganized capital, scare was brief.

VIGOROUS attacks on monopoly at home and promotion of interests abroad led "Teddy" to flood Capitol with "must" bills.

SOFT WALKING during Portsmouth Treaty negotiations earned Nobel Peace prize for fighting president.

ROOSEVELT'S INTERVENTION in Russo-Japanese war of 1905 brought a negotiated peace, but Japanese anger over denial of claims for indemnity embittered subsequent relations with U.S.

MRS. ROOSEVELT AS FIRST LADY

THE ROOSEVELTS OF OYSTER BAY

THE "ROUGH-RIDER" SIGHT-SEEING VIA HORSELESS CARRIAGE

THOUGH ABLY assisted by his two great Secretaries of State, John Hay and Elihu Root, Roosevelt took personal charge of foreign relations during his administration. When issue of the Alaskan-Canadian boundary—in dispute since 1898—flared up again, Roosevelt violently castigated Britain (who still controlled Canadian foreign affairs), forced the British Chief of Justice to decide in favor of the U.S. To prevent future European claims to territorial compensation for Latin American indebtedness, Roosevelt proclaimed as corollary to Monroe Doctrine right of U.S. to act as collector.

COAL MINERS PARADED in strike of 1902. Labor leader John Mitchell agreed to Roosevelt's demand for arbitration of the protracted walk-out, but the operators refused. Roosevelt's subsequent "big stick" threat to run the mines in the public interest, using federal troops to dig the coal, forced owners to accept arbitration and won T. R. new friends among workers.

ALARMED by German truculence at the Hague Conference of 1907 and by the sword-rattling of Japan in the Orient, Roosevelt ordered the "Great White Fleet" — 16 battleships and five destroyers — to sail on a good-will mission to the Orient and around the world, giving dramatic evidence of America's emergence as a world power. Above, Roosevelt reviews the fleet.

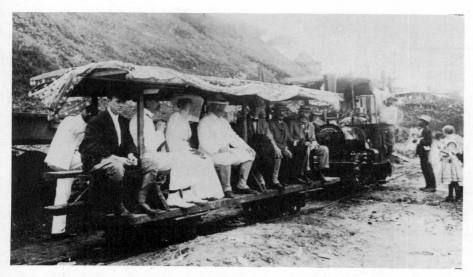

PANAMA DIGGINGS are inspected by the President. "I took the Isthmus, started the Canal, and then left Congress — not to debate the Canal, but to debate me" — thus Roosevelt summarized his role at Panama. Arguing the merits of Panama vs. Nicaragua as locale for an inter-ocean canal, Congress settled on the abandoned French Company site at Panama, territory then controlled by Columbia. When Columbians proved troublesome about terms, Roosevelt supported Panamanian insurrection. Minutes after news of the proclaiming of Panama's independence reached the White House, Roosevelt recognized new government and seven days later signed agreement for canal construction. The result: a canal, and an angry Columbia.

SUPPORTERS of William Randolph Hearst are shown demonstrating in 1906 New York gubernatorial race. Hearst lost to Charles Evans Hughes. He also made two unsuccessful bids for mayor of New York and backed Alton B. Parker against Roosevelt in 1904. Roosevelt won election in a landslide. On election night he declared opposition to a third term, a statement he later regretted.

AL SMITH (l.) played Annie Oakley at the Democratic Convention of 1908. The convention nominated Bryan on the first ballot for his third try.

WILLIAM HOWARD TAFT was hand-picked by Roosevelt as successor. Taft backed Roosevelt's policies, if not his methods, hoped to heal breach in ranks.

PROGRESSIVE MEASURES backed by President Taft were obscured by the commotion arising out of his growing differences with Roosevelt and by the great rift in the Republican Party. Ohio-born William Howard Taft was 27th U. S. President (1909-1913). He supported the League of

Nations in 1919, traveling throughout the nation on its behalf. In 1921 he was appointed Chief Justice of the Supreme Court, a position he held until his death in 1930. Taft is shown (l.) with Henry Cabot Lodge, senator from Mass., and (r.) with family. Son Robert (far r.) became U.S. senator.

TAFT ADMINISTRATION

Conflict between progressive and conservative wings splits Republican party

President William Howard Taft was the victim of the great conflict between conservatives and progressives in his party. Teddy Roosevelt had supported Taft for the Republican nomination in 1908 and a strong factor in his election was the belief that he would continue his predecessor's policies. When issues developed on which he took an opposing stand, Republican progressives turned against him.

Although not satisfied with some provisions of the Payne-Aldrich Tariff bill, Taft approved it in 1909 as the best the Congress had to offer. His support of this bill brought him heavy criticism for failing to keep his campaign pledge to reduce the tariffs. His stand in the Ballinger-Pinchot controversy

further antagonized the progressives. Again Taft's use of "dollar diplomacy" made him unpopular with many who believed this policy to be synonymous with imperialism and big business interests.

Although President Taft was the target of much criticism during the years 1909 to 1913, many important progressive measures went into effect during his term of office. They included the Mann-Elkins Act, Postal Savings Bank, Parcel Post, and creation of a Children's Bureau and Department of Labor. Trusts were vigorously attacked. Large tracts of oil, coal and timber lands were set aside as a move to conserve the nation's resources.

In 1910 Teddy Roosevelt returned from

Africa and openly opposed Taft. "Uncle Joe" Cannon, Speaker of the House, who had long blocked progressive legislation, was shorn of his power by amendment of the House rules in 1910. By 1911, the insurgent Progressive-Republicans led by Sen. Robert La Follette were campaigning for far-reaching political and social reforms and denouncing the President as a friend of big business. In the campaign of 1912, Taft was renominated on the Republican ticket. But the Progressives formed a third party, the Bull Moose, with Teddy Roosevelt as their candidate. The split in the Republican vote brought victory for Democratic candidate Woodrow Wilson, who received 435 electoral votes to Roosevelt's 88, Taft's eight.

CHIEF FORESTER GIFFORD PINCHOT

"FIGHTING BOB" LA FOLLETTE

T. ROOSEVELT AND HIRAM JOHNSON

PROGRESSIVES

Fired for insubordination, Chief Forester Gifford Pinchot was a key figure in the disastrous Republican party split. Pinchot opposed Sec. of Interior Ballinger for opening lands to private leasing which Teddy Roosevelt had withdrawn for conservation. Pinchot became martyr to the cause as Taft was attacked for dismissing him. Reformist Sen. Robert La Follette

seemed logical Progressive presidential candidate in 1912 until ex-Pres. Roosevelt announced: "My hat is in the ring." Conservatives in control of Republican convention nominated Taft. The Progressives formed a new party, the Bull Moose, naming as candidates, Teddy (with pince nez) and running mate, Calif. Gov. Hiram Johnson. Teddy attacked Democrat and Republican parties as being "boss-ridden" and "privilege controlled."

SCHOLAR AND IDEALIST, Woodrow Wilson campaigned for the presidency on the strength of his record as Governor of New Jersey and his New Freedom platform — advocating a tougher attitude toward Big Business — to win a decisive victory from both Theodore Roosevelt and William How-ard Taft (r.). His inauguration, March 4, 1913, began an era of social reform and strong Presidential government, infused with moral scruple. Country at large and business in particular soon felt pressure of increased regulations in banking, trade and commerce, anti-trust laws, income taxes.

WILSON AND REFORM

New president brings "New Freedom" to American people and government

Woodrow Wilson's inauguration as President of the United States did more than usher a new Democratic administration into office. It marked the beginning of a new concept in American government—a philosophy he chose to call the "New Freedom."

The New Freedom was Wilson's platform. Viewing monopolies as positive evils inimical to the existence of free competition, it called for a firmer attitude toward Big Business, a quest for social justice and strong Presidential leadership.

With Democrats in control of both House and Senate, and with party support for his program, the new President launched a series of drastic reform measures.

Among the key bills pushed through to enactment by Wilson were the Federal Reserve Act of 1913, which placed controls on the nation's currency supply; the Clayton Anti-Trust Act, to curb monopolistic practices in industry; and a measure providing regulation of "unfair methods of competition" by manufacturers in interstate commerce, with a Federal Trade Commission.

During his first term Wilson championed before Congress the eight-hour day and overtime demands of four Railway Brotherhoods threatening a countrywide strike. He signed the LaFollette Seamen's Act and obtained a disability compensation measure for civil service workers.

Aided by his program of accomplished reform legislation, Wilson won his battle for re-election in 1916, narrowly defeating Republican candidate Justice Charles Evans Hughes when California Progressives, under Hiram Johnson, cast their vote for him instead of the more conservative Hughes.

UNDERWOOD TARIFF of 1913, authorizing Congress to impose graduated income taxes on citizens, corporations, and joint-stock companies, was passed under Wilson's leadership as the first step in his reform program. The same year Wilson asked for, and got, passage of the Federal Reserve Act, significant for its steadying influence on nation's business and banking.

WILSON pushed his vigorous attack on privilege, which progressed with establishment of the Federal Trade Commission and organization of the Clayton Anti-Trust Act, and signed such measures as the Child Labor Act. Although later nullified by the Supreme Court, such reform acts amalgamated with others served as a valuable weapon in battle for re-election.

MEXICO'S internal troubles spilled across the border into the United States when Victoriano Huerta seized control of the Mexican government after assassinating President Madero. Huerta aroused Wilson's wrath by refusing him formal apology for the false arrest of U.S. Marines in Tampico, and Vera Cruz was occupied by American forces. More fuel to the Mexican fire was Pancho Villa, a bandit-general who led murderous raids across the border. In one foray he killed 17 Americans in Columbus, New Mexico. Wilson sent 6,000 troops under Gen. Pershing to get Villa (r., with Gen. Scott) but the hunt was a tedious failure. Wilson, faced by war with Germany, decided to compromise in order not to alienate Mexico and withdrew his troops. Huerta was exiled. Mexico continued its sporadic revolutions, maintaining neutrality during war.

GENERAL PERSHING (r.) DURING HIS 1916 SEARCH FOR VILLA

AMERICAN SAILORS AND MARINES AFTER OCCUPYING VERA CRUZ

RECOGNIZING THE IMPORTANCE of the Caribbean area for American defense and fearful of European intervention, President Wilson tooks steps to secure control of Nicaragua, the Dominican Republic and Haiti as American protectorates. When Haiti refused the protectorate, Marines landed to stamp out resistance. Treaties acquired from these three countries, along with the purchase of the Virgin Islands, gave the United States effective control over northern rim of the Caribbean "danger zone."

REPUBLICAN CANDIDATE for 1916 election was Charles E. Hughes. Wilson was criticized for Mexican and German policy, called a "pacifist." Democrats' slogan that Wilson had "kept us out of war," coupled with campaign blunders in California by Hughes offending Progressives, won the election for Wilson. Democrats once again captured both houses of Congress.

IMPERIALISM of European powers plunged countries into a world war that was unforeseen and unwanted. Germany's Kaiser Wilhelm did little to stem the conflict and boasted, "We can hold the sky on top of German bayonets." Wilson declared neutrality, appealed for impartiality "in thought as well as action." This proved impossible. Germany announced it would destroy all merchant ships caught in British waters. *Lusitania* was sunk without warning off Irish coast with a loss of 1,260 lives, 124 of whom were Americans. President's hardest decision, declaration of war, faced Wilson.

FIRST WORLD WAR

U. S. condemns Germany's unrestricted submarine warfare; declares war

Since the 1915 sinking of the *Lusitania* Americans had been recurrently shocked by U-boat attacks on passenger vessels. Wilson threatened to break diplomatic relations with Germany if attacks continued. They stopped for a few months, but recurred.

Acute tension gripped the country as William J. Bryan resigned as Sec'y of State, protesting that Wilson's stern protests to Germany might lead to U.S. involvement. He was replaced by Robert Lansing as Wilson unceasingly tried to bring peace by diplomatic procedures and through appeals in behalf of humanity. But all efforts failed.

Condemning German submarine policy as "warfare against mankind," President Wilson asked Congress for a declaration of war on April 2, 1917. With eight U.S. ships sunk in a three-month period prior to his message, an inflamed Congress declared war against Germany four days later. German Ambassador Johann von Bernstorff was given his passport.

U.S. entry into the war came at a time when prospect for an Allied victory took a decided turn for the worse. April was the peak month for German destruction of Allied shipping. Mutinies in the French army followed defeat in the Champagne and Aisne campaigns. A British offensive gained little ground and cost enormous casualties. Italians suffered disaster in the Caporetto campaign; Russia was reeling.

The declaration of war was Wilson's greatest decision in a year of decision. Re-elected the year before on the slogan "He kept us out of the war," his conscientious effort to steer a neutral course had failed. With an army of 200,000, lacking equipment and training facilities, America plunged into a war that proved to be the greatest conflict that man had yet brought upon himself.

Conscription in the U.S. began to call up millions as a small contingent of 14,500 men under General Pershing embarked for France. They helped boost French morale but suffered heavy casualties in their baptism of fire, due to inexperience. With combat seasoning and reinforcements, American troops and supplies tipped the balance of war in favor of the Allies.

TROOP SHIPMENTS to France aboard reconverted passenger ships such as the mammoth liner *Leviathan* were highly publicized. Soldiers soon crossed the submarine-infested Atlantic at the rate of 25,000 per month. Allied setbacks were compensated for by increased American industry, A.E.F. arrival.

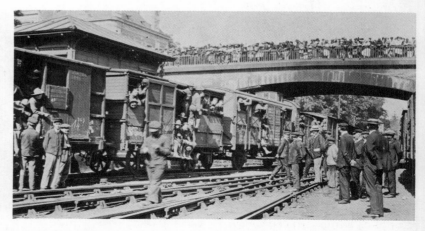

SAFELY IN FRANCE, Americans took fabled "40 et 8" car rides to the front. First U.S. troops to go to trenches were units of the 1st Division in the Toul sector. In all, 42 infantry divisions were sent to France, 29 took part in combat and the word "Doughboy" became synonymous with courage.

DOUGHNUTS and the inescapable ritual of pack inspection occupied soldiers before entraining for the trenches. Then mud and fighting became their prime consideration. Germans, aware of slowness with which America was mobilizing, made desperate attempt to overwhelm the French. They opened attack with 800,000 picked troops. Allies fell back, then held. Pershing offered his troops to French and British where they would help most and American troops won their first victories, storming Cantigny and defending Chateau-Thierry. By blocking the German advance at Chateau-Thierry the Americans helped French stem the German drive. The first big American action was at Belleau Wood.

TANKS, flame throwers and poison gas were used for the first time in World War I. Modern warfare weapons had begun to come into their own. Using such weapons Americans launched a series of offensives, driving the Germans from heavily fortified Belleau Wood, Bouresches and Vaux during June.

MEDICAL CARE was brought to the soldiers in the trenches whenever possible. Above, a front line dental clinic. Disease claimed thousands in spite of precautions as Americans fought the "muddiest war in history." Replacements poured toward Europe without loss of a ship on eastward voyage.

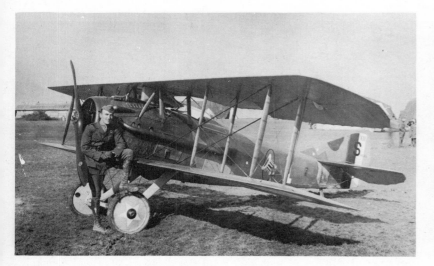

CAPTAIN EDDIE RICKENBACKER became America's leading ace with the 94th Pursuit Squadron. In the short time he was on the front he shot down 25 German planes. Other U.S. aces included Floyd Bennett, Billy Mitchell and Douglas Campbell. Germany's von Richthofen shot down 80 planes.

SUPPLY, as in any war, was a big problem. From June, 1917, until November, 1918, more than four million tons of cargo were shipped directly to France for the A.E.F. Mules and horses played a paramount role in getting supplies to trenches where Americans held down a quarter of the front.

HEAVY GUNS of the Allies helped stall the great March offensive launched by the Germans. Allies still fought on each front independently, U.S. troops were used where and when needed in spite of Pershing's theory that Americans should fight under American command. Success followed appointment of Marshall Foch, April, 1918, as supreme Allied commander.

DOUGHBOYS soon liberated French towns and won back French territory from the Germans. More than 85,000 Americans fought in the Marne-Champagne battles in July and the subsequent assault on the German front between Soissons and Chateau-Thierry. American forces were divided into two field armies, commanded by Generals Pershing and Robert L. Bullard.

OUTSTANDING achievements of American army were the reduction of the St. Mihiel salient and clearing of the Argonne Forest in the drive to the Meuse. American troops advanced, suffered heavy casualties in frontal assaults and patrol action (above). Germans fell back under onslaught.

GERMAN PRISONERS, above carrying U.S. wounded, were taken by the thousands. Meuse-Argonne drive alone produced 26,000 prisoners, 150 liberated towns and 560 miles of territory. The gain was invaluable, the price high. Casualties numbered 117,000, nearly half of the U.S. total.

FORTIFIED WILDERNESS, the Argonne Forest, was filled with machine-gun nests, crisscrossed with miles of barbed-wire. American troops, (resting, above, after fighting) cleared the Germans out of Argonne, broke German line of defense from Metz to Sedan. German retreat assumed larger proportions daily. Allies pushed forward on all fronts, German cause was lost.

DESTINY of millions of men rode with the decisions of Allied Generals. Pershing (center) was appointed commander of U.S. Army Aug. 10, 1918, retained command of A.E.F. As Americans pushed down the Meuse Valley, other forces under General Foch (l.) made emphatic advances. To Pershing's left, Generals Haig, Petain and Joffre welcoming President Poincare.

"MIGHTY GENERALS" who would "bring home the laurels of a glorious victory" were still talked of by the Kaiser, but superiority of Allies in men and supplies was increasing day by day. The German line became untenable when 1.2 million U.S. infantrymen slashed to the outskirts of Sedan, cutting the Germans from railway supply. Outpost duty or a few hours of prayer in a liberated church were about doughboy's only relief from grim fighting.

ADMIRAL KOLCHAK AND GEN. GRAVES IN SIBERIA

U.S. FLAG WENT TO SIBERIA WITH 9,000 AMERICAN TROOPS

U.S. TROOPS IN CHINA AND SIBERIA

Secretary Baker was informed by Wilson that "he was being urged to contribute American military forces to combined Allied expeditions to North Russia and Siberia" and that he felt "obliged to cooperate." Purpose was to assist White Russians and Czechs in revolutionary Russia, prevent Japanese seizure of eastern Siberia in accord with Wilson's policy of maintaining Chinese integrity, protect military stores at Archangel from falling into German hands. Russia was invaded from Black Sea, Archangel and Vladivostok by 4,500 Amer-

icans, British, French and 72,000 Japanese troops. Allied armies, including 9,000 Americans under Gen. W. S. Graves, later fought Bolsheviks, assisted White Russians under Admiral Kolchak and protected Trans-Siberian and Chinese Eastern Railway. U.S. troops were under British command at Archangel, stood with British and French against Bolshevik onslaught in winter campaign, suffered 400 casualties. Thousands of Russian peasants became indebted to Gen. Graves and his men for protection against Cossack chiefs subsidized by Japs.

"TAPS" FOR AMERICAN SOLDIER AT TSINGTAO, CHINA

AMERICAN TROOPS PROTECTED CHINESE INTERESTS

MEDICAL INSPECTIONS and inoculation of draftees continued as the military camps filled to overflowing. Such precautions failed to keep more than 62,000 Americans from dying of disease, in comparison to 39,000 combat deaths.

GERMAN IMMIGRANTS in America contributed gold and silverware to be melted to swell the coffers of Germany. Sinking of Allied ships was reaching apex as German U-boat warfare destroyed more than 850,000 tons a month in an effort to knock out England before American troops and industry could mobilize to aid her.

WAR SUCCESS was aided materially by leaders on the home front. Above, National Defense Council. Standing: second, third, eighth, Julius Rosenwald, Bernard Baruch, Walter S. Gifford. Seated (2nd, 3rd from l.), Navy Sec'y Josephus Daniels, Secretary of War Newton D. Baker. They channeled U.S. resources to the war effort.

Home Front
Industrial strength of nation geared to war

America entered World War I under the leadership of its idealistic President, militarily unprepared. But Wilson's battle cry, "The world must be made safe for democracy," stirred many patriotic hearts.

As two million troops sailed for France, the home front undertook its share of the burden of war. The U.S. went about the task of building and training a citizen army, conserving food, increasing industrial output and buying Liberty Bonds.

The Council of National Defense mobilized the nation's material resources and productive power, supplied food and equipment to the front.

Bernard Baruch's War Industries Board controlled U.S. manufacturing. The Food Administration under Herbert Hoover promoted conservation of food.

Americans bought bonds in the Liberty Loan drives, to come within $3 billion of paying for the total cost of the war. Instead of issuing bonds to the bankers, Secretary of the Treasury McAdoo went directly to the public, with spectacular success.

Women enlisted in the service by the thousands, filled vacancies left by men at war by working on farms and in factories.

The eight-hour day, equal pay for women workers and a living wage were achieved through the War Labor Policies Board under Felix Frankfurter.

Wilson's Program for Peace

As the pendulum of victory swung toward the Allies in early 1918 the need for a statement of Allied war aims became acute. When an Inter-Allied Conference in Paris was unable to agree upon such a statement Wilson was urged to issue a formulation.

Addressing Congress January 8, Wilson set forth his famous "14 Points" as the "only possible" program for peace from the U.S. standpoint. With the declaration, Wilson became the hope of all Europe as the one who would bring justice and equity to the peace tables.

The 14 Points were: 1. Open covenants with all nations. 2. Freedom of navigation. 3. Removal of economic barriers. 4. Reduction of armaments. 5. Adjustment of colonial claims. 6. Evacuation of Russia, free determination of own political policy. 7. Evacuation of Belgium. 8. Evacuation of French territory. 9. Redrawing of Italy's frontiers. 10. Freedom for Austro-Hungarian minorities. 11. Evacuation of Rumania, Montenegro, access to sea for Serbia. 12. Turkish, other nationalities of Ottoman Empire, given sovereignty. 13. Independence for Poland. 14. A League of Nations.

Germany, after Russia's surrender, transferred her troops from the Eastern Front to France in a concentrated effort to win the war, but fresh American troops and American industry were beginning to change the precarious situation of the Allies.

DRAFTEES AND VOLUNTEERS were sent to 16 camps in various parts of U.S. for training. Unprepared for major war effort, army trained new troops with wooden guns in lieu of artillery, and trucks were labeled as tanks on maneuvers.

DRAFT DODGERS were arrested (above) but were the exception rather than the rule. Army expanded from 200,000 men to more than four million by Armistice Day, 1918. The Navy, with a strength of about 500,000, convoyed troop transports, chased submarines, and helped the British keep German craft out of the North Sea.

PATRIOTIC SENTIMENTS of Americans were aroused by posters such as above, against hoarding. Herbert Hoover taught "hooverizing" — meatless meals and wheatless dishes, saving fats and oils for munitions and supplying food for European front. Women began to inundate war plants in addition to changing eating habits.

GREAT PARADES and grand slogans set the pace for the vigorous war effort at home. New York's Fifth Avenue became a pageant of uniforms, banners and flags, reverberating to the marching feet of soldiers off to war or Red Cross nurses (above) parading to promote Liberty Bond sales. Casualty reports from France served as added impetus for bond purchases as did personal appeals by movie stars. Women flocked to the colors, enlisting in such organizations as the Marinettes, Salvation Army and Young Women's Christian Association. Feeling ran high against all things Germanic, from German music to German school teachers. Teaching the German language was forbidden in most schools. War fever swept America.

WILSON BEFORE PREPAREDNESS PARADE

I WANT YOU
FOR U.S. ARMY
NEAREST RECRUITING STATION

A POSTER THAT RECRUITED THOUSANDS

AMERICAN WOMAN'S LEAGUE FOR SELF-DEFENSE

WOMEN WORKED AND PARADED WITH MEN

BITTER OPPOSITION to the war was raised by a small minority of pro-Germans, Socialists and pacifists. They agreed with Senator La Follette, who cast his vote against the war maintaining: "I say Germany has been patient with us," or Socialist Morris Hillquit who asserted "The country has been violently, needlessly and criminally involved in war." Their voices were lost in the crescendo of a country at war, with strong anti-German sentiments held by the majority. Ugly intolerance was bred, with Americans of foreign extraction suffering acutely, especially those "pro-German" in the neutrality period. The war became a holy crusade and conformity became the only true virtue. Refusal to conform bore a severe penalty. In response to this opinion, rather than for actual minority fear, the drastic Sedition Act of May 16, 1918, was added to the milder Espionage Act of 1917. Prominent critics of the war, including Eugene V. Debs, four times Socialist candidate for President, and Socialist Congressman Victor L. Berger, were given long prison sentences. Impediments to a complete war effort were not tolerated by the American public, eager for quick victory.

GEORGE CREEL was given the task of enlisting public opinion for the war, headed the Committee on Public Information. He flooded the country with millions of pamphlets, a daily *Official Journal,* and sent out thousands of speakers who addressed crowds in theaters, parks, meetings.

◄ **COLONEL** Edward M. House was Wilson's private diplomatic advisor and close friend. He twice went to Europe for Wilson to try and minimize the possibility of war. Wilson's 14 Points were partly based on consultation with House. Dispute at 1919 Conference ended the friendship.

"FIGHTING BOB" LA FOLLETTE opposed Wilson's foreign policy and as one of the "little group of willful men" (in Wilson's phrase) prevented passage of the armed merchant ship bill. Although voting against declaration of war on Germany, he supported most U.S. war measures. La Follette and his pacifist-isolationist group were hushed during war, later fought American participation in the League, World Court.

SECRETARY OF STATE William J. Bryan resigned office and was replaced by Robert Lansing of New York, Counselor of the State Department. His pacifist attitude, coupled with his refusal to sign Wilson's severe "notes" to Germany over merchant vessel sinkings, persuaded Germany that America would not fight.

THEODORE ROOSEVELT was a constant advocate of war with Germany, chastised Wilson for delaying action. He offered to raise a division for immediate service in France but Wilson declined the offer, asserting it "would seriously interfere . . . with early use of an effective army."

DELEGATION of peace-loving Americans sailed for Europe during war on ship chartered by Henry Ford to attempt to end the conflict. Boastful claims of an early peace and pictures of leap-frogging ministers at exercise on deck made the enterprise appear foolish to public.

PRESIDENT WILSON (shown leaving D.A.R. Hall with his wife) evoked considerable political comment in the early days of the war. Not only did he refuse Roosevelt's war services but relieved Gen. Leonard Wood from A.E.F. command in France, appointed Pershing instead.

INDUSTRIES AND FACTORIES were drained of men by the draft, and women stepped into the vacancies, performing arduous tasks with accuracy, skill and patience. Women also became increasingly in evidence in business and the professions. Their numerous wartime activities and spirit in meeting the emergency hastened the 19th Amendment.

MOST POWERFUL of all "war boards" was War Industries Board under Bernard Baruch (r.) which regulated U.S. production. Baruch confers above with (l. to r.) France's Louis Loucheur, Winston Churchill and Lloyd George.

FRENCH COMMANDER Gen. Joffre (above) became national hero after bearing brunt of early German attacks at Marne and bloody battle of Verdun. Here he is seen in Philadelphia during a tour of the United States in 1917 to develop enthusiasm for Allied cause.

FRANZ VON PAPEN, German military attache, and other diplomats were sent home in 1915 as climax to conspiracy revealed by briefcase left on street car by German espionage chief Heinrich Albert.

SOLDIERS AND SAILORS were entertained by camp shows and dances as a relief from the tedious routine of training and the painful boredom of hospitals. Fatigue duty and KP were terms becoming as familiar on the American scene as Berlin's *Yip, Yip Yaphank* and the equally popular *Hinky Dinky Parlay Voo?* Americans were proud of their Doughboys.

HERBERT HOOVER (right) practiced what he preached as U.S. Food Administrator. Shown with John D. Rockefeller (left) and Wm. F. Morgan, Hoover preached the "gospel of a clean plate" to Americans, urged them to conserve wheat and meat in facing the problem of sending increased food to Europe. High wheat prices led to the expansion of U.S. wheat acreage.

VICTORY PARADE through the Arc de Triomphe, Champs Elysees by Gen. Pershing, his staff and army marked an emphatic end to costliest war up to 1918. Germany did not surrender until the German fleet at Kiel had muti- nied rather than put to sea for a final attack on Allies, the Kaiser had abdi- cated and new leaders were in control of the government. Pershing opposed the armistice, asked for unconditional surrender as example for Germans.

ARMISTICE DAY in Washington, D. C., was greeted as elsewhere in America, with mingling wonder, prayer and wildly cheering crowds. Marshal Foch signed Armistice for Allies in a railroad car at Compiegne, Nov. 11, '18, 11 a.m.

FEAR of the "next war" was expressed in some quarters before ink was dry on armistice. Drawing shows that war cost more than $163 billion over the aggregate total of previous conflicts.

VICTORY OVER GERMANY meant peace and a happy ending to war's terror and strain to most people, but not to all. More than 10,000 citizens stormed an auditorium (above) to demand return of U.S. soldiers from Siberia and hear Hiram Johnson discredit proposed peace treaty.

DELIRIOUS WELCOME from a grateful country greeted soldiers as they returned from France and two million New Yorkers lined Fifth Avenue to cheer them in their triumphant march up the thoroughfare. Sobering thought, in face of the shouting, was the estimate that the war had cost America 130,000 men who would never march again, not to mention 12 billion American dollars. When the martial strains of the last parade faded into history the eyes of America and the world turned to Wilson as the man to save them from further catastrophies through his League of Nations.

IDEALISM OF WILSON was quickly challenged at beginning of the peace negotiations in Paris, Jan. 18, 1919. All major decisions were made by "Big Four" (left to right) Lloyd George of England; Vittorio Orlando, Italy; Georges Clemenceau, France, and Wilson. Orlando soon left, however, disgusted over his failure to enlarge Italy's frontiers. George and Clemenceau

then sabotaged every effort of Wilson to realize his 14 Points. His only consolation was agreement on his point of incorporating the League of Nations into the Treaty, after which he returned home (right) to face a hostile Congress and mounting opposition to the League in the U.S. Leading fight against Wilson and his League was Sen. Henry Cabot Lodge of Mass.

VERSAILLES TREATY

Wilson's attempt for American participation in League of Nations fails

Deeply stirred by the ovations of millions of Europeans, President Wilson received a different reception from the statesmen of Great Britain, France and Italy when he turned to the peace tables.

Wilson, accompanied by Sec'y Lansing, Col. House, Gen. Bliss and Henry White, soon realized that the delegates from 27 Allied powers in attendance bore diverse objectives.

France and Britain were determined to crush Germany, while Wilson stood for "peace without victory." France also wanted territorial concessions, reparations and military security against Germany. Further, the delegates formed an unwieldy body and were unable to conduct business with dispatch.

Confusion was relieved to some extent by formation of the Supreme Council of Ten, to do the important work. This in turn proved too large and gave way to the "Big Four" of Wilson, Georges Clemenceau of France, Prime Minister David Lloyd George of Great Britain and Premier Vittorio Orlando of Italy. Dissension became manifest in the group as Orlando quit the Conference after Wilson refused Italy the Austrian port of Fiume. From this point on, Lloyd George and Clemenceau hindered Wilson at every

turn in his relentless effort to obtain his 14 Points.

Wilson made concession after concession to save his League of Nations, finally compromised on his other 13 points to succeed in writing into the Treaty the Covenant of a League of Nations. The finished Treaty, signed June 28 at Versailles, forced Germany to admit war guilt; stripped her of her colonies; exacted reparations and substantially disarmed her.

Wilson returned home to face opposition to both the Treaty and the League. Republican forces had captured both houses of Congress in 1918.

Both the Treaty and League had to be approved by two thirds of the Senate before America could participate in them and Wilson began to realize, to his horror, that the Senate might not approve. Hiram Johnson and William Borah toured in opposition to the League and further led attack in Senate against it.

A heartsick Wilson set out from Washington, taking the issue to the people. Over-exhausted, he suffered a breakdown from which he never recovered.

An idealistic dream was shattered when, on Nov. 19, 1919, the Senate rejected both his treaty and his League of Nations.

LODGE led the fight in the Congress to defeat Wilson and his proposed peace treaty.

DISAPPOINTED over ▶ Harding's victory, ailing Wilson claimed, "The American people have repudiated fruitful leadership for a barren independence . . ." He fought on for League in spite of failing health, died an unhappy man on February 3, 1924.

◀ **JAMES M. COX** (right) with running mate Franklin D. Roosevelt, had Wilson's blessings in 1920 presidential election and made the League of Nations main issue of his campaign. Resentment against Wilson swung votes to Harding, who was elected.

CANADA'S TRANSCONTINENTAL railway, Canadian Pacific, was completed with a golden spike placed in position Nov. 7, 1885, by Donald Alexander Smith, one of Canada's first railroad tycoons. Associated with Hudson's Bay Company for 76 years, Smith's financing talent brought him control of Canada's Great Northern Lines, made him leading member of company which built Canadian Pacific, helped by gov't money, land grants.

CANADA GROWS

Building, industries, migration follow as Canadian-Pacific spans dominion

With the union of four provinces — Ontario, Quebec, Nova Scotia, New Brunswick — into a Dominion, the history of modern Canada had begun. British Columbia, at first reluctant to join the confederation, finally acquiesced with the stipulation that a transcontinental railroad be started within two years, completed within 10. Prince Edward Island followed. The Dominion government, under its first premier, Sir John Macdonald, agreed to assume the railway debt and readied contracts for almost immediate construction.

Canadian Pacific Railway cut through the wilderness in the wake of scandal which brought the resignation of Macdonald and resulted in the defeat of his Conservative government. Despite Macdonald's personal popularity, he was unable to withstand accusations of trading railroad construction contracts for election contributions. Partly responsible for his defeat was Donald Alexander Smith (later first Baron of Strathcona), who had earlier tried to mediate with Louis Riel and been imprisoned.

With Macdonald's fall, Smith turned his attention to railroading, gained control of the company which

JOHN A. MACDONALD was made Canada's first premier and knighted, in 1867.

completed Canadian Pacific (1885). He had acquired control of Canada's completed line, Great Northern, by 1878.

Alexander Mackenzie's Liberal government replaced Macdonald's Conservatives from 1873-78, when Macdonald returned to office, to remain until his death in 1891. His was an administration of protective tariffs, the organization and building of northwest Canada. A succession of Premiers followed him, culminating in Sir Wilfrid Laurier, whose Liberal administration was to rule Canada for the next 15 years (1896-1911).

In the first 10 years of Laurier's government, Clifford Sifton, minister of interior, offered free land to pioneers who would settle the West. This set in motion a migration which caused the formation of two new provinces, Saskatchewan and Alberta, whose self-government was patterned after the seven other provinces of the Dominion. The political framework of Canada from the Atlantic to the Pacific was completed. Canada's pioneers had accomplished the conquest of the West. In the future lay the power of an established union.

CALGARY STATION was way-stop for still incomplete Canadian Pacific Railroad in 1884, when Canada lent $20 million in addition to grants. On promise of a transcontinental railway, British Columbia had entered Canada Confederation in 1871. Coast to coast service started in May of 1887.

PIONEER GRAND TRUNK was Canada's first railway. In flurry of railroad building during latter part of the 19th century, Grand Trunk extended Montreal to Toronto link, proceeded on Canadian soil from Portland, Me., to Chicago, Ill. Other extensions followed. This is west of Edmonton.

DOMINION STATUS of Canada, granted by Parliament's passage of the British North America Act, was due largely to efforts of Sir John Macdonald (c. above, standing), who advocated strong bonds with England. First premier, he sent delegates to London for Britain's first colonial conference (r.), in 1887, during Queen Victoria's Golden Jubilee. Second conference, held in 1894, was in Ottawa, Canada's capital.

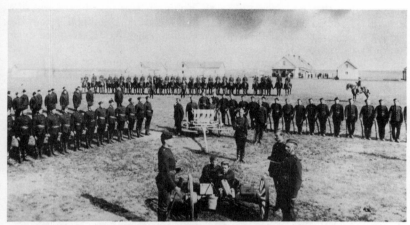

FORMED IN 1873, NORTHWEST MOUNTED POLICE CURB RIEL RIOT

METIS SCOUTS (FRENCH-INDIAN HALF-BREEDS) FOUGHT FOR LAND

RIEL REBELLION

Louis Riel, 41, tried for treason and hanged Nov. 16, 1885, led two epochal riots of French-speaking Indians and half-breeds in revolt against arbitrary British rule. A half-breed himself, Riel mobilized angry *Metis,* captured Fort Garry (Winnipeg), set up provisional government with himself as president in 1869. His murder of one prisoner, Thomas Scott, brought violent indignation from Ontario. Riel's government collapsed. He fled to U.S. until 1885 expansion of the Northwest inflicted further curbs on Indian and French half-breed life. *Metis* quickly gathered arms, recalled Riel to lead first burst of violence Mar. 26, 1885. Newly-organized Northwest Mounted

Police retreated before rebel numbers, hauled their wounded to Fort Carleton, and called up the militia. Volunteers, each with his own three-day supply of food, entrained at Ontario. Troops gathered in Winnipeg, fought on the plains of Saskatchewan. The three-day assault on Batoche, Riel's headquarters, ended the rebellion. Riel surrendered May 15, 1885. His death brought an outburst of radicalism to Quebec and Ontario which nearly overthrew Macdonald's Conservative government. *Metis,* Indians and French Canadians had wanted their own land, church, language and form of government. The Manitoba Act of 1870, making area a province, was a compromise, but provided Roman Catholic schools and religion.

UNCOMPROMISING FACES of Indian Chiefs Poundmaker, Little Bear and Big Bear, and *Metis* leaders who fought so bitterly to retain land and language rights in Canada's Northwest, mirrored French-Canadian resentment of Union, English rule. French-speaking half-breeds were dominant.

READYING FOR BATTLE Canadian militia encamped at Saskatchewan, joining strength to Northwest Mounted Police, whose organization in 1873 was designed to prevent Indian disorders. With original enrollment of 300 men, "Mounties" were organized to maintain order in Canadian Far West.

CANADIANS in World War I acquitted themselves admirably, and earned the praise of the world. As part of the British Empire, Canada entered the war on August 4, 1914. Except for an inadequately trained militia she had scarcely any fighting force. Yet the 1st Canadian Division in a convoy of 31 vessels left the Gaspe Basin on October 3. Some of those men are shown

above (r.) as they landed at Plymouth, England. This was the nucleus of a formidable force of 619,636 men who fought for the Dominion before the Armistice was signed. Of these it is recorded that 60,661 sacrificed their lives. The Canada Corps fought in the trenches in France (l. above) as assault troops, which accounted for unusually heavy number of casualties.

BEHIND THE LINES was a dressing station at the Old Mill near Vlamertinghe. Ambulances flowed endlessly over Europe's muddy roads. Canadians fought brilliantly at bloody Vimy Ridge in 1917. They were in the vanguard of the British Empire armies battling bravely during the epic "Hundred Days," beginning with Ameins in August and ending with German surrender Nov. 11, 1918.

CANADIAN WOMEN flocked to the factories and farms to replace the men who went to fight overseas. Munitions manufacturing became a giant industry from practically nothing. Ship building expanded. Despite enactment of income and excess profit taxes, the Government went into debt. "Victory bonds" were over-subscribed.

◄ **SIR WILFRID LAURIER,** was the first French Canadian to serve as Prime Minister (1896-1911). Left, in derby, he arrives at 1910 Vancouver Exhibition. Leader of the Liberals, he was skilled in promoting better relations between French and English.

SIR ROBERT BORDEN ▶ served as Prime Minister from 1911 to 1920, achieving greatness for himself and the nation during the war years. He pressed Canada's demands for its own foreign policy and diplomatic corps, leading up to change from British Empire to the British Commonwealth.

CANADA

Expanding industries, war hardships, bring birth of nationalism

As the 20th century dawned on the Dominion of Canada, 18 years of Conservative rule had been nearly forgotten in the rush of change under Sir Wilfried Laurier, whose Liberal administration was to linger until 1911 and the brink of the first World War.

A French Canadian, Laurier's long rule was dedicated to the growth of the Dominion. Under him, the western wilderness had been converted into richly productive farms. Population swelled with his policy of free land. Immigration and migration were further encouraged as railways and steamship service increased. The Klondike gold rush in 1896 had brought new thousands to the west, as had the opening of other mining areas, like the Laurentian Plateau.

Despite French Canadian reluctance to identify Dominion problems with those of Great Britain, Canadian contingents had fought in South Africa, paid by Britain, not Canada. Quebec, center of Laurier's support, not only did not participate but strongly protested Laurier's growing interest in sharing the Empire's problems of defense. Nonetheless, in 1910, he acquired two men-of-war training ships and in 1911 founded a small naval college at Halifax.

With loss of prestige in Quebec, Laurier's Liberal government fell over a reciprocity trade agreement with the U.S. in 1911, the same year in which Canada and the U.S. formed an international commission to consider questions about boundary waters.

Conservatives Return

Robert Borden, Conservative, succeeded Laurier in 1911, stepping into office in the shadow of gathering war clouds and Britain's apprehension over Germany's preparations. For two years, Borden tried in vain for naval appropriations. Then Britain declared war on Germany Aug. 4, 1914.

Canadians, generally believing the war to be just, sent 425,000 members of the Canadian Expeditionary Force overseas, mostly for service in northern France, made enormous contributions in munitions and food production, especially in wheat and beef. In 1913, Canada exported only $6 million of beef, sent $85 million overseas in 1918.

Living and government costs zoomed upward, only partially offset by income and excess profits taxes. Government loans in Victory bonds, war saving and thrift stamps were oversubscribed, but compulsory military service antagonized French Canadians.

At war's end, Canadians could evaluate the effects of war in practical terms. The pride of accomplishment could be explained away. It had roots in production figures. Less tangible, but of infinitely more value, Canada awoke to another pride, the first mighty stirrings of nationalism.

ICE CASTLE AT MONTREAL in 1887. These ice castles, which were built nearly every winter, were an architectural phenomena constructed entirely of ice. They stood as long as winter lasted. Usually the focal points of Canada's sparkling winter carnivals, they drew huge crowds of happy fun-seekers.

ON THE FERTILE PRAIRIES of midwestern Canada agriculture was coming into its own at the beginning of the Twentieth century. The threshing equipment pictured here was used in the Saskatchewan grain fields in 1905. Great influx of Ukrainian and Eastern European immigrants made the prairie states the Ukraine of North America and bread basket for Europe as well as for the British Empire.

LOGGING TRAINS were added to Canada's growing railroad network as the lumber industry continued to develop. By war's end, private business had met with intensive government regulation and, in some instances, participation. Formation of Canadian Railway Assoc., 1917, made possible later nationalization of railroads. By 1919 half the railway mileage had passed into government hands.

INCREASING DEMAND FOR HEAVY METAL led to the fabulous growth of steel industry. Largest single producer in world was Andrew Carnegie. He sold his entire business, including iron mines and railroads, for $447 million in 1901 to U. S. Steel Corp., trust organized by J. P. Morgan.

HENRY FORD (sitting in early 1900's car) put his Model T chassis on a moving assembly line in 1913 and turned out a finished car in 93 minutes, a job that had taken 14 hours before. Mass production meant lower costs, lower prices, more buyers. By 1920 one out of 13 Americans owned a car.

GIANTS OF INDUSTRY

Growth of trusts and business combines brings government intervention

The first 20 years of the new century saw the U. S. outproduce her three nearest competitors —Great Britain, France and Germany combined, and New York became financial capital of the world. This tremendous productivity was to a large extent the result of big business which, through standardization of parts and products, could produce more efficiently. Such giants as U.S. Steel— the first billion-dollar corporation, Standard Oil, American Sugar Refining and American Tobacco companies, virtually controlled their own fields. By 1914, 12 per cent of the manufacturing firms hired three-fourths of the workers, produced four-fifths of the nation's manufactured products.

The consolidation of American business and the resulting power which lay in so few hands aroused public demands for government intervention. President Theodore Roosevelt ushered in the attack. The Sherman Anti-Trust Act was invoked against mergers and holding companies in 1904 and laws passed to put the railroads and other carriers under the jurisdiction of the Interstate Commerce Commission. Pres. Wm. Howard Taft brought twice as many suits against trusts as had Roosevelt and broadened

JOHN D. ROCKEFELLER made a billion in oil, was second only to Morgan in finance realm.

the powers of the ICC. Woodrow Wilson entered the White House on a platform of effective restrictions on big business. He secured the Federal Reserve Act of 1913 to control the nation's currency (an outgrowth of the Bank Panic of 1907); the Clayton Anti-Trust Act, a further step in the curbing of unfair competition; and the establishment of the Federal Trade Commission, which was to investigate violations of anti-trust laws.

Meanwhile, in the great coal strike of 1902 the government marked its first successful intervention in labor-capital disputes. Organized labor, which by 1914 numbered 2,750,000 union members, had slowly improved working conditions since 1900, reducing the average work week in factories from 59 to 55 hours and raising weekly wages from $13 to $16. During the war it achieved an eight-hour day, equal pay for women workers and a living wage.

With the armistice, industry tried to take back the wartime gains made by labor and wholesale strikes resulted. Labor lost much of the ground it had gained. By the beginning of the Twenties over-expansion, speculation and high prices had combined to slip the country into a two-year depression.

TOP TYCOON was J. Pierpont Morgan, who virtually eliminated competition in nation's basic industries. He controlled vast financial empire through voting trusts but ran into increasing controls.

EARLY DU PONTS manufactured explosives. Under Pierre's (above) leadership, company developed scores of chemical products and bought control of other industries, including General Motors in 1920.

PHILANTHROPIST Daniel Guggenheim combined family interests with American Smelting and Refining Co. in 1901, headed an empire that mined tin in Bolivia, gold in Alaska, diamonds in Africa.

JUDGE ELBERT GARY organized U. S. Steel Corp. for J. P. Morgan, was board chairman, and in 1905 helped found Gary, Ind., the great steel center. Like Ford, he favored high wages and was anti-union.

JUDGE BEN LINDSEY pioneered in juvenile reforms. He founded one of the first juvenile courts—in Denver, Colo., and served as its judge from 1900 to 1927. His efforts brought about betterment in state's method of handling young offenders and secured legislation that held negligent parents and employers accountable.

WALL STREET EXPLOSION killed 38 persons ▶ and injured hundreds Sept. 16, 1920. At noon an old wagon halted across from J. P. Morgan & Co., and an instant later blew up. The driver escaped and cause of tragedy was never known, but was attributed to anti-capitalistic agitators.

CHILDREN under 16 composed 1,752,187 of U.S. labor force in 1900 and number increased steadily until 1910. Aroused public opinion led by Jane Addams and others secured congressional child labor law during Wilson's first term but it was nullified by Supreme Court in 1918.

PACIFIST EUGENE DEBS was perennial Socialist presidential candidate since 1900. In 1905 he helped found the IWW but soon withdrew. Sentenced to 10 years in prison in 1918 for anti-draft speeches, he polled 919,000 votes from Atlanta penitentiary in the 1920 elections.

DYNAMITE EXPLOSION in the offices of the *Los Angeles Times* Oct. 1, 1910, set off a fire which killed 21 working men. Labor radicals were blamed. Two McNamara brothers, defended by famous lawyer Clarence Darrow in sensational trial, pleaded guilty, drew long jail terms.

ABLE LABOR LEADER John Mitchell led the long deadlocked anthracite coal miners' strike of 1902. Operators finally agreed to arbitrate after Roosevelt threatened to have army take over and operate mines. Miners won wage hike, 9-hour day.

REVOLUTIONARY IWW fell into disrepute during the war. Organized in 1905 to unite skilled and unskilled workers to overthrow the capitalistic system, the IWW actively invited draft-dodging and crippling of industries producing war materials. Under Espionage Act of 1917 most of its leaders were jailed. Mob violence aided authorities in suppressing it — as in the deportation of 1200 members from Bisbee, Ariz., by armed citizens (l.). Best known woman trade unionist was energetic Rose Schneiderman (r.). She helped organize the Women's Trade Union League (1907-1919), later became its initial national president.

DR. LEE DEFOREST (above), was the inventor of the audion tube. The grid element which DeForest added to the "Fleming Valve" produced a device to amplify and generate radio signals. The three electrode tube and DeForest's later discovery of principle of regenerative feedback are two basic patents upon which modern radio, radar, and television are based.

FIRST TO THE POLE was American-born Robert Peary. Naval Engineer Peary made eight journeys to polar regions, demonstrating that white men may live in Arctic areas by following habits of Eskimos. Peary Arctic Club raised $5,000 for dash to Pole. Peary and Negro Matthew Henson stood at the North Pole April 6, 1909, climaxing many years of tragic attempts.

LITTLE GENIUS of General Electric Co. was German-born Charles Steinmetz. His greatest scientific contributions were hysteresis laws, studies of lightning and electrical transients, and mathematical concepts of a-c phenomenon.

PATHOLOGIST Theobald Smith was a pioneer in study of animal diseases and their relation to human beings. From professor of bacteriology at Geo. Washington Univ. he became Director of Animal Pathology at Rockefeller Institute.

MARCH OF SCIENCE

Research labs replace individuals as inventors

Mass research projects of the 20th century were rapidly obscuring the individual inventor. Among the last inventive giants of pre-World War I era were Lee DeForest and brothers Orville and Wilbur Wright.

At the turn of the century, principles of radio were well known. A practical device for the transmission and reception of radio signals, however, had not been found. Radio was condemned to the laboratory as a toy until this problem could be solved.

In 1883 Edison noted a flow of current from a heated filament to a charged plate, but was too engrossed with the electric lamp to follow this elusive clue. Sir John Fleming of England built a diode detector based upon this phenomenon, and there the matter rested. It remained for DeForest to grasp the tremendous implications of these two events. DeForest built a Fleming valve, adding a control grid, producing a vacuum tube capable of both amplification and oscillation. With these electronic principles in science's grasp, the potentialities of radio were ready to be developed.

The future of flying depended upon the solution of similar problems. A light, powerful aircraft motor was needed, and means of controlling the lateral movement of the aircraft were unknown. Until these problems were solved, heavier-than-air flight remained purely speculative. When the Wright brothers, working from basic concepts of Lillienthal and Chanute, solved these problems, the secret of flight was theirs. These basic riddles of nature were solved by individuals with no advanced knowledge or specialized training. Before many years had passed, however, aeronautics became too complex a field for the amateur inventor.

The early growth of the airplane was more spectacular than that of radio. In December, 1907, the U.S. Army Signal Corps purchased one Wright biplane, and soon started to train army officers as pilots. In 1910, Glenn Curtiss flew from Albany to New York City, establishing the airplane as a practical means of long distance transportation. Under the impetus of the First World War, the development of airplanes and engines was vastly accelerated. Within two years planes flying 100 miles per hour or more were common.

The war also provided impetus to radio communications. Using equipment developed during the war, the first commercial radio programs emanated from station KDKA in Pittsburgh, Pa., in 1920.

Many advances followed the war. Electric railways came into common use. The dial telephone system was inaugurated. The use of the steam turbine for power generation became general. Dr. Alexis Carrel developed new techniques for surgery and treatment of wounds. Dr. Irving Langmuir perfected the cathode-ray tube, the heart of modern television sets. The stage was set by these discoveries for even bigger developments that were to come.

FIRST FLIGHT

FIRST FLIGHT Wilbur and Orville Wright demonstrated flight in powered, heavier-than-air machine on deserted sand dunes of Kitty Hawk, N. C. In 1900, they performed man-carrying glider experiments at Kitty Hawk, then returned to conduct tests with wind tunnel models in their bicycle shop, Dayton, Ohio. Two hundred tests on wing surfaces, development of control systems preceded actual building of a powered plane (750 lbs., 12 hp motor). After parts failure and weather delays, a successful flight occurred Dec. 17, 1903. Four flights were made before Christmas, but the U.S. press generally ignored the event, believing the report to be a hoax. Years following Kitty Hawk were filled with many experiments to build a more air-worthy craft, and attempts were continued to master the technique of flying. Glenn H. Curtiss (Mrs. Curtiss above at the controls of early plane) worked with Alexander Graham Bell to produce first successful airplane to be flown before public in 1908. Curtiss developed a practical seaplane in 1911 and supplied many early aircraft to the embryonic U.S. Navy Aviation Section.

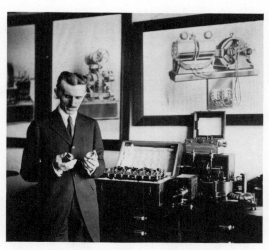

ETHNOLOGIST Franz Boas, anthropology professor at Columbia University (1899) studied the Indian and Eskimo tribes of North America. Curator at American Museum of Natural History (1901), Boas wrote many anthropological studies, in 1910 headed N.Y. Acad. of Sciences.

RADIO ENGINEER Nikola Tesla studied many of basic fundamentals of radio components between 1900-1914. His papers bridged gap between theory and production. Ideas set forth by Tesla enabled U.S. industry to mass produce radio equipment in time for World War I.

ERNEST ALEXANDERSON, Swedish-American radio engineer, did pioneer work on electric railroads, and invented high frequency Alexanderson Alternator, which made world-wide wireless possible. He also developed a multiple-tuned antenna and a different system for TV.

PANAMA CANAL

PANAMA CANAL Completion of a water link between the Atlantic and Pacific in August, 1914, gave America tremendous military and economic advantage in World War I. Conceived by the French, first attempts at canal building were failures due to typhoid fever and malaria. After political difficulties besetting canal were eliminated by Panamanian revolution, U.S. bought French property and started work in 1904. Disease was conquered in area, and army did construction work under Col. George Goethals. Tropical rains, landslides and cave-ins hampered work, but Canal opened in time for military use. Canal cost an estimated $400 million, but toll charges repaid original investment many times.

PRESIDENT TAFT visited Panama Canal as Secretary of War in 1908. Taft is shown on an inspection tour with General Goethals.

SUFFRAGETTES ON PARADE were a common sight around Washington in 1917. Marching at the head of the division, Mrs. Charles L. Tiffany (above) carried the flag for equal rights. Washington was headquarters for the National Woman's League, led by Mrs. Alice Paul. Suffragettes picketed the White House. Pres. Woodrow Wilson and politicians were given no rest until women's right to vote was passed. In August, 1920, when the required number of states approved it, the 19th amendment became part of the Constitution. Women won the ballot in time to vote for "Handsome Harding."

BIG-LEAGUE BALLPLAYER turned evangelist was Billy Sunday, an ordained Presbyterian minister. His huge revival meetings and dynamic speeches secured hosts of converts throughout the U.S. During the World War he devoted his talents to fomenting violent anti-Germanism.

RELIGIOUS SECT leader and faith healer, John Alexander Dowie built Zion City near Chicago. He had full control of Zion Bank, publishing house and devotees, declared the world was flat. In 1906 his followers suspended him from membership in Church on fraud, polygamy charges.

MUD-SLINGING cartoon of William Randolph Hearst appeared in *Harper's Weekly* in 1906. Defeated by exposure of Wall Street "plundering deals," Hearst lost election for governor of New York. He gave up dreams of becoming U.S. President, and formed biggest newspaper chain.

COUNTRY EDITOR William Allen White attained national fame in journalism, politics and literature without leaving his home town. He made the *Gazette,* of his birthplace Emporia, Kansas, tops in U.S. country newspapers. His liberal views and editorials became legendary.

MUCKRAKERS EVANGELISTS & EDUCATORS

The American band wagon rolled into an era of change, reforms, reactionary movements and high achievement at the start of the 20th century. Education, literature, religion and the press felt the nation-wide pressure of new ideas.

Corruption in politics and business developed a new school of protesting writers called muckrakers. The reforming zeal and search for social justice appeared in the magazines and books of the day. Prominent muckrakers of factual material were Ida M. Tarbell and her history of the Standard Oil Company, Lincoln Steffens, of *McClure's* magazine and Ray Stannard Baker. Upton Sinclair's *The Jungle* was the most successful of the muckraking books. Best sellers on the social revolt were written later by Jack London and Theodore Dreiser.

Newspapers became big money-making enterprises. Mass circulation, growth of great news services and syndicates tended to standardize the public's reading. By 1920, William Randolph Hearst was the biggest chain publisher in the nation. The New York *Times,* under Adolph Ochs, advanced pictorial journalism with use of rotogravure. The first American newspaper to have world-wide coverage, the *Times* won the Pulitzer Gold Medal for meritorious service in 1918. By the end of the first quarter of the 20th century the *Times* became the outstanding newspaper in the country.

Reform Sweeps Nation

The great reform fever sweeping the nation was evident in religion and education at the turn of the century. Modernism invaded the churches and colorful evangelists barnstormed the land. New sects of Zionists, the Assemblies of God, Nazarenes, Seventh Day Adventists gained popularity and followers. Billy Sunday, Mary Baker Eddy and Pastor Charles Russell were leaders in the religious crisis. New religions increased American church membership from 36 million in 1900 to 52 million in 1914.

Mass education problems of the period called for new theories of schooling. The little red schoolhouse gave way to new progressive education. Leader John Dewey emphasized the social efficiency of the student. Education came to include use of tools, play, contact with nature and the development of personal expression. Public school registration doubled and college attendance increased by 1920.

Millionaire philanthropists endowed schools of higher learning and other educational efforts. John D. Rockefeller and Andrew Carnegie, industrial tycoons, led the parade. Their example set the pace for educational research throughout the world. Education was established as the hope of democracy. Most American children aspired to at least a high school education in the post-World War I era.

FOREMOST POET of his era, Edwin Arlington Robinson was a master of blank verse technique. A three-time winner of the Pulitzer Prize for Poetry, his *Man Against the Sky* and *Town Down the River* brought him fame. His poetry stressed themes of tragedy and melancholia.

STARK NATURALISM reached a new high with the genius of Jack London and Theodore Dreiser. Reigning favorites of the readers during the first two decades of the 20th century, both authors revolted against evils of society. Both tried to picture life as it was, not as it should be. London is shown covering the Russo-Japanese War. Dreiser (above r. wearing cap) visits a "soup kitchen" in the Kentucky mine strike area. London's *Call of the Wild* and Dreiser's *The Titan* received wide American acclaim almost simultaneously. London also was the country's most famous writer of sea stories.

UPTON SINCLAIR'S packinghouse indictment, *The Jungle*, was the most powerful novel of the muckraking movement. This exposure led to stricter meat inspection and a new Pure Foods Act. Socialistic *Profits of Religion, Brass Check* followed.

EXPOSED CORRUPTION of municipal politics in 1902 by Lincoln Steffens set off the muckraking movement. On the staff of *McClure's* magazine, he gained success with *Tweed Days in St. Louis* and *Shame of the Cities*. Group above (l. to r. Clarence Darrow, Steffens, Edward A. Filene) fete writer at party.

NATURALISTS John Muir and John Burroughs are shown at Yosemite Park in 1909. Both, well-known nature writers, advocated the development of national parks in U.S. Muir's efforts aided growth of California's Sequoia, Yosemite Parks.

PRAGMATIC EDUCATOR John Dewey revolutionized U.S. teaching methods. Called the father of progressive education, Dewey opened his first "child-centered" school in 1900. A much-honored philosophy professor, he was a world influence in his field. He wrote several widely used textbooks on philosophy and ethics.

DANIEL COIT GILMAN was a prominent educator of 19th and early 20th century. President of University of California, he helped organize Johns Hopkins University in 1875, was its president till 1902. He was instrumental in founding the Johns Hopkins Hospital and Medical School, also edited New International Encyclopedia.

WORLD RENOWNED stateman and educator, Nicholas Murray Butler was a close friend of nine U.S. presidents. Butler (above with wife and daughter) raised Columbia to one of world's largest and most progressive universities in his 43-year presidency. His lifelong crusade for world peace increased American prestige abroad.

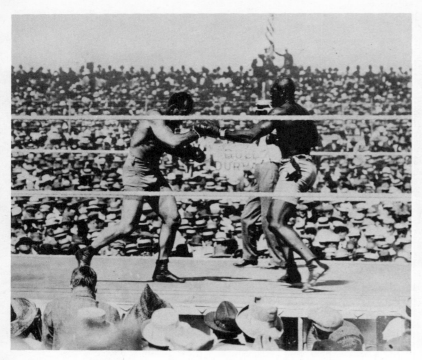

FORMER HEAVYWEIGHT title-holder Jim Jeffries (l.) came out of long retirement in 1910 to meet champion Jack Johnson (r.) in Reno on July 4th. Johnson held on to his crown by stopping the challenger in the 15th round. Jeffries had won the title in 1899, but after he retired it passed on to Marvin Hart. Hart lost it to Tommy Burns, who in turn lost it to Johnson.

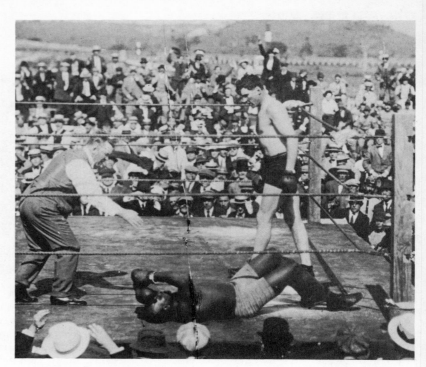

REFEREE TOLLED 10-COUNT over Jack Johnson in the 26th round of his fight with Jess Willard in Cuba in 1915. Willard was thus crowned the new heavyweight king, but there were those who claimed that Johnson took the easy way out while shading his eyes from the hot Havana sun. The new champ later defended the title successfully against Frank Moran in 1916.

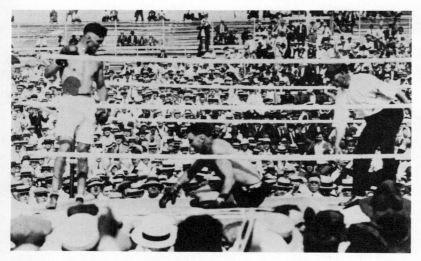

MANASSA MAULER, Jack Dempsey, was the most colorful heavyweight in ring history. Outweighed by more than 50 pounds in the title bout in Toledo in 1919, Dempsey knocked down Jess Willard seven times in the first round, and kept up such a merciless assault that Willard couldn't come out for the fourth. In five later fights Dempsey drew million-dollar gates.

SPORTS—1900-1920

Sports gained in popularity in the first two decades of the 20th century. World War I, with its emphasis on physical fitness, provided a new stimulus for sports-minded citizens before era ended.

Baseball flourished after 1903 when the upstart American League and the established National League ironed out their differences. The "Black Sox" scandal of 1919 shook confidence in the national pastime, but the election of Judge Kenesaw M. Landis as power-wielding high commissioner re-established public trust. Many of the stars in baseball's Hall of Fame shone in this era.

Football, dominated by the eastern universities, was somewhat revolutionized in the 1906 season when the more dangerous scrimmages were abolished and the forward pass was legalized. Boxing had its legal ups-and-downs until the passage of New York's Walker Law in 1920. Golf, tennis, polo, track and field, horse racing, automobile racing and swimming appealed more and more to a growing sports-minded public. The sports scene was colored by aggressive play and the crowd-pleasing personalities of Babe Ruth, Ty Cobb, Walter Johnson, Willie Heston, Jim Thorpe, Stanley Ketchel, Benny Leonard, Jack Dempsey, Bill Tilden, Bill Johnson and Walter Hagan.

STEALING HOME was all in the game to baseball immortal Ty Cobb, considered the best player of all time. In his long major league career, the "Georgia Peach" batted over .400 three times and holds a record lifetime average of .367.

FLYING DUTCHMAN of the diamond was Honus Wagner, unexcelled at shortstop and a top all-around team player. He held National League bat title eight years.

WIN-SOME TWOSOME of N. Y. Giants were mound marvel Christy Mathewson (l.) and mgr. John McGraw, 10 pennant winner. Matty won 373 games in his career.

GRAND OLD MAN of baseball, Connie Mack, was manager of Philadelphia A's for half a century. A former player, Mack piloted his teams to nine flags and five World Series victories, and was winning manager in first All-Star tilt.

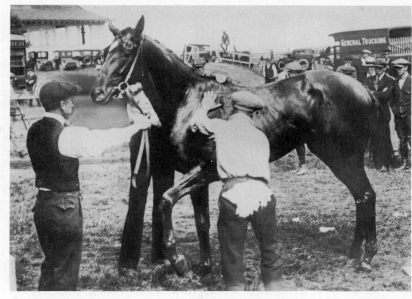

FIRST AMERICAN TEAM to win the international polo cup, in 1909, was composed (from l. to r.) of Devereux Milburn, Harry Payne Whitney, Monty Waterbury and Larry Waterbury. The rough and reckless style of the Big Four was criticized by many Britishers, but polo soon changed into a hard-riding, hard-hitting game, played that way the world over.

PURSE-SNATCHER of his day was Man O' War, the legendary Big Red of racing. In his two-year turf career, 1919 and 1920, Man O' War won 20 out of 21 starts, and his one loss was an upset to Upset. He earned $249,465 in purses for his owner, Samuel D. Riddle, and was retired to stud at the Faraway Farms near Lexington, Ky., where he died of heart attack in 1947.

OLYMPIC GAMES of 1912 featured dazzling performance of Jim Thorpe, who was acclaimed as the greatest all-around athlete in the world. However, Carlisle Indian's medals were later taken from him on charges of professionalism, and his Olympic records stricken from the book.

RACING SPARK among wealthy early automobile owners was generated in the 1900's by William K. Vanderbilt Cup Races held on Long Island. In ensuing years drivers included such favorites as Barney Oldfield, Ralph De Palma, Gaston Chevrolet, who popularized the sport.

SWING TO GOLF was set off in America by victory of 20-year-old unknown Francis Ouimet in U.S. Open of 1913. In a three-cornered playoff, he defeated top-heavy favorites Harry Vardon and Edward Ray of England. Above shows gallery following play of Ouimet, Brady in 1914.

BACKFIELD STAR Eddie Mahan played on Harvard team in 1913, 1914, 1915, and was chosen those three years for All-American honors by Walter Camp. Jim Thorpe called Mahan the greatest all-around halfback he ever saw in action.

FORWARD PASS came into its own in 1913 in hands of Notre Dame quarterback Gus Dorais and end Knute Rockne (above) who also scored as great Irish coach.

INCOMPARABLE Maurice Mc-Loughlin revolutionized lawn tennis with his power-laden serves and bullet passing shots down sidelines when he invaded East to win national title at Newport in 1912.

CATCH-AS-CATCH-CAN style of wrestler Frank Gotch made him powerful box office attraction from 1905, year he pinned Tom Jenkins for championship, until his retirement in 1913.

D. W. GRIFFITH'S "INTOLERANCE" outdid the successful *Birth of a Nation* by its magnitude, vast mob scenes (4,000 persons on the set for the fall of Babylon, above), and titanic settings, at a cost of $1.5 million. Although hailed as an artistic triumph, the film was not a box office success, since audiences found it difficult to follow the four parallel stories which portrayed the spirit of intolerance as it had been felt through the ages.

MOVIES BECOME BIG BUSINESS

Film industry provides mass entertainment, develops respectable art form

Movies began to take a strong hold on the public. The masses quickly became familiar with every mood and characteristic of their adored stars. Mary Pickford, Douglas Fairbanks, Gloria Swanson, Lillian and Dorothy Gish were famous celebrities. People laughed and cried at Charlie Chaplin, Marie Dressler, Mabel Normand, and the custard pie antics of Mack Sennett's Keystone Kops.

Children worshipped cowboy William S. Hart. Women secretly yearned to emulate the "vamp" of Theda Bara. Pearl White serials thrilled audiences week after week.

Such popular enthusiasm stimulated many enterprising business men to enter the field. Many companies, large and small, used indoor and outdoor "locations" to make films costing as little as $200 (in 1908). Soon stars' salaries, production and publicity costs rose tremendously, and exhibitors built million dollar picture palaces. Movies were becoming a major industry.

Story and camera innovations helped movies become an art form as well. Director D. W. Griffith introduced the mobile camera, the close up, the fade-in and fade-out, the flashback and other picture techniques.

"BIRTH OF A NATION" established Griffith in 1915 as the outstanding producer-director of the industry and persuaded millions to take the movies seriously. A sensational success, the film became the biggest money-maker in history.

GRIFFITH was the most revered creator and craftsman of his day, ranking as one of filmdom's "truly great." His innovations in camera and film techniques gave movies flexibility and dramatic force.

CHARLIE CHAPLIN, pantomimic genius of films, made his debut in 1913 with Sennett's Keystone Company. By 1915 he had become America's newest idol. Children promised to be good all week if they could see a Chaplin comedy Saturday. (Above, *The Adventurer.*)

MACK SENNETT, one of the three great early directors (with Griffith, Thomas Ince), made stars of unknowns, such as Chaplin, Gloria Swanson (c.) Phyllis Haver, Marie Prevost, Ben Turpin. He added sex appeal to his slapstick Keystone Comedies, with his daring "Bathing Beauty Brigade."

"WICKEDEST FACE In The World" was the title of seductive enchantress Theda Bara (above, *Cleopatra*, 1917). With her sensual face and exotic eyes the embodiment of mystery, she made the "vamp" famous, set new vogue for the woman of the world "whose passion is touched with death."

"AMERICA'S SWEETHEART" made charm, innocence, long golden curls her trademark. As leading actress of Zukor's Famous Players in 1913, Mary Pickford received a $2,000 weekly salary. In 1919 she joined Douglas Fairbanks, Chaplin, Griffith to form their own company, Allied Artists.

VITAGRAPH STUDIOS moved indoors in 1908 to speed up operations and outdo rival Biograph and Edison studios. Abandoning "locations" in city streets and public parks, they set up in skylight lofts of a tall building in Flatbush, Brooklyn, using mercury-vapor lamps for artificial lighting.

JESSE L. LASKY Feature Play Company was founded by Lasky (2nd from r.), Samuel Goldfish (later Goldwyn), and director Cecil B. DeMille (third from left). First to "discover" Hollywood, they set up in a barn, shot outdoors, scored financial success with their first film, *The Squaw Man.*

"GREAT TRAIN ROBBERY" in 1903 was a landmark film, the first motion picture to tell a connected scene-by-scene story. Directed by Edwin S. Porter, this dramatic narrative was imitated by all movie-makers and was the nickelodeon's most widely exhibited motion picture for many years.

CRYSTAL HALL, located on East 14th St., New York, was a popular Loew's picture house. Formerly Huber's Museum (featuring a penny arcade, vaudeville, museum of horrors), it showed the latest thrillers, retained the penny arcade and vaudeville show, all to be had for 10 cents admission.

ZIEGFELD FOLLIES

Beauty, extravaganza

ANNA HELD, imported from French music halls by Florenz Ziegfeld whom she later married, was reigning beauty. Highly publicized for taking milk baths, she starred in Ziegfeld's first *Follies*.

Dedicated to glorifying the beauty of American girls, temperamental showman Florenz Ziegfeld presented the first of his annual *Ziegfeld Follies* in 1907. It was the prototype of stylized musical revues which were to be invariably big box office successes for many years to come.

Ziegfeld's reputation for uncanny showmanship was won as each edition of the *Follies* surpassed its predecessor. Beautiful girls, lavish sets, scanty costumes, served as background for "unknowns" who made theater history under "Ziggy's" tutelage: Fanny Brice, Sophie Tucker, Nora Hayes, Ann Pennington, Mae Murray, the Dolly Sisters, Ina Claire, Marilyn Miller, Anna Held. Ziegfeld's judgment inspired the growth of new kinds of comedy and stellar comedians: Eddie Cantor, Bert Williams, Ed Wynn, Leon Errol, W. C. Fields, Frank Tinney, and leggy comedienne Charlotte Greenwood.

While the "Ziegfeld Girl" was becoming an American symbol, music halls and vaudeville stages flourished. Lillian Russell's talent and beauty made her the darling of New York's light opera stage; Eva Tanguay's audacity and her hit song "I Don't Care" brought her cabaret stardom, and music halls echoed to the songs and dances of 1900s shocking Floradora Sextette.

Blackface comics McIntyre and Heath shared popularity with another brand of American comedy—the dialects of Weber and Fields. Light opera took its place with Franz Lehar's *Merry Widow* (1907), lilting Victor Herbert tunes and George M. Cohan's *45 Minutes From Broadway*.

On the drama stage, the giants of U. S. theater paved their own paths to immortality: producer-managers Charles and David Frohman, Belasco, who pioneered the lasting trend toward realism, Klaw and Erlanger, and others who developed the "star-system."

LILLIAN RUSSELL, adored as theater's "American Beauty," was major star of the era. Equally popular in musicals or dramas, she won great personal success in *Wildfire*, a 1908 drama.

ANN PENNINGTON was a Ziegfeld dancing star who came to be known as "the girl with the dimpled knees." Her costumes, brief by standards of the period, were considered pert, saucy.

FUNNYMAN ED WYNN turned a high-pitched giggle and hesitant lisp into a comedy trademark. One of the century's great clowns, Wynn played in the *Follies*, George White's *Scandals*.

GEORGE M. COHAN capitalized on his July 4 birthday, later became known as the "Yankee Doodle Dandy." At turn of the century, he was just one of Four Cohans, vaudeville team with his sister, father and mother. Cohan (l.) was to become one of the most versatile successes in theater history, wrote WW I's most famous song "Over There," for which he was awarded the Congressional Medal.

WILD WEST was glorified with tall tales, sharp-shooting and whip cracking by Col. William "Buffalo Bill" Cody, Indian fighter, scout, showman and his "Wild West Show." Popular star of the show was sharp-shooter Annie Oakley. Famous Indian Sitting Bull named her "Little Sure-Shot" for her amazing accuracy with a rifle or pistol.

MAXINE ELLIOTT brought a sultry kind of beauty to the stage, was credited with being able to "out-sob" other stars. She was among the first actresses in the U.S. to open her own theater on Broadway, heart of the show world.

OLGA NETHERSOLE made headlines by being brought to court accused of violating public morals in play *Sappho*, 1900, for letting leading man supposedly carry her to her bedroom. "Not guilty" verdict helped assure the play's success.

MRS. LESLIE CARTER, fiery redhead, overcame critical disapproval for being a divorcee. Belasco's first star, she played *femme fatale* roles, won lyrical praise for her *Andrea* written for her by David Belasco and John Long, in 1905.

LOWER EAST SIDE'S Grand Street Theater flourished in 1908. Here, Jacob Adler, veteran actor of the Yiddish theater, made his English-speaking debut in *King Lear*. Off-Broadway theaters helped develop later Little Theaters in the U.S. In 1911 there were four — Toy Theater, Boston; Little Theater, N. Y.; Maurice Brown, Chicago; Plays and Players, Phila.

DAVID WARFIELD played burlesque with Weber and Fields before Belasco made him a drama star and matinee idol. In 1901, Warfield won instantaneous success in *The Auctioneer*, popularizing a Jewish peddler characterization. The show ran 105 consecutive performances in New York, two years on the road. In 1904, Warfield immortalized *The Music Master*.

DAVID BELASCO was to become almost legendary in American theater. Playwright, producer, director, manager, he fought stubbornly to break the theatrical monopoly, won by acquiring own theaters, writing and producing dramatic hits. Barred by Charles Frohman and the trust, Belasco leased theater, named it *Belasco*.

ETHEL BARRYMORE became a Frohman star in Clyde Fitch's *Captain Jinks of the Horse Marines*, Feb. 4, 1901. Just 21 years old, she had already played some minor stage roles.

DANCE DUO Vernon and Irene Castle helped to restyle ballroom dancing in U.S. They popularized tango, created "Castle Walk." Vernon was killed in plane crash in W W I.

COMPOSER VICTOR HERBERT, OPERETTA KING

JAZZ COMBOS reached a height of popularity after World War I, but the syncopated rhythms, born in New Orleans, were carried back to Chicago by itinerant musicians. Heavily dependent on improvisation, brassy in quality and possessed of a distinctive beat, the "new" music gained rapid favor among musicians. Originator of the "Dixieland" band was W. C. Handy, Negro musician whose composition, *St. Louis Blues*, earned him the title "Father of the Blues." In 1916, another orchestra (above) was given stellar billing as "Original Dixieland Jazz Band" at Reisenweber's Cafe, New York City night spot.

TENOR ENRICO CARUSO, OPERA'S GREATEST VOICE

MUSIC

New York, entertainment center of the U.S., was also the nation's music center. Boston, Philadelphia, Chicago and San Francisco had formed symphony orchestras, opera companies but New York's Metropolitan Opera under Gatti-Casazza had no equal. Artistically good, it was the fall social season's most glittering event. Music lovers paid $80 a pair for tickets to hear Italian tenor Enrico Caruso during his second season at the "Met," bravo'd hysterically after the sobbing *Pagliacci* aria. Wealthy cigar manufacturer Oscar Hammerstein opened the rival Manhattan Opera House in 1906. Even with such brilliant singers as Melba, Nordica, Tetrazzini, Schumann-Heink, John McCormack and Mary Garden, "Met" competition was too great. He sold out in 1910. Operettas by Victor Herbert won enduring popularity through such tunes as *Kiss Me Again*, made famous by Fritzi Scheff in *Mlle. Modiste* (1905). Irving Berlin wrote a "jazz classic" in 1912, *Alexander's Ragtime Band*.

THEATER HISTORY was to be made by this trio of men, but, earlier Irving Berlin (playing piano) wrote *Alexander's Ragtime Band*, "plugged" ballads; Eddie Cantor (l.) clowned for Ziegfeld (c.).

ANNA PAVLOVA made Russian ballet popular in the U.S. with enormously successful tour in 1911, showed technique in *Swan Lake*.

MUCH BELOVED concert singer, Madame Schumann-Heink, adopted America as her homeland. Patriotically, she raised Liberty Loan funds in World War I as sons fought in both the German and the Allied armies.

LUCREZIA BORI was to have a long and colorful career in opera, beginning with Caruso in Paris. From 1912 to 1915, she was leading soprano with New York's Metropolitan Opera Company, returned to same reigning position in '20s, was made a director of Association in 1935.

ROSA PONSELLE, American soprano, made her debut at the Metropolitan in 1918, with Enrico Caruso, singing Verdi's *La Forza del Destino*. She retired from active opera roles in 1937.

MARY GARDEN moved from behind the footlights of the opera stage in New York to the unique position of impresario in 1919, the first woman to take such production responsibility. The venture failed and she returned to starring.

REALIST JOHN SLOAN'S *THE WAKE OF THE FERRY*, PAINTED IN 1907

MORE "ASH CAN SCHOOL" REALISM IN BELLOW'S *STAG AT SHARKEY'S*

ART At the turn of the century, Americans' taste in art had been only mildly influenced by French Impressionism, despite publicity attendant on the first such showing by "Ten American Painters," in 1898. In the first decade of the century, U.S. painters clung to realism but expressed it in homely incident, based their techniques on European masters Goya, Hogarth, Daumier, and were critically derided as exponents of the "Ash Can School." Maurice Predergast (1859-1924) was known as leader of "The Eight," offshoot of this group, which included Robert Henri, George Luks, John Sloan, George Bellows. Sloan, rebelling against conservatism of the National Academy of Design, organized Society of Independent Artists, 1917. Bellows, whose *Stag at Sharkey's* (r., above) hung in the Cleveland Museum, revived the nearly lost art of lithography in America. With the New York Armory Show, 1913, Arthur Davies' Painters and Sculptors Association completed the break with conservatism.

"SEPTEMBER MORN," a "shocking" nude appeared in the window of a Chicago Art shop in 1912 and evoked a double-edged storm: from artists, who considered it bad art and from the public, who considered it indecent. Painted by Paul Chabas, it was his only claim to fame, was lithographed for calendars.

ALSO SHOCKING, but for different reasons, was this *Nude Descending a Staircase*, Marcel Duchamp's cubist impression, which had its U.S. debut in 1913 show.

JOHN D. ROCKEFELLER "sat" for John Singer Sargent, whose career as a portrait painter was aided immeasurably by his long-time association with one of America's richest and most colorful art patronesses, Mrs. John Gardner.

POPULAR ILLUSTRATORS glorified American girls of the period by accenting saccharine femininity. The "Gibson Girl," created by Charles Dana Gibson, for more than a decade was considered the "fashionable ideal of young womanhood." Typical is *The Sweetest Story Ever Told* (l.). Equally popular were the sketches of James Montgomery Flagg, whose sweet-faced girls were admired about 1907.

MARIN'S ISLAND was one of watercolorist John Marin's early studies, exemplified the influence of the Chinese school on artists who were seeking more original modes of expression. Marin's one-man shows were critical triumphs from 1909, when he was able to embody cubist and impressionist methods in Maine land and seascapes.

PASSING SCENE

ST. LOUIS EXPOSITION was held in 1904 commemorating the acquisition of the Louisiana Territory from France. A summary of the world's progress in knowledge was presented in the 15 large exhibit buildings arranged to form a fan. Noteworthy were the Congress of Arts and Sciences and the Government Building (c.), the anthropological exhibits from the Philippines, and the advances made in agriculture. Natives from foreign lands were part of exhibit. Pygmies, aborigines, and Eskimos were housed in authentic native buildings.

Cost was more than $31 million and recorded admissions totaled 19 million. Still standing, in St. Louis, is the City Art Museum erected for the Louisiana Purchase Exposition.

CONEY ISLAND was the most popular and populated resort of the day. Then, as now, its attractions were a hurly-burly of rides, freaks, elephants, food and sand. Shown above is section of former Luna Park in the amusement area.

LOUISIANA PURCHASE Exposition featured a huge parade. Visitors stood for hours in rain to see delegations from many nations march in parade. Chinese exhibit is seen at right, and the Fire Fighters Building is shown at the rear left.

EASTER PARADE on Fifth Avenue, New York, was display of latest fashions. Women's hats were adorned with birds, flowers, and grapes. Men sported derbys, top hats and Prince Albert cutaways. St. Patrick's Cathedral is visible (r.).

TYPICAL SCENE in midwest city was this street in Des Moines, Iowa. Traffic was sparse and the motorist or carriage-driver had no problems with parking meters, right-of-way, or which side of street to drive on. Policemen of the day were only casually concerned with traffic problems, issuing traffic violation tickets.

"NEARER TO HEAVEN" than any building, was description given Woolworth structure in 1913. Height of the building is 792 feet. It was awarded medal of honor as tallest office building.

MOUNT LASSEN erupted in 1914 and was intermittently active until 1921. It was the only active volcano in U.S. Stereopticons were not complete without at least one view of Mt. Lassen erupting.

WHITE FLAGS of surrender to congested and miserable living conditions wave in this tenement back-yard on Park Avenue and 107th Streets in New York City. These slums were the incubators of crime and violence, such as the Black Hand Society. Such living conditions as these were to exist until Mayor Fiorello LaGuardia's eventual clean-up of worst slums.

PUSH-CARTS on Mulberry Street in New York City were markets on wheels. Fruit, fish and clothing were sold to the teeming population at doorsteps and windows. Accompanying odors and flies they attracted were a constant nuisance. Playgrounds were non-existent and children were pressed into early labor. Life was coarse. Success was reserved for fittest.

IMMIGRANTS settled in cheap housing partly to be near people who spoke same language, mostly because they had little money. Many secured foothold in teeming cities, eventually moved to better areas. Outstanding men produced by the tough East Side included the late LaGuardia, Al Smith, and Walter Winchell, George Jessel, Jimmy Durante, and Eddie Cantor.

SLEEPING IN SHIFTS was common in slum areas. When alarm clock rang, one of these men relinquished his bed space to another. Shortage of adequate housing resulted in spread of disease and created hatreds. This resulted in high taxes to maintain hospitals and police forces. When fire occurred in these shack-cities, loss of life was often staggeringly high.

PALATIAL HOME of Wm. C. Whitney, financier and public official was tastefully furnished, avoiding the stifling heaviness of too much bric-a-brac, drapery, and pictures of half-remembered relatives. An excellent marble stairway was the showpiece of the home. Potted palms such as those shown were typical foliage in luxurious homes, restaurants and night clubs.

VANDERBILT MANSION was combination castle and museum. It housed priceless collections from Europe and the best work of American craftsmen. Note curved glass in chinacloset and intricate wood-carving throughout. Mirrors were backed with pure silver; ceilings trimmed with gold. Marble, tiles, and crystal were brought from Europe and Mediterranean countries.

NEW YORK TO PARIS by auto seemed impossible, but cars from several countries entered race in 1908. Route led across U.S., then by ship to Vladivostok, across Russia, then south and over to Paris. Men and machines fought mud, dust, bad roads and break-downs. Cattle were constant hazard, because cow-paths were the only roads in some areas. Two U.S. entries are shown above. Only one of the entries managed to finish the entire race.

LADIES DROVE AUTOS and sported top-heavy hats in 1910. Auto styles showed the square look, right-hand steering and squeeze horns. Milady's fashions made the most of the hour-glass figure, broad brims and the deceptive bustle. Although woman's place was still "in the home," she was breaking loose occasionally to "go for a pleasure spin" in the family car.

FIRST AIR MAIL was flown in 1911. Demonstration flights were beginning to impress the government and pave the way for federal appropriations. Earle Ovington is shown receiving mail from a Post Office official prior to pioneer air mail flight between Garden City Estates and Mineola, L. I. Later, in 1918, the first appropriation was made and service inaugurated.

GREATEST WOMAN FINANCIER was title given to shrewd Hetty Green who inherited a large fortune from her father and increased it to $100 million in stock manipulations. Hetty was usually surrounded by a battery of attorneys because of the many lawsuits which she had filed.

IMMIGRANTS were given extensive examinations on entry to U.S. at Ellis Island. Europe accounted for about 90 per cent of immigration. Heavy influx of German and Irish aroused native population in United States, and laws were passed to encourage quotas from other countries.

SANDOW, THE GREAT, strong man of the early 1900's, was versatile weight lifter and stunt man. Employed by various promoters, he lifted anvils, scale models of ferris wheels and assortment of back-breaking objects. His stunts required the use of brute force more than mere trickery.

HOUR-GLASS FIGURE and pearls were pride of Mrs. George Gould in 1905. Pearl embroidered dress was beautiful but proved impractical.

DIPLOMAT, JOURNALIST Whitelaw Reid and wife admire daughter on stairway of their New York residence. Reid held financial control of the *Tribune* in early 1900's, served as minister to France and special envoy to Great Britain.

FASHIONS

SOCIETY LEADER and wife of William K. Vanderbilt, Mrs. Vanderbilt typifies the fashionable woman at the turn of century. Besides being an influential society figure, she contributed to the style trends emerging in early 20th century.

SISSIES smoked cigarettes, contended men of pre-World War I days. Two-for-a-nickel cigars were a man's best smoke. Women of revolutionary mind sometimes smoked a cigar or cigarette.

PARIS FADS are displayed by Talmadge sisters Natalie, Norma and Constance on return from European tour. Skirt which Constance wore (r.) was latest innovation in women's apparel. Canes were *tres chic*.

NEW LOOK of 1910 was modeled by Marie Mulhearn. Although very few women could afford a sealskin and ermine stole, it gave them something to wish for.

CONEY ISLAND was the most concentrated area of massed humanity in the U.S. on hot Sunday afternoons. Beach pastimes were waist-deep wading, splashing water, and rubber-necking.

Huge baskets of food were standard beach equipment because of staggeringly big families. Difficult transportation made Sunday at the beach a special occasion and one to be remembered perpetually in the family album.

Beach fashions were becoming more audacious. Women had discarded stockings, and the hem line had crept up to the knee. Styles were beginning to show imagination through stripelines, checks and the middy top, but somehow the sack-look prevailed.

Men's swim suits allowed freedom when dry, but when wet the wool stretched and sagged, hindering effective swimming.

Chaperoning was still practiced by most mothers and romances thrived, in spite of it.

FIRE BROKE OUT seconds after San Franciscans were jolted by a severe earthquake at 5:15 on the morning of April 18, 1906. The water supply was destroyed by the quake and in a few hours flames had completely devastated the entire business and commercial section, reducing to rubble 60 years work of building San Francisco into one of the world's major cities. By dynamiting and back-firing, the flames were kept from spreading.

DISASTERS

MOVING LIKE A SCYTHE, a tornado cut a wide swath through the most thickly settled residential sections of Omaha, Neb., just at dusk, Easter Sunday, 1913. Casualties were 140 dead, 350 seriously injured. Path of destruction measured four and one-half miles long and from two to six blocks wide. Some 650 buildings were completely leveled and 1,250 damaged.

SPECTACULAR FIRE in the Equitable Life Building in downtown Manhattan Jan. 12, 1912, imprisoned insurance executives and killed six persons. Zero weather and a fierce gale froze the steam fire engines fast in ice. The building, an immense block which cut off light and air from its neighbors, brought about the first zoning law in 1916, regulating building size.

GALVESTON, TEXAS, was nearly washed from the face of the earth Sept. 8, 1900, when 135-mile-an-hour winds and tidal wave swept over it. One-sixth of the population and one-third of the city was lost — 5,000 dead, $17 million damage. To meet the emergency a commission of five was formed to run the city. The new type of government was so successful it was adopted permanently, spread to other cities. Sea wall saved city in '15.

ILL-FATED *TITANIC*, bound for New York from Southampton on her maiden voyage, struck an iceberg off Newfoundland on the night of April 14, 1912. Of the 2,207 passengers and crew aboard, 1,513 lost their lives, including 103 women and 53 children. Many Americans were among them. British White Star luxury liner, built at cost of $7.5 million, had supposedly been non-sinkable. A German artist depicted scene above from accounts.

to other sections of the city and after three days they were finally subdued. Nearly 1,000 persons had lost their lives in the disaster. Property damage topped $350 million. More than seven square miles had been razed. It was one of the greatest fires in history. Self-appointed vigilantes were quickly organized to prevent looting. Food, clothing were rushed in from all over the country. But for weeks homeless lived in streets or in makeshift shelters.

CRIME

Black Hand Society Terrorizes Italian Settlements

"BLACK JACK" DETCHUM was leader of one of the most desperate bands of train robbers in the West. He was tried and convicted not for murder — of which he was also guilty — but for train robbery, punishable by death in New Mexico at the time. Whole town of Clayton turned out for the hanging in March, 1901.

REFORM MAYOR of New York City, William J. Gaynor, was being routinely interviewed by reporters while embarking for Europe Aug. 8, 1910, when he was shot by discharged city employee. He never fully recovered, although he resumed his official duties, and died three years later at sea while enroute to Europe.

BLACK HAND societies created a reign of terror in "Little Italy" settlements throughout the country in the early 1900s. They preyed on their own race, living by robbery, extortion, kidnapping, blackmail and even murder. Bomb-throwing was their favorite protest when a victim failed to pay up. Police were baffled because honest Italians, afraid to complain, maintained an "omerta" — conspiracy of silence. New York detective Joseph Petrosino tracked the Black Hand to Palermo, Italy, where he was assassinated in 1909. Other detectives, following his trail, found most members were ex-convicts and had entered the U.S. illegally. With the help of the Italian government, the New York police secured the penal certificates of more than 700 Italians in the U.S. and moved to deport them. Political pressure, however, suppressed the certificates and the Black Hand thrived. In 1914, under a new commissioner, New York police cracked down with a policy of close surveillance and quick arrests which gained the confidence of the Italian citizenry. With the "omerta" broken, convictions and deportations soon broke the dreaded Black Hand organization.

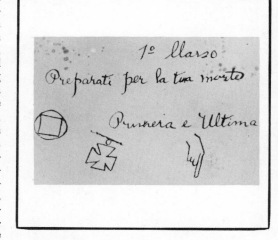

BOSTON POLICE WENT ON STRIKE Sept. 9, 1919, after their attempts to affiliate with A. F. of L. met with suspensions. Gov. Calvin Coolidge called out the state guard to curb lawlessness, said, "There is no right to strike against the public safety by anybody, anywhere, any time." Strike ended in three days but a new police force was enlisted to replace strikers completely.

BOOM AND BUST

Americans live high as mass production hits its stride in the Twenties; crash and depression bring F. D. R. and New Deal to hectic Thirties

By the end of World War I American capitalism had shown itself to be the most efficient economic system yet devised. With its vitality preserved by anti-trust laws, free enterprise was benefiting nearly everybody. It not only raised the standard of living, it revolutionized life itself. With a flivver in the garage and a radio in the parlor, almost all Americans were getting a touch of luxury. Materially, at least, the American way was proving a spectacular success.

The nation might have resisted the earthly temptations of a Golden Age, but deep spiritual roots which had nourished it for three centuries were under attack. Scientific knowledge had seriously challenged much of Christian theology. As churches clung fast to doctrine, they gradually lost influence with a skeptical generation. Those Americans who now doubted the existence of a literal Heaven or Hell were left with no compelling motive for doing good. And many churchmen were too busy defending the ramparts of faith, or contending with each other in their Sunday sermons on doctrinal questions, to raise an effective cry against the evils of the flesh.

So the nation accepted modern prosperity for all it was worth. This was no 20th Century Babylon; but it exhibited a huge zest for life which scorned restraint.

The Twenties brought the Golden Age of American sports — of Babe Ruth, Red Grange, of Jack Dempsey and Bobby Jones.

Rebellion at Conscience

It was also an age of booze and flaming youth, of civic corruption and the Teapot Dome. A burst of moral conscience had brought Prohibition. A still more powerful burst of resentment had killed it, and law-breaking became a social distinction, the Twenties an era of gangsterism. American literature caught fire again with such greats as Sinclair Lewis and Eugene O'Neill, but while they attacked the sham of a frivolous era, they offered no alternative but cynicism.

The newest art form, motion pictures, was showing its limitless scope of expression, but its impact on the nation exceeded its quality. It had the dubious honor of making such stars as Greta Garbo and Charlie Chaplin more familiar to Americans than the President.

Science and technology were conquering disease, shrinking the world and unloosening the secrets of the universe. Such daring flights as Lindbergh's trans-Atlantic hop encouraged airlines and air travel to distant lands; radio brought those lands into America's living room in an instant. Yet scientific knowledge was now so far beyond the reach of the average man that he began to rely more and more on the word of experts, to do less thinking of his own.

By the late Twenties, most Americans were happily engaged in credit buying and stock speculation. "Keeping up with the Joneses" was essential, and playing the risky bull market seemed a good way.

Babylon itself was better prepared for the day of wrath. When the stock market crashed in October, 1929, the nation panicked.

A TYPICAL 1930'S BREADLINE

Fortunes and lifetime savings were swept away. In the hasty retreat of business, millions were unemployed. President Hoover, who had inherited incipient disaster from his predecessors, tried to bolster credit with his Reconstruction Finance Corporation. But this was small comfort to those in the breadlines. In one of the greatest political reverses in history, Franklin Delano Roosevelt and the Democrats swept into power at the low point of the depression. This generation had, as F.D.R. put it, "a rendezvous with destiny."

To a paralyzed nation, the New Deal brought one thing — action. With his bank moratorium and other emergency measures, F.D.R. earned the esteem of the nation in the first "one hundred days." But as government control of the economy became established New Deal policy, he incurred the bitter enmity of U.S. business.

Labor's Power Increases

At the same time, organized labor, which had lost ground in the prosperous Twenties, gained new encouragement with the New Deal's Wagner Act, and reached a peak of power in the 1930's. The nation's farmers, who had suffered depression even in the boom years, were bolstered by government purchase of surplus crops. Roosevelt shocked the nation by his abortive attempt to pack the Supreme Court for declaring some of his measures unconstitutional. But so great was his popularity that he won an unprecedented third term.

By this time, foreign policy had taken a decisive hand in U.S. politics. Through the 1920s the nation had steered an isolated course, boosting its tariffs, demanding its war debts and avoiding international "entanglements." But in 1931, Hoover's Secretary of State, Henry Stimson, had tried to get international sanctions imposed on Japan for her invasion of Manchuria. Foreign cooperation was extended by F.D.R. and his Secretary of State, Cordell Hull, first with the reciprocal trade agreements and the Good Neighbor policy, later with Lend-Lease and other aid to a beleaguered Western Europe. The late 1930's saw a new awakening, economically and politically. "Isolation" became a subject of debate. More and more the United States began to realize that it could no longer remain aloof from the affairs of Europe and Asia. The nation was accepting its international responsibility — too late to prevent World War II, but perhaps in time to help win it.

So the "great bust" after the "great boom" had been beaten — not only by the artificial stimulus of war and government spending, but by the nation's basic vitality. Was this resort to paternalism an admission that the American system could no longer operate in a country grown as big and unwieldy as the United States? Americans still had faith in the competitive system, but they had learned a bitter lesson about letting it go unwatched. Whether they had also learned the perils of unabashed materialism was another question.

★ ★ ★

◀ **GIANTS OF AN AGE** were these three friends, who epitomized the inventive and productive genius of the 20th Century, (left to right) Thomas Alva Edison, Henry Ford and Harvey Firestone. In the American tradition, they rose from very modest beginnings and lived to see men's lives transformed and enriched by their work. To invention they added mass production and low unit cost. Lower prices plus advertising and salesmanship opened up a mass market. With the 1920's Americans became great producers and consumers, thus creating more time for leisure living.

HARDING MEETS EINSTEIN on early visit of the scientist to the U.S. Harding's inadequacies as President were numerous, but his affable personality won Harding the dubious distinction of being a well-liked incompetent.

WASHINGTON CONFERENCE in 1921-22, resulted in treaties designed to halt the competition between great naval powers in the construction of capital ships. This was greatest accomplishment of Harding regime. Delegates included: A. J. Balfour (l. c.), Britain; C. E. Hughes (r. c.), U.S.; Aristide Briand (next Hughes), France; Tekigawa (far r.), Japan.

LAST PICTURES of Harding show the President tired and grim after his trip to Alaska (above). He died suddenly in San Francisco, August 1923, sparing him embarrassment of Teapot Dome scandal. Caisson-carriage funeral (below) closed career of the "normalcy" leader.

BACK TO NORMALCY

Retrenchment and scandals mark Harding era

President Harding, a follower of the party whips, was elected by an impressive majority over the Democratic candidate, James M. Cox, in 1920. His promise to the nation was "normalcy in social and economic conditions." Conscious of his own limitations, Harding relied on a cabinet of "best minds" but unfortunately chose, for the most part, men who lacked public responsibility.

A major repercussion resulting from this poor selection was the Teapot Dome scandal. On area near Casper, Wyoming, had been set aside by Pres. Wilson in 1915, as an oil reserve for the Navy. By executive order of Harding, the Teapot Dome reserve was transferred to the Department of Interior, headed by Secretary Albert B. Fall. In 1922, Fall leased, without competitive bid, these and other oil fields in California to oil operators Harry F. Sinclair and Edward L. Doheny.

A Senate investigation conducted by Sen. Thomas J. Walsh led to the resignation of Fall and criminal prosecutions. A number of prominent individuals were involved. Although the court showed evidence of "gifts" to Secy. Fall, Doheny and Sinclair were acquitted. Sinclair was later convicted of a minor charge stemming from the investigation. The oil fields were restored to the government in 1927.

This and other scandalous irregularities gave the administration of Harding the reputation of being one of the most corrupt since the Grant Administration.

President Harding died suddenly in 1923, before the prosecutions occurred. His final days were not happy ones. Shuttled from place to place on distant trips, he traveled in an aura of constant anxiety.

He had been making a 39-day tour of western states and Alaska. His last speech, on July 27, 1923, at Seattle dealt with Alaskan problems. Then he was taken ill and was hurried to San Francisco.

He developed pneumonia and died Aug. 2.

TEAPOT DOME SCANDAL This affair contributed to the disrepute of the Harding Administration, and remains in history as a synonym for graft and corruption in government. President Harding (1) is shown with two friends who betrayed his confidence in them, Harry M. Daugherty (2) Attorney General, who failed to prosecute for graft in the Veterans Bureau, and Albert B. Fall (3) who illegally leased government oil reserves as Secretary of Interior. Investigation probed into Harry Sinclair's (r.) oil transactions with Fall, who was convicted and sentenced to one year in prison and fined $100,000. Sinclair was acquitted, but later imprisoned on another charge. Although Fall was convicted of accepting a bribe from Doheny, latter was acquitted. This may have hastened Harding's death.

IN CHAPS, Indian head-dress, or street clothes, Vermont born Calvin Coolidge was the frugally-spoken, ultra-conservative President of the United States. He was the complete opposite of Harding and inspired confidence in the American public after the Harding upheavals. Campaign directors equipped autos with radios to carry Candidate Coolidge's messages to remote areas in the 1924 election. Coolidge is shown in action at gymnasium with Indian clubs and matching wits with a trout. Even when he was fishing, Coolidge dressed in conservative business suit and hat.

KEEP COOL WITH CAL

Coolidge makes business the nation's business

At the death of President Harding, Calvin Coolidge was automatically placed into the role of Chief Executive, an unenviable position heaped with the unpleasant debris of the Harding administration.

Immediately, a policy of "The business of America is business" was put into effect by the repeal of excess profits taxes as contained in the Revenue Law of 1921, and the handing of The Interstate Commerce Commission and the Federal Trade Commission to private enterprise.

Industry boomed with the mass production of automobiles as pioneered by Henry Ford, and allied industries, glass, iron, fabrics, and steel.

A land rush in Florida during 1925 was one of the largest in American history. Speculation ran riot and real estate prices soared far above the value of the land.

Isolationist Sen. William Edgar Borah of Illinois, serving as Coolidge's Foreign Relations advisor and chairman of that committee, worked indomitably for freedom of press, world peace and disarmament.

When both the Harding and Coolidge administrations failed to pass a bill for government operation of the Muscle Shoals Development, Senator Norris of Nebraska and others attacked the Administration for its policies and said it catered to business.

The Progressive Party made a strong showing in the 1924 election. Backed by labor, liberals and the farm vote, Bob LaFollette of Wisconsin and Burton K. Wheeler of Montana garnered 4,823,000 votes for the Progressives.

Although Coolidge could have had the nomination again in 1928, he stated that he did not wish to run. Hoover was nominated.

COOLIDGE'S CABINET contained men whose names reappeared again in later administrations. Charles Evans Hughes (third from left) as Chief Justice in Roosevelt Administration, and Herbert Hoover (l.) as President in 1928. Henry Wallace, Sr., is standing third from left.

KELLOGG-BRIAND PACT was idealistic attempt to end wars. Signed by 15 nations and ratified by 62 in 1928, it helped prevent a war between Russia and China over Manchuria.

LA FOLLETTE, Progressive Party candidate, polled nearly 5,000,000 votes, about one sixth of those cast in 1924. Hiram Johnson was one of the founders of the Progressive Party.

CAMPAIGN BARBS were sharp and stinging, hitting strongly at Teapot Dome scandal, coddling of Navy Sec'y Denby, who was involved. Coolidge, atop elephant, allowed him to resign.

DEMOCRAT WM. McADOO was hard-hitting candidate for nomination in 1924. He was strong presidential timber, and son-in-law of the late President Woodrow Wilson. But a badly split Democratic party turned to conservative John Davis of West Virginia as a compromise candidate.

HOOVER announced his belief in "rugged individualism" as a boy, voicing an ambition "to be able to earn my own living without the help of anybody, anywhere." At 17 he had $300 and the desire to be a mining engineer. At 40 he was a little-known multimillionaire. At 54, he was the 31st President of the United States (left with cabinet, right with son, Allen). Born to Quaker parents of Pennsylvania Dutch origin, Hoover was orphaned before he was 10 and worked his way through Stanford to a degree as a mining engineer. From a job as day laborer in a mine he rose to control of international mine interests. Stranded in London by the outbreak of World War I, Hoover helped other Americans home, took over Belgian relief. He was appointed U. S. Food Administrator during the war and chief of Allied Supreme Econ. Council after Armistice. He was Sec'y of Commerce, 1921-28.

HOOVER

Stock market crash and resulting panic plunge nation into depression

Long pent-up forces of economic unrest struck blow after blow in the four years of Herbert Hoover's presidency. Immediate cause of the first crisis was the ruinous stock market crash of October, 1929, the result of hysterical speculation along with unregulated manipulation. Unprecedented panic closed banks and factories and cut already low farm prices. Farmers' plight was further aggravated by the 1930 drought.

To compound national disaster, a general European collapse struck in 1931, touched off by Viennese bank failure and runs on gold which forced Britain and 40 other nations off the gold standard. Overdue revision of war debts and reparations plus tariff barriers were problems underlying crisis.

Hoover hoped to introduce a broad social welfare program ranging from departmental reorganization through child care. Events forced him instead to devote his energy in an effort to avert total paralysis of the national and international economic structure. His approach to domestic events was to foster private enterprise and aid cooperative initiative, with recourse to federal intervention only as a last resort.

Democrats won control of Congress in 1930, but adopted Hoover's bills for an RFC and revision of the bankruptcy laws. Hoover also won support for a debt moratorium to meet the European crisis, but failed in plan he considered most vital to recovery, stabilization of international currency.

Business revival received a new set-back following the 1932 election. Rumors of inflationary fiscal policies and projected abandonment of the gold standard generated new panic and led to a paralyzing new run on domestic gold. Hoover asked Roosevelt's support of an international conference to take up the related questions of debts and currency stabilization, and again for aid in quieting fears of radical new monetary policies, but support was not forthcoming.

Bank runs and hoarding increased, until in the days preceding the inauguration gold hoarding had reached $86 million daily.

WAY WAS CLEARED for nomination of Hoover on the first ballot at party convention of 1928 when Calvin Coolidge "chose" not to run. In his first try for elective office Hoover faced as his Democratic opponent, Tammany's "Happy Warrior," Al Smith (l., c. l. at New York Governor's inaugural ball with F.D.R.). A widespread whispering campaign generated fear of the "Pope in the White House," since Smith was Catholic, and contributed to first Solid South break since the Civil War. Smith, born of poor parents on N. Y.'s East Side, had risen to be N. Y. governor. Hoover attacked Smith's farm and hydroelectric programs as "state socialism," supported prohibition against Smith's call for repeal. Former won by electoral vote of 444 to 87.

CRASH Worst New York stock market panic plummeted nation into black gloom. On October 29, 1929 the glittering bubble of unchecked stock speculation burst with repercussions felt around the world. In one day 16 million shares were dumped on the New York Exchange. Wall Street averages dropped 68 points in the next three days bringing speculative orgy to disastrous end. Hoover had worked to avert it by credit curbs. Industry ground to halt. Prediction of a "chicken in every pot" became a bread line in every city.

TO FORCE passage of special veterans' benefits, a "Bonus Army" (l.) marched on Washington in May, 1932. Despite pressure, bonus bill was defeated. At Hoover's suggestion Congress voted funds to send marchers home. But in July rioting broke out when local police were ordered to evict several thousand who stayed on. Use of pistols by police to quell uprising led the District Commissioners to call on federal troops to prevent more bloodshed. Cavalry, tank, and infantry troops under General Douglas Mac-Arthur marched on demonstrators (r.). forced dispersal with tear gas.

WORLD COURT role and collaboration with League were urged by Hoover, who also worked toward arms limitation. With British Prime Minister Ramsey MacDonald (center, with New York's Grover Whelan, left, and Secretary of State Stimson), Hoover laid the ground for the London Naval Conference, and a brief lull in naval construction. Strained Latin-American relations were eased by good-will tour and removal of troops from Haiti and Nicaragua. When Japan invaded Manchuria, Hoover offered League aid.

FRANKLIN D. ROOSEVELT, Governor of New York, and John N. Garner of Texas headed the Democratic ticket in 1932. Democratic platform called for federal aid to farmers and unemployed, reciprocal trade treaties, repeal, regulation of the stock exchange, and the "continuous responsibility of government for human welfare." Ills of the national economy were widely blamed on Hoover, who received crushing defeat, lost 42 states. Both houses of Congress passed to Democrats by an overwhelming majority.

SYMBOL of the depths to which the nation had plunged following the stock market crash of 1929 was the street corner apple vendor (left). Thousands of unemployed turned to this means of earning a livelihood as job opportunities vanished for 13 million Americans. Other marks of the times were the shanty towns, often called "Hoovervilles," which sprang up on the outskirts of many cities (right). To the apple sellers and the inhabitants of these primitive, packing case hovels, the New Deal proposals, advanced during 1932 campaign by the Democrats, had immense appeal.

DEPRESSION AND NEW DEAL

Famed "One Hundred Days" of Roosevelt's administration changes nation

Increased unemployment and the failure of thousands of banks had spread panic throughout the nation in the four months between Franklin Roosevelt's election and his inauguration. Such an emergency required stringent measures. Thus, on the second day after his inauguration, the President called a bank moratorium: on the fifth, a special session of Congress. One of its first acts was the passage, on March 9, of legislation confirming Roosevelt's action in closing the banks. When the banks reopened the panic had been checked.

The bold nature of this initial move became the model for an unprecedented decade of New Deal leadership. It began with the famous "One Hundred Days" session of the Congress. Before it had run its course

the face of America had quite literally been changed. Many long established precedents had been shattered. The government had assumed a full measure of responsibility for the welfare of all the citizens, and had injected itself into areas previously considered beyond the province of the Federal establishment.

The actual work of the New Deal fell into three main categories — relief, recovery and reform. With the Federal Relief Administration, the Works Progress Administration (WPA) and the Public Works Administration (PWA) the government provided relief for millions. With the Securities Exchange Act, the Banking Acts of 1933 and 1935, the Social Security Act and others, the government forced unprecedented reforms. With

such measures as the National Industrial Recovery Act (NIRA), Gold Repeal and the Tennessee Valley Authority (TVA), the Agricultural Adjustment Act (AAA), the government manipulated the economy in an attempt to restore prosperity. Labor made its biggest strides under New Deal legislation.

Many of the experiments tried by the administration proved unworkable, others were judged unconstitutional, and many fell into disuse and disrepute when the country returned to prosperity with the onset of World War II.

Although the New Deal shocked many with its radical approach to national problems, its roots were traceable to William Jennings Bryan, the Pragmatists, the Progressives and Woodrow Wilson's New Freedom.

MOST ACTIVE first lady in the nation's history, Eleanor Roosevelt early displayed an avid interest in the welfare of the people. Although the semi-official nature of her position raised criticisms of her activities in many quarters, she refused to heed them. She is pictured, equipped with electric-lighted miner's cap, below ground in an Ohio mine on one of her tours.

OFFICIAL FAMILY portrait was taken during Christmas, 1939. Shown with the President are his wife, mother, three of his five children and four grandchildren. The activities of the Roosevelt children, particularly of "Sistie" and "Buzzie" Dall, children of the President's only daughter Anna, provided much feature material for newspaper readers throughout nation.

ROOSEVELT INTIMATE Harry Hopkins exerted tremendous influence during entire life of the New Deal. In early years a direct participant in the work of administering New Deal measures, he later became the "right hand" of the President and his closest friend and advisor.

MANAGER of successful Democratic campaigns in 1932-36, Postmaster General James A. Farley later broke with Roosevelt on third term issue. An old-line Democrat whose interest was politics, Farley put the New Deal in power but was given very little voice in its councils.

PERSONAL FRIEND of Roosevelt, Louis McHenry Howe, worked for his election, became secretary, predecessor of Harry Hopkins, following victory. More conservative than "brain trust" advisors who quickly surrounded President, Howe's influence on policies was negligible.

CONFIDENT SMILE of Franklin D. Roosevelt, often satirized by his enemies, was important part of the New Deal. The man who promised the nation a relentless attack upon the forces of depression sought to instill confidence by his own example. He pledged a fight against "our real enemies . . . hunger, want, insecurity, poverty and fear." The smile, plus the assurance that "failure is not an American habit" restored citizens' morale, which had reached a very low ebb during the depression.

"LABOR'S MAGNA CARTA" (Wagner Act of 1935) guaranteed labor's right to organize and bargain, created National Labor Relations Board which could halt unfair practices of employers. With FDR are (l. to r.) Rep. Peyser, Labor Sec'y Perkins, and Sen. Wagner of N.Y.

RUNNING MATE of Roosevelt was John Garner, who proposed emergency powers for President but later broke with him over third term. He was replaced by Wallace.

"OLD CURMUDGEON" Harold Ickes was New Deal stalwart. Sec. of Interior 1933-46, he also bossed PWA agency which spent vast sums in its "pump priming" projects.

ELDER statesman Bernard Baruch did not become early cabinet member as expected. His advice and counsel, however, were continually sought by Roosevelt administration.

PWA was scheme to bolster private construction companies, create jobs. Administrator Ickes (at controls) and Mayor LaGuardia (center) are shown at ground breaking ceremonies for low-rent housing project.

EARLY FAILURE of the New Deal was the NRA. Admittedly an experimental measure, it sought to curb competition by forcing "fair trade" codes upon business. Legalizing of monopoly practices proved unworkable and the cooperation of business ended when administration sought to bring newspapers under code. Supreme Court ruled NRA unconstitutional in 1935.

MOST POPULAR of New Deal experiments was Civilian Conservation Corps (CCC). It took young men off streets and put them to work building roads, planting trees and clearing land for conservation purposes.

IMAGINATIVE minds of nation's youth, captured by New Deal idea, responded with such organizations as the American Youth Congress. Above group went to Washington in 1937 to urge the passage of an American Youth Act.

RECOVERY PANACEAS blossomed from many a rostrum during depression. One of wildest was advanced by "Kingfish" Huey Long of Louisiana. He wanted government to adopt "share the wealth" program—give everyone $5,000 a year.

STOP-GAP measure was the issuance of emergency scrip by clearing houses. Printed to meet shortage created by depositors' rush on banks, quick end of the panic and return of previous withdrawals terminated short-lived usefulness.

SUPREME COURT declared first AAA and NIRA unconstitutional, tumbling basic New Deal pillars. Roosevelt met challenge with "court packing" bill in 1937. Congressional opposition, led by Sen. B. K. Wheeler, defeated it.

FARM POLICIES of New Deal were carried out by Secretary of Agriculture Henry Wallace (right). He directed "slaughter of the little pigs" and plowing under of cotton, wheat, etc., as a means of reducing the farm surplusses.

"PUMP PRIMING" of PWA shifted emphasis from housing projects like Bronx development (above) after 1938 to bigger things. Hoover, Norris, Bonneville and Grand Coulee dams were brought to completion with PWA funds.

TEST of New Deal popularity was 1936 election. In spring Roosevelt estimated his chances at "no better than 50-50," was proven wrong when Gov. Alfred Landon of Kansas carried only two states. Roosevelt's popular majority, over 11 million, was greatest in U.S. history.

"GREAT CRUSADE" of Republican candidate Wendell Willkie (center, hand upraised) in 1940 fell short of mark. He based campaign on opposition to New Deal policies, as had Landon, but failed to take issue with peacetime draft (adopted Sept., 1940). Willkie carried 10 states and cut Roosevelt majority to five million.

EMPHASIS on domestic problems began shifting in late 1930's to concern over growing tension in both Europe and Asia. Signs of conflict already underway, such as German-American Bund (l.), stirred Americans to debate on issue of American involvement. America First Committee worked vigorously before Pearl Harbor against Lend-Lease and draft policies of administration. Leaders of this movement, Sen. Burton K. Wheeler and Charles A. Lindbergh (right, saluting flag), backed "let 'em fight it out" attitude toward war. Attack on U.S. by Axis forces settled the issue and united the nation in an all out war effort.

NON-AGGRESSION PACT between Hitler and Stalin in 1939 confused American Reds and forced them into turnabout agreement with America First objectives. Nazi attack upon Russia in June, 1941, restored "line" to previous Fascist menace.

WOUNDED SURVIVOR of Japanese bombing of U.S. gunboat *Panay* in Yangtze River (1937) is carried to safety. American protest brought immediate apology, but shortly thereafter Japan slammed "open door" in China, pointedly warning U.S. to get out of Asia. Deterioration of Japanese-American relations led to clash of arms initiated by sneak attack on Pearl Harbor.

FIRST PEACE TIME DRAFT in nation's history, freezing of Japanese assets, and call of President for "arsenal of democracy" production effort increased fear of involvement in developing world conflict. Debate on Lend-Lease Act in Congress (March, 1941) evoked mothers' sit-down strike in Senate corridor (above). But Act was passed and first of $50 billion in lend-lease goods (arms and other equipment) began leaving United States ports.

SPECIAL ENVOY Saburo Kurusu of Japan (front) and Ambassador Nomura (behind him) leave office of Secretary of State Hull on morning of Dec. 7, 1941. Kurusu mission was to make last try at peaceful settlement of American-Japanese differences. Failing, he stalled until the Pearl Harbor attack.

CHARLES A. LINDBERGH posed in front of his Ryan monoplane, the *Spirit of St. Louis* at Curtiss Field, Long Island, on May 15, 1927, as the craft was being prepared for a solo dash across the Atlantic to Paris. As one of a group of airmen competing for the Raymond Orteig $25,000 prize for the first to complete such a flight, Lindbergh took off from Roosevelt Field at

7:52 A.M. Eastern time on May 20, 1927, in his heavily-loaded airplane. Thirty-three hours and 30 minutes later he landed at Le Bourget Airfield at Paris. Capturing the respect and admiration of the entire world by his feat, Lindbergh returned to New York to one of the most enthusiastic and tumultuous receptions (right) ever accorded an individual American.

ROMANCE OF FLIGHT

Spectacular world flights and technical developments herald air age

Aviation entered the 1920's in a precarious state, still not nationally recognized as a practical approach to the problem of human transportation and not accepted from the standpoint of safety or good business.

Early flights like the coast-to-coast non-stop dash of Macready and Kelly in 1923 began to awaken people of vision to the potential offered by the airplane. The backers of the Air Force as a separate national defense arm, like Gen. "Billy" Mitchell, saw the military importance of the airplane and proved in 1921 and again in 1923 that the

"invincible" battleship was no match for a bombing attack from the air. For their enthusiasm and belief, men like Mitchell were persecuted and ridiculed by top Army and Navy figures. The advance of aviation through the 1920's and 1930's gradually pushed the airplane as a weapon of war to a position of national importance.

Lindbergh's flight across the Atlantic in 1927 was an inspiration to every air-minded youth. National interest in aviation was stimulated by the electrifying feat of the daring young aviator.

Perhaps the greatest progress through this period was made in the realm of air transportation. Starting the postwar period with 90 mph DeHavilland DH-4 mailplanes, the airlines of the country gradually increased their network of routes, the efficiency of their operations and in the late 1930s were operating 21-passenger Douglas DC-3 aircraft at speeds up to 200 mph with unexcelled passenger comfort and safety. The air age was beginning to shrink the globe, to change people's lives and to alter considerations of international politics.

MAGELLANS OF THE AIR were the six courageous U.S. Army Air Service Lieutenants who first flew around the world. Pictured above are Leigh Wade, Leslie Arnold, Lowell Smith, Henry Ogden, Erik Nelson and John Harding who took off from Seattle, Wash., on April 6, 1924, in Douglas biplanes and returned Sept. 28 in 15 days, 11 hours, 7 minutes flying time.

PROPHET OF AIR POWER was William L. "Billy" Mitchell of the U.S. Air Service. From his wartime experiences as head of America's air arm overseas, Brig. Gen. Mitchell fully appreciated the potential of the modern military airplane as a dominant weapon of war. For his outspoken criticism of national defense policies Mitchell was court-martialed and suspended.

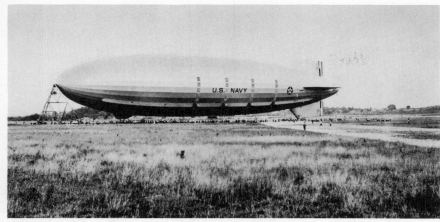

DIRIGIBLE "AKRON" is shown at launching in September, 1931. Built by Goodyear for U.S. Navy, this huge rigid airship featured storage space within hull for five aircraft and means of launching and recovering them. Conceived during the heyday of airship development the *Akron* was destroyed in April, 1933, during a storm at sea. Her sister ship, the *Macon* was lost in 1935 in a similar accident.

AMELIA EARHART, by her quiet but earnest enthusiasm for flying, cap-▶ tured the hearts of all America when she flew a Lockheed Vega monoplane solo from Harbor Grace, N. F. to Londonderry, Ireland, on May 20, 1932. Becoming the second person successfully to make the ocean flight alone she continued pioneering flights until 1937 when she was lost in the Pacific on a world flight.

ADMIRAL BYRD (center) and George Noville (right) are greeted by New York's "greeter" Grover Whalen during preparations for Atlantic crossing of tri-motor *America.* Flight started June 29, 1927, but adverse weather caused plane to crash near France June 30.

AIRLINE GROWTH was highlighted in 1938 when TWA inaugurated transcontinental service with the new Douglas DC-3. This airline had pioneered in the use of advanced aircraft types for passenger and mail service with the Douglas DC-1 and DC-2 series. Dwindling airmail subsidies forced the design and manufacture of more efficient carriers to attract revenue from passengers. These 12 DC-3s could carry 21 passengers each on 18-hour coast-to-coast schedules.

WILEY POST is shown just before take-off from Roosevelt Field, New York, on record shattering around the world flight June 23, 1931. With Harold Gatty as navigator, the *Winnie Mae* girdled the globe in eight days, 15 hours, 51 minutes while actual flying time totaled four days, 10 hours and 8 minutes for trip at an average 140 mph.

BENDIX RACE WINNER Ben O. Howard (center) is congratulated by Col. Roscoe Turner after Turner landed his Wedell racer only to find that Howard had beaten him from Los Angeles by a bare 23.5 seconds. This speed dash to Cleveland marked opening of the 1935 National Air Races held at Cleveland that year. Event encouraged design and construction of high speed aircraft in the U. S.

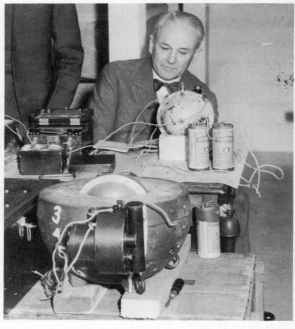

VANNEVAR BUSH, destined to become one of America's most celebrated scientists, won first acclaim for his work in building calculating devices. His differential analyzer, which solved complex equations, pointed the way toward the future's "electronic brain." An electrical engineer and physicist, Bush in 1939 was made president of Carnegie Institution, later directed the Office of Scientific Research and Development, became a leader in the field of atomic research.

ROBERT A. MILLIKAN won the 1923 Nobel Prize in Physics for measuring the charge on the electron and research in photoelectric effect. Head of California Institute of Technology, 1921-45, his "cosmic ray" and X-ray findings made history. He died Dec. 19, 1953.

SCIENCE AND MEDICINE

U. S. living changes as scientists produce cyclotron, nylon, sulfa drugs

While the people of the U.S. adjusted to the speed of the machine age, scientists across the nation emerged from their laboratories with discoveries and inventions which were to revolutionize the pattern of life throughout the world.

On the lighter side, men in the U.S. were slow to respond to the first electric dry razor, patented by Jacob Schick in 1928, but women flocked to beauty salons in 1924 to try the first permanent waves. The budding film industry flowered into color with Herbert Kalmus' Technicolor process

(1922) and to sound on film with Lee DeForest's invention in 1923.

On farm lands, farmers skeptically accepted the mechanical cotton picker of J. D. and M. D. Rust (1927), took more readily to the caterpillar tractor of 1931.

Across the U.S., "radio" and "autogiro" took their places in the nation's growing vocabulary, along with synthetic fabrics, vitamins, insulin, sulfa. Gilbert N. Lewis collaborated with Ernest O. Lawrence in inventing the cyclotron, which was to smash atoms, and helped to formulate the Lewis-

Langmuir theory of atomic structure and valence Pathologist Theobald Smith, whose contributions to animal pathology virtually wiped out epidemics among cattle, died in 1934, a scant year after being made president of famed Rockefeller Institute. To the widespread use of the first plastic, bakelite was added the first of the synthetic fabrics, casein, patented by Whittier and Gould in 1938. DuPont's nylon followed a year later. The speed of light had been remeasured, telephones had dials and psychoanalysis became popular among the wealthy.

SCIENTIST AND EDUCATOR Arthur H. Compton (above) with model of Piccard balloon-gondola, shared 1927 Nobel Prize in Physics with C. T. R. Wilson for discovery of "Compton effect," helped in development of atom bomb.

THIS HAPPY MAN INVENTED the cyclotron, first known as a "magnetic resonance accelerator," in 1931. For this, and studies in atomic structure and transmutation, Ernest O. Lawrence, at 38, won 1939 Nobel prize in physics.

MORE THAN 300 INVENTIONS in the realm of communications were credited to Dr. Lee De Forest (above, r.) "father of radio," whose audion tube led to development of "talking pictures," wirephotos, and television like this early model.

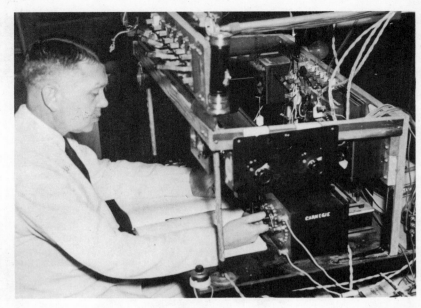

RADIO AND TELEVISION broadcasting owed much to Swedish-American scientist Ernst F. W. Alexanderson. His system of transoceanic radio telegraphy inspired the U.S., in 1920, to request formation of Radio Corp. of America to exploit it. Above, Dr. Alexanderson at home in 1928 with a radio picture receiver, forerunner of television he later helped to develop.

HAROLD C. UREY, who won the 1934 Nobel Prize in Chemistry for isolating heavy hydrogen, is shown here at work on the mass spectrometer which made isolation possible. Isolation of heavy isotopes of oxygen, nitrogen, carbon, sulphur followed. Authority on atomic, molecular structure, Urey directed research at Columbia; separated uranium isotope (U-235).

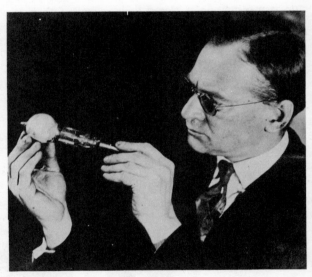

BRAZILIAN SWEET CORN, widely adopted by U.S. farmers, was one of many strains of hybrid corn developed by Henry A. Wallace, one-time editor of *Wallace's Farmer*. Like his father before him, he became U.S. Sec'y of Agriculture.

GEORGE WASHINGTON CARVER, Negro agricultural chemist, strove to better economy of South by soil improvement, diversified crops, use of by-products from peanuts, soybeans, potatoes.

ELECTRONIC WIZARD Vladimir K. Zworykin, subsequent inventor of TV's Iconoscope, first produced this thermionic photo-electric tube which, in 1925, he thought might make possible the transmission of motion pictures by radio. In 1933 he demonstrated television.

THOMAS HUNT MORGAN, GENETICIST

HARVEY W. CUSHING, SURGEON

ROSS G. HARRISON, BIOLOGIST

EDWARD C. KENDALL, BIOCHEMIST

MEDICINE
Medical research made enormous strides in the U.S. in the 20 years preceding World War II. The little-known subject of heredity was greatly clarified by the discoveries of Thomas Hunt Morgan, who won the Nobel Prize in Physiology and Medicine for his theory that hereditary characteristics are dependent on factors (genes) in chromosomes. Dr. Harvey Cushing was a pioneer of neurosurgery and neurology, proved that brain tumors could be removed successfully and did early research on functions and disorders of pituitary glands.

Also an author of note, Cushing won the Pulitzer Prize in 1925 for his *Life of Sir William Osler*, wrote numerous books on medical subjects. In the realm of biology, Dr. Ross G. Harrison's studies of tissue culture and peripheral nerves opened the way to the miracles of plastic surgery. Dr. Edward Kendall first gained recognition for his work with hormones in adrenal and thyroid glands, later discovered cortisone, used in the treatment of arthritis. He and another American, Dr. Philip Hench, were co-winners of the 1950 Nobel prize for medicine for their studies of hormones.

EDUCATION
BOOKS AND PRESS

Literary revolutionists of the 1920's, bitterly disillusioned by what now appeared a needless war, asserted that the old culture was dead. This "lost generation" maintained that their fathers' ideals had no relation to reality, that their values were outworn. Such writers as John Dos Passos and Sinclair Lewis, America's first Nobel Prize winner, attacked with bitterness and satire the smug complacency, the materialism and timid conformity of the middle class. Novelists such as James Branch Cabell sought escape in aestheticism and fantasy. Others, especially the group around Gertrude Stein (Ernest Hemingway most notably,) exalted the physical above the spiritual, and made a value of negation. F. Scott Fitzgerald and Thomas Wolfe pursued an anguished search for a body of beliefs in a cynical, hedonistic world.

With the depression of the thirties, writers such as James T. Farrell and John Steinbeck called the basic assumptions of American Society into question. Their descriptions of the pervasive spiritual poverty of people dehumanized by an industrialized society, were accompanied by earnest pleas for the betterment of mankind. The negative protests of the 1920s were replaced by the positive moral and social aspirations of the 1930s. Desperation and self-pity gave way to a belief in the potency of the state as the great instrument of social betterment.

Educational trends in the 1920's were being shaped by the revolutionary teaching methods of Columbia's John Dewey. He insisted that the principal aim of education should be socially useful adults "educated for life." Vocational education and manual training flourished as never before. Compulsory school attendance up to 16 and even 18 years of age was required by law in most states, and was strongly supported by public opinion. Accessible two-year junior colleges were provided in many states. State teachers' colleges multiplied, and graduate schools appeared in all larger universities. It was in the field of research that the universities' most successful achievements, in science and health, were recorded.

Paralleling trends in industry, merchandising and chain newspapers achieved their full stature in the post-World War I period. By 1933, despite the crush of the depression, and periods of unrest among printers and writers seeking better wage and working conditions, the Hearst chain had acquired some 30 newspapers, control of 2 wire services, the King Features Syndicate, 6 magazines, a newsreel, and a Sunday supplement, the *American Weekly*. The five other leading chains were Patterson-McCormick, Scripps-Howard, Paul Bloch, Ridder, and Gannett. These six controlled a total of 81 daily newspapers with a combined circulation of over 9,250,000.

STRIKING TEACHERS parading through the streets of Chicago in 1933 was a scene reenacted many times during the depression. Grossly underpaid, metropolitan teachers were yet often far better off than rural teachers. Many financially prostrate communities closed their schools. Others hired students as teachers.

JOHN STEINBECK'S deeply moving novel of American migratory workers in California, *Grapes of Wrath*, portrayed victims of the "Dust Bowl" and won the Pulitzer prize in 1940.

EDUCATIONAL TESTING and the measuring of differences in intelligence were developed in the U.S. by Columbia's Edward Lee Thorndike. He emphasized scientific methods.

POWERFUL MOLDERS of public opinion, Henry R. Luce (l.), editor of *Time, Life,* and *Fortune,* and Raymond Moley, *Newsweek,* helped to reshape news journalism. *Time* started in 1923, *Life* in 1936. *Newsweek* began in 1933.

SUCCESSFUL TABLOIDS featuring lurid crime, sex and feature stories were begun in 1919 by Joseph Medill Patterson with his New York *Daily News.* With liberal use of photographs, *News* topped all U.S. daily circulations by 1924.

IDOL-SHATTERING Henry L. Mencken (l.), editor of the *American Mercury* magazine from 1924 to 1933 ferociously attacked cherished beliefs and established institutions. Magazine was banned in Boston, causing his arrest (above).

FOUNDER of Chicago's famous Hull House, sociologist Jane Addams successfully experimented in improving civic, community life through settlement houses, the first of their kind in the U.S. Her writing on social reform and work for peace brought her the 1931 Nobel peace prize.

BITING SATIRE in Sinclair Lewis's *Main Street* and *Babbitt*, immensely popular novels of the 1920's, proved "Red" the most effective social critic of his generation. He was married to Dorothy Thompson (above), most famous woman columnist of the period, from 1928 to 1942.

BEST-SELLING novelist Edna Ferber's *So Big*, in 1924, *Show Boat*, 1926, and *Cimarron* in 1929, brought international recognition to the former newspaper woman who bypassed college for writing. She later turned playwright, collaborating on *Dinner At Eight* and *Stage Door*.

POET ROBERT FROST'S depiction of rural New England won him Pulitzer poetry prize in 1924, 1931, 1937, and 1943. Writing with a clarity and conversational ease that belied a richness in symbolism, Frost's *Mending Wall* exemplified his artistic grasp, belief in dignity of labor.

TRAGIC EFFECTS of World War I and the disillusionment that followed were most fully captured in the novels of Ernest Hemingway. Occupied with the theme of man mutilated by his environment, Hemingway's *A Farewell to Arms* expressed "lost generation's" cynical escapism.

GIFTED PLAYWRIGHT Eugene O'Neill's many successful plays all had complex psychological themes. Concerned with man's isolation and tragic illusions, such plays as *Strange Interlude* in 1928 were awarded the Pulitzer Prize. In 1936 he received the Nobel Prize in Literature.

NOVELIST-PLAYWRIGHT Thornton Wilder combined ingenious plotting with a polished style and won the Pulitzer Prize for his novel *The Bridge of San Luis Rey*, in 1928. Plays such as his 1938 Pulitzer award-winning *Our Town* were marked by intriguing touches of fantasy.

GONE WITH THE WIND, author Margaret Mitchell's (c.) only novel, won 1937 Pulitzer prize for its powerful narrative of Civil War and Reconstruction periods in Georgia. It was made into a highly successful motion picture starring Clark Gable and Vivien Leigh (above).

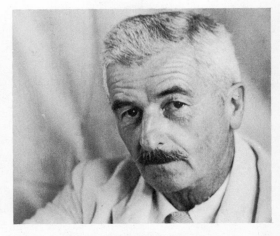

DECAY AND DISINTEGRATION of the Old South was the recurrent theme of William Faulkner, 1950 Nobel Prize winner. His highly stylized and complex novels, such as *Sound and the Fury*, 1929, were written in a subjective, often macabre vein, telling tales of violence.

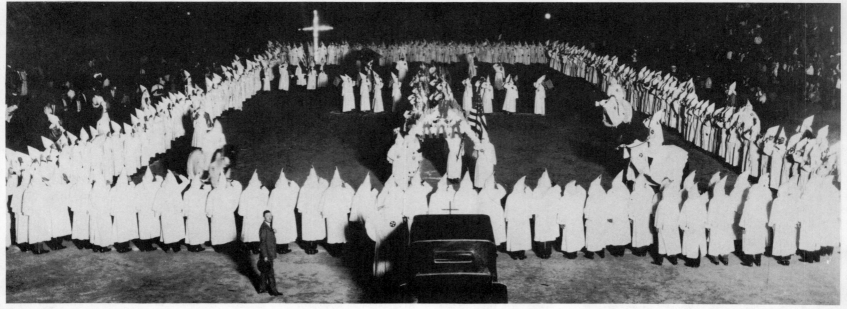

PREJUDICES garbed in cloaks and hoods and lighted by fiery crosses marked all the meetings of the Ku Klux Klan. Capitalizing on the period of unrest which followed World War I, the Second Ku Klux Klan was organized and with expert promotion expanded lucratively to four and one-half million members by 1924. It attempted to establish the supremacy of U.S. born, white, Protestant citizens. Its prejudices and excesses vented itself against Catholics and minorities in a program of fear and violence. States which had strong memberships were Oregon, California, Oklahoma, Texas, Arkansas, Indiana, Ohio. By 1930, public opinion denounced Klan and it dwindled. Attempts to revive it after World War II met police action.

AIMEE McPHERSON saved souls and "healed" the crippled with a new frenzied gospel which was publicized in neon lights. Involved in a kidnap hoax in 1926, Mrs. McPherson captured the headlines for several weeks and was brought to trial. She died in Oakland, Calif., in 1944.

RELIGION

Materialism vs. Church

With the end of World War I, people of the U.S. returned to peacetime existence in a highly materialistic world. The inroads of Prohibition and the general hysteria of the "flapper age" were symptomatic of an age restlessly in search of direction, hopeful of purpose, eager for miracle. The return to "formal religion" was less noticeable than the widespread popularity of "new" religions: Bahaists, who built a superstructure in Wilmette, Ill., 1931; Aimee Semple McPherson's "Four Square Gospel"; the accelerated growth of "Unity," "Christian Science," other philosophies with practical overtones helped offset growing cynicism.

MODERN RELIGIONIST, Harry Emerson Fosdick felt that creedal subscription to ancient confessions of faith was dangerous to church and individual's conscience. Given alternative to conform or leave First Presbyterian Church, N.Y.C., he left and headed Riverside Church.

SCOPE'S TRIAL Darrow and Bryan chatted amiably at test trial for teaching of evolution in schools. John T. Scopes, biology teacher, was the biology defendant in this test of the new Tennessee law in 1925. Bryan (r.), "silver tongued orator," took stand as Bible expert. Darrow was Scope's defender. The jury (r.) trial

was one of personalities and oratory rather than evidence. Expert testimony, both of science and religion, were excluded. At times the trial resembled a back woods debate. Scopes was convicted but sentence was set aside to prevent appeal to Federal courts. The trial was carefully reported to world readers who avidly read about Bible stories like Jonah and the whale.

WILSON DAM, the great Muscle Shoals project, was undertaken by the Federal Government during World War I. Power for making nitrates was the object. After the war, second dam was abandoned and completed dam became center of controversy. A bill for government operation was passed by Congress in 1928 (Norris Bill), but was vetoed by both Coolidge and Hoover. Power from dam was sold to private companies up to and during the depression. Norris Bill was signed by Franklin D. Roosevelt and the dam later became part of the larger Tennessee Valley Authority in 1933.

LABOR

Makes bid for strength

The struggle for power between labor and management was being fought strongly, sometimes bloodily, on the American industrial front between 1920 and 1940.

Breathing space for unionism was allowed through the Wagner Act of 1935 which guaranteed workers right to create and bargain through unions of their choice.

The CIO, a non-skilled labor union, evolved from AF of L trade unions in 1936.

Between 1920 and 1932 farm income declined from more than 15.5 billion to five and one-half billion dollars. By 1930 the total mortgage indebtedness of farms had risen to over 9 billion dollars. The American farmer was in grave difficulty and needed government assistance. Not until 1933 when the Agricultural Adjustment Act went into effect and Farm Credit was inaugurated, did "the nation's back-bone" receive a strong strong helping hand from the government.

Throughout the prosperous twenties child labor continued. The census of 1930 showed more than two million children under 18 years old were employed. Not until the New Deal were measures taken to end the scandal. Labor unions gained in strength during the 1930's after losing ground after World War I. Expanding unions became a political factor in elections during decade of the '30's.

LABOR LEADERS congratulate Sidney Hillman (c.), then member of the National Recovery Board. Hillman had just appeared before the Senate committee to testify for NRA. With him, A. F. of L.'s Green (l.), CIO'S Lewis (r.).

12,500,000 were unemployed in 1932 as the New Deal Administration tried to cope with immediate needs. U.S. was ripe for any radical ideology, Communism and Socialism gaining many members among hungry and unemployed.

LABOR GIANTS Philip Murray (l.) and John L. Lewis (r.), shake hands at CIO convention in Pittsburgh in 1937. Soft-spoken Murray and coal-miner's Bible-quoting Lewis were to guide the CIO for 14 years before Lewis broke away.

MIGRANT LABOR moved from the dust-bowl areas by thousands. Piling their possessions on autos, they traveled to other states following the crops and seeking work. Attracted by work leaflets and weather they swarmed to California.

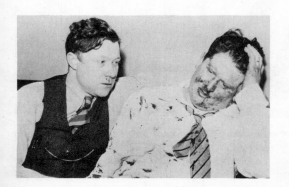

WALTER REUTHER comforts Richard Frankenstein (r.) after labor riot at Ford plant, in 1937. Reuther formed UAW-CIO which unionized auto and aircraft industry. Later, he was severely shot, but survived and became CIO president.

PREJUDICE was strong against everything foreign or radical. Sacco and Vanzetti were jailed for 7 years while trial for pay-master's murder progressed. Identification was never proven, yet the two men were executed for the murder.

BACK TO THE SOIL of Missouri went Thomas Hart Benton for his inspiration, after what he termed the "aesthetic drivelings and morbid self-concerns" of his Paris days. Shown here at his easel, the artist became one of the country's foremost painters of murals. His highly praised work in Missouri's State Capitol Building had at first brought him brickbats.

REGIONALISM gained impetus during the 1930's, after the example of such artists as Iowa's Grant Wood. His *American Gothic*, above, regarded as one of nation's best paintings, showed local scene could bear artistic fruit.

Modern Art Invades U. S.

American artists during the 1920's were still feeling shock waves generated by the Armory show in the previous decade. Many were employing the new French art forms — cubism, dadaism, fauvism, surrealism — with varying degrees of success, but finding little acceptance on the part of the general public.

Because it was understandable on sight, and needed no interpretation, the regional movement of Curry-Wood-Benton gained favor, but — critics asked — was it art, or merely illustration?

By the middle of the 1930's, however, the American public was becoming more sophisticated. Europe's new techniques were being assimilated and utilized by painters of the native scene to produce their own individual expressions. New forms in architecture and industrial design, in manufactured products and in advertising and packaging were familiarizing the layman with modern trends.

In New York, the opening of the Museum of Modern Art advanced the same cause. Of great importance was the creation of the Federal Art Project by the New Deal. Not only did it offer employment to some 5,000 artists in financial distress — it made the American public acquainted with living American art, by means of canvases and murals commissioned for government buildings, post-offices and courthouses throughout the country.

JOHN SLOAN'S meticulous etchings and oils (above, *Sixth Avenue El at Third Street*) and the water colors and tempera of Reginald Marsh (below, *Why Not Use the El?*) testified to the affection of both artists for New York in all its lively aspects.

SOCIAL REALISM as a school of painting came to the fore in the mid-30's. Then depression misery was exerting an emotional as well as economic effect on American artists, together with the threat of a second world war which loomed on the horizon. Ben Shahn's *The Passion of Sacco and Vanzetti* (left) was an excursion by the artist into earlier realms of social injustice. Philip Evergood, William Gropper, Jack Levine, Robert Gwathmey and Joseph Hirsch were other notable exponents of Social Realism, whose work had vitality and a sense of immediacy.

FROM KANSAS John Steuart Curry emerged with such sectional art as *The Tornado* (above) which gained popularity because it was instantly recognizable. Of perhaps higher quality was the work of another mid-westerner, Charles Burchfield, whose water-color depictions of the American scene were painted in the romantic tradition.

ORSON WELLES alarmed the U.S. in 1938 with a newsy radio-drama written as on-the-spot reporting of invasion from Mars. Show was a milestone in radio history, sparked trend toward suspenseful realism. With Welles, Dolores Del Rio.

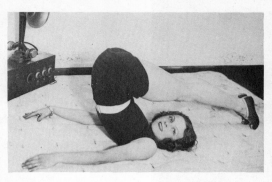

EARLY RADIO programming included a little of everything to keep the airlanes open. Of dubious popularity were daily "keep fit" shows announced to music. In 1925, actress Madeline Cameron helped to publicize radio's usefulness.

AMOS 'N' ANDY (Freeman Gosden, Charles Correll) started as *Sam 'n' Henry* on WMAQ, Chicago, 1928, became *Amos 'n' Andy*. They were networks' first nightly continuity show.

RADIO

Evolves major industry

In less than two decades, radio developed from an entertaining gadget to a major industry. Receivers changed from crude earphone and crystal sets to tubes and speakers, from battery-power to plug-in electricity. "Build-it-yourself" kits were snapped up by hordes of hobbyists. With the wider scope of "short wave," the amateur or "ham" emerged to build his own sending and receiving equipment.

The rapid success of KDKA, Pittsburgh, first radio station in the U.S. to air regularly scheduled programs, inspired a rash of small stations across the land. Resulting confusion brought formation, in 1927, of a Federal Radio Commission to assign specific wave lengths to the new stations.

In 1926, the first network, National Broadcasting Company, was organized as a subsidiary company of Radio Corporation of America. A year later, Columbia Broadcasting Company linked 16 stations. Its first broadcast Sept. 18, 1927, aired Edna St. Vincent Millay's "The King's Henchman" from WOR, New York, to KMOX, St. Louis.

By year's end, CBS had grossed $72,500.

TELEVISION Stations WGBS and W2XCR started regular broadcasts April 26, 1931, able to synchronize image and voice of performers like Fay Marbe. Same stations, NBC affiliates, were also first to telecast football (Sept. 9, 1939), used two cameras, one for closeups. Action was relayed from stadium to network's Manhattan transmitter by ultra short wave radio, then beamed out over a 50-mile radius from N. Y. C.

SPORTSCASTING and fast-talking Graham McNamee became synonymous as radio grew more mobile. To avoid "dead air" between innings, he interviewed sports stars such as Babe Ruth.

ELABORATE DRAPING in this 1922 broadcasting studio at KDKA was to serve as soundproofing. Radio officials even disguised microphones with lampshades as ruse to avert "mike fright."

CRYSTAL SETS like this one kept the nation spellbound in 1920-22. Table-model "tube" sets encased in box cabinets and powered by "wet" or dry-cell batteries supplanted these by 1923.

LAWRENCE COCKADAY, early radio engineer, lent his name to a circuit he devised which made this 1923 set possible. Cockaday circuit was standard equipment for "build-it-yourself" kits.

ROBERT LA FOLLETTE used radio in his 1924 Presidential try and polled nearly five million votes. First commercial broadcast in U.S. was Nov. 2, 1920 — KDKA aired Harding election.

RUDOLPH VALENTINO was the most sensationally popular of screen's great lovers. Women adored him as *Son of a Sheik*.

PEPPY DOUGLAS FAIRBANKS exemplified wholesome living in his brisk, athletic roles, unbeatable and undismayed in face of danger, fear.

THE TEN COMMANDMENTS established Cecil B. DeMille in 1924 as a director of the colossal superspectacle (in this case, with a simple moral). Theodore Roberts, holding staff, starred as Moses. Audiences thronged the box offices to see the parting of the Red Sea, and other DeMille techniques.

GLORIA SWANSON graduated from slapstick Mack Sennett comedy to roles of sophisticated woman of the world who "leads her own life."

SEX APPEAL, as criterion of personality, was glorified by Clara Bow, named "It" girl by author Elinor Glyn in 1920's.

MOVIES: FROM SILENT TO TALKIES

The Twenties glorified the screen's great idols. Public adulation was abundantly showered on Valentino, Gilbert, Barrymore, Fairbanks, Pickford, Colman, Swanson, Crawford and Garbo. Laughter created by Chaplin, Keaton, Lloyd, Rogers, Dressler and Mickey Mouse counteracted the heavy drama of Chaney, Cagney, Robinson, Hayes, and the spectacles of Cecil B. DeMille. Sex appeal (from flapper to sophisticated lady) was embodied in Bow, Harlow, West, Shearer. In 1927, the Academy of Motion Picture Arts and Sciences was founded, inaugurating its annual achievement awards.

A revolution occurred Oct. 6, 1927, when Warner Brothers' *The Jazz Singer*, with Al Jolson, introduced the "talkies." The silents were doomed and stars "without voices" would fade.

The Thirties and the depression created a demand for all-star casts, realism, social significance and glamorous musicals to America's theaters.

THE KID was Charlie Chaplin's longest and greatest picture to 1920. It introduced child star Jackie Coogan, who won overnight stardom as the waif who shared his woe.

HELEN HAYES won an Academy Award for her first film role in *The Sin of Madelon Claudet*, 1931, establishing her as one of screen's best actresses. (Above) *The Son-Daughter* (1932) with Ramon Navarro.

CHARACTER ACTOR Lon Chaney starred in off-beat macabre roles such as Quasimodo in Hugo's *The Hunchback of Notre Dame*, with Patsy R. Miller.

WILLIAM BOYD (later to become famous as Hopalong Cassidy) was a well-established star in 1929, appearing (c.) in *Painted Desert*. Bit player at right is Clark Gable.

HORN-RIMMED SPECTACLES were the familiar trademark of comedian Harold Lloyd, who won great popularity by playing a likable, earnest youth who always seemed to fall into unbelievable predicaments. Scene above, typical situation, finds him in *Hot Water*. *Grandma's Boy*, *Safety Last*, and *The Freshmen* were other hilarious hits.

WALT DISNEY first tried animation in 1920, making fairy-tale cartoons and series about Oswald the Rabbit. With his wife, he created a new character (1928) Mickey Mouse, who subsequently became an international favorite. *Steamboat Willie* had first sound.

LAUREL & HARDY began their zany comedy shorts in silent days, making films for Hal Roach. Their contrasting personalities and figures heightened comedy situations.

GRETA GARBO teamed with John Gilbert as the "screen's great lovers" in *Flesh and the Devil* (1927). A later triumph was her *Camille* (above) with the young actor, Robert Taylor.

HOMESPUN PHILOSOPHER and comedian was the dual role Will Rogers usually played, as in *Life Begins at 40*. With the talkies, his genial drawl, and warm comedy brought him fame.

JOHN GILBERT (r.) with his wife, actress Virginia Bruce (far left), Frederic March and Helen Hayes, failed in the "talkies," died tragically.

"COME UP AND SEE me sometime" was made famous by Mae West in Paramount's *She Done Him Wrong* (with Cary Grant), a remake of her bawdy play, *Diamond Lil*. Her first film was *Night After Night* in 1932.

SOPHISTICATED WOMAN of the world was one of many favorite characterizations of glamorous Norma Shearer (above, with Robert Montgomery, Herbert Marshall in MGM's *Riptide*). Married in 1927 to Irving Thalberg, Hollywood's esteemed producer, she starred with Leslie Howard in *A Free Soul* (1931) and *Romeo and Juliet* (1936).

PUBLIC ENEMY with James Cagney (l.) was typical of the "tough guy" films based on gangster crime of early '30's. Edward G. Robinson's *Little Caesar* set trend; later followed by dramatic G-man series.

THREE BARRYMORES (John, Ethel, Lionel) appeared together in 1932 in MGM's *Rasputin and the Empress*. Directed by Richard Boleslavsky, it was one of several films that dramatically treated former ruling heads of Europe as means of interpreting current social conditions in terms of the past.

JOAN CRAWFORD established the "flaming youth" type and her fame in *Our Dancing Daughters* (1928), then continued successfully in *Grand Hotel* (1932), and *Rain* (above, with Walter Huston).

KATHARINE HEPBURN, fresh from Broadway, disregarded Hollywood rules by making *A Bill of Divorcement* (1932) with John Barrymore, which was a hit. In 1933 she won Award for *Morning Glory*.

PLATINUM BLONDE Jean Harlow (with William Powell) personified fiery sex appeal when she rose from minor parts in 1930 to star in *Hell's Angels,* produced by unknown Howard Hughes. In MGM's *Dinner At Eight,* she held her own with Wallace Beery and the Barrymores. She died in 1937.

RUTHLESSNESS of big business journalism exposed in *Five Star Final* (1931), starred Edward G. Robinson, Boris Karloff. The same year, Robinson established himself in gangster roles in *Little Caesar.*

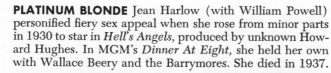

SHIRLEY TEMPLE sang, danced, charmed her way into the hearts of America to become the films' greatest child star in the 1930's. In *The Little Colonel* (1935) she danced with Bill "Bojangles" Robinson, and (above) performed with Jimmy Durante.

PRISON tyranny and brutality were exposed in the realistic and socially significant *I Am a Fugitive From a Chain Gang*. Movie was based on authentic experience and directed with vigor and conviction by Mervyn LeRoy. Paul Muni was starred.

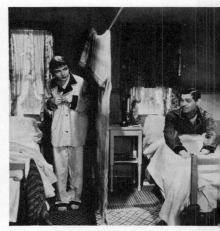

MARLENE DIETRICH became known as Director Josef von Sternberg's *femme fatale*. An obscure music hall singer when she sang *Falling In Love Again* in his German-made *The Blue Angel* (1930) opposite Emil Jannings, she later starred in six of his films made in the U.S.

TOPSY-TURVY went the movie industry when the "talkies" were made a success by Al Jolson in Warner Brothers' *The Jazz Singer*, 1927 (above with May McAvoy). Not an all-talking picture, it made Jolson a star, solved Warners' financial problems.

FAMOUS AUTO CAMP scene with the "Walls of Jericho"spiced Frank Capra's *It Happened One Night* (1934), with Claudette Colbert, Clark Gable. Film won five awards.

MAX REINHARDT repeated his opulent stage production of *A Midsummer Night's Dream* in a million-dollar-plus film version with music, ballet for Warner Bros. (1934). Mickey Rooney, Arthur Treacher, James Cagney, Hugh Herbert, Joe E. Brown starred.

SINGING TEAM of Nelson Eddy and Jeanette MacDonald delighted audiences for many years in such musical favorites as *Maytime* (above), *Bittersweet*. Her first role was with Maurice Chevalier in Lubitsch's *Love Parade* (1929).

GOLDWYN GIRLS, "the most beautiful girls this side of heaven," surrounded Eddie Cantor in the musical *The Kid From Spain*. Seated on left is Paulette Goddard. Cantor made screen debut in *Kid Boots*.

BORIS KARLOFF, succeeding Lon Chaney, made spines tingle as the monster *Frankenstein* (1931). Sequel followed.

OF HUMAN BONDAGE made young actress Bette Davis (with Leslie Howard) a star in RKO's production of W. Somerset Maugham's novel. She later won Oscars in 1935 for *Dangerous,* and 1938 for *Jezebel*.

SCREEN'S MOST FAMOUS dance team, Ginger Rogers and Fred Astaire, began their career in 1933 in *Flying Down to Rio* when Astaire's sister, his partner, retired. Other hits: *Top Hat, Gay Divorcee*.

TARZAN was played by swimming champ Johnny Weissmuller, whose large juvenile following made his sequels very successful.

JOHN STEINBECK'S *Of Mice and Men* was a powerful drama of migrant farm hands, directed by Lewis Milestone (1939) with Lon Chaney, Junior.

ALL-WOMAN, all-star cast gave spice and breezy comedy to Clare Boothe's satire *The Women* (1939). Director Cukor was kept busy with Norma Shearer, Joan Crawford, Rosalind Russell, Fontaine, others.

INTERMEZZO'S poignant love story was an excellent vehicle to display the talents of Ingrid Bergman and Britisher Leslie Howard.

GREER GARSON'S ladylike charm was introduced to America in English-made *Goodbye Mr. Chips* (1939) with Robert Donat. Above, *Remember*, with Ayres, Taylor.

BIGGEST MONEY-MAKER and winner of most Academy Awards (10) was David O. Selznick's *Gone With the Wind*, for which he won Thalberg Memorial Award. Named "Best Production" of 1939, it starred Vivien Leigh (c. "Best Actress"), Clark Gable (r), Leslie Howard, Hattie McDaniel ("Best Supporting Actress"). Victor Fleming's direction, Sidney Howard's screenplay won awards.

IDEALISTIC SENATOR was a tailor-made triumph for the youthful, family's favorite, James Stewart, in Frank Capra's *Mr. Smith Goes to Washington* (1939) with Jean Arthur. Foster's story won an Academy Award.

EARLY AMERICANA was the virile subject of *Northwest Passage*, which audiences enjoyed as much as they did Kenneth Roberts' best-selling novel, filmed by MGM in 1940 with Spencer Tracy (c.) and Robert Young (r.). Vidor directed, Stromberg produced.

DAVID SELZNICK'S *Rebecca* won the Academy Award as "Best Production" of 1940 due to Alfred Hitchcock's direction, expert acting by Laurence Olivier, Joan Fontaine (who emerged a star), and Judith Anderson.

AUDIENCES ENJOYED seeing small-town native Gary Cooper triumph over big-city business in the satirical, witty *Mr. Deeds Goes to Town* (1936). Frank Capra won the Academy Award for direction. Jean Arthur starred with Cooper.

GAY CABALLEROS, gunfighting in Old Mexico was the colorful setting of *Viva Villa*, an amusing biographical account of the Mexican bandit-revolutionist. Masters of rugged humor, Wallace Beery and Leo Carillo starred in the epic.

ANOTHER BEST-SELLER *Anthony Adverse*, was brought to the screen by director Mervyn LeRoy (r.). A vigorous craftsman, he is shown here examining the Hervey Allen saga with his stars, Fredric March and Olivia de Havilland.

LOUIS ARMSTRONG, rasp-voiced "great" of jazz music, won success as instrumentalist, composer. Flexible style with trumpet grew out of early *ad libs* in New Orleans jazz. Nicknamed "Satchmo," Armstrong formed his own band, played theater dates and amassed a fortune from recordings, radio, films. Here, he appeared in N. Y. stage show with Maxine Sullivan.

SWING MUSIC, another syncopated offshoot of "jazz," was the special province of clarinetist Benny Goodman (r.), known as "King of Swing" in late 1930's. In 1938, Goodman gained new recognition for his "Swing Concert" in N. Y.'s Carnegie Hall. Goodman's band was training ground for musicians. Here (l. with hat) Gene Krupa, next to Harry James.

SYMPHONIC BLUES received full treatment from Duke Ellington, whose musicianship and extensive wardrobe won him his lordly title. Composer of *Sophisticated Lady* and *Mood Indigo*, which were to become classics in the "modern" idiom, showman Ellington favored large bands, solo instrumentalists. His large repertoire included "sweet" and "hot" arrangements.

SYMPHONIC JAZZ, introduced by Paul Whiteman in the early '20's, earned him the title "King of Jazz." A pioneer in adapting jazz to symphonic arrangement and orchestration, Whiteman frequently used 100 pieces for dramatic effect. Whiteman is remembered for introducing George Gershwin's *Rhapsody in Blue*, which became jazz classic at concert in 1924.

"IS EVERYBODY HAPPY?" Ted Lewis' salutation to devotees, was as much a trademark for his popular band as were his battered top hat and prancing showmanship. His band followed popular trends and accented his clarinet solos.

TOMMY DORSEY specialized in smooth dance rhythms, jazz and swing. A trombonist, he differed with brother Jimmy, a clarinetist, whose interpretations were considered "sweet." The Dorsey brothers oftentimes combined talents.

CAB CALLOWAY made "hi-de-ho" part of jazz lingo. Star of N. Y.'s Cotton Club for years, he built loose-limbed dancing and acrobatic conducting into fame and fortune. Also a competent actor, he starred in premiere of *Porgy and Bess*.

RUDOLF FRIML contributed many successful light operas to American music, his *Vagabond King* (1925) among most remembered, partly because Rudy Vallee, U.S.'s first song stylist to be called crooner, used title-tune as theme song.

TUNESMITH Jerome Kern added film scores and smash-hit songs to his pace-setting musical comedies: *Showboat* (1929), *Cat and the Fiddle* (1927), *Roberta* (1933). Songs like "Ol' Man River," "Smoke Gets In Your Eyes" were hits.

GEORGE GERSHWIN'S influence on "modern" music was difficult to measure. From early jazz, piano-playing Gershwin created symphonic tone poems like *American in Paris*, moody piano concerto *Rhapsody in Blue*, opera *Porgy and Bess*.

STOKOWSKI capitalized on his expressive hands, conducted symphony orchestras with dramatic flourish. With Walt Disney, who tried to picture music mood on film with shades and color, Stokowski led huge orchestra for *Fantasia*, broke with "purists" in classic interpretations.

JAZZ AGE

Although American music had always been distinctive, it had never exerted noticeable influence outside the U.S. until World War I's "doughboys" carried the unique idiom of jazz to France. George Cohan's *Over There* went with them, small token of the infinite stream of ballads still to flow from his facile pen. The "Jazz Age" of the 20's arrived on a syncopated beat. A decade later, nationwide depression lent new meaning to the "blues." "Popular" music rose from dance floor to Carnegie Hall, where Benny Goodman gave new meaning to "swing."

Radio, in the same two decades, became a "name maker." From tenor in a trio with Gus Arnheim's band, a singer named Bing Crosby emerged to threaten Rudy Vallee's position as America's only "crooner."

Composer George Gershwin wrote folk opera; Deems Taylor put music to Edna St. Vincent Millay's long poem, "King's Henchman," and went on to more pretentious opera-fare in *Peter Ibbetson*. It was an era of "boom" and "bust," but one of the richest creative periods in U.S. music history.

TOSCANINI, Italy's reigning conductor, was also the most revered musician in America. Regarded as "The Maestro," he brought international prestige to N. Y. Philharmonic Orchestra, conducted opera orchestras at La Scala and N. Y. "Met." Here, in 1926, with daughter, wife.

XANTIPPE, as interpreted in 1928 by Sophie Tucker, America's jazz queen, at a charity affair in London. The indestructible Sophie, who was to become "the last of the red-hot mammas," made up in volume what she lacked in voice. She was honored for 50 years in show business.

CRITIC-COMPOSER Deems Taylor (l.) shared applause with Metropolitan Opera stars Lucrezia Bori, Edward Johnson, Lawrence Tibbett (r.) at 1933 debut of his opera *Peter Ibbetson*, which opened season in depression-struck N. Y. Taylor rated nationally as dean of music critics.

HOMEYNESS, a competent soprano voice and skillful management of Ted Collins (l.) lifted Kate Smith to radio's top-rated hour-long show. Among first women to announce or narrate a big network show, she was followed by others, most important being Mary Margaret McBride.

THEATRE

Experimental ideas tried on stage

Roaring Twenties saw an unparalleled exploration into the realms of literature and ideas in the theater.

There were musicals of all descriptions, from Irving Berlin's first *Music Box Review* in 1921, to George White's *Scandals* and Earl Carroll's *Vanities* in 1923, Vincent Youman's *Hit the Deck* and Rodgers' & Hart's *A Connecticut Yankee*, in 1926-27. But the honors (and three Pulitzer prizes) of the decade went to Eugene O'Neill. Pauline Lord played *Anna Christie* in his first popular success; after that came *The Emperor Jones* and *The Hairy Ape*, *The Great God Brown*, *Marco Millions*, and in 1928, *Strange Interlude*.

William A. Brady came out of retirement to produce the 1929 Pulitzer prize-winning *Street Scene* by Elmer Rice; Preston Sturges' *Strictly Dishonorable* also made a sensation.

The Green Pastures of Marc Connelly was 1930's unexpected smash. 1932 brought *Of Thee I Sing* by Morrie Ryskind, the Gershwins and George Kaufman. *You Can't Take It With You* was the collaborative effort of Moss Hart and Kaufman. Robert Sherwood came into his own with *Petrified Forest* and *Idiot's Delight*; the Group Theater produced such dramas as Clifford Odets' *Waiting for Lefty*. Thornton Wilder's *Our Town* won 1938 Pulitzer prize.

POPULAR IN AMERICA from her 1924 debut in Charlot's Review was English comedienne, Gertrude Lawrence (below). Talented singer and dancer, she excelled in sophisticated comedy, was tremendously successful in Noel Coward's *Private Lives* and *Tonight at 8:30*, hits of the mid-30's. Great charm came with her ability to project emotion, warmth, intimacy.

ETHEL WATERS' unique artistry developed over a long career of singing in cabarets during 1920's, came to full expression in her starring role in *Mamba's Daughters*.

TWO HAMLETS starred on Broadway in 1936. John Gielgud and Leslie Howard were rival Danes. Shakespearean success of 1937 was Maurice Evans' *King Richard II*.

MICHAEL TODD'S *Hot Mikado* featured an all-Negro cast, including Bill Robinson (wearing derby). 1939 was also the year of the N. Y. World's Fair, of Olsen and Johnson's *Hellzapoppin, The Philadelphia Story* with Katherine Hepburn, and Katharine Cornell's *No Time For Comedy. Life With Father* began its theatrical run.

"I GOT RHYTHM," sang Ethel Merman in 1930's *Girl Crazy,* and stopped the ▶ show. Lusty Merman style was surefire draw in *Anything Goes* to *Red, Hot and Blue, DuBarry Was A Lady, Panama Hattie.* Career of another personality, George M. Cohan, spanned years from vaudeville at turn of century to acclaim for acting in 1933's *Ah, Wilderness* and his song and dance stint in *I'd Rather Be Right.*

SCHMALTZ, burnt cork, and great showmanship enabled Al Jolson to become nation's favorite movie singer. The *Jazz Singer* and Warner's Vitaphone pioneered talking pictures. Jolson made comeback shortly before his death.

HENRY HULL was the first Jeeter Lester in *Tobacco Road,* the Erskine Caldwell play which confounded critics by playing 3,182 performances in the face of repeated attempts by church authorities to have it banned for what they termed obscenity.

"ISN'T IT A comfort to know they're married?" remarked one old lady in the audience of Alfred Lunt's and Lynn Fontaine's *The Guardsman.* Between Broadway plays, this favorite show couple went on road tours.

HER LEAST successful play was Tallulah Bankhead's *Anthony & Cleopatra.* Not until 1939, in Lillian Hellman's *The Little Foxes,* did she find a role completely suited to her talents. A spectacular "private" life contributed to her fame.

JOHN BARRYMORE'S *Hamlet* had a record run for Shakespearean performances in 1922. Away from theater for 18 years in Hollywood, he returned to do what critics called a painful caricature of himself in *My Dear Children.*

HELEN HAYES was a trouper from her childhood on. Jed Harris starred her in *Coquette* in 1928. Her most memorable performance was as *Victoria Regina* in 1935, wherein she performed feat of gradually aging 60 years during the play.

FABULOUS KING of the Roaring '20s, sports' golden era, was Babe Ruth. Babe did not invent the home run, but it became his trademark. The results were happy for baseball, which prospered as never before; for the Yankees, scourge of the majors, and for Ruth, whose $80,000 salary was larger than Pres. Hoover's. Babe hit 60 homers in his best season.

RECORD WORLD SERIES RALLY came in fourth game of 1929 classic when Connie Mack's A's scored 10 runs in seventh inning to beat Cubs, 10-8. Here, Al Simmons crosses plate on homer which started rally. Athletics took the Series in five games.

LARRUPIN' LOU Gehrig played in the shadow of the great Babe Ruth for years. Quietly, as became him, the "Iron Horse" built up reputation as one of the greatest first basemen. He played in 2,130 consecutive games before fatal illness.

SPORTS
In 1920's

PROFESSIONAL HOCKEY came into its own in this country in the mid 1920s. It was at this time that Boston, Chicago, New York and Detroit entered the league, and the World Series of hockey, the Stanley Cup playoffs, were instituted. A fast, rough game, ice hockey caught on quickly in United States despite fact that nine of every 10 players were Canadian-born.

TWO FIGURES dominated football scene during the 1920's — Red Grange as player and Knute Rockne as coach. Grange, the famed "Galloping Ghost," was All-American three years at Illinois before becoming one of pro football's biggest drawing cards. Rockne, born in Norway, starred in football at Notre Dame and took over the coaching reins of the Irish in 1918. In the next 13 years, until his untimely death in a plane crash in 1931, Rockne's teams won 105 games, lost only 12 and tied five. In that period five of his teams had unbeaten seasons. Rockne introduced Notre Dame shift and grid innovations.

CHANNEL SWIMMING made big headlines in 1926 when Gertrude Ederle became the first woman to swim the English Channel. She accomplished the feat in record time. Her swim was major event of golden era. She returned in triumph, was given traditional N. Y. ticker-tape parade, then quietly retired to sedate private life.

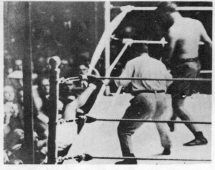

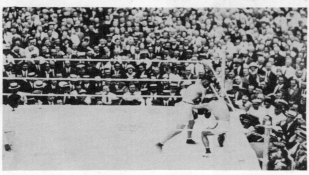

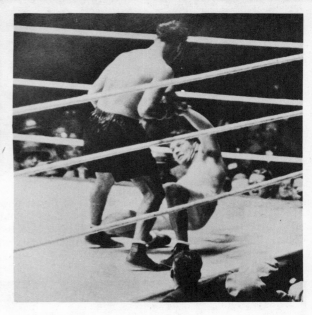

DEMPSEY

Boxing boomed during the 1920's, thanks largely to the smashing fists of the Manassa Mauler, Jack Dempsey. He was in three of the great fights of all time in this decade, and was largely responsible for the first million-dollar gates boxing had known. It was a golden era literally for the crowd-pleasing Dempsey, who earned more than $3 million. Left, Dempsey experienced one of his bad moments. He is shown just after being knocked out of the ring by Luis Firpo. Dempsey returned, disposed of his huge foe in second round in what was termed greatest fight of century. The first million-dollar gate resulted when promoter Rickard matched slugger Dempsey with boxer Carpentier (center). It was poor fight, but grossed $1,728,-238. Right, famous long-count begins in 1927 bout with Tunney. Dempsey hesitated . . . and lost.

BIG MAN IN TENNIS in an age of sports giants was "Big Bill" Tilden (l.). Tilden was 27 before he won first U.S. title, won seven in all, was ranked first nationally for 10 straight years.

GRAND SLAMMER extraordinary in golf was Robert Tyre Jones, greatest golfer of the '20s, who in 1930 startled the sports world by winning U.S. and British Amateur and Open titles.

MASTER PRO of golf was Walter Hagen, a winner of every major tourney at least once. He won U.S. Open twice, British Open four times, and was P.G.A. champ for four straight years.

GREAT AGE OF SPORT was not without its great horse and its great jockey. The horse, Man O' War, lost only one of 21 races. Earl Sande, the jockey, specialized in winning the biggest race of all, the Kentucky Derby. Here Sande is shown on his third Derby winner, Gallant Fox.

ROCKNE'S BEST TEAM was unbeaten 1924 aggregation with its famous "Four Horsemen." Backfield was nicknamed by the famous sports writer, Grantland Rice.

ORIGINAL CELTICS were considered the best professional basketball team of the 1920's. Originally organized as a New York Community House team, the Celtics played together with few personnel changes until 1928. Among Celtic players were Joe Lapchick and Nat Holman, who later gained fame as college, pro coaches.

QUEEN OF THE COURTS in the 1920's was "Miss Poker Face," Helen Wills, who won her first American championship in 1923, repeated in 1924 and 1925, then, after a lapse of one year, won three more championships from 1926 through 1929. She also dominated the European competition, winning Wimbledon tourney three straight years, starting in 1927.

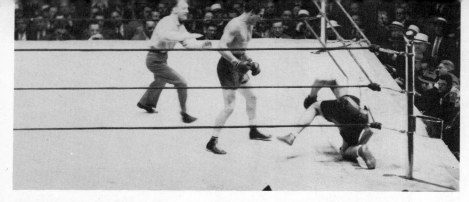

BIG QUESTION in boxing in the early 1930's was: how good is the Italian giant, Primo Carnera? Even after Carnera whipped Jack Sharkey for the world title in 1933, question persisted. Then, on June 14, 1934, Max Baer provided answer. He cut down the giant Carnera and the myth of invincibility with an 11-round knockout.

PLAYBOY Max Baer's heavyweight reign was brief. One year after Baer gained title, Jimmy Braddock came off relief in one of the ring's amazing comebacks to lift the crown. Braddock decisioned Baer, who "trained in night clubs," in a slow 15-round bout.

DOWN AND OUT went supposedly invincible Joe Louis in 12th round of his 1936 fight with Max Schmeling. Boxing had its biggest surprise of the decade and Louis his first loss, a temporary halt in rise to ring greatness.

Louis reached ultimate goal in 1937 with an eight-round KO of champion Jim Braddock. Then came return bout with Schmeling. Revenge was quick. Joe dances (above) as referee signals the end in 2:04 of first round.

SPORTS
In 1930's

"DREAM" MATCH RACE was held at Pimlico in 1938 to decide which was greatest horse — Seabiscuit, biggest money winner of 1930's, or 1937 triple-crown winner War Admiral. Seabiscuit set track record in pounding to victory to earn recognition as greatest since Man O' War.

JESSE OWENS ruled supreme among sprinters in 1930's. A triple winner in 1936 Olympics, Owens earlier had set three world's records and tied one in one afternoon in college competition.

LOUIS MEYER and Wilbur Shaw shared honors in Indianapolis 500-mile Memorial Day race classics during 1930's. Meyer (above after winning 1933 race) won in '33 and '36, while Shaw triumphed in '37, '39. Meyer was first triple winner, honor shared by Shaw with 1940 win.

PATTY BERG scored double triumph in 1938 by winning women's Western Amateur and U.S. Amateur titles. Earlier in decade Virginia Van Wie headed women's golf with three U.S. titles.

"LITTLE" grand-slam was feat of Lawson Little, who won U.S., British amateur titles in 1934-35. Later won U.S. Open as a professional.

GREATEST U.S. woman athlete of modern age, Babe Didrickson, first starred in track, then switched to golf. She is shown in the 1932 Olympics.

DON BUDGE scored tennis "grand slam" in 1937 by winning U.S., British, French and Australian amateur titles. He teamed with Gene Mako to take U.S., British doubles titles.

COLLEGE FOOTBALL reached new heights in popularity in 1930's while professional football came into its own as a major sport. One of the greatest of college stars was All-American Tom Harmon (above), of Michigan, whose feats led to inevitable comparison with immortal "Red" Grange. On best day against California Harmon had runs of 94, 72, 86, and 80 yards.

CENTER OF CONTROVERSY on U.S. 1936 Olympic team was swim star Eleanor Holm (r.), who was ousted from team for drinking champagne on ship while enroute to games in Berlin. She had won women's 100-meter backstroke title at 1932 Olympics in Los Angeles. U.S. stars dominated the two Olympics, winning 11 track championships in 1932 and 12 in 1936.

ONE OF GREATEST and most enduring pro football stars was Sammy Baugh, whose bullet passes sparked Washington Redskin offense. He first starred at Texas Christian U.

BRONKO Nagurski was not misnamed. He was pro football's most ferocious fullback in '30's, an all-league tackle on defense, also a well-known pro wrestler.

TARZAN AND THE DUKE (Johnny Weissmuller, left, and Duke Hananamoku) dominated the sprint field in swimming for 16 years. Here they pose during the 1932 Olympic swimming team tryouts. Weissmuller's record for the 100-meter sprint event withstood all challenges through the 1930's. Later he traded on reputation as swim king to star as Tarzan in movies.

SLUGGER Hank Greenberg helped Detroit win two pennants in the 1930's and led American League in homeruns with 58 in 1938, two short of Babe Ruth's all-time record.

TWO FACTORS in amazing record of four world's titles in a row by New York Yankees in 1936 to 1939 were sluggers Lou Gehrig (l.) and Joe DiMaggio. Domination of the World Series by New York led to a frantic cry of "break up the Yanks."

BOY WONDER Bob Feller joined Cleveland Indians in 1936 at age of 18. In 1938 he set new record for number of strikeouts in a game (18) and pitched one-hitter same year.

FABULOUS FIGURE of the '30's was Dizzy Dean. In 1934 Dean, with some help, principally from brother Paul, pitched Cardinals into the World Series, winning 30 games, a total unequalled since.

LINDBERGH KIDNAPPING

Nation was shocked March 1, 1932, when the infant son of flying hero Charles A. Lindbergh was kidnapped from his crib. Lindbergh paid $50,000 ransom to kidnapper, but child was not returned. Posters were circulated (c.) to speed search, but 72 days later the baby was found dead. Two years passed before Bruno Hauptmann (r., shown in center without tie) was arrested on Sept. 19, 1934, with part of the ransom money. Hauptmann, confronted by Lindbergh (l., entering courthouse to face suspect), maintained he was innocent. A jury, however, convicted Hauptmann and he was sentenced to die for murder. Trial excited the nation as radio and press capitalized on sensationalism. Hauptmann, after brief reprieve, was executed for crime April 3, 1936. Public indignation over the kidnapping resulted in Congressional passage of federal "Lindbergh Law" providing death penalty for convicted kidnappers.

CRIME

BENEFICIARY of 18th Amendment was Al Capone (c.) shown here in one of his brushes with the law before indictment for income tax evasion in 1931. "Scarface" terrorized Chicago in the 1920's with his crime syndicate which controlled vice and gambling, with enormous profit.

FAMED CRIMINAL LAWYER Clarence S. Darrow (center foreground) saved Richard Loeb and Nathan Leopold (behind Darrow) from death penalty after they pleaded guilty to the "thrill slaying" of young Bobby Franks in 1924. No Darrow clients were ever sentenced to die.

$30,000 FLORAL TRIBUTE in a procession of 100 autos blocked all traffic in Chicago's Loop, marking funeral of Vincent Drucci, Chicago gangster. Mass turnout included mobsters of all Windy City gangs, dignitaries, American Legionnaires, and Company B of Fort Sheridan.

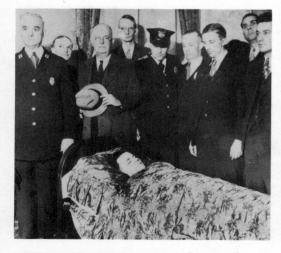

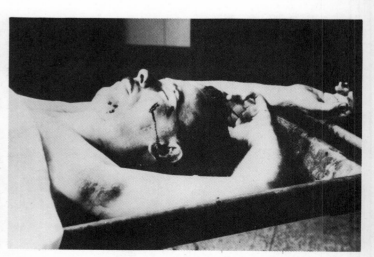

"PRETTY BOY" FLOYD wanted more than a farm could offer and tried to get it with a gun. Born on farm in Georgia, Charles Floyd was robbing banks in early 1930's. Eventually he was involved in murder, most notorious being machine-gunning in which five men were killed.

LIFE BY THE GUN resulted in death by the gun for John Dillinger, midwest bank robber and killer. Police and the F.B.I. hunted Dillinger as Public Enemy No. 1 in 1933-34. His many escapes and changes of identity marked him as no ordinary thug. Plastic surgery and altering fingerprints with acid were resorted to by the fugitive. He is shown at left with the wooden gun he used in making one daring jailbreak. End came in hail of bullets from F.B.I. agents' guns outside a Chicago theater, July, 1934. He and his gang were responsible for 16 murders and numerous thefts amounting to $300,000.

ANTI-ALCOHOL demonstration on Capitol steps by members of the Anti-Alcohol Congress explained that liquor was unhealthy and against American standards. 18th Amendment was enacted by pressure from such groups and the urgency to conserve grains and spirits during World War I.

LAST BOTTLES of liquor were sold before 18th Amendment became effective. Shelves were cleared and legal manufacture, sale, export and import were declared unlawful on Jan. 16,1920. Illegal sales and manufacture began immediately in such volume authorities were unable to control them.

CLEVER AGENTS were required to ferret out speakeasies and sly grog-shops. Izzy Einstein and Moe Smith posed as innocent drunks to gain entry; employed humor as shown by gag photo.

PROHIBITION
The era of speakeasies

Temperance societies developed rapidly in the 1900's. Since Carrie Nation, the most heart-tugging subject in literature and etching was the dissolute father and the pitiable child in the "Father, dear father, come home with me now—" theme. For 100 years, state and local government had experimented with prohibition in various forms. Maine had been a leader in the idea.

The 18th Amendment was passed on January 29, 1919, effective one year later. Its application over so large an area made it one of the most difficult experiments of modern times. Geography of U.S. protected illegal practice in some areas and the fact that government agents could not carry arms (until 1924) made enforcement a personal hazard. The law created crime syndicates, who, after repeal, turned their members loose on the nation to commit crimes of robbery, kidnap, and murder.

The Democrats adopted campaign planks in their 1928 and 1932 platforms calling for repeal of the 18th Amendment. The Republicans, although admitting changes were needed, continued to advocate prohibition.

In 1933, the 21st Amendment was ratified —the great experiment was over.

EXTREMELY FISHY cargo was discovered on the *Annie Louise* in 1924. Decaying fish covered "Scotch" whiskey from Havana worth $40 thousand. Quality was usually low, often deadly.

"RIGHT OFF THE SHIP" usually meant distilled in a local basement somewhere in the suburbs. This "rot gut" still was assembled from an assortment of laundry tubs and gas pipes.

BEER GUSHED like "Old Faithful" after being confiscated by federal agents. Millions of dollars worth of beer, wine, whiskey were destroyed, but the bootleggers still made huge profits.

DOWN THE DRAIN goes small confiscation while manufacturing, selling and hijacking continued on a large scale. Stills were being worked day and night to meet the demand. Crime increased accordingly.

"BOOZE BELT" was worn by returning tourists. This woman in a Havana cafe was one of thousands who broke 18th Amendment, but were otherwise law-abiding citizens. Liquor was imported by land, sea and air. Local police directed customers to speakeasies. The 18th Amendment became a farce.

REPEAL celebrants were well-behaved on the whole. Girls sitting on bar were posed for photo at Roosevelt Hotel in N.Y. Ratification of 21st Amendment in 1933 marked the end of 14 dry years.

FIRE RAZED the plush Breakers Hotel in Palm Beach, Fla., in March, 1925, at height of season; a tropical hurricane blew a Miami hotel off its foundations a year later, September, 1926.

DISASTERS
In the '20s and '30s, the U. S. survived boom and bust, fire and flood, tornadoes, hurricanes, dust storms, earthquakes and explosions. Two U. S. dirigibles and one German giant crashed and burned in the U. S., the *Macon* (1935); *Akron* (1933) and Germany's *Hindenberg* (above) which caught fire while mooring at Lakehurst, New Jersey, May 6, 1937. The giant ship (803 feet long, 135 feet at widest diameter) carried 97 across the Atlantic.

TRAGEDY STRUCK American steamship *Morro Castle* off Asbury Park, N. J., Sept. 6, 1934, when 135 perished in fire. Quick response to S.O.S. saved rest of 318 passengers, 231 crew.

ROOFLESS HOUSES and leafless trees were common sights around Miami, Fla., in Sept., 1926, when a tropical hurricane killed 472, injured a tabulated 6,381 persons. Dollar damage was estimated in the millions. With 21,500 families affected by freak storm, only 5,000 homes went down.

FARMER'S PLIGHT during the dark days of depression was made more tragic by dust storms which swept through Oklahoma in April, 1936. Black clouds of dust struck Cimarron County (above), drifted like snow, rendering land useless. Discouraged "Okies" migrated by thousands to California.

SPRING FLOODS paralyzed New England in March, 1936, when Connecticut River inundated Hartford and other cities. Manhattan, Kansas, had been similarly drowned out in June, 1935. Hartford flood (above) was called "worst in history," almost submerged main-artery railroad station.

CITIES WENT UNDER water throughout the midwest in 1937 as winter floods plagued dwellers in Allegheny, Mississippi and Ohio River valleys. Here, Cincinnati's Mill Creek District lies nearly submerged. From Portsmouth, O., flood victims were evacuated to take refuge in safer Columbus.

BUILDING The world's tallest, the 1,472-ft. Empire State Building in New York City was completed May 1, 1931, despite stock market crash and financial panic. Built by Starrett Bros. & Eken, from plans by Shreve, Lamb and Harmon, the structure had 102 stories, 69 elevators, could accommodate 25,000 tenants. Long owned by estate of John Raskob, it first was sold in 1951 for estimated $50 million.

JUST ONE of 15 buildings which make up Rockefeller Center in mid-town Manhattan is the RCA building. The Center, work of architect Wallace K. Harrison, covering 12½ acres, is mostly owned by Columbia University. In the Center, and underground, are 2½ miles of concourse; 24 eating places; 800-car garage; 20 foreign consulates; 12 landscaped sky gardens.

CRITICIZED AT FIRST for his extreme "functionalism" and freedom in building design was Frank Lloyd Wright, shown with model of early glass and concrete apartment he designed. Stressing "open" home architecture, he also was among first to believe in concrete slab construction. In 1948 he finally was awarded the American Institute of Architects Gold Medal.

VERY HIGH WINDS were but one of the reasons some thought the 4,200-ft. Golden Gate Bridge, with its towers sticking 746 ft. into the sky, couldn't be built. However, this longest single-span suspension bridge in the world was completed in 1937 under the direction of District Engineer J. B. Strauss. Four years under construction, it was built at a cost of $35 million.

CLOCHE HATS hid short-cut hair. After Lindbergh's flight, helmet-hats also hid the ears.

PLUNGER NECK white silk gown had heavily-beaded skirt. Wrap was white fox-trimmed.

FIRST LADY of the land, Mrs. Calvin Coolidge clung to more conservative formal attire of period 1924-28, but floor-length evening cloak bore fox trim.

MRS. HERBERT HOOVER, wife of the President, affected regal full-skirted gown in patterned silk with rows of ruffles. Beaded fringe decorated bodice.

FASHION

On the wraith-like boyish figure fashion decreed in the 1920's, designers hung rich fabrics, liberally ornamented with embroidery, beads, or both, used furs lavishly. Hemlines rose to the knees, waistlines fell to hips, or disappeared completely. Darling of the era, Clara Bow, "It" girl of films, cheated "long-look" with snug shirred sheath, knee flounce.

SCREEN STARS MODELED everything from bathing suits to evening gowns to whet public appetite for clothes during depression. Here, (l. to r.) Constance Bennett in 1933; Loretta Young, 1931; Tallulah Bankhead, 1932.

JOAN BLONDELL, popular screen star of the 30's, modeled revolutionary silk rubber swim suit sprinkled with multi-colored Indian figures, in 1936. Other manufacturers had come up with patterned bathing suits of shirred cotton. Very short, backless, one-piece designs were exceedingly popular.

LANA TURNER, later a blonde film beauty, here shown wearing a 1938 velvet jumper.

BATHING BEAUTIES of 1923 competed for honors in first contest held in Galveston, Texas. These lovelies, all winners, wore varied assortment of jewels, fabrics, never meant for water.

ROYAL VISITORS, England's King and Queen, center, leaving church with President Franklin Roosevelt (with cane) and family arrived for unprecedented goodwill tour of U.S. and Canada as 1939 World's Fair opened in New York. Six months later, Hitler marched on Poland; war was on.

DRAMATIC TRYLON AND PERISPHERE were theme structures of New York World's Fair which opened April 10, 1939. International displays covered two square miles of former city dump in Flushing Meadows, cost $150 million to build, attracted 45 million visitors. Participating were 62 foreign nations, 33 U.S. states and territories, more than 600 commercial and non-commercial firms. Exhibits and buildings reflected the future.

BERNARR McFADDEN, whose publishing of sentimental "true" story magazines made him rich, was most famous as a physical culturist. Here, in 1924, he won publicity by instructing U.S. Senators Capper, Dill, Magnus, Johnson and Brookhart, and Representative Nelson, in art of self-defense.

ECONOMIC DEPRESSION, waning in the late 30's, was keenly felt by housewives. Food prices, lowest since 1915 in 1933, had risen 20% by 1938, but big chain markets advertised porterhouse steak at 45 cents per pound; hamburger was 19c, pork chops 25c. Food, plentiful; salaries meagre.

UTILITIES TYCOON Samuel Insull, charged with fraud, embezzlement, fled to Greece, then Turkey, with collapse of his public utilities empire, 1932. Extradited, he was jailed in Illinois, then vindicated.

CHICAGO COED COMMENTARY on period of campus "sheiks," *circa* 1926, pointed up popularity of raccoon coats for college men during giddy days of the prohibition era. Same period saw collegians sporting "bell-bottom" trousers, boldly-striped blazer jackets. Girls, striving for "boyish" figures, were equally at home in boyish clothes, trousered slack suits. Here, a University of Chicago sextet, readies an original campus show called *The Mirror* which reflects college girl asking the proverbial "Where are we going?"

WAR AND COLD WAR

Global conflict makes America accept world leadership; challenge of Communism and atomic age forces nation to search its sources of strength

Americans entered the 1940s in a new and unfamiliar role — world leadership. It was a role they had been capable of assuming, but had refused to accept, since World War I. The nation was young — immature in spirit and outlook — and wanted nothing more than to be left alone to enjoy the fruits of freedom. It preferred to avoid a disagreeable responsibility.

But the responsibility was insistent. America was obliged to accept it, not by any deep-rooted conviction, but by circumstance. Even after World War II and Pearl Harbor had forced the decision, the nation often appeared convinced against its will. More than once in the years that followed, it seemed to be doing only what it must — meeting emergencies rather than preventing them.

First and biggest emergency was World War II. After mobilizing and equipping 12 million men, after fighting and helping to win two separate wars at once, after producing a terrifying weapon that virtually promised race suicide in any future world war, America had been reluctant to show the physical power it could command if it was necessary.

The war, in fact, left great vacuums of power in the world. When the United Nations was founded in 1945, as the great preserver of world peace, its success — and humanity's hope — hinged on the friendly cooperation of United States and Russia.

Once again America revealed its youth — and its naivete. It gave Russia strategic concessions in northern Asia; permitted the Soviets to occupy Berlin and North Korea; withheld aid to Nationalist China; stood by while the Communists spread their control over nearly one-half the earth's population.

But gradually the nation awoke to the danger, and to its responsibility. Russian troops were ordered out of northern Iran. Economic **aid** was sent to Western Europe. A North Atlantic military pact — **America's** first peacetime alliance — was formed. Arms were rushed to strategic Greece and Turkey. An "airlift" successfully fought the Russian blockade of Berlin.

Finally, American troops were sent to Korea on behalf of the U.N. to fight outright Communist aggression. This one bold act was enough to make a place in history for the man who didn't want to be President — Harry S. Truman.

Still more subtle decisions were forced on a nation which was growing up — fast. When the Chinese Reds were flung into the Korean War, the government had to choose between risking a third world war by retaliation, or fighting a stalemate war in Korea. When some Communist spies were uncovered in the government at home, Americans had to meet the challenge without succumbing to panic and demagoguery. Finally, as it appeared that the free world needed the military strength of its former enemies, the nation took steps to arm its former enemies, Germany and Japan.

Meanwhile, Moscow awaited the expected collapse of Western capitalism. Yet with American help, Europe was slowly recovering. Except for two short "recessions," the United States kept employment and production at a peacetime high. The greatest menace — inflation — was gradually controlled. While government still faced such problems as deficit budgets and farm surpluses, so long as industry was filling both military and civilian needs, there seemed to be little chance of an economic crisis.

Unintentionally, the Kremlin was strengthening America in other ways. The competition of ideologies was forcing democracy to set its own house in order. Racial discrimination, which denied the nation's basic precepts, was being vigorously attacked. Americans were going back to church — apparently from a vague understanding that this age of the atomic arms race called for deep soul-searching, for re-examination of human values and morality.

By 1954 the "cold war" still showed no signs of an end or a decision. There was no doubt that America was exercising its leadership. President Eisenhower's Secretary of State, John Foster Dulles, had engineered both a Pacific defense pact and a method of rearming Western Germany. But even these measures could not combat the Communist Fifth Column which was still infiltrating countries of Southeast Asia. The great hope was that America had not come of age too late to avert destruction.

Ahead, if the world survived this ordeal, lay an age of vast scientific progress. Already automatic appliances, television, wonder drugs and other medical advances were fulfilling prophesies of a post-war "dream world." Still greater strides in electronics and atomic power promised newer comforts, better health, longer life, perhaps even new frontiers.

TV REVOLUTIONIZED HOME LIFE

But hovering overhead was the spectre of the A-bomb and the H-bomb, reminding Americans that scientific invention could also destroy. Truth was the climate of freedom in U.S. and other democracies had fostered technical progress, but children of freedom had forfeited moral control. Man's brain had left his soul behind.

But there was a chance that America could rise to this greater challenge. Symptoms of national maturity were appearing—increased participation in the arts, new interest in enduring literature. The level of education was constantly rising, providing broader judgment in political and economic matters. Despite the country's bigness, the public was maintaining practical control over its own affairs by acting in groups—Americans were still the "joingingest" people on earth.

Yet group organization often meant the smothering of individual opinion. The American way could survive and develop only so long as the citizen kept his identity. The question was, could man still govern himself in 20th Century America? Beyond cold wars and H-bombs, this was America's gravest test.

★   ★   ★

WORLD WAR II broke with dramatic suddenness for the United States with the bursting of bombs at Pearl Harbor. Fighting on two fronts, American military might was spread around the globe. War in Europe consisted of massive invasions, large-scale campaigns and heavy bombing. Victory in the Pacific, however, came only after a series of naval engagements and costly, bloody "mopping-up" operations on dozens of Japanese-held islands by U.S. Marines (l.) and soldiers. By war's end U.S. had world's mightiest navy and largest air force, a tribute to the nation's industrial production.

ATTACK ON PEARL HARBOR caught U.S. forces unprepared. Five battleships and three cruisers were sunk or seriously damaged, several small vessels sunk or crippled, and 177 aircraft demolished. Casualties were 2,343 dead, 876 missing, and 1,272 injured. The USS *West Virginia* and USS *Tennessee* (above) were destroyed, having suffered brunt of attack. USS *Nevada* was only capital ship to escape from holocaust in "battleship row." Attack was without warning or declaration of war. President Roosevelt cabled to Hirohito on day previous urging him to preserve peace.

WORLD WAR II

Catastrophe turned to victory as United States wrests initiative in Pacific

On Dec. 7, 1941, Japan struck a surprise attack against the U.S. at Hawaii. War was declared by the U.S. on the following day. Japan, in an unbroken string of victories, conquered most of the important Pacific islands including Timor near Australia. Gen. Douglas MacArthur assumed command of Southwest Pacific forces on March 17, 1942, and the first reversals for Japan occurred in the naval battles of the Coral Sea, May 7, and Midway, June 4. Allies won land battles on New Guinea and the Solomons. From then on, Allied power recaptured, by hop-skip strategy, all important islands leading to the Philippines. Iwo Jima and Okinawa were secured and the final air assault against the Japanese mainland was started.

In Europe and Africa, the invasions of No. Africa, Sicily, and Normandy gave American and British power the necessary footholds from which to launch offensives against the Axis. In Europe, the capture of Cherbourg on June 27, 1943, gained a major port for unloading equipment and supplies. Liberation of Paris and the sweep up the Rhone brought the Allies into close organization for the assault on Germany. On April 26, 1945, American and Russian troops joined hands on the Elbe at Torgau, and on May 7, Germany surrendered.

The No. African campaign and battle for Italy broke the Fascist threat in the Mediterranean and released personnel for the invasion of Italy. The massive invasion of No. Africa brought Germany's Rommel to bay in Tunis and Bizerte on May 12, 1943.

The battle for Italy was a gruelling fight against stubborn resistance in mountainous country, and foul weather, with resolved itself into an unprogressive battle-line until the final collapse of Germany.

With the end of hostilities in Europe, the Allies concentrated on the Pacific Theater. American and British scientists secretly developed the atomic bomb which was dropped on Hiroshima and Nagasaki. This, and battle reverses on all fronts, compelled Japan to surrender on Aug. 14, 1945.

PILOTS aboard Japanese aircraft carrier received last minute instructions for attack on Pearl Harbor. Negotiations for peaceful settlement were under way at the time of the raid.

DECLARATION OF WAR was shouted by U.S. newspapers on Dec. 8. Overnight the U.S. was at war with Japan and Axis powers, and overnight the American spirit to fight was unified.

WAR VOTE against Japan was passed 388-1 by the House. Senate voted 82-0 in favor of war. Lone dissenting vote was cast by Rep. Jeanette Rankin, who also voted against war in 1917.

ATLANTIC CONFERENCE in August, 1941, brought Roosevelt and Churchill together on HMS *Prince of Wales* to discuss provisions of Atlantic Charter. Agreement was part of America's answer to the Tripartite Pact of Germany, Japan and Italy. Statement of principles was designed to encourage resistance and inspire renewed strength among the Allies against Axis. It also provided an eight-point proposal for world peace.

DEATH MARCH soldiers were assembled (above) prior to "walk in the sun" from Bataan to prison camps on Luzon, P.I. Besides brutality to prisoners, famine and disease, World War II caused 20 million displaced persons, 16 million deaths due to combat, and cost of 1,500 billion dollars. The U.S. lost 300,000 combatants. The war cost U.S. $350 billion. Approximately 30 million civilians were killed in all the theaters of war.

DEATH RATTLES of aircraft carrier *Lexington* were internal explosions set off by Jap dive bombers during the Coral Sea Battle. U.S. lost five aircraft carriers in the Pacific theater: The *Lexington, Yorktown, Wasp, Hornet,* and *Princeton.* Japan lost 20 carriers, 12 battleships, and 18 heavy cruisers. On the upper end of the world Japan invaded Kiska and Attu in the Bering Sea in an effort to prevent the construction of U.S. bases for air strikes.

PRELUDE TO LANDING in Solomons Aug. 7, 1942, was barrage by planes and ships. Same day Marines landed on Guadalcanal. Simultaneous drive was launched under MacArthur in New Guinea. Enemy, baffled by varied strategy, was caught off balance. Allies gained strength as ships, materiel poured from U. S. factories. Massing of personnel into South Pacific was major undertaking. The Allies were taking initiative on land, sea, and air.

AFRICA INVADED

A running warfare on the desert sands occupied the Australian and British forces against the Italians and Rommel's *Afrika Korps.* Assistance arrived with the gigantic invasion of North Africa under command of Gen. Dwight Eisenhower. Casablanca, Oran, and Algiers were struck simultaneously in November, 1942. Rommel retreated to the protection of the Mareth line,

doggedly followed by Eighth Army and U. S. Rangers (above, r.). In a last bid to hold Tunisia, reinforced Rommel seized vital Kasserine Pass but lost it to the Americans four days later. The final assault opened against Rommel in April, 1943. Two British armies, two French Corps, and a strong American Corps fought a dogged hill to hill battle to Bizerte and Tunis, subduing stubborn Nazi resistance. Complex prisoner roundup then began (above, l.).

ALASKAN BEACHHEAD was established on "D Day" at Quisling Cove, Kiska. On Aug. 15, 1943, a large amphibious force of Canadians and Marines landed, expecting stiff opposition. They found no enemy, merely notes threatening, "We shall come again." They never did.

WAR IN THE PACIFIC
Jungle fighting was toughest warfare in World War II. Mop-up operations on Bougainville (above) demanded strong nerves and fast shooting. The enemy might lurk in the trees just ahead or might aim down from behind. Safest procedure was to spray trees with submachine-gun lead if ammunition was plentiful. Climate and tropical diseases were sometimes greater trial to the soldiers than the combat itself. Boredom also was a problem in rear areas and on islands where soldiers were not in actual combat.

FINGERS WERE CROSSED as Doolittle's heavy-laden B-25's left deck of *U.S.S. Hornet* in April, 1942, for Tokyo. Hazardous return with limited fuel over Japanese-held sections of China was daring and costly. Raid, however, gave American morale a boost which was badly needed.

YARD BY YARD gains were made through palm stumps and 4,000 well-intrenched Japanese on Tarawa. In 76 hours the island had been taken and its defenders slain. Tarawa was the first fortified atoll assaulted by American troops, the first "impassable" reef for landing craft to be crossed under fire, and saw the first use of amphibious tractors as troop carriers. Valuable lessons were learned. It also taught the U.S. command that the enemy could not be destroyed by bombardment alone.

MACARTHUR, F.D.R., Nimitz, Leahy (l. to r.) met in Hawaii to discuss strategy in Pacific. Island-hopping plan, materiel and personnel allocation were items of discussion. Exchanges of views at this meeting co-ordinated Army and Navy plans, resulted in shorter, less costly war.

FLAME THROWERS eliminated enemy resistance with little cost of life to U.S. forces. Japanese entrenched themselves in block houses made of tree trunks. Coconut palms, which produced oils for American soap companies, also furnished Japanese with highly absorbent protection against bullet and shell fire. Flame throwers used by 7th Division on Kwajalein Island were answer to problem. Men in foreground "cover" flame operator. Method was safer than capturing the treacherous enemy.

DIGGING IN was important in holding perimeters. Unless solid entrenchment was made, Japanese could charge or infiltrate at night. Perimeter would be expanded next day and gradually enemy would be driven into pocket. Battle lines were flexible on island of Saipan.

LANDING PARTY crawls forward under sniper fire on one of countless islands on road to Tokyo. Invading troops (above in New Guinea) kept heads down and took advantage of every bit of cover. It was uncertain whether enemy was strong or had withdrawn, until rifles or artillery opened up. Training received in U.S. camps and instinct of self preservation made good soldiers. "One intelligent live soldier was worth 10 dead heroes."

KWAJALEIN FALLS and Marines take time out for butts and scuttle-butt. Japanese tanks were light and poorly armored, offering little protection for its crew. Enemy lost 8,122 before atoll fell to Marines. Kwajalein and Roi, which had an air-strip, were the first isles in the Marshalls to be recaptured. Main objective was to capture air-strip on most islands. Strips were converted for bombers and became spring-boards towards Tokyo.

HALSEY AND MITSCHER met on board flagship of Third Fleet to discuss battle plans. Admiral W. F. Halsey and Vice Admiral Mitscher (right) obviously "ribbed" each other in this meeting which preceded battle of Philippines.

CBI EXPERTS General Joseph Stilwell (l.) and Admiral Lord Louis Mountbatten confer about next move on the Burma front. Homespun "Vinegar Joe" and Mountbatten fought way back from India after the defeat by Japanese in 1942. The successful counter-attack in 1943-44 with construction of the Lido or Stilwell road, advanced CBI troops back into Burma. Pack mules (above) played important role in transporting equipment over rough mountain terrain and swollen rivers to the troops.

MACARTHUR RETURNS With the aid of U.S. and Allied forces, MacArthur waded ashore in the Philippines. Date: Oct. 20, 1944. Place: Leyte, P. I. It was two years and seven months after he escaped from Bataan by order of President Roosevelt. To defend the Army's movement in the invasion, Navy fought one of the greatest sea actions of history. The enemy's navy was severely damaged despite the murderous *Kamikaze* (suicide planes) attacks. Next came the battle of Mindanao and invasion of Mindoro, and finally troops on Luzon reached Manila. Stubborn street to street fighting went on for several weeks. At Rizal stadium a U.S. tank stood over the pitcher's box and lobbed shells into locker rooms where Japanese were "holed." After Manila, the enemy entrenched in and around Baguio. The process of island-hopping was resumed. Iwo Jima, only 750 miles from Tokyo, was taken for a base to bomb Japan. Resistance was crumbling.

INVASION OF ITALY

Following the invasion and capture of Sicily, July 10 to Aug. 16, 1943, the Allies struck Italy Sept. 3. Italy surrendered the first day of the attack. The biggest landing Allies made was at Salerno, Sept. 9. Although the Germans were entrenched as far south as Naples, they gave ground before the invaders until they reached the Gustav Line, anchored at Cassino, where they held fast. The Allies then attacked at Anzio, where a beachhead (left) was established Jan. 22, 1944. Little resistance was felt at first, but by mid-February, Nazi counterattacks had squeezed the Allies back to a small foothold. Picture (r.) shows Army Sec. Robert Patterson and Gen. Mark Clark congratulating officer of the 100th Inf. Battalion on the excellent job done by the entirely Japanese-American unit in the Italian campaign. Despite U.S. policy of interning Japanese-Americans in the States, many Nisei made outstanding combat records in Italian fighting.

BEFORE ITALY was invaded, B-24 *Liberators* of the 9th and 12th Air Forces in North Africa flew a 2,500-mile round trip to bomb the oil fields in Ploesti, Rumania on Aug. 1, 1943. American fliers played a big part in the Italian campaign, softening up German positions before assaults.

JACKASSES AND TANKS were almost equally important to Allies as Italian campaign progressed. Fighting over mountains and across rivers, lines of supply were tougher to maintain and more vital than usual to the Fifth Army. At left, a group of U.S. M-10 tank destroyers fire on German positions while at right, a muleskinner loads his animal with badly needed medical supplies for transporting up steep mountains to front-line aid station. The Allies began their final drive on the "forgotten front" (world attention was centered on Germany) April 9, 1945, and ended with Nazi surrender May 2.

STING of Yankee heavy bombers was felt often and hard by cities in the interior regions of Hitler's "Festung Europa" as the Allies softened Germany and her allies for the last drive. Here, Boeing B-17 *Flying Fortresses* drop their bombs on pinpoint target from very high altitude.

ALLIED LEADERS plotted final drives against the Axis at top-level meetings in 1943. At right, Stalin, Roosevelt and Churchill meet at Teheran, where the Russian dictator demanded a second front in Europe. Similar meetings in 1943: Casablanca (Roosevelt-Churchill-De Gaulle-Giraud) to unify the Free French; Cairo (Roosevelt-Churchill-Chiang Kai-shek) to coordinate the war against Japan. Left, invasion chief Gen. Dwight Eisenhower walks with Prime Minister Churchill at an English base where paratroopers were trained for their all-important jump into France during Normandy invasion.

D-DAY Men and materiel poured ashore at Normandy when the Allies breached the perimeter of Hitler's defenses June 6, 1944. At left, LST's with open bow doors have disgorged their loads of trucks and tanks onto the sand and pull back to sea for the return to England for another load. Barrage balloons were for protection in case of German strafing attacks. At right, American infantrymen have the Stars and Stripes displayed prominently against the cliffside above the landing beach to avoid shelling by their own ships off shore. In top of picture can be seen German prisoners taken in the assault on the fortifications lining the French shore. The first Allied drive was for Cherbourg, which the Germans destroyed before yielding. On Aug. 15, a second force of invaders struck France from the south, landing between Cannes and Toulon and driving 140 miles inland in eight days. Paris was liberated by the invaders August 25; the Allies reached the Marne and took Reims by September 1st.

GERMANS FLED frequently before advancing Allied armies, which were better armed, better supplied and had air superiority. However, in Dec., 1944 Gen. Von Runstedt made a counterattack from the Ardennes and drove well into Allied lines before being stopped in the Battle of the Bulge. Shown are American troops advancing with a tank into a German-held town in France. Germans often left snipers as they retreated to harass Allies.

PLASMA WAS GIVEN wounded men where they fell, resulting in many being saved who otherwise would have died before treatment could be given at rear hospitals. Medics distinguished themselves throughout World War II by heroic exploits and self sacrifice to aid the wounded; their efforts paid off in lower death totals, in comparison to numbers injured, than in other wars. Doctors operated nearer the battlefronts in this war than in past.

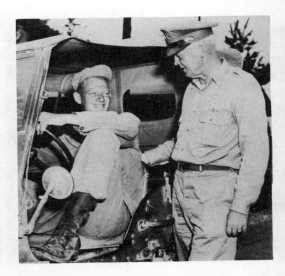

TOP COMMANDERS of the drive into Germany were Lt. Gen. George Patton (with his pearl-handled six-shooters); Lt. Gen. Omar Bradley and Field Marshal Sir Bernard (Monty) Montgomery. With his Third Army tanks, Patton raced across Europe to reach Czechoslovakia.

GREAT OVATION was given G.I.'s when once again American troops marched through the Arch of Triumph, down the Champs Elysee during the liberation of Paris. As war's tide turned, Nazis used V-weapons—flying bombs and stratosphere rockets, but did not change war's course.

VINDICATION for airpower came in World War II as U.S. Air Force under Gen. Henry H. (Hap) Arnold played tremendous part in reducing enemy's industrial potential and cowing civilians. Here, Arnold talks with his son Bruce. Biggest achievement — precision day bombings.

FAILING HEALTH of President Roosevelt was clearly evident by 1944. Yet he gave no serious thought to retiring from office. Fired with a determination to complete his "Grand Design," a plan of diplomacy based on personal contact with Winston Churchill and Stalin, he accepted nomination for fourth term. He declined to run again with Henry Wallace, picked

Harry Truman (right), who was nominated by the Democratic convention (center) despite strong sentiment for James F. Byrnes and Justice William O. Douglas. The fourth term which he won in a campaign based on wartime leadership, not New Deal, was only twelve weeks old when he died suddenly, on April 12, 1945, and Presidency was thrust upon Truman.

FDR'S 4th term

President's health is a big issue in campaign

CRUSHING DEFEAT of Wendell Willkie in the Wisconsin primary election caused him to withdraw from race for Republican nomination. The convention settled on former racket-buster, Governor Thomas E. Dewey of New York.

RUNNING MATES Dewey and John W. Bricker (c.), Republican governor from Ohio, ran a "high level" campaign. It failed to generate grass roots enthusiasm. Gov. Earl Warren of Calif. (r.) was earlier a presidential aspirant.

After four years of war-induced prosperity, the nation failed to respond to the half-hearted Republican efforts to make the New Deal a central issue of the 1944 campaign. Neither did it respond to the "high level" nature of Governor Dewey's speeches. A major Republican mistake also affected results: Party failed to capitalize on the "clear it with Sidney" statement of Roosevelt which linked the activities of the liberal CIO Political Action Committee with the Democratic Party. These handicaps, plus the fact that the Republican and Democratic platforms agreed on the need for a post-war international organization and on other points of foreign policy, reduced the real issues to two: should the nation "change horses in the middle of the stream", and was Franklin Roosevelt physically able to carry on his duties as President.

To capitalize on the former point, the Democrats emphasized Roosevelt's grasp of the international situation and his close personal relations with both Churchill and Stalin. To meet the latter argument, the President was forced to extreme measures. On one occasion he rode bareheaded through New York City in an open touring car during a driving rainstorm, which apparently did not affect him. In addition, Roosevelt's personal physician made a number of statements during the campaign declaring him to be in perfect health.

The Democratic efforts proved effective. The nation decided that Roosevelt was both "indispensable" and healthy enough to continue as President. But his popularity at the polls was reduced to its all time low — three and a half million votes majority.

MINOR PARTIES polled less than 200,000 votes in 1944. Gerald L. K. Smith, shown addressing delegates to Detroit convention, attempted to launch America First party. It did not catch on. Socialist Norman Thomas polled 80,000 votes.

CROWD in Pennsylvania Station, N. Y., waits to greet Communist Earl Browder after release from Atlanta prison on order of President Roosevelt in 1942. Reds did not put Browder up as candidate in 1944, as in 1936 and 1940.

YALTA

A secret pact whereby lands taken by Japan in 1904 were returned to Russia, who also got the Kurile Islands and guarantee of a naval base at Port Arthur, was signed in February, 1945, by F.D.R., Stalin and Churchill at a Crimea meeting. Russia agreed to help defeat Japan, pledged free elections in Poland, recognized the Nationalists as the true government of China. Stalin also agreed to the formation of the United Nations as planned at Dumbarton Oaks Conference.

GERMANY INVADED

Advancing Americans found most of the cities of Germany, especially the industrial ones, shattered masses of rubble from U.S. and British bombing raids. In the last days, Germany used very young teenagers and old men as soldiers. After Hitler committed suicide in Berlin, Adm. Carl Doenitz assumed command and surrendered unconditionally to the Allies May 7, 1945, ending bloodiest, costliest war Europe had ever known.

FRIENDLY HANDCLASPS and smiles were prominent as American and Russian soldiers met at the Elbe River, marking the cutting of Nazi Germany in half. The Allies agreed that Germany would, when conquered, be partitioned between the U.S., Britain, Russia and, over Red objections, France. Although Berlin was well inside the Russian sector, it too was divided. Russian and U.S. soldiers got along well before cold war started.

TRUMAN'S FIRST appearance on foreign soil as President of the United States was at the Potsdam Conference, where U.S., Britain and the Soviet Union formulated the terms of surrender for Japan. Churchill represented England in early part of the conference, but his government was defeated in elections at home half way through, and Clement Attlee, Labor Party leader, succeeded him in last sessions. Above, Attlee, Truman and Stalin.

ROOSEVELT'S SUDDEN DEATH April 12, 1945, shocked the U.S. and the rest of the free world. Shortly after the President's death in the "Little White House" in Warm Springs, Ga., Vice President Harry S. Truman was sworn into the important job (left) by Chief Justice Harlan F. Stone, as Mrs. Truman (c.) watches. It was Truman who made the decision to drop the atomic bomb on Japan and bring the war to a rapid end. At right, Roosevelt's casket is lowered into his grave at his Hyde Park, New York, home by an honor guard of soldiers, sailors and Marines. The nation's shock was not shared by those who had been close to the President before his unprecedented try for a fourth term. He had showed his failing health.

"MOPPING UP" after the main battle, had to be accomplished before islands were neutralized and ready for construction of air-strips. These soldiers on Okinawa had to blast and burn the enemy out of pillboxes and caves; sometimes fought hand to hand. Jap suicide planes made Okinawa casualties heaviest of war.

SCULPTURESQUE raising of flag on Iwo Jima by Marines is one of World War II's classic photos. Five days of gruelling battle took Mt. Suribachi after one of the costliest assaults attempted by the Marines (Feb. 23, 1945). Beach had been set up with cross-fire by Japanese, and invasion was made through soft volcanic ash.

JAPAN SURRENDERS

Nagasaki was reduced to rubble by an A-bomb on August 9th, 1945. About 75,000 people were killed or injured and more than one-third of city leveled. Hiroshima had been target for A-bomb three days earlier. Japan was tottering. Industrial cities had been devastated, the nation was suffering reversals in the islands. Russians were routing Japan's crack troops in Manchuria. Japan issued a statement to its people through Hirohito on Aug. 14, 1945, that it would accept Allied terms. Emperor's title was assured. The end of six years and one day of the Second World War had come. Formal surrender ceremonies on board *U.S.S. Missouri* brought war in Pacific to official close on Sept. 2, 1945. Mamoru Shigemitsu signed for Japan (above). MacArthur signed for the Allies. Historic moment was witnessed by large group of Allied officers. Lt. General Sutherland, U.S. Army Chief of Staff, Southern and Pacific Area, at left of table.

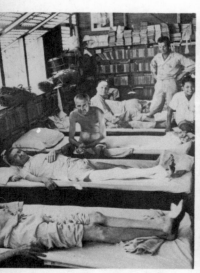

WAR CRIMES

Definition of war crimes included acts of aggressive warfare, actions against the peace, acts against humanity, and "the common plan or conspiracy." Acts against humanity and man's inhumanity to man were particularly rampant in World War II. Hospitalized soldiers (l.) were nourished back to health after rescue from concentration camp at Cabanatuan in the Philippines. Meagerly-fed prisoners sometimes ate sawdust to allay hunger pangs. At Nürnberg, 10 top Nazis were sentenced to death for war crimes. Goering (in white coat, c.), killed himself with a poison capsule on day of execution. Those sentenced to hang were: Von Ribbentrop, Keitel, Kaltenbrunner, Rosenberg, Frank, Frick, Streicher, Sauckel, Jodl, Seyss-Inquart, and Goering. Buchenwald (r.) was equipped with a strangling room, a neck-breaking shaft, and a body disposal plant with a capacity of 400 bodies per day. More than 51,000 people had been killed by brutal Nazi butchers.

RATIONING OVER and gasoline plentiful, attendant washed sailor's fender in Los Angeles. People massed in Times Square (r.) and elsewhere throughout nation to celebrate. Some smiled, some laughed, others became hysterical. General atmosphere was one of happiness. Unsuspecting females were bussed by males, familiar and unfamiliar. Lifting of rationing released cigarets, shoes, gum, soap, stockings, hundreds of small luxuries.

WORLD WAR II ENDS

Atomic bomb blasts punctuate end of the greatest conflict in history

Nuclear fission in the form of a gigantic mushroom was the awesome exclamation-point which punctuated the end of World War II. A war that was truly world-wide had ceased. If it acomplished anything other than to advance science, at a terrible price, it may have produced a stepping stone to world peace through: (1) fear of atomic destruction, (2) fear of retribution for war crimes through judgments of an international tribunal. By 1954, it was still an uneasy peace.

The first movement to punish criminals of war was contained in the Moscow Declaration of October 30, 1943. A list of top military, industrial, and political names was compiled. They were to be tried mostly for crimes committed in the USSR and to the Russian people. Shortly after, the United Nations Commission for the Investigation of War Crimes was formed.

In August, 1945, Great Britain, France, the USSR, and the United States adopted a statute for trying the principal Nazi leaders, both military and civilian. The trials at Nürnberg opened in

UNITED NATIONS met at San Francisco in 1945. Pres. Truman watched Stettinius sign for the U.S.

November, 1945, and voluminous evidence was presented to prove the plotting of aggressive warfare, the extermination of civilians, slave labor, the looting of occupied countries, and maltreatment and murder of prisoners of war. By 1950, 8,000 persons were tried and about 2,000 executed in both Germany and Japan.

The victors met in San Francisco in 1945 to set up the United Nations. It was not long, however, before the first friction developed—between U.S. and Russia during discussion of veto rights of the Security Council. Ultimate aim of the UN remained unchanged—to preserve world peace through social and economic justice. With this nobility of purpose, the UN prepared its charter.

On July 17, 1945, the "Big Three" met at Potsdam to formulate the demilitarization of Axis countries. Soon afterwards, all of eastern Europe was occupied by Russia. For much of the world, the fighting war was soon over. For the rest, the insidious threat of Communism foreshadowed another kind of war—a cold one.

GONE were dictators Hitler and Mussolini. Regardless of social and economic conditions which created them, their inhumanity to man left no doubt as to their guilt in creating war.

TOJO, as war leader and Prime Minister, was partly responsible for Japan's actions. He was sentenced in 1948, attempted suicide, and was executed upon release from Japanese hospital.

MUSSOLINI and his mistress, Clarette Petacci, were executed by a firing squad of Italian partisans April 28, 1945, and later mutilated in Milan. Thus ended the rule of Fascist dictators.

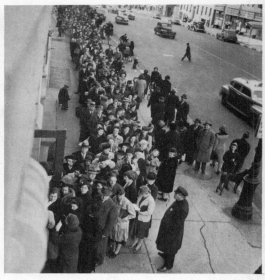

AMERICANS AT HOME adjusted to "war shortages" with good grace, bore up under the inconvenience of registering for ration books (r.), griped good naturedly when name-brand cigarettes disappeared from counters. They wrestled with red points, blue points, stamps, tokens, in exchange for meat, gasoline, shoes. Jobs were plentiful, incomes good. Prices, hours of work and rates of pay were "stabilized" by government order. Rents had "ceilings," but abuses were rampant as war-wives followed training or departing husbands. Gone "for the duration" were new houses, nylon hose.

WARTIME U.S.A.

Americans at home fought private wars with ration stamps, shortages

As World War II wore on, Americans at home settled into a pattern of living affected one way or another by the vast demands of war production. Factories, many once the exclusive province of men, were "manned," from welder's torch to drop-hammer, by women. Labor shortages, apparent everywhere, were especially evident in restaurants, beauty salons, department stores. Household help disappeared from the American scene and way of living.

The people of the U.S. became adjusted to standing in line for nearly everything, from ration books controlling purchases of meat, butter, sugar, gasoline, shoes, to transportation terminals where ticket agents juggled Government priority against personal urgency. Standing room was sold on

crack trains from Washington, D.C., to New York, New York to Chicago. Travelers slept and ate as they could. Train diners ran out of food. Hotels, even with three to five-day eviction policies, were booked beyond capacity, provided cots for servicemen in lobby alcoves, billiard rooms, laundries.

Wherever troops were stationed, war wives set up housekeeping, however temporary. They paid exhorbitant rents for furnished shacks, despite rental "ceilings," but found some compensation in patronizing military PX's where Hershey bars, cigarettes, cleansing tissues, were still obtainable.

Outside the military, bars closed at midnight, restaurants closed when food was gone, stayed closed two days a week to conserve dwindling meat supplies. "Sold Out"

signs hung on gasoline pumps, theater box-office windows, hosiery, tobacco and meat counters in indiscriminate disarray. Car pools lightened the burden of gasoline restrictions, but new cars, tires, and household appliances were gone "for the duration."

Victory gardens, war bonds, blood donations, were all part of the homefront. Never in American history had so many doughnuts been freely proffered or had so much chicory-laden coffee been brewed.

For the three years and seven months of war, people in the U.S. lived on the promise of tomorrow, the end of "duration," the return to *status quo*. Then the President died in office and an atom bomb was dropped. In the jubilation of war's end, no one cared to consider the shadow of a "cold war."

UNION STATION, Washington, D.C., July 7, 1942, seven months after Japan attacked Pearl Harbor, was unique in one respect — the lone woman. Across the country, civilian transportation bogged down under constant troop movements. Pullman trains and airlines met priority reservations, canceled or "bumped" passengers without notice when higher priorities applied. Trapped, travelers slept in train depots and airline terminal lobbies.

SHOW BUSINESS RALLIED to the plea for entertainment of GI's, gathered together its biggest "names" into USO overseas units. Most traveled comedian was Bob Hope (l.) who, with singer Frances Langford, performed on nearly every battlefront of war, often with guitarist Tony Romano, buffoon Jerry Colonna (r.). At home, USO units entertained in training camps, embarkation points, hospitals, set up Hollywood and Stage Door canteens.

DOUGLAS AIRCRAFT (above), largest airframe company, used 155,000 women in seven plants, many subplants, by 1943. Women went to war in their own way. Many joined Armed Forces open to them—WACs, WAVEs, etc. Millions streamed into industries, built ships, armament, aircraft.

ENEMY SUBMARINES SHELLED Santa Barbara, Calif., oilfields, February, 1942 (above), did little damage although coastal blackouts, air-raid alerts intensified. In Seattle, Wash., Jap subs sent "fire balloons" into timberlands, caused rash of forest fires. To the threat of Pacific coast invasion, civilians countered with volunteer defense corps, set up 24-hour "spotter" crews, air-raid alert systems, first-aid classes, fire protection equipment.

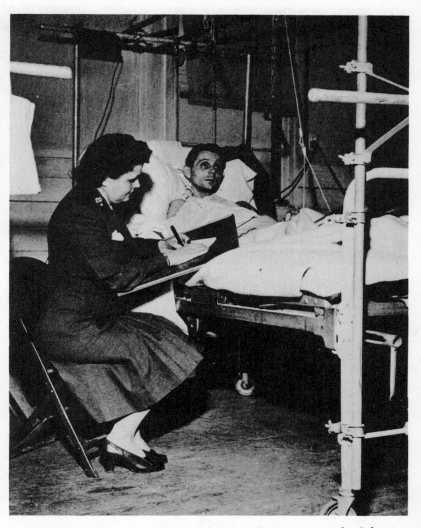

ANOTHER ARMY revered by GIs at home and overseas was the Salvation Army, whose "lassies" gave selfless war services without publicity (above). American Red Cross' uniformed ambulance drivers drilled and drove, Gray Ladies visited hospitals, canteen workers dispensed coffee and donuts to incoming and outgoing servicemen, set up and operated mobile blood units, launched strong campaigns for blood donations, new members, funds.

JAPANESE NISEIS enlisted in U.S. military service despite American hysteria which resulted in "relocation" of all Japanese from Pacific coast areas. By 1943, 110,000 Japanese had been shifted to inland War Relocation Projects. In Los Angeles confiscated property lay idle or was appropriated by hordes of Mexican and Negro war workers caught up in housing restrictions and shortages. Here Mrs. Hisako Tanouye, with six sons in service, is honored at Gold Star Mothers banquet in a Wyoming relocation camp.

"WAR NERVES" found outlet in turbulent race riots. Among worst in U.S. history was the June 22, 1943, uprising in industrial Detroit, Mich. Street fighting raged for 24 hours, was finally put down by armed troops who patrolled area in gun carrier (above). Riot left 34 dead, 700 injured; 1,300 were arrested. In the east, anti-German feeling exploded as American Bundists were squashed, and in Los Angeles military police broke up private wars waged by veteran GIs against taunts of zoot-suited *pachuco* gangs.

POTENTIAL POLITICIAN Gen. Dwight D. Eisenhower called on President Truman (l.) in December, 1945. Then Eisenhower was Army Chief of Staff, but he had already been promised Truman's backing in politics. Many Democratic leaders wanted "Ike" to head the ticket in 1948, but he declined. In 1951, at Truman's request, he commanded the NATO forces. Early in 1952, however, he returned to U.S. to seek Republican presidential nomination. Truman, President "by accident," became the seventh Vice President to succeed to the office when Roosevelt died April 12, 1945. Within 17 months he had replaced all department heads with appointees of his own choice. With few exceptions, his new Cabinet was filled with able men, most of them avid party supporters. In October, 1947, Truman posed (r.) with main advisors. They aided Truman's "Fair Deal" program.

TRUMAN'S TIMES

Post-war readjustment, the Fair Deal, and Cold War are vital issues

Harry S. Truman personified the American dream that any man can be President. Not trained for executive duties, as a senator his primary concern had been with domestic matters. Thrust into the Presidency upon Roosevelt's death in April, 1945, Truman took office with the nation still at war.

In his first hundred days as President, the man from Missouri found international events predominant. Hostilities in Europe ended, a conference was held at Potsdam, an atomic explosion was produced at Alamogordo, N.M., and the San Francisco conference to organize the United Nations was held. In September, Japan surrendered.

For a year Truman's home-town ways and simplicity, his humility and self-styled limitations made him extremely popular.

Problems of demobilization and economic readjustment reached a peak in 1946. The President's active role in management and labor disputes brought him criticism — as when he ordered seizure of the railroads. He was soon forced to lift controls except on rents. With strikes and prices in the headlines, the President's popularity declined sharply. Mid-term elections resulted in a Republican Congress.

An effective Republican alliance with conservative Democrats controlled Congress for Truman's next six years in office. His Fair Deal was only a paper program, being too liberal for the conservative legislators. Amid clashes with Capitol Hill, a bi-partisan approach to foreign policies was a singular achievement for the period.

To halt Soviet aggression in 1947, the Truman Doctrine was announced; economic and military aid was sent to Greece and Turkey. This was followed by the Marshall Plan of economic aid to Europe, which in 1948 became European Recovery Program.

Even before Truman's election victory in 1948, relations between the U.S. and the Soviet Union turned into a "Cold War." America rearmed, made tremendous strides in industrial production. With news of a Russian A-bomb, a race began for atomic supremacy. In 1950 Truman's use of American troops in Korea was instrumental in stopping Communist aggression.

Right in making big decisions, but often wrong in little things, evaluation of Truman's role rested in the lap of history.

NEW DEAL departure from Cabinet was completed Sept. 20, 1946, when Mr. Truman demanded the resignation of Henry Wallace as Sec. of Commerce. "A fundamental conflict" over policy caused break.

INDEPENDENCE for the Philippines came on July 4, 1946, and General Douglas MacArthur spoke at the ceremony. Then Supreme Commander for the Allied Powers in Japan, MacArthur was dismissed from his post in the Far East by Truman in the spring of 1951. The firing caused a furor.

POST MORTEM investigation of the Pearl Harbor disaster in 1946 by a Congressional committee brought forth volumes of testimony. During the Truman years committee probing was increased greatly.

OVER-OPTIMISM among Republicans in 1948 was encouraged by public opinion polls that showed Thomas E. Dewey an easy winner of the Presidency. The New York Governor was nominated at the G.O.P. convention in Philadelphia and Gov. Earl Warren of California was the candidate for Vice President. Campaigning on a theme of "unity," Dewey carried 16 states (189 electoral votes) in an election noted for general indifference.

SURPRISE WINNER, especially to the anti-Truman *Chicago Daily Tribune,* Harry S. Truman, the Democratic candidate, was elected in his own right as the 33rd President of the U.S. In a whistle-stop campaign which focused attention on the "do-nothing, Republican 80th Congress," Truman traveled 31,500 miles and gave 350 speeches. His popular vote was two million larger than Dewey's; he carried 28 states with total of 303 electoral votes.

"THE VEEP" was a title acquired by the Vice President, Alben W. Barkley. Nominated by the Democrats in an effort to retain the Southern vote, the Kentuckian proved he was an effective campaigner. In Congress, Barkley's legislative skill helped push enactment of Fair Deal bills.

WALKOUT of Alabama and Mississippi delegates from the 1948 Democratic convention came after Southerners opposed a civil rights plank. The Dixiecrats later formed a States' Rights Party whose presidential candidate, J. Strom Thurmond, received 39 electoral votes.

NEW PARTY, the Independent Progressives, held a national convention to nominate Henry A. Wallace and Sen. Glen Taylor as standard-bearers. In November, 1948, the I.P.P. won 1,157,100 popular but no electoral votes. Its strength kept some states from going Democrat.

G.O.P. LEADERS in the Senate during the Republican 80th Congress included (l. to r.) Homer Ferguson, Mich., Arthur Vandenberg, Mich., and Robert Taft, Ohio. As members of the Senate Republican Policy Committee in the next Congress, the above senators worked in alliance with Southern Democrats to stymie Fair Deal legislation. In the 1950 mid-term elections Republicans then campaigned on the record of the "Eighty-worst" Congress.

UNSUCCESSFUL ASSASSIN Oscar Collazo lies wounded at the steps of Blair House, the temporary residence of President Truman. On Nov. 1, 1950, Puerto Rican nationalists attempted to slay the President. One would-be assassin, Griselio Torresola, was killed in the attempt and a White House policeman lost his life. Collazo recovered from his wounds and was placed on trial. Found guilty, President Truman acted to spare him from death.

ALGER HISS, shaking hands with President Truman (l.) and confronted by Whittaker Chambers (above), was convicted on two counts of perjury and sentenced to five years in the penitentiary for denying under oath that he delivered secret documents to the Communist underground. Hiss, State Department official and Secretary General of the United Nations Conference at San Francisco, first claimed during 1948 Un-American Activities Committee session he had never heard of accuser, Whittaker Chambers. He was forced to retract when faced by Chambers. A furor developed later when Chambers produced copies of 48 State Department documents, four memos in Hiss' writing.

EVIDENCE that convicted 11 top U.S. Communists (above) came from FBI agents who infiltrated high party echelons. Reds were indicted under Smith Act for advocating and teaching overthrow of government by force and violence.

FAR EASTERN EXPERT Owen Lattimore (r.) denied Senator Joe McCarthy's charge he was "Russia's top spy." Indictment for later denial that he promoted Communist interests was dismissed by courts for failure to define terms.

REDS IN AMERICA

Theft of atom secrets alerts the United States

Charged by Federal Judge Irving Kaufman with having "altered the course of history to the disadvantage of your country," Ethel and Julius Rosenberg were executed June 19, 1953, as atomic spies. First civilians to receive the death penalty as traitors in the peacetime history of the United States ,the pair was convicted of recruiting members for, and transmitting information to, a world-wide ring which delivered inmost atomic secrets to the Soviet Union and cut the free world's atomic lead. The confession in Canada of Igor Gouzenko first exposed existence of the Soviet network in the U.S.

Congress, meanwhile, had unearthed other underground activity. Self-confessed ex-courier Whittaker Chambers gave dramatic evidence of his part in an extensive group which had worked in Washington during World War II. Chambers' testimony led to the perjury convictions of Alger Hiss, high Department of State official, and William Remington, Commerce Department economist. Additionally implicated by Chambers was Harry Dexter White, Assistant Secretary of the Treasury.

One result of the heated charges and denials which echoed in Congress was the introduction into all government agencies of Loyalty Review Boards to screen Federal employees. Loyalty questions became a po-

litical issue when Senator Joseph McCarthy made a succession of allegations concerning Communist coddling in government. His methods of handling witnesses during his probe of Reds in the armed forces resulted in a bitter hearing in which Army Secretary Stevens told McCarthy the Army could handle its own loyalty matters.

While rival politicians tried to use loyalty as vote-bait, American Communist Party officials began to feel the power of law. The Smith Act, making "advocacy of the overthrow of government by force and violence" a crime, was affirmed by the Supreme Court as constitutional and upheld conviction of the top 11 American party leaders. The FBI promptly jailed the second team. Bail-jumping before trials led the courts to impose unprecedented sums in an attempt to keep party leaders from fleeing abroad. Then, on Sept. 3, 1954, President Dwight Eisenhower signed the Communist Control Act, passed by the House Aug. 19, thus outlawing the Communist Party as "an instrument of conspiracy to overthrow the U.S. government."

By the time of McCarthy's death in 1957 the Big Red Scare had greatly diminished, but more because of America's increasing political maturity on matters of loyalty than because of that Senator's "crusade," which did not produce a single proven Red agent.

TOP SPY Col. Rudolf Ivanovich Abel (speaking into microphone) was first arrested for illegal immigration, then was charged with espionage. While posing as a Brooklyn photographer, he was said to head a farflung Soviet spy ring.

DEATH PENALTY was given to Ethel and Julius Rosenberg for giving atomic bomb secrets to Russia. They were the first to receive such a severe penalty in peacetime. They were executed on June 19, 1953 at Sing Sing Prison.

CONFESSED SPIES Jack and Myra Soble (with U.S. marshall, r.) who transmitted secrets to Russia, received comparatively light sentences (seven and four years respectively) because, unlike the Rosenbergs, they turned state's evidence.

TO BLOCK a Soviet drive on the Mediterranean via Greece, Turkey, the U.S. sent aid and Gen. Van Fleet during Greek guerrilla war. Truman Doctrine was started to stop the Red advance.

◀ **FAILURE** of American policy along with inflation, corruption, poverty and civil war led to the loss of China to Communist Party. Shown here, Marshall, Chiang and Madame Chiang.

IN GENEVA'S Palace of Nations, the Big ▶ Four (Russia's Bulganin, U. S.'s Eisenhower, France's Fauré, Britain's Eden) met July 18, 1955, conferring for the first time since WW II.

FOREIGN POLICY

Cold war blasts peace; U.S. aids, arms free world

Americans celebrated VJ Day not only with the wild abandon born of victory, but with high hope that totalitarian aggression had been forever abolished. They thought that through the new mechanism of the United Nations "One World" could be realized.

Forgotten in the intoxication of fevered plans for rehabilitation was the reality that among the victors was a totalitarian state based upon a philosophy inimical to the Western world, dedicated to its overthrow by force and violence, with a brutal record of aggression against weaker neighbors. But the subjugation—in violation of war-time agreements—of one after another of the Central European nations "liberated" by the Red Army, together with Soviet-inspired guerrilla war in Greece, pressure on Turkey, crisis in Iran, and violation of the terms of the Yalta Agreement served notice that the goal of Russian Communism remained world conquest by the destruction of non-Communist governments.

To meet this challenge of Cold War, the United States not only continued to press for collective security through the United Nations, but, when blocked by Soviet veto, contrived new methods. The Truman Doc-

trine of increasing the armed strength of anti-Communist nations was furthered by the offer of economic aid through the Marshall Plan and Point Four assistance. Other bulwarks were the Atlantic Pact and participation in NATO and SEATO.

Failure of the repeated attempts to secure a settlement for Germany except on Soviet terms led to the setting up a West German Republic in 1949 and admitting it to NATO. But the success of containing Soviet European expansion while—briefly—atomic supremacy balanced Soviet manpower was offset by failure in Asia. There the resistance of the West was not enough to prevent Communist success in China. A further blow was the loss of North Vietnam to the Reds in '54.

Revolts in Red satellites Poland and Hungary were brutally crushed. By 1957 Soviet influence was extending to the Middle East.

In Korea, U.N. action to meet aggression ended in stalemate, while a tense situation devloped in the Formosa Straits. Communist gains in Asia and Eastern Europe had brought one third of the world's peoples under totalitarian control. The great issue of American foreign policy remained th~ problem of averting atomic war.

ECA administrator Paul G. Hoffman is shown (l.) discussing plans for European economic rehabilitation with "roving ambassador" Averell Harriman. Conceived as an emergency aid program, ECA became the Mutual Security Adm.

PEACE TREATY with Japan was signed six years after war's end. The "peace of reconciliation" gave Japan the right to arm for self-defense, provided U.S. bases. Red propagandists used terms to fan Asian fear of resurgent Japan.

AT GENEVA, heads of government conferred in July, 1955. They are (l. to r.) Premier Bulganin of the U.S.S.R., President Eisenhower, French Premier Edgar Faure and Prime Minister Sir Anthony Eden of Britain. Question

of German reunification was a major stumbling block. Little was accomplished, but for a few months the comparitively amicable "Geneva spirit" led many to believe Cold War was easing. Russia's actions soon proved this false.

BERLIN BLOCKADE climaxed series of hostile Soviet moves designed to drive British, French, and American forces out of German capital. With rail and road facilities blocked, Western Powers used dramatic air-lift to supply sectors.

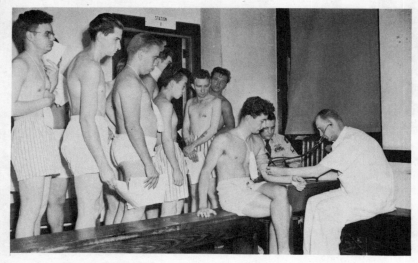

AMERICA'S MANPOWER again went to war via the draft, starting in 1950, after suspension of the involuntary calling up of men in 1948. When the North Koreans struck across the 38th Parallel on June 25, 1950, the South Korean forces were ill-equipped and ill-trained to stop charging Reds. U.S. troops from Japan were hurriedly thrown into battle to stem the tide.

WITHIN HOURS after Red forces invaded South Korea, the U. N. Security Council convened to take action. With Russia absent and Yugoslavia abstaining, resolution was passed 9-0 condemning attack, ordering cease-fire. Here, U. S. Secretary of State Dean Acheson (l.) blames war on Reds, as U.S.S.R. delegate Andrei Y. Vishinsky (r.) takes notes on denunciation.

KOREAN WAR

United Nations fights Red aggression, but war ends in tense stalemate

America surprised not only herself, but Russia and the world at large when she responded suddenly with men and arms against the Reds invading South Korea.

The Reds probably attacked believing the U.S. would hold aloof, having stated previously she would not defend South Korea.

For the first time in American history, a president committed U.S. troops to a prolonged war without approval of or consulting with Congress when Harry Truman ordered Americans into Korean battle.

The war cost America 142,277 dead, wounded and missing. In addition, after all POWs supposedly were exchanged after the truce, the Reds admitted they still held 917 American servicemen as prisoners.

The Korean War was the first time the

United Nations took military action against an aggressor. However, when the truce was signed, the battle line was close to the 38th Parallel; neither side was willing or able to press for a clear victory.

Mao Tze-tung claimed only Red Chinese "volunteers" fought in Korea, but most of his "volunteers" captured by the U.N. refused to go home after the truce, instead choosing Chiang Kai-shek and Formosa.

The fighting left the entire peninsula a wreck. With the help of U.S. and U.N. funds and advisors, South Korea began to rebuild. Reds started integrating North Korea into Red China's economy and rebuilt Communist war machine in violation of truce terms.

A new factor called "brainwashing," wherein POW's were subjected to intense

propaganda coupled with physical torture until they would admit anything, made its appearance during the Korean War. The Reds used it to make captured U.S. fliers say they engaged in "germ warfare," dropping disease-laden bombs on North Korea. Freed, men quickly repudiated confessions.

One provision of the truce was that a political conference to write a peace treaty for Korea be held within 90 days after shooting stopped. When a meeting finally was held, six months later, Korea was only a side issue. Indo-China, where the Reds then were conducting armed conquest, was the main issue and the Reds sought concessions there. They had their gains in Korea, and as a result, made no real attempt to write a treaty, leaving the uneasy truce in effect.

SUCCESSFUL INVASION was launched by the U.N. forces at Inchon Sept. 15, 1950, hundreds of miles behind Red lines. Pushed back to a small perimeter around Pusan by early Red attacks, the Allies mustered sufficient manpower to counterattack in three months. At left, Gen. MacArthur walks ashore at Inchon after the invasion. At right, he defends himself before U.S. Congress after President Truman summarily fired him in 1951 for his criticism of U.S. policy whereby Manchuria, the base of Red Chinese supply and air power, was spared from U.N. attack and provided sanctuary for buildup.

MORE THAN ANYONE ELSE, U.S. Gen. James A. Van Fleet, shown here with Korean orphan, was responsible for turning Republic of Korea Army from rabble, which fled at sight of Russian tanks early in war, into tough fighting group which, at truce time, held one-half of battle line.

WAR'S OLD STORY of mud, blood and men so tired from fighting they were almost prostrate, held true throughout the Korean campaign as battle surged up hill after hill in the extreme cold of winter and the heat of summer. At left, a group of U.S. Marines plods past wrecked vehicles on way north on central front. At right, riflemen fight in wrecked South Korean capital of Seoul, which changed hands four times during the war's course. As fighting progressed, American weapons, which almost exclusively supplied the soldiers of the 13 U.N. nations who had fighting forces in Korea, steadily improved until the smaller U.N. army successfully withstood "human sea" attacks of the fanatical Reds, to whom life meant very little.

RED PRISONERS, of whom the U.N. took thousands, were herded into compounds on Koje Island, where they rioted and almost seized control until U.N. put tough Gen. William Boatner in command. His severe policy ended the uprisings which Reds carefully staged for propaganda effect. Many thousands of POWs turned against Communism in captivity.

HELICOPTER came into its own in Korea as a vehicle of mercy, rescuing Allied fliers shot down behind enemy lines and evacuating wounded from the battlefield under fire. Use of "choppers" plus new medical techniques raised number of casualties saved to figures far beyond the best records achieved during World War II. Here, patient is loaded for trip to hospital.

TALES OF HORROR in Red prison camps were told by repatriated U.N. captives. Worst of all were the mass killings of Americans and South Koreans by retreating Reds which came to light as U.N. troops recaptured Communist-held areas. Evidence shown to the U.N. Assembly showed Reds cared nothing for rules of warfare.

IMPORTANT PART of the Korean War truce terms was agreement on handling POWs refusing repatriation. Here, Indian Gen. K. S. Thimayya (l.) talks with U.N. Commander Gen. Matthew Ridgway. POW provisions were point on which Reds stalled longest in truce talks, which covered two-thirds of Korean War time.

OFFICIAL signing of documents ending the war was done by Gen. Mark Clark, Supreme Allied Commander, who replaced Generals MacArthur and Ridgway. Officially, it never was a war, since Congress never declared war, but insurance companies were ordered by courts to pay double indemnity for death in police action.

CLEAN SWEEP of what Republicans termed the "mess" in Washington was promised by candidate Dwight D. Eisenhower, shown at left receiving a king-size broom. Above, Ike's hand is raised in the traditional winner's gesture by vice-presidential nominee Richard M. Nixon, 39, of California, at Republican Convention in 1952 after Ike won the nomination from Taft.

RETURN OF GOP

Eisenhower ends Korean War, cuts taxes, strikes middle course in policy

Thirty-nine states gave their electoral votes to Dwight D. Eisenhower in 1952's presidential election. It was primarily a personal victory for Eisenhower, as the GOP failed to muster more than a bare majority in either house of Congress. When GOP Sen. Robert A. Taft died, Republican control in the Senate was almost nil.

Eisenhower adopted the staff system, so familiar to a military man, in the conduct of government. Wide authority was delegated, to Presidential Assistant Sherman Adams, to other of his advisors, and to Richard Nixon, who grew into his job and enjoyed more influence than any previous vice-president. Political infighting was left to Nixon, Majority Leader William Knowland in the Senate, Speaker Joseph Martin and Floor Leader Halleck in the House.

That the people had elected Ike out of his personal popularity and not for party reasons was evinced by the 1954 Congressional elections when the GOP lost control of both houses. In 1956 Eisenhower and Nixon were swept to victory again, but for the first time in history both houses went Democratic, despite the election of a Republican administration. The President was "tremendously disappointed" by a Congress that enacted little of his program. Ike-appointed Chief Justice Earl Warren and the Court displayed an unusual regard for traditional American liberties and, in a series of notable decisions, upset numerous convictions.

Chief milestones in the Eisenhower age were passage of the long-delayed St. Lawrence Seaway Bill, establishment of a Department of Health, Education and Welfare, an end to the Korean War, passage of a civil rights bill and establishment of the Eisenhower Doctrine in the Middle East.

Falling farm prices plagued the administration and disapproval of Agriculture Secretary Benson mounted; but the President refused to fire him. Fear of an economic recession rocked the business world as demand fell off and unemployment spread in key areas despite a generally high standard of living.

Ike's serious illnesses in 1955 and 1956 were big news. While the Vice-President and Ike's personal staff carried on well during his absence and relieved him of some of the burdens of office after his recovery, the nation debated whether a vice-president should not be given greater responsibility and whether a president, partly incapacitated, should not resign.

Paramount among all Eisenhower's problems was that of maintaining world peace. The threat of Russian technical and scientific superiority led him to organize a greater national effort in behalf of science and education while simultaneously seeking an end to the arms race. As time went on, however, it became obvious that the Cold War would long remain to menace the world.

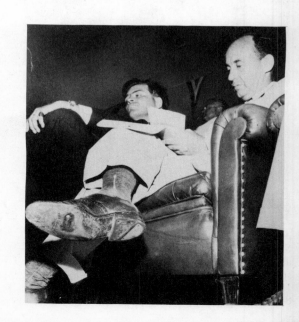

PULITZER PRIZE was won by photographer who shot this picture of witty and urbane Democratic presidential nominee Adlai Stevenson with a hole in his shoe. Illinois governor's 1952 and 1956 campaigns were vigorous but unsuccessful in the face of Eisenhower's overwhelming popularity. Stevenson returned to his law practice.

◀ LOSERS in the race for the Democratic nomination for presidency shake hands following 1952 convention. They are (l. to r.) W. Averill Harriman, Alben W. Barkley, Sen. E. Kefauver, Sen. R. Kerr and Sen. R. Russell.

IKE'S FIRST CABINET: Front, Atty. Gen. Herbert Brownell; Treasury Sec. George Humphrey; V-Pres. Nixon; Pres. Eisenhower; Sec. of State John Foster Dulles and Defense Sec. Charles E. Wilson. In Back (*l. to r.*), Budget Dir. Joseph Dodge; Health and Welfare Sec. Oveta Culp Hobby; Asst. to Pres. Sherman Adams; Comm. Sec. Sinclair Weeks, Postmaster Gen. Arthur Summerfield; Agr. Sec. Ezra Taft Benson; Labor Sec. Martin Durkin; Henry Cabot Lodge, Ambassador to U. N.; Special Asst. Harold Stassen.

STORMY PETREL of Ike's administration was Sen. Joseph McCarthy (R-Wis.) (shaking hands with the President). He won Eisenhower's backing in the 1952 campaign but in 1954 was the target of administration-directed censure hearings after his 36-day, nationally televised row with the Army over special treatment for his former aide, Pvt. G. David Schine. Chief criticism of McCarthy was his demagogic Red-hunting campaign. His influence slackened, and when he died in 1957 Joe McCarthy was little mourned.

"SENATOR FROM FORMOSA" was the nickname given Senate Majority Leader William Knowland (R., Cal.), who led the fight against recognition of Red China and was the leading champion of Chiang Kai-shek. Knowland said he would leave Senate, seek Cal. gubernatorial seat in 1958.

"ENGINE CHARLIE" Wilson's successor as Defense Secretary was Neil McElroy, appointed in 1957. Former president of Proctor and Gamble, McElroy came to office amid the furor over the launching of Russia's satellites. He promised to revamp the nation's backward defense setup.

EISENHOWER'S ILLNESSES (heart attack 1955, ileitis 1956, mild stroke 1957) caused grave concern about his ability to carry on. Many proposed that far greater responsibility devolve on the Vice-pres. During Ike's absence, Presidential Asst. Sherman Adams assumed a vital role.

JOHN FOSTER DULLES (l.), Ike's appointed successor to Dean Acheson, Secretary of State, took office on a "get tough" policy. Lawyer and foreign affairs expert, Dulles told Europe to defend itself against Communism, sparked 9-nation pact to rearm West Germany at London Conference (October, 1954) despite strong Soviet disapproval. In Asia, Dulles signed 8-nation NATO-type SEATO (South-East Asia Treaty Organization) pact.

INAUGURATION of President Eisenhower gave the Republicans their first chance to whoop it up in 20 years. Here, Ike is lassoed by cowboy actor Monty Montana during inaugural parade, one of the longest in history. Although Eisenhower carried many states, his personal popularity was not enough to gain the Republicans more than bare majority in Congress.

CANADIAN VISIT of reigning British monarchs, King George VI and Queen Elizabeth, shattered precedent in 1939. First to set foot on Canadian soil, King respected Dominion's constitution, deferred to Prime Minister Mackenzie King (back), opened Parliament.

HISTORIC DECISIONS on war strategy and diplomacy were made at the Quebec Conference, Aug., 1943, when Mackenzie King pledged Canadian support of Allied plans to open a "second front" on war-ravaged Europe. Absence of Russian representative, plus recall of Russian ambassador from Washington, D.C., during Quebec Conference led to speculation on possible rift among "Big Three." With King, Franklin D. Roosevelt and Winston Churchill, mapped tactics.

MODERN CANADA

In a quarter-century of progress, a new nation emerges, rich and powerful

Canada looked to internal problems at the end of World War I. She had signed the Versailles Treaty and joined the League of Nations. At home, she had gained industrial strength and, in the exploitation of her vast natural resources, she had begun to evaluate the economic means of the world around her and what they represented.

In the rosy light of a new nationalism, Canada's post-war economy spiralled into inflation and exploded in chaos. Food prices plummeted. Sales, income and "nuisance" taxes remained high.

After the spectacular stock market crashes of Oct. 29 and Nov. 13, 1929, the people of Canada were further unified by depression which spread over the country like a plague. With passage of the Statute of Westminster in 1931, the long-range evolution from British colony to autonomous nation was virtually complete. Bound only by allegiance to the Crown, Canada was now free to bolster her sagging economy by negotiating her own trade treaties. Further, she could now maintain her own diplomatic agents in other countries, including the United States.

Canada and the U.S. had other, more significant ties. Adjacent nations, boasting no armed border patrols, they were equally devastated by depression. In both countries, measures to restore economic "normalcy" were strikingly similar. Prime Minister Bennett's social program for recovery bore more than a chance resemblance to President Roosevelt's "New Deal."

In 1939, Canada once again mobilized for all-out war, this time dispatching troops, food and equipment for bloody fighting on three continents in support of the British Empire. Industry, agriculture and mines throughout the country kept pace with the catastrophic demands of an airborne war.

Canada had geared for war economy on a sound productive basis. When war ended, despite her later contributions to United Nations "police action" in Korea, Canada's enormous output had placed her among the world's postwar giants of industry.

TARIFF EXPERT Richard B. Bennett, leader of Conservatives, in 1930 offered preferential tariff rates to Great Britain against reciprocal concessions to curb U.S. competition during depression. Move helped make him prime minister.

AUTHOR-STATESMAN John Buchan was Lord Tweedsmuir, Canada's governor general 1935 to 1940. During his colorful career as director of Reuters News Service, publisher, lawyer, historian Buchan wrote *39 Steps, The Great War.*

RECOGNITION of Canada's growing importance as a nation came with the appointment of Vincent Massey as first Canadian minister to U.S. Nov., 1926. With Sir Robert Borden (l.), Prime Minister, he visited Pres. Coolidge, 1928.

FOR THE SECOND TIME in 20 years, Canada faced the decision to mobilize for war on European soil. Recovering from depression, building defenses, Mackenzie King's cabinet agreed to declare war if Britain did. On Sept. 10, 1939, Canada was at war with Germany; on June 10, 1940, with Italy; on Dec. 7, 1941, with Japan, Rumania, Hungary, Finland. On the home front, people listened (above), prepared for possible enemy air raids (r.).

MOBILIZATION OF TROOPS for World War II accelerated in 1942. U.S. troops aided Canadian Victory Loan drive in show of strength before Ottawa's Peace Tower, symbolizing high degree of cooperation between two neighbor nations.

VISCOUNT ALEXANDER of Tunis won this title Jan. 1, 1946, a few months after becoming governor general of Canada. A military career-man since World War I, he led Sicily conquest, became Mediterranean Chief Commander, 1944.

ONE DIVISION of Canadian troops went overseas in Sept., 1939. By June, 1945, 630,053 Canadians had seen active duty. Total casualties were reported at 102,954, of which 37,964 were presumed dead. Another cost: money, $7 billion.

ESSENTIAL SUPPLIES for Allies were assured by U.S. Lend-Lease Act of 1941. Planned first to aid Great Britain and China, it was amended the same year to include USSR. Britain signed a "master agreement" Feb., 1942; later reciprocal "reverse" lend-lease for aid to U.S. troops overseas was signed by Canada's Comm. Massey (l.); Russia's Gusev, U.S.'s Winant.

DREAMS OF PEACE for the world inspired delegates from 50 nations to meet at the San Francisco Conference of United Nations Organization where, June 26, 1945, Canada's Prime Minister, Mackenzie King, affixed his signature to the historic charter. With Canadian troops still in Europe, Canada pledged $90 million in supplies for UN Relief, Rehabilitation.

FRIENDLY RELATIONS between two mightiest nations in Western Hemisphere resulted in joint financing of $1.2 billion hydroelectric and waterways projects. N. Y.'s Gov. Thomas E. Dewey (c.) represented the U.S. as Prime Minister Louis St. Laurent and Ontario's Leslie Frost broke ground for power plant at Cornwall, Ont., part of Canada-U.S. $863 million St. Lawrence Seaway project, Aug., 1954. Welland Canal (above), was planned to provide more power, with locks and canals expanded to allow 27 ft. navigation from Lake Erie to Montreal.

BRIDGES SPANNED the wilderness of Labrador as Canada's newest province, Newfoundland, (1949) began full-scale development of natural resources. Ungava iron mines, among richest on N. American continent, found ready market in depleted U.S. forced to import iron for first time.

MEDICAL MACHINE for cancer treatment used radio-active cobalt instead of radium. Produced at Canada's Chalk River Labs., Dr. Ivan Smith named it Cobalt 60 "bomb," experimented at Victoria Hospital, London, Ont. Canada's plentiful cobalt, used in H-bomb, was at a premium.

BLACK RICHES poured from Alberta's growing oil fields, 239,000 barrels daily in June, 1953. By end of year, oil flowed through 771-mile transmountain pipe line into Vancouver, B.C. Across Canada, $200 million was spent to expand refining facilities, more millions for tankers.

HOOF AND MOUTH DISEASE resulted in widespread destruction of cattle and hogs as disease spread through livestock farms early in 1952; again, but less seriously, in spring of 1953. Animals were killed, covered with quick-lime and buried. In hard-hit Saskatchewan, farm cash income still rose to $697.5 million in 1952. Province mined eight million pounds of copper.

AWARD-WINNING MOVIE was Norman McLaren's documentary film of life in Canada. Titled *Neighbors*, story-line pointed up far-reaching results of hatred, what could happen when two men, living in adjoining homes, become enemies and build spite fences. Acted by non-professionals, story climaxed with death of men. Nat'l Film Board is country's major producer.

CANADIANS FOUGHT valiantly once more for the preservation of an ideal, this time in Korea as a member of United Nations. By 1951, when truce talks began, Canada had sent 8,500 men, three destroyers, into free world's fight against communism. Casualties listed 236 dead, 910 wounded. Dominion's defense appropriations, 1952-53, were $2 billion. After Defense Minister Claxton's 1953 report, military budget was upped to $5.7 billion.

PRINCESS ELIZABETH and Duke of Edinburgh included Canada in their 10,000-mile Royal Tour in the fall of 1951. World trip was cut short four months later when her father, King George VI, died, Feb. 6. Elizabeth was proclaimed Queen, Feb. 8, 1952, and was crowned on June 2, 1953.

JOHN DIEFENBAKER (*first row, fourth from left*), a progressive conservative, became Canada's Prime Minister in June, 1957. Here he poses with his Cabinet and Governor-General Vincent Massey (at Diefenbaker's right) after the oath-taking ceremonies in Ottawa. Diefenbaker's new government promptly made plans for increased trade within the Commonwealth.

CANADIAN STUDENTS in Toronto burned effigies of U.S. Senators Joe McCarthy, James Eastland and Senate Committee Investigator Robert Morris in demonstration against U.S. interference in Canadian affairs. Students blamed them for suicide of Herbert Norman, Canadian Ambassador to Egypt, after investigators publicized his alleged former Red connections.

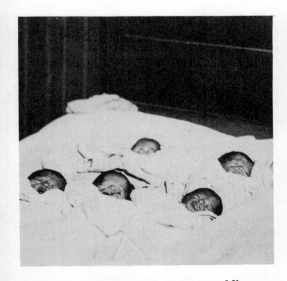

DIONNE QUINTUPLETS, were world's most publicized babies from moment Dr. Dafoe announced successful multiple birth May 28, 1934, in Callander, Ont. Living quietly, they had dropped from news until Emilie died in 1954.

NEWFOUNDLAND became Canada's 10th province Apr. 1, 1949. Discovered by John Cabot, 1497, the island was Great Britain's oldest colony. Strategically located, it was leased from Great Britain by the U.S. in 1941 as an air base.

LESTER BOWLES PEARSON, shown with India's Krishna Menon, was Canada's Foreign Minister until Conservative victory in 1957. A vital and familiar figure at the United Nations, Pearson won the Nobel Peace Price in 1957.

BIKINI ATOMIC TESTS occurred July, 1946. First controlled atomic explosions were joint Army-Navy-Air Force studies of after-effects of blast on machines and animals. Undersea explosion (above) created spectacular geyser several thousand feet high, smothering target ships in radioactive spray. Showers from 1952 tests burned natives of nearby atoll. Radioactive "fall-out" from 1954 hydrogen bomb tests injured Japanese fishermen.

A-BOMB CLOSES WAR

World celebrates peace as debris is removed and reconstruction begins

The world changed for better or worse on July 16, 1945, when the greatest triumph in the history of science was enacted on a cold, gray morning in New Mexico. The first man-made nuclear explosion was a success, raising a cloud of radioactive debris that was visible for miles, and raising seemingly insoluble political problems that became more visible as time passed. Since that date, bigger and better thermonuclear experimental explosions have occurred, and the political implications have kept step, growing in size and complexity with the atomic weapons.

The problem at first seemed clear. Mankind, having at last created the perfect weapon of self-destruction, wished to see it turned to more fruitful purposes. Used correctly, atomic energy could be a great boon to mankind. Misused, it would be a deadly scourge.

The United States, with a generosity hitherto unknown among big powers, offered the secrets of atomic energy to the United Nations, to hold as world custodian. In return, the U.S. requested reasonable and enforceable safeguards against possibility of clandestine use of atomic energy for war-like purposes. This proposal was placed before the U.N. by statesman Bernard M. Baruch on June 14, 1946.

To the dismay of the free world, the Soviet bloc turned down the proposal and countered with one of its own, suggesting that all existing A-bombs be destroyed, and an international control body be created, having limited inspection authority and being subject to the veto of the Security Council, of which the USSR was a member. The free world balked at this scheme. To strip themselves of their atomic shield, and to have no absolute control of surreptitious

H-BOMB AFTERGLOW in 1952 thermonuclear test shows deadly beauty of vast explosion that vaporized test island. In August, 1953, Russia's atomic experts detonated their first H-bomb.

atomic activities by nations of ill-faith was putting too much pressure on international trust and generosity. Not until August, 1955, when Eisenhower startled the world with his "Atoms for Peace" conference in Geneva, did Baruch's proposal seem realistic. In the Swiss Palais des Nations, 1200 scientists from 72 nations gathered "to explore means of developing peaceful uses of atomic energy through international cooperation." Basic objective was to share non-military data on application of atomic energy for fuel, food preservation, farming, medical care and research.

At home in the U. S., AEC's Dr. Walter H. Zinn described the dual-cycle steam reactor, under construction in Chicago for Commonwealth Edison Co., as capable of producing 200,000 kilowatts, enough power to supply a community of 150,000 persons. Other nuclear power-plants were in use or under construction from New York to California. Walter L. Crisler, president of Detroit Edison Co., now headed a 33-company organization known as Atomic Power Development Associates, Inc., formed to research means for making atomic power economically competitive with coal for civilian use.

Meanwhile, amateur and professional uranium hunters, armed with Geiger counters, swarmed hills and desert, staked claims on 2194 acres opened in California by U. S.

DR. EINSTEIN announced in 1953 that he had finished his greatest work, a Unified Field Theory which combined the Laws of Gravitation, Electricity, Magnetism and Relativity. He died in 1955 at age 76.

ENRICO FERMI showed in 1933 that streams of neutrons were ideal atom smashers. He fled Fascist Italy and came to Columbia U. where he built world's first atomic pile. He also helped build 1st A-bomb.

J. ROBERT OPPENHEIMER headed a group concerned with the critical size determination of an atomic bomb. As director of the Los Alamos Project he was responsible for assembly of the first atom bomb exploded at Alamogordo, N.M., in 1945. Security clearance was denied him by AEC at the height of McCarthyite hysteria, but he continued to do important research work.

GIANT BEVATRON in the radiation laboratory of University of California (Berkeley) was completed in 1954. The atom-smasher produced energy of five billion volts. Technician is shown at target area of huge circular machine. The radiation laboratory also had 184-inch cyclotron which had been in operation since 1948. Both these machines led in latest research concerning sub-atomic particles.

ATOMIC SUBMARINE *Nautilus,* launched in January, 1954, was capable of cruising almost indefinitely under water. *Nautilus,* soon followed by *Sea Wolf,* employed nuclear reactor to heat molten metal for boiler, generating steam for turbine. Use of atomic power in naval craft allowed unlimited operational radius. By 1957 atomic submarines were on mass-production basis and an atomic merchant ship was put under construction by the U. S.

FIRST ATOMIC CANNON fired a 1,000-pound projectile with an atomic war-head, carrying equivalent of 10,000 tons of TNT explosive. The test occurred at Nevada proving grounds, May 25, 1953. Giant weapon had barrel 44 feet long with 11-inch bore, and hurled three-foot atomic shell more than seven miles. Another new atomic weapon was "small" A-bomb which a fighter plane could carry.

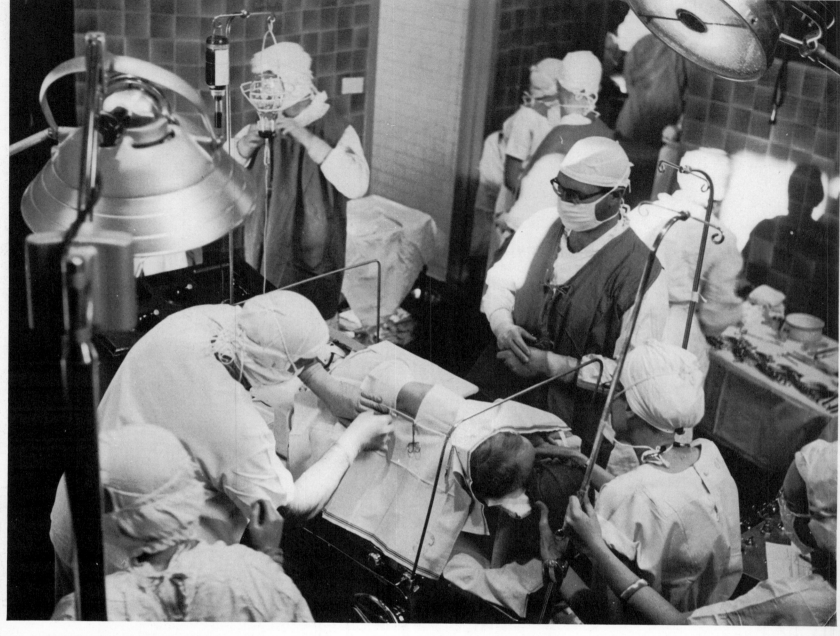

COMMUNICATING HYDROCEPHALUS in infant is cured by dramatic new surgical technique developed by Doctors Eugene B. Spitz and C. Everett Koop of Children's Hospital, Philadelphia. Abnormal accumulation of spinal fluid causes excessive pressure on brain, resulting in death or se-rious brain damage. Rapid growth of neurosurgery is emphasized by this operation. Excess spinal fluid is drained into abdominal cavity by means of a small plastic tube inserted in spinal canal. The operation is performed by two surgeons, through dual incisions made in small of back and abdomen.

MEDICINE
and
SCIENCE

Wartime research helps to provide nation with improved health and a higher living standard

The years following World War II reaped the benefits of important medical and scientific discoveries. The development of antibiotics — new sulfa compounds, penicillin, cortisone, aureomycin, and the use of radioactive isotopes, helped immeasurably in extending the human life span. Poliomyelitis was dealt a lethal blow with the Salk vaccine. Heart disease remained a great killer, but heart catheters and nylon Y-grafts brought relief to heart patients and made diagnosis more efficient. Greater time and money was spent in cancer research.

The electron microscope provided a new industrial tool, as did the electronic computer. The new theory of cybernetics was developed. Radar was employed for peacetime navigation, as well as in investigating the heavens.

Jet planes broke through the sonic barrier and attained speeds three times the speed of sound. Spurred on by Russia's immediate lead in the field, U. S. science and industry combined to work toward the production of superior ballistic and guided missiles. With the release of Russia's *Sputniks* the age of

space dawned. But as it dawned, it became apparent to the public, as it had been to scientists, that the U. S. could be falling behind in scientific knowledge. The evidence was to be found in Russia's lead in several fields, in the fact that most of the great scientists in the U. S. were foreign born, and by the fact that relatively few Nobel prizes in science went to Americans. President Eisenhower and scientists and educators throughout the country called for a complete re-examination of the nation's educational system, for higher salaries for teachers, and a change of attitude toward scientists and intellectuals.

Some of the most fascinating discoveries were made in physics. Einstein, before his death, announced completion of the mathematical formulation of his Unified Field Theory, in which he hoped to demonstrate that nature in all its manifestations, from the stars to atomic particles, follows the same basic laws. One of the "laws" of nature, however, that of the conservation of the parity, was disproved by professors Tsung Dao Lee and Chen Ning Yang in 1957

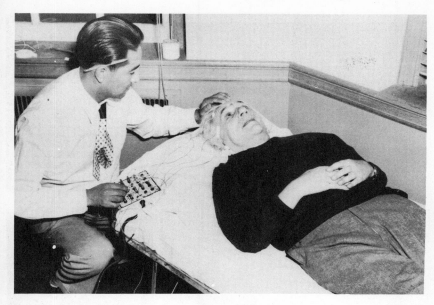

DR. ALBERT EINSTEIN, one of 20th century's most brilliant scientists, submitted to "brain wave" test at Massachusetts General Hospital where the electro-encephalograph was developed in 1950. Equipment recorded electrical fluctuations from brain activity on graph. Through study, scientists hoped to be able to use device as future aid in diagnosing brain damage.

MT. PALOMAR, leading U.S. observatory, houses the famous 200-inch telescope put into operation in 1948. It is capable of photographing objects at a distance of 200,000,000 light years. Responsible for many discoveries of the past decade, the reflector-type device will soon be rendered obsolete by the radio-telescope, which can operate without difficulty in any weather.

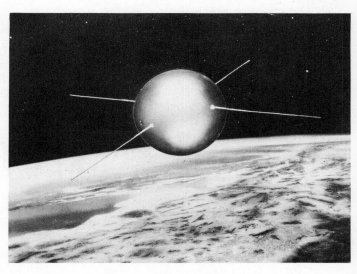

PARITY, a property of wave functions by which quantum mechanics described wave properties, was overthrown by Chinese-born professors C. N. Yang (*l.*) of Princeton and Tsung-Dao Lee (*r.*) of Columbia University, who showed that beta decay particles have both right and left handed spin. These principles, later proved by experiment, brought the 1957 Nobel Prize in physics to the two young professors who worked at Inst. for Advanced Study.

"SPUTNIK I," world's first artificial satellite, was rocket-propelled into outer space by the Russians in October, 1957. This, and "Sputnik II," which bore a live dog aloft, provided a tremendous challenge to American science and education. First U. S. efforts to launch a satellite proved to be dismal failures.

POLIO While research teams continued to ease crippling effects of polio with improved techniques and equipment like the "sit-up" respirator (right) developed at Harvard School of Public Health, Dr. Jonas E. Salk (left) continued work on his vaccine serum. Experiments begun at University of Pittsburgh developed into nationwide test-shots during 1954. By fall of 1955, results were still inconclusive, but new processes were producing purer serums. In August, Eisenhower signed the Poliomyelitis Vaccination Assistance Act of 1955, authorizing Federal Gov't distribution of $30 million in Salk vaccine free to states on basis of need. Topping list was Massachusetts, year's epidemic state, with 2274 polio cases reported by summer's end. All New England totaled only 643 cases in 1954.

FIERCE COMPETITION in autos resumed in 1954. Ford (1954 models, above) and Chevrolet fought for first place. At mid-year, giants General Motors and Ford held 80.7 percent of market. Chrysler was down to 13.5 percent. Independents 5.8 percent. Mergers united Hudson-Nash, others.

MASSIVE INGOT being forged in giant 7,500-ton press symbolizes expansion of steel production. Record output in war, post-war years depleted high grade domestic ores. Industry turned to better recovery processes with low grade Taconite ores; developed foreign deposits in Newfoundland.

INDUSTRY

Despite gloomy predictions, U. S. provides jobs for more than 60 millions

Expansion of the economy of the United States for a sustained period of 15 years (1939-1954) was perhaps the greatest phenomenon of the 20th century. Initiated by the world conflagration which began in 1939, it survived the ending of hostilities, a performance it repeated after the Korean War. It also survived a serious inflation, years of price ceilings and government controls, and three post-war adjustments.

The first adjustment, which came in 1948 following the end of World War II, threatened to be "the big one" many people expected. Unemployment passed 4 million mark, farm prices fell off sharply and industrial production dropped 17 percent. But consumer spending fell off only five percent and business confidence prevented a big drop in investment in new plants and equipment. By the summer of 1949 the boom was underway again, but not for long.

A second adjustment in early 1951 saw unemployment approach the 5 million mark. Then the Korean war changed things quickly. A buying spree by consumers anticipating war shortages of civilian goods reduced retail inventories and piled a backlog of orders on the books of most manufacturers.

The third shake-out began in the fall of 1953. A combination of factors produced it. The first was the "hard money" policy by which the government attempted to curb inflation; its credit shrinking effect accelerated the downturn when it came. Secondly the end of the Korean war produced immediate cuts in defense spending. Once again there was a well-stocked buyers' market.

By midsummer of 1954 some 4.5 million people were unemployed. Steel production had fallen to 63 percent of capacity. Coal production had dropped to an annual rate of 400 million tons — less than two-thirds the rate of 1948. Farm income, which had gone down $2.2 billion in 1953, slipped again in 1954. These were the worst spots. They set a downward pace, but the better part of the economy either did not follow at all or did so only in varying degrees.

In 1955 the U.S. economy moved away from the threat of recession which overhung the early months of 1954. The boom, aided by an expanding population, continued through the year. By 1956 employment rose to an unprecedented 66.7 million. And in spite of Eisenhower's tight money policy, the inflation spiral continued. Company mergers were plentiful.

In 1957 gross national product reached $438 billion although the boom was fading and industrial production was falling off. A definite business slump had occurred. Economic growth continued, but the rate of growth had begun to lag. By 1958, unemployment approached four million.

When Russia launched her *Sputniks* in late 1957 she performed an unintended service to the U.S. This surprising technological feat provided a stimulus for large increases in expenditure for national defense and thus promised to restore business to its pre-slump levels. Outlays for industrial research, which serves to create an "industry of innovation," were expected to exceed $10 billion by 1960, giving further impetus to economic expansion. Economists warned, however, that unless the complacency toward inflation was replaced with effective support for anti-inflationary measures, the national policy of "economic stability with growth" would have a grim future.

POST-WAR PHENOMENON, the television industry expanded rapidly, proved remarkably stable. By 1957 there were some 40 million sets in U.S. homes. Later development, tri-color tube (*above*) promised to start new buying wave if high cost could be reduced by mass-production methods.

SYNTHETIC FIBERS invaded soft goods field after World War II. Nylon (being spun above) all but eliminated silk hosiery. Orlon (also a DuPont development) created male ideal of wrinkle proof suit. Not so ideal was the effect on use of other fabrics. New England wool mills were in depression.

DOUBLE-DECKER passenger car was one innovation railroads used to meet airline competition. Others included Vista Dome cars, self-powered commuter cars, budget meals. Victory of Robert Young in gaining control of New York Central from Wall Street group was helped by Texas oil men.

WORLD'S LARGEST motor, built by General Electric Co., illustrates equipment that necessitated boosting electrical output from 82 million kilowatts in 1950 to an estimated 107 million kw in 1954. Doubling of capacity in next decade was forecast and would require $3.5 billion annual investment.

VAST NEW facilities, more efficient refining processes, emphasis on exploration, resulted in near doubling of U.S. petroleum production between 1944 and 1954. Even so, imports ($434 million in 1952) supplemented domestic output which reached 2.35 billion barrels of crude oil in 1953.

ATOMIC ELECTRIC POWER got under way at the Duquesne Light Company's Shippingport, Pa. plant in 1957. Home owners in the neighborhood were the world's first to benefit from this new power source. Technicians (*above*) prepare to lower the nuclear core containing atomic fuel into position.

SURPLUS, SURPLUS EVERYWHERE was the agriculture situation following World War II. Government price supports inspired increased production of farm commodities. As markets filled up, prices dropped below parity levels. The government had to buy and store the overproduction. Typical result (above), butter stocks piled to the beams of a Chicago warehouse.

"THE LITTLE FLOWER," Mayor Fiorello LaGuardia of New York, as director of the United Nations Relief and Rehabilitation Agency, distributed American surplus foodstuffs to the starving of many lands after the war. Above, he is shown with Secretary of Agriculture Clinton P. Anderson in 1946 examining a load of surplus wheat destined for shipment abroad.

FIRST TO DARE proposal of lower farm price supports was Ezra Taft Benson, Utah farmer named Secretary of Agriculture by President Eisenhower in 1953. His plan: a flexible support scale ranging from 82.5 to 90 per cent of parity. Congress approved flexible supports in 1954.

Agriculture
Amid surplus, high prices, income drops

In the years immediately following World War II, American farmers found themselves in an era of unprecedented prosperity, clouded by doubts of permanency.

Farm surplus, coupled with high prices in food stores, made the entire nation aware of farm policy. In 1954, Congress passed Secretary Ezra Benson's flexible support law. However, farm income already was dropping off, and farmers became more aware that increased consumption, rather than government aid, was the best insurance for a continued high standard of living.

Price supports were not the only reason for huge surpluses. Increased productivity resulted from mechanization made possible with high war incomes. Also, the continuing fight against crop-destroying insects progressed well, with chemists constantly improving compounds to safeguard the nation's crops against blights.

In 1957 Eisenhower signed a compromise Farm Bill with a Soil Bank provision, offering large grants to farmers in exchange for taking land usually sown in basic crops out of production. The Soil Bank plan, however, failed to lick the surplus problem. Farmers were still able to increase yields, and thus over-production continued.

Secretary of Agriculture Ezra Benson claimed lower prices would move crops to market rather than to storage bins. However, his proposal for accomplishing this — lower minimum price supports — raised a storm of protests from farmers. But the President supported Benson, and the declining political importance of the farm bloc made a lower floor on price supports a distinct possibility.

WORLD'S CHAMP at producing butterfat was Daisy Madcap, a Holstein owned by Carnation Milk Co. She produced 1,511.8 pounds of butterfat in a carefully supervised 365-day test. Advances in feed quality plus improved milking techniques boosted dairy products into surplus.

"WETBACKS," or illegal entrants into U.S. from Mexico, were used on many farms in the West and Southwest to ease the farm labor situation. America was so short on farm labor that an agreement was made with Mexico whereby that nation supplied thousands of workers each year to help with the harvesting of seasonal crops.

DROUTH, scourge of farmers for centuries, struck various parts of the nation several years running. Dryness was so extensive and farmers were so heavily hit that disaster conditions were proclaimed in several areas, making Federal funds available to the stricken. Even worse was loss of topsoil in floods which followed dry spells.

POLES APART in their professional lives were John L. Lewis (l.), president of the United Mine Workers, and Sen. Robert A. Taft, co-author of the Taft-Hartley labor law, which restricted unions to greater extent than at any time since early 1930's. They met here at a Senate hearing on mine safety regulations. One of the CIO's founders, Lewis later split with the leadership, briefly aligned his mine workers with AFL, but soon withdrew.

LABOR'S BIGGEST UNIONS joined forces when the AFL and CIO merged in December, 1955. Newly elected president George Meany (l.) and new vice president Walter Reuther celebrate the event. Meany faced the problems of organizing craft and industrial unions. Craft unions wanted to maintain their independence and jurisdictional disputes occurred across the country. Membership in the new federation totalled 15 million workers.

LABOR

Unions fight Taft-Hartley Law

From its struggling beginnings as an organized movement, American labor suddenly shot skyward in membership, finances and political strength during the New Deal of the 30's, the Second World War and the "Fair Deal" which followed it.

Following World War II, after a series of crippling strikes in basic industries, the Republican 80th Congress passed the Taft-Hartley Act, a law which reduced the extensive powers granted unions under the Wagner Act. The provision of Taft-Hartley most attacked by labor leaders was abolition of the "closed shop", meaning workers no longer were required to join the union in their respective plants. Although President Truman vetoed the act in 1947, Congress overrode the veto. From a favored position, labor was restored to a closer balance of power with management.

Twice during the post-war years Social Security was extended, first to cover farm and domestic workers, then self-employed and professional people. In 1954 the minimum wage was raised from 75¢ to $1.00 an hour. A guaranteed annual wage (with modifications) was won by the UAW at Ford and General Motors in 1955.

Unemployment reached all-time lows during World War II. Immediately afterwards, the pent-up demand for consumer goods kept everybody working. A slump followed in 1948-49, but the Korean War, in 1950, brought full employment again. The early Fifties witnessed a continuing boom, which began to run its course by 1957, however, and in 1958 unemployment reached four million.

The much-discussed merger of the AFL and CIO occurred in 1955 when their respective heads, George Meany and Walter Reuther, agreed to bring their giant, rival organizations together. Labor then spent vast sums to organize more workers and to prevent more states from adopting "right-to-work" (open shop) laws.

Labor's record was marred, however, by the widespread corruption in some unions that was uncovered in 1957 by the Senate Rackets Committee, headed by Sen. McClellan (D., Ark.). One of the worst of the labor bosses, Teamster Boss Dave Beck, lost his position and his union was ousted from the AFL-CIO as result of exposure of malfeasance on a grand scale. Even worse than corruption, however, was the proven connection of garbage collectors' and longshoremens' unions in the New York area with organized crime. Reuther emerged as labor's champion in the months following the exposures. He denounced corrupt union leaders, declaring that unless the unions cleaned themselves up, groups unfriendly to labor would do the job for them. He also called for increased production.

Despite glum predictions of recession, general prosperity continued as the Sixties approached, and that prosperity added new impetus to labor's biggest goals: higher wages and a four-day week.

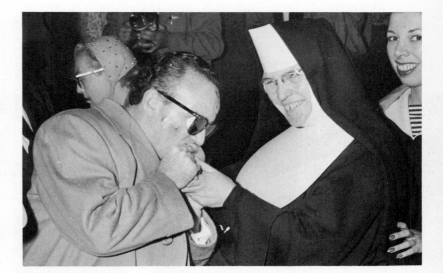

LABOR COLUMNIST VICTOR RIESEL, blinded in an acid throwing attack in 1956, is shown (r.) leaving hospital. Abraham Telvi, suspected acid hurler, was shot by the gang that paid him $1000. Johnny Dio, New York racketeer, was charged with arranging the attack. Riesel had been crusading against labor racketeers and continued to do so after the attack. Incident brought national attention to labor scandals, led to Senate investigation.

TEAMSTERS' UNION was investigated in 1957 by AFL-CIO Ethical Practices Committee and Senate Rackets Committee. Dave Beck (r.), then Teamster President, and Vice Pres. James Hoffa (l.) took 5th Amendment. Hoffa was made new Teamster boss in a disputed election despite exposure of corruption. Later, AFL-CIO ousted tainted Teamsters' and Bakers' unions. Beck was convicted of misusing funds, Hoffa tried for illegal wiretapping.

BRILLIANT COLUMNIST of the New York *Times*, Anne O'Hare McCormick won Pulitzer prize in 1937. She died in 1954. Her analyses of world events were usually based on personal observation and knowledge gained from travels.

WILLIAM OATIS, A.P. correspondent in Prague, was arrested by Czech police on charges of espionage. He spent two years in jail, despite all-out efforts by the U.S. State Department to obtain his release.

DISTINGUISHED publishing by Arthur Hays Sulzberger of the New York *Times* gave American journalism a distinctive yet conservative touch. Stress was laid upon accuracy, completeness and objectivity in news coverage, clarity in editorial columns.

PRESS

The significant story in newspaper publishing during and since World War II was the increase in circulation of large chain dailies — and the dropping away of many smaller, independent papers. The war helped to create a serious shortage of newsprint, and sent operating costs spiralling upward to such an extent that weaker papers were forced to consolidate with others in a stronger position. Inevitably, increased standardization of editorial opinion was a result.

Many major cities could boast only a single newspaper, often presenting only one side of local and national issues. The cost of starting a new metropolitan daily was prohibitive, running into millions. Just two were launched during the entire decade: the high successful *Newsday* of Alicia Patterson, published in Long Island City, New York; and Norman Chandler's Los Angeles *Mirror*, which continued to lose money. Another Chandler paper, the conservative Los Angeles *Times*, was an immense financial success.

Notable for excellence were the *Christian Science Monitor* of Boston, the *St. Louis Post Dispatch*, and the magazine, *U.S. News and World Report*.

SYNDICATION OF columnists like Walter Winchell (below) and Drew Pearson markedly increased. Additional dissemination of their views through radio and TV programs led to a concentration of opinion-molding in hands of top few.

GOSSIP COLUMNS of Hollywood's Hedda Hopper (below) and Louella Parsons were known throughout world. Often scolding stars, occasionally ecstatic in praise, such columnists wielded power in making or breaking careers.

JOURNALISTIC empire of William Randolph Hearst floundered and was recovered several times in his 64 years of publishing. After his death in 1951, his sons took over management of his publishing empire, ran his newspapers.

JOHN HERSEY

CARL SANDBURG

NORMAN MAILER

BOOKS

America's authors were writing about the things that concerned a majority of their fellow-citizens: the meaning of the war, and of their individual experiences in it. John Hersey's *A Bell for Adano* and *The Wall*, Irwin Shaw's *The Young Lions*, Norman Mailer's *The Naked and the Dead*, Herman Wouk's *The Caine Mutiny* — all were tough, realistic — yet vaguely tender — books with the war their central theme. Accompanying these was a spate of books on religion and guidance for the troubled: *Peace of Mind*, by Joshua Loth Liebman; the Overstreets' *The Mature Mind*; *The Power of Positive Thinking*, by Norman Vincent Peale, held top places on best-seller lists. War memoirs of Winston Churchill, Dwight Eisenhower, Harold Ickes and others made their appearance.

Poet-novelist-historian Carl Sandburg's definitive biography of Abraham Lincoln, begun in 1926, was completed in 1954. The Nobel prize was awarded to Ernest Hemingway the same year for *The Old Man and the Sea*.

Into the changing book world came the small paper-backed "pocket book," sold at drug counters, supermarkets, railway stations. Some were excellent reproductions of classics or former best-sellers. Emphasis was on mystery, adventure, "Western" stories, and their wide market affected "hard cover" sales. Comic books were popular with America's young readers. The onslaught of television seemed to hurt only the magazines, whose sales dropped off alarmingly. *Colliers, American* and *Woman's Home Companion* failed in 1956-1957, as did the music magazine *Etude* and *Town Journal*.

CLASSROOM WAS JAMMED on a day in January, 1949, when the famous stage star Judith Anderson modeled at the Art Institute of Chicago. She is posing as woman obsessed by revenge in Euripedes *Media*.

IN HER NINETIES "Grandma" Moses was America's best loved artist. She began to paint in her 70's. Her simple American primitive rural scenes were widely reproduced. Another favorite was Norman Rockwell for his skillful, nostalgic portrayal of small town life on the covers of the *Sat. Eve. Post*. He won acclaim for his World War II murals illustrating Four Freedoms.

ART
Public interest grows

JACKSON POLLOCK, leader of controversial "drip" school (*above*, "No. 1, 1948") died in August, 1956 auto accident. The canvasses of Pollock, acknowledged leader of New York school, have since increased enormously in their value.

BOLD, SATIRIC STYLE of William Gropper is evident in his *Don Quixote No. 1* which was awarded $500 third prize in Carnegie Institute Exhibition, *Painting in the United States, 1946*.

World War II and its aftermath saw a revival of public interest in the old masters and further development of abstract painting in America. The $15 million National Gallery of Art building, public gift from Andrew Mellon, was dedicated in 1941. Postwar travel exhibits of art treasures from abroad stirred public appreciation.

European artists came to the U.S. after the war and interested American painters in surrealist and abstract art. In the early 1950's most of the important exhibitions featured abstractionism. Its strangeness and spectacular quality found a wide if somewhat dubious public interest. A larger group of American artists painted representational observations but used distortions of form or color for interest.

Vivid portrayals of Chicago street scenes were done by Aaron Bohrod. Peter Hurd won acclaim for his realistic rendition of the spacious beauty of the great West. In the troubled Korean and cold war years, the example set by Eisenhower inspired many Americans to find relaxation and satisfaction in painting as a hobby.

END OF THE FESTIVAL colorful street scene by Louis Bosa was an award winner in 1949. The number and quality of awards and scholarships for artists increased greatly after World War II. Among the most coveted: the *Prix de Rome*.

GENERAL EISENHOWER poses for Jo Davidson whose works include busts of Woodrow Wilson, Franklin D. Roosevelt. His bust of former Army General John J. Pershing rests in the Pentagon Bldg. The famous sculptor died in 1952.

STRANGE AND EXCITING shapes in sculpture were viewed with equanimity during war and post-war years. *Enigma* (l.) is the work of Jose de Creeft. Center is Blanche Phillips' *Duo* and (r.) Henry Moore's titanic statuary. Dubious crushed-wire type of "profound interpretations" were constant set-back to public avantgarde sculpture acceptance.

RICHARD RODGERS, composer of musical comedies, collaborated with Oscar Hammerstein II in writing *Oklahoma!* in 1943. Their first operetta as a team, it won a special prize from the Pulitzer Committee in 1944. In 1947, they created *Allegro,* then *South Pacific* (1949), *King and I* (1951).

THE "MAESTRO," Arturo Toscanini, retired from the podium in 1953 after half a century of conducting symphonic and opera music. Considered the era's finest, Toscanini conducted on three continents, but never performed in Fascist countries. When he died in 1956 he was widely mourned.

MUSIC FOR MILLIONS

Radio, television, and motion pictures popularize symphony and opera

Music, from Metropolitan Opera to singing commercials, poured into American homes via television and radio. Vaster audiences than ever before saw top performers for the price of a receiving set, and the tolerance of commercials, in their own living rooms.

American composers gained importance. Music by Pulitzer prize winners Samuel Barber (*Overture to the School for Scandal,* 1932, *Commando March,* 1943) and Aaron Copeland (*Our Town,* 1940, *Appalachian Spring,* 1945) became increasingly familiar. Leonard Bernstein, young composer-conductor, won the Boston Symphony Orchestra Merit Award for 1949 for his *The Age of Innocence,* wrote scores for Broadway musicals, *Peter Pan* (1950) and *Wonderful Town* (1953). Ferde Grofe added *Aviation Suite* (1945) to his earlier works.

Cole Porter was still most famous for his melodies *Begin the Beguine* and *Night and Day,* and for his musical comedies: *Gay Divorcee* (1932), *Anything Goes* (1934), *Jubilee* (1935), and *Let's Face It* (1941). David Rose and Morton Gould wrote musical impressions of the twentieth century.

Smaller cities, such as Denver, Santa Monica, Tampa and Wilmington, Del., created orchestras from local talent and inaugurated family programs at popular prices.

Soloists Jascha Heifetz, Yehudi Menuhin, Zino Francescatti, Isaac Stern (violin); Vladimir Horowitz, Artur Rubinstein (piano); Gregor Piatigorsky (cello); and Wanda Landowska (harpsichord), played to audiences all over the world. Thor Johnson (Cincinnati), Alfred Wallenstein (Los Angeles) and Leonard Bernstein (New York) became the first native-born conductors of major U.S. symphony orchestras.

Singers Richard Crooks, Lawrence Tibbett and Lotte Lehmann went into retirement. Among other singers who went beyond opera to the musical comedy stage and other media were John Charles Thomas, Robert Merrill, Leonard Warren, Lauritz Melchior, Ezio Pinza, Kirsten Flagstad, Helen Traubel, and Patrice Munsel.

Motion picture composers received their share of prominence. Academy awards went to Alfred Newman for *Song of Bernadette* (1943), *Mother Wore Tights* (1947) and *Song in My Heart* (1952); to Max Steiner for *Since You Went Away* (1944), and to Dmitri Tiomkin for *High Noon* (1953).

Gyrating Elvis Presley became the adolescents' favorite rock n' roll singer, while Bing Crosby, Pat Boone, Frank Sinatra, Eddie Fisher, Perry Como and others led the field in popular song renditions. Biggest boon to musicians was the renewed public interest in recordings after long-playing high fidelity discs were made available.

REVITALIZED under Rudolph Bing's direction, N. Y.'s Metropolitan Opera Co. starred vivacious young singers like contralto Rise Stevens, a popular Carmen.

EASY performances were given by singers Frank Sinatra and Dinah Shore. Sinatra scored as an actor.

HELEN TRAUBEL replaced Kirsten Flagstad as leading Wagnerian singer, was guest artist on radio, night club programs.

HIGHEST PAID prima donna, coloratura Lily Pons and husband, conductor, Andre Kostelanetz, held concert stage successfully more than 20 years.

THEATER

Musicals and GI shows spur stage resurgence

Show business boomed during World War II. Widest-flung entertainment circuit of all time was that of U.S.O. Camp Shows, which played to GI's all over the globe. On its own, show business organized such soldier meccas as the American Theater Wing's Stage Door Canteen in New York City. It promoted mammoth bond rallies, lunch-time "Follies" for the entertainment of defense workers. Benefit shows like Irving Berlin's *This Is The Army* and Moss Hart's *Winged Victory* grossed millions of dollars for the Army Emergency Relief Fund.

New playwrights brought highly individual themes and treatments to the legitimate stage, from William Saroyan's *The Time of Your Life* (1941) and Mary Chase's *Harvey* (1945) — to Tennessee Williams' unusual *A Streetcar Named Desire* (1948), directed by Elia Kazan, and Arthur Miller's powerful *Death of a Salesman* (1949). All were Pulitzer Prize winners, as was Thornton Wilder's *The Skin of Our Teeth* (1943), starring Tallulah Bankhead, Frederic March, Florence Eldridge, Montgomery Clift.

A previous Tennessee Williams play, *The Glass Menagerie*, with Laurette Taylor, Julie Haydon and Eddie Dowling as its stars, had won the critics' award for 1944. Another off-beat success was William Inge's *Come Back, Little Sheba*, which brought stardom to Shirley Booth after 20 years as an actress. Carson McCuller's *The Member of the Wedding*, and the acting of Ethel Waters, Julie Harris and Brandon de Wilde created excellent theater.

Eugene O'Neill Dies

Long Day's Journey into Night, by Eugene O'Neill (who died in 1953) only hit Broadway in 1957 after premiering in Sweden.

Life With Father, adapted from the Clarence Day book by Howard Lindsay and Russel Crouse, was the play with the longest run (3,224 performances) in the history of the American theater, had a box office "take" of nearly $10 million.

Outstanding among war plays were: *Mister Roberts,* produced by Leland Hayward and Joshua Logan, starring Henry Fonda; *Tomorrow the World,* with Ralph Bellamy, Shirley Booth, Skippy Homeier. John van Druten's *The Voice of the Turtle* was a producer's dream; it called for a single stage set and only three actors.

Popular musicals were *Something for the Boys* with Ethel Merman, *Pal Joey* by Rodgers and Hart, written in 1940 and revived in 1952, *Guys and Dolls,* whose plot was woven from collected Damon Runyon stories, *Gentlemen Prefer Blondes,* from the famous Anita Loos book.

But perhaps the greatest innovations took place in what might be called the "serious" musicals. Such productions as *Oklahoma!,* *South Pacific* and *My Fair Lady* carved a place high above the former songs-and-skits type of Broadway revue popular in the 1930's.

STUNNING LEGS of Katharine Hepburn were a little known facet of her talents until she appeared in *As You Like It,* 1950. She had previous light comedy success in Philip Barry's *The Philadelphia Story.*

TOUR DE FORCE was performance by Vivien Leigh and Sir Laurence Olivier, on alternate nights, of Shaw's *Caesar & Cleopatra,* Shakespeare's *Antony & Cleopatra.*

ETHEL MERMAN hit the mark in uproarious 1946 success, *Annie Get Your Gun,* book by Dorothy & Herbert Fields, music by Irving Berlin. The Berlin-Merman team scored another hit in 1950, *Call Me Madam.*

PRIZE-WINNING play *Inherit the Wind* was based on the Scopes trial of the 20's. It brought Paul Muni (r.) back to Broadway scene in 1955 after a six-year absence.

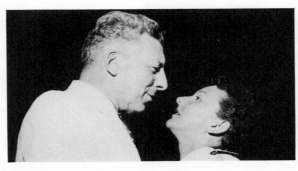

983 ENCHANTED evenings were spent by audiences at Rodgers' & Hammerstein's *South Pacific,* based on the James Michener book. It was triumph for versatile Mary Martin and opera star Ezio Pinza, whose virile role created vogue for older actors in romantic parts.

1952 AWARDS are presented by Helen Hayes (c.) to co-authors Rodgers and Hammerstein for *The King and I,* musical starring Gertrude Lawrence (l.), who died during run; Yul Brynner (far r.).

"MY FAIR LADY," based on Shaw's *Pygmalion* was Broadway's greatest hit in 1957. Rex Harrison (l.) as Prof. Higgins played in his first musical. British Julie Andrews (r.) made a charming Eliza Doolittle.

AGAINST ADVICE of Broadway sages, the Theater Guild's Theresa Helburn produced *Oklahoma* in 1943. It turned out to be most successful musical in history.

MOST PROVOCATIVE and discussed film in many years was *Citizen Kane* (1941), which young Orson Welles (l.) wrote, produced, directed and starred in with Joseph Cotten (r.). Its advanced camera technique, unorthodox lighting earned many critical raves.

MRS. MINIVER, story of wartime England, won major awards for 1942: Best production, screenplay, cinematography, direction (William Wyler), acting (Greer Garson, Teresa Wright). Walter Pidgeon played middle class Britisher, Mr. Miniver.

LANA TURNER was a prime example of the Hollywood legend that an unknown can become a star by being "discovered" at a soda fountain. In 1938 she was the object of Mickey Rooney's affection in an *Andy Hardy* movie. Soon she graduated to title, screen's glamorous "sweater girl."

WELSH MINING town was realistic setting for 1941's best film, *How Green Was My Valley*, for which director John Ford and cameraman Arthur Miller won awards. Walter Pidgeon and Maureen O'Hara were starred.

JOAN CRAWFORD returned to screen in 1945 after several years' absence to capture her first Oscar as the sacrificing mother in Warner Brothers' much publicized *Mildred Pierce*, with Zachary Scott.

INNER STRUGGLE of an alcoholic was dramatically portrayed by Ray Milland in *Lost Weekend*, 1945's best production. The role won Oscars for Milland and Billy Wilder.

MOVIES

Boom days of 1947's sky-high profits ended all too soon. The threat of television, studio-theater divorcement and foreign monetary restrictions took their toll. By 1952, a movie-TV battle royal raged as the country bought 12 million TV sets and 5,500 theaters had closed since 1946. The movie attendance dropped, and only popcorn-candy sales kept exhibitors "out of the red."

The shot-in-the-arm came in 1953 with third dimension, an old novelty, revived. Audiences thronged box offices in unprecedented numbers to see "bigger and better" pictures on wide screen with stereophonic sound. CinemaScope (ratio 2.55:1) became the standardized medium, rivalled by Vista-Vision, Cinerama. Prosperity was reborn.

PINOCCHIO followed overwhelming success of *Snow White* as Walt Disney's second feature-length cartoon. Its skillful animation, score *(When You Wish Upon a Star)* were standouts.

LARRY PARKS created perfect illusion, simulating Jolson's style to recorded songs in *The Jolson Story*.

AT WAR'S END real-life veteran Harold Russell (l.), amputee, won Hollywood's Oscar for his portrayal of G.I. readjustment in *The Best Years of Our Lives* in 1946. This was his only movie.

NEGRO-WHITE RELATIONS, a subject hitherto taboo, was treated frankly in several 1949 films: Stanley Kramer's *Home of the Brave* and 20th Century's *Pinky* (below) with Ethel Waters and Jeanne Crain.

DEAF MUTE, played by award-winning Jane Wyman, was central character of the poignant drama, *Johnny Belinda*, with Agnes Moorehead, C. Bickford, L. Ayres.

JOHN HUSTON won screenplay, direction awards (1948) for his great *Treasure of Sierra Madre*, with father Walter, Humphrey Bogart, Tim Holt.

POLITICAL DICTATOR (resembling Huey Long) was the central figure of 1949's best film, Robert Rosson's *All the King's Men*. Broderick Crawford, Mercedes McCambridge won awards.

INSANITY was given shockingly realistic treatment in 20th Century-Fox *The Snake Pit*. Olivia de Havilland, star, won Academy Award for her role in *To Each His Own*.

SCHIZOPHRENIC actor was played by Ronald Colman in the Garson Kanins' *A Double Life* (1947). It earned him his first Oscar. Another went to Miklos Rozsa for musical scoring. Film gave Shelley Winters her first big chance.

DEFT COMEDIENNE Judy Holliday stole all comedy honors from Katharine Hepburn and Spencer Tracy in her first film, *Adam's Rib* (1949). The next year, in a starring role, she repeated, this time winning an Academy Award for playing brassy, culture-seeking Billie Dawn in *Born Yesterday*. This was Columbia's film version of Judy's hilarious stage success of the same name, with William Holden (l.) and Broderick Crawford, co-stars.

BEST PICTURE of 1950 was 20th Century-Fox's sophisticated drama of a scheming actress, *All About Eve*, with Anne Baxter, Bette Davis, Marilyn Monroe (soon to be 20th's delight). Cynical George Sanders won Academy Award.

DANNY KAYE'S jet-speed comedy delivery made him an overnight hit in Broadway's *Lady in the Dark*. History repeated itself in his first picture, musical *Up In Arms* (1943) and again in Goldwyn's *The Secret Life of Walter Mitty* (above, with Virginia Mayo) in 1947.

CATTLE DRIVE over an unknown trail was the story of Howard Hawks' *Red River*, one of the best Westerns ever made. It starred John Wayne (l.), Montgomery Clift (r.) who had made hit in *The Search*.

INGRID BERGMAN was impressive in lavish *Joan of Arc*, 1948. Actress won Academy Award in 1944 for performance in *Gaslight*.

DUEL IN THE SUN proved to be one of producer David Selznick's greatest successes. Jennifer Jones and gun-toting Gregory Peck made their fiery love conflict one of the production's highlights. Film grossed $9 million to join all-time top money makers in the movie industry.

GLORIA SWANSON made a great comeback in *Sunset Boulevard* (1950), an offbeat Hollywood drama about a silent-movie queen who murders the writer she loves (William Holden). Film won story, art, set decoration and also music awards.

VIVIEN LEIGH'S ill-starred heroine won her an Academy Award in *Streetcar Named Desire* (1951), co-starring Marlon Brando, Karl Malden, Kim Hunter.

HIGH NOON was highlight of 1952. Gary Cooper (with Grace Kelly) as a town marshal who single-handedly fought four desperadoes, won the "Oscar."

LOVE AFFAIR between hardened skipper (Humphrey Bogart) and spinster (Katharine Hepburn) sparked the wartime plot of John Huston's *The African Queen.*

JOHN FORD won fourth "best director" award for *The Quiet Man* (1952). Filmed in Ireland, the cast included Barry Fitzgerald, John Wayne, Maureen O'Hara, Abbey Players.

DETECTIVE STORY, film version of Sidney Kingsley's hit play, rated as tense melodrama, exposing the inner workings of a detective bureau. William Bendix, Joseph Wiseman and Kirk Douglas shared honors.

GENTLEMEN PREFER BLONDES proved to be an excellent vehicle to display the dancing and singing charms of Marilyn Monroe and Jane Russell. Named the "fastest rising star of 1952," Miss Monroe enhanced her popularity with a provocative walk and "come-hither" look, then modified her approach. Miss Russell, famous for her performance in censored *The Outlaw,* invited chastisement again with her dance in *The French Line.*

CIRCUS SAWDUST and melodrama under the big top featured Cecil B. DeMille's *The Greatest Show on Earth,* voted best production and film story of 1951. An all-star cast included Cornel Wilde, James Stewart, Betty Hutton, with C. Heston and Gloria Grahame supporting.

CINERAMA was the first technical change that helped revolutionize movie production and revitalize an ailing industry in 1952. Projecting three images side-by-side on one huge screen, the Lowell Thomas-Merian Cooper process gave a vivid feeling of third dimension. Roller coaster scene (above) electrified viewers.

HOUSE OF WAX was one of the first 3-D films, a box office success for Warner Bros. Requiring polaroid glasses, it abounded in "3-D gimmicks" that tickled audiences, annoyed critics. After the first flurry of 3-D films viewers settled for good shows.

SHIRLEY BOOTH made a clean sweep of best actress awards (Academy, Cannes, New York) repeating stage success for Hal Wallis' *Come Back, Little Sheba,* in 1953.

ALL-GERSHWIN musical score, exciting choreography set in Gay Paree love story gave MGM's *An American in Paris* the best picture, screenplay (Alan Jay Lerner), photography, and other awards in 1951. Ballet dancer Leslie Caron made her film debut, teaming with Gene Kelly in brilliant ballet.

MOULIN ROUGE led the field of biographical movies in John Huston's 1952 story of the deformed Parisian artist, Toulouse-Lautrec, starring Jose Ferrer, Zsa Zsa Gabor (below) Colette Marchand. Art direction, costume design, set decoration were outstanding and won awards. Huston's color sublety was achieved with filters.

ALAN LADD had the best role of his career in George Stevens' *Shane,* a rugged conflict between homesteaders and strong cattlemen.

FRANK SINATRA won an Oscar for dramatic role in 1953's most honored film, *From Here to Eternity*, with Montgomery Clift, Lancaster, Deborah Kerr.

RITA HAYWORTH added another sultry heroine to her credit as the torrid nightclub singer in *Miss Sadie Thompson*. Somerset Maugham's classic story of moral reformation in the South Seas, *Rain*, was remade in "3-D" color by Columbia Pictures.

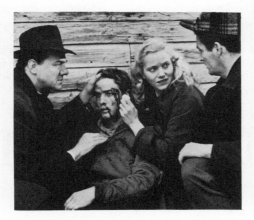

HERMAN WOUK'S *The Caine Mutiny* (Pulitzer Prize) earned acclaim as film, starring Fred Mac Murray, Robert Francis, Van Johnson, and Bogart.

MARLON BRANDO added another brilliant role to his list in Budd Schulberg's brutal story of waterfront racketeers, *On the Waterfront* (1954). Movie was directed by Elia Kazan and starred Karl Malden (left) and Eva Marie Saint.

JUDY GARLAND made a great "comeback" in Warner Brothers' handsome three-hour re-make of *A Star Is Born*. Her singing, dancing emoting brought her popular and critical acclaim in the sympathetic role of the young actress who reaches stardom as her matinee idol husband (James Mason) loses his fame and becomes an alcoholic. Judy's husband, Sid Luft, produced; George Cukor directed; co-starred Charles Bickford, Jack Carson.

ALCOHOLISM was treated with sensitivity and warmth in Paramount's film version of Odet's fine play *The Country Girl*. Bing Crosby, Grace Kelly and William Holden were distinguished cast.

UNLIKELY CASTING of Marilyn Monroe with Laurence Olivier resulted in romantic comedy *The Prince and the Showgirl* (1957). Olivier, as regent of mythical country, sought Miss Monroe's companionship.

ANOTHER ALL-STAR cast turned MGM's *Executive Suite*, produced by John Houseman, into one of 1954's most successful films. Cast: Louis Calhern, Paul Douglas, Frederic March, Barbara Stanwyck, William Holden, Nina Foch, June Allyson.

ROVING ROMEO (Gary Cooper) falls in love with naive, but determined French girl (Audrey Hepburn) in charming 1957 comedy *Love in the Afternoon*.

"MARTY," by TV playwright Paddy Chayevsky, was first U.S. film to win Cannes Grand Prix (1955). Picture starred Ernest Borgnine.

"EAST OF EDEN," John Steinbeck's novel, was filmed by Elia Kazan in 1955. A Cannes Festival winner, it told of the clash between a devout man (Raymond Massey, *r.*) and his twin sons, one "good", the other "wicked" (James Dean, *c.*), who discover a starting fact about their mother, believed by them to be dead.

AFRICAN SAFARI and a love triangle made John Ford's *Mogambo* first rate entertainment. Top acting honors went to Ava Gardner (l.) and Grace Kelly (c.) for their roles as competitors for the affection of Clark Gable (repeating original role he played in 1932; Jean Harlow was co-star).

FIRST CINEMASCOPE film, *The Robe*, justified 20th Century-Fox's gamble to convert entirely to the new medium. Other studios followed suit, as *Robe* made millions.

DISTINGUISHED REPORTING of Edward R. Murrow on CBS' *See It Now* gave line and form to TV's spotty newscasting. His 1952 example encouraged other top reporters like Walter Winchell to try TV. Murrow's *Person to Person* combined "live" remote interviews with use of film.

"ARTHUR GODFREY and his Friends", a popular variety show, featured Godfrey touches of casual commercials and ukelele strumming. He made headlines when he fired a number of his "friends" on the grounds that they did not show proper "humility." But his fans remained loyal.

HERO TO CHILDREN across the nation through his role of *Hopalong Cassidy*, Bill Boyd — star of stage and silent films — shared pinnacle with puppets. "Naturals" for TV medium, popular even with adults were *Howdy Doody* (insert below), *Kukla, Fran, and Ollie, Time for Beanie.*

TELEVISION BOOMS

A phenomenon in American life, it revolutionized U. S. living habits

After World War II, television emerged from the laboratory and became a commercial reality, bringing perceptible changes in American family life. Conversation went into a decline as U. S. rooftops sprouted TV aerials. Vintage movies and wrestling were, at first, the major fare of the 10- or 12-inch screens.

In 1945 10,000 sets were in production. On September 4, 1951, 16,000,000 sets in America were tuned to the Japanese Peace Treaty Conference in San Francisco. It was the first coast-to-coast telecast. Today such telecasts are very common. Many shows seen in New York originate in Hollywood, and some, like the Academy Award presentations, switch back and forth from Hollywood to New York.

In 1951 too, CBS aired the first commercial color telecast using its" non-compatible" system. During the Korean War, RCA stepped up experimentation with a "compatible" system which allows color telecasts to be picked up by black and white receivers. On December 17, 1953, the FCC granted permission for the first color telecast of a commercial program: Menotti's television opera *Amahl and the Nightvisitors* on December 21. Incidentally this opera was so successful that it became a television Christmas classic.

As television has grown, with larger screens at lower cost, the fare has improved considerably. There are dramatic programs which allow the talents of new playwrights and actors to be displayed. Variety shows, westerns and situation comedies abound. The most popular type to emerge is the quiz show. It has either a single contestant, a pair of rival contestants or a panel of celebrities answering questions. Prizes on these programs have reached astronomical proportions, for example top prize on *$64,000 Question* is $256,000.

Although quiz shows have certain educative features, they stress the capacity to remember isolated detail. The great hopes for educational TV have not been fulfilled yet, although there has been tremendous progress. All over the U.S. there are closed circuit programs for those who cannot attend school in person. In New York there was an English literature course, *Sunrise Semester*, given by New York University in 1957-8.

News coverage is an important feature of television. Through this medium everyone can see as well as hear history in the making, such as U.N. proceedings, Senate investigations, and so on. Charity benefits reach millions of potential donors as well as provide entertainment for them in mammoth proportions—the "telethon"—when the particular benefit has been given unlimited air time.

NIKITA KHRUSHCHEV was an unexpected television personality in 1957 when he appeared on "Face the Nation" in an unrehearsed interview situation. He was unpredictably frank in his responses to queries by top CBS reporters concerning political issues between the U.S. and the U.S.S.R.

LACK OF STAGE PRESENCE apparently made Ed Sullivan (*l.*) especially endearing to audiences and CBS changed the name of his variety program to *The Ed Sullivan Show*. It specialized in big names, such as Jack Benny (*c.*) and Groucho Marx (*r.*), who appeared in comedy or dramatic skits.

PEABODY AWARD and five "Emmies" were among the honors given to *Requiem for a Heavyweight*, a "Playhouse 90" production for CBS. Rod Serling received the Peabody Award, which was for the first time in its history, given to a television writer. Jack Palance (*c.*) starred and former comedians Ed (*l.*) and Keenan (*r.*) Wynn showed artistry in dramatic roles.

"I LOVE LUCY" featured energetic and versatile talents of Lucille Ball with real-life band leader husband, Desi Arnaz, as TV husband, "Ricky Ricardo." Hilarious weekly show soared to top popularity rating in 1952. Desilu Productions made by-product fortune lending name "Lucy" and "Ricky" to husband-wife twin pajama sets, "Ricky" dolls; produced other TV shows.

NOSTALGIC VAUDEVILLE routines of Jimmy Durante and Eddie Jackson found ready TV audience. Margaret Truman rehearsed one of many appearances during father's Presidency.

MILTON BERLE clowned in outlandish costumes and thrilled the new audience of T.V with famous guest stars on "Texaco Star Theater." "Mr. T V" signed 30 year contract with NBC.

DRAGNET, Jack Webb's underplayed series, dramatized actual police-file cases, evolving an enormously popular formula. Derived from radio it was first TV show to become a movie.

TV'S FIRST STAR Faye Emerson set pace for fashion-conscious performers and record for plunging neckline. She conducted relaxed informal interviews with many professionals, **served Pepsi Cola.**

TOE TWISTS AND NECK LOCKS held undiminished fascination for viewers, though careers of individual protagonists were markedly short-lived. Early wrestling sensation was Gorgeous George, of marcelled hair fame. Boxing matches, especially championship bouts, also had enthusiastic viewers.

GAMBLING & BRAINS are exciting combination Jack Barry (*c.*) used to create quiz show *21.* English instructor Charles Van Doren (*r.*) easily defeated opponents until lawyer Vivienne Nearing (*l.*) turned tables.

IN "$64,000 QUESTION" contestant picked a category and then tried to answer questions, read by emcee Hal March (*r.*), which doubled in value up to $64,000. Another series of questions enabled one to win $256,000. Robert Strom (*l.*), 10-year old science wizard, won $192,000, then retired.

CLOWNING BY SID CAESAR was great attraction of *Caesar's Hour,* a comedy with Carl Reiner, Nanette Fabray (1957 Emmy winners for their parts) and Howard Morris. Caesar, one of television's most inventive comedians, lost his show at end of the 1957 video season, much to his fans' sorrow.

PERFECT BASE BALL GAME, first such in World Series history, was pitched by Yankee Don Larsen in 1956. Television enabled millions to see the game and the jubilation shown when Yogi Berra, wearing No. 8 uniform, jumped into Larsen's arms. Most important sports events are televised, thus allowing those who do not live near such arenas or who are unable to acquire a ticket to share in the excitement of *seeing* them in comfort.

"WHAT'S MY LINE?," a favorite panel show for years, had as its moderator, John Daly, a newscaster (*right*). There were four members of the panel (the three "regulars" are shown); the fourth was some guest celebrity. The "gimmick" of the program was to guess the occupation of the guest.

RADIO CONCENTRATES ON NEWS AND MUSIC

Radio sales reached an all-time high during the late postwar period. Although threatened by the phenomenal expansion of television, technical improvements such as transistor radios, high-fidelity and FM brought a resurgence of interest in invisible entertainment.

Radio manufacturing boomed as the high-fidelity fans demanded and got special equipment for their radio-phonograph combinations such as three-speed record players. Pocket and wrist radios were experimented with and promised much to radiophiles. Millions of car radios assured networks of additional listeners.

Programming on local stations changed from expensive-to-produce shows to a "music and news" format, thus introducing a new type of entertainer — the disc jockey — who wove small talk between the records he played. The music heard depended upon the station's predeliction and ranged from "rock n' roll" to classical. Five minutes of news was presented at least once every hour. Soap operas continued, however, to enthrall housewives and such personalities as Arthur Godfrey held on to their sponsors and fans.

ONE MAN'S FAMILY had its inception during 1931 in San Francisco. Transplanted to Hollywood in 1936, the serial moved to TV in 1951, eventually taking a firm hold in that medium. In 1954, still under guidance of creator Carleton E. Morse, personal tragedies cut original cast to five: Father, Mother, Hazel (J. Anthony Smythe, Minetta Ellen, Bernice Berwin, c.); Jack (Page Gilman, standing, left); and Paul (Michael Rafetto, right).

EXPLOSIVE BAT of Ted Williams, Boston Red Sox outfielder, kept him among batting leaders. Williams led parade of sports stars serving in World War II, Korea.

FIREBALL PITCHING of Bob Feller made Cleveland Indians consistent contenders for American League pennant. Feller fanned 348 batters in 1946 for record.

TOUCHDOWN TWINS Felix (Doc) Blanchard (r.) and Glenn Davis sparked wartime teams for Army. Both were All-Americans three years in a row. Wartime college football was unpredictable. Navy and Army and colleges with service training programs had manpower to field good teams, but schools lacking such programs had to rely on 17-year-olds and "4-F's."

"JOLTIN' JOE" DIMAGGIO joined the New York Yankees just as Ruth and Gehrig were beginning to fade. In 13 seasons with the Yankees he became one of the greatest center fielders in baseball history. The "Yankee Clipper" set majors' record for hits in consecutive games (56 in 1941). He won American League batting crown in 1939 and 1940; retired in 1951.

WHIRLAWAY, one of the first of the Calumet Farm's famous super horses, took racing's Triple Crown in 1941. Above, Whirlaway in the winner's circle after winning Preakness. Eddie Arcaro, who rode him in all three races, is up.

WARTIME SPORTS

Best men taken by the services; college, professional athletic programs in decline

GOLF, like many other sports, felt the impact of the wartime emergency but continued on a restricted basis. Sam Snead, Craig Wood, Lawson Little and Byron Nelson were among the professional golfers who kept championship play alive to provide the golf fans with some relief from the strain of war. Such major events as the Masters Tournament, U.S. Open and the U.S. Amateur were cancelled in 1943-1945. Byron Nelson (left) won the PGA championship in 1945 and was leading money winner two years straight, 1944-'45.

HEAVYWEIGHT CHAMPION Joe Louis contributed boxing talents for Army and Navy Relief funds in 1942 in bouts with Buddy Baer and Abe Simon (above). Louis served in army during World War II, touring camps and bases to present boxing shows.

EXODUS of ball clubs from New York took place in 1957. Giants' directors decided to move to San Francisco because of poor revenues in N.Y. Dodgers' directors and stockholders decided to move to Los Angeles in '58. Above, clown Emmett Kelly sheds a tear on bench beside Roy Campanella as Dodgers wind up last Ebbets Field game.

BEDLAM reigns as Milwaukee Braves return home after taking the 1957 World Series from the N.Y. Yankees. Pitcher Lew Burdette (*left*) and Warren Spahn wave to crowds as they ride down the parade route. Braves enjoyed heartier support than any team.

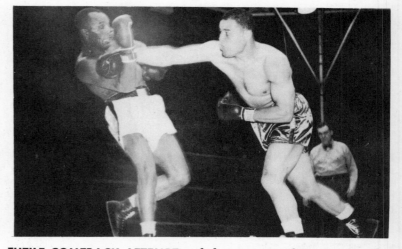

NEW ERA IN BASEBALL began in 1947 when Branch Rickey signed Jackie Robinson to Brooklyn Dodger contract and opened the door to Negro players in majors. Robinson (r., above) was National League batting champion in 1949. His teammate, Roy Campanella, nabbed senior loop's Most Valuable Player Award in 1951, 1953, as Negroes became part of big league baseball.

FUTILE COMEBACK ATTEMPT ended retirement of Joe Louis as he sought to regain heavyweight crown he had vacated. Ezzard Charles, who had won title in bout with Jersey Joe Walcott, defeated Louis in Yankee Stadium, Sept. 27, 1950. Later, Charles lost title to Walcott. 1948 Louis-Walcott fight, above, was Brown Bomber's last as champ.

POSTWAR
SPORTS

SUGAR RAY ROBINSON deserted the welterweight ranks to win middleweight crown from Jake LaMotta in Feb., 1951. On July 10, he lost it to England's Randy Turpin. Robinson (l.) regained crown in rematch on September 12.

ROCKY MARCIANO lifted the world's heavyweight crown from head of Jersey Joe Walcott in 1952. He knocked Walcott out in 1953 rematch. Marciano (r.) won decision over leading challenger Ezzard Charles in 1954 (above).

MILDRED "BABE" DIDRIKSON ZAHARIAS, one of history's most versatile women athletes, died in 1956. In golf she won virtually every existing women's title between 1935-54, winning a total of 82 tournaments. She also excelled in track.

BASKETBALL SCANDAL rocked nation in 1951 as players from several leading college teams admitted taking bribes from gamblers to regulate game scores. Players from NYU, CCNY, Bradley, Kentucky were among those implicated. Kentucky-Loyola game (above) was allegedly "fixed."

DECATHLON CHAMP Bob Mathias (r.) shattered his own world record with 7,887 points in 1952 Olympic Games held in Helsinki. The Tulare, Calif., athlete led American team to victory despite determined opposition from the Russian delegation. The U.S. team scored a total of 614 points.

CALUMET FARM'S Citation became first equine millionaire on July 14, 1951. Jockey Steve Brooks piloted "Big Cy" to a four-length victory over his stablemate Bewitch in the Gold Cup race at Hollywood Park, Calif. The $100,000 purse skyrocketed horse's earnings to total of $1,085,760. Citation, the 1948 Triple Crown winner, was retired after this victory.

BANTAM BEN HOGAN hit the pinnacle of his career as a professional golfer when he won three top tournaments in 1953 — The Masters, U.S. Open, British Open. Experts considered feat equal to, if not better than Bobby Jones' famous grand slam in 1930. It climaxed comeback which the Fort Worth, Texas, golfer had made since near fatal auto accident in 1949.

ROSE BOWL officials completed agreement in 1946 between the Pacific Coast Conference and the Big 9 to match their champions in annual New Year's game at Pasadena, Calif. Michigan met California (left) in 1951.

ALTHEA GIBSON, first Negro to win women's singles championship (1957) at Wimbledon, is bussed by runner-up Darlene Hard. The two then teamed up to capture the women's doubles championship.

STOLES of real and imitation furs were more and more a part of the wardrobe of the fashionable woman in the mid-20th century. They were worn with daytime suits as well as with evening attire. The stole at the

left was one of the more spectacular, made in white and dark mink to form a breathtaking contrast. At the *right*, a Ceil Chapman dress of champagne silk satin is highlighted by the popular pale mutation mink stole.

FASHIONS Released from fabric limitations of war economy, women of the U.S. rushed to acquire the New Look, a feminine one. Instead of square shoulders, severe lines, they adopted another era's "Gibson Girl" styles. This was later replaced by the "bare," "covered-up," and "sack" looks. Shoes harmonized in fabric and hue with the costume, a fad for a while: glass-like shoes. Influence of 20's was strong.

SUITS showed the emphasis on fabric just as all other phases of the clothing industry. Casual wear was still dominated by tweeds (*l.*), but they had the luxury of being lined with fur, alpaca, in this case. De-

signers added another feature: a suit which was not a suit, but a dress with a jacket, which, if closed, made the ensemble look like one. The "suit" (*r.*) is made of black silk brocade and is chic and dressy.

"VENUS" WAS THE NAME given this wrapped-to-the-figure bathing suit by Cole. Designed to drape up or down for torso adjustment, this suit was not far from the most popular patterns. Bathings suits varied in amount of nakedness, some even had sleeves; materials ranged from elasticized metallic fabrics to "velvet." U. S. women were not taken by bikini at all.

FABRICS from the most casual to the most elaborate, were used in fashions in the 1950's. The burlap used in the coat (*l.*) is a far cry from the utilitarian potato sack material. The

wedding dress (*r.*), influenced by Mexican Empress Carlotta's clothing, has a covered up look, but the figure is not hidden as was the fashion in the 1957 faddist "sack."

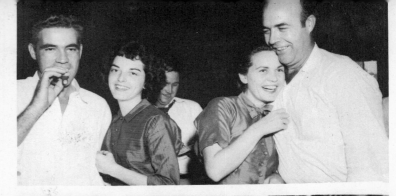

CRIME Lucky Luciano (*l.*) was still considered underworld czar despite his deportation in 1946. In Italy he lived lushly without visible means of support, was believed to be head of numbers racket and narcotics traffic in U. S. Frank Costello (*r.*), reigning king of gambling, was shot but only slightly injured in 1957. He refused to speculate on the identity of his assailant. Vincent Gigante, finger-man of rival gang, was indicted.

MONEYMAN of the syndicate's Chicago "outfit," Jake "Greasy Thumb" Guzik refused to answer questions before 1951 Senate Crime Investigating Committee because he might incriminate himself; was imprisoned.

TWO MASKED MEN walked into a N.Y. barbershop on Oct. 25, 1957 at 10:20 a.m. and killed Albert Anastasia, one of N.Y.'s most notorious gansters. Dist. Atty. Hogan assumed a tie-up between the murder and Havana gambling.

SHAME OF A NATION, the race issue erupted in the "Wolf Whistle" murder. Emmett Till, 14-year-old Negro from Chicago, visiting in Mississippi, allegedly whistled at wife of Roy Bryant (*l. above*). That night, he was kidnapped by Bryant and his half-brother (*r. above*). Till was found in a river, shot in the head. All-white jury, acquitted the kidnappers, seen celebrating. Below, mother receives boy's casket.

JUVENILE DELINQUENCY reached enormous proportions in the 1950's. This defiant young hoodlum stabbed a teacher. Tough New York gangs fought bloody "rumbles," attacked passers-by.

PRISON RIOTS broke out throughout the nation. One of worst was at Jackson, Mich., in 1952, when 2,600 prisoners mutinied (above). Main complaint was overcrowding. Prison population since war had outgrown living quarters.

TELEVISED Senate crime hearings helped state and local police to dig up what Sen. Kefauver's (*r.*, at long rear table) committee had unearthed. Costello got 18 months for contempt; got out to go in again for income tax evasion.

SENSATIONAL VICE TRIAL of $3 million oleomargerine heir Minot "Mickey" Jelke, 23 (*r.*), in New York, February, 1953, ended in a 2 to 6 year sentence to Sing Sing prison. Jelke was found guilty of pandering by all-male jury. Pat Ward (*l.*, with attorney), was state witness.

RECORD RANSOM of $600,000 was paid by frantic father of 6-year-old Bobby Greenlease to kidnappers Mrs. Bonnie Heady and Carl Hall (above) Oct. 4, 1953. But boy was dead, shot by Hall shortly after being lured from a Kansas City, Mo., school. Both were executed Dec. 18.

"MAD BOMBER" of New York was finally captured in 1957 after eluding police detection for 16 years. He had repeatedly terrorized New Yorkers by placing bombs in congested areas. George Metesky blamed Con Ed for his TB, used bombs to draw attention to his grievance.

DISASTERS
Abandoned ice boxes and wells proved death traps for so many children that some towns passed safety laws. First tragedy brought to nationwide attention was that of three-year-old Kathy Fiscus. She fell into an old well at San Marino, Calif., April 8, 1949, setting off a three-day rescue attempt by volunteers. Climax came when doctor (being hoisted into tube) descended 94 feet to find her dead.

TEXAS CITY, TEXAS, was rent by explosions April 16, 1947, when the French freighter *Grandcamp* loaded with nitrate fertilizer blew up in the harbor, touching off the Monsanto Chemical Co. plant, warehouses and oil tanks (above, still burning out of control for second day). Spreading to the city itself, fires and explosions brought the death toll to 512 with property damage at $50 million. Within year most of the damage had been repaired.

"ANDREA DORIA" LISTS SHARPLY to starboard after being rammed by Swedish liner *Stockholm* in mysterious collision at sea (1956). The *Ile de France* rushed to the rescue. The toll was 4 dead, 51 missing. Investigation was launched to find which captain was at fault for the mysterious crash.

TORRENTIAL RAINS AND FLOODS on Oct. 14-17, 1955 brought destruction to 7 eastern states. Connecticut was the hardest hit with 13 dead and 6 missing. Floods isolated many towns (Danbury, Conn. *shown*). Almost $52 million was given for flood control and an extensive relief program.

USS BENNINGTON was ripped by between-decks explosions and fire May 26, 1954, killing 93 and injuring 201 (above, attempts are made to identify dead). Worst peacetime U.S. naval disaster occurred when aircraft carrier *Wasp* rammed and sank destroyer *Hobson* April 26, 1952, killing 178.

BOSTON NIGHT CLUB, the Cocoanut Grove, swiftly turned into an inferno Nov. 28, 1942, when flimsy decorations caught fire. Only exits for capacity crowd of 750 were two revolving doors. Hysteria and fire killed 491 persons, injured scores. It was one of worst disasters in show history.

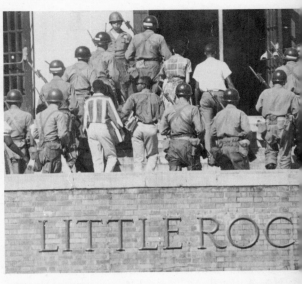

NEW METHODS of learning came to the home and classroom with educational TV. Dentists taking brush-up course at University of Illinois College of Dentistry were able to watch new techniques simultaneously in five laboratories.

EX-GI CRAFTSMEN in New York learned art of making handwrought jewelry from Arnold Ghinger. Millions of former soldiers after World War II and the Korean conflict had chance for schooling in trades, crafts, on U. S. GI education bill.

INTEGRATION of schools was the decade's gravest domestic crisis. When, in 1957, Ark.'s Gov. Faubus stationed National Guard at Little Rock's Central High School to bar Negroes, Eisenhower sent 101st Airborne to enforce integration.

EDUCATION

Never before had the nation been so beset by school problems. During the decade and a half when soldiers went to war and came back to school, education grew painfully. There were not enough classrooms, teachers, or funds to go around. While public schools and universities squeezed record numbers of pupils into converted Army barracks, plane fuselages and trailers, educators prepared for a postwar baby crop of 32 million students in 1957-58.

The "GI Bill of Rights" made higher education possible for thousands who otherwise wouldn't have had a chance. Big enrollments brought headaches and 5,000 citizens' groups looked for a cure. Businessmen rejected federal aid to education, formed donor plans to help staggering private schools. Worried school boards, needing 105,000 elementary teachers yearly while only 35,000 were graduating, courted and kept teachers with better pay, more personal freedom and training funds from Ford Foundation.

"What should be taught and how?" parents asked. A California court upheld university professors opposing loyalty oaths; most educators felt a Communist was not a free teaching agent. A history-making decision came when segregation of white and Negro pupils was banned by the Supreme Court. Objections, flare-ups and threatened defiance marked the attitude of many states, especially in the South, to the decision.

Russia's advance in the field of scientific education, dramatized by the launching of the *Sputniks* in 1957, forced Americans to make an "agonizing reappraisal" of their own educational systems. Reforms promised to load curricula with basic scientific courses to prepare youth for space age.

BILLY GRAHAM, eloquent and dedicated evangelist, was one of the great religious figures of the postwar years. His crusade took him to cities and towns all over the world. Above, he preaches to crowd in Frankfurt/Main, Germany.

MADE BISHOP by Pope Pius XII June 11, 1951, Fulton J. Sheen became television personality with regular Sunday sermons. He headed Catholic Church's Society for Propagation of Faith, became noted for number of "famous" converts.

WORLD COUNCIL of Churches opened Second Assembly at Evanston, Ill., Aug. 15, 1954. More than 1,500 delegates, observers from 161 communions and 48 countries attended the meeting under banner, "Christ—the Hope of the World."

RELIGION

During World War II and the postwar period, the United States was caught up in a religious revival and 92 million members swelled church rolls to an all-time high.

Church leaders offered a return to the Christian faith as a weapon against Communism and destruction of the world by atomic force. Evangelist Billy Graham, like Billy Sunday, spurred thousands to make "decisions for Christ," while Roman Catholic Bishop Fulton Sheen became an emissary of the Church on television. Protestant churches also turned to network television in a TV version of the radio show, "World Churches."

In a return of religious festivals, 150,000 persons jammed Chicago's Soldier Field for a Marian Year Mass and Jews marked the 300th Anniversary of their landing at New Amsterdam. Young people joined the "Youth for Christ" crusade to combat problems of juvenile delinquency.

Americans contributed a record amount ($1.4 billion) to churches and bought the new Revised Standard Version of the Bible. An era of self-examination made audiences for inspirational best-seller books and movies.

Men of religion were not set apart. The "Red Dean" of Canterbury was attacked by fellow churchmen, while Congress rejected charges against Methodist Bishop G. Bromley Oxnam. Forty per cent of the country's Christians united as the National Council of Churches of Christ in the United States. The World Council of Churches, at Amsterdam and Evanston, sought grounds of theological agreement and probed possible church unity. As Council put it, "The real battles of faith are being fought in factories, shops, offices and farms, in political parties and government agencies."

SOURCES OF PICTURES

The following list credits the source of each picture used in YEAR's Pictorial History of America. Credits are listed picture by picture for each page – left to right, top to bottom. Each picture starting a new line across a page is preceded by a dash (–); each picture following on same line is preceded by a comma (,).

Abbreviations used are:

WW–Wide World; **INP**–International News Photos; **UP**–United Press; **U & U**–Underwood & Underwood; **BB**–Brown Bros.; **LC**–Library of Congress; **NA**–National Archives; **AMP**–American Museum of Photography.

2–Historical Society of Montana (Helena)
5–Columbia University
8–drawn especially for YEAR by Gerardus Leeflang of Rotterdam
9–YEAR
10–by Frederic Remington from LC–by Carl Brodmer from LC, American Factors Ltd. (Honolulu)
11–by Ernest Henry Griset from Peabody Museum of Harvard Univ., by Paul Kane from the Royal Ontario Museum of Archaeology (Toronto)–same, Missouri Hist. Soc.–by Carl Brodmer from LC, same, same
12–The House of Seagram (Montreal)–Smithsonian Institution –Nasjonal Galleriet (Oslo)
13–reproduced from *Pageant of America* © Yale Univ. Press–YEAR, AMP, Obra Ortega from Ampliaciones y Reproducciones (Barcelona)
14–drawn especially for YEAR by Arseny Spilewsky, LC–reproduced from *Pageant of America* © Yale Univ. Press, BB
15–YEAR, by W. R. Leigh from Woolaroc Museum (Bartlesville, Oklahoma)–YEAR, WW–YEAR, Boston Pub. Lib.
16–YEAR, drawing by J. D. Kelly from BB–AMP, same
17–Buffalo Hist. Soc., by J. N. Marchand courtesy of the Singer Sewing Machine Co.–BB, Chicago Hist. Soc., YEAR–AMP, same, YEAR
18–by C. W. Jeffreys courtesy of *Pageant of America* © Yale Univ. Press, Chicago Hist. Soc., Mrs. Robert E. Treman (Ithaca, N.Y.)–Minnesota Dept. of Administration, Missouri Hist. Soc., YEAR–State Hist. Soc. of Wisconsin, Public Archives of Canada
19–BB, Public Archives of Canada–New York Hist. Soc.,The House of Seagram–"Harry Shaw Newman, The Old Print Shop"–Boston Pub. Lib., same, YEAR
20–New England Mutual Life Ins. Co.
21–John Hancock Mutual Life Ins. Co.
22–BB, YEAR–BB, by John White from British Museum (London), drawn especially for YEAR by Gerardus Leeflang (Rotterdam)
23–BB–LC, YEAR, YEAR–Maryland Hist. Soc., Enoch Pratt Free Library
24–LC, Boston Pub. Lib.–same, same, same
25–YEAR, New England Mutual Life Ins. Co.–LC, Metropolitan Museum of Art–LC, YEAR
26–Picture Post Library (London), YEAR–YEAR, YEAR, BB –BB, Camera Clix
27–BB, New York Pub. Lib.–YEAR, YEAR, YEAR–BB, BB
28–by J. L. G. Ferris from Harold L. Fischer (St. Paul, Minn.) –painted by Alfred Fredericks courtesy of Title Guarantee & Trust Co., painted by John Ward Dunsmore courtesy of Title Guarantee & Trust Co.
29–painted by John Ward Dunsmore courtesy of Title Guarantee & Trust Co.–by Stanley M. Arthurs from Univ. of Delaware (Newark), Hist. Soc. of Pennsylvania
30–drawn especially for YEAR by Gerardus Leeflang (Rotterdam)–National Life Ins. Co. (Montpelier, Vt.), same, same
31–Essex Inst. (Salem, Mass.)–New York Pub. Lib., Boston Pub. Lib.–L. J. Bullard Co. (Cleveland), painted by E. L. Henry courtesy of Title Guarantee & Trust Co.
32–Boston Pub. Lib.–Pennsylvania Academy of Fine Arts
33–Continental Distilling Corporation (Philadelphia), L. J. Bullard Co. (Cleveland)–Frick Art Reference Library–AMP, Picture Post Library (London), by J. Luis Mora from New York Pub. Lib.
34–New England Mutual Life Ins. Co., City Art Museum (St. Louis)–BB, Boston Pub. Lib.
35–AMP, Glen Falls Ins. Co.–BB–Royal Ontario Museum of Archaeology (Toronto), Virginia Museum of Fine Arts–Royal Ontario Museum of Archaeology, Public Archives of Canada
36–National Life Ins. Co. (Montpelier, Vt.)–drawn especially for YEAR by Gerardus Leeflang (Rotterdam)–Washington Univ. (St. Louis)
37–M. H. De Young Memorial Museum (San Francisco), from *Pictorial History of California* courtesy of M. H. De Young Museum, California State Lib.–same, Security First National Bank (Los Angeles)–M. H. De Young Memorial Museum, same, INP–Bancroft Library from Univ. of California (Berkeley), same, same, same
38–National Life Ins. Co. (Montpelier, Vt.), same–same–same, same, same
39–New York Pub. Lib.–Bettman Archive, YEAR, BB–LC, YEAR, Culver Service
40–Colonial Williamsburg–reproduced from *The Pageant of America* © Yale Univ. Press, LC, LC–L. J. Bullard Co. (Cleveland), Camera Clix, Colonial Williamsburg
41–Essex Institute (Salem, Mass.), BB, courtesy of Yale Univ. Art Gallery–YEAR, YEAR, Columbia Univ.–LC–Harvard College Lib., YEAR, LC
42–Boston Pub. Lib., LC–by F. C. Yohn from Essex Institute (Salem, Mass.), American Antiquarian Society–Boston Pub. Lib., LC
43–Boston Pub. Lib., YEAR, LC–YEAR, BB–LC, YEAR, AMP
44–New York Pub. Lib., AMP–National Life Ins. Co., same, YEAR–BB, same
45–New York Pub. Lib.–NA, same–YEAR–New York Pub. Lib.
46–LC, courtesy of the Mabel Brady Garvan Coll. from Yale Univ. Art Gallery–BB–AMP, drawn especially for YEAR by Miss Edith Sully, YEAR
47–New York Pub. Lib., same, AMP–BB, New York Pub. Lib., YEAR–Continental Distilling Corp. (Philadelphia)
48–Continental Distilling Corp. (Philadelphia), BB, BB–BB, YEAR, American Antiquarian Soc.–Boston Pub. Lib., National Life Ins. Co., Colonial Soc. of Massachusetts
49–YEAR, YEAR–from Pyle's *Book of Pirates*, same–"Harry Shaw Newman, The Old Print Shop," YEAR
50–by F. C. Yohn © Charles Scribner's Sons
51–Museum of Fine Arts (Boston)
52–Picture Post Libary (London), Colonial Williamsburg–BB
53–Franklin Institute, New England Mutual Life Ins. Co.–BB, YEAR, America Fore Ins. Group–Picture Post Library (London), BB, National Portrait Gallery (London), Africa House (London)
54–WW–BB–AMP, Picture Post Library (London)
55–American Telephone & Telegraph Co., YEAR–YEAR, Bibliotheque Nationale (Paris)–LC
56–New England Mutual Life Ins. Co., by John Ward Dunsmore courtesy Sons of the Revolution (Fraunces Tavern, New York City), same–INP, New York Pub. Lib.
57–Picture Post Library (London)–America Fore Ins. Group, YEAR–YEAR, YEAR
58–Stackpole Co. (Harrisburg, Pa.)–BB, LC
59–AMP
60–LC–Wadsworth Atheneum (Hartford, Conn.)
61–New England Mutual Life Ins. Co.–Museum of Fine Arts (Boston), BB–LC, YEAR, painted by John Ward Dunsmore courtesy of Title Guarantee & Trust Co.
62–Stackpole Co. (Harrisburg, Pa.), WW, Essex Institute (Salem, Mass.)–YEAR–National Life Ins. Co., LC, YEAR
63–INP, Essex Institute (Salem, Mass.)–LC–LC–YEAR, The America Fore Ins. Group
64–BB, YEAR, Title Guarantee & Trust Co.–same, same, YEAR –by John Ward Dunsmore courtesy of the Sons of the Revolution (Fraunces Tavern, New York City), BB, YEAR–by John Ward Dunsmore courtesy Sons of the Revolution (Fraunces Tavern, New York City), U. S. Naval Academy, New York Pub. Lib.
65–Metropolitan Museum of Art–Wadsworth Atheneum (Hartford, Conn.), Yale Univ. Art Gallery–Somerville Pub. Lib. (Somerville, Mass.), By John Ward Dunsmore courtesy Sons of the Revolution (Fraunces Tavern, New York City)
66–Royal Ontario Museum of Archaeology (Toronto), BB–Continental Distilling Corporation (Philadelphia)–drawn especially for YEAR by Arseny Spilewsky, BB
67–Painting by F. C. Yohn Utica Pub. Lib.–by F. C. Yohn from The America Fore Ins. Group, Rome Pub. Lib. (Rome, New York), by John Trumbull from LC–National Life Ins. Co. (Montpelier, Vt.), by John Vanderlyn from Wadsworth Atheneum (Hartford, Conn.), National Life Ins. Co.
68–City Art Museum of St. Louis, YEAR–New York State Hist. Assoc. (Cooperstown), LC, YEAR–YEAR, YEAR, YEAR–YEAR, YEAR, YEAR, YEAR
69–by John Ward Dunsmore courtesy Sons of the Revolution (Fraunces Tavern, New York City)–YEAR, LC, LC–Continental Distilling Corp. (Philadelphia), WW, Boston Pub. Lib.
70–Smithsonian Institution, Franklin Technical Institute–Mariner's Museum (Newport News, Va.), National Life Ins. Co. –Boston Pub. Lib., AMP
71–Seelbach Hotel (Louisville, Ky.)–The Filson Club (Louisville)–America Fore Ins. Group, Indiana Hist. Bureau–LC, by Benjamin West from National Gallery of Art, YEAR
72–by John Ward Dunsmore courtesy Sons of the Revolution (Fraunces Tavern, New York City), YEAR–Yale Univ. Press, Massie (Missouri Resources Division)–New York Pub. Lib., by Gilbert Stuart from Independence Hall Collection (Philadelphia), New York Academy of Medicine
73–LC, LC–YEAR, New York Pub. Lib.–YEAR, by John Ward Dunsmore, courtesy Sons of the Revolution (Fraunces Tavern, New York City)
74–YEAR, by Richard Morrell Staigg from Sleepy Hollow Restorations Inc.–YEAR, Picture Post Library, LC–by Benjamin West from Boston Pub. Lib., BB–BB
75–by Robert Trumbull from Colonial Williamsburg–BB, Picture Post Library–LC, "Harry Shaw Newman, The Old Print Shop"
76–drawn especially for YEAR by Gerardus Leeflang (Rotterdam), YEAR, BB–YEAR, BB
77–Franklin Technical Institute–by Ezra Ames from New York Hist. Soc., LC–YEAR, YEAR, YEAR
78–NA
79–by Junius Brutus Stearns from Virginia Museum of Fine Art –BB, YEAR, BB–WW, BB, Colonial Williamsburg, YEAR
80–by Edward Savage from National Gallery of Art, BB–LC, LC –by Junius Brutus Stearns from Virginia Museum of Fine Arts, same–by John Ward Dunsmore courtesy Sons of the Revolution (Fraunces Tavern), New York City), same, same
81–BB, YEAR–by Daniel Huntington "In the Brooklyn Museum Collection" – WW – YEAR, Continental Distilling Corp. (Philadelphia), YEAR
82–by Howard Chandler Christy from Ohio Development and Publicity Commission (Columbus), YEAR–NA, BB–by Gilbert Stuart from Metropolitan Museum of Art, YEAR, National Life Ins. Co.
83–by Mather Brown from Museum of Fine Arts (Boston)–YEAR–YEAR–New England Mutual Life Ins. Co. (Boston), YEAR, LC
84–by Hippolyte Sebron from Tulane Univ. (New Orleans)
85–by Thomas Sully from West Point Museum U.S. Military Academy
86–by Gilbert Stuart from The Bowdoin College Museum of Fine Arts, LC–YEAR, LC, YEAR
87–Mariner's Museum (Newport News, Va.)–YEAR, New York Pub. Lib.
88–BB, "Harry Shaw Newman, The Old Print Shop"–LC
89–by Charles Russell from Hist. Soc. of Montana (Helena)–Missouri Hist. Soc., Oregon State Highway Commission (Salem)–John Hancock Mutual Life Ins. Co. (Boston), Missouri Hist. Soc.
90–by Ezra Ames from Union College (Schenectady, N. Y.), YEAR–AMP, LC, YEAR
91–YEAR, by Asher B. Durand from New York Hist. Soc.–Peabody Museum (Salem, Mass.), YEAR–BB, Buffalo Hist. Soc., by Charles B. King from Corcoran Gallery of Art
92–YEAR, by Carlton Chapman from New York Hist. Soc.–by Thomas Birch from Museum of Fine Arts (Boston)–by Thomas Birch from LC, Chicago Hist. Soc., YEAR
93–New York Public Library, YEAR–Sigmund Samuel Canadiana Gallery Royal Ontario Museum of Archaeology (Toronto)–Chicago Hist. Soc., NA
94–by William H. Powell from LC–AMP–Massie (Missouri F sources Division), LC
95–LC, Enoch Pratt Free Lib.–U.S. Army Photograph–AM National Collection of Fine Arts & Smithsonian Institution
96–LC, LC–YEAR, YEAR, YEAR
97–Boston Pub. Lib.–Hist. Soc. of Pennsylvania–LC–Califor State Lib., by Thomas Birch from Wadsworth Atheneu (Hartford, Conn.)
98–New York Hist. Soc.–BB–Chicago Hist. Soc., YEAR
99–LC, Oregon State Highway Commission (Salem), WW Peabody Museum Harvard Univ., LC–Missouri Hist. So American Factors Ltd.–LC, BB
100–Maryland Hist. Soc., by Charles Russell from Peter A. Jul & Son (New York)–courtesy Mabel Brady Garvan Coll. Ya Univ. Art Gallery–by C. Giroux from Museum of Fine A (Boston), YEAR, New York Pub. Lib.
101–Smithsonian Institution, BB–Hist. Soc. of Pennsylvania–L Burton Hist. Coll. Detroit Pub. Lib., New York Pub. Lib.
102–LC, Courtesy Mrs. John C. Giriat–National Life Ins. C Essex Institute (Salem, Mass.), NA–John Hancock Life In Co. (Boston), National Life Ins. Co., same–LC, LC
103–New York Pub. Lib., "Harry Shaw Newman, The Old Pri Shop"–YEAR, New York Pub. Lib., Continental Distilli Corp. (Philadelphia)–same, BB
104–YEAR, Pennsylvania Hist. Soc., National Life Ins. Co.– Henry Sargent from Museum of Fine Arts (Boston), Conti ental Distilling Corp. (Philadelphia), Metropolitan Museu of Art–Daughters of the American Revolution, Bettmann A chive, Metropolitan Museum of Art
105–by J. A. Woodside courtesy Mr. Henry T. Peters Jr. and Metr politan Museum of Art–National Life Ins. Co., same, same Continental Distilling Corp. (Philadelphia), same
106–Chicago Hist. Soc., Metropolitan Museum of Art–Mrs. Geor M. D. Kelly of "Melrose" (Natchez, Miss.), LC–Came Clix, LC
107–Wyeth (Philadelphia, Pa.)–same
108–Museum of Fine Arts (Boston)–The Art Institute (Chicago –Museum of Fine Arts (Boston)
109–Pennsylvania Academy of Fine Arts (Philadelphia), Fog Museum of Art Harvard Univ.–New York State Hist. Assoc City Art Museum (St. Louis), Gallery of Fine Arts Yale Uni –Fogg Museum of Art Harvard Univ., The Newark Museur Pennsylvania Academy of the Fine Arts
110–LC, New York Pub. Lib.–Museum of the City of New Yor YEAR–National Life Ins. Co., YEAR, from the Elmer Clark Coll. (Lake Junalaska, N.C.)
111–National Life Ins. Co., BB, National Life Ins. Co.–"Har Shaw Newman, The Old Print Shop", Chamber of Commer (Ft. Wayne, Indiana), John Hancock Mutual Life Ins. C (Boston, Mass.)–National Life Ins. Co., LC, BB
112–LC, LC, YEAR–YEAR, YEAR, YEAR
113–YEAR–American Antiquarian Soc., Buffalo Hist. Soc.–YEAI Chicago Hist. Soc., YEAR
114–LC, American Antiquarian Society–BB, New York Pub. Lil –same, American Antiquarian Soc.
115–Woolaroc Museum (Bartlesville, Okla.)–"Harry Shaw New man, The Old Print Shop"–BB, Black Star
116–BB, YEAR, YEAR–YEAR–YEAR, New York Pub. Lib., His Soc. of Pennsylvania
117–LC, Commonwealth of Virginia–Chicago Hist. Soc., LC Metropolitan Museum of Art, BB
118–by F. C. Yohn from America Fore Ins. Group–AMP, Elliso Photo Co. (Austin, Texas), same, LC
119–San Jacinto Memorial Museum, WW–John Carter Brow Lib., San Jacinto Memorial Museum–Ellison Photo Co. (Aus tin, Texas), same
120–Oregon State Highway Commission (Salem), same, Orego State Hist. Soc.–E. B. Crocker Art Gallery (Sacramento) LC, University of California
121–Missouri Hist. Soc., California Gold Label Beer–Denver Pub Lib. Western Collection, same–Nebraska State Hist. Assoc (Lincoln)–by John Mix Stanley Peabody Museum Harvar Univ., by John Mix Stanley from Detroit Institute of Arts same
122–N. Y. Pub. Lib., AMP–Church of Jesus Christ of Latter Da Saints–BB, LC
123–LC, LC–LC–YEAR, LC
124–NA, LC–LC, LC–LC, LC–BB, LC, YEAR, YEAR
125–YEAR, YEAR, New York Pub Lib., California State Lib.– Bancroft Library of Univ. of California–YEAR–BB, YEAR BB, Wine Institute (San Francisco)
126–LC, YEAR–LC, LC–LC
127–painted by Harold Von Schmidt for John Morrell & Co. (Ottumwa, Iowa), same–same, same
128–painted by Harold Von Schmidt for John Morrell & Co., same same–Wells Fargo Bank history room, California State Lib. University of California, Society of California Pioneers (Sar Francisco)–painted by Harold Von Schmidt for John Morrel & Co., California State Lib.
129–University of California, NA–University of California–same California State Lib., same–Wells Fargo history room, Society of California Pioneers–California State Lib.
130–The Parker Gallery (London), LC–California State Lib., M H. De Young Memorial Museum–LC, Missouri Hist. Soc.
131–YEAR, by Charles T. Webber Cincinnati Art Museum (St Louis)–LC–by Caleb Bingham National Gallery of Art, BB
132–LC–John Morrell & Co. (Ottumwa, Iowa)–LC, LC, by George P. Healy from Museum of Fine Arts (Boston)
133–AMP, LC, LC–LC, LC–YEAR, California State Lib., same
134–"Harry Shaw Newman, The Old Print Shop", LC–INP, LC, LC–BB, Corcoran Gallery of Art
135–LC, YEAR–State Hist. Soc. of Wisconsin, Chicago Hist. Soc., AMP–Univ. of California, LC, BB
136–by Thomas Hovenden Metropolitan Museum of Art–AMP, YEAR, YEAR
137–New York Pub. Lib., Museum of the City of New York–LC–Smithsonian Institution, YEAR–New York Pub. Lib.
138–America Fore Ins. Group–National Life Ins. Co., New York Pub. Lib., AMP
139–LC, Corcoran Gallery of Art–LC, Soc. of Calif. Pioneers–BB, "Harry Shaw Newman, The Old Print Shop"
140–LC, YEAR–Chicago Hist. Soc., same–LC, Chicago Hist. Soc.
141–New York Hist. Soc., same–Mariner's Museum (Newport News, Va.), New York Pub. Lib.–Enoch Pratt Free Lib.–Missouri Hist. Soc., Mariner's Museum (Newport News, Va.)
142–New York Pub. Lib., YEAR, "Harry Shaw Newman, The Old Print Shop"–Oregon State Highway Commission (Salem), painted by Harold Von Schmidt for John Morrell & Co.

—INP, John Hancock Mutual Life Ins. Co.—LC, "Harry Shaw Newman, The Old Print Shop"—LC, LC
—Wyeth (Philadelphia, Pa.)—George Eastman House (Rochester, N. Y.), BB
—John Hancock Mutual Life Ins. Co., BB—YEAR, BB, YEAR—Smithsonian Institution, International Harvester Co., Goodyear Tire & Rubber Co.
—New York Pub. Lib., BB—Essex Institute, LC, BB—BB, L. C. Page & Co. (Boston), BB, BB
—New York Pub. Lib., WW, BB—Enoch Pratt Free Lib., LC, LC, BB—BB, LC, BB
—LC, LC—LC, BB—Missouri Hist. Soc., YEAR, LC
—LC, John Hancock Mutual Life Ins. Co.—LC, Calif. State Library, "Harry Shaw Newman, The Old Print Shop"—LC, LC, BB
—YEAR, New York Pub. Lib.—YEAR—Pennsylvania Hist. Soc., "Harry Shaw Newman, The Old Print Shop", LC
—"The Edward W. C. Arnold Collection, The Metropolitan Museum of Art, photograph courtesy Museum of the City of New York"—LC, YEAR—YEAR, LC
2—National Life Ins. Co., LC—YEAR, YEAR—YEAR, YEAR
3—LC—Bettman Archive—YEAR, LC
4—"Harry Shaw Newman, The Old Print Shop," YEAR, YEAR—YEAR, "Harry Shaw Newman, The Old Print Shop"—Hist. Soc. of Pennsylvania, New York Pub. Lib.
5—YEAR—John Hancock Mutual Life Ins. Co., by James E. Buttersworth from Museum of Art (Providence, R. I.)—LC, New York Pub. Lib.
6—BB, BB—M. H. De Young Memorial Museum (San Francisco)—YEAR, LC, New York Hist. Soc.
7—New York Pub. Lib., LC—YEAR—Picture Post Libary (London), BB—Wells Fargo Bank History Room, Soc. of California Pioneers, LC
8—Museum of Fine Arts (Boston), BB—New York State Hist. Soc. (Cooperstown)—Washington Univ. of St. Louis
9—City Art Museum of St. Louis—Smithsonian Institution, De Witt Clinton Bontelle Museum of Fine Arts (Boston), Smithsonian Institution—LC, National Gallery of Art, Univ. of California, YEAR
0—by Eastman Johnson courtesy Stuart Collection New York Hist. Soc., WW—LC, Philharmonic Symphony Soc. of N. Y.—YEAR, New York Pub. Lib., YEAR
1—"The Edward W. C. Arnold Collection, The Metropolitan Museum of Art, Photograph courtesy Museum of the City of New York", "Harry Shaw Newman, The Old Print Shop"—LC—YEAR, YEAR—"The J. Clarence Davies Collection, Museum of City of New York", LC
2—NA
3—YEAR
4—YEAR, LC, LC—Historisches Bildarchiv (Bad Berneck, Germany), YEAR, NA
5—NA, YEAR, YEAR—YEAR, State of Alabama Dept of Archives & Hist.—NA, LC, Richmond Chamber of Commerce
6—Chicago Hist. Soc., National Park Service, LC—Lincoln National Life Ins. Co., LC, *Collier's*—BB, LC, WW—NA, LC, LC
67—YEAR, LC—YEAR—BB, BB—Black Star, INP
68—New York Pub. Lib., LC—YEAR—YEAR, YEAR
69—LC, YEAR, NA—LC, Museum of City of New York Coll. of Edward W. C. Arnold—YEAR
70—LC—LC, YEAR, NA, ANSCO (Binghamton, N. Y.)
71—Historisches Bildarchiv (Bad Berneck, Germany), INP—WW, AMP—YEAR, LC
72—LC, New York Pub. Lib.—LC—YEAR
73—LC—LC, LC—NA, *U.S. Army*
74—LC—YEAR, LC—NA, LC
75—LC—NA, LC—LC, LC
76—NA—LC, YEAR
77—NA—LC, INP, LC—INP
78—LC, Harper & Bros.—LC—U. S. Army Photograph, YEAR
79—YEAR—LC, YEAR—New York Pub. Lib., Cyril Nast
80—LC—LC, NA—NA—LC, LC
81—LC—LC, WW
82—LC—LC, Pennsylvania Hist. Soc.—LC, NA, LC
83—Gettysburg National Military Park—Military Service Publishing Co. (Harrisburg, Pa.)—WW, INP
84—Lincoln National Life Ins. Co.—Gilbert Paper Co. (Menasha, Wisc.), NA, Lincoln National Life Ins. Co.
85—LC, NA—AMP—NA, AMP, NA
86—NA, LC—LC, LC—NA, LC—LC, LC
87—NA, Handy Studios (Washington)—NA—LC, WW, LC
88—NA, LC—LC—California State Lib., same, LC
89—Harpers Weekly, NA—LC—NA, NA
90—LC, LC—INP—by David G. Blythe from Museum of Fine Arts (Boston), LC
91—LC—YEAR, YEAR—YEAR—YEAR, YEAR
92—YEAR, LC—NA, LC—YEAR, NA, NA
93—YEAR, U. S. Army Photograph—BB, LC—LC, LC
94—LC, LC—New York Pub. Lib., LC, LC—LC, LC
95—Wells Fargo Bank History Room, National Park Service—same—B. H. Ward, INP—Frank Leslie's Illustrated Newspaper, California State Lib.
96—LC—YEAR, YEAR, LC—LC, YEAR, LC
97—NA, NA—LC—LC, NA
98—Assoc. of American Railroads—WW, Corcoran Gallery of Art—Virginia Military Institute, same
99—LC, LC—LC—The State Hist. Soc. of Wisconsin, NA—NA, LC
00—LC—LC, LC, LC
01—NA—LC
02—LC—YEAR, YEAR, Confederate Museum (Richmond, Va.)
03—LC, LC—NA—NA
04—LC, Black Star, YEAR, YEAR
05—LC, YEAR—YEAR, BB
06—LC—AMP—LC, LC
07—LC, LC—YEAR, Metropolitan Museum of Art—LC, BB
08—AMP, INP—LC—AMP, BB, BB
09—LC, YEAR, LC—BB
10—New York Pub. Lib., YEAR, YEAR—Handy Studios (Washington, D. C.), BB
11—"by Eastman Johnson from Mildred Anna Williams Collection, California Palace of the Legion of Honor, Lincoln Park (San Francisco)"—BB, BB—LC, LC
12—WW—Paramount Pictures—LC, YEAR, YEAR, BB
13—Smithsonian Institution, LC—WW, BB, LC—BB, LC
14—LC—BB, INP, NA, NA—NA, NA, NA, NA
15—Historical Soc. of Montana, LC—BB, BB, BB, Wells Fargo Bank History Room—U & U, INP, YEAR
16—Wittle Memorial Museum—LC, Hist. Soc. of Montana (Helena), Calif. State Lib.—LC, YEAR
17—Union Pacific Railroad, Boatmen's Nat'l. Bank of St. Louis—Wells Fargo Bank History Room, same, Calif. State Lib.—Washington State Hist. Soc., Union Pacific Railroad, John Morrell & Co.
18—BB—ANSCO (Binghamton, N. Y.)—Harper & Bros., BB, BB
19—LC, LC—LC, LC, New York Pub. Lib.—YEAR, LC, U & U
20—U & U
21—LC
22—LC—LC, LC—YEAR, BB
23—BB—LC, LC—LC, LC
24—F. W. Woolworth Co., Montgomery Ward & Co.—LC, LC—LC, New York Pub. Lib.
25—INP—LC, LC—LC, LC, YEAR
26—Public Archives of Canada—Los Angeles Public Lib., same
27—Public Archives of Canada, Los Angeles Public Lib.—Canadiana Gallery Royal Ontario Museum of Archaeology, same, Public Archives of Canada—Canadiana Gallery Royal Ontario Museum of Archaeology, same, Mayor's Office (Toronto)
228—Public Archives of Canada—Los Angeles Public Lib., same—U & U—Canadiana Gallery Royal Ontario Museum of Archaeology, same, Royal Ontario Museum of Archaeology
229—Public Archives of Canada—New York Pub. Lib., LC—Public Archives of Canada, Canadiana Gallery Royal Ontario Museum of Archaeology
230—New York Pub. Lib., "Harry Shaw Newman, The Old Print Shop"—N. Y. Historical Society—LC—Royal Ontario Museum of Archaeology
231—University of California, "Harry Shaw Newman, The Old Print Shop"—LC, "Harry Shaw Newman, The Old Print Shop"—Royal Ontario Museum of Archaeology, Public Archives of Canada—Royal Ontario Museum of Archaeology
232—Wyeth (Philadelphia)—Keystone View Co.
233—BB, BB—LC, WW, LC—YEAR, LC, YEAR
234—LC, WW—LC, INP, BB, WW
235—LC, INP—LC, John Hancock Mutual Life Ins. Co., LC, YEAR—Fogg Museum of Art, LC, YEAR, LC—WW, WW, WW, YEAR
236—BB—National Gallery of Art—BB
237—"Phyllis Rankin, Harry Davenport Collection", YEAR, INP—LC, LC—LC, LC, LC
238—LC, LC, LC—LC—LC, LC—Missouri Historical Soc., LC
239—LC, Wells Fargo History Room, LC—LC, LC—LC, New York Central System
240—LC, LC, BB—LC, Utah Hist. Soc., LC
241—YEAR, Harper & Bros.—LC, BB—BB, LC, YEAR
242—YEAR, New York Pub. Lib.—by John Whetton Ehninger from Museum of Fine Arts (Boston), "Harry Shaw Newman, The Old Print Shop"—same, same
243—INP, New York Hist. Soc.—Institute of Aeronautical Sciences, LC—Los Angeles Public Library, New York Hist. Soc.—Wells Fargo Bank History Room
244—LC, BB—Chicago Hist. Soc.—YEAR, YEAR
245—LC, LC—NA, NA
246—LC, NA—Chicago Hist. Soc., BB—New York Hist. Soc., Nebraska State Hist. Soc.
247—LC—BB, LC—BB, LC
248—LC, LC—New York Hist. Soc.—Keystone View Co., LC
249—BB—NA, NA, Union Pacific Railroad—LC, LC, LC, YEAR
250—BB, LC—BB, LC
251—LC, YEAR, LC—YEAR, LC, LC—WW, WW
252—NA, YEAR—LC, YEAR
253—AMP, New York Pub. Lib.—AMP, George F. Harding Museum—LC, LC, INP
254—U & U, LC—LC, George F. Harding Museum—LC, NA
255—LC, Metropolitan Museum of Art—LC—LC, INP
256—NA, Boston Pub. Lib.—NA, New York Pub. Lib.—Boston Pub. Lib., BB, LC
257—LC, LC—California State Library, Seattle Hist. Soc.—LC, Keystone View Co.—Seattle Hist. Soc.
258—WW, BB—NA—LC, NA, LC
259—LC, INP—LC, LC—BB, YEAR
260—U & U—The Thomas Alva Edison Foundation Museum, NA—Peoria Public Library, WW
261—U & U, WW, U & U—Society of California Pioneers, LC—Smithsonian Institution, INP
262—BB, by Weir from Metropolitan Museum of Art—BB—LC, WW
263—Metropolitan Museum of Art, INP—BB, LC—LC, WW, BB
264—Wyeth (Philadelphia)—same, WW
265—YEAR, BB, BB—LC, LC—BB, BB—BB, BB
266—YEAR, LC, National Women's Christian Temperance Union—LC, LC, LC
267—WW, LC—LC, LC—BB, BB, LC
268—LC, WW—WW—Bettman Archive, LC
269—Peoria Pub. Lib.—LC, LC, WW—LC, LC, AMP, AMP, LC
270—LC, INP, WW—LC—INP, INP, INP, INP
271—LC, LC, LC—WW, Museum of Modern Art Film Lib.—INP, BB, BB
272—Metropolitan Museum of Art, LC—Philadelphia Museum of Art, Metropolitan Museum of Art, same—same, BB, WW
273—Cincinnati Art Museum—Metropolitan Museum of Art, George F. Harding Museum—M. H. De Young Memorial Museum, Museum of the City of New York
274—Museum of the City of New York, LC, LC—LC, LC, U & U
275—LC, Black Star—LC—LC, LC
276—New York Pub. Lib., LC—Chicago Hist. Soc., LC—LC, LC—INP, YEAR
277—LC, INP—LC, BB—LC, BB
278—Institute of Aeronautical Sciences
279—NA
280—LC, LC, LC—LC, LC, LC
281—BB—LC, LC, INP—LC, LC, LC
282—BB, INP—WW, LC—BB, Museum of the City of New York, LC
283—LC, LC—WW, BB, LC
284—INP, INP—YEAR, INP
285—LC, LC—LC—INP, BB—BB, U & U
286—WW, WW—BB, BB
287—Keystone View Co., same—NA, NA—NA, NA
288—NA, NA—NA, NA—NA, WW
289—NA, NA—NA, NA—NA, NA
290—INP, INP—INP, INP—BB, LC
291—BB—Harris & Ewing, LC, INP
292—LC, BB—The State Hist. Soc. of Wisconsin, Culver Service—INP, YEAR, LC
293—BB, LC—BB, INP, YEAR—WW, BB
294—NA—INP, LC, INP—BB, WW
295—BB, WW—LC—Harris & Ewing, WW
296—Canadian Pacific Railway—Royal Ontario Museum of Archaeology—Canadian Pacific Railway, Archives of Saskatchewan
297—Public Archives of Canada, same—Canadian Pacific Railway, Archives of Saskatchewan—Canadian Pacific Railway, Archives of Saskatchewan
298—BB, INP—WW, LC—YEAR, Los Angeles Pub. Lib.
299—LC—Archives of Saskatchewan—Los Angeles Pub. Lib.
300—BB, Black Star—LC—LC, BB, U & U, WW
301—LC, BB—BB, U & U, BB—BB, BB, BB
302—BB, BB—WW—U & U
303—Air Force Photo, LC—BB, BB, BB—BB, INP
304—WW—INP, INP—YEAR, BB
305—WW, BB, INP—BB, U & U, LC—WW, BB, U & U
306—BB, U & U—INP—INP, LC, WW, BB
307—Bettman Archive, BB—LC, INP, INP—INP, LC, LC, WW
308—Film Library Museum of Modern Art—same, WW, Photoplay
309—WW, WW—LC—BB, Jesse Lasky—WW, BB
310—WW, BB—Town & Country (N. Y.), BB—INP, BB, INP
311—INP, WW, INP—photograph by Byron from The Byron Coll. Museum of the City of New York, Town & Country, courtesy Irene Castle Enzinger
312—INP, LC, U & U—WW, WW, INP—U & U, WW, U & U
313—Phillips Collection, Keystone View Co.—International Studio, Philadelphia Museum of Art, BB—LC, Scribner's Magazine, Philadelphia Museum of Art
314—WW—Keystone View Co., LC, LC—LC, INP, C. A. Perry (Healdsburg, Calif.)
315—LC, LC—U & U, LC—LC, WW
316—LC, LC—WW, INP—INP, Keystone View Co., LC
317—LC, BB, INP—LC, WW, INP—Keystone View Co., same
318—LC—BB, BB—BB, BB
319—INP, BB—BB, INP
320—U & U
321—U & U
322—LC, INP—LC—LC—INP, LC, WW
323—WW, WW, LC, WW—LC—Harris & Ewing—LC, LC, WW
324—U & U, WW—WW, WW, LC
325—U & U, U & U—U & U, U & U—WW, INP
326—U & U, U & U—WW, WW
327—WW, WW—WW—WW—WW, WW, WW, INP
328—INP, WW, WW—WW, WW WW—WW, WW, WW
329—WW, INP—INP, U & U, WW—WW, INP, INP
330—Institute Aeronautical Sciences, Packard Motor Car Co.—Douglas Aircraft Co., INP
331—Goodyear Tire & Rubber Co., INP—U & U, Douglas Aircraft Co.—INP, WW
332—WW, WW—BB, INP, U & U
333—WW, BB—WW, BB, BB—WW, WW, WW, WW
334—WW—WW, WW—WW, WW, INP
335—WW, WW, Black Star—WW, INP, WW—WW, WW, Black Star
336—LC—INP, WW—WW, BB
337—WW—WW, WW—BB, LC—WW, WW
338—Black Star, BB—Whitney Museum of American Art—same, BB—Whitney Museum of American Art
339—WW, U & U, WW—WW, WW, WW—BB, BB, LC
340—Academy of Motion Picture Arts and Sciences, same, BB, Academy of Motion Picture Arts and Sciences, U & U—INP, BB, Academy of Motion Picture Arts and Sciences—WW, BB, Walt Disney, U & U
341—WW, BB, Academy of Motion Picture Arts and Sciences—WW, Academy of Motion Picture Arts and Sciences—Warner Bros., Academy of Motion Picture Arts and Sciences, same—same, BB, Academy of Motion Picture Arts and Sciences
342—Academy of Motion Picture Arts and Sciences, same, Warner Bros., BB—Academy of Motion Picture Arts and Sciences, same, WW—Academy of Motion Picture Arts and Sciences, same, same, WW
343—Academy of Motion Picture Arts and Sciences, same, same—same, WW—Academy of Motion Picture Arts and Sciences, same, same—BB, MGM, U & U
344—WW, WW—BB, BB—BB, BB, BB
345—INP, WW, INP—Black Star, U & U—WW, WW, Black Star
346—BB, BB—BB, BB, WW
347—WW, BB—BB, WW, BB—BB, BB, BB
348—WW, WW, WW, WW—LC, WW, WW, Bettmann Archive
349—INP, BB, INP—WW, WW, WW—WW, WW, WW—INP
350—WW, WW—WW, WW—WW, WW, WW—INP, INP, WW, WW
351—WW, WW—WW, WW, WW—WW, WW, WW, WW
352—U & U, U & U, U & U—INP, WW, U & U—WW, WW, WW
353—INP, BB—INP, BB—BB, U & U—BB, WW, BB
354—INP, BB, WW—BB, BB—BB, BB
355—U & U, BB—U & U, BB
356—Culver Service, BB, BB, LC, LC—WW, WW, WW, WW, WW, LC
357—BB, U & U—U & U, U & U—BB, U & U
358—Black Star
359—YEAR
360—Official photograph U.S. Navy—INP, Black Star, BB
361—U.S. Navy Photo, WW—BB, BB—BB, BB
362—LC, Official photograph U.S. Navy—BB, WW, WW—U.S. Army Photograph, LC
363—U.S. Army Photograph, LC—WW, Dept. of Defense, U.S. Army Photograph—WW, U.S. Army Photograph
364—U.S. Army Photograph, same—Air Force Photo, BB, Red Cross Photo by Atkins—Air Force Photo, WW, Official Photograph U.S. Navy
365—BB, U.S. Army Photograph—same, same—WW, UP, INP
366—WW, WW, WW—WW, WW—WW, WW
367—BB, Black Star—U.S. Army Photograph, BB—WW, WW
368—BB, BB, WW, U.S. Army Photograph—WW, WW, WW
369—WW, WW—WW—WW, WW, WW
370—Black Star, same, WW—WW, U.S. Army Photograph
371—Douglas Aircraft Co. Inc., Salvation Army—WW—LC, WW
372—WW, WW—INP, WW, INP
373—INP, INP—WW, WW, INP—WW, INP
374—WW, WW—WW—WW, WW—UP, WW, WW
375—WW, WW, WW—WW—WW—UP, WW
376—WW, WW—WW, WW, WW
377—WW, WW—WW, WW—WW, WW, WW
378—WW, WW—WW—WW, WW
379—WW, WW—WW, WW, UP—WW, INP
380—WW, WW—Canadian Pacific Railway, National Film Board, WW.
381—Black Star, same—WW, WW, WW—WW, WW
382—WW, WW—National Film Board from Canadian Consulate General (Los Angeles), Jeanne Graham from London Free Press, National Film Board—Dept. of Agriculture (Ottawa), Arthur Mayer and Edward Kinsley
383—National Defense Photo (Canada), INP—INP, INP—WW, National Film Board, UNATIONS
384—BB—BB
385—WW, BB, Black Star—WW, Atomic Energy Comm.—UP
386—Gus Pasquarella
387—WW, WW—UP, WW—Virus Laboratory of the Univ. of California, YEAR
388—Ford Motor Co., INP
389—RCA Victor, DuPont Co.—Chicago Burlington & Quincy RR, Bureau of Reclamation—Shell Oil Co., WW
390—USDA Photo, WW—USDA Photo, Robert Hare (Carnation Co.)—UP, INP
391—WW, INP—WW—INP
392—*The New York Times*, UP, *The New York Times*—ABC Photo, WW, UP—INP, WW, Rinehart & Co., Inc.
393—WW, WW—Mus. of Modern Art, Illinois Univ.—WW—U.S. Army Photograph, J. W. Russell Photograph (NYC), WW, Curt Valentin Gallery
394—Black Star, NBC—WW, NBC Photo by Herb Ball, WW, WW
395—WW, WW—WW, WW—WW, WW—WW, WW
396—MGM, Academy of Motion Picture Arts & Sciences, same, same, Warner Bros.—Academy of Motion Picture Arts & Sciences, same, same—same, BB, Warner Bros.
397—Columbia Pictures Corp., Academy of Motion Picture Arts & Sciences, Columbia Pictures Corp.—20th Century Fox, Academy of Motion Picture Arts & Sciences—20th Century Fox, RKO Pictures, United Artists—RKO Radio Pictures, Academy of Motion Picture Arts & Sciences, WW, Warner Bros.
398—20th Century Fox, United Artists, same, Republic, Paramount—same, Cinerama, Warner Bros.—"Come Back Little Sheba", Academy of Motion Picture Arts & Sciences, United Artists, Paramount
399—Columbia Pictures Corp., same, Warner Bros.—Columbia Pictures Corp., 20th Century Fox—Paramount, Warner Bros., MGM, Allied Artists—Hecht-Lancaster Org., Warner Bros., MGM, 20th Century Fox
400—CBS, CBS, UP—CBS, INP
401—CBS, CBS—WW, NBC, NBC—INP, WW, CBS
402—INP, INP—INP, CBS—NBC
403—WW, Cleveland Indians, U&U—INP—WW, WW—INP
404—INP, INP—INP, WW—Keystone Pictures, Inc., UP—UP
405—WW, INP—UP, WW—Univ. of California at Berkeley, INP
406—Eleanor Lambert, same, Couture Group of the N.Y. Dress Inst.—WW, Couture Group of the N.Y. Dress Inst.—Cole of California—WW, Traphagen School
407—WW, INP, INP—WW, INP—INP, UP, WW—WW, UP, INP
408—WW, WW—INP, WW—WW, BB
409—WW, WW, INP—WW, WW, WW

INDEX

413

AMERICAN HISTORY ATLAS

FOR

PICTORIAL HISTORY

of

UNITED STATES AND CANADA

by The Editors of

CONTENTS

Pictorial Chart Credits: Graphic Institute, N.Y.C.—Plates 19 and 23—Pictograph Corp., N.Y.C.—Plates 9, 15, 16, and 18

MAPS COPYRIGHTED MCMLIII

BY

C. S. HAMMOND & CO., INC.

Maplewood, N. J.   New York, N. Y.

PLATE 1

The map at right illustrates the conception of the Western Hemisphere held by Europeans on the eve of Columbus' first voyage. The pink land areas are from Behaim's globe of 1492. The white outline shows the true shape of the land area of the hemisphere as we know it today. The two maps coincide at one point—the Strait of Gibraltar. Behaim's globe depicts vividly the lack of geographical knowledge prior to the age of discovery. While his shape of the west coast of Europe and Africa roughly approximates the true coastline of these continents, the east coast of Asia is quite fanciful and is misplaced by a third of the distance around the globe. Of course, the American continents do not appear because their depiction on a map awaited the great voyages of discovery shown on the map in the center of this page.

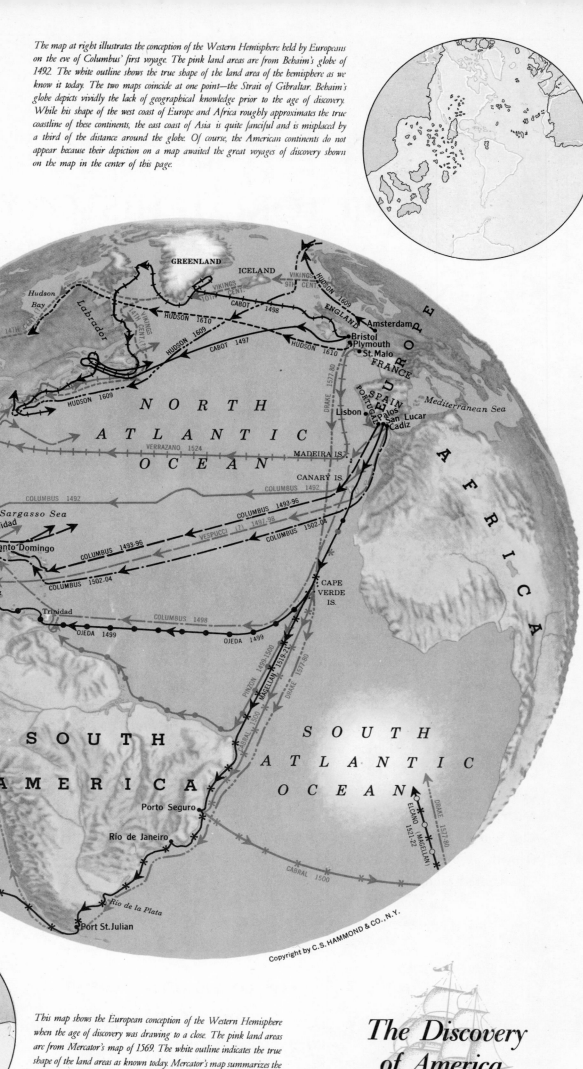

Copyright by C.S. HAMMOND & CO., N.Y.

This map shows the European conception of the Western Hemisphere when the age of discovery was drawing to a close. The pink land areas are from Mercator's map of 1569. The white outline indicates the true shape of the land areas as known today. Mercator's map summarizes the results of nearly eighty years of exploration after Columbus. The American continents appear in their true position though exaggerated in size. The eastern part of Asia is no longer shown in the hemisphere but is replaced by the Pacific Ocean. The overestimated size of the Antarctic continent would not be clarified until a much later date.

The Discovery of America

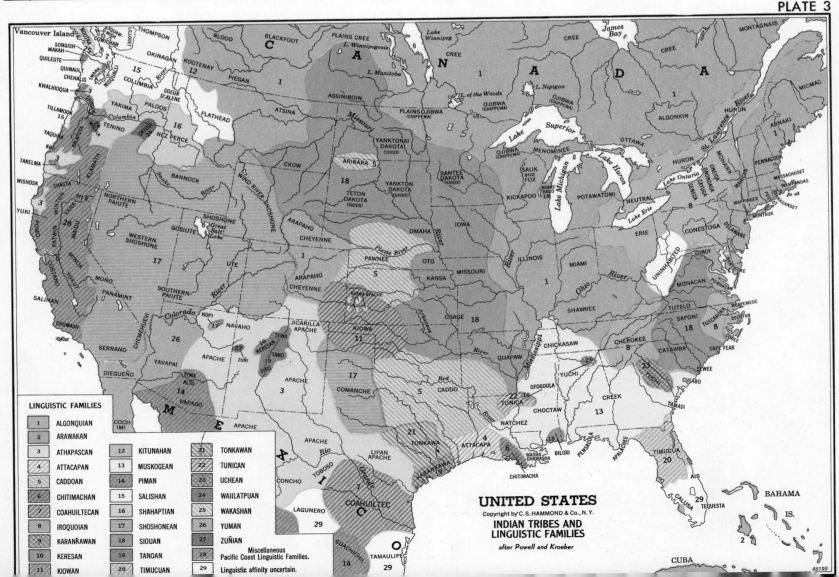

PLATE 4

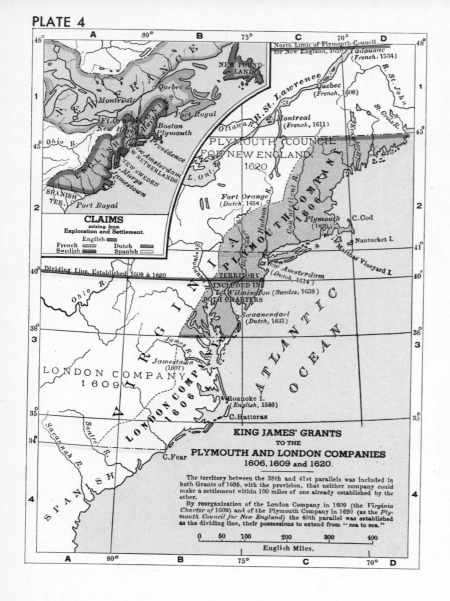

CLAIMS
arising from
Exploration and Settlement.

English — French — Dutch — Swedish — Spanish

KING JAMES' GRANTS
TO THE
PLYMOUTH AND LONDON COMPANIES
1606, 1609 and 1620

The territory between the 38th and 41st parallels was included in both Grants of 1606, with the provision, that neither company could make a settlement within 100 miles of one already established by the other.

By reorganization of the London Company in 1609 (the *Virginia Charter of 1609*) and of the Plymouth Company in 1620 (as the *Plymouth Council for New England*) the 40th parallel was established as the dividing line, their possessions to extend from "sea to sea."

0 50 100 200 400
English Miles.

PLATE 5

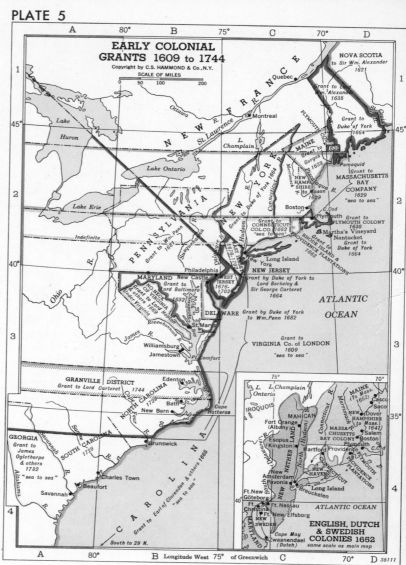

EARLY COLONIAL
GRANTS 1609 to 1744
Copyright by C.S. HAMMOND & Co., N.Y.
SCALE OF MILES

ENGLISH, DUTCH
& SWEDISH
COLONIES 1652
same scale as main map

PLATE 6

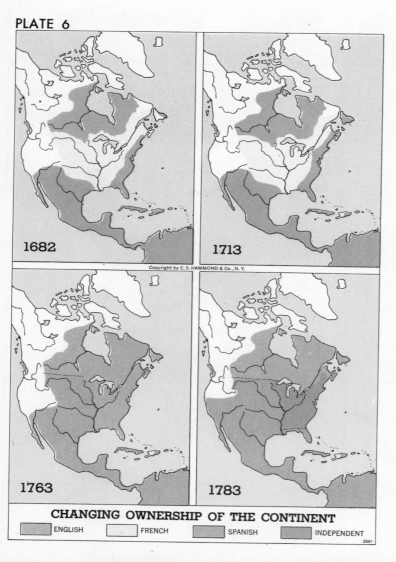

1682

1713

Copyright by C.S. HAMMOND & Co., N.Y.

1763

1783

CHANGING OWNERSHIP OF THE CONTINENT

ENGLISH — FRENCH — SPANISH — INDEPENDENT

PLATE 7

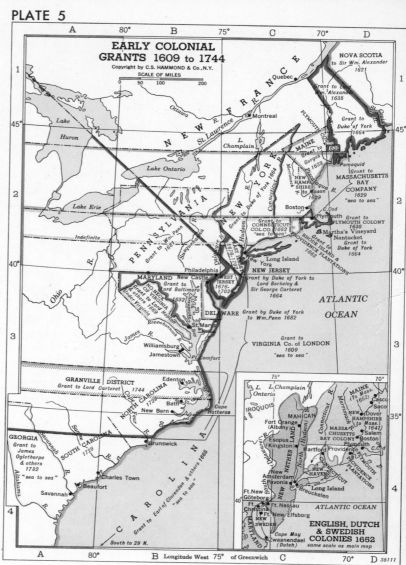

BEFORE THE
FRENCH AND INDIAN WAR
English Statute Miles

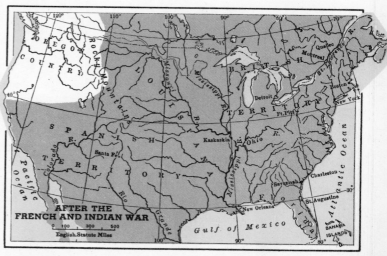

AFTER THE
FRENCH AND INDIAN WAR
English Statute Miles

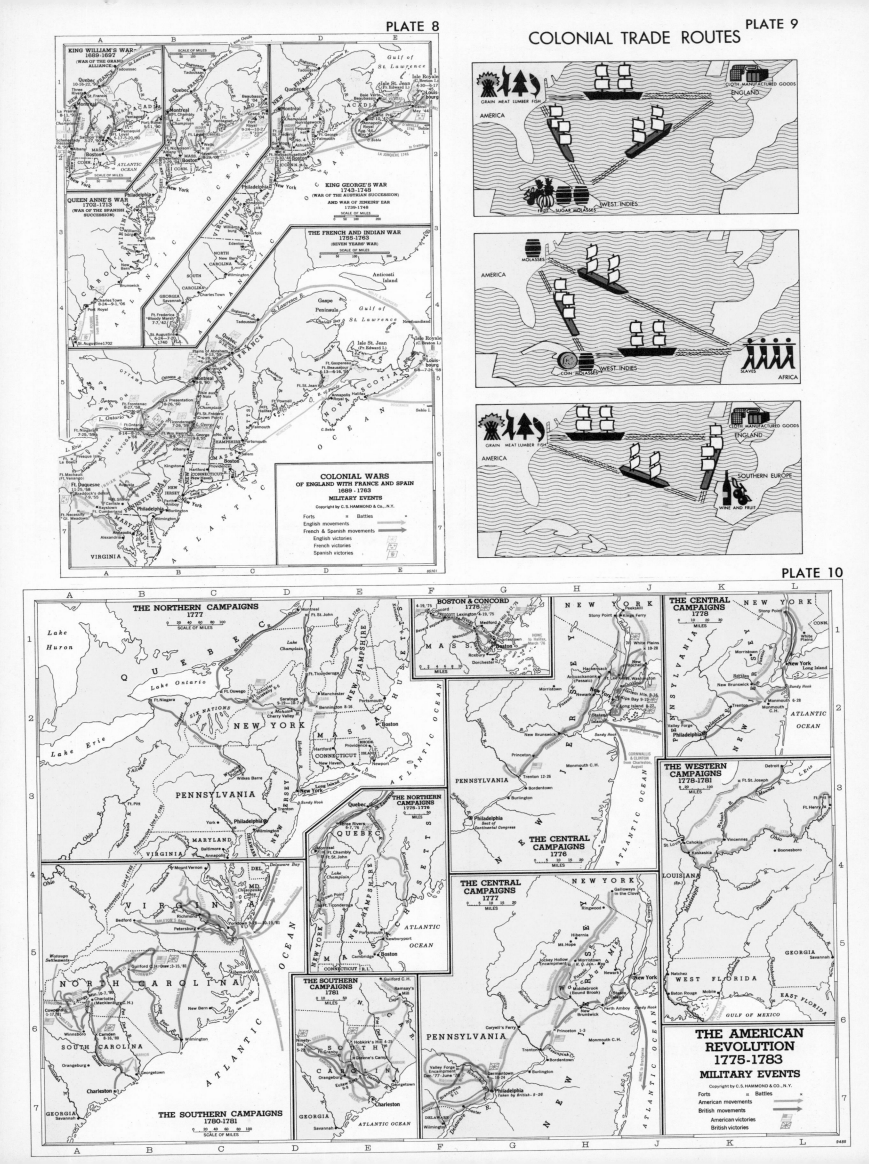

PLATE 11

THE NORTHERN FRONTIER CAMPAIGNS 1812-1814

SCALE OF MILES
0 10 20 30 40 50 60

¤ Ft. Mackinac
Taken by British
July 1812

Manitoulin
Island

Lake Huron

Georgian Bay

MICHIGAN TERR.

UPPER CANADA

Saginaw Bay

Lake Ontario

York (Toronto)
Taken & burned
by Americans
April 1813

Kingston

Sacketts Harbor

DEARBORN 1813

Oswego

Mohawk R.

Albany

NEW YORK

Ft. Niagara
Lundy's Lane × Chippewa
Draw; Sept. 1814 × 7-5, '14
1814
Ft. Erie
Buffalo

Genesee R.

Montreal
PREVOST 1814
Chateauguay 10-26, '13
×
Chrystlers Farm
11-11, '13
HAMPTON
1813
Plattsburg
Naval Battle of
Lake Champlain
Lake Champlain

St. Lawrence R.
WILKINSON 1813
MULCASTER

× Battle of the Thames
10-5, '13

Detroit
Surrendered to British Aug. 1812
Recaptured Sept. 1813

Lake
St. Clair

Thames R.

¤ Ft. Malden Taken by Americans
Sept. 1813

Raisin
R. 1-22, '13
Frenchtown

BARCLAY

¤ Ft. Meigs

¤ Ft. Defiance

Maumee R.

HARRISON

¤ Ft. Stephenson

Naval Battle of Lake Erie
Put-in-Bay
9-20, '13

PERRY 1813

Erie

Cleveland

Lake Erie

OHIO

HARRISON
from Cincinnati 1813

PENNSYLVANIA

Allegheny R.

Delaware R.

NEW JERSEY

New York
Hudson R.

MISSISSIPPI TERRITORY

Tennessee R.

Huntsville

Ft. Deposit

JACKSON

CREEK WAR 1813-1814

Horseshoe Bend
3-27, '14

Coosa R.

Fort Jackson

Ft. Confederation ¤

Tombigbee R.

Alabama R.

Yazoo R.

Vicksburg

Mississippi R.

Pearl R.

Ft. Mims Massacre ¤
8-30, '13

Mobile

JACKSON

FLORIDA

L. Pontchartrain

Borgne

New Orleans
Dec.-Jan. 1815

LOUISIANA

Ft. St. Philip

PAKENHAM

Ft. Bowyer

Pensacola
Taken by Americans
11-7, '14

GULF OF MEXICO

THE GULF CAMPAIGN 1813-1815

SCALE OF MILES
0 20 40 60 80

THE CHESAPEAKE CAMPAIGN 1814

MARYLAND

Patapsco R.

Baltimore
Ft. McHenry ¤
9-12
North Point

Chestertown

Dover ★

NEW JERSEY

Delaware R.

Centerville

Delaware Bay

Milford

Potomac R.

Annapolis

St. Michaels

DIST. OF COL.
Washington
Taken & burned
by British 8-24

Bladensburg
8-24 ×
COCKBURN & ROSS

Alexandria

ROSS

¤ Ft. Washington

Patuxent R.

Tilghman
(British base)

Easton

Denton

Salisbury

Berlin

Benedict

Cambridge

La Plata

King George

Rappahannock R.

Mattaponi R.

Pamunkey R.

VIRGINIA

King and Queen

Williamsburg

Yorktown

James R.

Hampton

Norfolk

Chesapeake Bay

Princess Anne

Pungoteague

Cape Charles

Cape Henry

Lynnhaven Bay

COCKBURN

MARYLAND

DELAWARE

Lewes

BRITISH BLOCKADE

ATLANTIC OCEAN

SCALE OF MILES
0 5 10 15 20

THE WAR OF 1812
MILITARY EVENTS
Copyright by C. S. Hammond & Co., N.Y.

Forts ¤	Battles ×
American movements	
British movements	
American victories	
British victories	

85110

PLATE 12

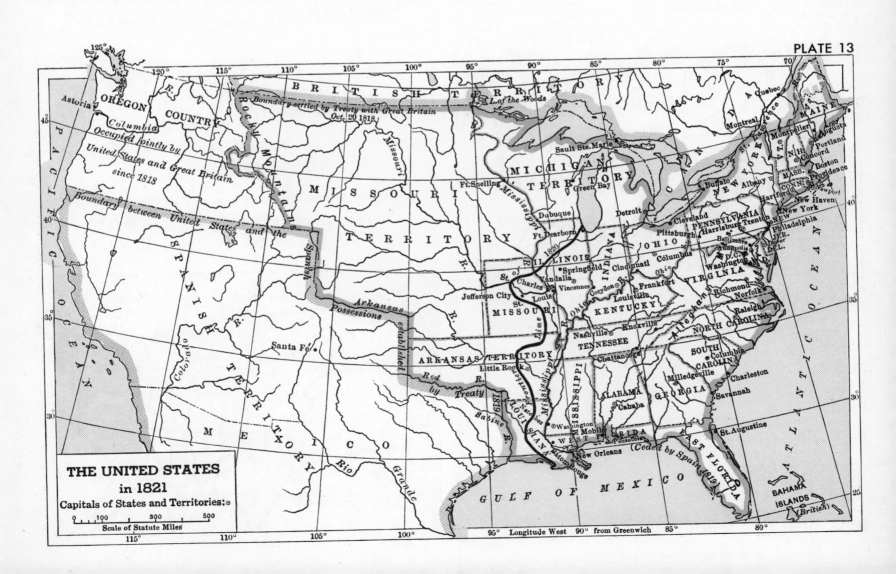

THE GROWTH
of the
UNITED STATES
From 1776 to 1867

MILES
0 50 100   200

The acquisitions made by the United States from
1776 to 1867 are shown by different colors.

The boundaries of the States and Territories at the close
of 1867 are outlined by blue lines:

The Capitals of the States and Territories in
1867 are shown on map by: ⊙

Copyright by C.S. HAMMOND & CO., N.Y.

WASHINGTON TERRITORY
OREGON COUNTRY
Acquired by Treaty with
Great Britain in 1846

THE MEXICAN CESSION OF 1848
THE GADSDEN PURCHASE 1853

ALASKA
Purchased from
Russia in 1867

LOUISIANA Purchased from France in 1803

Annexed in 1845

Acquired by Spain in 1819

PLATE 13

THE UNITED STATES
in 1821
Capitals of States and Territories: ⊙

100   300   500
Scale of Statute Miles

OREGON COUNTRY
Columbia
Occupied jointly by
United States and Great Britain
since 1818

Boundary between United States and the

BRITISH TERRITORY
Boundary settled by Treaty with Great Britain
Oct. 20 1818

SPANISH POSSESSIONS

Arkansas established
Red R. by Treaty 1819

PLATE 14

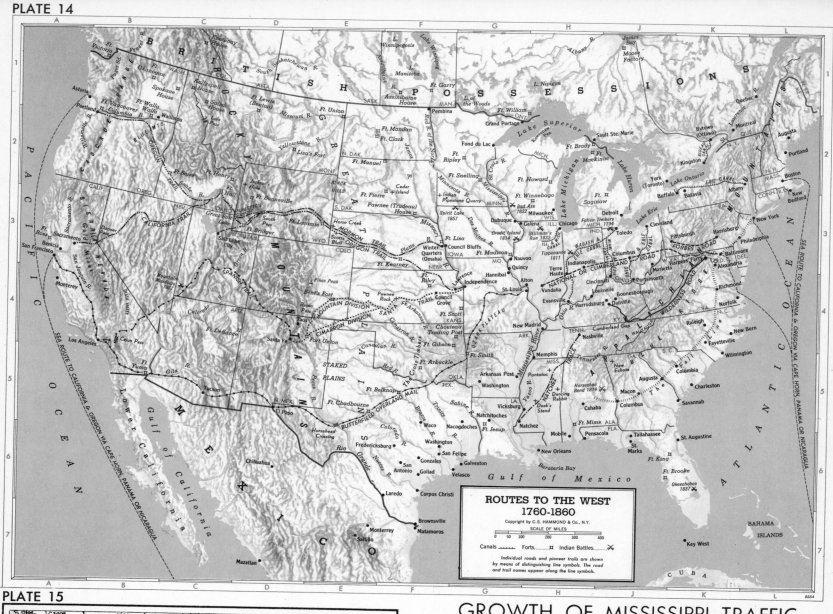

ROUTES TO THE WEST
1760-1860

Copyright by C.S. Hammond & Co., N.Y.

SCALE OF MILES
0 50 100 200 300 400

Canals ••••• Forts ⌂ Indian Battles ✕

Individual roads and pioneer trails are shown by means of distinguishing line symbols. The road and trail names appear along the line symbols.

PLATE 15

The date of admission of States to the Union, between 1821 and 1840, is marked under name of State

0 100   300   600
English Statute Miles

THE UNITED STATES IN 1840

GROWTH OF MISSISSIPPI TRAFFIC

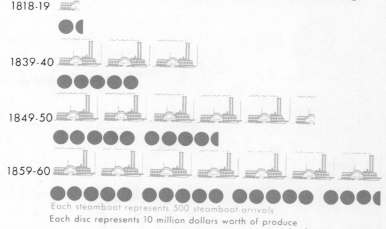

1818-19

1839-40

1849-50

1859-60

Each steamboat represents 500 steamboat-arrivals

Each disc represents 10 million dollars worth of produce
received at New Orleans

PLATE 16

POPULATION GROWTH IN THE WEST

1820   1850

1820

1840

1860

1890

Each man represents one million people

The date of admission of States to the Union, between 1840 and 1850, is marked under name of State

0 100 300 500
English Statute Miles

THE UNITED STATES IN 1850

PLATE 17

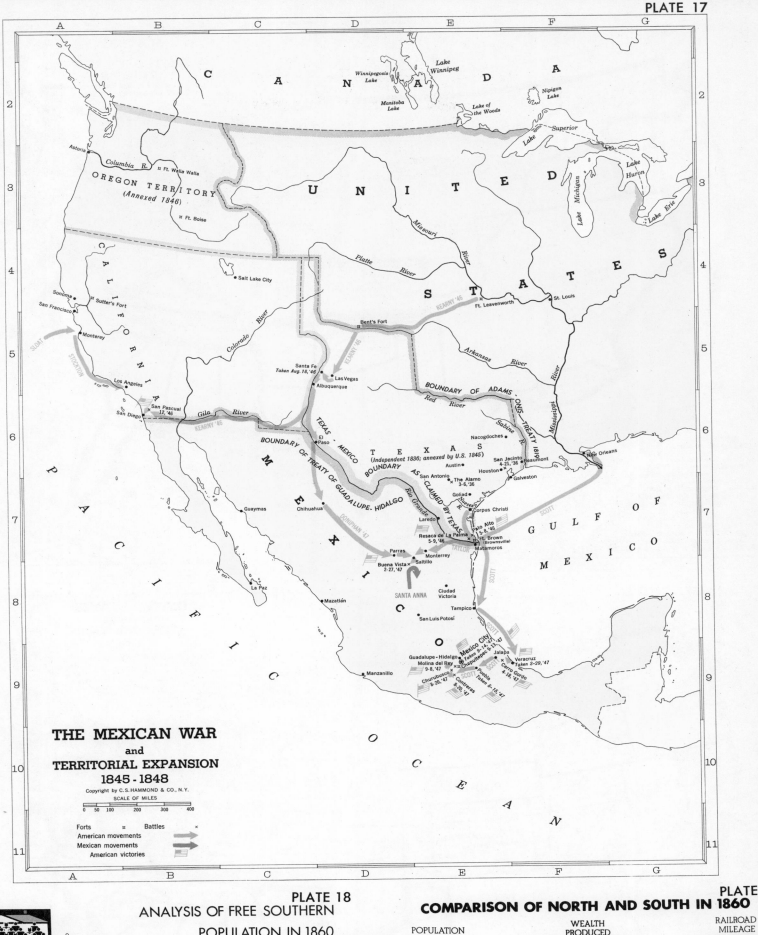

THE MEXICAN WAR
and
TERRITORIAL EXPANSION
1845 - 1848

Copyright by C.S. HAMMOND & CO., N.Y.

SCALE OF MILES

0 50 100 200 300 400

Forts ¤   Battles ×
American movements →
Mexican movements →
American victories

PLATE 18

ANALYSIS OF FREE SOUTHERN

POPULATION IN 1860

The free Southern population in 1860 is shown
quantitatively according to the number of slaves held.

20 OR MORE SLAVES ← 200,000

10 TO 20 SLAVES ← 300,000

1 TO 9 SLAVES ← 1,400,000

NO SLAVES ← WHITE 6,000,000   NEGRO 200,000

Each symbol represents 200,000 people

PLATE 19

COMPARISON OF NORTH AND SOUTH IN 1860

POPULATION
NORTH 61%
SOUTH 39%

WEALTH
PRODUCED
NORTH 75%
SOUTH 25%

RAILROAD
MILEAGE
NORTH 66%
SOUTH 34%

FACTORIES
NORTH 81%
SOUTH 19%

BANK
DEPOSITS
NORTH 74%
SOUTH 26%

FARMS
NORTH 67%
SOUTH 33%

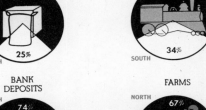

PLATE 20

A 120° B 110° C Longitude 100° West from D Greenwich. 90° E 80° F 70° G

BRITISH POSSESSIONS

SLAVERY
IN THE
UNITED STATES
1775–1865

Free by Action of National Government: ▭▭▭▭
" " voluntary Action of States.

0 100 200 300 400
English Miles

Free, Oregon Act, 1848
Slave, Dred Scott Decision, 1857
Free, Territorial Act, 1862

Columbia R.

Free, Oregon Act, 1848
Slave, Dred Scott Decision, 1857
Free, State Act, 1859

Snake R.

Free, Missouri Compromise, 1820
Slave, Kansas-Nebraska Act, 1854
" Confirmed by Dred Scott Decision, 1857
Free, Territorial Act, 1862

Missouri R.

Free, State Act, 1858

Free, Mo. Comp., 1820
Slave, Kan.-Neb. Act, 1854
Slave, Dred Scott Decision, 1857
Free, State Act, 1858

Free, by North West Ordinance, 1787

Free, State Act, 1848

Free, State Act, 1836

Free, Mexican Law
Slave, D.S. Dec. 1857
Free, Terr. Act 1862

Free, Mo. Comp., 1820
Free, State Act, 1846

Free, State Act, 1799

Free, State Act, 1780

Free, State Act, 1804

Free, State Act, 1780 Mass.

Free, State Act, 1784

Free, State Act, 1784

Free, by Mexican Law
Slave, Compromise of 1850
" Confirmed by Dred Scott Decision, 1857
Free, Territorial Act, 1862

Free, Mo. Comp., 1820
Slave, Kan.-Neb. Act 1854
Slave, Confirmed by Dred Scott Decision, 1857
Free, State Act, 1861

Free, State Act, 1818

Free, State Act, 1816

Free, State Act, 1802

Free, State Act, 1863

Free, 13th Amendment 1865

Ohio R.

Free, State Act, 1865

Free, 13th Amendment 1865

Free, by Mexican Law Confirmed by State Act, 1850

Colorado R.

Free, Territorial Act, 1862

Arkansas R.

Free, State Act, 1865

Free, Mexican Law
Slave, Annexation, 1853
Free, Terr. Act, 1862

Rio Grande

Free, by Proclamation of Emancipation, Jan. 1, 1863.
Confirmed by Acts of States.

Free, State Act, 1864

Mississippi R.

REFERENCE
TO LETTERS ON MAP.

A. Free, Mexican Law.
Slave, Comprom. of 1850.
" Added to Kan., 1860.
Free, State Act, 1861.

B. Free, Compromise of 1820.
Slave, Kansas-Neb. Act, 1854.
" Confirmed by Dred Scott Decision, 1857.
Free, Territorial Act of 1862.

C. Free, Compromise of 1820.
Slave, Added to Missouri, 1836.
Free, State Act, 1864.

D. Free, District of Columbia Act, 1862.

NOTE.— Portions of Virginia and Louisiana were excepted in the Proclamation of Emancipation of Jan. 1, 1863. The whole State of Tennessee was also excepted.

MEXICO

GULF OF MEXICO

PACIFIC OCEAN

ATLANTIC OCEAN

CUBA

B 110° C 100° D 90° E 80° F

H 120° J 110° K 100° L 90° M 80° N 70° O

BRITISH POSSESSIONS

UNITED STATES
at the Beginning of
THE CIVIL WAR
1861

Union States and Territories : ▭▭▭▭
Confederate States ....
The Territories are shown in outline color.
That part of Virginia called West Virginia refused to secede and was admitted as a State in 1863.

WASHINGTON TER.

Astoria
Portland
Columbia R.
OREGON

Ft. Benton
Missouri R.
DAKOTA TER.
Yellowstone R.

Snake R.

MINNESOTA
St. Paul
Minneapolis
WISCONSIN
Milwaukee
MICHIGAN

MAINE
VERMONT
N. HAMP.
Boston
MASS.
CONN. R.I.
NEW YORK
Buffalo

CALIFORNIA
Sacramento
San Francisco

NEVADA TER.
Virginia City

Salt Lake City
UTAH TER.

NEBRASKA TER.
Missouri R.
Omaha

IOWA
Des Moines

Chicago
ILLINOIS
Indianapolis
INDIANA
OHIO
Cleveland
Cincinnati
Detroit

PENNSYLVANIA
Gettysburg
Philadelphia
NEW JERSEY
MD.
DEL.
Washington
Bull Run
Cedar Creek
Antietam

COLORADO TER.
Denver
Colorado Springs

KANSAS
Kansas City

St. Louis
MISSOURI
Wilsons Creek
Ft. Henry

Ohio R.
Louisville
Perryville
Bowling Green
KENTUCKY
Chancellorsville
Appomattox C.H.
WEST VA.
VIRGINIA
Richmond
Fair Oaks
Hampton Roads
Norfolk

Los Angeles

Santa Fé
NEW MEXICO TER.

PUBLIC LAND
Arkansas R.

INDIAN TER.
Little Rock
ARKANSAS
Memphis

Ft. Donelson
Nashville
Cumberland Gap
TENNESSEE
Chattanooga
Chickamauga
Resaca
Shiloh
Corinth

NORTH CAROLINA
Raleigh
Beaufort

SOUTH CAROLINA
Columbia
Charleston
Ft. Sumter

San Diego
Yuma

TEXAS

Red R.

MISS.
Vicksburg
Kenesaw Mtn.
ALABAMA
Montgomery
Atlanta
GEORGIA
Savannah

Rio Grande

MEXICO

Austin

LOUISIANA
New Orleans
Mobile
FLORIDA
Jacksonville

Galveston

GULF OF MEXICO

PACIFIC OCEAN

ATLANTIC OCEAN

CUBA

0 100 200 300 400 500
English Miles

J 110° K 100° L 90° M 80° N

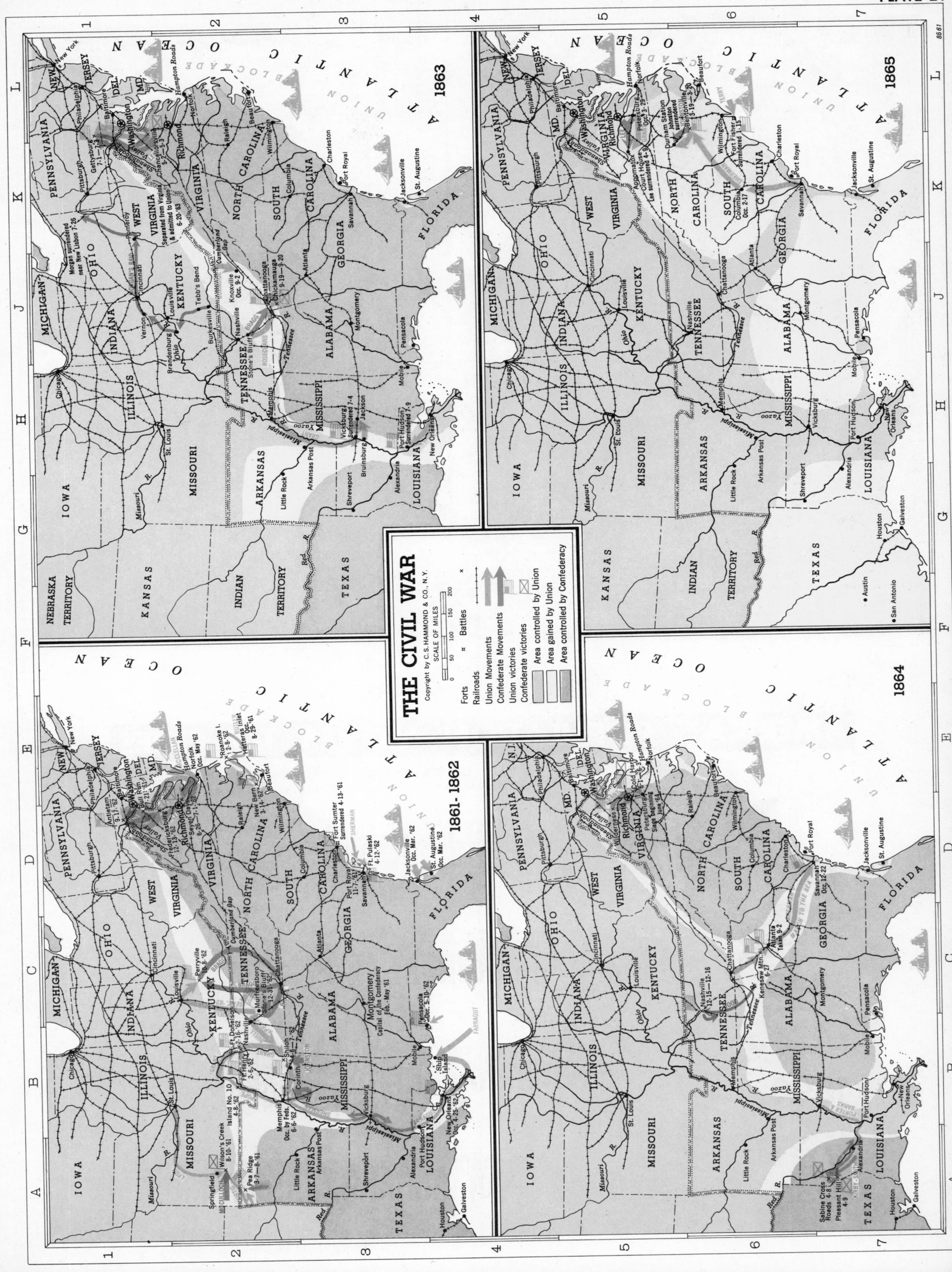

PLATE 21

THE CIVIL WAR

Copyright by C.S. HAMMOND & CO., N.Y.

SCALE OF MILES
0 50 100 150 200

Forts
Railroads
Union Movements
Confederate Movements
Union victories
Confederate victories
× Battles

Area controlled by Union
Area gained by Union
Area controlled by Confederacy

1861–1862

1863

1864

1865

PLATE 22

THE WEST 1860-1910
Showing Railroads and Federal Land Grants
Copyright by C.S. HAMMOND & Co., N.Y.

Frontiers of Settlement in 1860 _____ Forts .... ⊔

Trails .... Indian Battles ...... ✗

Pony Express .....

TRANSCONTINENTAL RAILROADS

Constructed 1860-1870 —— Constructed 1870-1880 - - - -

Constructed 1880-1890 —·—·— Constructed 1890-1900 ----

Constructed 1900-1910 ....

Major Federal land grants to railroads.

NOTE-Within land-grant areas, no more than half the land-grant sections belonged to the railroad.

PLATE 23

AMERICA'S POPULATION MOVES TO CITIES

PERCENT OF POPULATION LIVING IN RURAL AREAS   **PERCENT OF POPULATION LIVING IN URBAN AREAS**

1790
94.9% 5.1%

1840
89.2% 10.8%

1890
64.9% 35.1%

1940
43.5% 56.5%

Cities Or Other Incorporated Places
Having 2500 Or More Inhabitants

PLATE 24

DISTRIBUTION OF FOREIGN BORN
PER CENT OF POPULATION OF EACH
STATE BORN IN PRINCIPAL FOREIGN
COUNTRIES 1910

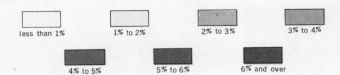

less than 1% — 1% to 2% — 2% to 3% — 3% to 4%

4% to 5% — 5% to 6% — 6% and over

Immigration to the United States in the nineteenth century was largely made up of Western European peoples—Germans, Irish, Swedes, English, etc. In the twentieth century the largest number of immigrants came from Southern and Eastern Europe—Italians, Poles and natives of the Russian and Austro-Hungarian Empires. Therefore, the year 1910 has been chosen as a base year for these maps because at that time both groups were present in sufficient numbers to be statistically significant.

ENGLAND, SCOTLAND & WALES

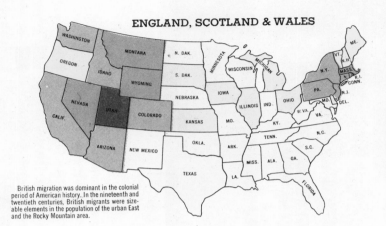

British migration was dominant in the colonial period of American history. In the nineteenth and twentieth centuries, British migrants were sizeable elements in the population of the urban East and the Rocky Mountain area.

IRELAND

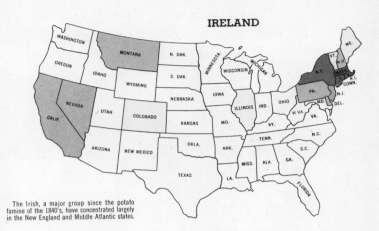

The Irish, a major group since the potato famine of the 1840's, have concentrated largely in the New England and Middle Atlantic states.

GERMANY

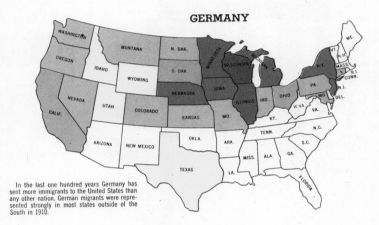

In the last one hundred years Germany has sent more immigrants to the United States than any other nation. German migrants were represented strongly in most states outside of the South in 1910.

CANADA & NEWFOUNDLAND

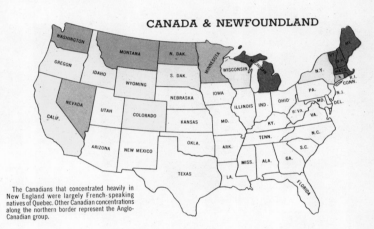

The Canadians that concentrated heavily in New England were largely French-speaking natives of Quebec. Other Canadian concentrations along the northern border represent the Anglo-Canadian group.

NORWAY, SWEDEN & DENMARK

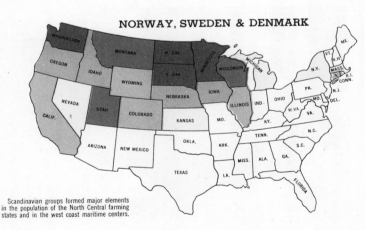

Scandinavian groups formed major elements in the population of the North Central farming states and in the west coast maritime centers.

AUSTRO-HUNGARIAN MONARCHY

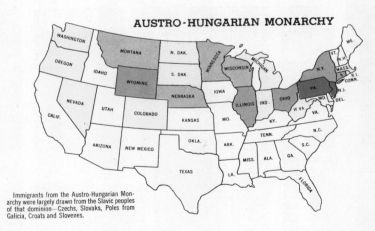

Immigrants from the Austro-Hungarian Monarchy were largely drawn from the Slavic peoples of that dominion—Czechs, Slovaks, Poles from Galicia, Croats and Slovenes.

RUSSIAN EMPIRE

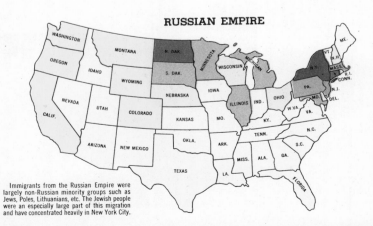

Immigrants from the Russian Empire were largely non-Russian minority groups such as Jews, Poles, Lithuanians, etc. The Jewish people were an especially large part of this migration and have concentrated heavily in New York City.

ITALY

Italians arrived in great numbers after 1900. The majority have concentrated in the urban centers of the Northeast.

4661

PLATE 25

DEVELOPMENT OF POLITICAL PARTIES
PARTY STRENGTH IN PRESIDENTIAL ELECTIONS 1796-1952

Legend:

FEDERALIST
DEMOCRATIC-REPUBLICAN
INDEPENDENT REPUBLICAN
FUSION
NO PARTY (J.Q.ADAMS)
NO PARTY (JACKSON)

CAUCUS (CRAWFORD)
NO PARTY (CLAY)
JACKSONIAN DEMOCRAT
NATIONAL REPUBLICAN
INDEPENDENT DEMOCRATIC (FLOYD)
ANTI-MASONIC

DEMOCRATIC
WHIG
WHIG (WHITE)
WHIG (WEBSTER)
INDEPENDENT
REPUBLICAN

AMERICAN-KNOW NOTHING-WHIG
DEMOCRATIC, SOUTHERN (BRECKINRIDGE)
CONSTITUTIONAL UNION
DEMOCRATIC, NORTHERN (DOUGLAS)
INDEPENDENT DEMOCRATIC (HENDRICKS)
DEMOCRATIC (BROWN)

DEMOCRATIC (JENKINS)
DEMOCRATIC (DAVIS)
POPULIST
PROGRESSIVE (T.ROOSEVELT)
PROGRESSIVE (LA FOLLETTE)
STATES' RIGHTS DEMOCRATIC

★ J.Q.Adams chosen president by House of Representatives as no candidate received majority of electoral vote.

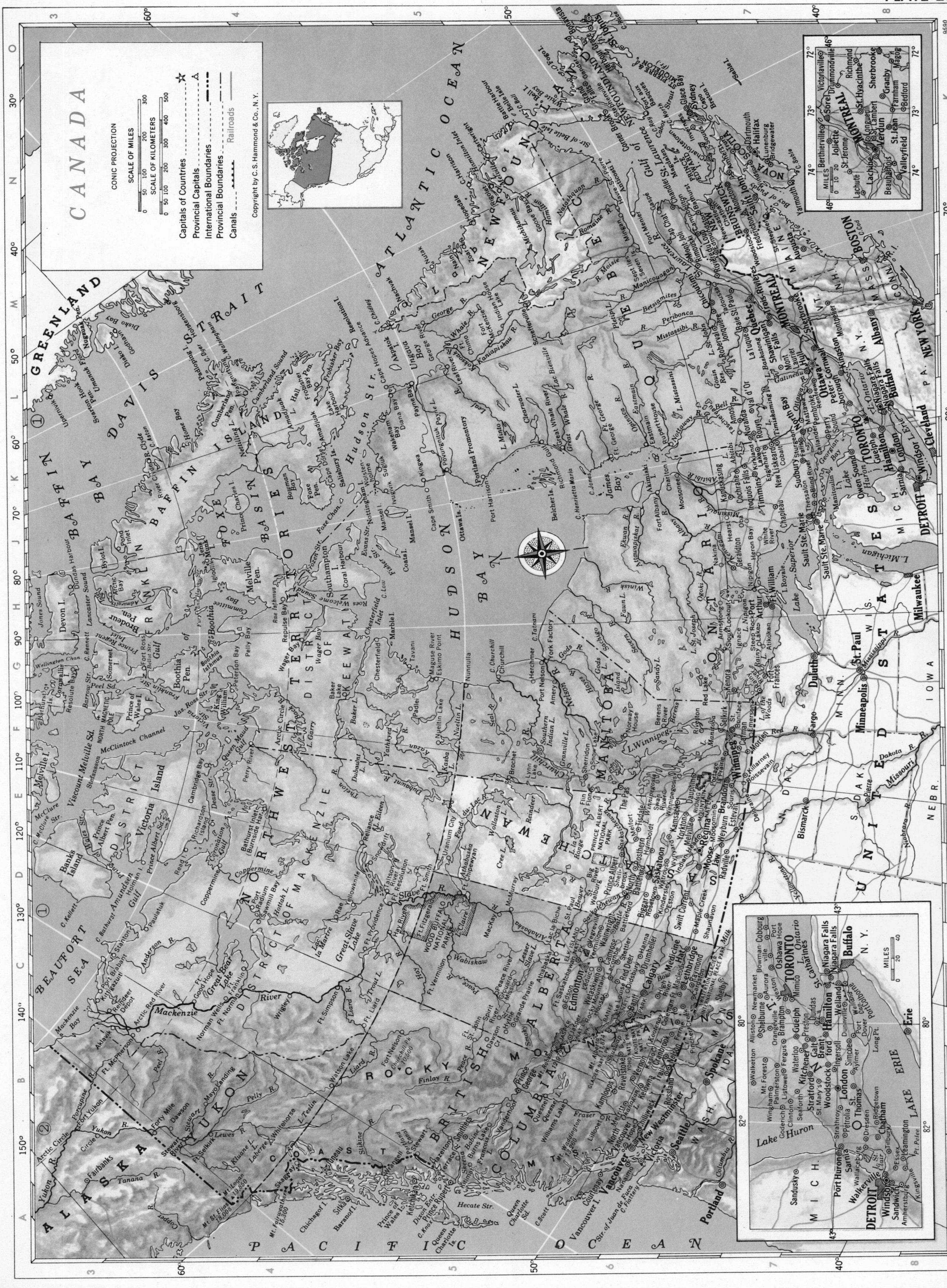

PLATE 26

CANADA

CONIC PROJECTION

SCALE OF MILES

0 50 100 200 300

SCALE OF KILOMETERS

0 50 100 200 300 400 500

Capitals of Countries ★
Provincial Capitals
International Boundaries
Provincial Boundaries
Railroads
Canals

Copyright by C. S. HAMMOND & Co., N.Y.

GREENLAND

BAFFIN BAY

DAVIS STRAIT

ATLANTIC OCEAN

BAFFIN ISLAND

FOXE BASIN

FRANKLIN DISTRICT

NORTHWEST TERRITORIES

DISTRICT OF KEEWATIN

HUDSON BAY

DISTRICT OF MACKENZIE

BEAUFORT SEA

ALASKA

YUKON

ROCKY MOUNTAINS

BRITISH COLUMBIA

ALBERTA

SASKATCHEWAN

MANITOBA

ONTARIO

QUEBEC

NEWFOUNDLAND

NEW BRUNSWICK

NOVA SCOTIA

MAINE

UNITED STATES

PACIFIC OCEAN

Longitude 90° West of Greenwich

MILES 0 20 40

DETROIT

Windsor

LAKE ERIE

TORONTO

Niagara Falls Buffalo N.Y.

Lake Huron

MICH.

MONTREAL

Sherbrooke

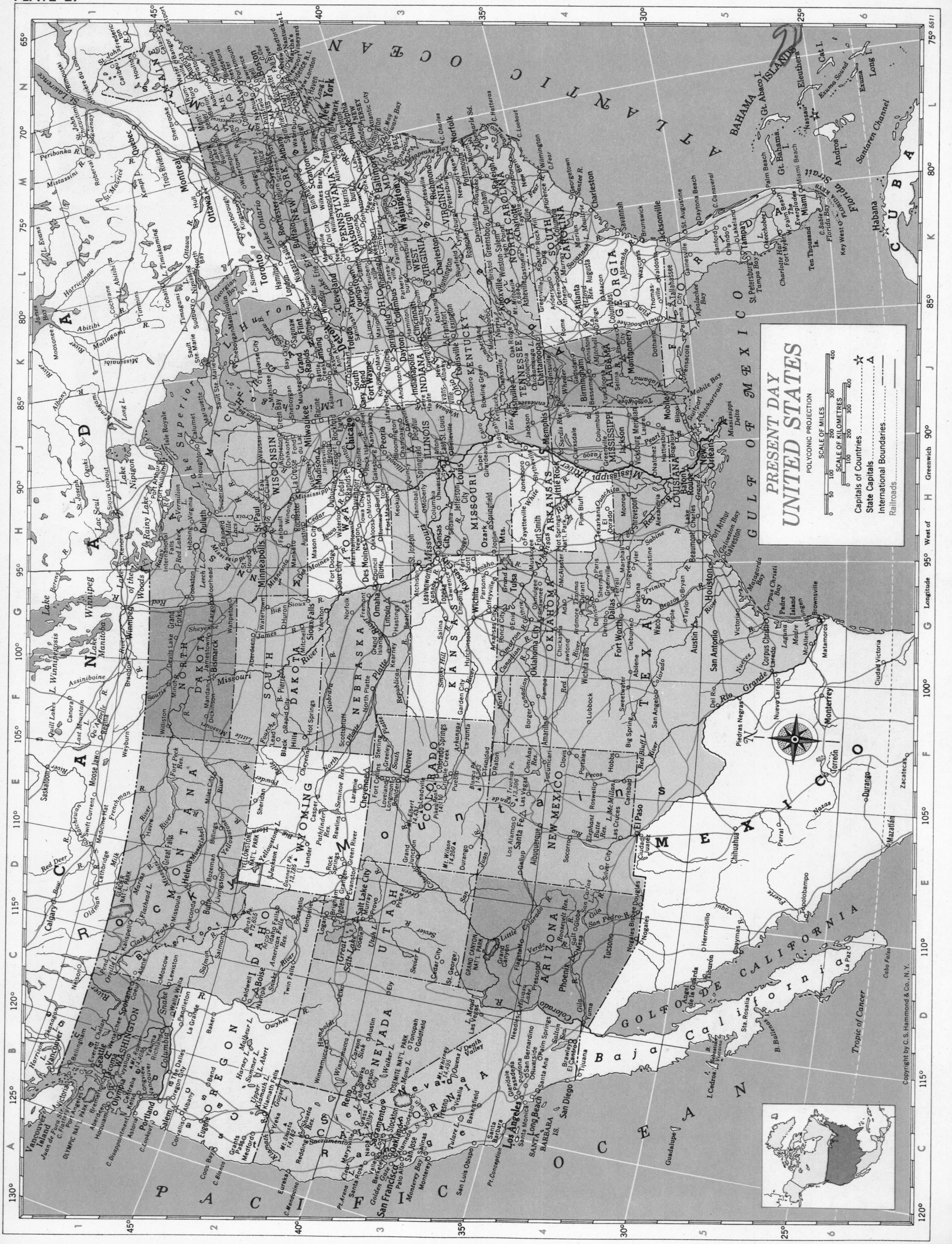

PLATE 27

PRESENT DAY
UNITED STATES
POLYCONIC PROJECTION

SCALE OF MILES

SCALE OF KILOMETRES

Capitals of Countries .... ☆
State Capitals .... △
International Boundaries ....
Railroads ....

Copyright by C. S. Hammond & Co., N. Y.

ATLANTIC OCEAN

PACIFIC OCEAN

GULF OF MEXICO

CANADA

MEXICO

CUBA

BAHAMA ISLANDS